The Restaurants of New York

1982-1983 Edition

THE
RESTAURANTS
of NEW YORK
1982 – 1983 Edition

SEYMOUR BRITCHKY

RANDOM HOUSE NEW YORK

The following reviews appeared, in somewhat different form, in *Seymour Britchky's Restaurant Letter*: American Charcuterie, Andrée's Mediterranean Cuisine, Balkan Armenian, Ballato, Le Bistro, Bistro do Brasil, Bread Shop Café, Broadway Joe Steak House, Black Sheep, Box Tree, Bruno, Cabana Carioca, Café des Sports, Café 58, Café San Martin, Café Un Deux Trois, Camelback & Central, Canton, Cent'Anni, Chanterelle, Le Chantilly, Le Cherche-Midi, Chez Pascal, Le Cirque, Claude's, La Côte Basque, Csarda, Danieli, Devon House, Dézaley, Divino, Elio's, Felidia, Foro Italico, Four Seasons, La Gauloise, Gibbon, Gin Ray, Home Village, L'Hostaria del Bongustaio, Huberts, Le Jacques Coeur, Joanna, Joe & Rose, K.O.'s, Laughing Mountain Bar & Grill, Le Lavandou, Lavin's, Lello, La Louisiana, Le Madrigal, La Maison Japonaise, Malaga, Manhattan Market, McFeely's, Michael Phillips, Mr. Chow, Mitali, Il Monello, Nadia's, Nicola's, Il Nido, Nishi, Odeon, Oenophilia, Oyster Bar & Restaurant, Palace, Pamir, Paris Commune, Parma, La Petite Ferme, La Place, Post House, Primavera, Raga, Le Refuge, Restaurant Raphaël, La Ripaille, Sabor, Say Eng Look, Shezan, Shun Lee West, Sichuan Pavilion, 65 Irving Place, Swiss Inn, Table d'Hôte, Tenth Street Café, Toscana, Tres Carabelas, Uzies, Vanessa, Vienna Park, Vienna 79, Wings, Wise Maria.

The following reviews appeared, in somewhat different form, in *New York* magazine: Alfredo, Alfredo the Original of Rome, Ambassador Grill, Ararat, Arirang, Auberge Suisse, Barbetta, Berry's, Bizen, Broome Street Bar, Café des Artistes, Café Loup, Café New Amsterdam, Casa Brasil, Chalet Suisse, Charley O's Bar & Grill & Bar, Copenhagen, Le Cygne, Da Silvano, Dimitri, Elephant & Castle, Fiorello's, Frankie and Johnnie's, Gage & Tollner, La Gamelle, El Gaucho, Ginger Man, Gloucester House, Hoexter's Market, Jane Street Seafood Café, J. G. Melon, Jim McMullen, Joe Allen, Lion's Head, Marchi's, Il Menestrello, La Métairie, Mon Paris, Il Mulino, O'Neals' Baloon, Oren and Aretsky, Pantheon, Le Paris Bistro, Le Petit Robert, P. J. Clarke's, Il Ponte Vecchio, Ravelled Sleave, Le Relais, El Rincón de España, Rio de Janeiro, Russian Tea Room, Sea-Fare of the Aegean, Simon's, Sloppy Louie's, Sweets, Les Tournebroches, La Tulipe, United States Steakhouse Co., Le Veau d'Or, Wally's, Woods.

The following reviews appeared, in somewhat different form, in the *SoHo Weekly News:* Coach House, Grotta Azzurra, Hunam, Palm and Palm Too, Raoul's, Smith & Wollensky, Sparks, Vašata.

81-644170
ISSN 0277-9005

Manufactured in the United States of America
24689753
First Edition

To David, Nicholas, Lis and John

CONTENTS

Preface   ix

Ten Sensible Rules   x

A Note on Using This Book   xii

The Ratings   xii

Listings of Restaurants

  by Type of Food   xiii

  by Rating   xvii

  by Neighborhood   xx

  Open on Sunday   xxiii

  Open Late   xxiv

  Suitable for Large Family Groups   xxv

  Outdoor Dining and Enclosed Gardens   xxv

  Enclosed Sidewalk Cafés   xxv

  Bring Your Own Wine   xxv

Restaurant Reviews   3

PREFACE

Heavy demand from Japanese and Arab sporting interests has driven the price of thoroughbred horses beyond the reach of American mere millionaires. You can still turn a basement invention and hard work into a lifetime of first-class food, clothing and shelter, but you may not be able to swing a racing stable for a hobby.

To the rescue a new game—Restaurant—which any number can play (though to do it right will require six figures). Folks are trying their luck all over town—even on streets where nobody lives, or works, or ever passes by. Entire new neighborhoods pop up, built on ruins, consisting of nothing but eating places and a few shops specializing in old clothes. Operating restaurants, once just a way of making a living, has become so mature an industry that into interstices hitherto not perceived as such middlemen have inserted themselves, these the so-called restaurant brokers. Come one, come all. If you're not in it, you're out of it.

The climax of the game, of course, is the novice restaurateur's discovery, one fine day, that his new toy has been allocated space in the pages of this book. This year the new eating places could have filled a book all their own. Merely to accommodate those most worthy—by virtue of excellence, silliness or a particularly well-preserved stamped-tin ceiling—it has been necessary to produce the most extensive revision of *The Restaurants of New York* ever published. More than 35 percent of the articles in this edition are new. And, of course, as in every previous edition, we have made timely all information on credit cards, days open, meals served, liquor licenses, reservations, telephone numbers. Still, it does not hurt to call ahead. When all the colts and fillies are gone, representatives of the Eastern Hemisphere may move in on the eating game—with, probably, unpredictable results.

TEN SENSIBLE RULES ABOUT GOING TO, EATING IN, PAYING AT AND DEPARTING FROM NEW YORK RESTAURANTS

1. RESERVATIONS. Before going to a New York restaurant, telephone to make a reservation. True, reservations are often not accepted, but this is sometimes because the restaurant no longer exists. By telephoning you determine whether the place is still in business, and if so, whether you can get a table when you want one.

2. NO RESERVATIONS. If a restaurant does not accept reservations, it is probably because it is so busy that it can get away without offering the convenience. Ask if the place is likely to be crowded when you want to go. Sometimes you will get a helpful answer, sometimes an honest one, sometimes both.

3. COMPLAINTS. It's no fun to complain throughout your meal. After all, you go to a restaurant to enjoy yourself, your food and your companions. But it's a good idea to complain about *something* early on. People who complain are people who seem to know what they want and what they are about, and they get better treatment than the timid or unsure. If you are shy or diffident, or don't know what you want, that's too bad, but it need not be a guarantee that you will not enjoy eating in New York restaurants.

4. SENDING BACK. If you don't like something you ordered, tell the waiter it tastes terrible and send it back. Do the same thing if what should be hot food is cold or if there is anything else clearly wrong with what is brought to you.

5. WINE. If you like wine but don't know much about it, order an inexpensive bottle. Modestly priced wines are the most reliable ones in restaurants. They are what they are. Restaurants are not the places to give yourself a wine education; it is much too expensive and unreliable. Expensive wines in restaurants may be too young or too old, or damaged from poor storage, and if you're unsure of yourself, you may not know why you don't like what you get and whether you really ought to return it. If there is a sommelier (the man with the chain around his neck), his business is to sell you wine (after suitable discussion), pour your first glass, and generally convert the purchase and consumption of a bottle of mild booze into an important event. Few New York restaurants have sommeliers any more, but those that do generally have pretty good wine stocks. If the sommelier seems like a decent sort and if you want to spring for a fancy bottle, tell him how much you are willing to spend, and he will recommend a bottle at the price, and probably a good one.

6. EMERGENCIES. If you need service at once and are unable to catch your waiter's or captain's eye, the best system is to rise from your chair and approach the nearest responsible member of the staff. The late English conductor Sir Thomas Beecham used to brush dishes to the floor to get attention, but as most dining-room floors in New York restaurants are carpeted, this ploy might go unnoticed. Flinging dishes against the walls or ceiling, however, is a sure-fire way to bring the help.

7. YOUR CHECK. Review it. It's wrong about one time in ten; in your favor

about one time in a hundred. Ask for a menu to check the prices if you think you have been overcharged or charged for a more expensive item than the one you ordered. Check the addition. Of course you may have had a few drinks and a bottle of wine, while the waiter is probably sober, so he may be right, and you may be wrong.

8. TIPPING—HOW. Don't leave your tip under a plate. It simply is not done. If you want to give someone a tip, hand it to him. If you don't spot him, leave the money out in the open where it is easy to see. If you're tipping on a credit-card voucher, write in the tip *and write in the grand total.* If you do not, an emendation may be made favoring the waiter and penalizing you. This is so common that the credit-card companies have a name for it; they call it an "override."

9. TIPPING—HOW MUCH. Par is 15 percent of the before-tax food total, plus some lesser percentage of the liquor and wine. If you are served by both a waiter and a captain, 20 percent is fair, most of it to the waiter, the exact proportion depending on whether the captain did no more than cursorily take your order or if, at the other extreme, he thoroughly explained the menu, prepared sauces and desserts, and helped with the selection of wine.

Reasons for tipping more: You ate the least expensive items on the menu and occupied the table for three hours; the service was terrific; you are feeling expansive.

Reasons for tipping less: The reverse of the above, except that waiters should not be penalized for your depression unless it is their fault.

Sommeliers should be tipped $2 per bottle, but no less than $3 in total if they have been really helpful.

10. DEPARTURE. Leave when you are good and ready. It is your right to eat at your own pace, including lingering over a second cup of coffee. Enjoy possession of a table that others are waiting in line for. Later they will.

A Note on Using This Book

Of the 205 restaurant reviews in this book, 73 are articles appearing for the first time—35 are of restaurants new to the book, and 38 are complete re-evaluations of restaurants that appeared in the last edition or in earlier ones. While reasonable efforts have been made to assure the factual accuracy and timeliness of the information in all of the reviews, any of these places may have changed appreciably since this edition was prepared for publication, for the New York restaurant scene never holds still. Be prepared.

The restaurants in this book have been classified as "inexpensive," "medium-priced," "expensive" or "very expensive."

When the book went to press, these categorizations were roughly defined as follows, for complete dinners for two, with wine or some other suitable beverage, tax and tip included:

Inexpensive: $40 or less
Medium-priced: $40 to $65
Expensive: $65 to $80
Very expensive: More than $80

By the time the book is printed, bound, distributed and purchased by you, these definitions, in many instances, will no longer be accurate. First, prices in all restaurants seem to go up steadily—that is inflation. Second, if an inexpensive or medium-priced restaurant is doing very well, it may shift from one category to the next—that is the profit motive. A press-time $40 dinner may run to $50 by the time you eat it.

In some few instances specific prices of dishes or drinks or wines are referred to in the text. They are meant to give an impression of the restaurant's pricing policy. The information was correct when written, and the impression is probably still correct, even if the exact price has changed.

The Ratings

★★★★ Excellent
★★★ Very good
★★ Good
★ Good (but not *as* good)
● Acceptable
○ Unacceptable

Listings of Restaurants

BY TYPE OF FOOD

AFGHAN

Pamir   **209**

AMERICAN

Ambassador Grill   **6**
American Charcuterie   **7**
Berry's   **21**
Billy's   **22**
Bradley's   **30**
Bread Shop Café   **31**
Broadway Joe Steak House   **33**
Broome Street Bar   **34**
Camelback & Central   **50**
Charley O's Bar & Grill & Bar   **66**
Christ Cella   **71**
Coach House   **76**
East-West   **98**
Elephant & Castle   **100**
Four Seasons   **108**
Frankie and Johnnie's   **111**
Gage & Tollner   **112**
Gloucester House   **123**
Hoexter's Market   **131**
Jane Street Seafood Café   **141**
J. G. Melon   **142**

Jim McMullen   **143**
Joanna   **144**
Joe Allen   **146**
Joe & Rose   **147**
K.O.'s   **151**
Lavin's   **156**
Lion's Head   **159**
La Louisiana   **160**
Manhattan Market   **169**
McFeely's   **174**
O'Neals' Baloon   **200**
Oren and Aretsky   **201**
Oyster Bar & Restaurant   **202**
Palm   **207**
Palm Too   **207**
P. J. Clarke's   **226**
Post House   **230**
Ravelled Sleave   **237**
Sardi's   **254**
Sea-Fare of the Aegean   **256**
Sloppy Louie's   **269**
Smith & Wollensky   **270**
Sparks   **272**
Sweets   **275**
Tavern on the Green   **281**
"21" Club   **291**
United States Steakhouse Co.   **296**

Wally's 308
Windows on the World 309

CHINESE

Canton 52
Cuisine of Szechuan 86
Home Village 132
Hunam 137
Mr. Chow 181
Phoenix Garden 220
Say Eng Look 255
Shun Lee Palace 259
Shun Lee West 260
Sichuan Pavilion 262
Silver Palace 264
Uncle Tai's Hunan Yuan 294

CZECHOSLOVAKIAN

Vašata 302

DIVERSE OLD AND NEW WORLD

Ambassador Grill 6
American Charcuterie 7
Berry's 21
Black Sheep 27
Bread Shop Café 31
Café des Artistes 39
Café Europa/La Brioche 42
Café New Amsterdam 46
Camelback & Central 50
Coach House 76
Four Seasons 108
Huberts 135
Joanna 144
Laughing Mountain Bar & Grill 153
Lavin's 156
Lion's Head 159
Manhattan Market 169
Maxwell's Plum 171
Michael Phillips 179
Oenophilia 198
Simon's 266
65 Irving Place 267
Table d'Hôte 279
Tavern on the Green 281
Tenth Street Café 283
"21" Club 291
Windows on the World 309

ENGLISH/IRISH

Charley O's Bar & Grill & Bar 66

FRENCH

Le Bistro 23
Box Tree 28
Café des Sports 41
Café 58 44
Café Loup 45
Café Un Deux Trois 49
La Caravelle 54
Casa Brasil 57
Chanterelle 62
Le Chantilly 64
Le Cherche-Midi 67
Chez Pascal 68
Le Cirque 72
Claude's 74
La Colombe d'Or 78
La Côte Basque 82
Le Cygne 87
Devon House 93
Four Seasons 108
La Gamelle 114
La Gauloise 117
Gibbon 118
Ginger Man 120
La Goulue 125
La Grenouille 127
Le Jacques Coeur 139
Le Lavandou 154
Lutèce 161
Madame Romaine de Lyon 164
Le Madrigal 165
La Maison Japonaise 167
Maxwell's Plum 171
La Métairie 178
Mon Paris 186
Odeon 196
Oenophilia 198
Palace 204
Le Paris Bistro 214
Paris Commune 215
La Petite Ferme 217
Le Petit Robert 219
La Place 227
Raoul's 235
Le Refuge 238
Le Relais 239
René Pujol 241

Restaurant Raphaël   243
La Ripaille   247
Tenth Street Café   283
Les Tournebroches   286
Tout Va Bien   287
La Tulipe   290
"21" Club   291
Le Veau d'Or   303
Wings   311
Woods   314

GREEK

Dimitri   96
Pantheon   210

HUNGARIAN

Csarda   85

INDIAN/PAKISTAN

India Pavilion   138
Mitali   183
Nirvana   193
Raga   233
Shezan   258

ITALIAN

Alfredo   3
Alfredo the Original of Rome   4
Angelo's   11
Ballato   18
Barbetta   19
Bruno   36
Cent'Anni   59
Danieli   90
Da Silvano   91
Divino   97
Elio's   101
Felidia   104
Fiorello's   106
Foro Italico   107
Grotta Azzurra   129
L'Hostaria del Bongustaio   133
Joe & Rose   147
Joe's   148
Lello   157
Marchi's   171
Il Menestrello   176

Il Monello   185
Il Mulino   188
Nadia's   189
Nicola's   190
Il Nido   192
Parioli, Romanissimo   212
Parma   216
Pietro's   222
Pinocchio   225
Il Ponte Vecchio   229
Primavera   231
Salta in Bocca   251
San Marco   252
Toscana   285
Uzies   297
Il Valletto   298
Vanessa   300
Wally's   308
Wise Maria   312

JAPANESE

Bizen   25
East-West   98
Gibbon   118
Gin Ray   122
Kitcho   150
La Maison Japonaise   167
Nishi   195
Sushiko   274

KOREAN

Arirang   14

LATIN AMERICAN

Bistro do Brasil   24
Cabana Carioca   38
Casa Brasil   57
El Gaucho   116
El Parador Café   211
Rio de Janeiro   246
Sabor   249

MIDDLE EASTERN

Andrée's Mediterranean Cuisine   9
Ararat   13
Balkan Armenian   17

xvi

RUSSIAN

Russian Tea Room 248
Ukrainian Restaurant 293

SANDWICHES/LIGHT FOOD

American Charcuterie 7
Broome Street Bar 34
Café Un Deux Trois 49
Charley O's Bar & Grill & Bar 66
Elephant & Castle 100
Fiorello's 106
Ginger Man 120
J. G. Melon 142
Joanna 144
Joe Allen 146
Lion's Head 159
Madame Romaine de Lyon 164
Maxwell's Plum 171
McFeely's 174
O'Neals' Baloon 200
P. J. Clarke's 226

SCANDINAVIAN

Copenhagen 81

SEAFOOD

East-West 98
Gage & Tollner 112
Gloucester House 123
Jane Street Seafood Café 141
Oyster Bar & Restaurant 202
Sea-Fare of the Aegean 256
Sloppy Louie's 269
Sweets 275

SPANISH/PORTUGUESE

Café San Martin 47
El Faro 102
Malaga 168
El Rincón de España 245
Tres Carabelas 289

STEAK HOUSES

Billy's 22
Bradley's 30
Broadway Joe Steak House 33

Charley O's Bar & Grill & Bar 66
Christ Cella 71
Frankie and Johnnie's 111
Gage & Tollner 112
Hoexter's Market 131
J. G. Melon 142
Jim McMullen 143
Joe Allen 146
Joe & Rose 147
K.O.'s 151
Oren and Aretsky 201
Palm 207
Palm Too 207
Pietro's 222
P. J. Clarke's 226
Post House 230
Smith & Wollensky 270
Sparks 272
"21" Club 291
United States Steakhouse Co. 296
Wally's 308

SWISS

Auberge Suisse 15
Chalet Suisse 60
Dézaley 94
Swiss Inn 277

VIENNESE

Vienna Park 305
Vienna 79 306

BY RATING

★★★★ EXCELLENT

Chanterelle **62**
La Grenouille **127**
Lutèce **161**

★★★ VERY GOOD

Auberge Suisse **15**
La Caravelle **54**
Chalet Suisse **60**
Le Chantilly **64**
Chez Pascal **68**
Christ Cella **71**
La Côte Basque **82**
Le Cygne **87**
Gloucester House **123**
Madame Romaine de Lyon **164**
Le Madrigal **165**
Mon Paris **186**
Il Nido **192**
Parioli, Romanissimo **212**
Phoenix Garden **220**
Pinocchio **225**
Raoul's **235**
Restaurant Raphaël **243**
Russian Tea Room **248**
Les Tournebroches **286**
La Tulipe **290**
Le Veau d'Or **303**

★★ GOOD

Alfredo **3**
Andrée's Mediterranean Cuisine **9**
Angelo's **11**
Arirang **14**
Ballato **18**
Le Bistro **23**
Bizen **25**
Box Tree **28**
Bread Shop Café **31**
Bruno **36**
Cabana Carioca **38**
Café des Artistes **39**
Café des Sports **41**
Café Europa/La Brioche **42**
Café 58 **44**
Café Loup **45**
Café New Amsterdam **46**
Canton **52**

Casa Brasil **57**
Cent'Anni **59**
Le Cherche-Midi **67**
La Colombe d'Or **78**
Copenhagen **81**
Cuisine of Szechuan **86**
Da Silvano **91**
Dézaley **94**
Dimitri **96**
East-West **98**
Elio's **101**
Felidia **104**
Foro Italico **107**
Four Seasons **108**
Gage & Tollner **112**
La Gamelle **114**
El Gaucho **116**
Gin Ray **122**
La Goulue **125**
Hoexter's Market **131**
Home Village **132**
Huberts **135**
India Pavilion **138**
Le Jacques Coeur **139**
Jane Street Seafood Café **141**
Joe's **148**
Kitcho **150**
Le Lavandou **154**
La Louisiana **160**
Manhattan Market **169**
Il Menestrello **176**
La Métairie **178**
Mitali **183**
Il Mulino **188**
Nirvana **193**
Odeon **196**
Oenophilia **198**
Oyster Bar & Restaurant **202**
Palace **204**
Le Paris Bistro **214**
Paris Commune **215**
La Petite Ferme **217**
Le Petit Robert **219**
Pietro's **222**
Il Ponte Vecchio **229**
Raga **233**
Le Refuge **238**
Le Relais **239**
René Pujol **241**
El Rincón de España **245**
Sabor **249**

Salta in Bocca **251**
San Marco **252**
Say Eng Look **255**
Sea-Fare of the Aegean **256**
Shezan **258**
Sichuan Pavilion **262**
Sushiko **274**
Swiss Inn **277**
Table d'Hôte **279**
Uncle Tai's Hunan Yuan **294**
Uzies **297**
Il Valletto **298**
Vašata **302**
Wally's **308**
Wise Maria **312**

★ GOOD (BUT NOT AS GOOD)

Ambassador Grill **6**
American Charcuterie **7**
Ararat **13**
Balkan Armenian **17**
Barbetta **19**
Berry's **21**
Billy's **22**
Bistro do Brasil **24**
Bradley's **30**
Broadway Joe Steak House **33**
Broome Street Bar **34**
Café San Martin **47**
Café Un Deux Trois **49**
Charley O's Bar & Grill & Bar **66**
Le Cirque **72**
Claude's **74**
Csarda **85**
Danieli **90**
Divino **97**
Elephant & Castle **100**
El Faro **102**
Fiorello's **106**
Frankie and Johnnie's **111**
La Gauloise **117**
Gibbon **118**
Ginger Man **120**
Grotta Azzurra **129**
L'Hostaria del Bongustaio **133**
Hunam **137**
Joanna **144**
Joe Allen **146**
Joe & Rose **147**
K.O.'s **151**
Laughing Mountain Bar & Grill **153**

Lavin's **156**
Lello **157**
Lion's Head **159**
La Maison Japonaise **167**
Malaga **168**
Maxwell's Plum **171**
McFeely's **174**
Nishi **195**
Palm **207**
Palm Too **207**
Pamir **209**
Pantheon **210**
Parma **216**
La Place **227**
Primavera **231**
Le Refuge **238**
Rio de Janeiro **246**
La Ripaille **247**
Shun Lee Palace **259**
Silver Palace **264**
Simon's **266**
65 Irving Place **267**
Smith & Wollensky **270**
Sweets **275**
Tenth Street Café **283**
Toscana **285**
Tout Va Bien **287**
Tres Carabelas **289**
Ukrainian Restaurant **293**
Vienna Park **305**
Vienna 79 **306**
Windows on the World **309**

●ACCEPTABLE

Black Sheep **27**
Camelback & Central **50**
Coach House **76**
Devon House **93**
J. G. Melon **142**
Jim McMullen **143**
Marchi's **171**
Michael Phillips **179**
Il Monello **185**
Nadia's **189**
Nicola's **190**
O'Neals' Baloon **200**
Oren and Aretsky **201**
El Parador Café **211**
Post House **230**
Ravelled Sleave **237**
Shun Lee West **260**

Sloppy Louie's **269**
Sparks **272**
"21" Club **291**
Vanessa **300**
Wings **311**
Woods **314**

○ **UNACCEPTABLE**

Alfredo the Original of Rome **4**
Mr. Chow **181**
P. J. Clarke's **226**
Sardi's **254**
Tavern on the Green **281**
United States Steakhouse Co. **296**

BY NEIGHBORHOOD

DOWNTOWN, INCLUDING LITTLE ITALY AND SOHO

Angelo's **11**
Ballato **18**
Berry's **21**
Bizen **25**
Bread Shop Café **31**
Broome Street Bar **34**
Canton **52**
Chanterelle **62**
Elephant & Castle **100**
La Gamelle **114**
Grotta Azzurra **129**
Home Village **132**

Laughing Mountain Bar & Grill **153**
Odeon **196**
Phoenix Garden **220**
Raoul's **235**
Say Eng Look **255**
Silver Palace **264**
Sloppy Louie's **269**
Sweets **275**
Windows on the World **309**
Wings **311**
Wise Maria **312**

GREENWICH VILLAGE, INCLUDING THE EAST VILLAGE

Black Sheep **27**
Bradley's **30**
Café Loup **45**
Café New Amsterdam **46**
Cent'Anni **59**
Coach House **76**
Da Silvano **91**
Dézaley **94**
East-West **98**
El Faro **102**
El Gaucho **116**
La Gauloise **117**
Jane Street Seafood Café **141**
Joe's **148**
K.O.'s **151**

Lion's Head **159**
La Métairie **178**
Mitali **183**
Il Mulino **188**
Le Paris Bistro **214**
Paris Commune **215**
Le Petit Robert **219**
Il Ponte Vecchio **229**
El Rincón de España **245**
La Ripaille **247**
Sabor **249**
Tenth Street Café **283**
La Tulipe **290**
Ukrainian Restaurant **293**
Vanessa **300**

EAST SIDE, 14TH STREET TO 33RD STREET

Balkan Armenian **17**
La Colombe d'Or **78**
Cuisine of Szechuan **86**
Huberts **135**
Joanna **144**

La Louisiana **160**
Marchi's **171**
Mon Paris **186**
65 Irving Place **267**

EAST SIDE, 34TH STREET TO 41ST STREET

Ambassador Grill **6**
Ararat **13**
La Maison Japonaise **167**

El Parador Café **211**
Salta in Bocca **251**
Tres Carabelas **289**

EAST SIDE, 42ND STREET TO 50TH STREET

Box Tree 28
Chalet Suisse 60
Christ Cella 71
Gin Ray 122
Gloucester House 123
Hunam 137
Joe & Rose 147
Lutèce 161
Oyster Bar & Restaurant 202
Palm 207
Palm Too 207
Pietro's 222
Sichuan Pavilion 262
Smith & Wollensky 270
Sparks 272
Swiss Inn 277

EAST SIDE, 51ST STREET TO 59TH STREET

Alfredo the Original of Rome 4
Auberge Suisse 15
Billy's 22
Le Bistro 23
Bruno 36
Café Europa/La Brioche 42
Café 58 44
Le Chantilly 64
Le Cherche-Midi 67
La Côte Basque 82
Le Cygne 87
Felidia 104
Four Seasons 108
La Grenouille 127
L'Hostaria del Bongustaio 133
India Pavilion 138
Lello 157
Le Madrigal 165
Manhattan Market 169
Il Menestrello 176
Michael Phillips 179
Mr. Chow 181
Nadia's 189
Il Nido 192
Palace 204
P. J. Clarke's 226
Shun Lee Palace 259
Toscana 285
Les Tournebroches 286

EAST SIDE, 60TH STREET TO 72ND STREET

Le Cirque 72
La Goulue 125
Le Lavandou 154
Madame Romaine de Lyon 164
Maxwell's Plum 171
La Petite Ferme 217
La Place 227
Post House 230
Le Relais 239
Uncle Tai's Hunan Yuan 294
Il Valletto 298
Le Veau d'Or 303
Vienna Park 305
Woods 314

EAST SIDE, ABOVE 72ND STREET

Andrée's Mediterranean Cuisine 9
Bistro do Brasil 24
Café San Martin 47
Camelback & Central 50
Casa Brasil 57
Chez Pascal 68
Claude's 74
Csarda 85
Devon House 93
Divino 97
Elio's 101
Gibbon 118
Hoexter's Market 131
Le Jacques Coeur 139
J. G. Melon 142
Jim McMullen 143
Malaga 168
Il Monello 185
Nicola's 190
Oren and Aretsky 201

Pamir 209
Parioli, Romanissimo 212
Parma 216
Pinocchio 225
Primavera 231
Ravelled Sleave 237

Le Refuge 238
Table d'Hôte 279
Uzies 297
Vašata 302
Vienna 79 306

WEST SIDE, 14TH STREET TO 41ST STREET

Danieli 90
Foro Italico 107

Lavin's 156
McFeely's 174

WEST SIDE, 42ND STREET TO 50TH STREET

Barbetta 19
Broadway Joe Steak House 33
Cabana Carioca 38
Café Un Deux Trois 49
Charley O's Bar & Grill & Bar 66
Frankie and Johnnie's 111

Joe Allen 146
Kitcho 150
Pantheon 210
Raga 233
Sardi's 254
Wally's 308

WEST SIDE, 51ST STREET TO 59TH STREET

Alfredo 3
American Charcuterie 7
Arirang 14
Café des Sports 41
La Caravelle 54
Copenhagen 81
Nirvana 193
René Pujol 241
Restaurant Raphaël 243

Rio de Janeiro 246
Russian Tea Room 248
San Marco 252
Sea-Fare of the Aegean 256
Shezan 258
Sushiko 274
Tout Va Bien 287
"21" Club 291
United States Steakhouse Co. 296

WEST SIDE, ABOVE 59TH STREET

Café des Artistes 39
Dimitri 96
Fiorello's 106
Ginger Man 120
Nishi 195

Oenophilia 198
O'Neals' Baloon 200
Shun Lee West 260
Simon's 266
Tavern on the Green 281

BROOKLYN

Gage & Tollner 112

OPEN ON SUNDAY

Alfredo the Original of Rome **4**
Ambassador Grill **6**
Angelo's **11**
Ararat **13**
Arirang **14**
Auberge Suisse **15**
Berry's **21**
Billy's **22**
Bistro do Brasil **24**
Bizen **25**
Black Sheep **27**
Box Tree **28**
Bradley's **30**
Bread Shop Café **31**
Broadway Joe Steak House **33**
Broome Street Bar **34**
Cabana Carioca **38**
Café des Artistes **39**
Café des Sports **41**
Café 58 **44**
Café New Amsterdam **46**
Café San Martin **47**
Café Un Deux Trois **49**
Camelback & Central **50**
Canton **52**
Cent'Anni **59**
Chez Pascal **68**
Coach House **76**
Csarda **85**
Cuisine of Szechuan **86**
Danieli **90**
Da Silvano **91**
Devon House **93**
Dimitri **96**
Divino **97**
East-West **98**
Elephant & Castle **100**
Elio's **101**
El Faro **102**
Fiorello's **106**
Gage & Tollner **112**
La Gamelle **114**
El Gaucho **116**
La Gauloise **117**
Ginger Man **120**
Gloucester House **123**
Grotta Azzurra **129**
Hoexter's Market **131**
Home Village **132**
Hunam **137**

India Pavilion **138**
Le Jacques Coeur **139**
Jane Street Seafood Café **141**
J. G. Melon **142**
Jim McMullen **143**
Joanna **144**
Joe Allen **146**
Joe's **148**
Kitcho **150**
K.O.'s **151**
Laughing Mountain Bar & Grill **153**
Lion's Head **159**
La Louisiana **160**
Madame Romaine de Lyon **164**
La Maison Japonaise **167**
Malaga **168**
Manhattan Market **169**
Maxwell's Plum **171**
McFeely's **174**
La Métairie **178**
Michael Phillips **179**
Mr. Chow **181**
Mitali **183**
Il Mulino **188**
Nicola's **190**
Nirvana **193**
Nishi **195**
Odeon **196**
Oenophilia **198**
O'Neals' Baloon **200**
Oren and Aretsky **201**
Pamir **209**
Le Paris Bistro **214**
Paris Commune **215**
Parma **216**
Le Petit Robert **219**
Phoenix Garden **220**
Pinocchio **225**
P. J. Clarke's **226**
La Place **227**
Il Ponte Vecchio **229**
Post House **230**
Primavera **231**
Raga **233**
Raoul's **235**
Ravelled Sleave **237**
Le Relais **239**
El Rincón de España **245**
Rio de Janeiro **246**
Russian Tea Room **248**

Sabor **249**
Sardi's **254**
Say Eng Look **255**
Sea-Fare of the Aegean **256**
Shun Lee Palace **259**
Shun Lee West **260**
Sichuan Pavilion **262**
Silver Palace **264**
Simon's **266**
65 Irving Place **267**
Smith & Wollensky **270**
Tavern on the Green **281**

Tenth Street Café **283**
Tres Carabelas **289**
La Tulipe **290**
Ukrainian Restaurant **293**
Uncle Tai's Hunan Yuan **294**
Uzies **297**
Vanessa **300**
Vašata **302**
Vienna 79 **306**
Windows on the World **309**
Wings **311**
Wise Maria **312**

OPEN LATE (until midnight or later each night the restaurant is open for business)

Ambassador Grill **6**
American Charcuterie **7**
Barbetta **19**
Berry's **21**
Bradley's **30**
Broadway Joe Steak House **33**
Broome Street Bar **34**
Café Loup **45**
Café Un Deux Trois **49**
Camelback & Central **50**
Charley O's Bar & Grill & Bar **66**
Dimitri **96**
Divino **97**
Elephant & Castle **100**
Elio's **101**
El Faro **102**
Fiorello's **106**
Frankie and Johnnie's **111**
La Gamelle **114**
El Gaucho **116**
Ginger Man **120**
Grotta Azzurra **129**
Hoexter's Market **131**
Home Village **132**
J. G. Melon **142**
Jim McMullen **143**
Joanna **144**

Joe Allen **146**
Laughing Mountain Bar & Grill **153**
Lion's Head **159**
La Louisiana **160**
Malaga **168**
Maxwell's Plum **171**
McFeely's **174**
Mitali **183**
Nicola's **190**
Nirvana **193**
Nishi **195**
Odeon **196**
O'Neals' Baloon **200**
Oren and Aretsky **201**
Parma **216**
P. J. Clarke's **226**
Primavera **231**
Raoul's **235**
Russian Tea Room **248**
Sardi's **254**
Simon's **266**
Tavern on the Green **281**
"21" Club **291**
Vanessa **300**
Wings **311**
Wise Maria **312**

SUITABLE (by reason of economy/menu/accommodations) FOR LARGE FAMILY GROUPS

Alfredo the Original of Rome   4
Canton   52
Gage & Tollner   112
Home Village   132
Jim McMullen   143
Malaga   168
Marchi's   171
McFeely's   174

Oyster Bar & Restaurant   202
Raga   233
Say Eng Look   255
Shun Lee Palace   259
Shun Lee West   260
Sichuan Pavilion   262
Ukrainian Restaurant   293
Uncle Tai's Hunan Yuan   294

OUTDOOR DINING AND ENCLOSED GARDENS

Barbetta   19
Café Loup   45
Da Silvano   91
Fiorello's   106
Lutèce   161

Le Paris Bistro   214
La Place   227
Le Relais   239
65 Irving Place   267
Tavern on the Green   281

ENCLOSED SIDEWALK CAFES

Ginger Man   120
Maxwell's Plum   171

O'Neals' Baloon   200

BRING YOUR OWN WINE (or whatever)

Andrée's Mediterranean Cuisine   9
Canton   52
Casa Brasil   57
Cent'Anni   59
Cuisine of Szechuan   86
East-West   98

Home Village   132
India Pavilion   138
Phoenix Garden   220
Silver Palace   264
Sloppy Louie's   269
Table d'Hôte   279

The Restaurants of New York
1982-1983 Edition

★★ ALFREDO

240 Central Park South
LUNCH, MONDAY TO FRIDAY; DINNER, MONDAY TO SATURDAY. CLOSED SUNDAY.
Reservations, 246-7050.
Credit cards: AE, CB, DC, MC, V.
Expensive.

This kind of overstuffed posh is so passé it may be up for a revival: pearly banquettes, mirrored columns, pleated gauze curtains that are framed in tied-back drapes and carved valances. The leather is held to the armchairs by brass upholstery nails. The thick carpeting simulates marble. Some walls are faced with floor-to-ceiling wine racks, others are covered with elaborately patterned wallpaper. From overhead, gentle light falls through panels of frosted glass that are built into the ceiling—they look like pieces from a jigsaw puzzle, but are meant to suggest clouds.

The lady who checks your coat is better-dressed than you are, in her smashing little frock. Her hair is drawn severely back. Her makeup is impeccable. The minute you meet her you feel frumpy. The captains and waiters are in black-and-white formals. Only your host himself is of sufficient eminence to look a little sporty. He is suave, silver-haired, in gray slacks and a double-breasted blazer with brass buttons. He will put you in mind of the ingénue's older lover in Italian movies of a couple of decades ago. Now and again he embraces an arriving female guest, careful not to disarrange her coiffure. Of course, jackets are required. A rumpled sweater, however, so long as it is on the back of a friend of the house, is taken for a sport coat. And the times being what they are, jeans are overlooked.

This is the kind of place in which it is well to be known. You will not otherwise be rudely treated, but it is possible to sit with your menu for fifteen minutes, without so much as a drink, while a dozen members of the floor staff hover around a tenor. (Alfredo is favored by certain members of the Metropolitan Opera.) But once you have spent well here a couple of times, you will be treated with the kind of genuine respect that only money can buy. Alfredo gets a crowd that has purchased a lot of that kind of love—pairs of guys occupying large booths and talking big deals; the staff of the Italian consulate establishing good relations with the community; heavyweights from ABC.

They favor the marvelous stinging sauce of sour capers and strong mustard that dresses this establishment's carpaccio, a five-inch circle of tender, raw, just-sliced filet mignon. They like the frutta di mare al vino bianco (an order for two is the minimum), in which fresh squid, scallops, and mussels and tiny clams in their shells are served in a salty broth that is fortified with an abundance of chopped garlic and made fragrant with a green blizzard of fresh parsley—a terrific appetizer that commands a mere $18 for two. The menu describes the crostini di polenta con Fontina as a specialty of the house. The sandwich-like logs of cornmeal and cheese are notable more for their hot, moist lightness, for the creaminess of the melted-cheese filling and for the delicate, almost fugitive crispness of the pale-brown crust than for any vividness of cheese or grain flavor—still, a good dish. Be advised that if you wish to begin with pasta, half-orders are available only with meat sauce or tomato sauce. But if you have a companion who will eat what you eat, share a full order of spaghetti al salmone. Pasta-and-salmon dishes are suddenly showing up all over town, but few of them work as well as this one—the smoked salmon is puréed into a creamy, garlic-flavored sauce that clings to the tender noodles. Better still is the spaghettini al Stefano, in which the noodles are served in a black sauce of olives and anchovies, garlic and oil—it is sharp, heady, rousing.

Alfredo's sautéed shrimp are sweet, crisped, seemingly saturated with butter and garlic, garnished with a couple of fresh mussels in their shells. Its good chicken forestiera consists of morsels of nicely browned, moist chicken in a well-seasoned wine sauce. But if you want the best chicken, you will need a partner again, for the chicken in beer is a whole bird, which makes up an order for two. It is prepared from scratch, so you must wait about half an hour for it, whereupon it is wheeled to your table and carved. The bird has picked up a good bit of brisk beer flavor, which heightens the taste of the pale meat. The tangy beer sauce is enriched by the juices of the chicken. The loin of veal that the menu promises will come in a "paper bag" actually arrives in a little puffed-up pillowcase fashioned of aluminum foil. The balloon is cut open, steam escapes and you are served the pale, tender, very moist and slightly fibrous eyes of two veal chops in a dark and winy sauce. The dish is garnished with almost weightless fried zucchini. Do not conclude that this kitchen is a whiz with veal. Its version of veal alla zingara is of good enough veal, but the other ingredients—tongue, mushrooms, peppers —have not been cooked with the meat. They have been combined with it so late, in fact, that they reach you still cold. The lightly floured and sautéed sweetbreads are as airy as soufflés. The four slices of loin of lamb are deliciously flavored with garlic and idiotically surmounted by canned artichoke hearts. Presumably no one orders à la carte vegetables here. They, and most of the vegetable garnishes—other than that fried zucchini—are delivered, most of the time, in a condition that can be achieved only by hours of exposure to a Turkish bath or a steam table.

No mention of cheese on the menu, but some flinty, aged Parmesan can usually be had, the kind of which a little will hold you—it is sharp and will clear your ears. Of the desserts, Alfredo's cheese cake is a hybrid of ricotta and cream cheese—it is smooth, solid but airy, lightly lemoned, its browned top like a zest to the sugary cake. The rum cakes, zuppas, and chocolate confections are the usual excessive sweets. There are ice-cream items, and there are dishes that arrive flaming.

○ ALFREDO THE ORIGINAL OF ROME

153 East 53rd Street
LUNCH AND DINNER.
Reservations, 371–3367.
Credit cards: AE, CB, DC, MC, V.
Medium-priced.

Alfredo the Original of Rome may in fact, as it claims, be the New York branch of a venerable Roman restaurant, but the food it purveys, albeit unmistakably Italian, is in a sense American, for it duplicates faithfully the red-and-dead cooking of the Main Street Italian restaurants you would do well to avoid in cities of 50,000 or more in the eastern United States. The place has become vastly popular from the sad day of its grand opening, for it is the perfect attraction for tourists and for what certain Manhattan restaurant staffs refer to as BBQ people (Bronx, Brooklyn and Queens). The

Original, as it will hereafter be called, is the perfect out-of-towner restaurant. It flatters visitors with the titillating suggestion that they are here embarking on a culinary adventure of Roman-holiday proportions, while serving them precisely what they have been eating on Saturday nights at Joe's Place ever since they started dating during their high school days.

This is much the largest restaurant in the Citicorp Building, but search as you may within its L-shaped vastness, you will find little that is Italian about its appearance beyond the Italian face of the host (of the restaurant in Rome) smiling out at you from dozens of photos of his famous customers and him.

You are greeted by one of the young hostesses. She does not so much lead you to your table as join you in the search for one. She and you wander over brown carpeting; through narrow, clogged aisles that run between lengthy rows of smallish linened tables and foursquare modern oak chairs; under oak-beamed ceilings; to, if you are lucky, a table beside a wall, far away from the congestion around the constantly swinging doors that lead to the kitchen—an area of particular commotion that has been set aside for the most hapless misfortunates who chance on this place. The Original is an eating factory (done up in California Motel), but there are kinks in the assembly line.

The specialty of the house, of course, is fettuccine all'Alfredo, made, if publicity releases mean anything, according to a seventy-four-year-old family recipe. By the age of seventy-four, it must be concluded, even a recipe may not remember so well, for one night the sauce that graces your noodles is barely moist, the ground cheese gravelly, so that the pepper you grind on bounces about on the pasta like jacks on a sidewalk; but on another occasion the sauce is lavalike, thick and buttery. Either way, this does appear to be the best dish in the house, the wide fettuccine firm but tender, the sauce made with fresh, sharp cheese. The linguine with white clam sauce, though made with similarly decent pasta, would be improved by the substitution of tasteless canned clams for whatever it is they are using—the dish is strong without having any flavor, surely not that of fresh clams from the sea or garlic recently out of the ground.

A handful of veal dishes are offered, and they offer nothing: a saltimbocca of harsh ham that is glued to tasteless veal with an herb paste; veal parmigiana that would be leaden even if it were not breaded, which it is; a scaloppine alla pizzaiola in which this establishment's tasteless veal is just a carrier for this establishment's undistinguished red sauce; and a scaloppine alla cacciatora that is abundant with mushrooms that are utterly without the flavor of the original article.

The rum cake and cheese cake taste like something you would find inside a chocolate-covered candy, and the gran coppa di macedonia all'Alfredo like something you would find inside a Del Monte can.

Pastas are the only first courses, and the half orders are substantial.

★ AMBASSADOR GRILL

1 United Nations Plaza (First Avenue and 44th Street)
LUNCH AND DINNER.
Reservations, 355–3400.
Credit cards: AE, CB, DC, MC, V.
Very expensive.

The Ambassador Grill, at the United Nations Plaza Hotel, is a design descendant of the Four Seasons—luxurious comfort in a setting of glinting, hard-edged modernity, stark and posh, striking and familiar, like a big black limousine. The room is dark, with dark walls and charcoal-gray mirrors; the floor is of large marble squares, white and deep, deep green; and the banquettes are of burgundy velvet, cushy as the fur of a fat cat. On each table there is white linen, polished crystal, a long-stemmed flower in a slender glass vase; at each place there is a broad copper serving plate that shines in the glow of the candles that make each table an island of light. Overhead, an arrangement of glass, mirrors and ivory frames reflects itself and the scene below in an infinitely repeating pattern that recedes upward and away from view—an inverted, glittering geometric cascade. Very romantic.

First you are brought the bread basket, which is an ordinary thing in itself. But the breads and rolls that are stuffed into it prop up a standing matzoh the size of the *Daily News,* creating little structures that look like unleavened, single-masted junks—this is an international restaurant.

The Ambassador Grill, which was a dreadful restaurant when it opened, has advanced to a point at which it now does simple things well—on occasion, very well. You get good, fresh oysters and unimpeachable Scotch smoked salmon. But those oysters, when converted to oysters Rockefeller, are little more than a warm juxtaposition of oysters and spinach, neither doing anything for the other. And the cucumber soup, though cool, creamy and bright, and prettily adorned with a caviar-topped crouton, is undone by an excess of dried tarragon.

An excellent sirloin steak of tender beef accurately prepared is served with a perfectly baked potato and a Béarnaise sauce that is thick, herby and rich. And the broiled prawns, done, happily, with their shells on, are buttery and fragrantly garlicked. But the roast duck is little more than nice enough, the skin a bit limp, the orange sauce like liquored candy. And the poached bass (you get a serving the size of a baby's hand), though of fresh fish that is flaky and moist, is accompanied by a dill sauce that is absurdly overpowering.

If you have eaten simply thus far, keep it up, with ice cream or berries, and avoid assiduously the cakes, which manage to be heavy without being rich.

The United Nations provides an international set that crowds the long bar in the handsome cocktail lounge. There is a striking display of illuminated bottles against a mirrored wall. A grand piano is tinkled by a cocktail pianist who concentrates on reverent pop—much from Rodgers and Hammerstein's holy-as-hell period; and at least three times a night the clowns are sent in.

★ AMERICAN CHARCUTERIE

51 West 52nd Street
LUNCH AND DINNER. CLOSED SUNDAY.
Reservations, 751-5152.
Credit cards: AE, CB, DC, MC, V.
Medium-priced.

The American Charcuterie provides midtown Manhattan with a Jewish delicatessen while promoting the notion that what its customers are really sampling is an international array of cultural experiences. Come one, come all! You don't have to be Jewish to love the Charcuterie's grilled pastrami and mozzarella on onion rye. All it takes is $6.95.

The front page of the restaurant's menu proclaims that the American Charcuterie is Italian, Polish, Hungarian, Swedish, Jewish, Irish, Russian, Greek, French, Scottish and German (as well as American). But of these dozen national origins (one a creed, actually), there are three that cannot reasonably be connected with anything on the lengthy menu, while several others are represented by only an item or two. Of course the true sire of this restaurant is not a nationality or a religion at all. It is Zabar's—with a few genes thrown in by Ratner's and the Second Avenue Deli. There is very little here that you cannot obtain in one of those places.

But a way had to be found to get the goyim to come. Oh, sure, non-Semites have been sold for years on Nova Scotia salmon and bagels for Sunday brunch. But Hebrew food any day of the week?

So the marketing men were called in, and the big meeting was held, and the creative thoughts and ideas were shuttled back and forth. But all anyone could come up with was the direct approach, simple-minded at that, false at that. Let's pretend the place is not Jewish at all was the idea. Let's call it the *American* Delicatessen. But that would not quite do. For, especially in New York, there are many who feel—some bitterly—that the word "American" has been worn down to a point at which it has taken on a certain commonality of meaning with the word "Judaic." And so, instead of the word "Delicatessen," it was decided to use the word "Charcuterie." A charcuterie, you understand, is a pork store.

The Charcuterie is a great high-ceilinged, dumbbell-shaped establishment that extends clear through a block-long Sixth Avenue skyscraper. The 52nd Street room houses the massive three-sided bar, high circular tables for stand-up drinking and sandwich eating, smaller tables that are in use mainly at lunchtime. This is the room to which you enter, and when you do so at night, you may think the place is deserted. Running north from the bar is a long skinny room and a row of cushy booths, partially glass-enclosed, on one side; on the other side is a long white marble counter, on which are displayed, on ice, the innumerable cold foods that are much of the stock-in-trade of this place. The 53rd Street room is where dinner is served, hefty armchairs surrounding tables that are covered with white linen. Walls of dark stone or brass rise like cliffs on all sides. The soaring windows, around three stories high, are shaded with delicate chains. Huge abstract paintings hang on the walls. Palm trees stand in big pots and reach halfway to the ceiling. A large suspended mobile of big steel spangles and steel rods seems to float in midair. And glowing lamps of green glass hang low over the tables (a few of them shrewdly positioned to shine directly into unprotected eyes). Despite these efforts to break up the space, the room retains much of its grand and imposing starkness. It could do with a little more of that, and a lot less of the misplaced art.

Within this lofty room, some quite earthy food: borscht, purplish pink, cool and creamy, sweet and sour, crisp beets at the bottom of the bowl, a dish of thick and velvety sour cream on the side; a sometimes available gazpacho, the puréed vegetable soup of Spain (this is a guest appearance for Spain—"Spanish" is not on the front of the menu), which is thick, pleasantly textured, polished with oil, spicy—and easy on the garlic, which will please some, distress others. Earthier still is the chopped chicken liver, a chunky version, not a mousse, flecked with bits of hard-cooked egg and coarsely chopped parsley, bound in fat, served with matzohs and raw onions. The herring in mustard dill sauce is at once tart and sugary, but its sweetness almost overpowers the mild sauce. Much better is the matjes herring, the shiny brown slab of salty fish as smooth as oil, firm and tender, its combination of richness and sharpness almost confusing—wonderful food to eat with bread and butter. Texas purists will quarrel (or shoot it out) about this establishment's so-called Texas chili—most of the beef in the dish is ground almost to a mush, the chunks of beef are but few, and the dish is lightly studded with irrelevant beans. The chili is spicy and strong but short on flavor—the garnishes of sour cream and minced onions are essential.

Cured fish, of course: silken Nova Scotia salmon, tender and delicate, perfect as is, a little more exciting if you squeeze on lemon, a little more mellifluous if you moisten it with oil; but to eat it with onions, or with cream cheese between slices of a coarse roll, is to advertise that you are not in touch with what you are having. The saltier smoked salmons are here too, and they are fine if you like the loud stuff. And there is Scottish smoked salmon as well, though what the Charcuterie is serving is much stronger than the light, almost fugitive pink fish Scotland sometimes exports. Sturgeon is soapy stuff. Some people love it. It is here, it is slightly dry, lacking a little of the usual oil. The big absentee is smoked whitefish, which, like the proverbial onion, would be a delicacy if only it cost a whole lot more.

New York's deli staples are pastrami, tongue and corned beef. The Charcuterie's pastrami is coarse, almost harsh; its tongue is bland and dry, as if it were machine-sliced in advance; only the corned beef is about right—moist, fatted, resilient but tender. The meats are served as platters or assorted platters; or as plain sandwiches or complicated ones. The sandwich section of the menu lists the restaurant's most imaginative offerings, well-chosen combinations of ingredients rarely found together between slices of bread. One of the big winners is No. 10: grilled Gorgonzola, Naples salami and red peppers—the cheese becomes really strong when it is heated up, the meat adds a little gaminess and a bit of texture, and the red peppers add slippery sweetness and strength. Very good on French bread.

The chicken in the pot consists of well-seasoned broth, powerfully flavored of fat, but not fatty, substantial chunks of moist chicken that has lots of flavor for a chicken of these times, vegetables in among the sections of meat. The dish is, unfortunately, served up foolishly, so packed into a tight little tureen that you can only insert the wrong end of the ladle.

Avoid resolutely the lasagna, when that is the pasta of the day—the noodles may be as hard as flint around the edges, waterlogged and sodden near the center.

Each day a different sausage platter is offered. The servings are gigantic, and they are supplemented with hillocks of good rice. The bratwurst is bland but satisfying; the chorizos spicy but somehow lacking in meaty character. The sausages are inundated in sautéed peppers and onions in a light tomato sauce.

There are a number of good desserts, so skip rapidly by the cheese blintzes, which consist of greasy casings around cheese that has been cooked to mush. Have instead the apple walnut pie—simply a sweet apple crumb pie on a well-baked crust, with nuts in among the chunks of fruit. Or have the so-called Old Fashioned strawberry shortcake (which is really New Fangled, for it is made with sponge cake rather than shortcake), a giant three-sided block of layers of cake and cream under ripe berries. The bread pudding is too much bread and too little pudding, but the white bourbon sauce amounts to an after-dinner drink. The big winner is one of the two house cheese cakes, specifically the one called S & S—as solid, sugary, rich and uncompromisingly weighty a cake as you will find, with no such gestures to the delicate as a graham-cracker crust, or preserves at the bottom, or fruits on the top.

★★ ANDRÉE'S MEDITERRANEAN CUISINE

354 East 74th Street
DINNER, TUESDAY TO SATURDAY. CLOSED SUNDAY AND MONDAY.
Reservations, 249-6619.
No credit cards.
No liquor.
Expensive.

Good cooking is all that Andrée's is about. It is not quite a restaurant otherwise. You enter to the downstairs hall of an old, well-preserved brownstone, from which a stairway leads, presumably, to the bedrooms above. You turn left, through a broad portal, into what would be the living room if this were a one-family dwelling, but which is instead the dining room of this quasi-restaurant. At the front a couple of small sash windows are open to the quiet noises of the street, and at the back a wall of shutters shields you from the sights, but not the sounds, of the kitchen—the clatter of dishes and the whirr of the Cuisinart are noticeable constants on quiet nights here. Two large rugs hang on the long brick wall. A chest of drawers between the front windows is adorned with a candelabrum and flowers; a shelf at the back with still more flowers, in a pretty pail, a bowl of fruit, and other homey odds and ends. There are only nine tables, most of them small and covered with white linen, but one of them is a large, oblong, unlinened, of dark wood, in the Spanish style, which can easily accommodate six or even eight. The ceiling is low, the acoustics are superb and when business is slow, as it sometimes is, a conversation across the room is as intimately audible as a conversation across a living room anywhere. It takes a full house to dispel the impression that you are an interloper eating in someone else's abode. But Andrée has her following—a highly civilized and international set they are—and when they show up in numbers, this odd little place can be cheerful.

You are waited on by young women of approximately high-school age who, it is said, are scions of the boss. They are cheerful and willing, but never inform you in advance which dishes are not available (on any given night Andrée prepares fewer than all the dishes she lists), and it is entirely possible to study the menu, make your choices and not learn until you place your order that you have been wasting your time.

But the food—most of it of the Near East, some of it French—is almost all worth the bother. From France: a velvety salmon mousse of fresh red fish, of buttery richness and consistency, coated with a smooth, cool mayonnaise. From elsewhere: baba ghannoush and hommus, the well-known eggplant and chickpea pastes, respectively, light and delicately spiced and yet substantial, with all the sparkle of food just made; mushrooms à la Grecque, the tired old dish in sprightly good form, firm mushrooms in their marinade of superb oil, lightly touched with Eastern spices and herbs; tabbouleh, the mixed salad of crushed wheat, parsley and scallions, in a lively dressing of oil and fresh lemon; and the hot kobeba or falafel, crusty little deep-fried cakes, the one filled with a moist pine-nut filling, the other with seasoned chickpeas.

As part of your dinner you are entitled to soup. There is a soup of the night, but the one to have is the always available mulokheyyah, a marvelous Egyptian chicken broth that is thick with the rare herb of the title (something between spinach and mint), studded with bits of chicken and pungently seasoned—a striking dish.

Seafood appears to be the least of Andrée's enthusiasms, for the shrimp Alexandria, though touched with lemon and exotic spices, is hardly more than shrimp in tomato sauce, like Italian food with a slight accent; and the striped bass Corfu, which is the size, shape and color of a single blintz, is a kind of flaky fish tart, prettily browned and light, but insubstantial, and almost devoid of the quality of seafood. However, the couscous here is a terrific stew: big slabs of lamb, moist, coming away from the bone; sections of juicy hot chicken; turnips in large slices; squash and chickpeas and carrots; sweet black raisins and onions—the flavor of each element vivid, a mound of gentle grain a foil to the meats and vegetables. A fiery black paste is served with the dish as a pungent sharpener.

Andrée makes a good rack of lamb, the herbed and spiced breading with which the meat is coated cooked to a dry crispness in the roasting—the meat is pink and tender and strong. A dish given as tournedos Izmir consists of two slices of tender filet mignon around a dark and sweet eggplant paste that is studded with crisp slices of zucchini —good food. And she manages to convert Cornish hen into a good dish—the roasted bird is filled with a sweet-spiced, nubbly and steamy stuffing of nuts and grain and raisins—the bird itself is about as moist as Cornish hen ever manages to be.

The mocha crème royale is a sharp, sweet and very creamy coffee ice cream studded with bits of black chocolate. The baklava is delicate, lightly oiled, the pastry wrapped around a perfumed filling of honey and pistachio nuts. You may find the basboussa a bit too much like your basic corn muffin, but the chocolate walnut torte is fine—a fresh, strongly flavored chocolate nut cake. And the fruit salad does not come out of a can —the stewed apricots and prunes and raisins are served in a winy rose water syrup that is populated with pistachio nuts and pine nuts and slivered almonds.

Special main courses may be ordered in advance for groups of four or more.

★★ ANGELO'S

146 Mulberry Street (near Grand Street)
LUNCH AND DINNER. CLOSED MONDAY.
Reservations, WO 6–1277.
Credit cards: AE, CB, DC, MC, V.
Medium-priced.

Just inside the door is a hatcheck facility, the simple appearance of which is no clue to the turmoil that can develop around it. We have here an aisle, three feet wide, formed by the door and the wall opposite. Mounted on the wall are coat hooks—six feet of them, about fifty in all. About fifteen inches from the wall (we are still in the three-foot aisle) there is a Formica counter, long as the row of hooks, and six inches deep. The condition between the counter and the wall, when the coat hooks are all in use, is one of not enough space for anything more, certainly not for the plump young thing whose post is, technically, between the counter and the coats. (Conditions on the other side of the counter are equally dense when customers arrive in groups of more than two normal or one stout. And as customers not only arrive here but also leave, the scene is frequently one of direct confrontation, unalleviated by right-of-way guidelines.) What happens, of course, is that the attendant must contort herself wickedly to hang or retrieve a coat. As she stretches, her short sweater rises above her skirt, revealing a band of well-filled skin. This attracts the attention of the waiter at the front table, whose customers, in a moment, find themselves giving their order to empty air because the waiter has stuck his pencil behind his ear, to free his right hand to caress the revealed skin as he shares a whispered country thought with the harried soubrette. When things ease up she comes out from behind her counter and parks on a chair near the door—here she scratches herself a lot (perhaps she is allergic to coats) and pretends to read the *News*. The natty host (he constantly buttons and unbuttons his velvet jacket) keeps her company with suggestions about what they might undertake after work. She levels a look of transcendent boredom, then giggles and turns a page.

Farther inside is a restaurant. It is a comfortable if overdecorated place. There are three rooms, back to back, and a kitchen that is visible from the street through a steamy window. The front room is red-flocked; the second one is done in crazed mirrors and illuminated, framed beachscapes; and the back room is dominated by a hazy mural, the central feature of which is a mosque—it's hard to figure. The food is good, the service serviceable, and the price tolerable. The customers are expansive and well-fed.

Before you get to the pasta and main courses you may want to have something light —the Angelo Special Antipasto di Mare. It is light stuff, but you get a heavy amount of it—a foot-long platter of squid, conch, shrimp, scallops and celery cut into small pieces, dressed in garlicky oil and a little lemon, and sprinkled with coarsely chopped fresh parsley. The ingredients are fresh-tasting and the dish is stimulating, but you can't be sure that the conch will not be leathery—but for this occasional flaw, the salad is a wonderful and stimulating first course. If you don't wish to take a chance on tough conch, or if you want hot food right from the start, the hot first courses include Eggplant Provenzana (thoroughly sautéed eggplant, browned, soft and oily, in a tomato sauce flavored with garlic and herbs); there are also stuffed mushrooms—they are fresh, and the stuffing of bread crumbs, oil and chopped red peppers is tasty without overpowering the mushrooms; as part of the Home Made Hot Antipasto you also get a couple of whole bell peppers, sautéed in oil until there are little black spots here and there, which add a strong accent to the hot, limp and oily vegetable.

This place has something of a reputation for its linguine with clam sauce. It is served here with the clams still in their shells, the pasta dressed with oil and plenty of garlic. Theoretically this should be a wonderful dish—as the clams are steamed separately from the preparation of the sauce, they can be tender; and because they arrive still housed in and attached to their shells, you know they are fresh. But despite the advantages, the clams are sometimes tough, which makes the whole dish an absurdity. The linguine, however, is good and not overcooked, and the garlic has not been browned, so it has the strong flavor of the barely adulterated genuine article. There are also some quite eggy homemade noodles here, served in a variety of sauces, including a frankly southern mushroom sauce—a thick tomato sauce, very spicy, combined with plenty of sautéed fresh mushrooms. (About 90 percent of New York's Italian restaurants now call themselves "northern," no matter what kind of Italian food they serve —it's the fad. In Little Italy that fashion would be suicide, as the population down here, after lifetimes of powerful sauces, is largely unable to detect the flavor in anything that lacks garlic and/or hot red pepper.) For a noodle made with potatoes instead of flour, the Gnocchi di Casa alla Napoletana are pleasantly gummy and amorphous little morsels—the sauce is, of course, strong and red, with sautéed onions, and over the whole dish there is a layer of melted cheese. Hard to beat.

The Veal Pizzaiola is served in a hearty sauce that is made with lots of red peppers and oregano and mushrooms; but you can't be certain of getting tender veal in the scaloppine dishes. The fish, on the other hand, is reliable—fresh, moist and flaky—and the Bass Livornese, in its sauce of capers, olives, onions, tomatoes and, you guessed it, garlic, is a good choice if you have already had a couple of courses, because there is room for a light fish where a heavy meat will not fit. If you are not having that problem, then try the Calves' Brains Arreganata—the brains are white, rich, tender, lightly breaded and browned, and they are served with a sauce that includes *whole cloves* of garlic and an abundance of oregano.

Some of the vegetable dishes at Angelo's are well above average, and in the city-wide deep-fried-zucchini contest, the crisp and moist zucchini you get here maintains a respectable position. For an item you will not encounter all over town, try the Escarole alla Monachina—the strong green leafy vegetable is sautéed in oil with garlic, black olives, pine nuts, strong and salty anchovies, and sweet black raisins. The result is an amazingly well balanced dish, despite the unbelievable diversity of its elements.

The pastries come from Ferrara, of course, so if you have been to Ferrara, you know that the cheese cake is a compromise—the menu refers to it as Torta di Ricotta, and sure enough, there is a little ricotta cheese in it, but mostly cream cheese. The cake is fairly moist, studded with candied fruit and flavored slightly with lemon. The rum cake is a rum-moistened sponge cake with whipped cream on top—a meaningless item.

This is a spotty restaurant with a mixed clientele: families, with children; hirsute East Villagers on a spree; the gay; SoHo artists and hangers-on. It is just for a few hours, so they all get along.

★ ARARAT

4 East 36th Street
LUNCH, MONDAY TO SATURDAY; DINNER, DAILY.
Reservations, 686-4622.
Credit cards: AE, CB, DC, MC, V.
Inexpensive.

Harem technicolor is the decorative idiom of New York's Near Eastern eating places, and Ararat is right in style. Red carpeting, wallpaper that simulates hammered copper, carved wooden screens, antiqued mirrors, crystal chandeliers. The tables are covered with white linen; the waiters are in red jackets. You sit on banquettes with backs that are onion-shaped, like Byzantine domes. What could be pasha?

The menus of New York's few Armenian restaurants are virtually interchangeable, but Ararat's offers a couple of dishes you will not find on the others: chi kufta, lovely, plump little nuggets of just-ground raw lamb moistened with oil and buried in chopped onion, parsley and green pepper; and pasterma, a powerfully spiced dry beef served in hefty strips—the meat is gamy, just short of rank, and it leaves a pungent aftertaste. There is good börek, flaky pastry filled with warm mild cheese, and good imam bayildi, cool baked eggplant saturated with oil and tomato, strongly garlicked, mingled with onions. Unfortunately, the stuffed grape leaves and mussels have a clammy quality, and the marvelous things Armenians do with artichokes are not done here—if the enguinar appetizer is not made of canned artichokes, it might as well be.

For simple tastes there is lamb steak, of mildly marinated meat, charred and juicy and tender. The shish kebab is of the same good lamb, skewered with slices of pepper and onion and tomato, the meat rare, the vegetables at once charred at the edges and close to raw at the center. One of the best dishes in the place is called harpoot kufta —balls of ground lamb coated with a mixture of lamb and bulgur wheat. The meat is flavored with sweet spices, made crunchy with pine nuts and served in a strong meat broth that is touched with tomato. More of that bulgur in the choban pilaf: a great mound of grain in which chunks of this establishment's good lamb are buried—the oiled and spicy dish is studded with whole okras, and the odd assortment of flavors and textures, though not immediately appealing, has the unmistakable stamp of authenticity. The hot stuffed grape leaves have no resemblance to the cold appetizer—tender vine leaves are wrapped around a spicy mixture of ground lamb and rice that is just slightly lemoned. Many of the other main courses are stewlike combinations of lamb, eggplant, tomato, rice—substantial items, all well made.

Armenians take fruit compote seriously, and the mélange of stewed prunes, apricots, apples and pears served here comes in a strong, sugary syrup that is like spiced wine. The most intense dessert on the menu is ekmek kadayif—a sturdy, breadlike cake that is saturated with honey and garnished with kaimak, a remarkably thick cream of the Near East that seems like pure butterfat, though it is rich rather than cloying. Baklava, bourma, chekma—the familiar flaky and nutted pastries—are here, and they are fine.

The wine list is dreadful, the bread is usually stale and the background music is dreary. Some of the waiters have been around a long time, and they are nice; others of them are new to the profession, and they are punks. The brevity of their answers effectively discourages the flow of questions, and they set food before you with all the politesse of a turnkey delivering bread and water.

★★ ARIRANG

28 West 56th Street
LUNCH, MONDAY TO FRIDAY; DINNER, DAILY.
Reservations, 581-9698.
Credit cards: AE, CB, DC, MC, V.
Medium-priced.

The granddaddy of New York's Korean restaurants puts forth its exoticism with Madison Avenue polish. The rough wooden walls and the dim lighting are like something out of an old pirate movie. And the misty Oriental art that hangs on the walls seems to be peering not only out of the fog but out of the past. All you need is a gentleman in a hat and dark glasses, sitting silent at the bar, to complete the picture.

Instead, the scene is fleshed out with a host in a tux and a half-dozen waitresses in brilliantly colored floor-length dresses—they are like floating shafts of light in this dark setting. The service these angels provide is as gracious as anything in town.

Koreans and Japanese make up about half the restaurant's clientele, low-budget Broadway types much of the balance. Arirang is not greatly admired in national guidebooks, so—happily—the tourists have not found it. But the food is consistently good, and since many of the dishes are based on beef, sampling this locally rare Oriental cuisine is hardly experimental.

The food seems just-made. When the appetizer called wanja is placed before you, the meatballs are still sizzling, the crusted meat nutlike, spicy and moist. And when you receive your mandu tuikim—pastry dumplings that are filled with spicy ground meat and vegetables—they have the lightness and fragility of something just taken from the deep fat. One of the main courses, yauk hae, makes a good appetizer for two. Yauk hae is shredded raw beef, long strands of it, dressed with clear oil and flecked with sesame seeds, which add texture and brightness to the meat. And there is a wonderful soup here, duenjang kuk, a thick, strong broth that is heavily populated with scallions and bean curd and chunks of beef—very hot and very hearty.

If you eat at Arirang but once, the dish to have is kalbi chim, maybe the best rib dish in town. The little slabs of beef are rich meat in a meaty gravy that is at once salty and sour and herbed. The firm and tender beef is sweet, saturated with the oil and soy sauce it was cooked in—a tiny ascetic could dispatch six orders of the succulent stuff. There is a good dish called san juk: skewered carrots and celery and marinated beef in a thin, strong sauce that is dominated by the earthy and lively flavors of vegetables.

If you are entertaining visitors from, say, west of the Hudson, know that excursions to the big city are incomplete without at least one *frisson* per exotic dinner. To bring on the shivers of excitement at Arirang, order sin sullo. Not only does this dish arrive in a pot shaped like a doughnut, but there are flames shooting up through the hole. Your waitress bisects the toroid by lifting off the upper half, revealing, around the blazing core, a circle of steaming broth populated with vegetables and mushrooms, bits of beef and slices of omelet, slivers of liver and globes of meatball, a partylike mélange in which each participant is clearly itself. To prevent client incineration, the food is spooned from doughnut to plate by the help.

Whole fish, deep-fried, are available in Chinese restaurants all over town, so the red snapper here is automatically compared with hundreds of similar preparations—and suffers thereby. It is perfectly good food, fresh and crisp, but it is overcooked and a little mushy, its sauce undistinguished. The most far-out dish is sea cucumber, a rather slimy beast-of-the-deep—the predominating fatlike texture in an otherwise crisp assortment of vegetables, including water chestnuts and cloud ears; chunks of beef add a startling, chewy note to the land and sea elements.

All the main courses are served with cool vegetables: wonderfully fresh spinach, bean sprouts, and the sharp, carrot-colored root vegetable of Korea called doraji. They are dressed in oil and sesame, and they are lovely foils to the sturdy food. For even sharper relief, you may order kimchi, the strong, soured cabbage of Korea.

For dessert there is fruit or ice cream. To drink, there is tea, beer or sake, which is very good with this food.

★★★ AUBERGE SUISSE

153 East 53rd Street
LUNCH, MONDAY TO SATURDAY; DINNER, DAILY.
Reservations, 421–1420.
Credit cards: AE, CB, DC, MC, V.
Expensive.

Two small rooms—fewer than a dozen tables in each—and a short bar are the whole of Auberge Suisse. The look of Swiss modernity is neutrality and variations thereon. This rendition is silvery and sleek and just a little soft, with glinting walls of charcoal-gray glass, walls and banquettes of chestnut-colored suede, gray suede booths, modern bentwood chairs. The tables are set with beige linen and beige china. You walk on brown carpeting under a ceiling of metallic acoustical tiles—they reflect the room back with a somber glow. It is a perfect rendering of a cool style, it eschews ornament, and it can be forbidding. But when the restaurant is busy, the sight and sounds of people dress it up. And the vivid food this kitchen turns out is all the more dramatic, in look and taste, for its cool setting.

The sparkling food includes a refreshing salade de boeuf bouilli, strands of cool, rare beef and crisp vegetables in a tangy vinaigrette; fillets of boned smoked trout, cool, flaky and a little oily, served with a horseradish sauce that has the head-clearing pungency of the just-grated root—the sauce is cut with slivers of apple, but the fruit makes little impression in this fiery context; and viande de Grison et jambon cru, thin slices of mahogany-colored air-dried beef, chewy and a little gamy, and smoky ham, the pink meat rimmed with delicate white fat, served with slivered onions—just cut, strong and crisp—a vivid foil to the high-flavored meats.

This place makes snails in a version they call escargots "Café de Paris." This is a singular preparation, in which the plump and tender snails are baked in brandy and flavored butter. What they put in that butter is a mystery—your waiter questions the chef and returns with the dubious advice that the recipe calls for twenty herbs and spices—but sweeter spices and the perfume of green herbs dominate. The snails are served in shells in a little pot; just before serving, the entire production is lightly covered with good cheese and browned. A wondrous dish.

Good soups, mostly, including a hot, clear and profound oxtail broth that is livened with the sharpness of minced chives; and an item given as potage balois, a creamy beef soup that has a strong and earthy flavor of whole grain. There is a cold apricot soup as well, but it may strike you as little more than liquefied preserves.

More trout (Switzerland is sweet-water country), this one poached in wine, boned, skinned and served in a creamy white sauce that is dotted with fresh herbs—the fish is immaculately fresh, and the sauce has the smoothness and polish of a thing just made.

It is unlikely that you will get a better cheese fondue in New York than the one served here (for two people or more). It is brought to you in a broad ceramic pot, within which it is bubbling; on your table it is kept hot and active over a little burner; and as is the way with this dish at its best, its flavor deepens as it continues to bubble, darken and grow thick. There are wine, garlic and seasonings in this dish, but in such judicious dosages that they heighten the flavor of the melted Gruyère cheese without intruding their own. You are supplied with long forks and a copious mound of chunks of crusty bread. You pierce the bread with the forks, dip it into the seething cheese, and eat. If you are normal, you will frequently burn your lips and palate with the hot tines and molten cheese.

Emincé de veau Zurichoise is a wonderful veal dish in which slivers of delicate veal and chunks of fresh mushroom are served in a dark sauce. The veal is accompanied by rösti potatoes, the marvelous Swiss potato tart that has a crust of browned potatoes, a core that is soft and moist. The plat Bernoise is the low point of the place, a leaden collection of sausages, meats and sauerkraut. But the saucisse de veau grillé is fine— a substantial veal sausage, pale, smooth and rich, served under strands of onion that are sweet and dark from long braising. Sausages again, this time as a garnish to the elegant calf's liver that arrives with dark-brown grill marks on the outer surfaces of the pink meat—the accompanying little sausages are chippolatas, strong and charred, the dark, spicy meat filling heavily fatted, just about bursting from the crackling cases.

A complex steak production is served up here. It is styled tournedos cordon-rouge, and it is a stack of things—the steak, foie gras, ham, a big mushroom, Béarnaise sauce —and it is served with a gravy that is so winy it is purple. The foie gras is not first class, but everything else is okay, and the dark gravy is marvelously suited to the salty buttered noodles that accompany this dish. The production more than survives its overdesign.

If you did not scorch yourself on cheese fondue, you get a second chance with chocolate fondue, bubbling milk chocolate that is studded with nuts—you scoop it out of its pot on chunks of cake or pineapple, or on strawberries or grapes. There is a superb excess called coupe rouge et blanc, a mousse of white chocolate that is mingled with whipped cream and liquored strawberries—for all its richness it is light. And there is a good carrot cake, nutty and substantial and moist. The most elegant dessert is a sherbet item for some reason called "Le Colonel"—the lemon ice is soaked with pear brandy, and the dish has a strong sweetness that seems to glisten.

Swiss wines are perfectly decent, but not especially interesting if you are used to sampling the best of France and California. If you are curious, this place offers about a dozen that are perfectly drinkable.

★ BALKAN ARMENIAN

129 East 27th Street
LUNCH AND DINNER. CLOSED SUNDAY.
Reservations, MU 9-7925.
Credit cards: AE, CB, DC, MC, V.
Inexpensive.

Did you know that Charles Aznavour, Alan Hovannes and Lucine Amara (as well as lots of other people) are Armenian? That there are 600,000 Armenians in the United States? That the Berberian family bought this restaurant in 1948 and has been running it ever since? These and other analgesic facts may be picked up by reading the inaccurately titled ("A Little About Armenia") back page of the award-winning (a fact from the front page) menu. It is therefore ironic, though not surprising, that no more justice is done here to the real breadth of Armenian cookery than in any other of the handful of Armenian restaurants in New York. In that regard some places do a little better. Which is not to say that within the narrow range of the Balkan Armenian's repertoire the performances are bad, rather that the tedious chauvinism is all the more boring for being strictly public relations.

Get right into the spirit by starting your Armenian dinner with some Greek feta cheese and black olives—the substantial slabs of cheese are firm and sharp, and the olives are strong and oily. Or with some tarama (Greek again), the paste of red caviar and bread, here served in a salty and well-lemoned version that is light, almost fluffy. The hommus is good (albeit borrowed by the Balkan Armenian from the cuisines of the Arab restaurants in its neighborhood)—it is smooth and thick, with more sesame, and less chickpea and garlic, than in most versions, so that it tastes faintly like halvah. And the imam bayildi is so good you would never guess it is really a Turkish dish— the eggplant is rich, red, spicy, succulent. Some of the cold appetizers, however, should be eschewed—the white bean salad is dull, the stuffed grape leaves are cinnamoned beyond reason, and the rather clammy mussels were past their prime when prepared. Cheese boerek is the one hot appetizer, mildly spiced cheese in an exceedingly light and flaky pastry—a wonderfully satisfying little dish.

The hot soup and the cold soup are both yogurt soups, and if you chilled the former, heated the latter, and reversed their places, it is unlikely a non-Armenian would know the difference. Both are white, pleasantly sour, weighted with grain.

Shish kebab, of course, herbs on the charred meat, which is alternated on its skewer with slices of blackened onion—the lamb has been carefully marinated, and it has strong flavor without being bloodless. The burgers here are of lamb, they are called scara kufte and they are crusty, solid, weighty without being heavy, tasty winter food. Mantar kebab is a stew-like dish of lamb and vegetables in which the dominant flavor is of sautéed green peppers—sweet onions offset their tartness, and mushrooms give the dish a woodsy earthiness. You can get a good lamb shank—kouzou dolma—baked until the juicy meat is falling from the bone. It is served with lightly oiled rice that is studded with nuts and currants. Kabak dolma consists of hollowed-out zucchini that are filled with ground meat, rice and onions. It adds up to dull stuff until, for an additional 90 cents, you add cool yogurt—this yogurt is the real thing, at once sour and rich, and its cool bite is perfect against the somewhat heavy stuffed squash. Most of the main-course menu is lamb, and most of the dishes are fine.

Pastry, walnuts and honey are the principal ingredients of almost all the desserts, so, of course, they are sweet, nutted, flaky. An exception is the ekmek kadayiff, which is prepared by baking bread and honey to a paste of almost brandy-like intensity. It should be ordered with kaymak, an extreme reduction of cream, the thickness of which is in nice contrast to the honeyed sweet.

Your waiter hands you the menu and goes away. He returns, and you attempt to order, only to learn that half your selections are unavailable. You mention to him that when you were a waiter, you always informed customers in advance about the dishes that were unavailable. "You were better waiter than me," he shrieks, and laughs so hysterically at his howler that you offer him a chair lest he injure himself. His partner in incompetence moans audibly and implores the ceiling for justice when you send back a bottle of wine—unopened—because it is plainly too old. This is a small restaurant, and its appointments—including hanging Oriental rugs, antiqued mirrors and brass-filigree lanterns—are standard Motel Middle-East.

★★ BALLATO

55 East Houston Street (near Mott Street)
LUNCH AND DINNER. CLOSED SUNDAY.
Reservations required for dinner, CA 6-9683.
No credit cards.
Beer and wine.
Medium-priced.

Mrs. Ballato now presides over the late Mr. Ballato's famous hideaway. The old gentleman was something of a professional character; his survivor is anything but. She is slight, blue-haired, courteous, sweet. She helps you off with your coat, apologizes for the weather. If she fails to embrace you on your arrival because she does not know you very well, she will at least place a hand on your shoulder when you leave, now that you are old pals. Except that the restaurant is a little more relaxed than it was under the governance of its occasionally bristling founder, the change in proprietary style has changed it very little.

You enter to a small anteroom, wherein a shelf of books and magazines has been installed for the diversion of customers waiting for tables. Your coat is put in a closet, the portal of which is hung with amber beads. There is a glass icebox stocked with wine, cheese, fruit. Farther back the oblong dining room holds two rows of square tables, eleven all told, four chairs at each. The walls are surfaced with broad panels of plain cloth, and they are hung with scores of photos and pictures of John Ballato, framed articles about the restaurant, a Sinatra poster, a good number of Warhol prints, and other assorted contemporary graphics (when SoHo decided to come into existence, it chose a site not far from this place). The rear wall of the dining room hardly exists, for it is wide open to the brightly lit and immaculate kitchen (into which you must enter for the facilities and the pay phone).

The uptown set that used to crowd the curb outside with waiting limousines has deserted Ballato in favor of the slumming that has in recent years been provided for them on their own Third Avenue. But Ballato is still busy. Many of the gentlemen who come regularly look as if they ought to be the mayor of Brooklyn. You would swear that others are off-duty policemen, except that their ladies wear more jewels than a cop's salary can account for. Large families come here (a couple of tables are pushed together), and Greenwich Villagers in search of a better bargain than their own pricey nabe offers. It is a comfort-loving rather than a luxury-loving crowd, and they are here for the familiarity of the surroundings, the reliability of the food, the straightforward service.

The baked clams and the mussels reganate are browned and crisped, their breading easy on the dried oregano—they come in pools of parsleyed and buttered broth. Roasted green peppers are stuffed with a pungent meat-and-cheese filling, and they are dressed with a spicy tomato sauce—satisfying food.

Good pasta: lovely green noodles in a sauce that is little more than cream and cheese, the dish ornamented with a sprinkling of sharp red pepper; very good linguine with fresh clams, cloves of browned garlic and much parsley in the briny butter; excellent manicotti, the pillows of pasta stuffed with pully cheese and covered with an honest red sauce that is still bubbling when the casserole reaches your table.

If you can bring yourself to do it, order the octopus. It is served, be warned, in rather undisguised long shafts, but the slightly rubbery meat has a sharp gaminess that is worth learning to like, and the strong red sauce, thick with garlic and onions, will help. On occasion this establishment has served bass that would have pleased much more a couple of days earlier, in a sauce livornese devoid of the olives and capers that title leads you to expect. But the scampi are good—big and crunchy shrimp in a creamy tomato sauce that is thick with rice.

You get a giant portion of brains, and the rich meat arrives sizzling, crusted with seasoned breading. A small spoon protrudes from the dark marrow of the osso buco, the tender meat barely clings to the bone, a thick and gravylike mushroom sauce moistens the meat and its garnish of rice. But better than almost anything in the place is the rolatine of veal, the browned cylindrical packages filled with a spiced stuffing of strong cheese, sausage, herbs, the meat moistened with a sturdy brown sauce.

The menu lists "assorted cheeses," but a decent Fontina is all you usually can get. The zabaglione is the usual hot and winy froth, but it comes with a bonus of tissue-wrapped macaroons. When the restaurant is busy your waiter may discourage the zabaglione on the grounds that it takes twenty minutes. It takes five. The cheese cake is distinctly Italian—wet, light and sugary.

★ BARBETTA

321 West 46th Street
LUNCH AND DINNER. CLOSED SUNDAY.
Reservations, CI 6-9171.
Credit cards: AE, CB, DC, MC, V.
Expensive.

In New York the best food to be had by the light of moonbeams is served at the venerable Barbetta, an upper-crust restaurant distinguished from its prestigious Italian competitors by the elegance of its posh interior, and from every restaurant in town by its serene backyard—a luxurious dining garden that is like a spiffy glade in a sylvan setting. The food, however, is not invariably superior, and the pre- and after-theater crowds that often beset this place on summer nights can undo the tranquillity.

You enter to a wood-paneled room—cocktail tables of green marble, cushy chairs upholstered in silk velvet. You pass a marble bar on the way to the big dining room —large, well-spaced tables in a room of arched windows hung with silken drapes, everything softly lighted by the glow of crystal chandeliers. A portal leads to the garden —a circle of snowy tables and cushioned iron chairs under white umbrellas that have tops like minarets; at the center, an illuminated pool, into which four streams gently tinkle; around the sides, trees and vines, the restaurant itself, and stone walls patrolled by thoughtful cats.

You are greeted by Mediterranean captains. They ooze, each in his own way, self-possession. Take, for example, the patriarch among them, a gray-topped chap who receives you with his right hand in his trousers pocket, a Buddha-like smile of infinite wisdom on his well-fleshed face, as if he were posing for an elder-statesman portrait. (He develops a problem, of which foot to put before the other, at the sight of fetching blondes one-third his age.) The captains are the keys to eating well here, and if they know you, or if you look important, or if they are prodded, they will disseminate their knowledge of what is good on the menu and off.

On the menu you will find peperoni with bagna calda—sweet roasted red peppers flecked with black, doused with a heavily oiled anchovy sauce, and a salad of fresh mushrooms, the crisp woodsy article, sliced thin and livened with oil and lemon. Off the menu there is raw veal: chopped, dressed with oil and lemon, garnished with minced raw garlic—a vibrant dish. Cold trout is listed as a main course, but a serving of it is a good appetizer for two or three people—the clear-tasting fish is firm and flaky, tart from its vinegared marinade, strewn with cool vegetables. What Barbetta calls vitel tonné (the rest of the world calls it vitello tonnato) is another main course which you might do better to start with. The pale, cold veal is spread with an oiled, salty tuna purée that is studded with capers; the moist sauce is lovely against the dry meat.

Your captain does not want you to order risotto: He tells you it will take 30 minutes. You insist. He tells you it will take 35 minutes. You do not relent. Shortly after the conclusion of the auction you receive your risotto alla Piemontese: sautéed rice that has been cooked in stock until it is earthy and rich, studded with bits of mushroom and meat—pungent, long-lasting food. Somewhere this place obtains green noodles—in the thin strands called tagliarini—so powerfully flavored with fresh, grassy spinach that its perfume rises from the dish like heat. It is served with an utterly melded sauce—solid without being heavy—of mushrooms, meat, tomatoes and oil. This is a fabulous dish, not always available.

The main courses can be comedowns. The scaloppines of veal are impeccable. But the fritto misto Piemontese is a dull assortment of deep-fried organ meats and vegetables; the duckling à l'orange a good excuse for jumping to conclusions about Italians who essay French dishes; and the chicken preparations indictments of precooking and the modern chicken.

When there are berries, they are plump and firm, and you can have them with zabaglione sauce. The peach in wine is ripe fresh fruit deeply imbued with the flavors of red wine and cloves. Pass up the chocolate mousse (little more than heavy syrup) and the liquored cake (wet cake). The gâteau St. Honoré, the French dessert of Grand Marnier–flavored pastry cream on two kinds of pastry is not bad, but all wrong at the end of an Italian meal.

★ BERRY'S

180 Spring Street (at Thompson Street)
LUNCH AND DINNER. CLOSED MONDAY.
Reservations, 226-4394.
Credit cards: AE, MC, V.
Medium-priced.

This is a good place to cure a hangover, for it is cool and dark, and comfortable in a turn-of-the-century way. There is much dark wood, four-bladed fans hang from the stamped-tin ceiling, ornate mirrors hang over the dark, intricately patterned paper that covers the walls. Plants in the windows filter the light that shines in and falls on an old barbershop-tile floor. The front room is most of the restaurant: on your left a bar that can comfortably lubricate fifteen—there is a mound of crushed ice at its center, into which beer mugs are forced to keep them cold until they are used; on your right and at the back, enough small, dark-wooden tables with candles on them to feed a couple of dozen. A tiny room with a handful of tables has been added at the rear— this part of Berry's, because of its closeness, can be painfully noisy when it is crowded.

When things are slow, as they sometimes are, Berry herself stands at the far end of the bar, drawing on a cigarette, sipping a glass of wine or something stronger, watching the door, or glancing toward it suddenly when it opens. Berry is nice, giving the waitresses a hand when things pick up, hustling a drink if she sees a glass that is not working, answering customers' questions about the dishes that are listed on the brief, constantly changing blackboard menu. That menu has a footnote: "Chef Paula de Lancey." And when Berry really wants to lay on a little lather while describing a dish, she soups-up her British accent until she sounds like Winston Churchill, furrows her brow, and, in a veritable transport of explication, applies the trowel: "You see, what Paula has done [pause] is take the *entire* flounder [long pause] and *cut it in half* [long, very significant pause] the *lawng* way [intermission] and then . . ." At each full stop she eyes her questioner sharply, to determine if it is all getting through. You would think she was describing a recipe by Beethoven.

Many of the dishes have cute names and are composed of unexpected combinations of ingredients. Despite this, many of them are good to eat. A misguided groping for the unusual came up with blue shrimp kiev, in which the shrimp are deep-fried in a batter that is made with blue cheese—this dish would be nowhere even if the shrimp were not a little off. But "duck and sausage sizzle" transcends its title: discs of strong sausage, chunks of duck liver and duck meat, and fresh spinach are sautéed together and tinctured with the flavor of sweet pork fat, the crispness of the spinach good against the rich meats. The salade chinoise is an assortment of items—scallions, cress, baby corn, sprouts and more—in a sesame-oil dressing; the elements are fine, but they do not add up to a dish.

Simple food like calf's liver with shallots is sometimes prepared perfectly here, the meat lightly floured so that it comes out of the pan delicately crusted. And do not be scared off by filet mignon with oysters, for the steak is perfectly grilled, and the oysters are gently warmed in the steak's sauce and combined with the filet just before the dish is served—the oysters are fresh, they are not toughened in the cooking, and the two delicate meats are artfully married by a sauce that is derived from both. The pomegranate and walnut duck is notable for a sauce that is thick with walnuts and lightly sweetened with the seeds of the fruit. And the grilled swordfish is fresh, firm and juicy. Do not experiment with the steak tartare—the meat is ground long before the dish is prepared.

The mint flavor in the chocolate mousse is a variation that is hard to fault, but the chocolate surprise is a chocolate cake that, with its thick icing and layers of raspberry, is rather heavy, gooey going. The fruit tarts always seem to be good, and the cranberry upside-down cake is marvelous for the effect of the berry juice soaked into the dark-brown, nut-flavored cake.

Someone has peddled this place a really dreary wine list, but there is usually a tolerable bottle or two among the losers.

★ BILLY'S

948 First Avenue (near 52nd Street)
LUNCH, MONDAY TO FRIDAY; DINNER, DAILY.
Reservations, 355–8920.
Credit cards: AE, CB, DC, MC, V.
Medium-priced.

Billy's is like P. J. Clarke's, but without the drunks. Also without the jukebox, preserved decay, bouncer and ice blocks in the urinals, for which blessings you pay through the trunk, for the prices here are an object lesson to P. J.'s of what you can get away with if you don't have to fill three large rooms to pay the real estate taxes.

You come here for your shrimp cocktail, for your sirloin steak, for your hamburger steak for the lady, for your lamb chops, for your Irish coffee. And you eat and drink these ingestibles amid furnishings and fixtures that graced Billy's at the old spot four blocks from here, for doth not the sign read "Established by Michael Condron Way Back in 1870," and is that not Michael's bar, the same one as was in the old place, and are not these the old gas lamps wired up for electric, and don't the wooden doors and panels with the brass knobs and hinges seem to be the same ones as Michael knew? Sure. And isn't there a bottle of ketchup on the red-checkered tablecloth, same as in the old place? Sure. And isn't that Michael's own begotten son, Billy, behind the bar? You bet it is. And even if the place does look like a saloon, the waiters wear those little long-sleeved vests so you can tell them from the customers, and the only loud talking is from the kiddies some folks don't mind bringing here because this is a family-type restaurant, even if it did forget to close during Prohibition.

The menu is painted on a slate, and occasional daily specials are indicated by little signs tacked on the wall. Tomato juice is half a dollar, the onion soup is pretty ordinary, and the shrimp cocktail consists of four carefully cooked shrimp and cocktail sauce (you can add horseradish).

Eschew the pork chops (cooked to the point where you not only will not get trichinosis, but anything else either). Pass up the lobster tails (either for political reasons—they are from South Africa—or for personal ones—they had a tough trip). Do not order the broiled filet of sole (it may be broiled, but it is gently broiled, so it tastes as if it has been stewed in butter; the coloration is paprika, not natural browning by fire). Whatever you order, do not order the sautéed onions. They are limp (as such onions should be), but they lack the accent of burnt grease that can make this dish a kind of sinful pleasure.

Do order the steak. It is thick, cooked exactly the way you ordered it, tender and tasty. Or order the chopped steak—large, made of freshly ground meat, and excellent with the steak sauce that is a companion to the ketchup on your table. Or order the steak tartare—the meat is freshly ground, and you can ask for the pepper mill or whatever if you want to adjust the seasoning. The broiled chicken seems to be of a fresh bird, and the lamb chops are as carefully made as the steaks. Fair French fries (they are the kind you put ketchup on, not the kind you put salt on), baked potatoes that seem to be made in a slow oven, so the skin, instead of being flaky and slightly blackened, is merely a tired container.

The apple pie is a fair commercial variety, but the cheese cake is dreadful.

★★ LE BISTRO

827 Third Avenue (near 50th Street)
LUNCH, MONDAY TO FRIDAY; DINNER, MONDAY TO SATURDAY. CLOSED SUNDAY.
Reservations, 759-8439.
Credit cards: AE, CB, DC, MC, V.
Expensive.

The checkroom attendant is a happy lady with the approachable smile of a jolly good sport and a French accent of piping, clarion musicality. Here people do not mind eating by themselves, and of an evening you will usually see one or two tables of one gentleman per, a newspaper in the left hand, a fork in the right. Le Bistro is the kind of restaurant to which people repair more for their own talk than for the restaurant's food—for though what you get to eat is almost invariably of good quality, these dishes are so familiar, to frequenters of New York's older French restaurants, that they call little or no attention to themselves.

But the physical place commands a glance or two, for it is handsomely appointed: two foursquare rooms slightly separated by etched-glass partitions; the front room equipped with a small stainless-steel simulation of a zinc-topped bar; both rooms rimmed with a tufted red banquette, along the back ledge of which runs a brass rail that is about as thick as a pencil; just above the banquette, odd-shaped mirrors in sinuous mahogany frames; above those a continuous mural of butterflies and flowers and hanging vines and innocent turn-of-the-century ladies, all in a muted, rosy, dream fantasy. The intended effect is art nouveau, but, happily, it is not laid on thick. You eat off white linen. You walk on a floor of pegged oak. And you are served by waiters in black jackets, white shirts and long white aprons.

Of course there is country pâté, and this one is powerfully laced with cognac. And of course there is saucisson chaud, and these slabs of hot fatted meat, spicy and loud, are garnished, oddly, with warm lentils—the beans make a fine buffer to this coarse sausage. What the menu refers to as saucisson d'Arles will look like salami to you: thin slices of fat-studded purple meat, peppercorns in every slice, fragrant with garlic—very good with bread and butter. The leeks are fresh, but a little overcooked and therefore limp—a pungently mustard-flavored vinaigrette redeems them. The céleri rémoulade is crisp, slightly acidic, clearly fresh. And you get good mussels—they are cold and tender, and their mustard sauce, if used sparingly, just emphasizes their sweet oceanic flavor.

The poached salmon is fresh, firm, only slightly complicated by the warm, rich and lemony hollandaise that comes with it. The frogs' legs, though plump and tender, artfully breaded and crisped, are a little bland—they have slight flavor of their own, and not much of the garlic that their "Provençales" billing suggests. At one time chicken crêpes were a familiar item on French menus in New York, but the abundance of rich sauce that is part of the dish puts it out of fashion now. Le Bistro unabashedly offers a hefty version, nevertheless: lots of chicken in a thick sauce, wrapped in a crêpe like a large pillow, covered over with a Mornay sauce that is pungent with cheese, the whole works baked onto the plate on which it is served, handsomely browned—plain food that is sturdy and utterly satisfying. If that crêpe will not hold you, try the cassoulet: mild sausages and extremely hot ones, chunks of lamb and bird, all buried in the firm white beans and their pungent sauce—winter food. The veal chop is beautifully browned, garnished with hot sliced apple, and moistened with an apple-brandy sauce that is studded with mushrooms. The steak au poivre comes in a lovely cognac sauce, but the pepper and meat seem at odds, and the beef, even when quite rare, is chewy.

Except for an item styled "la ganache au sabayon"—an exceptionally fluffy chocolate cake that is moistened with a creamy sauce—none of the desserts will be new or surprising to anyone. You get a good strawberry tart; a pleasant coffee-flavored parfait served in a tulip-shaped cup of icy metal; a solid rice cake moistened with liquored vanilla sauce; a coupe aux marrons of icy chestnuts that are crunchy and tender in their cold vanilla cream. And there is cheese—the Roquefort is good, if not the subtlest you ever had.

The cost of your dinner is determined by the main course you choose, but a handful of appetizers and a few desserts command premiums.

★ BISTRO DO BRASIL

1373 First Avenue (near 74th Street)
DINNER.
Reservations, 734-8318.
Credit cards: AE, DC.
Medium-priced.

An honest but somewhat bumbling restaurant is now housed in the unaltered premises left behind by the finally departed Bagatelle. The place is as pretty as ever, softly lit, colorful, aglow, aglint. The walls are of pale mottled tiles and of colored tiles formed into rectangular illustrations that, placed like paintings, adorn them. Those "paintings" alternate, along one side of the room, with built-in mirrors that tilt forward at the top, affording the voyeuristic diner an overview of the room and the people in it. Another wall is bejeweled with windowpane mirrors. Fluted-glass lamps hang low on brass chains. You walk on gay green-and-blue carpeting. You sit on bentwood sidechairs at tables that are clothed in pale-pink linen and adorned with fresh flowers. You are waited on by young gentlemen from Brazil. They are unfailingly polite, if not invariably hip to what the kitchen is up to.

The kitchen is up to preparing considerably less than all the items listed on the menu. It does, however, send forth a rousing escabeche, a warm one at that, the little side of fish crusted and browned after its marination, then dressed with the cold, tart vegetable marinade just before it is served. Or you may begin with a firm and ripe half-avocado, over which much good lobster meat has been mounded—it is mingled with hearts of palm (canned) and minced red peppers in a creamy dressing. You will do well to avoid the other first courses, some of which not only include, but are dominated by, canned ingredients. The onion soup, tomato soup and chicken soup "Brazilian style" are like those soups anywhere.

Much of more interest is to be found among the main courses: a big slab of striped bass, browned and moist, lemoned and buttery, strewn with parsley and slivered almonds; fresh sole, nicely sautéed, with shrimp and mussels in a creamy sherry sauce that converts the seafoods into a rich mélange of high flavor. Codfish dishes—oddly for a Brazilian restaurant—are not listed, but on occasion a codfish casserole is offered in which big chunks of salty fish, juicy tomatoes, browned potatoes, green and red peppers and plenty of onions are all baked together into a hefty jumble. It is particularly satisfying with the rice and black beans that come with all main courses here. You may have shrimp prepared in the manner called paulista—the little crustaceans are sautéed in their shells, and they are garlicked, moist with oil, sweet, crunchy. Or you may have them in the manner called baina, in which they are buried in a garlic-flavored sauce that is thick with tomatoes and green peppers. What Bistro do Brasil lists as lobster thermidor consists of much good lobster meat and a creamy sherry sauce in which the alcohol has been only partially cooked off—for some reason the quality of raw alcohol is very good with lobster meat. Meat dishes and chicken dishes are listed, but the only nonseafood item you may be fairly certain of finding is feijoada, which, as everybody knows, is the national dish of Brazil. It is served as a pot of black beans in which are buried chunks of beef, on the bone, and deep-red blood sausages. The sturdy stuff comes with sliced oranges, crinkly green kale and the ground root of the manioc plant, a zest traditionally eaten with feijoada. This is solid and satisfying food, but its slim variety of meats, and its fairly dull bean flavor, make it one of the less interesting versions around town.

The carioca pudding is custard and pineapple. The plum pudding is custard and a stewed prune. Cheese and fresh fruit are sometimes available.

★★ BIZEN

171 Spring Street (near Thompson Street)
DINNER. CLOSED MONDAY.
Reservations, 966-0963.
Credit cards: AE.
Inexpensive.

Bizen provides you with a printed menu, but what is available at the restaurant on any given day depends, in part, on the best foodstuffs available at the markets. For brightness, clarity, purity and freshness of seafood and vegetables, nothing in SoHo surpasses Bizen. And the simple Japanese preparations that are applied to the foodstuffs reveal and emphasize—sometimes dramatically, but never falsely—the food's essence.

When you have, for example, a sardine at Bizen, it may seem as if you are having your first sardine.

Like many SoHo restaurants, this one is carved out of lofty commercial space. But here the fact is not emphasized, and the spare lines and pale-wood tones that dominate seem at once Japanese and Scandinavian, rather than the favored downtown look, which is Great Barn. Bizen is both an eating place and a gallery, the front of the store given over to displays of Bizen pottery, which, a spiel on the back of the menu informs you, is the "finest pottery in Japan." At the back there is a small bar on your right, polished maple-stained tables on your left. *Sumi-e* paintings (of horses, grasses, calligraphy, birds, branches) by local students of a local master adorn the walls. The dining room and bar are tended, usually, by a couple of Occidental gentlemen who speak Japanese and are apparently conversant with that culture. The Japanese women who prepare the food emerge at quiet times and receive with much pleasure the compliments of the customers at the tables.

First sardine or five-thousandth, when sardine sashimi is offered, have it. Glistening and silvery little filets of firm fish, dark and oily, a bit salty, are garnished with just-shredded radish, the crispness and sharpness of which is lovely against the rich meat. Mackerel sashimi is available more regularly—this is milder, but just as slick, just as vivid and just as stimulating. There are raw scallops served as a first course, the rich meat slivered into discs, sprinkled with sesame seeds and moistened with a lightly oiled lemon sauce that is at once gentle and lively. An item called green sashimi consists simply of half an avocado, cool but not cold, ripe but firm, cut into thin slices that are prettily arranged on your plate and dressed with a dark, slightly sharp sauce that is almost chocolatey. When lotus root is available, do not pass it up—the cross-sectional slices are marinated in vinegar that has a bit of sugar in it, giving the crisp tuber a vaguely melonlike flavor. The hot first course to have is the squid teriyaki—firm but never rubbery circlets of squid, just touched with blackness in their cooking, in a syruplike dark sauce that is flecked with bits of fresh ginger.

The steamed bass is moist and fluffy and firm, the mushrooms that adorn it a pungent contrast to the simple fish. The baked shrimp arrive, as the menu promises, sizzling, the breaded and browned crustaceans crunchy and sweet. Something called sea nabe is a nice enough stew of seafood and vegetables, but simpler—purer—dishes are what this restaurant does best.

Seafood is not all. Chicken tsukimi, for example, is an elemental and elegant dish of boned morsels of white meat, breaded, buttered and baked until the crust is nubbly and brown—the meat within the breading is hot and juicy. And what the menu, in a burst of English, calls rolled beef is constructed by wrapping little sheets of meat around shafts of scallion, bits of mushroom and garlic. The resulting rolls are cooked dry, then cut into sections about an inch long, of which more than a dozen are arranged on one side of your plate, with three great slices of roasted green pepper on the other. The presentation looks like opposing forces on a field. Every morsel is lively, the peppers sweet in their ginger-flavored black sauce.

The desserts are ice cream items—dark, winy butterscotch or slightly sweetened red beans on good vanilla.

• BLACK SHEEP

344 West 11th Street
LUNCH, SUNDAY. DINNER, DAILY.
Reservations, 242-1010.
Credit cards: AE, CB, DC, MC, V.
Medium-priced.

You eat copiously here rather cheaply. You choose your drink from an international wine list of more than 100 bottles, almost all of them offered at well under the usual Manhattan restaurant prices. The place is, moreover, of the snug, dim, bare-brick-and-lantern-light school, to which you bring your most casual ease. Accordingly it is popular. You will never get a bad meal here, nor ever a memorable one. The Black Sheep is the quintessential neighborhood joint, very much part of its community, with just enough kooky about it to make it right at home in this remote corner of the far-west Village. The art on the walls, for example, is right out of a nightmare.

You enter and get your hand pumped by a waiter who thinks he remembers you from last time. At the little front-room bar gentlemen embrace as they arrive, form groups, are then led to their tables. Boy-girl types come too, for the Sheep's out-of-the-way situation and cozy appointments make it very much the standard romantic hideaway. The restaurant is two high-ceilinged rooms, plain wooden floors, paraphernalia on the walls, red cloths on the tables. Near where the two rooms connect, on an ancient, enameled breakfront gas range, a selection of the restaurant's good desserts, illuminated by a couple of long tapers, is displayed on the stove-top level. Not far from there, most evenings, a young man on a chair strums a guitar—he is miked, amplified, carried to all corners of the rooms. When he takes a break, recorded music stands in for him. The aproned waiters are chatty. You learn, for example, that the Sheep has this real fine medical plan. Each waiter seems to have been given a short course in wine magic. "I'm going to let this breathe," goes one, "and I'll present it when it's ready." (You beg for a glass right away, and it comes with a set of injured feelings.) They will decant anything that predates the 80s, and they are horrified when you drink the perfectly clear heel first.

The abundance of these dinners is a function of the format of this restaurant's menu. Your dinner consists of six courses—three of them are fixed, you usually select your soup from a choice of two, your dessert from among a handful. The price of your dinner is determined by the main course you choose from among a dozen or so.

At once you are presented with a slightly gargantuan bowl of *crudités,* a big jigger of garlic sauce at the center. The vegetables—variously carrots, zucchini, florets of cauliflower, mushrooms, squash, with halves of hardcooked eggs—are fresh but often icy, seem to have been cut up and refrigerated well in advance of the dinner hour. And the sauce varies from time to time from creamy to wet, from tart to sour. Then you are served a leek-and-watercress soup (sometimes thick, sometimes watery) or a soup of the day (the onion-and-potato soup is substantial, sharpened by the flavor of potato skin; the zucchini-and-bacon soup is just as solid, the meat a nice accent). The weakness of these soups is the absence of a strong stock base—they are as much like purées as soups. Course three is a somewhat overbaked and dry pâté that is dominated by an excess of sweet spice.

You select your main course from among those your waiter does not warn you off. He recommends some salmon one night, and sure enough it is fresh and moist within its harmless pastry. Good scallops are sautéed with whole mushrooms, and they are served in a pale sauce that is lightly lemoned—the dish is a little heavy, but not leaden. You are warned that there is lots of Pernod in the provençal fish stew, but you are unable to detect its impact on the rather watery broth in which are assembled broad spectra of overcooked seafood and overcooked vegetables. Stuffed breast of chicken is offered on the regular menu and, with alternate stuffings, off the menu. The version that is filled with cheese and spinach is a winner; the big fist of white meat—it looks like chicken Kiev—is browned outside, moist within. The roast leg of lamb sometimes lacks pinkness, but it is good strong meat. The steak au poivre is not prime beef, but its heavily peppered surface and strong brandy sauce make it a tasty if inelegant dish. Course number five is a green salad—it is sometimes limp, and regulars often skip it.

If you have had poor luck, the desserts will cheer you up. The chunks of apple in the golden brown tarte Tatin are touched with caramel and a hint of acid. The double chocolate cake is of chocolate studded with chocolate. A so-called Sicilian rum cake is nutted, dotted with chocolate, weighted down with a layer of cheese cake, subtly liquored. The raspberry preserves in the beautifully browned pastry of the linzer torte are thick and of an almost liquor-like strength. The bits of hazelnut in the cheese cake are a nice surprise—you wish the cake were not cold.

★★BOX TREE

242 East 50th Street
LUNCH, MONDAY TO FRIDAY; DINNER, DAILY.
Reservations, PL 8-8320.
No credit cards.
Wine.
Very expensive.

If you arrive early for the second (9:30) dinner sitting, you must ring a bell to be admitted. You are let into a minuscule anteroom. Because you walked in the vicinity of building construction to get here, your shoes have picked up a bit of plaster dust. You note that your faint white footprints are swept from the carpet as soon as you deposit them, by a lad who follows you around with a carpet sweeper. If your arrival coincides with the departure of the 6:30 shift, you and they minuet to avoid collision, for this vestibule is at best a one-lane walkway between East 50th and the wee exquisiteness that is the Box Tree's dining room. The place accommodates, when every seat is taken, 24.

The walls have been enameled a deep emerald green, the intensity of which is dramatically set off by the pairs of tiny lamps, on wall sconces, that glow in deep-red shades. In the front part of the dining room you sit at bare, quasi-antique wooden tables, on chairs of pale bentwood and bamboo. At the back, you sit in an alcove, on a banquette upholstered in a multicolored, lightning-pattern, gleaming cloth. The banquette rises behind you a couple of feet higher than your head. It is positioned around four white-linened tables that are tightly assembled into the shape of a U along the three walls of a space that is no larger than a standard subway change booth. Back here everyone's back is to the wall, and no one is more than easy whispering distance from anyone else. Four unrelated couples at 9:30 are, perforce, by the end of the evening, an involuntary dinner party. (When you reserve, ask for a table in the front.) The restaurant is adorned with pewter and prints, pastoral scenes depicted in large, mostly deep-green stained-glass panels. Here there is a brass candelabrum, there flowers in a niche. A dark wooden beam circles the room along the wall, just below the ceiling— decorative plates and pottery are displayed thereon. A fancy plate is at each place setting, a napkin on it, next to that a red rose, which is intended for your lapel, your cleavage, your whatever. If you simply put the rose aside, however, your waiter comes to its rescue. Says he, with a straight face, "I'll put this in water and return it to you after dinner," which he does, with your check. Presently you order a bottle of wine, and, as you are now getting into the spirit of the place, you feel offended when the cork, when it is brought for your olfactory inspection, arrives in a small wineglass instead of on a silver tray. If you wish to retain your sense of reality, reserve the very front table—it is right beside the curtain that hangs over the front window, and you may peer through its lace at 50th Street.

Everyone is handed a menu, but only the apparent host or hostess a menu with prices written in. From it you may select the mousse of smoked haddock—finnan haddie, that is, salty and smoky and cool, bound together by perhaps too much gelatin, but very nice anyway. The serving is adorned with a dab of red caviar, which is pretty, but otherwise undetectable in this setting. Some very well-chosen shrimp—of clear, sweet flavor—are served mounded up in a small oval ramekin—their creamy wine sauce seems almost brandied. A perfectly nice, rather tart vinaigrette is wasted on an arti- choke that, though carefully poached and firm, is ice cold. The pâté of duckling livers is blenderized to the point at which its character is more or less aerated out. Presumably for fear that some liverishness may nevertheless be detectable, brandy is added until the mixture reaches approximately 40 proof. Special attention is given to the service of this dish: a youngster holds forth a cocotte as he lifts off its lid (the handle of which is in the form of a duck); your captain then scrapes out a curl of the stuff with a large spoon, lays it seriously on your plate and repeats the process until you stop him. Stop him. If you come here only once, begin your dinner with the snails. They are plump, tender, strongly flavored of the stock they were cooked in, and the rich and heady Pernod-flavored butter in which they are served is nicely moderated by a dusting of cheese that is browned just before serving. A plate of good soup follows your first course.

Salmon is poached in strong broth, so its fresh flavor is intensified. The moist and flaky fish is served covered over with a creamy—and very lemony—sauce mousseline. Your lobster is removed from its shell, cut up, returned to its half-shell, dressed with a sauce Mornay, which seems to have not only cheese in it, but a touch of liquor, and browned in the broiler. This is good lobster, but that sauce is a little too much for it —it obscures the shellfish as much as it emphasizes it. The calf's liver has a rare intensity of liver flavor, which is nicely set off by the polished madeira sauce—thick with minced truffles—in which it is served. The rack of lamb—served as four chops —is prepared with so thick a coating of herbs and fennel seeds that the flavor of the two end chops (whole faces of which are so coated) is solely of the herbs, not at all of the otherwise fine lamb. The mint sauce—little more than a purée of the herb—is intense, but redundant in the circumstance. If you must have red meat, have the filet of beef instead. The thick steak is perfectly grilled, then butterflied. The two resulting medallions are served with their rare (ungrilled) surfaces up, a dark wine sauce poured over them. The flavor of charring is emphasized in the sauce, which sets off the juicy and tender meat perfectly.

In this table d'hôte dinner, your main course is followed by a crisp salad of lettuce and watercress in a good mustard dressing, a few slivers of apple, Stilton cheese (the quality of which depends on the freshness of the wheel the night you come) and what the menu refers to as "Old Port." "Old Port," you understand, is not an *appellation contrôlée.*

Though half a dozen desserts are listed, the vacherin Box Tree is what everyone has. This is a construction of layers of white, crisp, chewy hazelnut meringue, airy whipped cream, and ripe raspberries that are firm and plump and juicy. It cannot go wrong. The light crème brûlée has the distinction of a touch of nutmeg. A sometimes available chocolate délice is a nutted combination of dark cake and chocolate mousse—a little cloying. The so-called cocotte of raspberries is a nice custard, raspberries buried within.

When new, the restaurant attracted an upper-crusty crowd, but people who get to the top are often aided in their ascent by their appreciation of the value of money, and these days that set is able to find more interesting places than the Box Tree at which to spend top dollars. Accordingly the crowd here is in large measure special-occasion once-in-a-lifetime celebrators. Still, most of the menu is first-class food, and the restaurant, for all its pretension, is striking.

★ BRADLEY'S

70 University Place (near 11th Street)
LUNCH AND DINNER.
No reservations (CA 8-6440).
Credit cards: AE, CB, DC.
Expensive.

Bradley's is a small, dark, wood-paneled saloon-with-back-room that specializes in burly bartenders and smashing waitresses, fresh clams and thick soups, plump hamburgers and plumper chopped steaks, a good green salad and tender sirloins, immaculate fish on Fridays, and strong coffee, rich cheese cake and good ice cream— and ice cream concoctions—all week long. Bradley's is used for literary lunches (Farrar, Straus and Giroux and the *Village Voice* are nearby) and smoky jazz dinners (the Baldwin grand piano was bequeathed to Bradley's—on condition that it be used in Bradley's—by the legendary saxophonist Paul Desmond, and the ivories and ebonies are burnished nightly by the fingertips of the best jazz pianists in New York).

Occasionally the density of humanity at the long front bar is such that achieving the dining room at the back is as problematic as getting to the back of an M3 bus at 59th and Madison at 5 P.M. on the Friday afternoon before a four-day weekend. But the back room is the place to be, for the linened tables are commodious, and the experience of being one of the few at one of them, in the class society that is Bradley's, may pleasantly fan your fantasies of status.

Throughout the place, the mahogany-colored walls are hung with spotlighted art of modern schools, including a stunning, mostly orange David Young, which hangs behind the bass player's place, setting up, thereby, a striking silhouette. High over the bar and running the full length of it is a strip of mirror, tilted forward at the top so that anyone mired in one part of the barroom may survey those mired in other parts.

The ruler of Bradley's is an actual person named Bradley, a gentleman who stands several stories high and who wears, alternately, a glower or a radiant, benedictory smile on the considerable expanse of his rugged complexion. If you want to be certain to meet Bradley, it is best to arrive late.

The menu goes well beyond the aforementioned items, but venturers into those territories proceed on their own courage. The safest byways are the clams casino, lamb chops, fillet of sole (hold the almonds), and, when available, the pecan pie.

The music, which begins at around ten, continues, officially, until 2 A.M. By that time, those who nurse one beer per set are gone, those who have or have not made social arrangements for the night are gone, some of those who have offices waiting at nine in the morning are gone, the cloths have been stripped from the tables in the back room, there is only one bartender behind the bar. At this hour the thinned crowd consists of restaurant and saloon people whose places closed earlier, a few theatrical types down from uptown after the performance, solitary drinkers whose long thoughts describe ever broader circles with each succeeding drink. And sometimes at this hour, Bradley himself sits down at the piano and plays dreamily.

Early in the week the crowd is not so dense.

★★ BREAD SHOP CAFÉ

157 Duane Street (near West Broadway)
LUNCH, MONDAY TO FRIDAY; DINNER, DAILY.
Reservations, 964-0524.
Credit cards: AE, MC, V.
Medium-priced.

Like the casual crowd it gets on a summer evening, the Bread Shop Café is a little undressed, revealing, as it does, for all to see, a part of itself that is private in most public eating places. The rectangular dining room is fitted, at one end, into the angle of an L-shaped kitchen, but no wall separates the two. You can, if you wish, send your compliments to the chef by smiling at him (though the rather athletic gents who, bareheaded, and with sleeves rolled up, turn out the stuff, do so with a kind of grim determination that does not invite comment).

The Bread Shop is long and lofty. Where it broadens at the back to take in the kitchen, it is a little like wide open spaces. The distant ceiling is of stamped tin, the floor underfoot of old hardwood. A brick wall runs along one side. The pay phone on the wall is right near the coat pegs. The place is lighted by white glass globes, and it is fanned by slowly turning, four-bladed ceiling fans. The white-linened tables, which are adorned with wildflowers, are big and well-spaced. One of them, at the front window, looks out on a wall of torn posters, across Duane Street. But little of the neighborhood's urban grimness seeps into this calm and cheerful place. The waiters and waitresses, who are civilized and helpful, actually appear to enjoy working here. And you can always get their attention, for they are never out of sight—when they "go to the kitchen," they are simply stepping up to a counter that is right in the dining room. The place is one big worker/customer commune.

What you are offered to eat is less a menu than a state of experimentation indefinitely prolonged. Accordingly, the choices are not printed on paper, but are written on white slates, one of which is brought to your table shortly after you are seated. On occasion it offers a ceviche of scallops, in which the raw seafood is "cooked" by marinating it in spiced citrus juice, with chopped vegetables. The scallops are served cool, and the tender little morsels are lovely in the tangy marinade. When tomatoes are good, the Café serves slabs of them—dark-red, glistening and juicy—under a mound of strands of strong red onion, in a smooth and mustardy vinaigrette. The so-called Gorgonzola dip seems to be little more than that pungent cheese softened—it is served with crisp sticks of carrot and celery. On your lucky night you will encounter this establishment's carpaccio, juicy slices of just cut raw beef, moistened with lemon juice and good oil, sprinkled with fresh herbs and crisp chopped vegetables and strewn with strong cheese that is just ground—rich meat made a little tart and very sparkling by its dressing. Sometimes there is good ham, but it is wrapped around melon that is insufficiently ripe. On happier occasions it is wrapped around a sheaf of slender asparagus spears, buttered, sprinkled with grated cheese and baked until the cheese is slightly browned, all of which adds up to a dish that is at once pungent and delicate. One of the best pesto sauces in town is made here, wildly fragrant of fresh basil, and the oiled and nutted sauce, sharpened with cheese, is served on perfectly cooked, tender but firm linguine. And one of the most unusual lobster bisques, its distinction being that its rich flavor is derived from an abundance of sweet lobster meat.

Utterly fresh fish, but the orange sauce that adorns the crisped and flaky snapper, though it does not clash with it, does not improve it either, and what sounds like a dramatic concoction turns out to be a rather harmless little surprise. But the so-called piccata of swordfish, in which scallops of the fresh fish are spread with a buttery sauce of lemon and capers, and then baked, is an elegant composition, in which the very tart sauce offsets the natural fibrousness and weight of the swordfish. The curried chicken is a creamy stew, its spices mainly sweet ones, surmounted by sliced fruit—hot peaches and apples. The veal scaloppine with fresh rosemary is not of the most buttery veal, and the lightly lemoned herb sauce seems a little misplaced on the slightly coarse meat. The loin of lamb, with fresh thyme and port, is a slab of charred meat that is rare and juicy inside—it is moistened with a dark and winy sauce that is very much a match for the strong lamb. And a beef dish rather frighteningly titled "roast filet mignon with gravlax sauce" turns out, happily, not to be smothered in marinated salmon. The powerfully flavored sauce is of dill and capers, and it is fine on the beef, though it would probably be even better on a stronger-tasting cut than filet mignon, which, because of its relative delicacy, is almost obliterated by the strong flavors of this sauce.

Often there are odd kinds of sherbet, such as grapefruit-campari, mint-pineapple, both of which, like the more familiar lemon ice, are sweet and clear and rousing. And almost always there is on hand the unlikely-sounding salted almond ice cream, which is perhaps more of a surprise than a delight—the salted nuts that are dotted throughout are startlingly consonant with the rich, sweet cream. The apple pie is tart, sweet, spicy, and the pecan pie—mostly nuts, very little filler—is sharp and crisp. The orange-flavored brandy cake is really little more than a good pound cake soaked in booze—fun, but not classy. Even more fun is the mocha-dacquoise, in which layers of mocha-flavored cream alternate with chewy meringue—a black icing is painted across the top of the multi-storied structure.

At a little after eleven the boys and girls of the dining room and kitchen staffs push a few tables together near the back of the store, uncork a bottle of red and one of white, and sit down to eat. While they do so the last parties hang around over coffee.

★ BROADWAY JOE STEAK HOUSE

315 West 46th Street
LUNCH, MONDAY TO FRIDAY; DINNER, DAILY.
Reservations, CI 6-6513.
Credit cards: AE, CB, DC, MC, V.
Expensive.

Broadway Joe has been around for decades, but in recent years it fell into near disuse. New interests now run the place, and some improvements are evident. This is a steak house, and its steaks—as well as some of the traditional accompaniments thereof —are now first-rate. More, however, could be done.

You enter to a clubby barroom, paneled with broad beams of polished honey-colored wood. Most of one long wall is still occupied by a huge painting entitled "100 Years of Broadway Theatre," which consists of full-color caricatures of famous faces, including the likes of John Garfield, Pearl Bailey, Marlon Brando, George Gershwin, Bette Davis, Al Jolson; for the new management knows that this is the Theater District, and that showgoers love memories even more than nostalgia itself. But the new team is mindful also that this is the New York *Times* District as well, so when you take the path through the open kitchen to the two dining rooms at the back, you will note that not only are the rooms freshly painted, their heavily grained oak beams gleaming, but that they have been hung with Hirschfeld drawings of men of letters that subsequent men of letters have made into legends, among them A.J. Liebling, G.S. Kaufman, R.W. Lardner. (A.M. Rosenthal is inexplicably omitted.) The good-old-days theme is echoed in the background music (Billie Holiday, Frank Sinatra, Artie Shaw) which is turned off only for foreground music. A white upright you may have spotted threatening when you entered the front room is, late in the evening, had at by a character actor doing this really terrific imitation of a certain now extinct Broadway type—tux, handkerchief in breast pocket, silver hair combed close to the pate, just hum a few bars and he'll fake it from there. That, however, is not so bad. But among the Reporters (the full title is Hardboiled Reporter) who congregate at the brass rail (and congratulate one another for being whoever they are) there is sometimes one or another who is persuaded by his refreshments that he is not only a great writer, but a crooner too. He tosses a song title at the pianist, leans (necessarily) on the instrument, puts the microphone to his lips and you know the rest. Men of letters have an obligation, to themselves and to their public, to stay in touch with local, national and world affairs, so the color television set in the barroom is turned on (without sound, to be sure) whenever a major league contest is being broadcast. Sometimes the piano, an inebriated crooner and the Yankees are going all at once.

Very little of interest to hold you while you are waiting for your plank of medium-rare. The herring is sour and mealy rather than tart and fibrous. The jumbo shrimp cocktail is of contemporary jumbo shrimp. Many oldtimers begin with salad. The one named for Caesar, of crisp romaine lettuce and slivers of anchovy, with much ground cheese, is fine, despite the crumbled slice of toasted white bread that substitutes for the usual croutons. But another night the so-called Roquefort salad is of two-toned lettuce (green and brown) that is soaked in its oil-and-cheese dressing.

Of course meat is your major. Broadway Joe now serves up sirloin that is the equal of the best in town, the blood-juicy beef of strong flavor within its expertly seared surfaces. The filet mignon is good too, but less of a standout. The veal chop is huge, the buttery meat browned, cooked to the perfect point. And the lamb chops, lightly charred, have a stout and gamy taste. Stop right there. Do not order the broiled chicken, which is beautifully crisped and utterly tasteless. And do not order the steak tartare, which is of meat ground in advance—and it continues to advance, is already heavily flecked with brown. Much is made of the potato shells à la Scanlon. (On an early version of the menu they were entitled "Shells à la The Laundry, East Hampton.") These are potato shells, baked (or something) until they are not quite as crisp as slate, in the hollow of each shell a bit of chopped parsley and crumbled bacon. They are not food, but they are fun. The hash browns are powerfully seasoned, nicely greased, crusty, ample. The lyonnaise potatoes are superior—big slabs of browned tuber, with sections of blackened onion that retain much of the strength of the raw article. The huge mound of French-fried onions is dark, a little resilient, sweet within their crisp batter. The exhausted baked potatoes seem not to have been scrubbed before they were put in the oven—the skins of some of them are a bit moldy. Your baked comes with a half-pint container of sour cream—sometimes Breakstone's, sometimes Friendship—into which chives have been stirred.

The cheese cake is cold, lemon-flavored clay. The chocolate cheese cake is cold, chocolate-flavored clay. You may figure out the cherry cheese cake for yourself. There is ice cream.

★ BROOME STREET BAR

363 West Broadway (at Broome Street)
LUNCH AND DINNER.
No reservations (925-2086).
No credit cards.
Inexpensive.

At the Broome Street Bar you can often get a table even when the crowd appears to exceed the Fire Department limit. The habitués are crowded twelve deep at the bar of this tight, gamy joint, disporting themselves. Overt sexuality, overt alienation, overt youth, overt bitterness, overt desperation, overt sinister menace even. Laid back, you understand, does not come here. Thumbs are hooked in the belt loops of tight jeans. Fingers snap and behinds wiggle to the rhythmic jangle and thump of a perpetual tape deck. Whole bodies jiggle like paper dolls controlled by invisible strings. Sullen men pump smoke through their nostrils and stare balefully at the untouchable scene. There are baseball hats on some, leather jackets on others, opaque plastic eyeglasses with thin slits in their lenses over the eyes of those who can stand only so much of the visible world. The bartender regards you from behind bangs that have grown down to his upper eyelashes—when bent forward (a position in which he spends much of his working day), he can see very, very little. Your worldly waitress seems like a naïf in this crowd. And the busboy/sweeper/general aide—a slight gent in a ponytail, chin beard, vest, jeans and running shoes—scratches the seat of his pants while he chats with the regulars. But when Mayor Koch drops in, everyone wants to shake his hand and grin at him, just like political groupies anywhere.

Those who sit down to eat are largely another set—uptown slummers, NYU and Cooper Union collegiates, suburban gawkers, even leftover flower children, defiantly poor, sharing sandwiches and drinking draft beer, fancying themselves tragic. You may sit in the back room (which is large enough for a double bed and a bureau, but which is furnished, instead, with more than a dozen tables and a suitable number of chairs) or in the front room (which is somewhat larger, and where you get a good view of the action at that famous bar).

Throughout the restaurant the walls are dark, in some places of slate, and pieces of colored chalk are left in the chalk troughs so that customers may express themselves in dull graffiti (e.g., "Peron lives") or in tic-tac-toe. Dim, low-hanging factory lamps light the restaurant, four-bladed fans cool it. The floors are of unfinished wood. Hanging green plants filter the light that comes through the ancient, small-paned windows that look out on West Broadway.

Your board is set with paper napkins, milk in a steel pourer, ketchup in a glass bowl with a glass lid (ketchup in a bottle with a screw-on top would be a collectable). You select your repast from a listing that is chalked, in iridescent colors, high on the walls: such items as blue cheese, pear and sprout salad, a serving of food about the size of a major league basketball, the fruit perfect, sweet and crisp, the cheese creamy and sharp, the sprouts fresh, an abundance of peanuts, and an oil-and-lemon dressing that is not bad despite its dried herbs; or the mushroom and watercress salad, the only dish in SoHo (perhaps in all of lower Manhattan) that is served topped with Triscuits—and if that does not make it singular, then the mandarin orange sections do, especially in combination with a clump of watercress that is complete but for its rubber band, enough chopped tomatoes to make a pint of juice, lots of good mushrooms, and sprigs of dill here and there for an unexpected intensity of flavor in every fourth bite or so.

The chili is sprinkled with strong chopped onions and layered over with triangles of an orange cheese that looks stronger than it tastes—the meat and beans that are the bulk of the dish are nubbly, thick and fiery. The hungry and relatively insolvent have been known to make a meal of this chili, augmented with thick slices of the firm, moist, and crusty rye and pumpernickel breads you get here. The burgers are not bad, the best of them served in pita with a slice of tomato, unmelted blue cheese, and a slab of strong onion. The contents of an unfortunate grilled sandwich, unfortunately named pigwhich, are a slice of ham cut from a waterlogged block, Swiss cheese from Brooklyn (or perhaps Austria), slices of tomato and (for an additional half dollar) that orange cheese —the dish is almost rescued by the toasted brown bread within which it is assembled.

The Broome Street Bar is a busy place, and the desserts are always fresh: moist, honeyed carrot cake; pecan pie with lots of nuts and too much corn syrup; rich, sugary cheese cake; ice creams.

★★ BRUNO

240 East 58th Street
LUNCH, MONDAY TO FRIDAY; DINNER, MONDAY TO SATURDAY. CLOSED SUNDAY.
Reservations, 688-4190.
Credit cards: AE, DC, MC, V.
Expensive.

Bruno has enough help. And during its busy hours (nine P.M. seems to be the peak) the aisles between the rows of tables are seething with scurrying gentlemen delivering little trays of drinks and big platters of food, transporting buckets of ice and replenishments of linen, tearing slips from their order pads as they tear for the kitchen. The choreography has been so arranged that as one hastener passes another in the narrows, waists are sucked in, loads are gracefully lifted high, or swung out over tables, and carriers pass each other, bodies not quite kissing, like adagio dancers in a speeded-up movie. Still, calm rules. All the while other gents are standing at tablesides—pulling corks from bottles, tilting purple wine into crystal glasses, spooning ground cheese onto mounds of steaming noodles—with equanimity, with utter confidence that the action at their backs will never collide with their postures.

The waiters are in white, the captains in black, and it is with the latter you have most of your truck. These are mellifluous fellows, suave in several Italianate manners, ranging from imperious to sweet. And while the least of them will raise a dubious eyebrow if he disapproves what you choose to eat—or murmur a slightly condescending "of course," or "very good," when you do better—others among them take you through the menu with such enthusiasm and detail, underscoring their descriptions with Toscaninian gestures, pinching and caressing the air before your eyes, that when a selection is finally made, it is the harmonious decision of a unison captain-and-customer chorus.

Bruno himself presides over all, looking a little young for one so successfully along in the restaurant business, a tall, slender, handsome, mustachioed figure in an Italian suit. He goes, occasionally, from table to table to ask if all is well. Usually it is.

His restaurant is housed in a long, low room. There are a couple of little marble-topped tables just inside, under the storefront window; further along there is a small, handsome bar—fixtures of glinting brass behind it—a few tables more across the way; and beyond that the restaurant proper, rows of ample, white-linened tables that are surrounded by simple bentwood chairs. The walls are of trowel-marked pale-ivory plaster or dark-brown mirrored glass. The room is softly lighted, carpeted, casually adorned with botanical prints in plain wooden frames and with displays of Italian wine. Little bursts of bright flowers on the tables add a gay note. And so do the customers, for they are a happy lot. There is no false pretension about the way they dress and adorn themselves. Their costumes and jewelry are chosen, quite simply, to attract attention. Broad-striped shirts are seen on many of the men, broad-brimmed hats, throughout dinner, on some of the ladies; multiple rings on hands of either gender; silk shirts and blouses, open at the neck, tucked into tailored denim that fits like the skin on a plum. When the restaurant is filled, around $10,000 worth of hair-care is on display, ten million strands of human keratin, each one coaxed and fixed into its proper gleaming place. But this is a knowing crowd. They know the difference between Bruno and the places closer to home—in Queens and Fort Lee. And when they want a good dinner, they leave home for Bruno. Their evident financial well-being derives from the fact that they are nobody's fools.

For neither in Queens nor Fort Lee, nor almost anywhere else, are you likely to discover the equal of Bruno's zucchini ripieni, six shafts cut from a laterally bifurcated green squash, hot, crisp and juicy, mounded over with a lightly browned stuffing—of veal and ham, cheese and wine and herbs—of such fluffiness, such freshness of taste, as to make other forcemeats seem petrified. The dish is moistened with a simple tomato sauce that has just a slight tartness. The same tomato sauce is served on hot clams, eight fresh cherrystones, sold as vongole alla capri—the clams have been warmed a little too long, and they have lost some of their tenderness, but none of their freshness. Good spiedino alla romana made here, that repeating sandwich of bread, ham and cheese, battered and deep-fried until the contents are hot, the cheese pully. It is served as a great glistening block, in a sauce—of herbs, oil and anchovies—that makes the dish at once less heavy and more powerful. For an easy start you may begin with the mushroom salad—crisp slices of woodsy fungi, mingled with strands of sharp red onion, in a delicate and lightly herbed oil. The mushrooms soak up the dressing and its flavor, but remain dry.

Bruno cooks packaged pasta, not the moist fresh stuff that is the last word, but it is boiled with care, it reaches you firm but tender, and the sauces are splendid: a pesto that is sharp, strong and, especially, perfumed, the scent of the basil fragrant and fresh even out of season, the garlic and cheese clear but not too strong; the smoky red sauce called matriciana, its pungency that of good prosciutto ham, its sweetness that of sautéed onions; and a briny seafood sauce, also red, studded with plump mussels, squid, thick slivers of garlic and, unfortunately, shrimps of little flavor—still, a good sauce.

For the most primitive kind of pleasure, order the risotto milanese, a gigantic mound of rice, each grain separate, almost hard, but cooked not a moment too briefly. The buttered grain is made red and exotically spicy with much saffron; you add ground Parmesan cheese to the rice and toss the two together, adding more and more cheese until just short of the point where it takes over the dish.

The red snapper is a great slab of snowy fish, just out of the sea, garnished with little clams and covered over with a marinara sauce that is thick with vegetables and polished with oil. Superb veal paillard, the thin steaks of buttery meat grilled until they are flecked with mahogany, just barely cooked through and still juicy. When you squeeze on the lemon the meat comes to life. Do not go near the veal parmigiana, which is apparently on the menu to alienate those who would order it. And think twice about the sausages, for though they are buried in a marvelous stew of onions and peppers and solid tomato sauce, the sausages themselves are gray and rather coarse. They do better in the pollo alla contadina, chunks of chicken, discs of sausage, those peppers again and halved cloves of garlic in great amount—in this setting those sausages are just an accent to the moist and oily meat of the bird.

For dessert there is a smooth and sugary cheese cake, lemony and light; a rum cake that is the usual boozy confection; a hot zabaglione that is prepared publicly at the back of the dining room in a round-bottomed copper pot—but that is all you can say for sure, for the wininess, frothiness and heat of the concoction vary with the whim of the maker.

★★CABANA CARIOCA

123 West 45th Street
LUNCH AND DINNER.
Reservations, 581-8088
Credit cards: AE, CB, DC, MC, V.
Inexpensive.

Life in Brazil is ever gay, or so you may conclude from depictions of it in the brilliantly colored murals that adorn the walls of the stairway leading to this primitive second- and third-story eating place. One flight up, through the parti-colored door, and you are at the pea-green plastic lunch (and dinner) counter and bar, which is lined with stools upholstered in plastic the color of Sunkist oranges. The ancient coffee urn looks like a public triumphal sculpture in stainless steel. The nailed-up wooden shelves suggest the carpentry in a general store in a jungle clearing. Here at the counter New York's Brazilian bachelors eat with dispatch and drink Brazilian beer from the bottle. And nearby, at most times, one or both of this restaurant's bosses—gentlemen in white shirts (sleeves rolled up), neckties and aprons—are to be found. Either of them is a candidate for mayor of New York's Brazilian community. They know half the customers who walk in (the other half are not Brazilian), but are sweet and hospitable to everyone. The dining room proper has varnished wood walls, garishly colored paintings, a density of tables (most of them occupied most of the time) covered with blue cloths, and steel chairs upholstered with red, white and green plastic. The front windows are overgrown with greenery, which filters somewhat the overhead view of 45th Street continuing downhill. The third-floor dining room is more of the same, but no counter. Cabana Carioca is not a quiet restaurant. But, happily, much of the noise is the sibilant and singsong sound of the Portuguese language spoken with polite passion. New York's seekers after ethnic curiosity come here too, to broaden themselves by contact with another culture and to fatten up on the immense servings purveyed here at low prices.

Two of you can share a single order of ameijoa à bulhao pato, twelve giant cherrystone clams (almost as big as full-size quahogs), served in a huge iron pot that holds also three inches of oiled, parsleyed and briny broth. Clams this big can be chewy, if not tough, and these are such that you may want to have at them with a knife and fork, to eat them in two or three bites. What the Cabana calls a special appetizer of shrimp, you will, on inspection, identify as a lunch and a half. The many shrimp are mingled with black olives, and the dish is singular for the strength of the olive and olive-oil flavors that the hot shrimp have absorbed. The fried sausages are spicy, crusted and pleasantly greasy, and the lettuce on which they are served is, in effect, dressed—and wilted—by the fat that drains out of the sausages onto the leaves. The caldo verde (green soup) is thick with potato, studded with chunks of strong sausage, laced with sharp kale.

About a quart of black beans and a platter of rice in which you could bury a small mammal are delivered to every table. As an accompaniment to those try the bacalhau à braz, a primitive dish, at once vigorous and homey, of salt cod mingled with black olives, sautéed onions, eggs and plenty of potatoes. The paella here is not a standout.

It is, of course, copious, half a lobster tail and plenty of shrimp, scallops and squid, sections of chicken, sausages and green peas buried in the rice, but the seasoning does not bring out the individuality of these ingredients, though the chicken, which has absorbed the seafood flavors, is thereby converted into an interesting item. There is an odd lobster dish here—listed as lagosta à cheff—that probably has more allure to those with Brazilian memories than to the rest of you. The decent crustacean is covered over with a seasoned and browned bread paste, giving it an undetectable charm. A menu entry of "carne porco alentejana" is described as "pork bits with clams." Actually the chunks of meat are the size of paving stones, which is to say almost as large as the clams. Both are delivered to you in a pot of sufficient girth to hold a dozen of each, as well as more of those sausages, all in a buttered broth—the meat is tender, the clams fresh, the broth powerful, the entire production adorned with the coarse but good fried potatoes that garnish many of the main courses here. The fried chicken carioca style is a good, moist bird, well crusted, saturated with the flavor of garlic. Of course there is feijoada, which, as all the world knows, is the national dish of Brazil—buried in the black beans are joints of meat, chunks of meat, ribs of meat, sausages. The dish is garnished with slices of raw orange, buttered kale and manioc, the tangy zest always served with feijoada.

The flan differs from those you get in Spanish restaurants in that it is the color of salmon. The desserts of guava, guava paste, caramelized milk and hard cheese may well be skipped. The Brazilian coffee, of course, is strong and good.

★★ CAFÉ DES ARTISTES

1 West 67th Street
LUNCH AND DINNER.
Reservations, 877-3500.
Credit cards: AE, CB, DC, MC, V.
Expensive.

Dozens of young ladies, unclothed, and in the rosy florescence of youth, still cavort in the Café's woods, just as they did when Howard Chandler Christy first painted the sylvan murals that transform the walls of this place into a young man's fancy. Along the length of the main dining room, tall casement windows face out on 67th Street, and the dozens of plants that stand and hang just inside them repeat in living three dimensions only, unfortunately, the flora of Christy's fantasies. Where the murals are not, the walls are mirrored, adding a jewel-like glint to the lush scene. A second room, a few steps up, has a big three-sided bar at the back, around which the large booths and tables afford more commodiousness and privacy than you will find (or, probably, seek) in the cheerfully populous main room.

You do see people here (even young men) who hardly glance at the art. They have come for the mostly good food, and to be part of the gaiety of the contented crowd around them. The Café is popular. The clientele is West Side—middle-class, to be sure, but their concern with the dollar is revealed more in the care with which they spend it than in its display. Magnates do not come here much. The place gets shrinks and professors, proprietors of Broadway shops, solvent authors of non-best sellers, ladies in fedoras, young marrieds whose budget for an evening out can cover this establishment's reasonable tariffs if they skip cocktails, drink carafe wine and share a dessert.

Some of them begin with eel, though the name frightens others away. It should not, for the cold fish—marinated in lemon and wine, and served with the onions that were part of the marinade—is no more frightening than marinated mackerel, and just as refreshing. You get a platter of cold salmon four ways: The smoked salmon is red and strong, not the pink and delicate best, but good; the Scandinavian marinated salmon called gravlax is salty, powerfully flavored with dill, much better straight than with the rather sugary mustard-and-dill sauce that comes with it; the poached salmon is fresh and firm, very good with its rich, smoky, tarragon-flavored mayonnaise; and the so-called salmon tartare—chopped salmon mixed with oil and dill and much seasoning—is nice, too, though its intense flavoring seems to obscure rather than enhance its rawness, and the avocado on which it is served makes no sense at all with the fish. Nor does another slice of avocado have any business associating with the otherwise fine cold mussels in their lightly curried mayonnaise. Many of the restaurant's appetizers and desserts are displayed on a big, two-tiered table at the center of the main room. You will spot thereon a large glass bowl. Eschew its contents, lumps of olive-cured mozzarella, which, if you do order the dish, are ladled onto your plate in bounteous excess, as if the help cannot wait to be done with the evening's supply—the stuff has the flavor and texture of oiled, hard-boiled, denatured egg white. You will much prefer most of the items that make up the assortment of charcuterie. The nutted country pâté, though heavily fatted, is of good, coarse flavor. The sausage is garlicky and strong. The chicken-liver pâté, is well brandied. The headcheese is the big winner—chunks of sweetbread and tongue and cartilaginous meats, mingled with peppercorns, in a firm, dark jelly. The rillettes—pounded pork—could use more seasoning to offset the fat. The Café's bresaola is a rather mild version of the Italian air-dried beef, good, but lacking some of the toughness and gaminess of this stuff at its best; the melon with which it is served is sometimes not at the peak of its ripeness.

A hefty slice from a huge fresh bluefish is served slightly crusted, a disc of parsleyed butter melting on it, anchovies adorning it. In a splendid dish of bay scallops the little morsels of seafood are combined, in a buttery sauce, with crisp walnuts and herbs. The poulet casserole is a stew-like item of browned chicken, with onion and mushrooms, green peppers and tomato, in which the flavor of the good bird is heightened by the vegetables and seasonings. Duck confit is duck preserved in its own fat. It is served hot, and it is salty, rich without being fatty, the pieces of bird very dark, blackened a bit in places, resilient, almost leathery, of powerful, seemingly intensified duck flavor. What the house calls a "lightly toasted curry tartar steak" is not just a redesignated hamburger. The seasoned ground meat is cool, its surface barely singed. It is moist, studded with pine nuts, and garnished with capers, chopped onion, and chopped tomato, but the curry the menu leads you to expect is at best an obscurity. The beans of the cassoulet are tender yet firm—just the right texture—but the chunks of lamb and sausage hardly compose the feast of variety you hope to find buried in a dish of that name. The so-called mignon of lamb is two tournedos of fat-rimmed, strong-flavored, juicy broiled meat, served with an intensely tarragon-flavored sauce béarnaise. The sirloin steaks are fine if not first-class—order yours lyonnaise and it arrives covered over with good sautéed onions.

A couple of those ladies in felt hats nibble their way gingerly through their dinner, all the while anticipating the climax—"The Great Dessert Plate," $10 for a slice of every cake, tart, torte and pie on display. Their appetites lift as soon as the production arrives. They like the sweet-spiced carrot cake, the clear citrus flavor of the orange savarin cake, the velvety black icing on the moist chocolate cake, the lovely coffee flavor and the pleasantly chewy meringue in the nutted dacquoise. Skip the dates "stuffed" with cream cheese—little blocks of hard cheese wedged into the dried fruit. There are many flavors of ice cream, fruits and berries of variable quality.

The menu changes a little from day to day, so you will not always find what you seek.

It is often impossible to get a reservation in this place. But nine times in ten, if you just show up, you will have a table in ten or fifteen minutes.

★★CAFÉ DES SPORTS

329 West 51st Street
LUNCH, MONDAY TO FRIDAY; DINNER, DAILY.
Reservations, 581-1283.
Credit cards: AE.
Medium-priced.

Your waitress is not shocked when you ask to have your red wine chilled. She would not be shocked if you asked her to mix it with tomato juice. Café des Sports is a restaurant in which the customer is right simply because he is the customer. The place is, in fact, so taken with the idea of satisfying its clientele that it offers fair value for your money. And to ensure that satisfied customers will be satisfied again on return visits, the restaurant prepares its good food the same way, year after year. In such a changeless establishment it is easy to relax. You find yourself concentrating on your thoughts and conversation rather than on the event of going out. Dozens of French restaurants dot the West Forties and Fifties. They have for decades. And many of them, despite tempting new styles that flourish on the other side of Sixth Avenue, stick, either by fanaticism or habit, to old ways. Café des Sports is one of these.

The restaurant is clearly a family enterprise. The woman who greets you does not lead you to your table in the manner of an overworked usher marching you to a seat behind a pole; she may even linger awhile, in case your assigned spot does not please you. And the silver-haired gentleman behind the bar reads his French newspaper in the at-home manner of a burgher on his Sunday off. He folds it up when his Gallic cronies come in for late drinks.

In the old days the waitresses in these West Side bistros were, almost uniformly, bulky, businesslike and cheerful, easily adjusting their French-peasant manners to their urban jobs. Today a second generation of them works the floor at Café des Sports, young women who have not yet developed the monumental solidity and earthy savvy of their predecessors, but who seem to have inherited their no-nonsense facility for extracting your order in a trice, and that purposeful, thumping walk for delivering your instructions to the kitchen and your food back to you. If you seek ceremony, this is not the place.

Café des Sports is spiffy in a roadhouse manner. The floor-to-ceiling knotty pine is stained walnut and burnished to a velvet sheen. A few copper utensils hang on a few square feet of exposed brick. There are colorful plaid cloths under the white table linen. A case of athletic trophies in the front room and some flashy sporting prints in the back seem to have no other purpose than to make the place appropriate to its name.

The familiar food includes cold marinated mackerel, firm and sour in its jelly—it wakes you right up; saucisson à l'ail, five discs of the cool sausage, well fatted, spicy and loudly garlicked—very good with sharp mustard. Unfortunately, the asparagus may be overcooked when in season, canned when not; the leeks, however, are susceptible only to the former mishap; and the vinaigrette that is served with both of these is bright and mustardy and just about rescues the vegetables on better days. The snails are pretty good, their garlic butter pungent and salty, but they are small and lack the voluptuousness of really first-class escargots.

What the Café does best is the kind of thing you probably yearn for least. Tripe, for example (à la mode Bretonne, by word of the menu)—gummy and firm slivers of the soft white meat, mingled with bits of carrot, in a thick broth that is hot and oily and startlingly fragrant of clove. Tête de veau, for another—chunks of brain and little slabs of meat that are anchored to jellied cartilage and rimmed with fat, the cloying richness of the steaming dish mitigated by the simple boiled potatoes that garnish it and by the tart vinaigrette, laced with onions and parsley, with which you dress it. The breaded and garlicked and sautéed frog's legs are browned and crusty, tender and moist—a very well made dish. When bass is available the fresh fish is done meunière—lightly floured and sautéed in butter—and the flaky white meat is lovely within its light brown crust. The duck, of course, is prepared à l'orange, and it is good, crisped, rich but not fatty, rather foolishly adorned with sections of mandarin orange; its sauce is a little candylike, but this is decent food despite its flaws. The grilled chicken is perhaps more interesting —it is made when you order it, it is a simple dish, seasoned and blackened, with the softness and juiciness of chicken just cooked; the bird is garnished, happily, with thin, salted French fries, at once crisp and tender—the real thing, they even taste like potatoes. The steaks and chops are of tender, tasty meat, accurately prepared. The vegetable garnishes that accompany the main courses are kept waiting in a steam table, and you may do well to suggest that your portion remain there.

The coupe aux marrons is a hopelessly silly combination of candied nuts and vanilla cream. The crème caramel is reliable, the chocolate mousse forgettable. The items on the pastry tray are harmless, filled with creditable custards and perfectly OK pastry creams. The winner is the apple ($.80)—it arrives still attached to the corer/slicer that has divided it into ten convenient sections—you can have the fruit alone, or, at a premium, with some fair Roquefort cheese.

This place can be very busy just before the nearby curtains go up. Thereafter regulars come in at a slow but steady rate for leisurely dinners.

★★CAFÉ EUROPA/LA BRIOCHE

347 East 54th Street
LUNCH, MONDAY TO FRIDAY; DINNER, MONDAY TO SATURDAY. CLOSED SUNDAY.
Reservations, 755–0160.
Credit cards: AE, CB, DC, MC, V.
Medium-priced.

This is one of the simplest and most straightforward neighborhood restaurants in New York. It is also reasonably priced. The present site is its third since the restaurant first opened as Peter's Café Europa more than a decade ago. The present expanded name reflects an expansion of the menu by an additional menu of large, stew-filled brioches which are good value for some imaginative food.

There is a quasi garden wherein it never rains—a small room in the back which, with its skylight, glass wall, floor of simulated red tiles, and plants, feels very much like a garden. The main dining area, with space for about twenty tables, has the dim, soothing atmosphere of a cool, deeply shaded house in some hot part of the world. The walls are of bare plaster, overlaid here and there with stripped cabinetry, tapestries and cracked oil paintings. The illumination is from a couple of pewter chandeliers with dim lanterns, and from candles on each table. Oriental rugs fail to absorb the shock of the heavy-footed; the wooden floor is creaky, and when a customer or waiter goes by, you may feel it through your chair.

Mussels Marinière are the always available appetizer, and they are well made—in a buttery broth of wine, seasonings, abundant fresh parsley and, adding an unusual tang, minced scallions. The alternate first course varies from week to week, and it is rarely a humdrum item: on occasion there is something the house refers to as Shrimp Castillo—a little hot sandwich of minced shrimp, flavored with spices and lemon, between two slices of well-browned French toast; at times a very decent ham-and-asparagus quiche. The invariable soup is gazpacho. This dish has too often been called a liquid salad, but the version made here really merits the description. It consists of very finely minced vegetables—tomatoes, celery, cucumber, onions, etc.—in their own juices, with very little oil, no thickening of bread and hardly any garlic, all very fresh, refreshing, nourishing and thinning, but it should be listed as V-8 Maison. Among the alternate soups one is likely to prefer is a mulligatawny that is sometimes available cold, sometimes hot, sometimes both ways; but hot is best because the soup is a thick, curried, puréed vegetable made with a chicken base, and curry when it is cold is a little queer. There is also, on occasion, a cucumber soup (sometimes hot, sometimes cold) which is very thick and has a strong flavoring of dill.

Broiled lamb chops, it would seem, should not be tampered with. Get some good chops and broil them, but not too long. The result, as everyone knows, is a simple, perfect dish, and anyone who can't consume sixteen baby ribs at a sitting is a sissy. Well, you don't get sixteen ribs here, and they are tampered with, but in such a way that the simple dish is actually improved. The chops are marinated in soy sauce, sake and ginger before they are broiled. The marination lasts only long enough to flavor the outside of the meat, and the subsequent broiling creates a brilliantly flavored crust—the lamb on the three-rib chops is excellent, but even better are the highly flavored bits and pieces one finds when the nearly denuded bones are finally picked up and nibbled at. Amazingly, the chops are served with *fresh peas.*

The Duck à l'Orange here, as in almost every restaurant, has a sauce that is too candied; its sweetness is not as exaggerated as in some places, but it is a bit excessive. The bird is perfectly roasted, however; the sauce is served in a separate dish, and using just a little helps. There is also Chicken Kiev (yes, the butter spurts out when you cut into it), and Beef Wellington (no, it is not overcooked).

Then there is this matter of the brioches. Each one is the size of a cantaloupe. The conical top is pulled out of the brioche, the center is hollowed and filled with the stew of your choice, and the plug replaced. Among the available fillings is an excellent Chicken Basquaise—chicken cooked in wine, with strong ham and green peppers. There is also a good Veal Marengo, made with fresh sautéed mushrooms, onions, celery and tomatoes; a spicy Curried Beef (with nuts, fruits and chutney); Crab Gumbo; and something named Shrimp & Mushroom Polonaise. In all of these the flavors of the ingredients are preserved, and the combinations are well balanced. You will get more brioche than gravy with which to moisten it—spread the remainder with butter and eat it that way.

The salad is nothing special. Among the desserts, there are several good reasons to pass up the chocolate mousse. It must be on the menu because it sells well, and it is made with good, dark chocolate, but it is airless, like a pudding rather than a mousse.

Have, instead, the macédoine of fresh fruit—the apples are crisp, as if they were just cut; the strawberries are ripe and juicy; the blueberries are large and firm; the orange sections are seeded and sweet; there is no sugar added, and the fruit arrives in the juice that comes of cutting it up—very pure, though a little bloodless. Better still are the crêpes, in a sauce of wine, lemon and sugar. Best of all are the bananas au rhum—bananas baked soft in a custard—very sweet, with just a suggestion of the edgy flavor of cooked milk, and a strong flavor of dark rum.

If every part of New York had a handful of sensibly priced neighborhood restaurants like this one, the supermarkets would be reduced to their natural commerce—dog food and soap.

★★ CAFÉ 58

232 East 58th Street
LUNCH, MONDAY TO SATURDAY; DINNER, DAILY.
Reservations, 758-5665.
Credit cards: AE, CB, DC, MC, V.
Medium-priced.

The jollity that pervades this place, it is certain, has to do at least in part with the fact that one may dine here rather cheaply (for a French restaurant, in New York, in the East 50s, in the 1980s). People whose backgrounds or circumstances have given them an undue respect for the value of the dollar come here. You see young lawyers with their dates—while they are still in the five-figure bracket, their salaries go entirely to their landlords. You see pairs of widows of a certain age—they arrive in carefully cared-for furs, wear hats throughout dinner, nibble, tipple a little and gossip a lot for a couple of hours, for only a double sawbuck apiece. Middle Europeans who never learned the technique of living on next year's luck spend many of their infrequently scheduled evenings-out in this comfortable establishment. Gents who must eat alone come with the paper. Even college students come here—their allowances could cover higher prices, but when Dad drew up the budget, he did not figure in certain habits. (Anything *really* worth ingesting costs more than dinner anywhere.) Café 58 looks like the kind of place one may just wander into for a casual meal. But, especially at peak hours, and on weekends, you are out of luck without a reservation. For not only are the prices nostalgic, the food is good.

This store has been many restaurants. When this latest occupant arrived, the place was given its new identity by covering almost everything in sight with a dark plaid cloth. Then the lights were lowered and the front door was opened for business. The caramel-colored banquettes and the red carpeting escaped the treatment. What you notice mostly is the tinkle of glasses and dishes, and the hum of conversation.

You will recognize the menu, Theater District French, the fixed price of your dinner determined by the main course you select. You would, of course, have to pay a premium for the snails, so skip them, for they are leathery, the worst item in the house. You are somewhat better off with the littlenecks, perfectly fresh, but they suffer—are a little flat —from being opened in advance. Begin instead with the cool leeks, in a tart dressing touched with tomato; or with the tangy mackerel marinated in white wine; or with the saucisson sec, thin slices of hard dark sausage, peppery, fortified with garlic; or with rillettes, pounded pork and fat, herbed and heavily seasoned, rich but not cloying.

You may, of course, have decent-to-good versions of steak au poivre, rack of lamb, duck à l'orange, sole meunière, &c. But as long as you are here, why not do what you so rarely get a chance to do? Have a pig's foot. It is much jelly around a solidity of bones, breaded and crusted, charred here and there—you eat it with mustard, and with the good French fries this place serves with many of its main courses. Or have tripe, the huge serving of which comes in a big red pot that is placed on your table, so that when you have downed, say, half the glutinous slivers of innard, and their peppery oil, there will be that much more where they came from. Or have the boudin, two big, fat, purplish-brown blood sausages, in crackling casings, the soft filling rich and hot and weighty. For sissies there is choucroute, pickled cabbage studded with black pepper-corns, three good varieties of sausage, a pink and tender pork chop and a slice of dreadful ham. Or have the rabbit, big nuggets of tender meat, on the bone, with mushrooms and boiled potatoes in the thick mustard sauce. There is bouillabaisse on weekends. It is much more expensive than anything else on the menu, but it is superior to some dearer versions elsewhere in town. It contains many varieties of fish, 50 percent of a rather small lobster, clams and mussels. You get much to eat, none of it over-cooked, the saffroned broth is stout, and there are a pepper sauce and a garlic sauce with which you may strengthen it further. (When you add garlic to the hot soup, its fragrance reaches out to six or eight tables in the vicinity.)

For an extra $2 you choose from the pretty good cheeses. The oeuf à la neige is light, moistened with a smooth vanilla sauce, adorned with strands of candied citrus rind. The bombe praliné, studded with hazelnuts, is icy and refreshing. The chocolate mousse is no more than chocolate pudding. Anyway, almost everyone has the good apple tart, which is listed as the tarte maison.

★★ CAFÉ LOUP

18 East 13th Street
LUNCH, MONDAY TO FRIDAY; DINNER, MONDAY TO SATURDAY. CLOSED SUNDAY.
Reservations, 255–4746.
Credit cards: AE, CB, DC, MC, V.
Medium-priced.

A ten-stool bar at the front and a dozen or so tables in the back are all of Café Loup, but if every neighborhood in New York had a dozen like it, the supermarkets would fold and the mom-and-pop stores would go back to the middle-of-the-night sandwich trade. The food here is simple and good, if never wondrous; the prices are reasonable, if not exactly low; the surroundings are comfortable; the service is efficient, friendly and unpretentious (though occasionally a waiter will sniff a cork); and the people at the next table do not grunt. This is a civilized place, and one senses no generation gap between the young people who wait on tables and tend bar and the contented middle-aged crowd that has made this its neighborhood joint. The walls are beige and hung with prints. Pots and pans and little vases of dried flowers are on display on little shelves. The bar and tables are of unstained wood, and at every place setting there is a deep-blue napkin in the bowl of a large wineglass. Blackboard menus circulate to where they are needed—when it is time for you to look at one, one is placed on a blond bentwood chair near your table.

You are offered different soups on different days—sometimes pea soup, ham and noodles in it, thick, only mildly seasoned, Germanic, a good first course if you missed lunch. Otherwise try the mushrooms à la Grecque, very crunchy, in an herbed and onioned marinade that is perhaps a bit too sweet, but good. Splendid snails are served without shells, with mushrooms, in a thick and garlicky sauce, a hefty chunk of toast buried therein, which makes for a lovely hardness against the rich food.

The place is a bird house: good duck Montmorency, the skin crisp, the dark meat rich, the cherry sauce not excessively sweet; and good poulet moutarde, a simple dish of nicely browned chicken with a mild mustard sauce; and, best of the lot, Cornish hen aux fines herbes, the skin of the little bird almost black without being burned, intensely flavored with the taste of herbs.

The sautéed calf's liver is okay, strewn with sautéed onions, the meat pink and moist, though it could do with a crisper surface. And the almost excessive richness that is natural to sweetbreads is leavened by the sharp dark sauce and strands of ham that are served in this version. The steaks, at around $15, are the most expensive items in the place.

Fresh vegetables, simply prepared, are served with all the main courses.

The desserts have cute names, like "Peter's Pan Chocolate Cake," which, name aside, is memorable for the raisins and nuts the rich cake is studded with. The cheese cake is the heavy, cream-cheese variety—it is brightly lemoned, sweet and extremely thick. There is carrot cake, and it is spicy, moist, pleasantly pebbly. And there is strawberry shortcake, made with plump ripe berries and good whipped cream—it would be better still on a biscuit instead of this pallid sponge cake. Very good coffee.

A near-singularity for these days: juice for sours and such is squeezed from fresh fruit, at the bar, when the drinks are ordered.

★★ CAFÉ NEW AMSTERDAM

284 West 12th Street
LUNCH, SUNDAY; DINNER, DAILY.
Reservations, 242-7929.
Credit cards: AE, MC, V.
Expensive.

A two-room corner store in the oldest part of the Village, but, though the place is very much in the tradition of eating places in that part of town—it is den-like, snug —its dramatic lines and snappy food are very up-to-date. The deep-garnet walls of the dimly lit place are hung with dozens of engravings of old New York, behind glass, handsomely gold-framed, individually lighted, so they seem to glow a little in the dark. Underfoot, the floor has been painted a gleaming ebony brown. The big, square front room is rimmed with white-linened tables. A round table at the center is laden with desserts, graced with a burst of flowers, spotlighted from above. The back room is smaller, noisy when it gets a noisy table. The service is intelligent, by young men and women who know well the details of the constantly changing bill of fare. Your hostess, an imposing redheaded lady with a cigarette, is a worried-looking ever-presence.

She has little to worry about if her associates in the kitchen continue to send forth these lovely cold meats: roast beef at room temperature with a cold and tangy tomato chutney; slices of fat-rimmed roast pork alternated on your plate with slivers of glistening mango, the two strewn with white grapes and crisp pine nuts. Stilton cheese shows up often on the first-course list. Sometimes it is made into a paste and stuffed into a pear that has been poached in wine, the whole served surrounded by slivered almonds —a little pallid, in part because the Stilton has been mixed with milder cheese. And sometimes Stilton is commingled with apples and walnuts and served hot in a light turnover—a lovely dish in which the moist fruit tempers the sharpness of the nuts and cheese. The terrine of duck liver is polished and rich, studded with sweet black raisins —a striking note.

A slab of sole, surmounted by plump scallops and fresh vegetables, is baked in paper and not freed from its bag until it is under your nose—a light broth is liberated with it. Poached fresh salmon, firm and flaky, smooth and buttery and well seasoned, is served in a red-wine sauce that is brightened by red peppercorns. You get a good veal chop here, fat and juicy, lightly seasoned, the sage with which it is sprinkled singed on the surface of the meat. And you get good lamb chops, of loud lamb flavor, whole shallots in their stout, slightly sweet-and-sour tomato sauce. If the steak is not of America's foremost beef, it is well made, and the winy sweetness of its Madeira sauce almost substitutes for the blood-juiciness the sirloin lacks. Barely grilled calf's liver is served with a dollop of sharp horseradish butter—this, like most of the Café's unexpected combinations, is a surprisingly successful juxtaposition. The sautéed veal kidneys are clean, crunchy, their dark sauce touched with good mustard. A simple pasta dish is always on the menu.

Both the chocolate cake New Amsterdam and the cheese cake are shot through with finely chopped hazelnuts—these are superb desserts, but you must get them the day they are made, or they are a little leaden. The hazelnut dacquoise is crisp and nutty, a coffee-flavored cream encased within a slightly chewy meringue. The tarts are of fresh fruit on gentle custard and firm crust, and they are garnished with straight, rich whipped cream.

★ CAFÉ SAN MARTIN

1458 First Avenue (near 76th Street)
LUNCH, SUNDAY. DINNER, DAILY.
Reservations, 288-0470.
Credit cards: AE, CB, DC, MC, V.
Medium-priced.

Almost nothing about this restaurant, except the help and half the food, is Spanish —anyway, not Spanish in the New York manner. There is nary a bullfight poster on the walls. Black wrought iron is nowhere in evidence. The rooms do not simulate a stone-walled wine cellar in a medieval Castilian castle. The restaurant is, in fact, airy, all white, with greenery standing in the front windows (right next to the piano—which is harmlessly tinkled—and not far from the glittery little bar, and the handful of tables that are arranged in an L around it). There is more greenery hanging from the skylight that is centered over the two-steps-down main dining room at the back. Colorful, ornately framed oils adorn the walls, and handsome cane-and-bentwood chairs surround white-linened tables that are set with painted plates and pale-blue napkins. When the place fills up—with a prosperous but not flashy uptown crowd—it hums and bustles. The hard-working waiters (in white shirts and vests and long, striped aprons) and the captains (in dark suits) are all courtesy, and they keep the place running smoothly.

Café San Martin is not an especially expensive restaurant, but for $10.50 you may discover for yourself that a small plate of baby eels—these are virtually embryonic eels —looks like a small plate of short spaghetti. And with the sizzling oil, browned garlic and blackened and fiery red peppers in which the creatures are served, they as well could be, for the forthright flavors of the sauce conceal whatever subtle merit this rarity might have to disclose. More of that garlic in the garlic shrimp—but it fails to obscure the iodine that ruins these poorly chosen crustaceans. Opt instead for xangurro, which arrives in the little dish in which it was cooked. The food consists of crabmeat, sherry and a powerful dose of clove—a substantial patty of the flavored seafood is baked under a breading until the crust is browned. It must be told that this establishment does no better shopping for mussels than it does buying shrimp. The green sauce is good— smooth, creamy, loaded with fresh parsley—but there are, among these mostly lovely mussels, a few that are considerably louder than that piano. Discs of Spanish sausage, with slivers of red and green peppers, are sealed—with seasoned red wine and oil—in a little pillow fashioned of aluminum foil, and then heated. The shiny balloon is placed before you and cut open. Steam pours forth. The morsels of spiced meat are good with the salty wine and vegetables. Of course there is black bean soup—it may not be as thick as you like it, but it has a deep flavor, and the onions that come with it are recently chopped, so they are strong.

The Café serves one of the best paellas in town—barring the occasional mischance of encountering those less than perfect shrimps or mussels. The rice is oiled and red and spicy, studded with chunks of exceptionally sweet and peppery sausage, plump scallops, mussels and shrimp, clams that are sometimes a bit tough for having been cooked too long, red pimentos, green peppers and glistening sweet green peas. The paella is prepared only for two. If you want lobster in yours, there is a surcharge. All those items of shellfish, as well as a substantial slab of fresh striped bass, make up the zarzuela de mariscos, which—in its broad pottery dish—is immersed in a creamy sauce. Parillada is that same collection again, this time broiled, all the elements of vivid flavor, served with a pitcher of spicy tomato sauce. Hake, a cousin to cod, is a big item in Spanish cookery. Here it is served in a manner given as "à la Vasca," in which the hefty, flaky fish is buried in a thick, green sauce that is both lemony and spicy. The pale meat is garnished with clams and mussels and halves of hardcooked eggs, all of which are usually fine. But the entire production is served over a few shafts of canned white asparagus, which, perhaps at the sacrifice of some authenticity, could be omitted to excellent effect. A so-called grain-fed chicken is roasted artfully on a spit when you order it (you must allow time). The skin is crisp, the meat is moist, but the flavor of the bird, though a little better than most contemporary chickens, is still shy of the real thing. Much of the rest of the menu is given over to French and Italian dishes—

entrecôte au poivre, fettuccine Alfredo and the like—but that is not what this restaurant is about.

Happily, the deviations from Spanish restraints extend to the dessert menu: a tart of slivers of ripe banana, creamy custard, crumbly crust; a kiwi tart much like it, the green fruit glistening and sweet; a raisin-studded bread pudding that is made tangy by strands of lemon rind; claufouties of cherries or blueberries, in which the stewed fruits are buried in, and stain, the dark cake; an intense and airy chocolate mousse cake; a whole orange, peeled and sliced, served under strands of orange rind that have been marinated in Grand Marnier. None of the sweets is extraordinary, but all of them are more than decent.

★ CAFÉ UN DEUX TROIS

123 West 44th Street
LUNCH AND DINNER.
Reservations, 354-4148.
Credit cards: AE, MC, V.
Medium-priced.

This is a great big place, with a long bar just inside the door, and rows and clusters of little tables—"linened" with white butcher paper and set up with paper napkins and plain water tumblers—that accommodate, in every far corner of the dining room, at lunch, cocktail time, dinner and supper, scores of mostly young people who come here for the simple menu, the colorful crowd of which they are a part, and the café rules of the casual house. You may dine extensively or lightly, drink or have coffee—for though this is a restaurant, it is primarily a place to which people come to talk.

The proprietors have done little to renovate the battered premises left behind by La Bourgogne, former tenant at this address. The floor is of ancient tiles. The ceiling is of cracking black plaster, from which hangs, in splendiferous disregard of its frayed surroundings, a glittering chandelier. Framed and unframed mirrors hang here and there on the aged walls; harshly colored perspective paintings of the streets and rooftops of Paris add to the general clutter. During the day much of this room's light floods in through the big front windows on 44th Street. But at night most of the illumination is provided by the bare bulbs that protrude from pillars and walls like the bright lights around the mirrors of theatrical dressing tables.

A slightly out-of-place crowd stands at the bar: posing dancers who raise glasses to their lips with the kind of sweeping gesture that usually accompanies a florid toast; hysterical young women wearing frizzled hair and little else; and ordinary pathetic singles. The bartender is your basic hip cynic. When he needs both hands he sticks his cigarette between his teeth.

Most of the people who come here are gregarious and friended—and though their garb extends from T-shirts with baggy pants to the suits and ties and wraparound skirts and blouses of the business side of magazine offices, and the logistics side of the theatrical world, they have in common that optimistic enthusiasm you may just be able to recall.

Your host, in shawl-collar blazer over a yellow athletic shirt, shows up at the front door approximately every five minutes to greet the customers who arrive every thirty seconds. He betrays not a suspicion that impatience has been devised, much less gained currency.

The din in this restaurant can be so intense (particularly when the air conditioner is roaring) that the intimate relationship of adjacent tables must remain purely physical —no communication (much less eavesdropping) is possible. But if you and your companion have said all you are going to say to each other, you have an out—you may pass your time doodling, in color, on the paper that covers your table, for a glass of crayons is provided to every party.

Food is secondary, so you are not distressed if the pâté de canard à l'orange is rashly overflavored with orange and orange rind, never mind the excess salt and pepper— perfectly edible food, nevertheless. Nor will you be surprised that the stuffed mushrooms are rather obviously previously cooked and recently reheated—these are something less than passable. The Roquefort salad, however, is a happy mélange of crisp apples, crunchy walnuts, abundant fresh romaine lettuce and much good cheese— though it is not French Roquefort; the dressing, too bad, lacks life. A sometimes soup of the day, the gazpacho, is tired.

Les plats du jours—which are posted up on pillars—are the safest main courses. A plate of cold sea trout consists of firm, just about perfectly fresh fish, garnished with rich mayonnaise, tomatoes and a light rice salad studded with crisp vegetables. And the couscous, which is *du jour* both Thursday and Friday, is an enormous platter of warm, oiled and seasoned grain surmounted by chunks of chicken from a big bird, and great sections of lamb that have been cooked to moist tenderness, the two meats mingled with chickpeas and vegetables, the entire production a gluttonous hour's diversion. You can get steak pommes frites—a decent slab of grilled meat served with salty French fries that are distinctly crisper and lighter than the New York average. And the liver is nicely crusted, livened with garlic, garnished with the same fries. Avoid with passion the steak tartare, which seems to be a blenderized syrup of beef and Worcestershire sauce.

The slightly burnt pastry of the apple tart adds a nice carbon note to the dark winy fruit. The orange tart is juicy and acidic, a layer of light custard between the citrus and the pastry. And the charlotte aux fraises—layers of white cake, chocolate and meringue, moistened with a thin crème Anglaise that is studded with strawberries—is an inoffensive, sugary sweet.

As the evening wears on, the crowd becomes more theatrical and more bohemian —hair over one shoulder, mini-skirts, double-breasted, unlined, unpadded, wrinkled, natural linen jackets worn directly over hairy chests, argyles and sandals.

• CAMELBACK & CENTRAL

1403 Second Avenue (at 73rd Street)
LUNCH AND DINNER.
Reservations, 249-8380.
Credit cards: AE, CB, DC, MC, V.
Medium-priced.

It is as if the place were designed by a programed automaton into which certain essential information was not fed. A menu is printed up, for example, but you are not provided with enough light by which to read it (a condition that is aggravated by the fact that the document is printed in ink lighter than black, on paper darker than white). Single tables are provided with plural chairs, but you may as well come alone, for within the hard surfaces that contain, reflect and seemingly amplify the noise in this place (most especially the bandshell, wraparound corner windows), it is possible to converse only in writing. Just in case everyone discovers his inaudibility all at once, and shuts up, thumping background (foreground) music is incessantly in place. When a cash register rings repeatedly behind the bar near the front, it sounds like a fire drill near the back. And except for the bare oak floor, the mirror behind the bar, and the front windows, the place is painted a uniform battleship gray, presumably to offset any light that may be showing through the cracks in your depression. Look around you, and you may conclude that the people who come here are trying both to compete with the clangor of the place and to undo its gloom. They wear too much makeup, too-loud neckties, suits with copper threads running through the bold plaids, earrings down to the shoulder, hair the color of metal-plastic alloys not yet invented. You see matching sets of shoes, belt, handbag, nail polish, lipstick. Her high heels would make her taller than he is, but for his gravity-defying pompadour. The place is popular.

And the food, though far from immortal, is the best thing about it. The faintly legible menu is augmented each day by several additional dishes, which are announced to you by means of a little framed sign that is placed on your table on a small stand. (It is understood that a speech from your waiter would be inaudible). The sign manages not to topple over in hysterics even when its lists Mozzarella Tempura Marinara. Actually the pully cheese is not bad in its crisp crust and thick, red sauce. But the hot seafood diablo is a silly dish, served, as the menu puts it, on a "bed" of spaghetti (the Italian-American manner is being revived). It is also a nearly inedible one, the conch rubbery, the shrimp imbued with iodine. The chicken liver appetizer is as copious as a main course, the chunks of meat in a nice winy sauce, white grapes and almonds cool and crunchy notes. The skewered pork arrives very promptly, is clearly precooked and reheated—its peanut sauce helps, but not enough. Bad as the shellfish was in the hot appetizer, it is fine in the cold seafood salad, wherein it is dressed with a tangy, herbed vinaigrette. A salad of papaya and orange, slices of the two fruits arranged to form, respectively, the circumference and spokes of a wheel, has walnuts and watercress in the triangles thereby formed—good ingredients, dull salad.

Pasta primavera is on the menu, and pasta puttanesca is sometimes offered—neither sauce quite comes together. Idiotically, a good filet of beef is served up to its knees in a wine and mushroom sauce, and also cloaked in Béarnaise—halving the number of sauces would double the quality of the dish. The chicken paillard is tasteless. A couple of simple dishes—grilled swordfish and a grilled veal chop—are close to perfectly made.

The strawberry peach pie is fine when it is not ice cold. Something called chocolate sin is served. Save your virtue for a better offer. The berries are good but not perfect —they come with very nice whipped cream, which is available with the other desserts as well.

Camelback and Central is an intersection in Phoenix, Arizona.

★★ CANTON

45 Division Street (near Market Street)
LUNCH AND DINNER. CLOSED MONDAY.
Reservations for large groups only (226-9173).
No credit cards.
Beer.
Medium-priced.

Legendary belletrists, architects of international repute, prize-winning play-wrights, world-class photographers, literary critics with hyphenated names, potent behind-the-scenes editors, byline journalists and, even, headliners from the world of sport—all these types get themselves to Canton and, if necessary, wait, along with everybody else, on the street, or in the little alcove just inside the front door, for a turn at a table. Once within, they are at the next table to clusters of gents in jeans and plaid flannel shirts—their leather jackets are draped over the backs of their chairs, and their noses are three inches from their plates when they eat. Pop-eyed, purple-complected fat men come here, sweating and breathing hard, raving eaters, apparently let loose on one-night passes for an oral binge. You see silver-haired academics in rimless spectacles, Hispanics in sunglasses. And when the invading hordes from Queens hit Chinatown on weekend nights, discriminating defectors slip away from the squads of Szechuan addicts for something more subtle here. But what is unique about Canton's clientele is that, invariably, at least a few of the tables are occupied by mixed groups—of Chinese and Occidentals. And thereby depends some lowdown: though this restaurant has had a menu printed up—complete with such categories as Soup for One, Soup for Two, Chop Suey, Chow Mein, Egg Foo Young—production of this document was clearly just a gesture to the suchness of the situation, for the composition of almost every meal consumed here is determined not by consulting a list, but by conversation with the proprietor—a woman whose youthful appearance fails to signal the mature calm and good cheer with which she efficiently governs this place. Her English is as good as yours. But without a satisfactory written summary of the kitchen's real repertoire, white folks and other non-Asians often feel the need for some almond-eyed support during their encounters with the lady of the house. Unless you are unusually persistent, or have been here often and are known, singsong inquiries in native Chinese will yield more information than tuneless, grunting queries in New York English. Still, splendid dinners have been had on first visits by blonds. And if you feel that you must command —rather than ask questions—there are some swell orders in the paragraphs ahead.

Canton is a big, brightly lit, high-ceilinged, boxlike store, a cash register at the front, a stainless-steel coffee urn and some steel shelves at the back, and enough Formica-topped tables—some of them the huge round kind suitable for banquet dinners—to seat around sixty. This place has a Chinatown bare-necessities elementality about it, but it is in no way tattered or ramshackle or improvised. The walls are faced with a cheerful yellow quasi-cloth covering; the tables do not rock; the waiters are in crisp jackets; everything looks clean; and a lovely stained-glass fish adorns the front window— seafood is Canton's specialty.

But first, the first courses, a number of which your hostess and the regulars refer to, in English, by code names. "The lettuce," for example: one of those dishes consisting of flavored ground meat which you make into a bundle by rolling a spoonful of it in a lettuce leaf, which package you then hold in your fingers and eat. What particularly distinguishes this version from that available in other restaurants is that the leaves of lettuce are large and unperforated, so the operation can be carried out without spillage. What further distinguishes it is that the meat is mingled with fresh green peas for sweetness, water chestnuts for crispness, strong garlic for flavor. The mixture is light, with a hint of charring in its flavor. Something called "buns" consists of three small slices of meat—lean pork, sweet ham and tender white chicken, all lightly oiled and a little blackened—impaled on a wooden skewer, the meats accompanied by a two-part muffin of barely baked dough. You make a light, tasty sandwich of the "bun" and the succulent meats. The fried dumplings are fine, but they are much the standard thing, not notably superior to what you get in many places.

Seafood. Pan-fried butterfish: two whole fish, impeccably fresh, each the size of a gentleman's hand, strewn with scallion greens; the skin of the fish—which is crisped to a light, brittle flakiness—is a zest to the light meat within it. This is an easy fish to eat, for the side bones are delicate enough to swallow. The steamed flounder is big; it arrives spread out on a great platter in a pool of oily broth that is so hot that the fish continues to cook on the table—you must eat it quickly, while it is fluffy and retains its subtly fibrous texture. The flounder is strewn with scallions and ginger, which are striking against the gentle white meat.

Sturdier seafood. Conch: slightly cartilaginous slices and morsels of the oceanic meat, mingled with ginger and scallions and bits of pepper that you encounter as a surprise every third bite or so, all vibrant in their peppery oil. Squid: the tubular shafts of the fresh, tender meat scored, as if by strokes of a sharp-pointed fork, darkened by a black-bean sauce, made tangy with little discs of scallion and bits of fresh, loud ginger, the whole a dish that is powerful but never weighty.

The roast duck is simple: a half bird cut into slabs that an expert can hold in chopsticks while chewing the crisp skin and moist meat from the bones—an occasional peppercorn adds a touch of fire to the rich meat. The herbed chicken is more complex, the skin coated with herbs that have been blackened in the cooking, the meat moistened with a black sauce that is salty, sweet, a little hard, but hardly too much for this chicken —for Canton obtains chickens that are as flavorful as the chickens of your memory.

Lotus root, that crisp, vaguely perfumed and prettily perforated legume, is mixed with meats here: pork and lotus root, the pork juicy and sweet, with crunchy snow peas, whole cloves of garlic, and ginger in the oily but not heavy dish; beef and lotus root, the slivers of beef medium rare, microcosmic steaks, water chestnuts and snow peas and mushrooms the bulk of the multitextured dish. Canton is capable of turning out such things as roast pork with wide noodles, one of those complicated assemblages the components of which are identifiable only by sight. But one of the simpler noodle dishes is superb, the thin strands of rice noodle moistened with dark oil and dotted here and there with bits of scallion and bits of ginger—as elegant as the most refined Italian pasta. You get terrific string beans: the vegetable barely cooked, crisp and hot and oiled, tossed with slices of red pepper, ground pork, and garlic, all in a gravylike and pungently seasoned dark-brown sauce. Many dishes are not always available. Skip dessert, unless you want some cool canned fruit.

The house sells Oriental beers, but booze of all nations—Scotch whiskey, Wild Turkey, California rosé, cognac—adorns the tables, for you may bring your own.

★★★ LA CARAVELLE

33 West 55th Street
LUNCH AND DINNER. CLOSED SUNDAY.
Reservations, JU 6–4252.
Credit cards: AE, CB, DC, MC, V.
Very expensive.

Perfections and a well-bred lid on passion have been the marks of the Caravelle kitchen. But the latter is hard to take without the former. It was never the business of this place to dramatize the flavors of the produce of the earth and the waters, but rather to demonstrate how elegantly they could be tamed or transformed or concealed. That is a kind of magic that is, if it is executed artfully, its own excuse. But magic, to justify itself, must work perfectly. The failure is total, not partial, if while sawing the lady in half you draw even a little blood. The crimson droplets have been spotted at La Caravelle. It is no longer a great restaurant. Plenty of wonderful food, and you may have a delightful time, but the magic is gone.

Which is a pity. M. Meyzen, the portly and—to some—frightening proprietor who operates this institution, will be sorry to learn it. For Meyzen, who is actually a courtly pussycat, is no happier than when his customers are happy. And thereby, maybe, depends the key. They are happy no matter what.

La Caravelle is banker-and-broker heaven, the most sanitary clientele in town, and a very well-educated lot. They know the names of things, and they know which names are better than which names. But they do not know the substances the names represent. In this way of life, substances do not matter, only that they have the right names. La Caravelle, of course, has one of the right names. It is therefore, by definition, marvelous. With customers like these, it may be humanly difficult to maintain standards. From a financial point of view no standards are necessary. The customers come to the name "La Caravelle," never mind what it is.

Take, for a for-instance, this well-tailored jurist on your left. He would like a bottle of Château d'Yquem with his dinner (no objection from his frau), and you wonder if he would have tasted it clearly enough to have regretted his choice had not his captain steered him to something sane. International clusters of businessmen glare at each other in four languages, stuck with one another's company until the big deal is made. Matrons and their patrons, every hair nailed into place, sip their 1945 châteaux casually, not because it is a lifetime habit, but because they do not realize they are drinking something special. (The bottles are selected, of course, by their three-figure price tags.) On Friday and Saturday nights there is a bit of gaiety in the air, a smile at this table, an actual tune of laughter at that one. But the rest of the week ladies in print dresses stick out like gypsies at a bishop's funeral, gentlemen in plaid suits are taken for bookies.

You enter to a red-velvet anteroom, where a display of hors d'oeuvres and desserts is reflected in a great polished mirror. Your coat is taken by a demure clerk whose smile remains engraved in place for as long as you wish to gaze at it. You are led first through a mural-lined corridor, tables along each side, with seating on banquettes of that same red velvet. Ordinarily, in restaurants of this rank, front tables like these are the choice spots, from which the lucky holders thereof may see, and be seen by, all who come and go, with particular attention to the celebrated. But this pass is too nakedly exposed and close for that, it is front-row orchestra—a bit vulgar, don't you know—not the grand tier, and it is given over to families with minors, females without males, strays. The rest of us march grandly through, looking neither to the left nor right, colonial governors between ranks of native mendicants.

The main dining room is your basic posh. More of those velvet banquettes rim the room and are formed into semicircular settees around large tables in the center. Mirrored walls and columns reflect glowing sconces. Murals of the parks and streets of Paris save the scene; they are pale, they glow with the soft light of that city, and they are made bright with spots of strong color—the Tricolor waves in all of them. Glowing linen, shining solid flatware and gleaming china, stemware with sailing ships engraved on the bowls—"Les Caravelles" made water crossings before they were fitted out with jet engines.

Your captain will be with you in a moment, for he is at work serving a silver bowl of Le Caviar de Béluga to your neighbors. *Zing.* He has scooped up and swallowed a spoon of the stuff so quickly that only the bright eye of a clear-headed observer catches it. Confronted by you moments later with the fact that he has been caught out, he shrugs and allows that he really does not much like the stuff. What may be made of all this? Much, actually. The dining-room staff does its job well, but not seriously, reflecting a commitment to efficiency but not to excellence. They are cheerful and friendly as well. But no one here is shocked if a thing goes wrong.

Les Moules Caravelle have gone a little wrong. They are perfectly fresh, you understand, almost every one of them free of grit, and they are dressed in a pinked mayonnaise that is smooth and rich, but totally forgettable. Much better La Cervelle Vinaigrette, cool chunks of calf's brains that have been cooked with bit of vinegar, the tartness of which eliminates the otherwise cloying richness of this organ meat—the dressing is light, made spiky with bits of minced red pepper and parsley. Your captain suggests that a dollop of Le Céleri Rémoulade would garnish the cervelle nicely. The root is crisp and nutty in the lightly lemoned dressing, but there is missing the clear flavor of fresh celery that characterizes this dish at its best. Le Pâté Toulousain is splendid, fatty and loud, garnished with cool jelly and powerfully sour little pickles. La Caravelle has always listed as its first-course specialty Le Pain de Brochet, a mousse of pike prepared as if for quenelles, but cooked in a loaf and served by the slice. They are still at it, the mousse is light and the flavor of the fish is vivid, but a trace of fishiness has been detected on occasion, and it is not undone by the lightly tomatoed white-wine sauce that is poured over it, or by the crunchy little button mushrooms or plump white grapes therein—a superb dish with a slight but devastating flaw.

Le Homard Washington, Friday's lobster (the listing of main courses changes a little from day to day), is a crustacean elegance of tender and fresh lobster meat that has been poached to the perfect point; it is then served in a white sauce that has been fortified with bourbon whiskey and port wine. If you are a lobster freak, this dish is not for you, for the lobster, as such, is not glorified in this treatment—the heady sauce is the dominant element of this dish, the strength of the liquor tamed to the point at which its hard edge conflicts superbly with the seafood. It is a magical dish, at the expense of the magic of lobster.

Half the house, it seems, orders duck, and the birds flow from the kitchen in their copper pans by the dozen, to be ritualistically carved by assiduous waiters who go through the motions hardly looking. The house is famous for its sauce Smitane, of sour cream and green pepper, but on certain nights it offers instead Le Caneton rôti au

Poivre, a winy sauce that bristles with nodules of the pungent spice, making an excellent slight harshness against the rich bird. But the kitchen makes those birds by the score, and they do not get the attention each one deserves, and once in a while the bird is underdone—red and a bit tough near the bone. The duck is garnished with a mound of wild rice that is unsullied by ordinary rice—it is the plain thing itself, and its strong, grainy flavor is a perfect foil for these rich sauces. Pigeons, too, including a Véronique —you are served the entire bird, crisp skin and supple dark meat, with a sauce that has the depth of a good stock. There are warm white grapes in the sauce, and their juiciness is a pleasure against the rich bird.

L'Escalopine de Veau au Citron is like a song that is sung unaccompanied in a hall with clear acoustics. If anything goes wrong, you cannot miss it. This is a simple dish of veal sautéed in butter, a bit of sauce made in the pan by the addition of lemon and seasoning. Perfect veal, admirably browned, but you cannot taste the lemon for the salt —magic in reverse, sleight-of-hand ruination. You console yourself with the little balls of roasted potato—golden skins of browned butter around soft, steamy potato cores— and with the chopped spinach, which is strong, spicy, smooth. Excellent steaks of all shapes and cuts.

Fine apple tarts and banana tarts, fresh berries filmed over with a light crème Anglaise, a Bavarian cream that is purple with the juice of dark berries, lofty soufflés. But Les Crêpes "Ma Pomme" (for two) are the specialty of the house. If you order them, Meyzen himself may trot over to finish the dish at your tableside. But first you learn, as the menu does not state, that this dish takes time. Your captain suggests you sample the half-dozen cheeses with half a bottle of wine while your dessert is working (the menu does not even mention their availability), and you find that they vary from good to super, and later you learn that there is no extra charge. Meanwhile, back in the kitchen, chunks of apple are being sautéed in brown sugar, for your crêpes, until they are candied and crusted; they are brought to the dining room when you have dispatched your cheese, and Meyzen wraps them in large, thin pancakes, and then cooks the bundles very slowly and long in cognac and calvados, until they are soaked and browned in the brandies. He explains that he invented the dish himself, which explains his concern for their preparation. While he works he continues his friendly lecture, pointing out that anyone can flame a crêpe dish to the ceiling, but that it is the slow preparation that achieves the desired concentration of flavor. It turns out a very good dessert, spirited and perfumed, and you tame it with big dollops from the pitcher of whipped cream. You are brought a plate of glazed fruit to nibble on, the grapes and berries and orange sections encased in sugar that is as clear as glass.

★★CASA BRASIL

406 East 85th Street
DINNER. CLOSED SUNDAY.
Reservations essential, 288-5284.
No credit cards.
No liquor.
Very expensive.

Around twenty years ago a lady by the name of Madame Helma did a slightly revolutionary thing. She started a restaurant, on East 86th Street—it is now on East 85th—in which a customer had little to say about what he ate, not much choice as to when, no control at all over how much he spent. If he wanted a drink, he had to bring it with him. A splendid and extensive dinner was a flat $5.

Madame Helma made no effort to charm her patrons into coming back. Her manner was aloof, almost mechanical. A regular customer was treated with the same marginal, schooled correctness as a stray. This is the way I run my restaurant, she said, in effect, and if you like it, you will return; if not, you will not. She crowned her indifference to the conventions of public accommodation by calling her place Casa Brasil. It was as if someone named a restaurant the Italian Pavilion, then served spaghetti and meatballs on Sundays, the rest of the week the food of Szechuan. For Casa Brasil, since its inception, has served Brazilian food on Wednesdays, the other days almost none of it. Madame Helma did not just break with tradition, she ignored it, and her place was booked up weeks in advance.

Today the nonprofessional restaurant is no novelty. There are dozens of neighborhood places in which some culinary ability is combined with one or more of various efficiencies and economies—simple wooden chairs, bare tables, uncarpeted floors, limited menus, customer-supplied alcohol, fixed seating times, informal service—to give the public the pleasure of eating out without the pain of great expense or the discomforts of attendant formalities (there have always been many to whom even such minor matters as waiters in black tie, menus in foreign languages, and esoteric wine lists are unsettling). Madame Helma is no longer sharing many of those economies with her clientele. You still bring your own wine, but dinners just like the ones she served in 1963 are now $30. Still, as amateur restaurants go, this one is probably the best in New York—it flashes a perfection or two at almost every meal.

Ten tables in the front room and four in the back make up Casa Brasil. The place is a little cramped, cluttered with mementos, testimonial photographs, knickknacks, patterned tablecloths, fresh roses on all the tables. Even the air is cluttered—with background music, often the Latin strains of a few decades ago. Recognition of "Amapola" ("my pretty little poppy") and "Bésame Mucho" will give away your vintage. Casa Brasil has always attracted a disproportionate share of boors, and when they occupy one of the tables in the small back room, their noise ruins all. It is well to specify the front room when you reserve.

You are provided with tall glasses of thin crystal for the wine you bring, but you are given no printed menu. As soon as you are seated you are served hearts of palm in a creamy cheese sauce—the palm is canned, but it is merely a carrier for the thick sauce, which is studded with bits of ham and chopped egg. "Now you have crabmeat or papaya," your waiter informs you. The melon is unexceptional, as is the ham that accompanies it, so opt for the crabmeat, great tender chunks of it in a cool and creamy dressing, the seafood sweet, moist and utterly fresh. In France it is unheard of to consume a croissant after breakfast. In Casa Brasil they have always been served with the second course. These are not the lightest croissants west of Paris, but they are nicely browned, seem just-baked and turn out to be elegant bread even with other than butter and confiture. It is a good idea to dawdle over a course or two, for the service is executed with stunning rapidity, and if you have not contrived to delay the process, instantly after your crabmeat you receive a salad of impeccable, crunchy lettuce in a dressing thick with scallion greens.

Now—if it is not Wednesday—Madame Helma herself may approach, to itemize the three or four main courses. She does not, however, tell you that the roast veal, served in quasi-cutlets with a buttery white sauce, suffers by the automatic comparison to sautéed veal served this way; nor that beef Wellington, despite the rareness and tenderness of this filet mignon, is really a dopey dish of beef fancied up with pâté and a pastry wrapper, the only function of all the trouble being, it seems, to prevent the crusting of the steak, which is essential if filet mignon is to have much flavor. But the rack of lamb breaks down into lovely baby chops, pink and delicate, and Madame's roast duck is masterful, rich without being fatty, the skin parchmentlike without being dry. It is served without sauce, a bowl of warm cooked fruits providing the expected sweet. These dishes are served with fresh vegetables, carefully prepared—little beets, hard and crunchy, in butter; rice that is firm and fluffy, herbed and lightly spiced; puréed fresh peas; creamed cucumbers.

On Wednesday Madame does not stop by, for only feijoada, the national dish of Brazil, is available. In most Brazilian restaurants in New York, what goes by this name is an assortment of meats buried in black beans, but in Brazil the beans and meats are served separately. At Casa Brasil an intermediate position is taken: the beans, thick, polished and winy, are mingled with chunks of sausage and tongue, and two beef dishes are served separately. One of them consists of slices of rare meat with sautéed onions and a bit of thin, sharp sauce that is little more than blood; the other is a hefty stew of coarser, fibrous meat and small whole onions. This repast is accompanied by slices of raw orange, honeyed hot bananas, rice and a fine powder ground from the root of the manioc plant—this subtle zest, which you spoon onto the beans, seems to lighten, almost to carbonate, the sturdy food. The Wednesday dinner is a singular meal.

For dessert there is a lovely and airy lemon mousse with a vivid citrus flavor, ripe strawberries in a syrupy raspberry glaze, raspberries with thick whipped cream. But the dessert to have is the tapioca—not the bland pudding you know, but pellets of that starch (which is extracted from the manioc plant) that are cooked in wine and served under a simple (vanilla-flavored) and satiny crème Anglaise. The reddened beads are like juicy, skinless berries, a cool foil to the rich sauce.

If you bring two wines, you are supplied with a change of glasses. If you feel a draft, you are brought a wrap (ladies only). But when your seating has not yet used up its allotted time, the lights are brusquely turned up to remind you that you are not at home. And if you arrive early, you may have to wait in the street.

★★ CENT'ANNI

50 Carmine Street (near Bleecker Street)
DINNER. CLOSED MONDAY.
Reservations, 989-9494.
No credit cards.
No liquor.
Medium-priced.

Umberto, your host, is tall, suave, darkly smiling. His arrival in this land some years back reintroduced to America the practice of handkissing. (Ladies only.) There is apparently a market for the press of warm Mediterranean lips to the sere, weatherbeaten backs of northern palms, for no sooner did Umberto open his doors and start kissing than folks began making their way to his obscure site. Of course, the food is good too.

Cent'Anni has the clean and brightly lighted lines of a trattoria: white walls, white-linened tables surrounded by chairs of pale wood, here and there a potted palm, at the center of the room a display of cold foods, at the back a coffee machine, an espresso machine, the little bar. Clusters of paintings by local artists function only as splashes of color. The room holds a few more than a dozen tables, including some big round ones, one of them just inside each of the two front windows.

There is a handwritten menu, but Umberto, during the little conferences he holds at each table (if he knows you well, he takes a chair), urges dishes that availabilities in the market have suggested for the day. His seafood salad, however, can be had almost any time: chunks of sweet shrimp, lobster, squid, not dressed in the usual seafood-salad way, but just moistened with an intensely garlicked vinaigrette, in an amount that is almost entirely absorbed by the pale meats, so they seem powerfully flavored but not otherwise changed. Thin slices of smoked mozzarella (some people like it) and thinner slices of fatted, tender, fibrous prosciutto are dressed with drops of a spectacular olive oil that seems like an earthy perfume. Chicken livers and chicken hearts, sautéed and seasoned and herbed, are made into a hot paste and served—as crostini—on warm, lightly toasted slices of Italian bread. Sometimes there is ribollita, a weighty bean soup that is leavened a little with leeks, onions, cabbage—the sturdy stuff has a meaty undertone, the accent of judicious seasoning, the fragrance of herbs. It is served in a ceramic pot, a chunk of hard bread buried within it.

Cent'Anni sometimes offers a pasta dish that is described as "alla Medici," because it traces its origins to Renaissance times. The item has lasted well. It consists of rather hefty tubular noodles that are dressed with a creamy sauce that is thick with chicken and wild mushrooms and lightly brandied, a substance at once sturdy and high. Another house rarity is made with the broad noodles called pappardelle in a sauce of rabbit giblets. In this restaurant's version of the dish, the nubbly, flagrantly herbed, oily and red-spiced sauce is brightened with slivers of tomato—an extraordinary plate of food. Cent'Anni makes a briny and thick red seafood sauce for linguine; a creamy sauce of peas and wild mushrooms—it has a nice touch of coarse saltiness—for the cork-screw-shaped pasta called fusilli. If you are prepared to wait a little while, there is risotto, the mound of warm grain dark, moistened with oil, well seasoned, dotted with wild mushrooms.

In the kitchen there is an open grill whereon what you want is brushed with olive oil, seasoned and cooked. If you want striped bass, you get fresh, moist fish that is crusted and browned in the grilling. An immense veal chop, leaves of fresh sage pressed to the surface of the meat, is charred in the grilling—the herb makes the buttery, juicy meat fragrant. The seasoned and oiled steak (a T-bone, served for two) is lemoned as well—this slow, low-heat cooking of beef over coals reveals the pink meat at its tender best. If you think Cornish hens have no flavor, you are right. But when they are marinated in oil and rosemary for a couple of days, and then grilled, the charred bird is the equal of a pre-war chicken. Not all the main courses are grilled. Sautéed scallops and shrimp, lobsters, scaloppine dishes are all made well here. When there is osso buco the big knuckles of tender spiced veal are served in a meaty red sauce that is loaded with fresh parsley.

The zabaglione is abundantly liquored, and it is served over good strawberries. The cheese cake is fresh, light, textured, its black raisins little bursts of sweet fruit within the cake's solidity.

★★★ CHALET SUISSE

6 East 48th Street
LUNCH AND DINNER. CLOSED SATURDAY AND SUNDAY.
Reservations, 355-0855.
Credit cards: AE, DC, MC, V.
Expensive.

Chalet Suisse has been in New York for around a half century. A few decades ago it changed hands, and a dozen years ago it moved from its original 52nd Street site to the present one on East 48th. Restaurant guidebooks from the 1930s reveal that some of the dishes served now were served then. But during its long and consistent history, Chalet Suisse has never been the rage. It is, and for years has been, simply a marvelous restaurant, characterized by the most fundamental restaurant virtues. Enough people know about the place to keep it quite humming, but they do not make a lot of noise about their knowledge. Chalet Suisse is not mentioned in the gossip columns. Faces seen on television are not seen here. And the city's culinary avant-garde have never discovered the restaurant's merits (though the hot new places they tout every year cannot, ten times in eleven, warm this one up).

Chalet Suisse has the look of an old-fashioned European country inn. Its comfort derives from its simplicity. Rough plaster walls, the color of aged ivory, are hung here and there with oil paintings and pottery. The ceiling beams are of dark wood. Ironwork and suggestions of arches and pillars divide the room into snug areas, and the banquettes along the sides are fitted into niches. The tables are surrounded by slat-back chairs that have loose cushions on the seats. The restaurant is softly lighted by sconces that give off an amber glow.

Much of the pleasure of eating at Chalet Suisse traces to its civilized service. The standard is set by your host, a gentleman who seems to take pleasure in touring his restaurant floor to fill a glass here, provide a fresh plate there, answer questions, whatever. Happily, the waitresses follow his example. They are dressed in what are, presumably, native Swiss costumes, brightly colored, trimmed with lace, protected by gaily striped aprons. And they attend to their tasks with alertness, intelligence and good will. It is enough to make you cry.

At lunchtime, the most tasteful executives of the least frivolous industries decorously crowd the place to the rafters, filling it with the soft, cheery tinkle of ample coin. At night, vintage New Yorkers, sometimes whole families of them, relax here in a manner most at-home. The Chalet is also well-known to visiting European businessmen, Stockholmers and Amsterdammers and Düsseldorfers, who have found here the little plot of Manhattan Island that is *echt* home away from *Frau.*

Swiss food, as all the world knows, derives in large part from German, Italian and French cooking. It is, however, less ponderous than German, less emotional than Italian, more forthright than *haute cuisine,* more dramatic than *cuisine bourgeoise.* So much for eminently destructible generalizations. Whatever its provenance, much of what the Swiss eat is *sui generis*—like bündnerschinken and bündnerfleisch, the salted-and-dried ham and beef of Switzerland. The ham is pink, smoky and high, with fiber in its texture, fat around its rim; the beef is a stronger red but a paler flavor, rather gentle for a cured raw meat. Each is served in abundant portions, the rosy slices spread across broad plates. The so-called cervelat salad is humbler stuff, discs of porky sausage adorned with marinated onions and moistened with a light vinaigrette. The meats and the sausage are especially good with the strong, salty breads and the splendid sweet butter served here, and they may be nicely supplemented with an order of mushrooms Ascona, in which the chunks of fresh mushroom are served in an herby and slightly sour sauce that is thick with morsels of tomato.

Among the hot appetizers, the sleeper is the ravioli Milanese. It is not like what you get in your neighborhood spaghetti joint. These tender pasta envelopes are filled with fluffy ground meat, greens and grain; they are bathed in buttery consommé; and they are strewn with just-ground strong cheese and fresh parsley. The dish is airy, it seems to sing a little and it disappears weightlessly, miraculously. There are wondrous snails, deeply flavored by the stock they were poached in, served in an herbed and well-salted butter; a cheese-and-onion pie that is actually a hefty quiche larded with sautéed onions; and délice d'Emmenthal, crescents of strong Swiss cheese that have been breaded and deep-fried until the cheese is hot, soft and pully, the crust brown and crisp.

When your enchanting waitress spoons some medaillons de veau aux morilles onto your hot plate, she always asks, "May I keep the rest of this warm for you?" And when she delivers the balance (having observed that you vanished the first helping in a twinkling), she brings a fresh hot plate as well. This second delivery, if you forget to expect it, can render you deliriously happy, for this delicate veal, in its polished brandy sauce, studded with woodsy wild mushrooms, is at once easy, earthy and rich. Then there is the veal chop sauté au marc du Valais—a large eye of meat on a long bone that is dressed in a little paper pant, the meat white, flecked with glistening brown, and moistened with a dark sauce and dozens of hot, sweet white grapes. There is a crusty rack of lamb, touched with garlic, utterly tender, juicy and slightly high—racks of lamb are not roasted better within a day's drive of this restaurant. Liver and kidney à la Suisse is composed of bite-size chunks of the meats in a stout, herbed, gravylike sauce. Another dark sauce, this one winier and more polished, is served with slices of tender beef as filet de boeuf à la mode du chef. Whatever you do, do not pass up the rösti, the remarkable Swiss potato dish in which partially cooked potatoes are formed into broad pancakes that are then fried until golden. At Chalet Suisse the pancakes are crusty and tender, and if you are not yet in love with your waitress, you will capitulate completely when she comes around with a second plate.

The outstanding, low-priced main course is a cheese fondue called Neuchâteloise. It is perhaps a bit more work than eating in a restaurant ought to be, but this dish, brought to you bubbling over a flame in an enamel pot, dispels quibbles. The soft, slightly pully, nutmeg-flavored mixture of Emmenthal and Gruyère cheeses, mingled with wine and kirsch and a little garlic, is solid and heady, and it thickens and becomes stronger as it simmers. A basket of bread cubes is supplied, and you eat the dish by dunking the bread in the hot and fragrant stuff.

If you wish to continue dunking, the chocolate fondue (for two) is yet another bubbling pot, this one filled with chocolate that is at once creamy and sharp and sweet, slightly liquored, into which you dip slices of fruit—pineapple, banana, apple—thereby creating your own hot little candies. Chocolate is prominent throughout the dessert list. The chocolate mousse has an emphatic, almost naked chocolate intensity; the coupe chocolat is little more than a perfect sundae: vanilla ice cream and the kind of rich and fluffy, unsugared whipped cream that is just about unobtainable in restaurants these days—you pour a strong, hot, nutted chocolate over the two white creams and eat. The apple tart, a simple pastry filled with crisp fruit, is a good vehicle for more of that whipped cream—as is Aargauer rüeblitorte, a lightly liquored carrot-and-almond cake —as is the surprise Valaisanne, a crisp meringue that is mounded over with fresh strawberries that have been cured with Grand Marnier. The dessert menu is long, and all the sweets are pure and fresh.

★★★★ CHANTERELLE

89 Grand Street (at Greene Street)
LUNCH AND DINNER. CLOSED SUNDAY AND MONDAY.
Reservations, 966-6960.
Credit cards: AE, MC, V.
Very expensive.

Everything about this place may be found elsewhere (except, of course, the chef's original dishes), and yet the restaurant is reminiscent of no other. Chanterelle puts you in mind not of some other place at all, but of another era. Its essential quality is that it is outside its time and place. But it is in no way a stylized period piece. Its isolated situation on a remote corner is not coy. You can think of it as an ivory tower in which everything is done solely for its own sake. People go out of their way to eat here, sure enough, and they are just New Yorkers eating out. But they could as well be travelers who have come to observe something rare, that exists nowhere else in quite this form.

Fewer than a dozen large, white-linened tables are arranged, luxurious space around them, in a lofty store. The room has been stripped to its elements, restored in such a way as to give it the stately spaciousness—the grandeur, almost—of the grandest room in a great old house. The tall front windows are framed in columns of dark-stained wood that are faced with old mirrors. The ceiling overhead is a triptych of elaborately patterned stamped-tin panels, painted white, and fitted out—at the central, focal point of each section—with glinting brass chandeliers. The pale-apricot room is otherwise unadorned, except for two big sprays of branches—one is on a simple table that occupies the small anteroom between the dining room and the kitchen at the back; the other is high up on the honey-colored antique armoire at the front, in which your coat is hung—and a burst of flowers on the desk near the armoire, whereat telephone calls are received, the reservation book consulted, checks prepared. It all adds up to civilization—as it existed before progress took over.

This is so advanced a civilization, in fact, that your hostess greets you with the cordiality of a merchant welcoming a patron. If that does not floor you, the waiters and waitresses will, for they are thoroughly familiar with the dishes on the menu—even though the listings change from week to week—and they share the information with you neither in the manner of reciting robots nor in the vernacular of old buddies. (You never suspect for a moment that your shoulder is going to be leaned on during the recitation of the specials.) It is quite enough to make you blink your eyes. And if you try to make trouble (that is, if one member of your party orders à la carte, while the other chooses the fixed seven-course menu), the complication is finessed by serving both meals in seven stages—an extra plate for sharing is brought when only a dish from the prix fixe is being served. It is made to seem quite easy. It is not surprising that the place gets the most tasteful crowd in town.

From the extensive repertoire, less than all of which may be available at any one time: an egg-shaped scoop of squab mousse prettily served on an impeccable leaf of red-tipped lettuce, the enriched, buttery meat seasoned with restraint, brandied with care, dotted with crunchy bits of truffle—you spread it on toasted French bread; a salad of duck, the slivers of dark meat strongly flavored of the fat in which they were preserved, moistened with marvelous olive oil, garnished with leaves of crisp, sharp endive; a grilled seafood sausage, pale and browned, plump with the sweet meats of fresh shellfish, pine nuts in among the morsels, the whole in a sauce the honey-like sweetness of which is almost startling against the seafood; ravioli of lobster, the tender little packages served in a tangy tomato sauce that is wildly fragrant with cilantro; crayfish tails, small shrimp-like items that come in tiny carapaces much like those that house lobsters—the bodies are removed from the shells, sautéed, and served under crisp strands of root vegetables in a buttery sauce touched with tomato; lotte livers, the surprisingly substantial pink meat of the angler fish, its texture grainy but not sandy, its flavor like red-blood meat that is just touched with sea-gaminess, served in a smooth vinegar sauce with a bit of fresh spinach; a crayfish bisque of intense seafood and seafood-shell flavor, deep, rich, polished and strong.

Chanterelle houses a trout tank in its below-ground recesses, so truite au bleu is sometimes offered. The fish is pink—a salmon trout. Of course it is fresh, and it is served in a gentle sauce that is little more than butter sharpened with chives, but it lacks the slightly shocking vinegar tartness you expect from this dish. A broad expanse of filet of striped bass is presented to you in a creamy but stout dill and mustard sauce that is slightly gentled with bits of tomato. A block of poached salmon, pink and moist and of strong flavor, is served up in a pool of sauce that is almost metallic of its sorrel. In shad season this place sometimes serves the roe in a striking sauce, sour and earthy, of rhubarb and leeks—the roe itself is of minuscule grains that are so juicy they seem plump. Chanterelle's roast squab is a simple dish—perfectly moist and browned chunks of bird in a smooth truffle sauce. The rack of lamb is of tender, tasty, rosy meat in a sauce of coarse mustard that seems to be flavored of grain as well. The sirloin steak is velvety meat, seared, moist, accurately prepared, its wine and marrow sauce restrained, so the flavor of the excellent beef is undisguised.

Brought to you on a tray of white marble is New York's best cheese board—the walnut-and-onion bread you get with it is made on the premises, and it works well with everything from mild cottage cheeses to the gamiest goats.

The simpler sweet desserts include an exceptionally icy lime sherbet—very tart, sugared just a little; coffee ice cream—its texture creamy, its flavor that of strong espresso; a poached pear—firm and still faintly gritty, served in its cooking syrup of sweet-spiced red wine. The warm rhubarb tart is a little sour and a little sugary on its buttery pastry—it is graced with a dollop of perfect whipped cream. Something given as chocolate pavé is of a chocolate mousse and a chocolate cake that are concentrated without being heavy—it is moistened with a light vanilla cream. The reine de saba is a slightly orange-flavored chocolate cake in which the citrus acidity seems to dramatize the substantiality of the chocolate—it is covered with a silken black icing and garnished with more of that solid whipped cream.

★★★ LE CHANTILLY

106 East 57th Street
LUNCH AND DINNER. CLOSED SUNDAY.
Reservations, 751-2931.
Credit cards: AE, CB, DC, MC, V.
Very expensive.

"Originality," it has been written, "is the absence of style." The absence of style, however, is not originality. It should not be expected of every restaurant that it be original, different from all others. For if one good restaurant of a kind is good, surely two may well be twice as good. (The reasoning cannot be extended indefinitely.) But respect for tradition is one thing, imitation another. The really good spots always reveal at least a trace of individuality. Le Chantilly is standard New York–haute cuisine and taking no chances, thank you. Its food is excellent, the service more than able, the accommodations comfortable. But there is no art in the place, nothing personal. It could have been assembled from parts supplied in some modular French-restaurant kit. Le Chantilly is the B. Altman of New York's restaurants (as La Grenouille and Lutèce are Lord & Taylor and Bloomingdale's), an example of instant senescence, for the place is only a couple of years old.

Le Chantilly is rimmed with a tufted red banquette, illuminated by crystal chandeliers and tear-drop sconces, sheathed in mirror, carpeted with broadloom and adorned with hazy murals (including one of the blue-domed château at Chantilly, and another of a field of horses out on the famous track). Bunches of brightly colored flowers on the white-linened tables relieve a little the formality of gleaming crystal and polished flatware. And the staff of thousands, workingmen in black-and-white uniforms, relieves the garish posh of the crowd that comes here—fat ladies in print dresses, bald gentlemen with silken suits on their backs and high-school dropouts on their arms. From among this crowd the management has attempted to extract an elite, in order to simulate the hierarchical structures that obtain in those restaurants in which the famous are seated in "choice" locations, the ruck in the rear. Since the noteworthy do not frequent this place in any great numbers, the privileged are drawn from among the ordinary. All you have to do to become a Chantilly celeb is come often and spend big. The weakness of this system is that unknown celebrities are hard to recognize, so that when the boss host is briefly away from his post, underlings inadvertently seat important clients near the kitchen. When his eminence returns from the facilities and sees what has been done, he hustles his misplaced favorites to one of the tables in the corridor near the front (which leads into the dining room proper), carrying their martinis and their Kent Golden Lights in his own hands. So when you enter Le Chantilly and pass through this aisle of greats, you are sized up, from the left and the right, by people whose only distinction is that Le Chantilly is their favorite restaurant.

Very likely none of this will affect you one way or the other when you address yourself to your food, which can be utterly distracting: an ivory-colored mussel soup that manages to be both vividly and subtly briny, fragrant of saffron, buttery—a single plump mussel is at the center of the bowl; an assortment of hors d'oeuvres that includes a truly nutlike shredded celery root in a sharp and glistening dressing, and a country pâté that has all the essential gaminess and fat; a salty terrine of sweetbreads that is studded with nuggets of crunchy truffle, adorned with cool jelly, and garnished with an herbed whipped cream that is no more weighty than froth. The snails are very much the usual thing (despite the menu's designation, "à ma façon"), but many of the hot appetizers are memorable: a so-called mousse of two fish that consists of two dumplings, each with a sparkling flavor of fresh seafood that is somehow intensified while bulk and heaviness are almost eliminated—the airy substances are moistened with a sauce that is honeylike in both its flavor and its polish; huîtres au champagne, in which the plump oysters are served, in their shells, in a creamy sauce—of wine and the oyster liquor—that is lightly browned just before the delicate dish is brought hot to your table.

There are dishes here that are like the place itself, richness for the sake of richness. Such is a sometime special of sole stuffed with lobster, the entire enterprise bathed in a sauce that is nothing but opulence—the dish is fine, but it is a production number and nothing more, its excellent ingredients almost irrelevant to its effect. But when that lobster is served as cassolette de homard au whisky, the lightly bourboned sauce—at once sweet, syrupy and spicy hot—dramatizes the lobster meat without concealing any of its delicacy. The frogs' legs are fresh-tasting and tender, crisped and garlicked, garnished with a dense and oily tomato purée. There is a pale roast veal, delicate and almost without fiber, served with a thin, dark sauce that is like strong blood against the milky meat. The veal chop is sturdier stuff, the hefty rib strewn with woodsy chanterelles and a pan sauce that is dark and winy. The noisettes d'agneau are sturdier still, the nuggets of gamy lamb dressed with a strong sauce that is studded with whole green peppercorns—a powerful dish.

Good cheeses at room temperature, six or eight different ones on any given night, ranging from loud, chalky goats to buttery Brie. The sweet desserts have a kind of mechanical perfection, layers of fluffy cake, crisp and chewy and tender meringues, mellifluous pastry creams, silken icings, flaky crusts. The chocolate mousse cake is intense and sharp, great sails of chocolate leaf rising from its top. The nutted mocha meringue chestnut cake is dazzling in the way its elements play off against each other. But the tarte Tatin seems to be made with pallid apples, and as they are not caramelized, there is almost nothing to it. All the cakes and pastries are served with a light and lightly liquored crème Anglaise. The unexpected winner is the cut fresh fruits, which seem not only to have been cut moments before serving, but picked only moments before that, in citrus juices and a touch of booze—the dish is as refreshing as cold spring water.

★ CHARLEY O'S BAR & GRILL & BAR

33 West 48th Street
LUNCH AND DINNER. CLOSED SUNDAY.
Reservations, 582-7141.
Credit cards: AE, CB, DC, MC, V.
Expensive.

Charley O's was created by Restaurant Associates (which no longer owns it) as a slick Irish saloon, with the smell of beer out, the polish of mahogany paneling, the solidity of deep-hunter-green walls, the sparkle of great cut mirrors, the elegance of etched glass and the brilliance of white linen in. Where your neighborhood joint has photographic mementos of neighborhood guys casually hung about, this place is bedecked with big, snappy photos of the famous, in shimmering frames and behind glass, some clever utterance of the subject quoted below. The tone of Charley O's is old-fashioned masculine, and if you really want to live it all the way, you step up to the sandwich bar and you order your clams, oysters or shrimp by the piece, or your roast-beef or corned-beef sandwich, and you eat, in your trench coat, at the circular stand-up counter, watching the parade of stock-market quotations on the television screen at the end of the liquor bar, while showing no emotion. The shellfish is good, if not pristine; the sandwiches are hefty, their meat tasty.

At cocktail time the place is mobbed with office guys and gals brandishing their gender. A recent survey indicates that a preponderance of the ladies still stall until a gent offers to buy a drink. There are tables near the bar where newly-mets can sit down and get better acquainted. If drinks lead to sandwiches or (this is rare) dinner in the back room, things are going very swimmingly indeedy.

The back-room food is serious stuff: those aforementioned shellfish; pea soup that is thick and good, although not meaty; big, crusty prawns in ale batter, with a slightly fruity mustard sauce; a gamy and satisfying lamb stew that has the edgy taste of cooked bones and the richness of lamb fat; steaks and lamb chops that are seared, plump and accurately prepared, albeit not of the finest meat; boring broiled scallops; and a fish of the day that often seems to be just a millimeter shy of fresh. Bassett's Irish-coffee ice cream is a perfect dessert of its simple, sweet kind, and the chocolate-mousse pie is just like good chocolate ice cream in pie form. The chocolate cake and cheese cake are rich but not distinguished.

★★ LE CHERCHE-MIDI

936 First Avenue (near 51st Street)
LUNCH, MONDAY TO FRIDAY; DINNER, MONDAY TO SATURDAY. CLOSED SUNDAY.
Reservations, 355-4499.
Credit cards: AE, MC, V.
Expensive.

Two narrow stores, connected at the back, and almost everything within them très, très Provence. The tall, spare, trowel-stroked dead-white plaster walls suggest the rigors of sun-baked life in the French subtropics. Some of the few furnishings have been handed down from generation to generation (or were picked up in Bleecker Street antique shops). On a single red wall, old mirrors in plain wooden frames. At the back a rough-hewn table whereon the cheeses and desserts are prettily illuminated by two lighted tapers. An ancient three-drawer bureau that has not been painted in a century is piled with napkins. Straw baskets are stored on a high shelf—*so* convenient when you are making a trip to the market. There are wildflowers in little crockery mustard jars on the rather small, white-linened tables that stand in rows along the walls. But a handful of posters and prints, here and there, in simple, modern frames, concede the suchness of this New York enterprise. Altogether, of the many eating places in town that have commissioned their architects to do them up in French rustic, this one got the least corny job.

You find on your table a dish of marinated Mediterranean olives, small and black. Sometimes they are simply moist with oil and wildly garlicked. Sometimes they are flavored with herbs, mingled with citrus rind, fortified with fiery spices. They are always delicious, and when you dispatch your allotment, it is not replenished. So you consider the menu, which is changed frequently, and you console yourself with moules à la moutarde, about a dozen fresh ones, out of their shells, in a little mound, cool and of vivid flavor in their smooth mustard dressing. Or with some of the nicest smoked trout around, the meat of the entire fish separated from its bones and put back in place within the gold-colored skin—a dollop of light, mildly seasoned crème fraîche is the sauce for the moist fish. When there are leeks, they are judiciously poached, so that they are firm, and the inch or two of greens still attached to the bulbs is pleasantly fibrous. They are served in a good mustard vinaigrette, and you wish they were more thoroughly separated from their sand. You may well conclude that a few leaves of lettuce, a handful of walnut meats, and a bit of dressing are not much of an excuse for the substantial price tag, but this is red lettuce, tender yet crisp, the walnuts are crunchy, and the dressing—of walnut oil and a superb vinegar that manages to be strong but not truly sour—is like velvet. The terrine of duck is ordinary, loud rather than tasty, a little leaden. Far better is the saucisson en croûte, four thick discs of glistening red sausage, rimmed with a dark, well-greased pastry—the spicy meat is resilient, even chewy in parts, very nice with this establishment's biting Dijon mustard and some cold red wine.

A great slab of swordfish is served with a dollop of butter—to which herbs and minced capers have been added—melting over it. The fish is fresh, firm, rich even without its added butter. In a deep plate of hot, buttered broth, many fresh mussels, an abundance of tiny bay scallops and a few crisp shrimp make up the ragoût de fruits de mer. The pungent fish stew is herbed, saffroned, studded with little chunks of tomato, and fortified with a good dose of Pernod. On occasion Le Cherche-Midi makes a version of a dish that is more famous than familiar. In it chicken is roasted with many whole cloves of garlic. When the chicken is made well, as it is here, there is nothing obvious or gross about the concentrated garlic flavor. The bird is moist, and its meat and dark sauce produce an aroma that heats the room. The cloves of garlic themselves—which are still in their skins when they are served—are soft and moist and eminently edible. A fine roast duck is offered in a tart sauce made with sherry vinegar. More of that good duck, as well as pork, lamb and strong sausage, is to be found in the cassoulet. The meats are gamy, the white beans tender but still firm. The heavy dish addresses itself directly to the provocations of gluttony. The gigot is of marinated lamb—tender, rare, strong—served, in many thin slices, in a tart and very peppery sauce poivrade that seems to be leavened a little with fruit.

Cheeses are always available, and if now and again a few of them are further from pristine than a few others, you can figure out which are which by inspection. A basket of fruit—ripe pears and juicy clementines have been served—goes with the cheese. You may prefer a salad of some utterly fresh watercress, endive that is sharp and almost hard, more of that lovely walnut oil.

The apple tart is thin, delicate, hardly more than a breath of pastry. Your slice of dacquoise is as if cut from a pie, its meringue is chewy, coffee-flavored, and it is spread with a sweet lemon cream—you wish the item were a little less candy-like. The strong chocolate cake—under an almost syrupy icing—has sharp bits of hazelnut throughout.

★★★ CHEZ PASCAL

151 East 82nd Street
DINNER.
Reservations, 249-1334.
Credit cards: AE, CB, DC, MC, V.
Very expensive.

This place is like a laboratory product in which are combined elements not found together in nature. The place is a low-ceilinged, brick-walled, candlelit side-street hideaway that does little to call attention to itself—just the thing when what you want to effect is an occasion of comfort, informality, intimacy. Chez Pascal purveys the kind of stylish food that is usually gobbled up by New York's trendiest go-getters in the day's flashiest joints. Yet it is frequented by as starched a crowd as may be found outside the boardroom of Morgan Guaranty. On occasion every last gentleman in the place is clean-shaven; is attired in polished black shoes, blue or gray trousers that are of the same goods as his jacket, a tasteful four-in-hand under a small collar; is accompanied by a wife who, if she is to be judged by her appearance, spends the length of her days preparing to be perfect in the evening. And she *is* perfect. There is hardly a woman in the place who, if she learned to hold still, could not get a job in a Saks window. In fact, everyone here—boys and girls together—has access to all the latest in cosmetic, tonsorial, vestmental, dental, medical and—you may be sure—spiritual advances. If you want to get away from it all, do not go to this year's tropic isle. Come, instead, to Chez Pascal. In this little world, no one has a care in the world. Don't knock it. There is much to be said for money well spent. Many people waste more money in their lives than is spent well here in one evening.

The walls are of rosy brick, with sidings of old wood paneling set before them here and there, from behind which indirect light steals. The stamped-tin ceiling has been finished to look like old copper. The floor is of worn wood. The tables are ample but proximate, they are covered with pink linen, and they are set with big wine goblets, slender vases that hold a single flower each, and stout candles, the flames of which burn down into the core, so that the white wax cylinders glow like frosted lamps. You sit on banquettes or armchairs of gray suede, or on French period chairs of carved wood and caning. You are attended to by articulate gentlemen in natty blazers and smart neckties who look very much as if they were dressed for dinner themselves.

The establishment is not without its disharmonies. Among them are certain members of New York's international set—they smoke brown cigarettes and raise their voices a little when inserting foreign phrases in their English conversation. Interlopers from the Sun Belt come as well, to pick up pointers about the eating habits of natives in cold climates. One visitor, betraying a veritable naturalist's keenness of observation, notes that chocolate mousse, though you can eat it with either a fork or a spoon, is really not a form of Jell-O. Sour notes from nearby also creep in—a helmet-haired gent, in a suit of vivid stripes, and his companion, in a two-piece outfit of fool's-gold lamé, manage, remarkably, to be overlooked by the entire house. Then there are the paintings —an extensive collection of mostly sad people in mostly revelrous situations in mostly strong colors. They do not adorn and seem to be hung so as to strain the shapes of the walls. Withal this is an attractive place; its flaws do not undo.

You are served, the moment you sit down, a disc of saucisson en croûte. The meat is like a profound salami, warm and spicy and fatted; it is rimmed with flaky pastry, and it is garnished with a dollop of mustard that is sharp enough to relieve the solidity of the sausage. That tidbit is the last you get for free. For money you may try the pâté de gibier à l'Armagnac—two rectangular slabs the size of your hand, dark jelly around their edges, the salty forcemeat studded with chunks of game and whole peppercorns, all prettily garnished with a twirl of tomato and a floret of cornichons. The dish is perhaps too powerfully seasoned, and the brandy of the title is certainly applied with restraint—it is the kind of food with which you might want beer rather than wine. The fish pâtés that you get around town are almost invariably pallid. It can be said for Pascal's terrine de brochet aux pointes d'asperges that it is less so, and that its rich herbed mayonnaise just about rescues it. There is a nice first course of cool string beans mingled with goose liver and mushrooms in a creamy dressing. And another that, though its ingredients read like a put-on—kiwi, avocado, crabmeat—is made quite for-real by a slightly fruity pink dressing that brings the elements together. Strawberries and slices of grapefruit liven the dish.

But for something you will not forget, begin with the cassolette d'huîtres au champagne. The dish is served to you in a small tin-lined copper saucepan in which the hot and gentle oysters, and a few slivered mushrooms, are covered over with a buttery wine broth and surmounted by strands of crisp vegetables—each element is clear and itself, and the food, though elaborate, has a comforting quality usually found in simpler food. In another saucepan just like that one you are served Chez Pascal's snails—about a dozen of the plump nuggets, mingled with mushrooms and little morsels of sharp Roquefort cheese, in a hot polished oil that is fortified with Pernod.

If Chez Pascal is known for a single dish, it is for its bouillabaisse, probably the most dramatic version of this fish stew served in New York. (Purists will point out that for including some of the seafoods included here one would be shot in Marseilles.) To serve the bouillabaisse, the boss himself sometimes steps in, first displaying to you—in a great "bowl" that is actually a hardwood plank roughly bent into a trough—the glistening fish and shellfish that have just been cooked in the soup. Then, stationed in the aisle, he skins and bones the fish. Thereupon he serves you the shellfish on one end of a huge oval platter, the cleaned fish—in a deep soup plate—on the other end. Over the fish, from a large conical pot, he ladles the thick brown soup, spreads grated cheese over that, then crusts of toasted French bread, on which he spoons the pink and peppery garlic sauce called rouille. The fish is moist and fresh and flaky, the clams and lobster and mussels are juicy and tender, the almost opaque soup is dazzlingly fragrant and spicy—at once earthy and oceanic—and the rouille is about as pungent and strong as such essences can be, short of violence. If you come here once, the bouillabaisse is the thing to have. At the other end of the seafood spectrum is the grilled Dover sole—the fillets are elegantly browned, but they lack some of the buttery sweetness of this fish at its best, and the tangy mustard sauce served with them brightens the dish but cannot improve the sole.

You get a splendid veal chop here, thick and tender, its exterior browned to a glistening shade of reddish walnut. The chop comes to you on a layer of fresh spinach, it is adorned with crunchy fluted mushrooms, and it is moistened with a sauce that is a little like warm brandy. Veal again, this time thin overlapping slices of it alternated with circles of peeled lime, the sautéed meat and the tangy fruit in a sauce that has a touch of citric acidity—light food, but strong. The steak—entrecôte poêlée à la moelle —could be of tastier, more tender beef, but the meat is redeemed by its perfect cooking and by the winy depth of its marrow sauce, which is sharpened with pepper and sweetened with shallots. The duck is fresh, its flavor is strong; there is fat in the meat but it is not fatty. You wish the skin were more crisp, but you cannot fault the slightly sweet and slightly tart raspberry sauce. Most of the main courses are served with a grand array of vegetables—among them scalloped potatoes that are creamy and browned, a sharp purée of turnips or a sweet one of carrots, braised endive or braised fennel, strong and crinkly spinach, grilled tomatoes and zucchini.

Good desserts. The apples on the tarte Tatin are almost purple from their long cooking; they are sweet and a bit sour, and they are graced with perfect, rich whipped cream. The bombe glacée is a block of ice cream, the sweetness of which has an almost liquorlike intensity—it is veined with meats of hazelnuts. The sorbet cassis comes in a huge wineglass—three balls of plum-colored sherbet, icy, sweet, winy, refreshing, vivifying. The mousses are impeccable—the one of chocolate creamy and a little sticky, mingled with chopped nuts; the pink raspberry mousse exceptionally rich, its smooth fluffiness pointed up just a bit by the pleasant grittiness of raspberry seed.

Ladies are presented with menus on which prices are not shown.

★★★ CHRIST CELLA

160 East 46th Street
LUNCH, MONDAY TO FRIDAY; DINNER, MONDAY TO SATURDAY. CLOSED SUNDAY.
Reservations, OX 7–2479.
Credit cards: AE, CB, DC, MC, V.
Very expensive.

You are greeted by a host who, when you reject the first couple of tables he shows you to, does not, directly or by suggestion or by gesture, imply that Christ Cella can do without fussy customers. This is remarkable because Christ Cella *can* do without fussy customers. It has plenty of all kinds, and they pay more than liberally for the pleasure of eating in this establishment. But your host listens to your objections carefully, no sooner does he grasp them than you are escorted to the bar, and as soon as a table is available that meets your specifications (not in the traffic, not near the door), he comes to get you. The amazing policy of this restaurant is: you pay your money and you take *your* choice.

That bar where you waited for your table is very much of the place. The downstairs of this two-story restaurant is made up of many small rooms, and one of them is the handsome wood-paneled barroom, the bar the length of one wall, the three tables opposite spaced well apart. There are no stools at the bar (this is not primarily a drinking place), and the polished walls and the mounted antelope head notwithstanding, the room is not clubbily masculine, just comfortable. Then there are all the other rooms, with their pale-green walls hung with prints and photographs. At the back is the immaculate kitchen, open to view, with accommodations for a handful of regular customers who find that eating in the kitchen at an unlinened table, under the clamor of the pots and pans and kitchen patter, is a fillip that spices the simple pleasures this restaurant provides. Upstairs the rooms are large, bare and forbidding—a good place for big parties, where your companions are also your scenery.

Christ Cella has an Old New York feel to it, like a restaurant born in the Depression; it is Spartan in its appointments and lavish of quality, as if it knew and remembered the value of a customer and never learned the show-biz side of the food biz.

The customers have more than a touch of class—conservative but not stuffy, people who do not brandish their individuality, who are not dazed by their own success. The clothes worn here are neither uniforms nor political statements. (Of course, that is at dinner. At lunchtime the restaurant is just another place in the midtown business district, and the place is loaded with guys who seem more important outside their offices than at their programmed tasks performed at standard desks.)

There is no printed menu. The waiter tells you what there is, all of which is simple food. The crabmeat cocktail is copious, tender, fresh, with a brightly flavored cocktail sauce—not inherently a great dish, but as good as it can be for what it is. Shrimp and lobster cocktails of comparable quality, but no clams or oysters.

Perfectly broiled fish is available, on occasion roast beef, good liver. But the standard dishes here, making up probably 90 percent of the main-course orders, are steaks and lobsters, and they are more consistently excellent than in any other steak/lobster house in this Steak Row neighborhood, or, for that matter, in New York. The steaks are fibrous, tender, seared (but not burnt), so the juice of the meat is sealed into the center of the steak. The filet mignon is at least three inches thick, adorned with a few fresh mushrooms; the sirloin is not that deep, but it is substantial enough to be cooked for more than a moment and still come out rare. By and large, the degree of doneness of your steak is as you request it in this restaurant, and deviations are slight. The steaks are sprinkled abundantly with fresh parsley.

The lobsters are big but not huge, they are broiled, and they are fresh, unbelievably moist, faintly imbued with the taste of the charred shell. Unrequested, your waiter separates most of the lobster from its shell, so that even a child can eat it with a knife and fork; the meat from the claws is brought to you extricated from its housing and served up in a little bowl. Still, grown diners are up to their elbows in drawn butter by the time they have worked their way through one of these things, their wineglasses coated with the stuff, as if it wouldn't be a lobster without the mess. The hashed brown potatoes are lightly blackened and crunchy outside, soft within. The baked potatoes are done perfectly. The salads are of fresh, unblemished greens in a tart, limpid dressing —the arugula, for example, has a full, strong fragrance, as if it were just picked.

Excessive desserts, but good of their kind. The cheese cake at this restaurant is not what it was a few years back, but it is one of the best of its type in town—extremely rich and creamy, very heavily lemoned. The napoleon is made up, elementally, of thick layers of custard between very flaky layers of pastry. If all of that sounds like too much, which it should be if you have eaten well to this point, there is a more than decent raspberry sherbet served in more than indecent quantity.

★ LE CIRQUE

58 East 65th Street
LUNCH AND DINNER. CLOSED SUNDAY.
Reservations, 794-9292.
Credit cards: AE, DC.
Very expensive.

The voluminous dresses on the ladies glitter with metallic appliqués. The suits on the rounded gentlemen fit like the jackets on baked potatoes. And each night, hordes of these well-feds are inserted into this place like eggs into a carton, are handed menus that have been printed up in a language almost none of them can read, get 10 percent of the document explicated during a two-minute allotment of the captain's time and, after gladly agreeing to his suggestions, are rewarded with a compliment each—"A *very* good choice, madame," and then, "An *excellent* choice, monsieur"—by their deft handler before he heads for another table and another quick kill. Still, contentment and even delight fill the air. In fact, if you are not suffocated by the imported fragrances that heavy the atmosphere in this place, you may wish to hold your napkin before your face to thin the odor of self-satisfaction. For to the ladies and gentlemen who pack this restaurant nightly, eating at Le Cirque is not just dinner (if it is that at all), it is the public display of the material rewards fate has conferred on them for their inner goodness. And though bad guys cannot come to Le Cirque (they simply do not have enough money), the good guys are forever suspiciously sniffing for sinners. Wear the wrong kind of clothes, for example, and you get the feeling that the lady at the adjacent table, who is seated beside you on the banquette, would inch away if there were room.

Presently she forgets about you, for her French captain has come. "What is the spay-see-al-ee-tay?" she asks him. "Dover sole, ah-knee-way," he answers. "I'll have that," goes she. "How?" goes he. "Ah-knee-way," goes she, now a little confused. He suggests that she have it poached, with white grapes, and she is rescued. The name of the restaurant (The Circus) is not, however, a reference to the clientele. It makes allusion to the pale trelliswork wallpaper, which incorporates within it unfunny depictions of animals doing human things—hunting, dining at table, dancing, flirting. The look of the place is that of posh that pretends to be nothing but posh for the sake of posh, with thick carpeting, mirrored columns, tentacled wall sconces with glowing bulbs at the end of each limb. A banquette of mauve-colored suede rims the room. There are great bursts of flowers here and there and bunches of them on each white-linened table. But posh is not luxury. There is not quite enough of this fancy place. Throw your arm over the back of your companion's chair, and it will be clipped by the next passing busboy. The waiters are forever backtracking into small sidings of space to permit other waiters to pass them in the aisles. There are restaurants where that kind of crowding engenders a sort of tumultuous gaiety. But this place gets too stodgy a set for conviviality ever to take over. All you can do at Le Cirque is enjoy your own company and the mostly very good food.

Some of which is trilingual, including the "Seviche of Red Snapper au Coriandre," a sparkling dish in which chunks of the raw, fresh fish, "cooked" in a lime-juice marinade, are served under strands of sweet red pepper—the strong seafood is vividly flavored of citrus and cilantro. But Le Cirque's mussel salad, albeit a good idea—fresh mussels in a smooth cream sauce that is thick with crunchy, just-chopped red onions —suffers from the fact that a number of the mollusks are (at Le Cirque!) rank. The duck pâté is fine—nutted, well seasoned, fragrant with herbs, at its center a core of buttery foie gras—but it is short on the flavor of duck itself. Far better is the pâté of rabbit, which is pale, of a rich animality of flavor that has been subtly heightened by its seasoning, but not at all disguised. Some splendid plump snails are mingled with nuts, sharp strands of scallion and hard croutons in a sauce that is little more than sweet butter—the disparate elements work perfectly together. A couple of delicate crêpes, wrapped around morsels of hot, fresh shellfish, are served in two sauces, a mild curry sauce and a spicy sauce, all of which add up to a complicated but not fascinating production. Simpler but far more enthralling are the poached oysters, the warmed morsels returned to their half shells and adorned with a pale wine sauce that is laced with fresh spinach.

At just about every Le Cirque dinner one little thing will go startlingly wrong. Take, for example, the "Fricassée de Lotte Baies des Singes," a title that makes reference to the ugliness of the fish called lotte, but not to the fact that in its preparation at Le Cirque, the otherwise yummy fish—the big chunks of it firm, of clear flavor, moistened with a smooth sauce that is fragrant with saffron, mounded up in a pastry shell, dotted with a thick tomato purée and garnished with buttered snow peas and steaming grilled tomatoes—is gritty. It probably does not occur every day. You may have a sautéed chicken that is elegantly browned, in a dark tomato-flavored sauce that is laden with mushrooms and sharp with the heady flavor of fresh ginger. The rare-cooked duck is served as numerous thin slices, rosy and glistening, but there is very little flavor to the meat, and the garnishes—tart cranberries and crisp slices of Granny Smith apples that have been lightly battered and fried—improve but cannot redeem the dish. Le Cirque's sweetbreads are rich, tender, light and lightly browned—they are touched with the sharp flavor of fresh watercress and garnished with woodsy wild mushrooms. An excellent veal chop, of delicate, almost white meat, is seared, moistened with a glistening red-brown sauce, garnished with a brimming-over pastry cup of wild mushrooms in a creamy, sharply salted sauce. Le Cirque was one of the first places in New York to serve carpaccio—raw beef in the Italian manner. It has been graduated from appetizer status to main course, but nowadays it is served in cursory fashion: the thin slices of red meat are cut in advance, and they are icy, wet rather than blooded, and it takes a pint of this good green sauce—sour and crunchy—plus a blizzard of grated Parmesan cheese to obscure those conditions. The menu promises two mignons of lamb, but you are delivered only a single large one—this is a perfectly nice disc of perfectly medium-rare meat, strong-flavored and tender, and its thick and slightly tart sauce has a nice subtlety of rosemary about it; but your doggy bag plans for that second tournedos have been foiled.

Clear your head for what is to come with some bracing Parmesan cheese. You may, of course, then proceed to one of the soufflés, for they are well made—the raspberry-flavored number is deep pink, light, moist but firm, berry-flavored almost to the point of winimess, better by far unsullied than with the unforgivably icy raspberry sauce your waiter spoons onto it. But these days almost all of New York's more pretentious French restaurants turn out first-class soufflés, whereas this establishment's dessert cart is at least a level or two above most of the others. The chocolate mousse cake will probably kill you, or at least knock you down, for it is light, pungent, covered with chocolate flakes that are polished and intense—the rich mousse that is half its bulk is in dramatic textural contrast to the dark cake that is the other half. The butter-cream cassis cake is a startling balance of fruit and cream, nuts and light cake, velvet and air. The banana papaya tart is smooth, polished, the two oddly matched fruits very easy on each other. And if the lemon meringue tart is not on the level of the aforementioned, it is probably the best lemon meringue pie you have had since grandma's.

Your check arrives unrequested.

★ CLAUDE'S

205 East 81st Street
DINNER. CLOSED SUNDAY.
Reservations, 472-0487.
Credit cards: AE, CB, DC, MC, V.
Very expensive.

Broad vertical stripes of dark-red glass alternate on the walls with equally broad stripes of polished mirror (in which are reflected identical striped walls on opposite sides of the room). The banquettes are dove gray, the carpeting plush crimson. The place has what used to be called "looks," a quality characterized by an attention-getting appearance and no beauty. Claude's is a two-color cosmetics ad in a glossy magazine, a painted redhead in a silver dress. Withal it is sterile. There is much of the hospital in its clean, quiet lines and its colorless use of color. The premises consist of a couple of identically appointed rooms, small but not cozy. Blessedly they are dimly lit.

A few of the tables are so small that the base of your wineglass is necessarily under the lip of your plate. When your waiter must add one more item to those before you, there is much minuscule moving, of the tiny vase half an inch this way, of the ashtray half an inch that, so that a pepper mill or some such may be snugged in. If you are an unknown party of two, you will probably be shown to one of these midgety accommodations—you must demur firmly, in favor of something more commodious, for at $50 an hour you may feel that you have the right to place your elbow right beside your spoon.

Almost everybody who comes to Claude's gets dressed up for the event. These are occasions for dark three-piece suits, black dresses and strings of pearls. And if you do not like it here there must be something wrong with you. Everyone who arrives is sized up by everyone who has already arrived. If you want to be really looked over, come in tight pants, a loose shirt, a sweater tossed across one shoulder. The guessing games will go on all night about who you might just possibly be.

If you happen to be a favored regular, the captain, when he enumerates for you the special—unlisted—dishes of the day, will mention all of them. But if you are unknown, a choice item or two may be withheld, pending the possible later arrival of friends of the house. Claude's is not alone in this practice, other restaurants do it, but it is an especially stupid policy in a restaurant where the captain's spiel to one table is audible, in all the rudeness of its favoritism, to three or four others.

If you have wondered all your life just what is meant by "Carolines d'escargots à l'aïl doux," know that the expression refers to snail sandwiches. At Claude's the standard serving of six snails arrives between halves of six little cream puffs, looking very much like six little hamburgers on a plate. The sandwiches are buttery (no one said "Hold the butter") and herbed (in place of lettuce). It is one of New York's few witty dishes, but no one knows for sure whether the humor is intentional, whether everyone in the kitchen has a good laugh every time they turn out the production. Anyway, the dish is pretty good, but those snails really do not mix with chou pastry.

Then there is the salade dinardaise, nothing more than several dressed seafoods on a plate: shrimps in cocktail sauce, lobster meat in Russian dressing, crabmeat in a lovely green sauce that is bright with fresh herbs, one oyster with an excessively peppery mignonette, and a couple of mussels in a creamy mayonnaise that is flavored with saffron and adorned with a couple of threads of the fragrant spice. This is nice food, but hardly what you came to Claude's for. But there is a kicker, sea urchins, an organism much like tan, gamy, slimy dust, the experience of eating which is probably akin to drowning at sea.

But do not rush to generalize about this place. The appetizer called mille feuille de roquefort au celeri is a remarkable block of pastry, solid but flaky, interlarded with the strong and creamy mousse of the blue cheese, and garnished with crisp celery root, walnuts and dill, the three of which are lightly moistened with oil—a wondrous dish. And when shad roe is available this French establishment does a better job with it than any American restaurant in town—the roe is served between the halves of a kind of pastry box, with strands of vegetable in the sandwich, under a pale sauce that is heightened with sprigs of heady dill and sharpened with strong pepper. The roe itself, sealed in its glistening membrane, has been gently cooked, so that each tiny egg is a burst of rich moisture.

It is remarkable that a restaurant capable, for example, of that roe can send out of its kitchen a dish that is barely one remove from the frozen precooked dishes that are the specialties of roadside chains. Such is the ballotine de poularde florentine sauce pistache, chicken wrapped around spinach, cheese and pignoli nuts, to no end—the sauce is winy, the pistachio nuts in the sauce are fun and the dish is overwhelmed by the taste of the spinach, for the chicken, which is most of the bulk, provides no flavor and might as well be white bread. The veal chop is decent, spread with a purée of rice and a mousse of duck liver, neither of which does anything for the meat, with which they merely argue. But you need not look far (the menu is brief) for a winner—the carré d'agneau en chemise aux herbes de provence is a rack of lamb that has been spread with a layer of fresh herbs, wrapped in a thin pastry and roasted just a little—the purpose of the pastry is to hold the herbs against the meat and to keep the meat moist without the expedient of searing it. This method eliminates all charring, so the flavors of the herbs are mingled with rare lamb—the ultimate meat—adding to it a quality of wild mystery.

You are shown a cheese board, and you point at one of the cheeses thereon and inquire of the waiter as to its characteristics. "It is a cross between Brie and Camembert," says he. It is not, but they sell a lot of cheese this way. The half-witted salesmanship notwithstanding, the board is worth sending for. All the cheeses are in good shape, and there is usually an aged Parmesan available—hard and flaky, sharp as spice, head-clearing—good goat cheeses and Roquefort as well. The salad you may choose to have with your cheese is made of impeccable greens, and it is heightened with nuts and with strands of shredded scallion.

Not only is the tarte Tatin but a step or two removed from humdrum apple pie, but the alleged crème fraîche with which it is adorned might just as well be sour cream. The principal excuse for trying this establishment's oeufs à la neige is that the meringues are adorned with violets. After all, how many restaurants sell violets? But the succès au chocolat is swell, layers of cake, cream and mousse, studded with candied fruits and nuts and wrapped in chocolate leaf—a splendid sweet. The poached pear requires twenty-five minutes to prepare, three or four to eat, and just about forever to comprehend what all the fuss is about—just a nicely cooked fruit, irrelevantly wrapped in harmless pastry, served in a pool of thin pear-brandy sauce.

Specialties of the house—main courses and desserts—are available on two days' notice, but only if each dish is ordered for four people or more. With so unpredictable a kitchen, the recommended risk is different dishes for different people.

• COACH HOUSE

110 Waverly Place (near Sixth Avenue)
DINNER. CLOSED MONDAY.
Reservations, SP 7-0303.
Credit cards: AE, CB, DC, MC, V.
Very expensive.

What sets the Coach House apart from other New York restaurants is the unquestioning reverence with which it is regarded by this city's culinary hierarchy. Venerable food gods and "controversial" restaurant critics cross themselves when they pass the Coach House, and rival restaurateurs suspend hostilities when the name of the beloved old place comes up. Even heretics contribute to the awe. They reveal their dirty little secret—that they find the Coach House tiresome—in a manner best described as confessional, as if they were unburdening themselves of a secret distaste for caviar, or Haydn.

There is a simple explanation for all this. The Coach House always provides exactly what its customers seek, which is nothing more than the experience of having been to the Coach House. The satisfaction is in the occurrence of the event. You need not be comfortable, or eat well, or be well served to enjoy eating at the Coach House. You simply need to have done it. It is something like having laid eyes on Franklin Roosevelt or Marilyn Monroe, so that you can tell your grandchildren about it, or the boys in the office. Eating at the Coach House is a rite at which the participant establishes himself as the right kind of person, one who does the right kinds of things. (There are plenty of other restaurants to go to when all you want is a good hot meal.)

The place does have its physical charms, though they are not unalloyed. But not one dish in ten is superb—none at all consistently so. And the discourtesy that unfamiliar customers sometimes suffer at the hands of the host and a few of his underlings suggests that they take the establishment's star status as seriously as do the restaurant's mindless devotees. (This last condition is somewhat improved of late, owing largely to the frequent absence from the premises of the proprietor, who is also the resident scorn. He is given to looking at his customers as if that forced him simultaneously to control his stomach.)

You are greeted by a sign on the outer door: RESERVATIONS ONLY. This deters the timid and helps keep the riffraff out. But if you enter anyway and appear to be the right sort, and if there is a place to sit you down, the house will happily exchange its brand of hospitality for your style of American money.

You enter to a dining room that is a heavy dose of Olde Colonial, well done, with great, airy chandeliers hanging from beamed ceilings, still lifes on brick walls and horsey paintings of red-coated gentlemen hopping hedges on their steeds. The tables are set with pink linen, napkins of brilliant cherry red, fresh flowers. The room is rimmed with banquettes of gleaming maroon. Food and wine are displayed here and there. It is all brightly but gently lit, so that it glows. But when the room is filled, the noise borders on the thunderous. And there are juxtapositions of tables between which even the sveltest waiter cannot easily pass—if you are seated at one of these points, your shoulder may regularly get clipped just as you are aiming your fork for your mouth. A few of the tables for two have tops no larger than chessboards. But a broad stairway at the back leads up to a better—albeit plainer—room. This so-called Hayloft is paneled with dark wood, adorned with inoffensive art and furnished with tables of human proportions, luxurious space between them.

Banking, medicine and law provide most of the moneyed clientele, the Seven Sisters most of the professionals' wives. They come here in tiers of generations, and they settle in with the contentment of elders in their pews. There is rarely a beard in the place, never an unfettered female bosom. Occasionally top-level international business negotiations are celebrated here, American hosts showing off America's alleged best to visitors who would have much more fun in Little Italy. And sometimes Great Plains visitors come by, having counted the stars in the *Mobil Guide*. They are blank, washed, proud to be here. All in all you hear very little laughter at the Coach House.

The final myth is that this is an American restaurant. The menu is about as American as a cast at the Metropolitan Opera House.

If this establishment has one strength, it is the quality and freshness of its seafood; and since all the kitchen does to the raw oysters is split them open and serve them on ice, they are the most reliable dish in the place—plump, sweet and briny, the ultimate mollusk. But the equally fresh clams, served as clams Provençale—in a buttery sauce flavored with garlic and parsley—are invariably toughened in the cooking. (Really first-class kitchens—Le Cygne and La Grenouille are two—can bake hundreds of clams a day and not toughen a single one.) The place serves snails in a similar garlicky sauce, and they are pretty good, though it is unsettling to drop $8 for a couple of orders of escargots and get them served over croutons that are toasted until black. The grilled shrimp with mustard sauce suffer for being contemporary shrimp—they are a little loud, though perfectly cooked—and the sauce is obvious, as if it were meant for a hot dog. The famous black bean soup is sometimes claylike, sometimes tepid, sometimes both, no match for certain Cuban soups around town.

The Coach House has always specialized in bloodless red meat, bloodless even if it is rare. The roast beef is ample, picturesque, tender and tasteless. The steak au poivre is flat, sometimes inaccurately cooked, barely peppered despite the title, and served in a gorgeous-looking plum-colored sauce that tastes of bouillon rather than stock. The menu refers to "Rack of Lamb, Roasted to a Crisp," and if you are lucky you know that means "Burnt to a Cinder." The dish is tasteless but for the flavor of carbon. If you like that lamb, you will love the duck, which is wrecked in much the same way.

So the Ivy League will feel at home, the Coach House makes available college cafeteria food: American chicken pie, in which good chicken is converted to something that seems to be built around canned soup; and crabmeat au gratin, in which perfect crabmeat is magically transformed into macaroni and cheese.

You can get baby lobster tails in garlic butter, and whatever these lumps of white meat may be, they lack the oceanic sparkle and sweetness of fresh shellfish. But the striped bass poached in broth is fine, a giant slab of fresh fish in a tomato-flavored broth —good, simple food.

Eat early and the baked potatoes are fine; later in the evening they have turned to powder in their jackets. The vegetables are dull, often arriving in puddles of their cooking water. There are good salads these days, crisp greens in a simple dressing made with excellent olive oil.

Over the years the apple tart has gone through changes. In its present state it is an apple-sauce tart. The best desserts are the spectacular chocolate cake, which has a profound intensity of chocolate flavor, and the hot fudge ice-cream cake, which is little more than a terrific sundae—rich ice cream and warm, heavy fudge over a thin layer of cake. The pinch of salt in the published recipe for the dacquoise seems to be a handful in the ridiculous execution. Avoid whipped cream with any of the desserts—it seems to have been made of cream that was processed to yield eternal shelf life.

★★ LA COLOMBE D'OR

134 East 26th Street
LUNCH, MONDAY TO FRIDAY; DINNER, MONDAY TO SATURDAY. CLOSED SUNDAY.
Reservations, MU 9–0666.
Credit cards: AE, DC, MC, V.
Expensive.

Bored we are, and novelty is a virtue. La Colombe d'Or is unlike any other French restaurant in New York, and we fall into it in relief, like dogged Christmas shoppers taking the consolation of an after-Altman's cocktail.

There is more to French food than Manhattan Island's familiar extremes—*haute cuisine et la cuisine bourgeoise*—and local eating places often put themselves forward as "Normand," or "Brittany," or "Périgord," et al. But their justifications are little more than the odd dish or two among the dozens of familiars. You could, for example, collect all the menus of the French restaurants in New York's theater district, shuffle them and redistribute them at random—those kitchens, despite their suddenly "new" bills of fare, could continue operations without skipping a beat. But drop this establishment's menu on an uptown chef, and you send him to his books.

La Colombe d'Or has named itself, though it does not model itself, after a legendary eating place in the town of St. Paul, in Provence—a land of sunshine and olive oil, herbs and garlic, bouillabaisse by the sea, spicy stews of meats, fowls, sausages, vegetables in the fertile countryside that lies inland from the Mediterranean. Like the restaurants in that part of the world, this one on East 26th Street offers no duck à l'orange, no tripe à la mode de Caen, no Dover sole—neither real nor imagined. The listings are so relentlessly southern, so free of deference to local custom, that reading through them engenders—are you ready?—curiosity! But there's too many a slip, alas. The singularity of the undertaking is matched by the variability of its success—the food here is never less than OK, mind you, but from such heady promise the more than occasional disappointments are commensurately disappointing.

La Colombe d'Or is a charming little place. When it was new, its ivories and beiges and freshened sand-colored brick gleamed a bit brightly. But The Golden Dove has been around awhile now; it has been—if not lived in—eaten in, it is humanly scuffed here and there, its edges beveled by brushes with human sleeves, an orderly clutter around its dozen or so tables. There are clumps of flowers here and there, the vividly colored forms of Léger prints on the walls, benchlike banquettes with cushions in a French country print of small florets on a dark-green field—which goods is repeated in the curtains on the front windows, repeated again in the pinafores on the nubile waitresses. At lunchtime the place is frequented by the gentle editors of the genteel publishing houses that have eschewed uptown in favor of this old neighborhood. And resident Gramercy Parkers have discovered the place, some of them now eating in a restaurant within walking distance of their own town houses for the first time since they got the sulks when Madison Avenue was made a one-way street.

Everyone goes for the cold spinach appetizer, given as Epinards à l'Huile d'Olives, the fresh leafy vegetable in smooth olive oil, accented with browned sesame seeds and the little black olives of southern France—sometimes the dish is crackling and vibrant, but now and again it is limp. The Mousse aux 4 Poissons, a pale-green fish pâté that is studded with bits of whole fish in among the otherwise thoroughly ground meat, is powerfully flavored with fresh dill, which accounts for its color; and it is garnished with a tomato-flavored mayonnaise and crushed black and green olives. Unfortunately, the mousse itself is strong but short of character; it has flavor but not the distinctive liveliness of fresh seafood. The Brochette de Crevettes is a simple dish of shrimp that are herbed and broiled—the shrimp are plump and crunchy, and the herbing is delicate but sufficient to liven the shrimp. A good, spicy ratatouille is available, too, and it, like all the appetizers, is wonderful with the strong, sour bread you get here—served with sweet butter and with an alternative spread, a tapenade of anchovies, tuna, oil and olives, ground fine to a vibrant paste.

Along the Mediterranean they eat a lot of fish, one of them an especially ugly variety called *lotte*. The *lotte* never actually swims across the Atlantic, and the dish that Colombe d'Or gives us in French as Lotte à la Façon du Pétit Nice, is very freely translated by them as "monk fish, scalloped & sautéed à la provençale." The monk fish, better known as angle fish or anglerfish, is a fairly close approximation of its subtropical swimmer cousin, both in the horribleness of its appearance and the light sweetness of its flavor. In this preparation it arrives in a thick and slightly oily sauce that is studded with capers and black olives; the sauce is peppery, the flavor of its tomatoes heightened with fresh herbs, the whole dish strewn plentifully with fresh parsley. Bass is on the menu in a simple preparation—braised with tomatoes and herbs, the braising liquid then made into a sauce that is spiked with anchovies and olives—and the bass is good that way, for the fish here is always fresh. But on occasion you can have your bass in a buttery sauce that is aswim with mushrooms, onions, parsley. The seasoning is artful, bringing out all the flavors in the sauce and fish without overpowering them—it is a subtler, more balanced preparation. These are both good bass dishes, but once in a while the fish is under- or over-cooked.

When the highest-priced main course on a menu is a kidney dish, you figure they do something special with that unpopular organ, and in fact Rognons aux Morilles is one of the best items in the place. The kidneys have been carefully cleansed of their acids, and they are sweet and crunchy; the forest flavor of the wild morel mushrooms is heightened by the brandy that fortifies the creamy and slightly fatty sauce. The steaming dish is wonderful in the clarity of its textures—crisp kidneys, tender mushrooms, the two bound together by a sauce that is at once thick and polished.

Not every dish is an obscure one. Cassoulet is sold all over town, but this is an especially good one: a couple of sausages and hefty chunks of lamb and duck buried in a little pot of white beans, the top of which has been breaded and crusted. And the coq au vin, though a familiar title, is of better-than-average quality, the chicken thoroughly stewed, after browning, in wine and vegetables, the cooking liquid then made into an earthy sauce to which mushrooms and little onions are added late, so that they stand out in a lively way from the solid, sauced meat. The vegetable garnishes can be swell—thin, crisp French fries; or dreary—limp zucchini; or very interesting— dandelion in broth, with bits of pork fat adding body to the leafy greens.

A good selection of cheeses at room temperature may be had with a variety of salads, all of which are fresh and crisp. Many of the sweet desserts are supplied by outsiders, and they are fine, but the Paris Brest is made here, and it is a rather remarkable cassis-flavored airy cream between layers of light pastry. The pear, poached in wine, is firm but cooked thoroughly, and its winy syrup is sweet and refreshing. Good coffee.

If you drink wine by the glass, your needs are taken care of during the periodic trips taken through the dining room by a member of the staff, carrying a bottle—he or she refills your glass at the nod of your head. The wines by the bottle are mostly overpriced, but half a dozen inexpensive and quite drinkable ones are available.

★★ COPENHAGEN

68 West 58th Street
LUNCH AND DINNER. CLOSED SUNDAY.
Reservations, 688-3690.
Credit cards: AE, CB, DC, MC, V.
Expensive.

This is the only restaurant in town in which you may sample the full range of Danish cooking—but only sample. Danish food may, for convenience, be divided into three parts: (1) *Det koldt bord,* a buffet of foods from which one may assemble a complete meal—the term actually means "cold table," but in practice it often includes hot food as well. (Everyone calls it *smörgåsbord,* but that is the Swedish name.) (2) *Smørrebrød,* the open-faced sandwiches that are available in almost limitless variety in restaurants in Denmark, consisting of buttered bread on which all sorts of meats, fish, eggs, cheeses, vegetables and assortments thereof are assembled. (3) Everything else, including stews, roasts, broilings, sautés, egg dishes.

The popularity of Copenhagen rests principally on the buffet, and almost everyone who patronizes the restaurant does so for the privilege of making repeated trips to the circular table at the center of the dining room, where something on the order of forty discrete foods are arrayed on trays, on plates, on boards, in bowls.

You begin by taking a plate from a stack. You assemble upon it a harmonious selection, repair to your table, consume what you have chosen, put the used plate aside to be picked up by a member of the staff, and return to the buffet to repeat the process. Continue until sated. Select first some gravlax, a particularly delicate version of this sugar-and-salt-cured salmon, which you moisten with a gentle dill sauce. Beside it place some cold poached salmon and mayonnaise, fresh fish and very rich mayo. Leave a spot for the smoked eel, shafts of firm white meat in a leathery skin; for the curried herring; for the silvery, smeltlike Norwegian anchovies, slick and tart; for the strong matjes herring, at once sweet and salty; for the tomato herring, slightly chewy in its thick, red tomato sauce. The weighty potato salad, the cold stewed tomatoes and the cool buttered beets make striking garnishes for the cured fish.

If you have trouble keeping up with the marathoners who have developed eight- or ten-trip capacities, help yourself along with the Carlsberg beer you get here. And for especially trying moments, order a shot of aquavit, the Scandinavian caraway-flavored liquor traditionally drunk during meals—the waiters pour it at your table from bottles that are encased in blocks of ice.

On subsequent sorties to the buffet, sample the spicy chicken salad, the rare roast beef with its pungent and creamy horseradish sauce, the fine ham, and the meaty headcheese in its polished jelly. There is a liver pâté that is about as rich as a malted milk. And there is roast duck (which turns out to be a fine bird to eat cool) and cold chicken in a cool jelly.

The hot foods on the counter—such things as party frankfurters, or beans, or fish cakes—are poor substitutes for second helpings of the items you liked the first time around. Then there are fruits and cheeses, including a perfectly decent Danish blue that simply does not stand up to blue cheeses from certain other parts of the world.

The *smørrebrød* menu (offered only if requested) lists thirty-four sandwiches, on either light or dark bread—a negligible selection by Danish standards, but enough to daunt the tyro. In Denmark these sandwiches are usually small, so one may comfortably eat several at a light meal, but here they are more like little main courses spread across a slice of well-buttered bread, so two of them will satisfy. Most of the sandwich ingredients are available on the buffet table, but in addition there is a lovely little chopped steak with onions, like a super hamburger without a lid. And the scrambled eggs that garnish ham sandwich No. 25 are fluffy and creamy, as eggs nowadays almost never are. But the big winners are Nos. 28 and 48, the former a sandwich of spiced veal that seems to have been cured the way pastrami is—the meat is adorned with strands of jelly and garnished with cold beets—the latter a sparkling combination of duck, apples, prunes and red cabbage.

On the menu, the down-home cooking of the Danish kitchen: a so-called Copenhagen omelet, in which tiny shrimp and mushrooms are encased in the steamy interior of a firm and browned egg pillow; homemade sausages, big and spicy and profoundly meaty, dry until you inundate them with the house gravy; frikadeller, the meatballs of Denmark, one of the best meatball dishes in town, sweet and moist and crusty; pork chops, browned until seared and sealed, sweetened by their own pork fat, buried in wonderfully greasy onions; and boiled chicken in horseradish sauce, very salty, the kind of dish you love if you grew up with it, and not bad otherwise.

Whether you eat from the buffet or from the menu, desserts are served from the cart—cool apple cake, a commendable chocolate mousse and a lemon chiffon among them, all fresh and elemental sweets. Your waiter will spoon whipped cream, the genuine article, onto them until you call a halt.

Most of the waiters sound like Victor Borge. They are nice, but accustomed to diners who eat from the buffet. If you want much service, you may be frustrated, for the gentlemen often wander around like clouds.

Copenhagen is a relaxed place, with wood paneling, soft lighting, comfortable banquettes, large tables, and, throughout the restaurant, paintings and photographs of the city of Copenhagen—reminders of a civilized, happy and beautiful place.

★★★ LA CÔTE BASQUE

5 East 55th Street
LUNCH AND DINNER. CLOSED SUNDAY.
Reservations, MU 8-6525.
Credit cards: AE.
Very expensive.

There is, apparently, a plot of East 55th Street that is for ever La Côte Basque. During the seventies the place seemed to die, slowly and unattractively, pretending to be its living self after the spirit had departed. But here it is again, in place and healthy, with perhaps more of the spirit than ever.

In the beginning no one would have guessed that, of all New York's more pretentious restaurants, this one would become the keeper of all that is stuffiest in the manners that attach to getting a bite to eat. After all, the restaurant was conceived, by Henri Soulé, as relief to the formal rigors and high seriousness of his Pavillon. Unfortunately, Soulé failed to live forever, and the lady friend who got the place on his demise preserved it in superb ignorance of what it was. In its last years it was populated by properly dressed customers (she permitted no others) and snooty help, ignoring each other. That clientele did not complain, for that would have amounted to admission that things had changed; instead they died out. At the end the misplaced came as well: tourists from all over (beckoned by four stars in the *Mobil Guide*); and locals with fresh money and outmoded notions of where the action was. The restaurant never lost its looks, but in its last days under Soulé's survivor, no one in the place was in it for the right reasons.

Happily, she sold. And, more happily, the buyer has preserved and done well by the physical plant he bought. For if there is, say, a handful of eating places in New York that, in some parlor game, must be given the protection of landmark status, surely La Côte Basque is one of them. It is not merely that the place is commodious and good-looking, a well-made confluence of form, function and theater. Lots of restaurants are that. It is, rather, that La Côte Basque is at once grand and human. (Which is not to say that it is of "human scale," for there is room in here for a herd of giraffes to stand up or lie down.)

The place is dominated by the famous murals of Bernard Lamotte. Much art on the walls of New York's eating places is pretty, or smart, or even evocative. But none of it is painting of such loving detail as this, such spirited affection for what it depicts. These renderings were fed by memory, longing and delight, and they have miraculous effects. Look at the view of the harbor of St. Jean de Luz, as it is depicted in the huge mural that enwraps the back of the main dining room: thousands of little boats at rest, their flags flapping in the breeze in the brilliant sun; cafés along the blue water's edge; red-tiled roofs on the tiers upon tiers of houses that, clustered like barnacles on the hills around the town, extend to a luminous horizon. Anyone seen against this backdrop— or before any of these large waterside scenes—becomes lovely to look at. Well, almost anyone.

Black-brown timbers rise along the columns and up the ivory-colored walls to a distant ceiling. There are simulated stone arches over the false windows "through" which you see Lamotte's smaller views of the Basque coast. Flowers are on the tables in pottery pots, big bursts of them around the dining room in bigger pots. There are sconces on the walls, of black bent-iron, supporting soft lights in parchment shades— they give off a golden glow. Palm trees stand here and there. A garish red banquette rims the room and forms islands of tables near its center. The place has a contented clutter of which the staff is a part—they are serious, easy, busy, always on the purposeful move. An unfortunate note: once upon a time the table linen at La Côte Basque was gaily, brightly striped, but today it is white—a disharmonious note that is, fortunately, easy to ignore.

Inevitably, some of the food is at least something of a comedown. What you eat is presented, in the spirit of the place, garnished to a fare-thee-well on prettily patterned china. Much of it, moreover, is delicious, even moving. But not all, and definitely not the assortment of pâtés and terrines. When platters of this kind succeed, it is in part because of the surprising contrasts among seemingly similar foods. But this assortment —of a pâté de campagne that is strong and fatty without being distinctive, of a pâté de foie gras that lacks richness and is encased in a doughy pastry, and a pickle-studded exercise in the mosaicist's art that is raw-salty and little else—manages to come off as almost homogeneous despite the disparities among the shortcomings. The best thing on the plate is a cool jelly garnish that has an intense flavor of herbs and vegetables. A seafood terrine, which arrives as a pastel-striped rectangular slab looking like the flag of some effete nation, should be thoroughly doused with the accompanying green sauce, for the sauce is vividly, pungently herbed, and the seafood is tasteless.

But then there is the ragout de homard aux morilles, which, like many of the hot dishes here, is placed before you under a great silver dome. When the lid is lifted, you see before you, on one side of your plate, the meat of a small lobster, strewn with shredded leeks, surrounded by black, crinkly morels, all in a pool of a dark, honeylike sauce; the other side of your plate contains only a film of pale sauce, in which the features of a flower have been drawn—complete with stem and leaves—with the darker sauce. Very pretty. The lobster is perfect, tender, warm and moist, and those morels are a subtle, dark, woodsy contrast to the oceanic white meat. Or you may start with half a brace of quails, the lone bird clothed in a perfectly tailored pastry jacket, the meat inside dark, almost chocolate-rich, the bird encircled on its plate by plump, warm white grapes, positioned around the perimeter like the numbers on a clock, the entire production bathed in a smooth, sticky and peppery sauce that is flecked with truffles.

English sole is served here—now one way, now another. However they do it, no better fish comes out of the sea, and it is prepared here flawlessly, in one rendition the long, pale fillets encasing eight warm oysters, the mild, sweet acidity of which emphasizes the buttery quality of the fish. The poularde is rare chicken, a big bird with a nutlike flavor that chickens had in pre-chicken-factory days. The breast of the chicken is sliced into large slabs that are rimmed with crisp skin, and the white meat is moistened with a buttery wine sauce in which there are about a dozen of the morels that this restaurant uses up at the rate of around one long ton per evening. Crisped, sautéed noisettes of pale and juicy veal are served with yet another morel sauce, and in this one the wild mushrooms seem as sweet as raisins—but there are two slices of veal, and so there are two sauces, the second one dark and creamy and flecked with truffles (a short ton per evening). You can have firm chunks of kidney, crunchy and sweet, in a mustard sauce that is fiery with green pepper. And you can get roasted rack of lamb of almost unspeakably succulent red meat, in an herbed crust, moistened by yet another truffle sauce, this one viscous and winy. The main courses are adorned with vegetable purées of intense color and high flavor, sheaves of asparagus tips in cucumber bracelets, mounds of rice, more.

If your captain observes that you have done well by your dinner thus far, he may offer you the cheese tray before the dessert (no extra charge). An item or two thereon has perhaps been in and out of the refrigerator a time or two too often, but you can judge by looking or sampling.

You may order a soufflé for one; they are available in sundry flavors, and they are eggy and light and prettily risen above their white pots. Each has a sauce of its own —your waiter cuts away a section of the browned top, spoons in the sauce, and puts the carved-out portion back in its place. The raspberry soufflé is a particular winner, the red sauce studded with whole, hot berries. The pear soufflé is enriched with an apricot sauce that has a brandylike intensity. There is a creamy and smooth Grand Marnier mousse, one dollop of which has in it the equivalent of an after-dinner drink. The flaky pastry of the napoleon is dark, the sugar in it slightly caramelized, and the custard between the layers is silken and thick. The fruit tarts sparkle. And the clafouti —of black cherries in a dark cake—has a homey solidity without being heavy. The staff will cooperate if you wish to sample more than one item from the dessert cart.

★ CSARDA

1477 Second Avenue (at 77th Street)
LUNCH, SATURDAY AND SUNDAY; DINNER, DAILY.
Reservations, 472-2892.
Credit cards: AE.
Medium-priced.

This is a high-ceilinged white-plastered cube of a place, its walls hung with objects of Hungarian folk art, rugs, pottery, oil paintings depicting scenes of the old country, artifacts of life on horseback (Hungarians are great horsemen and cattle herders). Under the white linen covering the tables there are cloths decorated with red-and-black embroidered stripes. The chairs are rustic, of dark wood—they appear to have been carved into shape by ax.

The restaurant is situated where New York's Central European enclaves are clustered, and it lures the homesick immigrants with the flavors of their pasts. Brooding Magyars come to Csarda, their dark mustaches hanging down at the ends, in the company of lipsticked blond ladies who know better than to interrupt their thoughtful moods. For on occasion every other table in the place is actually a small government in exile, dreaming. Respectable burghers come and remove their jackets for the heavy dinner, but neither loosen their ties nor roll up the sleeves of their white shirts—when they have finished eating, their napkins are used not to dab their lips, but to mop their faces. (The wives manage not to work up a sweat.) The waitresses, cheerful red-uniformed hefties from the other side, understand their clientele. They warn foreigners (Americans) away from dishes that only a Hungarian can love. But a Csarda waitress gives her most complaisant attention to the men without women who come here for some home cooking. She listens carefully, almost maternally, as a gentleman grips her wrist, looks a couple of miles into her eyes, and explains in detail how to roast his chicken.

While waiting for his chicken he has an order of brains and eggs—a rich hot mush, strongly fortified with strong paprika, deeply satisfying. Or he has some lecsos Kolbasz, a stew of peppers and onions, powerfully seasoned, slivers of spicy sausage in among the vegetables, all in a hot red broth. The stuffed cabbage is unexceptional, though its salty meat filling is solid stuff, the cabbage crunchy. You get good chopped liver here, textured, eggy, fresh, oiled but not oily. The cold cherry soup, however, is more candylike than this odd, creamy fruit soup at its best.

If you visit Csarda only once, the thing to have is the beef goulash. This is ultimate stew: great chunks of dark beef, fibrous and moist and tender, in a sauce that is profound in its winy and peppery depth. The dish comes with nockerl, tiny dough dumplings, over which you spoon the powerful gravy. The dish is not, however, a sign of a far-reaching talent for dealing with that particular meat, for the boiled beef is pallid, most of its juiciness and some of its flavor cooked away. Choose instead the stuffed roast chicken, the bird's skin crisp and dark, its meat tasty and tender, the giblet stuffing—which is inserted in an incision in the breast meat—spicy and livery. The roast duck is just the simple thing—garnished with apple sauce—but almost perfectly done. One of the restaurant's singular essays is something given as "garlic medallions of veal." The cutlets are lightly breaded and sautéed, and they are buried in a thick sauce of such naked garlic intensity that the restaurant is filled with its fragrance whenever an order comes out of the kitchen. This is a good dish, and despite all that garlic, there is no harshness or crudeness to it. One of the items your waitress will probably try to warn you away from is the veal knuckle. There is no meat on the knuckle, just a crisp breading around a thick jelly. It is rich without being at all fatty, it is low on flavor, its principal appeal the texture of the crust against the stickiness of the goo. You may squeeze on lemon for a little zing, or you add mayonnaise—a dish of creamy homemade mayo is provided—though that will almost surely seem redundant to the unaccustomed palate.

The apple strudel is warm, light, flaky, the fruit filling heavily sugared. The palacsintas consist of crêpes that are covered over with apricot preserves, sprinkled with ground nuts and adorned with powdered sugar. The slight acidity of the fruit and the crunchiness of the nuts relieve a little the syrupy sweetness of the good dish. A chocolate version is also available, but your waitress admits that fact with a show of scorn.

★★ CUISINE OF SZECHUAN

33 Irving Place (near 16th Street)
LUNCH AND DINNER.
Reservations, 982-5678.
No credit cards.
No liquor.
Inexpensive.

If the nation's shortage of resources engenders utilitarian chic, Cuisine of Szechuan will, to its astonishment and without so much as the flick of a warped chopstick, find itself aglitter with galaxies of awards of three- and four-star ratings for undécor. From the white plastic frame just inside the door, wherein the pay telephone once rested but which now serves as a resting place for your elbow when there is a wait for tables, to the twisted metal hangers waiting for your coat on the flaking, formerly chromed pipe rack, this little place is a hair-down, jeans-up, boots-on repair from the pretensions of Gramercy Park—plain white walls and strands of plain white air-conditioning duct across the dreary acoustical ceiling, an enameled red rear wall echoes the plastic red of the booths along the sides. (In recent years the paper place mats on Formica tabletops have been replaced by white linen—a dangerous trend.) Functional, and the shirt-sleeved waiters merely function—they record, deliver and bill. Consultants they are not. But as in many neighborhood Chinese restaurants around town where each copy of the printed menu serves its purpose through a full cycle of the four seasons, you get your advice from clients who have come before—they leave check marks next to recommended dishes (valuable restaurant lore: this is usually sound guidance), the urban equivalent of the Welcome Wagon.

One of your predecessors has checked Aromatic Sliced Beef, so you send for a platter of this cold dish while you and your companions determine the highest check-mark scores among four menus. You have plenty of time for the arithmetic, since the platter of cold beef is rather immense, which is nice because the dark slices of tender, fibrous meat are saturated with the flavor of peanut oil (though the meat is not oily) and accented with the sharpness of the chopped scallion greens that have been sprinkled over.

Three check marks out of a possible four to Smoked Duck with Camphor and Tea —the duck, in the Chinese manner, cross-sectionally slabbed through skin, fat, meat and bone, the outer layer crisped and dark-brown, plenty of fat just under it, the meat saturated with the smoky flavor of tea, some of the bones crumbly enough to eat, all served with a thick plum sauce and shafts of glistening scallion.

In a tie with the duck for the three-check-mark lead is the mis-Anglicized "Dried Sautéed String Beans." Fear not—the string beans are not dried but dry-sautéed, which means they are stirred about in a barely oiled and very hot pan. This process yields beans that are cooked, but as firm and bright-green as raw ones, at once crisp and chewy. They are served tossed with heavily seasoned ground pork, the earthy and oily meat a perfect garnish for the vibrant freshness of the beans.

Many, many two-check-mark entries, including Bean Curd, Szechuan Style—a fiery, weighty porridge, inexplicably not flagged with the red asterisk that denotes "Hot Spiced Flavor" (doubtless a typographer's oversight). It is like the rice, potatoes or noodles that are the starchy bulk of meals designed in other sections of the world. To a Szechuanite, of course, such stuff would be undetectable (if not unpalatable) in the context of this blazing cuisine. The ubiquitous scallions are present.

For $2.50 you get a giant bowl of two-check-mark Cold Noodle with Sesame Sauce. By the time the dish reaches your table, the sesame oil, peanut oil and soy sauce will have drained to the bottom—stir the noodles well in the liquid, even go so far as to obtain a spoon with which to ladle the salty mixture over the firm strands. The dish has an intensity of peanut flavor almost like that of peanut butter, and of course, this richness is offset with a sprinkling of, you guessed it, minced scallions.

Now you have grown confident. You are no longer dependent on and therefore shun the advice of the early pioneers who left their marks and went on. You hack out a path of your own—Hot Spiced Sautéed Kidney. Really have to credit those first settlers, don't you? Next time, it's back to the check-mark system, right? Nothing actually wrong with the food, what with its crisp water chestnuts, tender mushrooms and impeccably rinsed kidneys all in a spicy brown sauce, but nothing special.

Hurry to Cuisine of Szechuan before they lay in a supply of clean menus. Bring enough beer (it is not sold on the premises), which, with this food, is about a quart per person.

★★★ LE CYGNE

55 East 54th Street (new address)
LUNCH, MONDAY TO FRIDAY; DINNER, MONDAY TO SATURDAY. CLOSED SUNDAY.
Reservations, PL 9-5941.
Credit cards: AE, CB, DC, MC, V.
Very expensive.

In December of 1977 the *Times* reported that the food at Le Cygne was "the best haute cuisine French fare in the city." The verdict had been reached, the article said, after research over a six-month period.

The bells had hardly stopped ringing when, ten weeks later, the same paper was compelled to report that Alain Sailhac, Le Cygne's chef, had become Le Cygne's former chef. (The incident was reminiscent of 1841, when, after a heroic military career and a rip-roaring political campaign, William Henry Harrison ascended to the Presidency and, thirty-one days later, demised.)

But opinion, when challenged by events, becomes dogma, and on May 12, 1978, the *Times* was back on the subject, reporting that a return visit to Le Cygne "indicated the top rating is still well deserved." (*HARRISON STILL ALIVE.*) In June 1980 the four-star rating was reaffirmed again.

If Le Cygne was once arguably—albeit not actually—one of the best French restaurants in New York, only a rare affection for consistency can explain that finding since then.

Le Cygne today is an effort to replicate and perpetuate what it was, whereas really great restaurants are re-created, afresh, every day. At its best the place was full of surprises. It flourished on the constant exercise of imagination. To eat at Le Cygne was to be bedazzled. Every time, just about, no matter how high your expectations, a thing or two would awe you in a way you could not possibly have expected.

It is still impossible to get bad food at Le Cygne. Of a handful of dishes one or two will be spectacular. But it is a rare meal that does not include something ordinary. Le Cygne is a wonderful restaurant—undeniably one of the best in New York—but it is a disservice to the curious, and to the establishment itself, to set up disappointment by pretending it is what it was.

The two proprietors are real restaurant people. They seem always to be present and watching—not in the manner of martinets looking for faults in their staff, but as hosts looking after guests. They are not above pouring wine, taking an order, clearing away used dishes, when the often crowded place is straining its capacity. The busboys, waiters and captains are alert and polite, and they do their jobs in a way that suggests they consider them important. That is a rarity.

The céleris rémoulade is something of a rarity also, for the julienned celery root is fresh and crunchy, its tangy flavor clear even in this sharp, mustardy sauce. If you ask for the special terrine maison, you are generally awarded a slice of pâté de campagne as well. The latter is strong without being excessively spiced—it has the nice gamy quality of exaggerated meat. But the premium-priced terrine, a truffled core of foie gras surrounded by a forcemeat that is studded with nuts, lacks drama in the contrast between the two components. The dish seems like perfectly decent food that has been pointlessly fancied-up. The house obtains excellent smoked trout—salty, smoky and strong—and serves it with thick cream that has been sharpened with fresh horseradish. This is an excellent version of a familiar dish, and only a handful of places in New York serve it up this well. You can have littlenecks or oysters on the half shell, and they are invariably as sweet and lively as these mollusks ever are, but for the sacrifice of a premium you can have either of them prepared "des Gourmets"—the clams or oysters are baked under a fine-grained mushroom hash, so carefully that the seafood, though warmed through, is as tender as raw clams or oysters can be. The pungent and earthy mushroom flavor is a striking foil to both the briny clams and the sweet, rich oysters—these dishes are still Le Cygne at its best. Naturally there are escargots, made in the usual manner, and though the sauce is powerfully flavored and still subtle, the snails are less than perfectly plump and tender—this dish is the new Le Cygne, good, but no more than that. A sometimes available vol-au-vent of seafood is a lovely little pastry, with scallops, shrimp and lobster meat in a gentle and buttery sauce—a simple and unimpeachable dish.

But le suprême de bass à l'oseille is flatly uninteresting. The slender serving of fish is rather too browned, the meat a bit dry, but the real disappointment is the sorrel sauce, which is more like a pallid and tepid soup than the concentration of richness and sharp flavor this sauce must be if it is to do much for any fish (Le Cygne at its worst). On the other hand, the minor miracle of Le Cygne's quenelles de brochet seems still to be intact. The huge dumplings, the size of small fists, are fluffy almost to the point of flimsy airiness, and they sparkle with the clear flavor of sweet fish. At lunchtime they are served à l'armoricaine, in a startling sauce that is like honeyed crayfish.

A couple of slightly unfortunate ducks: both of them are a little overcooked, a little dry, a little stringy. The orange sauce on one is balanced and avoids tasting candied, but it lacks depth or body; the green-pepper sauce on the other is hot and strong and silken, but it cannot undo the coarseness of the bird. The excellent sweetbreads are sliced down to small cutlets and browned so that the extremely rich meat is enveloped in a light, seasoned crust, but they are buried under chanterelles that are almost ruined by an excess of salt.

It is possible that the present kitchen of Le Cygne errs in addressing itself mainly to so-called haute cuisine, for it seems to be better at heartier food. A sometime lunch special of osso buco, no less, is quite possibly a better version of that dish than any New York Italian restaurant has ever served. The meat on the bone is firm and wet and flaky, roasted to a glistening deep ebony brown; and the dark gravy, with wine and mushrooms, is a meaty intensity lightly weighted with fat. A plat du jour of roast lamb that has been marinated in the manner of venison is served with a polished venison sauce that is at once sweet and tart, and garnished with a slightly sweetened purée of chestnuts. Even le tournedos aux cèpes, despite the delicacy of filet mignon, succeeds because it is sturdy. The excellent beef is seared and crusted, and the great chunks of wild mushroom have been sautéed until their fibrousness is rich with the flavor of fat.

The cheeses are varied and ready, including a particularly good Brie. And the bread for your cheese arrives warm.

"Soufflés tous parfums" is the familiar legend on the dinner menu, and the soufflés are lofty, browned, airy and moist. The raspberry soufflé is served with a liquored sauce studded with globules of the fresh berry. But the winner is the calvados soufflé, with a slight taste of tart apple. Its sauce, with crisp slivers of the fruit, is laced with hard brandy, which is stark against the cloudlike dessert. Sometimes there is a cherry clafoutis, an almost custardy cake that is baked with the fruit in it—this is a homey, reassuring kind of dessert. And on occasion there is a strawberry mille-feuille, which is quite the opposite thing—whipped cream and strawberries in among leaves of sugared, flaky pastry. The chocolate mousse is light, intense and sticky. The frothy mousse of Grand Marnier is lightly liquored and strongly flavored of fresh orange. Both are perfect sweets. If you cannot choose between the mousses, you are served both.

At one time Le Cygne was something of a discovery, and it was frequented by a mixed and casual crowd that came for the good food. Lately the restaurant has been given high marks in the press, which has attracted some stuffier folk. But the original customers still come too, and all that binds this clientele is the wherewithal to eat in the place.

★ DANIELI

320 **Eighth Avenue (at 26th Street)**
LUNCH, MONDAY TO FRIDAY; DINNER, DAILY.
Reservations, 807-0977.
Credit cards: AE, CB, DC, MC, V.
Medium-priced.

If French bistros thrive in the West Fifties, and English pubs on the Upper East Side, why not a Queens ristorante in darkest Chelsea? It is as if a kosher restaurant were to show up in Beirut and, *tout de suite,* the place is hopping with gentlemen in yarmulkes. For no sooner did this gaudy little eating place come upon the scene, than some very dressed-up folks who order Kahlúa-and-cream before dinner found it. A frequent topic of conversation in this crowd is the drinking capacity of companions not present. But some of the food here is good, there is no double-digit pasta on the menu, and Italian restaurants in this part of the world are scarce, so the more casual folks who live on Chelsea's side streets have also found the place.

Danieli is all beige and brown, brass and glass. It is mirrored and gilded and carpeted. The pale bottom-cloths on the tables hang to the floor, as on tables at which magicians do tricks. The top cloth is dark brown, laid over the bottom one on the bias, so that the corners of the dark cloth form big scallops around the table's edge. A brass four-bladed fan over the bar (which is in the dining room) spins slowly, but in a myriad places, for the mirrored walls on opposite sides of the room reflect each other into infinity—or at least as far as Kew Gardens.

It may be assumed that the site was chosen for its modest rent. The two young gentlemen in charge are very nervous hosts with, you suspect, no great reserves of capital. When one of them aims a frozen smile of fearful ingratiation at you, you know it is because his life depends on it. At a guess, it will be five years before these gents relax.

Relax over an order of Carpaccio Harry Bar (the exact title). The good raw beef is served with a thick green sauce, at once tart and spicy, that is powerfully flavored with Italian parsley. Or over the sometimes available cold seafood salad, in which shrimp, chunks of conch, slivers of squid, a few mussels and a bit of crisp celery are moistened with a lightly garlicked lemon dressing. Proceed to cappelini con frutti di mare, extremely thin pasta dressed with more of that seafood, in an herbed and garlicky tomato sauce. The noodles are firm and tender, but the clear flavors lack strength; and the dish is a little watery, as if the capellini were not adequately drained before the sauce was added. In this department there is a big winner called fettuccine Danieli, in which the red-peppered sauce that moistens the flat noodles is thick with sharp green olives and tart capers, and briny with bits of anchovy—a rousing dish.

Some rank mussels mar the bass in brodetto and the zuppa di pesce. The bass is nicely poached in white wine, browned and then served in its cooking liquid surrounded by a few clams and mussels. The zuppa is an assortment of seafood and fish in a creamy red sauce. Both dishes are decent, but, oh, those mussels. You get an immense platter of chicken scarpariello, the chunks of browned chicken mingled with sweet sausage and slivers of fresh garlic, the whole lightly moistened with a bit of red sauce. The veal piccata is an okay version of the standard dish—a little veal, a little lemon, a little butter. The liver veneziana is a bit better than that—the meat is tender and strong-tasting, the onions are buttery and sweet, and the sauce is smooth and carefully seasoned. But the lamb chops stand apart, for the little ribs are tender and rare, and they have a powerful flavor, which is emphasized by a potent sauce of capers and olives, a bit of tomato, garlic.

One of those slightly clownish hosts tells you what cheeses are on hand. The smile on the other, when you attempt to order those very ones, is of sympathy for your stupidity in thinking they are available. You finally get some Bel Paese, which, of all Italian cheeses, is the one that could most easily be from anywhere at all. You may have it with the so-called salad Danieli, a nice assortment of what is on hand—crisp watercress, endive, bibb lettuce, green peppers, celery, black olives and/or green ones—in a tart dressing.

The lemon mousse is notable for the strands of rind therein—you wish it were colder. The tartufo—ice cream, candied fruits and pineapple, all wrapped in chocolate—will bring the children to attention. The cheese cake is made of cream cheese.

★★DA SILVANO

260 Sixth Avenue (near Bleecker Street)
LUNCH, MONDAY TO FRIDAY; DINNER, DAILY.
Reservations, 982-0090.
No credit cards.
Very expensive.

Silvano is the proud and stocky gentleman wearing an unbuttoned shirt and a left earring. His bearing could be called regal, but he is a couple of inches too short for that. Instead, it is often referred to as Napoleonic. Which is misleading, for he smiles more than he glowers. You can understand why, for his is the best Italian restaurant in Greenwich Village. Sometimes. When he takes a day off (Silvano likes his days off), it may be the second best, or the fourth. And when he is away for a stay of some weeks' duration, you may obtain in his restaurant such delicacies as mussels that worked up a sweat hiking there from the Fulton Fish Market, their shells all zippered up, while the boss was resting in California. Still, his achievement cannot be reasonably gainsaid.

His store is softly lit and simply laid out. Within walls of plaster and brick, rows of white-linened tables are separated by aisles of such subtlety that only the slenderest waiters (in the tightest trousers) perceive these interstices as passages. The odds and ends on the walls look like nothing so much as gestures to the tradition of having odds and ends on restaurant walls. Greenery stands or hangs in the front windows, just inside of which the largest and most commodious tables are situated. Plants and flowers adorn the little coffee and service bar. The proliferation of flora does much to make the place more comfortable than, by the ratio of chairs to space, it ought to be. In summer tables are set up out front, on the sidewalk, where they afford a panoramic view of Sixth Avenue traffic struggling north.

There is a printed menu, but many pay no attention to it, for sometime after you are seated 15 SPECIALS 15 are rattled off to you. If you are lucky, you will have overheard the spiel delivered at nearby tables before your own performance. The soundness of your choice depends on your ability to concentrate. (Do not drink before you come here.)

The seafood salad is of fresh squid and mussels in a lemony garlic dressing. Usually it is sparkling, occasionally it is a little flat, a comment that applies as well to the panzanella, a singular cold salad—of peppers, onion, tomato—in which chunks of bread are mingled with the vegetables in their strong, almost sour vinaigrette. The crostini consist of chopped chicken livers, made flagrant with capers and anchovies, served spread on slices of bread; sometimes they are garnished with powerful Italian salami and stout ham. When white (tan, actually) truffles are in season, you may have a few drams deployed across a field of chopped celery for a little under $20. This is probably the most you can pay, per ounce, for anything you ingest that does not alter your consciousness. God knows the stuff has a heavenly flavor, as of the whole earth, but food, to be satisfying, must have volume. However, when the truffles are grated onto pasta they suffuse the dish, are more like food and less like dubious evidence.

Silvano's meat sauce is deep, nubbly, spicy, weighted with cheese, served on the heavy pasta tubes called penne. His puttanesca sauce—of anchovies and tomato, capers and black olives and garlic—is dark, oceanic, intense, and he serves it on carefully cooked spaghetti. Sometimes he offers fresh green pasta—taglierini—in a crabmeat sauce that is fragrant with parsley. His all-time winner in this department is not pasta at all, for the light but substantial egg-shaped green gnocchi are composed of fresh spinach and creamy ricotta cheese. The dumplings are served in black butter, which dramatizes the almost overwhelming richness, directness and stunning simplicity of the homey but elegant dish.

When fresh sturgeon is available, Silvano obtains same, broils and browns it, and serves the flaky fish in a buttery herb sauce. He gets West Coast shrimp, calls them shrimp Monterey—they are sautéed in their shells, and they are in a light wine sauce that is strongly herbed and dotted with bits of tomato. He procures abalone, pounds it down until it is the size and shape of a great big cookie, breads it, sautés it, sprinkles it with parsley, serves it with lemon—its flavor is fugitive, the citrus essential. He roasts fresh duck vertically, so the meat is neither fatty nor overcooked. He serves pheasant in a cacciatore sauce that is tangy and winy and thick with onion, the skin of the bird loaded with the flavors of the sauce, the pale meat in simple contrast to them. He marinates venison and sautés scallops of the sweet meat until they are browned, sends them to you in a striking sauce of pears and mushrooms. He chooses huge veal chops —they are juicy, tender, moistened with a white-wine sauce to which chicken livers, tomato and peas add their diverse flavors. He braises beef until it is tender, and serves it in a red sauce that is dense and winy.

You can usually get some good Italian cheese. The grape tart is of white grapes in a dark, crumbly crust—if you come the day it is made, it is super. The crème caramel and the chocolate mousse are not notable examples.

If you order from the announced specials, ask the price of what you choose. Mostly, the prices are consistent with similar items on the menu, but there have been anomalies.

• DEVON HOUSE

1316 Madison Avenue
LUNCH, SUNDAY; DINNER, DAILY.
Reservations, 860-8294.
Credit cards: AE, DC.
Very expensive.

One would have thought that derision from all sides had finally driven high religiosity out of eating-and-drinking establishments. But, perhaps encouraged by the recent nationwide oscillation to the right, it appears to be essaying a comeback. Take, for example, Devon House, which is now open for solemnity, services every evening. Proper attire, of course. The suggested contribution is appropriate to the purpose. Full license.

You are dealing here, however, with mail-order ministers, new in the business. They learned the rituals from a book, so they do not know the style. They know the notes to the tunes, but not how to make them swing. In New York, as soon as someone fills your water glass from a silver coffee pot he has lost you. And when you find on your table a couple of cigarettes in a shot glass, you are painfully reminded of what putting on the ritz was like at wedding and confirmation parties in 1950s catering establishments.

The restaurant consists of two rooms connected by an entrance foyer that is down a few steps from street level. The walls are dusty blue. Nonfunctioning fireplaces, dark and polished, are the only adornments. Pleated gauze, pulled tight, covers the windows. The floors are of polished parquetry. The white-linened tables are large, graced with long red tapers that are held by pottery renditions of turned candlesticks, and with cut-glass crystal. You sit on high-backed chairs of cane and wood. They were aiming for stark elegance, and this stiffness comes fairly close.

The dark-jacketed gentlemen who usually greet you, and then wait on you, have the bearing and expression of robots programed for politesse. When one of them tells you that such and such is "flambéed" with Pernod, you know that, had it been his instruction, he would as readily tell you it was sautéed with tobacco. These fellows have no waiterly finesse. They hold a plate like a court clerk holding a Bible.

The boss, however, is something else. She flounces over after you are seated, on heels that effectively double the distance between her knees and her parquetry. As such encumbrances render useless the ankle, her backward-leaning, bow-shaped posture and mincing gait are those of the terrified bather approaching the icy water's edge. If she has not seen you before, she will say, "This is my restaurant. Thanks for coming in," or words to that effect, a speech she delivers with, understandably, both hands gripping the edge of your table.

The prix-fixe menu is brief, and it is changed often. Some of the food is very nice. But not the moules au safran, for the thick, smooth and creamy sauce, powerfully seasoned with saffron, cannot conceal that the mussels are gritty and past their peak. You are expected to remove the mussels from their shells with a full-sized fork, and seemingly in cognizance of the problem this may create, you are provided with a postmussel finger bowl, which turns out to be soapy water complete with suds (you should get a bowl of fresh, for to rinse) but not with a new napkin. The terrine trois couleurs, like most striped seafood terrines, has no seafood quality, and is meant merely to dazzle—who, after all, will not jump up and down at the sight of something made of fish that looks just like spumoni? The spinach pâté is a block of spinach. The pâté of duck, however, nutted and slightly sweetened with orange, is solid and moist, with a clear strong flavor of the meat. Better still is the bouchée d'escargots, plump snails in a creamy sauce laced with parsley and tomato, served in a cup fashioned of delicate pastry, complete with lid.

One day you get an overcooked duck, with a dark sweet sauce that clings to it like syrup. At the same time you get a rack of lamb that, though it seems like less to eat than that billing suggests—three thin chops (in pink pants)—is of good meat, accurately cooked. Some splendid shrimp come in a Pernod sauce that is touched with tomato and herbs. And a nice dish of sweetbreads and whole shallots in red-wine sauce is succulent, earthy and well seasoned.

You are served salad from a bowl of greens that are beginning to wilt in the room temperature. Your waiter describes the two dressings—one of which consists of oil and vinegar—with the seriousness of a Cadillac salesman comparing two option packages. While at it, he spoons out a quantity of dressing and permits it to dribble back into its bowl. This is meant to entice you.

Then there is the cheese. If you are lucky, the owner herself will come by for this course and tell you that one of the offerings is a chevron. There are four or five cheeses, and they are of a quality you would find in an ordinary grocery store anywhere, among them, on occasion, a dreadful goat cheese that has been studded with peppercorns. Pears and apples come with the cheese, as well as the excellent bread that is served in bite-size morsels to each diner about every twenty minutes. A basket of bread on the table, you understand, would be gross. Undistinguished port accompanies this course.

The fruit tarts are good, the fresh fruits impaled on a stick are colorful, and the strawberry mousse—you are introduced to it with yet another display of dribbling—is loose.

Do not dismiss this place. Everyone has an austere type in his life who must occasionally be entertained, but not, heaven forbid, with a good time.

★★ DÉZALEY

54 East 58th Street
LUNCH, MONDAY TO FRIDAY; DINNER, MONDAY TO SATURDAY. CLOSED SUNDAY.
Reservations, 755-8546.
Credit cards: AE, CB, DC, MC, V.
Medium-priced.

This is a Swiss restaurant, but when you enter you may figure that you are in the wrong place, for Dézaley has for some years now been selecting the members of its dining room staff from among young Southeast Asians in New York. These folk have made something of a home of this place, and they are given to congregating peacefully around the little bar that is just inside the front door. As waiters they are perhaps not as nifty as those who have been trained in Swiss colleges of hotel management. These fellows roll up their sleeves and move around as effortlessly as possible, as if New York were tropical Asia all year around. But they are available when wanted and they know the menu. If they put you in mind, sometimes, of the bored stolidity with which many Chinese waiters in New York regard their puzzling customers, that does not alter their efficiency, or the quality of Dézaley's mostly excellent food.

The restaurant is softly lit, simple, modern, furnished with handsome wooden booths, bench-like banquettes, comfortable wooden armchairs. The pale-amber-colored walls are adorned with great big Swiss travel posters that were created in a strong, expressionistic style. The small front room sometimes gets too much noise from the bar, so you may prefer the larger room farther back.

Wherever you eat, you will appreciate the snails. They arrive in the six dents of a ceramic pan, in a brandied, liquorlike butter, under a skin—which covers the snails and the entire pan—of buttered and browned herbs and spices. You will appreciate somewhat less the hot oysters, which are served in a rather coarse mushroom duxelles—lemon lightens and improves the dish, but the character of the oysters and the mushrooms is mostly lost in this preparation. Much better is the raclette valaisanne: you are brought a little pan in which there is nothing but melted cheese, bubbling, and a few slices of potato. The thick, soft cheese seems both spicy and winy, but that is simply the flavor this cheese takes on when it is hot. Dézaley's tortellini are meat-filled, they are mingled with fresh mushrooms and they are bathed in a densely creamy cheese sauce that is dark pink from its admixture of tomato. The so-called Plat Grischun consists of many slices of bündnerfleisch—the strong, mahogany-colored air-dried beef of Switzerland—and good prosciutto, arranged around the circumference of a large plate: this is an abundant platter of cold cuts, garnished with strands of strong raw onion and little pickles, and one serving is sufficient for two.

The Swiss have a way with sweetwater fish, and this establishment's trout is perfectly poached, so the fillet reaches you firm and moist and flaky, in a velvety white sauce that is tangy with minced chives. Lovely boiled potatoes accompany the fish, and you sincerely wish the trout were absolutely fresh, instead of ever-so-slightly off. Bone a breast of chicken, but leave it attached to the leg, and you have created a kind of chop, which Dézaley stuffs with ham and cheese and nuts, and serves, browned and even a little charred, in a salty wine sauce, with buttery noodles on the side—a strong, hearty dish. The veal steak is just right, cooked through but not dry, and it comes in a brandied cream sauce that is thick with woodsy morels. The dish manages to be at once fancy food and country cooking. You can get liver here—a large, thin, elegantly grilled slice of it—under hot, sweet bananas that are firm but soft: a stunning dish. Even more unlikely is the tournedos of peppered beef, upon which a few shrimp and several smoked oysters are disguised—as what?—in a polished and winy sauce that just manages to bring the seafood and the juicy beef together. This is good meat, accurately prepared, in a far-out dish that, miraculously, just about works—miraculously, because smoked oysters are an asset to no dish, but in this instance they are at least made harmless.

If you are parched you may have a lovely lemon ice soaked in vodka. If you are still hungry, you may have a mousse of white chocolate, one of the six or seven richest substances on earth. If you are concerned about vitamins, you may conclude your dinner with fresh berries. If you are simply oral, you may have the frozen soufflé, which is just like ice cream—it is submerged in several ounces of amaretto, which your waiter pours on right under your gaze. And if you are none of the above, you may go for the meringue glacée, which consists of chewy little meringues, good vanilla ice cream, thick whipped cream, and a hot chocolate sauce of a deep, cocoa-like strength—a very grown-up sundae.

Bottled wines from four nations (Switzerland, France, Italy and California) make up the list.

★★ DIMITRI

152 Columbus Avenue (near 67th Street)
LUNCH, MONDAY TO FRIDAY; DINNER, DAILY.
Reservations, 787-7306.
Credit cards: AE, CB, DC, MC, V.
Medium-priced.

This one has the attributes of a neighborhood restaurant. It is innocent, without gimmicks. You enter to a bar on your right, tables on your left, more of them at the back. The tables are covered with white linen, the walls with shiny gray paint. The restaurant is brightly lighted. Half the people who walk into the store know the boss by name, and you conclude that the two otherwise inexplicable framed representations that hang on the walls—one of Ingrid Bergman and Humphrey Bogart in their *Casablanca* days, the other of Greta Garbo as Anna Christie—were foisted on him by a relative who would have been offended if they had not been hung.

That proprietor is always around, and the earnest waitresses are always sweet to the customers. When every hall at Lincoln Center is working, you will not find an empty seat here between 6:30 P.M. and ten minutes before the downbeat. During that time the bar is filled, too, with people who are waiting for the tables they know will open up at eight. The popularity of the place is, of course, in part a function of its eminently reasonable prices. But the food, most of which—and the best of which—is Greek, is good, too.

The Greek salad, for example, is a big platter of cool chopped tomato mingled with the strong whites and greens of crisp scallions, cucumber and green peppers, pungent chocolate-brown olives, salty anchovies, chopped feta cheese and chopped hard-cooked egg. Chunks of cheese and quarters of hard-cooked eggs garnish the salad, which is in a cool, acidic, well-seasoned dressing. Your waitress warns you when you order it that it is enough for two. There are not quite as many ingredients in the platter of Greek hors d'oeuvre, nor are they tossed together. The rice-filled grape leaves are firm, fresh, oiled, lemoned, the green wrappers resilient. The tarama—the paste of red caviar and moistened bread—is tart and sparkling. The eggplant spread is thick, glistening, powerfully garlicked. There is more of that strong feta cheese on this plate, as well as spinach pie, a hot turnover of flaky pastry filled with spiced spinach. Among the restaurant's more successful essays beyond Greek borders are the mussels marinières, fresh, tender mussels that have been steamed in a buttery broth that is thick with chopped garlic. There are a few pasta dishes on the menu. The linguine seafood verde (lots of parsley makes it green) is of good ingredients, but it somehow lacks the character of Italian food.

Dimitri's shrimp taste strongly of iodine (most restaurants in New York have the same problem), and that is the undoing of the otherwise refreshing cold seafood salad, in which those shrimp, fresh mussels, scallops, and chunks of octopus and squid are served in their cool marinade of seasoned and lemoned oil. The red snapper, "skaras," is a whole fresh fish, brushed with oil and grilled until it is lightly charred. It is cooked through but still moist, served lemoned and strewn with parsley—the preparation yields a fish of clear, sweet flavor within its crisp skin. Dimitri's steamed salmon is a big log of fish, none of its natural oil or juiciness cooked away, in a shallow pool of butter, sprigs of fresh dill spread across the pink meat—you squeeze on lemon, which livens the lovely, elemental fish. A small card is placed on each table each night, listing the specials of the evening. Mostly they are seafood, and sometimes steamed sea bass is among them, the whole fish, snowy meat within a silvery skin, in a broth that is shot through with scallions and lightly flavored with fresh ginger. Occasionally the card lists osso buco, and if the house does not always get Italian food to seem Italian, in this instance it does, for the meat is tender, flaky, barely clinging to the bone, spicy. The so-called chicken scarpariello is a perfectly nice broiled bird, but not the chunks of herbed, sautéed chicken the name will probably lead you to expect. You get good lamb chops here, three big ones, blackened and juicy, of strong lamb flavor. The flavor of the sirloin steak is just as good, its preparation just as accurate, but sometimes the beef is a little tough.

No Greek desserts. The fruit tarts are either good (a lovely one of peaches), or not so good (a dull one of apples). The chocolate mousse is slightly coffee-flavored, sugary, smooth, fresh, but lacking in airiness, or chocolate intensity, or any of a number of things that might raise it above chocolate pudding. The cheese cake is of the solid, rich, cream-cheese type, lemon-flavored, sweet, silken; if you like that kind of cheese cake, you will like this one.

★ DIVINO

1556 Second Avenue (near 81st Street)
LUNCH, MONDAY TO SATURDAY; DINNER, DAILY.
Reservations, 861-1096.
Credit cards: AE, CB, DC, MC, V.
Medium-priced.

If you remember the period between the wars, you remember that ladies' hats used to be decorated the way this restaurant is today. You have here your rough plaster archways over walls of rosy brick. You have your striped wallpaper. You have your plates and pots and pans, your hanging greenery and bursts of flowers, your prints and paintings and posters. You have your wine and liquor bottles here and there on your little wooden shelves. Brown linen peeks out from under the beige linen. The seat of your chair is flamboyantly floral. The restaurant is small, but tables are tucked into every odd corner. And the entire production is bathed in the rosy glow of the pink lights in the ceiling. Some of that light falls, of course, on the heads of the diners. It illuminates blue-blacked hair, hennaed hair, bleached hair, enameled hair, teased hair, permed hair, rugs. Divino was praised in the press when it was new, and the clientele it has retained —and they are legion—are those whose received opinions never suffer modification through experience. These comers consist in substantial measure of folks from the outlying counties who, when they go into "the city" for a night out, sometimes choose this as their destination. Often they stand in line to sit down when they get here. The food is not really bad. You just have to know how to order in a restaurant in which most of the prepared dishes are prepared well in advance.

The vitello tonnato, for example, is too clearly of cold veal that was put back in the icebox after it was sliced, under a tuna purée that was whipped up before the slicing session. But the hot squid appetizer called calamari nettuna is fine at its age, the shafts of seafood tender in a spicy oil that is studded with capers and lots of garlic. You may have a half order of any pasta except the one made with a seafood sauce, but this is one of the dishes in which the house exceeds itself. The thick, tangy and well-garlicked red sauce is heavy with fresh clams and mussels in their shells, scallops and squid, and —the dish is not perfect—shrimp that are tainted with iodine. The preassembled cannelloni is reheated to your order—it is blackened and crusted and bubbling, but the ground-meat filling lost its sparkle earlier in the day. The fettuccine Alfredo is rich, but lacks any bite—the ground cheese does not help, for it was grated at an indeterminate time past and has grown flat.

You receive your red snapper al cartoccio in the sealed aluminum-foil bag in which it was baked. The foil is cut away, and you are left with a big slab of fresh fish up to its gills in a red sauce that is thick with onions and morsels of shellfish—a good dish. If you are here the day the house has good shrimp, you will do well with the scampi dragoncella—this is just a dish of shrimp in tomato sauce, but one that has been aggressively flavored with spices and tarragon. The "Veal Divino" is not very divino. The veal chop, pale and charred and lightly lemoned, is only slightly dry. The big veal winner is the inexpensive one—stuffed breast of veal, the kind of dish that improves, up to a point, with age. The butterflied meat is rolled around an herbed, chunky vegetable stuffing, baked, and served in slices in a deep and pleasantly fatty sauce. The chicken contadina, a collection consisting of chunks of browned, garlicked chicken, mushrooms and red peppers in a dark and winy sauce, has been held so long that the garlic has given up its stuff—an abundance of smoky sage in the dish gives it some life.

The rum cake is an icinged, booze-soaked, layered affair of white cake and chocolate mousse. It lacks only maraschino cherries. When the fruit tarts are fresh they are lively. They are not always fresh. The Italian cheese cake is old-fashioned, bread-like and solid, dotted with candied fruit, satisfying. You can get a very frothy zabaglione sauce, powerfully liquored, over ripe strawberries.

★★ EAST-WEST

105 East 9th Street
DINNER.
Reservations, 260–1994.
No credit cards.
No liquor.
Inexpensive.

Natural food, health food, organic food. Who is not put off by the antiseptic phrases? Yet this stuff need not taste like undoctored shredded wheat. Set aside for the moment the fact that the terms are vague at best, meaningless most likely, that they suggest plain food, unsauced food, intact food, unbleached and nonchemicalized food, berries and nuts, salads of weeds and stews of tubers—in short, medical repasts; and call to mind for the same moment your knowledge that things take on identities only when they are given names: had the pizza parlors leaped onto the health-food bandwagon at the beginning (whole-grain crust, vine-ripened tomato sauce, certified-milk cheese), we would associate lithe bodies and clear eyes with the red-and-white pies. But no particular kind of food has monopolized the fad, and though there is a pretty consistent tendency in the movement to eschew red blood, there are natural-food restaurants in New York where you can get steaks and chops with your seaweed. Perhaps because Japanese food, as perceived by Americans, has a Spartan quality, it is a natural for the sound-body freaks, and this restaurant serves up its health à la Japanese, with a preponderance of tempura on the menu. Tempura, of course, is deep-fried food, usually shrimp, fish, vegetables. Wasn't fried food once the antithesis of health food?

East-West is a low-luxury but comfortable little place, perfectly suited to its youthful clientele. They come in their sandals, jeans, long flower-print skirts, sleeveless tops, splendiferous hair; they park themselves on the ledge under the hanging plants at the front window to wait patiently for one of the little tables, even more patiently for one of the burlap-upholstered booths along the side. The walls are of raw redwood clapboard, the slat ceiling is vaguely Japanese, there are white paper place mats on the red-clothed tables.

This is a bring-your-own-wine-or- beer establishment, but the innocents drink mostly tea or tap water or spring water from the water cooler, just like the one in your office, or mineral water.

The food is rather elegantly made; it has, it cannot be denied, freshness, purity, life; you eat it with chopsticks (the little Japanese ones that come joined and wrapped) unless you want to advertise yourself as an alien.

There is a charge for bread with miso spread (soybean paste). Pay the charge. The bread is extraordinarily assertive in its vibrant scent and flavor of wheat, and the miso, warm and oily, is the perfect succulent foil to it.

Begin with shrimp tempura. The shrimp (several) seem to be fresh, as are the broccoli, carrots and green peppers, and they are all very artfully battered and rapidly deep-fried in very hot and, it must be, frequently changed oil. The ingredients of the dish are just barely cooked, and the batter is crisp and airy, all in all the equal or superior of the same dish in Japanese restaurants that are actually run by Japanese. Move on to a soup of the day, which, when it is split-pea and zucchini soup, is a substantial bowl of thick pea soup, rather heavy, relieved by chunks of moist zucchini —a nice idea.

In line with the "East-West" theme, there is a dish called Scallops Champignon, the Orientalism of which is in the dish itself, the Westernism in the title. This is a gigantic stew of scallops (the big ones from the ocean, not the little ones from the bay), mushrooms and other vegetables, in a briny broth. The food lacks character, but the excellence of the ingredients and the straightforward preparation yield a pretty satisfying plate. Better is the broiled fish—immaculately fresh bluefish, for example, broiled in butter and flavored with rosemary; flaky and moist, the rich fish retains its robust character, and the browned skin, crisp and buttery, is like a built-in sharp seasoning. As a garnish to whatever you eat, there is (are you ready?) seaweed du jour.

Domestic desserts, displayed on a counter just below the window at the back of the room, through which you may observe the activity in the bustling kitchen. The banana cake consists of a dark, moist, banana-flavored cake, a banana-flavored icing and chunks of banana-flavored bananas. Excellent. Good pies, and pretty good apple strudel, with crisp apples and lots of cinnamon, wrapped in a flaky pastry.

★ ELEPHANT & CASTLE

183 Prince Street (near Sullivan Street)
LUNCH AND DINNER.
Reservations, 260-3600.
Credit cards: AE, CB, DC, MC, V.
Inexpensive.

Elephant & Castle draws the plaid-skirt crowd and the fellows in sweaters and slacks, daters who appear to have been introduced by their parents. You probably thought that element no longer existed, at least not in SoHo.

There is much of the tearoom in this most unlikely of SoHo eating places. The floor of the restaurant's foursquare dining room is of old marble, scrubbed daily, you may be sure. A mirrored wall is hung with glass shelves on which jars of preserves are displayed. The rest of the place is white, the lower walls of dark-brown wainscoting varnished to a high sheen. Windowpanes make up the front wall of the store, from floor to high ceiling, letting in abundant light under the restaurant's broad canopy. Elephant & Castle would be airy and commodious if the tables were not so tiny, and if they did not stand as close together as books on a shelf. Place is not set aside for coats, so they are tossed over the backs of chairs, where they obtrude on the slight space between the tables; or they are folded onto the wooden bench that rims the room like a banquette, where they further constrict the cramped seating space. (Never mind what happens when umbrellas have to be disposed of.) Elephant & Castle is a little uncomfortable and a little antiseptic, the kind of place in which one is automatically disinclined to smoke, drink or entertain libidinal thoughts. It is the perfect place to take a clergyperson for lunch.

The waiters and waitresses are in black (the latter in black stockings, even, and black hair ribbons, if any). The lone gesture to relief is the slogan imprinted, in white, on the backs of the help's T-shirts: I LOVE OMELETTES. All part of the fun. Service is slow when the restaurant is crowded, for though the help is earnest, the young cooks observable at their labors through a hole in the rear wall cannot keep up with the pressure. In other regards they have been trained well, for the food you are served here is always satisfactory, often delicious, never bad.

There is not much sustenance in the corn, spinach and bacon chowder, a light and creamy soup with many yellow kernels and just a touch of bacon, to which lightly cooked fresh spinach is added. Much better is the seafood rice bisque, a sometime soup of the day, the briny broth edged with the sharp flavor of cooked milk, an abundance of seafood in small chunks at the bottom of the bowl. You get a splendid Caesar salad here, composed of utterly crisp greens, crunchy croutons, whole anchovies (salty and oily), strong grated cheese and a thick dressing. The quiches of the day are fluffy every day, sharpened with nutmeg, their crusts well browned. And the omelets are great yellow pillows, artfully turned, just browned outside, the insides steamy and moist.

Portuguese sausages are on the menu, glistening red-brown shafts of spiced and fatty meat, split and grilled, and thereby marked with black lines and accented with charcoal flavor. A high-flavored chicken dish goes as chicken Niçoise, not much bird, but lots of green olives and pungent Mediterranean black ones, onions and peppers and celery, all flavored with herbs and served over good rice. Beefsteak du jour is one of the odd menu entries—the meat comes with onions one day, mushrooms another and so on, but this is hamburger meat unground, very tasty, but sometimes tough. You can get hamburgers eight ways here, and the silliest-sounding of them is something of an unlikely winner—the standard sandwich is augmented with curried sour cream and tomatoes for moisture, cheddar cheese and bacon for flavor, scallions for sharpness. That item is called an elephant burger, and you have to eat it to like it.

What is billed as the "world's best cheesecake" is the usual sweet, lemoned, creamy, rich goo that much of the world loves. Get some Indian pudding instead—it is like a hot cereal flavored with sweet spices, a lump of cool ice cream at its center; or frou frou, just a bowl of plain yogurt, a lot of fresh fruit and walnuts; or the simplest of the sweet crêpes, delicate pancakes folded around warm strawberry jam, confectioners' sugar sprinkled thereon; or a banana split, made with ripe bananas and your choice of Häagen-Dazs ice creams. The mousse pie is little more than unexceptional, albeit rich, chocolate mousse in the shape of a wedge.

Grilled sandwiches, eggs, fancy coffees and herb teas are always available.

★★ ELIO'S

1621 Second Avenue (near 84th Street)
DINNER.
Reservations, 772-2242.
Credit cards: AE.
Expensive.

Be sure you have the exact address, as no sign calls attention to this establishment's existence. The purpose, of course, is to create a brand-new former speakeasy. The place is clubby, insular. It receives you a little better if you are known than if you are not. It is an immediate old hangout, no sooner in business than folks drop by as if by ancient habit.

You enter to a bar on your left, wood paneling all around (it is wonderful the effects that can be achieved with stained plywood), a plain hardwood floor. Sconces on the walls and old-fashioned milk-glass globes that hang from the ceiling provide the ample illumination. There is white linen on the tables, simple bentwood chairs around them. The waiters, in white shirts (sleeves rolled up) and black four-in-hands, are cordial and hard hitting—they give it to you fast and get going. As the menu is unexplicated and in large part incomprehensible (spaghetti gaeta, sole mugnaia, bass riviera, chicken alba), you must have ready an extensive list of questions when your drinks are delivered if you are to make informed choices. Though the restaurant has something of a reputation for attracting the occasional celebrity (it is the most recently identified symptom in the Elaine's-Nicola's-Parma syndrome), you are surrounded mostly by prosperous Upper East Side professional and entrepreneurial well-feds. The winter tan is not unknown here.

Those who are mindful of their silhouettes begin with the raw mushroom salad, a great mound of sliced, utterly fresh and earthy mushrooms, which have soaked up their light dressing of good olive oil touched with tart vinegar. The seafood salad—of octopus, sweet shrimp and slivers of tender squid—is cool and refreshing in its lightly garlicked oil, even better when you add lemon. The vitello tonnato is of good cold veal spread with a heavily oiled tuna purée that is studded with capers and adorned with strands of roasted red pepper. In what is referred to as polenta & gorgonzola, a tomato purée is spread sparingly, as in a thin sandwich, between two slices of hot polenta. They are moistened with a tomato-tinctured Gorgonzola sauce—not bad.

Elio's will not serve half orders of pasta, but you will not mind consuming a full order of spaghetti gaeta, in which the very thin al dente noodles are almost blackened by their pungent sauce of ripe olives and anchovies. Or you may have your pasta with a sauce puttanesca, in which those same ingredients are incorporated in a thick tomato sauce that is pleasantly soured by its admixture of plump capers.

Sometimes the fish of the day is tilefish—it is fresh, moist, firm, flaky, sweet, altogether a splendid slice of fish—and it is served in an oiled broth to which anchovies and capers, chopped fine, have been added. The gamberoni, grilled in their red shells, are not the world's sweetest shrimp (though they are among the largest), but they are served with a vividly peppered sauce of hot butter that is fragrant with herbs and thick with the capers that this place probably acquires in carload lots. The zuppa di pesce is a deep bowl of bass and snapper, clams and mussels, shrimps and scallops, all in a hot, saffron-flavored broth that is thick with plum tomatoes—a wonderfully hearty dish. Chicken scarpariello is various things in different restaurants. At Elio's it has the advantage of being made from a good bird—the chunks of moist chicken are lightly browned, filmed with butter, strongly flavored of rosemary, strewn with parsley and just subtly touched with garlic. Sometimes the house offers suckling pig. Its moist and succulent meat is wrapped in layers of baby fat, those in turn in crisp pig skin. The veal chop is charred and pink, but dry and chewy. The huge beef paillard is rather thick, more like an ordinary steak than the very quickly grilled real thing—still, this is nice beef.

You are not informed about cheeses unless you specifically ask, but good Gorgonzola and Parmesan may be had. The cheese cake is the real Italian thing, weighty, wet, browned, lemoned just a little, sprinkled irrelevantly with pine nuts—it would be better still if it were not served cold. The lemon tart is a pleasant lemon custard on a decent pastry. Unexpected chunks of pineapple make the zuppa inglese a surprise, but not a delight—it is the usual many-layered, rum-soaked excess. The big winners are the strawberry tart—big, ripe, juicy berries; and the crème brûlée—an airy custard under a light crystallized caramel.

★ EL FARO

823 Greenwich Street (at Horatio Street)
LUNCH AND DINNER.
No reservations (WA 9–8210).
No credit cards.
Medium-priced.

El Faro means "the lighthouse," which is probably the least appropriate name this place could have. El Faro is situated in a section of the West Village that is virtually dead after sundown, and the place does not call attention to itself. To find it you must know where it is, with confidence; for years more people have been finding it than the place knows what to do with. This is one of the oldest and most popular restaurants in Greenwich Village, and it is an astonishment to approach it down dim, deserted streets to discover, when you go in, that the place is clamorous. You enter into a small, low-ceilinged barroom, complete with beer-sign clocks, juke box, coatrack, cigarette machine, air-conditioning machine, and customers at various points of alcoholic contentment, depending on how long they have been waiting for their turn for the next available table.

The dining room is small, efficiently filled with Formica-topped tables, and somberly, anciently muraled with grimed-over flamenco dancers. Between the tightly packed tables skip the red-vested waiters—more of them than you will find in other restaurants this size, but they are busy all the time.

It is the way of these busy places—to keep you quiet they bring your salad right away; but in a way that is *not* the way of these places, it is made of fresh lettuce and crisp red cabbage, in a thick, red, peppery Spanish dressing. ("Our Salad Dressing is available to Our Customers," it says on the menu.)

The food here is usually good; the first courses always best. The Broiled Chorizos are discs of spicy Spanish sausage, crisped and browned on the outside, served in warm, peppery oil—they make you thirsty. Ham and olives is referred to as Ham and Olives Spanish Style. Well, they look like ham and olives, and they taste, respectively, smoky and salty—they make you thirsty. Salpicon is crabmeat salad, a piquant and peppery mélange of crabmeat, minced eggs, green peppers, raw onions and parsley in a lemony dressing. It will *not* make you particularly thirsty, though the Galician Soup may— this is the familiar Caldo Gallego, the thick bean soup made with meats or sausages and turnip greens. The version served here is thick and loud.

Your waiter refers to the Cornish hen as *perdiz*. It is the only word you know in Spanish, but you leap at the opportunity to insist that he not misrepresent a domestic hen as a partridge. He's impressed with your knowledge of the Romance languages and waffles uncomfortably for a bit. The minor misrepresentation notwithstanding, this is a splendid dish—you get a big enameled iron pot in which there are several moist, plump parts of a moist, plump bird, in two inches of an oily gravy that is powerfully and fragrantly flavored with clove, onions and bay. If you're going to come here once, the hen is the dish to have. There is, of course, pork with almonds. It is pretty good, the thick slices tender and moist and all that, but the almond sauce lacks an edge, so the dish is satisfying without being exciting. There are shrimp dishes and there are lobster dishes. If you want seafood, eschew the latter in favor of the former. Lobsters do not suffer well the perils of freezing and casual cooking. To overcook a frozen lobster is to add toughness to fibrousness. The green sauce you can have it in is thick and winy, but it does not rescue the lobster. The Shrimp al Ajillo, however, is something else— the shrimp themselves are just OK, but the sauce has character: it is fiery and spicy, redolent of garlic, and uncompromisingly oily.

Spanish desserts are, admit it, dull. Perhaps not to Spaniards. Anyway, the ones you get here are about as good as they ever get: firm, red, crunchy guava shells with a chunk of cream cheese and crisp saltine crackers, for example, can be simple and delicious if all the elements are fresh; the flan is cool, firm and nicely flavored with the lightly burnt sugar; and there is natilla, the *other* custard, gooey and vanilla-flavored and very sugary.

★★ FELIDIA

243 East 58th Street
LUNCH, MONDAY TO FRIDAY; DINNER, MONDAY TO SATURDAY. CLOSED SUNDAY.
Reservations, 758-1479.
Credit cards: AE, CB, DC, MC, V.
Expensive.

You are greeted by Felix and/or Lydia, who have named their new restaurant for a contraction of themselves. They were restaurateurs of considerable success in the county of Queens, and their move to Manhattan is an effort to make it in the big time. Though, clearly, they are going to succeed, just as clearly they are going to do it without picking up the high style. For Felix and Lydia are a somewhat countrified duo. Their portliness, it strikes you, is their way of proudly letting their success show. They are still obtaining their clothes on the other side of the East River. And they are at once reserved, as if waiting for a signal, and then friendly, all openness when addressed and when they have come to know you. It is difficult to imagine that either of them will ever develop the hauteur, or brusque efficiency, or false humility that are the standard shields with which your host in many big-town establishments insulates himself from those he despises for being essential to his livelihood. Felix and Lydia exhibit no such neuroses.

The quarters they have established for themselves, however, reflect none of the modesty of their demeanor. The place is, in fact, baronial. You arrive to a sign that informs you that jackets are required. You enter (properly dressed) to a dimly lit barroom—a comely official at a desk near the door, wood paneling all about, the solidity of the installation an instant clue to the seriousness of this enterprise. Just beyond the massive bar, the first dining room, more of that polished, honey-colored paneling, floor to ceiling, a handful of dining tables and a display table of cold fish, fruits and vegetables, cheeses and ham, desserts, bottles of wine. Farther back, the rear of the restaurant, on two levels; and back here the chalk-white walls, floors of red tiles, potted palms, interior brick with vines adhering, and overhead glass admitting the glow of day add up to the look of luxury in the Mediterranean subtropics.

Felidia's principal idiocy is its printed menu, which is composed exclusively in Italian. Even mastery of that tongue will help only a little, for such entries as "scampi Felidia" and "insalata appetitosa" mean nothing in any language. Not only would it require a twenty-minute interview (and a terrific memory) to get yourself into a position to make an informed choice, but when Felix or Lydia—or, less often, one of their staff —come by for explication, a substantial list of additional choices is announced, items that happen to be available the day of your visit. Getting to know Felidia is a three-credit course.

But getting to know the cold appetizers is comparatively easy, if you are on the lower level—a selection of them can be wheeled to your table for inspection. Some are on the menu, some are not: trippa vinaigrette is—the lovely strands of cool tripe, meatier and less gummy than most tripe, tasting almost like chicken, in a gentle vinaigrette that you rouse by the addition of lemon; seafood salad, chunks of conch (a little tough), squid, shrimps, exceptionally tender octopus, all in a lightly garlicked dressing; cold mussels, nicely adorned with chopped red onions and pimentos, all in a light dressing, but to no end, for some of those mussels are well past their peak. The so-called antipasto rustico is not much above the cold antipasto you learned to avoid in Italian restaurants when first you started making distinctions—the meats and cheese are fine, the raw vegetables quite fresh, but the presence of a canned sardine on any plate is dismaying.

Two listings of pasta: fresca fatta in casa (fresh, "home"-made); and asciutta (dried). Among the former, fuzi alla fortuna del cacciatore, diamond-shaped slivers of noodle adorned (on this occasion) with sections of quail (yes, quail), the pasta soft but firm, the bird—on its toothpick bones—browned but juicy, and the thin, dark-brown sauce fragrant with clove: a stunning dish. Also fresh are the sometimes available green tortellini, served in a spicy tomato sauce that is thick, smoothed by oil, heavy with mushrooms, onions and peas—strong, fresh Parmesan cheese is grated onto the pasta until you say stop. Dried noodles are used in the dish called occhio di lupo alla boscaiola, heavy tubes of pasta, cooked just past the point of toughness, served in a sauce that is thick with cheese, powerfully flavored of strong sausages, lightened a little with sweet peas and mushrooms.

Rice (risotto) and cornmeal (polenta), variously prepared, have a position in Italian eating that corresponds roughly to that of pasta. Felidia serves blocks of warm polenta under melting Gorgonzola cheese. And they serve risotto all'amiraglia, the polished rice mingled with mussels and shrimp, squid and juicy scallops, the marvelous mush alive with garlic and moist with the strong broth in which the rice was cooked.

Sometimes there is striped bass, and though it is impeccably broiled, it could stand having lost its life somewhat more recently—you get a small pitcher of garlic-and-lemon-flavored oil, which you apply according to your taste, and which almost redeems the fish. The chicken roasted with rosemary and brandy is a big bird, very unsubtly flavored with the stated ingredients, good to eat just the same. The huge veal chop valdostana, which is stuffed with, and oozes, melted cheese, is rather ponderously heavy, albeit of good meat carefully cooked. But the scaloppine alla Felice, thin slices of pale veal, powdered with cheese, sautéed in butter, and served parsleyed in a pan sauce made with white wine and lemon, is a rarity—meat that is at once light and full of strong flavor. The sweetbreads are prepared similarly, but with breading rather than cheese—a rich dish that is simple, even homey. When asparagus is in season, thin stalks are served here under strong cheese that has been melted and browned into a thin blanket across the tender shoots.

Usually there are several good cheeses on hand. And on occasion you may have them with a salad of Italian radish greens—radicchio—of a variety that are not normally available here, and which the proprietors are able to provide because they import seeds and grow their own in their own garden. The flavor is vaguely like that of arugula, but much milder.

The cream puffs are light little balls of puff pastry, filled with airy custard and apricot preserves, powdered with sugar. The Italian cheese cake is wet, sugary, cool, actually refreshing despite its substantiality.

At this writing the food at Felidia is a little less expensive than at most of this neighborhood's seriously intended Italian restaurants. And dozens of the dishes are like nothing you have tasted before.

★ FIORELLO'S

1900 Broadway (near 63rd Street)
LUNCH AND DINNER.
Reservations, 595–5330.
Credit cards: AE, MC, V.
Medium-priced.

Glaring neon confronts you whether you face front or rear—the outside sign glitters through the front window, and there is a green, glowing FIORELLO'S over the brightly lit tile-and-copper pizza kitchen visible at the back. Fiorello's was designed to distract; its appearance alone can keep you awake. The walls are diagonal stripes of masonry and mirror, the tabletops are of copper, the floors of red tile, the Italian posters on the walls exclusively of primary colors. A jukebox glows and broadcasts. Waiters and waitresses must be spunky and quick with a quip to work here. When the weather is fine, many people prefer the tables that are set up under umbrellas out on the sidewalk, where the scenery and traffic are comparatively soporific. The prices are low, so Fiorello's serves not only Lincoln Center patrons but also thrifty West Siders avoiding their kitchens for a night. Many come here alone with a book—if you can read on the subway, you can read anywhere. Sometimes they encounter friends, and if they do not, they can put their solitude in a bottle—the drinkable house wine is cheap.

You will never get great food—you hardly expect it, for the place is more a café than a restaurant—but much of it is tasty and satisfying. One comes here for such as the crisp first-course salads, including the cold string beans and raw onions in a dressing that is mostly oil and a little lemon. For good pasta you have to get lucky—if very little lasagne has been served one day, it may have become claylike by the time you order it, though its meat sauce is decent. Fiorello's calls the tortellini its specialty, and it is a fine plate of food, firm little pasta packages stuffed with seasoned meat, in a creamy sauce that is studded with slivers of strong prosciutto—you liven the dish with the fresh cheese that is supplied. Eschew religiously anything high-flown, such as spinach-soufflé crêpe, for which the best that can be said is that it looks like one of the posters. And skirt the veal—the parmigiana, for example, resembles ballast. Choose instead the very good pizzas. The pizza supreme, crisp and hot, covered with sausages and mushrooms, peppers and onions, all of them lightly charred, is a minor adventure. The desserts are sundaes on plates, and the unfortunate whipped cream, which is a component of most of them, is machine-made and sugared. But the ice creams are fine, and the fruits ripe and ready. The café coffees are hot and strong.

A good place for dessert and coffee, but there is a $5 minimum at dinnertime.

★★ FORO ITALICO

453 West 34th Street
LUNCH, MONDAY TO FRIDAY; DINNER, MONDAY TO SATURDAY. CLOSED SUNDAY.
Reservations, 564-6619.
Credit cards: AE, CB, DC, MC, V.
Expensive.

A situation that is remote from everywhere except the Lincoln Tunnel, appointments that would do credit to the second-best Italian restaurant in a suburb of Des Moines, Iowa, prices that are far from bashful, and a brief menu that is original solely in its orthography, should have conspired, you would think, about thirty days after the grand opening, to close this place down. But years have passed since then, and Foro Italico has not: one begrudged point for the tiresome position that if you serve good food, people will come and get it.

Red jackets on the waiters, red carpeting on the floor, red plastic upholstery on the chairs. The walls are of wood paneling, exposed brick, dark mirror. The ceiling is beamed, the art is ornately framed, the wall sconces give off an amber glow, and the fifteen tables are snowy with white linen. A wrought-iron partition segregates the small bar from the dining room. If you have not seen all this before, you have not lived.

The tuxedoed captain (not always on hand) pronounces the names of the dishes in an Italian that is accented with Spanish-accented English, which is marvelous to hear. But he has the answers to all your questions, he explains patiently, and he is well-meaning and sweet-tempered, like all the help here.

As soon as you are seated you send for an order or two of deep-fried zucchini, with which to pass the time while you consider the menu. The squash could be crisper, but the batter is delicate, the strands are hot and subtly salted and display a clear flavor of the vegetable. Seven littleneck clams are tiny, sweet and fresh. Or you can get six of them, baked and breaded. They are gently cooked, so they retain their tenderness; the breading is just touched with oil, so it has a pleasant browned crispness; but the abundance of oregano is unfortunate, for it is the dried herb.

Those who know this restaurant best usually start their dinners with pasta: tortellini alla panna, the tiny dumplings stuffed with a meaty, nutmeg-flavored filling, covered over with a thick, eggy sauce that manages to fall just short of excess; spaghetti bolognese, the thinnest noodle to go by that name, *al dente,* in a textured, spicy, lightly tomatoed meat sauce that is abundantly oiled without being oily; that svelte spaghetti yet again, this time with tender clams, crunchy shrimp, soft mussels and chunks of sturdy conch, their flavors all distinct in a red sauce that is briny, tart, almost gamy of the sea.

The bass brodetto is put under the broiler briefly after it is steamed, which gives the white meat a dark crust—the fish is served in the buttery brine it was steamed in, and it is surrounded by steamed mussels and clams. Frozen shrimp are used in the scampi alla veneziana, so there is less of their flavor than you want, but the shrimp are huge and firm, and their flavoring—of red pepper and garlic—is powerful, making for a satisfying dish.

Veal francese used to appear on more menus than it does now. Foro Italico makes as good a version as you could ever get in New York. The cutlets of pale veal are coated with a lemon-flavored flour-and-egg batter and then sautéed, yielding a gentle, moist crust around the tender meat—the dish is at once acidic and sweet. An occasional special of the day is the veal chop valdostana, the immense chop butterflied, stuffed with cheese, breaded and sautéed—its crust is crisp, the cheese pully and tasty, the meat substantial and juicy. The steaks are well prepared—rare, seared until crusty—but this is not America's finest beef.

Eschew the cheese cake, which clings to the roof of the mouth like mortar. The tartufo is an adult candy, but a good one: excellent ice cream sheathed in a dark coating that has the sharpness of good bitter chocolate. Best of all is the zabaglione, which is prepared in the dining room—a hundred strokes or so of the whisk against the inside of the copper pot. The golden froth is hot, sweet, very winy; it is poured over ripe, sugared strawberries just before it is served.

★★FOUR SEASONS

99 East 52nd Street
LUNCH AND DINNER. CLOSED SUNDAY.
Reservations, 754-9494.
Credit cards: AE, CB, DC, MC, V.
Very expensive.

The world is changing fast (*too* fast, some say), but the Four Seasons is determined to keep up. The Seasons have gone so far as to "redefine," as they put it, their "Bar Room," formerly the Grill Room. The aim is to get two restaurants out of one reputation. The new one is targeted at the hip crowd that these days is packing the gaudy and casual eateries that are being switched on all over town like street lamps at dusk. Well, not *that* crowd exactly, not the Odeon or Joanna types, but folks who want to keep up with the latest fashions in going out to eat while wearing other than burlap and tiaras.

The Bar Room's printed menu is sprinkled with the buzz words that identify the right places—tartare and paillard, fettuccine and grilled fish, steaks and chops. And of course the Four Seasons has been successfully serving these things to the communications industry at lunchtime for several years now. But that is lunchtime, and when daylight filters through the famous rippling chains that festoon the three-story windows, much of this establishment's built-in solemnity is dispelled. At night, however, it would take not only the Ringling Brothers, but also Barnum and Bailey to make this a café. No one will ever come to the Four Seasons to be amused by the crowd, to show off a new pair of silken pantaloons, to pick up a stranger at the bar. It may be fun to go to the Four Seasons, but that does not mean you will have fun while you are there. And except for that lunchtime executive session, this restaurant has always been too much of a tourist attraction, and too filled with boobs, to attract a sophisticated New York set.

You know the layout. Up the grand stairway to where a tuxedoed gent stands at a high desk. On your right the Bar Room, complete with the big square bar. The walls of the room rise like the faces of cliffs, the inner ones faced with great panels of burnished wood the color of dark copper, its grain as dark as port wine. The thousands of brass- and copper-colored chains that are draped across the lofty windows unfortunately ripple in the moving air (which was discovered only when they were installed), disturbing the intended stillness of the huge, stark room. The bar is separated from the dining room proper by dark, vine-covered panels. The tall trees positioned here and there are changed with the seasons—bare ones in winter, leafy ones in spring. Elsewhere potted flowering plants are clustered like tonsured shrubbery. Over a mezzanine of tables at the east side of the room hangs Part I of the Lippold stabile of brass rods and their supporting wires. The larger Part II is suspended over the bar. If you turn left when you reach the top of the stairs, you enter a glass-and-marble corridor. Through one of its transparent walls you get a view of the Seagram Building's monumental lobby and, beyond its front doors, the plaza on Park Avenue. Through the opposite wall you may observe the air-conditioned repose of several thousand bottles of well-chosen wine. At the end of the tunnel is the so-called Pool Room, the posher half of the Four Seasons, another huge block of very valuable air space, with again the polished mahogany-colored walls and the tall windows trying so hard to look stately, but unable to stop the flow of their shades. A square, shallow pool, about the size of a second bedroom, and rimmed with a white marble ledge, is brightly lighted and gurgling at the center of the room. The four rubber trees positioned at the pool's corners seem dejected in this monumental setting.

In whichever room you eat, you are seated—on modern chairs or sofas of chocolate-brown leather and stainless steel—before large tables that are covered with lightly starched beige cloths. They seem to have the bulk and resilience of actual linen. You are waited on by (mostly) young ladies or gentlemen in identical uniforms of gray, long-sleeved vests (the Four Seasons insignia of four trees on the breast pocket), black trousers, and white shirts with black bow ties. To the extent that the Bar Room attracts New Yorkers at all, it gets the kind who avoid the Pool Room for the same reason one owns a Bentley rather than a Rolls Royce. Anyway, you do not see many poor people here. The Pool Room gets the honeymooners. "Ooh, honey, look what they're doing," says she, grabbing his lapel. (They are transfering food from a pan to a plate in the presence of a flame.) Few here are habitués. Though the Four Seasons is a New York landmark, the Pool Room and its crowd of an evening could be anywhere. The place has never quite become Manhattan; the locals have never taken it up as their own.

Some of the Bar Room food appears on the Pool Room menu as well, but not the sirloin tartare, a deceptively named mainstay of the businessman's lunch. It shares with tartares you have known only the uncooked condition of its beef, which is entirely unalloyed when served. The few ounces of red meat are pounded thin and fitted, edge to edge, to the surface of an oval platter more or less as icing is applied to the top of a cake. You peel away sections of the fresh, tender, bright-red beef, dip it in—or otherwise apply—the thick, eggy, slightly sour and altogether superb mayonnaise with which it is served, and eat. That will be $12, please. The menu in both rooms changes with the solstices and equinoxes, and the wild boar pâté (offered only in the Pool Room and, presumably, only when in season) suggests itself—by its aggressive title as much as by its pungent character—for cold-weather consumption. It is a nutted mosaic of meats and organ meats, fat and jelly, of myriad textures, well seasoned, very striking against the sour lingonberries that garnish it. The Pool Room's cassoulet appetizer consists of some rather too resilient preserved goose, dark and strong, buried in the white beans—those beans are firm, and the sauce is thick with many turnings under of the crusted top. The Bar Room's shrimp are prepared on an open grill, are crisp and sweet, are suffused with the flavor of charring. But its fried Camembert is only a proof nobody asked for that good cheese is convertible into fair fun food. Its spaghetti Four

Seasons consists of noodles that have been sautéed in the oil that is the base of the sauce; peppers and onions, wild mushrooms and ham are the bulk—strong cheese is grated onto the dish until you say stop. Either room will sell you the onion soup—it comes in the usual crock, and the dark, sturdy broth, abundant onions and chunk of toasted bread reach you under a seal of browned and pully cheese.

In the Bar Room grilled fish is very much the thing. The snapper is touched with citrus, slightly crusted, and its white meat is fresh, juicy, tender—it is served with a tomato-flavored tarragon sauce that is powerfully fragrant of the herb. Chopped lamb steak is a good dish—but not so good when the ground meat is sweet-spiced, mingled with pine nuts, somewhat overcooked. A so-called chutney served with it, though composed of many fruits, is indistinguishable from apple sauce. The scallops of veal are nicely browned, surmounted by perfectly good ham, and served in a sauce that is lemony and smooth—still, the dish comes off like Italian food without Italian character, and the veal itself is less than buttery. What the house calls venison paillard are really tournedos, for the two little steaks have not been pounded into sheets. Anyway, the game meat is fine, very sweet, with some of the richness of organ meat, and it is garnished with a peppered and fruity sauce that is like a slightly thin hoisin, and with spiced, sugared and citrus-flavored lingonberries.

Over in the Pool Room, things are a bit more elaborate (and considerably dearer). But once you try the $26 fricassée of beef tenderloin and oysters, you may conclude that high prices and good eating are not incompatible. The slivers of beef are browned, tender and blood-juicy. The oysters are fresh, plump, light, subtly oceanic. And the sauce in which they and a few pistachio nuts are combined is dark and rich, at once gravy-like and elegant. You can get a slice of calf's liver as thick as a three-rib lamb chop. It is broiled over charcoal, and its somewhat blackened and crusted surface is like a zest of the intense flavor of the velvet meat—a couple of dollops of scallion butter surmount the meat and slowly melt thereon. You order the pheasant, and you are delighted to receive a muffin of polenta that is studded with dark, sweet raisins; are happy with the gingered cabbage; enjoy the candied gooseberries; but despair of the dull bird—it is dry, almost without flavor, and its peppered wine sauce cannot rescue it.

Cheese is served in the Bar Room only—a wagon on which ten kinds are displayed, with several kinds of fruit, is wheeled to your table. The help will give you the names of the cheeses, your eyes will determine which are in good shape. Soufflés for one are served in the earless cups in which they are baked—they are browned, triumphantly risen, occasionally a bit dry. The coconut soufflé, with its quality of hot nuttedness, is a nice departure from the more common flavors. The dessert cart displays an orange mousse pie that is sometimes a bit too jellied—but the glistening white mousse, wrapped in almost paper-thin slices of orange, is a good sweet that is nicely set off by the tang of the orange rind. The chestnut mousse is liquored and leaden, the amaretti cake a big soft macaroon, the chocolate velvet cake an almost ridiculously rich one-step remove from unadulterated chocolate, the chocolate pistachio cake a nutted, layered item—green alternates with brown—of rather obvious appeal. The so-called Four Seasons fancy cake, which is always displayed on the top level of the three-tier cart, is a cinnamoned chocolate and hazelnut concoction loosely clothed in sheet chocolate. All the desserts are fresh, all are probably just what they are meant to be—elicitors of oohs and ahs from the once-in-a-lifetime celebrants who come here to be wowed.

Then there is the wine list, more than 200 still wines from six countries (including around 70 from California), at $7.50 to $350 the fifth. You will have no trouble finding a good bottle at a price you can pay. By and large the wine prices here are lower than at the rest of midtown's more pretentious restaurants.

★ FRANKIE AND JOHNNIE'S

269 West 45th Street
DINNER. CLOSED SUNDAY.
Reservations, 245-9717.
Credit cards: AE, CB, DC, MC, V.
Very expensive.

A narrow stairs takes you up to Frankie and Johnnie's. The restaurant was once a speakeasy. Its windows, which face Eighth Avenue and 45th Street, still have their shutters in place, and the low ceiling and the dull light from red-shaded lamps create a slightly sinister effect, which is not undone by the theatrical posters that hang on the stained-wood walls. At the east end of the dining room there is an open kitchen— stainless steel and bright light, clutter and clatter, and multilingual work talk. When things slow down, the cooks lean on the counters and look out over the dining room, which is often crowded with theater people (not the younger set), studiously hard-boiled journalists from the nearby *Times,* visiting buyers and local sellers, detectives and ticket brokers. There is nary a Bendel bonnet nor a Brooks Brothers flannel in the gay and gaudy crowd, certainly not on the gruff Greek waiters who patrol the place in limp tuxedos.

You may begin with cold fresh clams, or oysters, or with rich chopped liver served in a pool of schmaltz with a garnish of raw onions. But about half the customers start with the special salad for two, an inelegant but tasty mix of iceberg lettuce and raw mushrooms, strong onions and crisp green pepper, with salted anchovies for strength, ripe tomato for color and tart dressings.

Those waiters carry knives, and knowledgeable habitués order the giant charred, double-rib lamb chops, the eyes of which, in an ancient Frankie and Johnnie's ritual, are cut away from their bones with the sleeved steel the waiters secrete in their inside jacket pockets. Those chops are the best main course in the house, and though the sirloins and filets mignons are good too, they are a notch below the best steaks in town. The veal chops are immense, the broiled chicken nicely charred and the chopped steaks juicy, but nothing here measures up to the terrific lamb.

Few places around still serve potato pancakes. This one does, and does them the right way, starting with raw grated potatoes that are heavily seasoned and cooking them in plenty of hot grease, so that they are at once acidic, rich and crusty.

Frankie and Johnnie's sells lots of old-fashioned blueberry pie, probably for reasons of nostalgia, for it is little more than cold berry preserves in a glazed lard crust. The cheese cake, on its graham-cracker crust, is fine. Sometimes there are good strawberries.

After the nearby curtains go down, the place fills merrily with guys clutching girls clutching *Playbill*s.

★★GAGE & TOLLNER

372 Fulton Street (near Borough Hall), Brooklyn
LUNCH AND DINNER.
Reservations, 875-5181.
Credit cards: AE, CB, DC, MC, V.
Expensive.

Of New York's more venerable eating places, Gage & Tollner is the one that, more than any other, reveals its antiquity not only in well-preserved appointments but also in food that is prepared, at least in large measure, according to old, mostly forgotten recipes: crabmeat Virginia and crabmeat Dewey, lobster thermidor and lobster Maryland, scallops Baltimore, soft clams Chicago, more. And, of course, if you pump your waiter until the patience of his other customers runs out, you can find out what all those names mean. The menu is without explanatory annotation. It is as if today were truly yesteryear, when an oyster celery cream broil, for example, was as identifiable as spaghetti primavera.

This is turn-of-the-century splendor, dark and handsome and a little bit grand. The room is about half a block long, and wide enough for four rows of mahogany-colored tables—spread with white napkins—and two broad aisles. On walls of dark flocking, tall mirrors with arched tops run the length of the place. In them are reflected the intricate chandeliers—equipped with both electrical and gaslight fixtures—that glitter in a great overhead column from the front of the big room to the mirrored wall at the back.

There is more of antiquity here than the appointments and the American-heritage recipes. An entry on the back of the menu reads, "Our Waiters Wear Service Emblems: Gold Eagle—25 years; Gold Star—5 years; Gold Bar—1 year." And almost all the waiters are of color. It is as if somewhere back there in history, someone replaced the plantation system with an incentive program. Presumably it is supposed that a fellow would never leave the old homestead if an eagle were just a couple of years off.

G&T is deep in the heart of downtown Brooklyn, so Brooklyn business lunches here and sometimes crowds the place. But in the evening the restaurant is quiet, albeit far from deserted. Members of the borough's old families come here, most of them from Brooklyn Heights—they are distinguishable from their Manhattan neighbors by virtue of their serviceable Abraham & Straus clothing, which has been avoiding calling attention to its wearers for generations. That old crowd has been augmented the last ten years or so by the restorers, young people who have been buying up and fixing up old brownstone houses in various parts of wildest Brooklyn. They are distinguishable from the Old Guard by virtue of their L. L. Bean garb and the freshness of their revealed optimism.

Such things as raw clams and oysters, and the shrimp, crabmeat and lobster cocktails, are fine here, but it would be pointless to mount an expedition all the way to Brooklyn and then not sample the native dishes, among them crabmeat Virginia, in which a small platter of crabmeat is moistened with lemon, buttered, and baked until the surface of the sweet white meat is a glistening reddish brown—a superb dish. Soft clam bellies are clams with the tough part removed, and G&T makes them a dozen and a half different ways. A good introduction is the soft-clam-belly-broil appetizer—lots of tender bellies, with buttery crusts, on toast. They are good as is, which is to say plain and homey, with just a hint of ocean flavor, and they are good with lemon, which livens them. You get splendid steamers here, tender, free of sand, submerged in broth in a copper pot, on the side a monkey dish of hot butter in which to dip them. The clams Cassino arrive on a layer of hot rock salt. These are hefty cherrystones, and they can be a little tough, which is a pity, for they have a sweet tang, and the hot clam juice in the half-shells has taken on the flavor of the bacon, peppers and onion with which the clams are sprinkled. Rock salt also keeps the oysters Rockefeller warm, and these are tender, buried in spinach that has the vivid tang of Pernod without the alcohol rawness that is often the undoing of this dish.

There is a distinctly American quality to the scallop celery cream broil, tiny bay scallops mingled with little chunks of crisp celery in a thick and spicy cream sauce, served on toast—utterly satisfying food. Crabmeat Dewey is a famous dish served almost nowhere in town but here. This is college casserole cookery—crabmeat and red and green pepper in a creamy sauce. It is unfortunate that the crabmeat is imperfectly divorced from its cartilage, for you must therefore eat in a state of alertness, and this pleasantly gooey and highly flavored food is not the kind of thing you want to pick at.

When there are soft-shells, this place sautés them elegantly, and they arrive crinkly and delicate and sweet. The lobsters are perfectly broiled, the juicy meat touched with the flavor of the charred shell—butter is apparently poured over the beast just before it is served, a superfluous and slightly unfortunate adulteration. You get perfectly cooked boned bluefish, but—disaster in a place like this—on a Saturday night it is faintly, but clearly, less than fresh. Lemon sole is a delicate fish, somewhat undone here by overbroiling. And the fried seafood combination—fish and shrimp and scallops and oysters—is beautifully battered and crisped, but that cannot rescue it from poorly chosen shrimp (from certain waters) that taste of iodine to the point of inedibility.

Gage & Tollner characterizes itself as a steakhouse as well as a seafood restaurant. You are shown your meat before it is broiled, the sirloin steak looking very much like a sirloin steak, the so-called single mutton chop looking like a small rack of lamb sheathed in fat. The steak is fine, the mutton—split after the viewing—rather mild; both of them are charred, and cooked a little drier than what medium-rare usually means in Manhattan. The broiled meats come with rather leaden French fries. This is an unmixed blessing, for it gives you an excuse to cancel them in favor of a crusty loaf of well-seasoned hashed-brown potatoes, served waist-high in hot cream—superb. Ascetics, of course, may have theirs dry. The lyonnaise potatoes are browned, blackened a bit here and there, moist with butter, interleaved with slivers of sautéed onion. The grilled sweet potatoes are firm, soft, slightly burnt. The slabs of fried eggplant are greasy. The big, hefty corn fritters are studded with kernels of fresh corn, and they are served with thick syrup. You can even get fried tomatoes, three hot red slabs, each of them sandwiched between layers of crisp, eggy breading.

Not a first-class dessert house: The lemon mousse shakes like jelly; the cheese cake is that clay-like cream-cheese item, which, if it is to be appreciated for its unabashed excess, must not be served ice-cold—this is. The brandy-Alexander pie is exactly what it sounds like, loudly liquored, under a blizzard of cocoa (an unhappy departure from the nutmeg that goes on the cocktail of the same name). Something given as Wade's birthday cake is a rather soggy chocolate cake with redundant chocolate sauce—its whipped cream is perfect. Get that cream with the pecan pie instead—chewy and sharp, an abundance of crunchy nuts and only a minimum of filler, the surface of the pie just a little caramelized.

★★ LA GAMELLE

59 Grand Street (near West Broadway)
DINNER.
Reservations, 431–6695.
Credit cards: AE.
Medium-priced.

Gutted space, sleek and stagy, with a touch of color here, a spot of warmth there
—such is the SoHo look, and such is the look of Grand Street's La Gamelle, albeit in
small, and in French.

The front room is the barroom, and you enter it between storefront windows that
are twice your height and filled with plants. Just within the door, to either side,
surmounted by globular white lights, stand a pair of old City of New York lampposts,
ten feet tall, like totems of this upside-down part of town. SoHo is not only where there
are streetlamps indoors, but also where the bohemians have cash in the pockets of their
jeans and not a revolutionary thought in their apolitical heads. It is an artists' quarter
in which "commercial art" is not a dirty word, and the people you encounter in the
front room of La Gamelle are quite at ease in this not inexpensive place. They deck
themselves out jauntily, often stylishly. And in this nifty setting, which seems more like
Technicolor than the real world, everyone looks at least a little smashing, just like in
the movies.

Track lighting shines down on walls of white-enameled brick, or slate-blue smooth,
or French Provincial cotton—big sweeps of it—in a blue-and-white pattern. Quirky
photos and oddments hang on the walls, in one corner simulating the at-random
arrangement of a bulletin board. The bar itself is of hammered copper that glints.
Behind it there is a tall white cabinet, framed in warm wood, that is stocked with crystal
and brandy. To each side of that are big framed mirrors that tilt forward at their tops,
giving everyone in the room a pretty good view of everyone in the room—drinkers at
the bar or loungers at the four marble-topped tables, at which you may drink, or eat,
or pass the time while waiting for a table in the dining room. No. 59 Grand Street is
an old building, and a row of its ancient support columns extends from the barroom,
through the foyer that bypasses the kitchen, into the skylighted dining room a few steps
up at the back.

Things are simpler back here—just a dozen of those marble-topped tables and simple
bentwood side chairs—so that the survey of Western music, from J. S. Bach to our very
own day, that is broadcast throughout the premises can sometimes be heard with
painful clarity. If you ask, you can get it turned down. That cotton print on the walls
looks delicate when it is hung with restrained posters and blackboard menus, but the
food that is chalked on the slate is anything but.

You are brought a basket of good French bread, wrapped in linen, warm, its corners
lightly toasted, its crust falling to crumbs, and a ramekin of fluted white porcelain filled
with sweet butter. They are fine with the pâté de campagne, very much the standard
thing, but good, coarsely ground and porky, heavily spiced and salted, sprinkled with
parsley, and served at well above icebox temperature, so that its flavors are clear. There
is an odd first course called salade Gamelle, which consists of fresh greens, strands of

Swiss cheese (the real Swiss thing), and walnuts, in a thick and mustardy dressing. It reads like one of those abominations you get at some of the fast-food salad bars opening around town, but this is real food, of ingredients that contrast simply and strikingly with one another, and its tangy dressing makes it stimulating.

An appetizer given as "tarte aux légumes" is a pungent, quiche-like dish, in which sautéed vegetables—celery, green peppers, onions and fresh mushrooms—are buried in warm cheese on a dark and flaky crust. Just before serving, the tart is sprinkled with more cheese and browned. This is food in which there is no absence of finesse, for none is intended, and it is utterly satisfying. The gentleman in the kitchen does well when he cooks with cheese, and his coquille St-Jacques, which he makes with fresh scallops and mushrooms, comes in a mild sauce, the cheese topping browned and strong, the entire production picturesque in its big scallop shell. The soupe aux courgettes, which is intended as zucchini soup, is little more than a potato base and a remoteness of the green vegetable.

The main courses are as conventional as the appetizers, and just about as successful. One of the more charming blackboard listings is "poisson, bleu," by which is meant bluefish. The grilled fillet is fresh, moist and browned, and it is virtually buried in a buttery and heavily peppered sauce that is thick with sautéed shallots, lightly herbed with parsley and dill. Even a dish like veau à la Normande, of which one expects a certain lightness, is prepared here in a strong—almost obvious—version that is nevertheless successful. The veal is pale and buttery, and the thick cream sauce, fortified with wine and cognac, is dense with smoky tarragon—somehow it works. You get a good steak here called "entrecôte aux échalotes," something of a bargain at $8.50. It is accurately grilled and tender, the beef tasty, spread with the peppery sautéed shallots this place seems to favor. For the few of you out there who when solvent will eat kidneys, La Gamelle serves a pretty good dish of them, blackened and herbed, garnished with grilled tomatoes. The gigot d'agneau is unfortunately of lamb that does not taste like any specific meat at all. All the main courses are served with a mélange of crisp fresh vegetables—green beans, mushrooms, zucchini.

Among the desserts there has been a simple and sweet raspberry crêpe, syrupy and rich, with whipped cream; a chocolate mousse that is deep-brown and as solid as fudge, its topping of whipped cream and strawberries actually a leavening; a conceit called "délice maison," which is a froth much like zabaglione, but made with Grand Marnier instead of Marsala—it is hot and well liquored, and it is served over good strawberries, but it amounts to little more than a grownup's sundae. The bowl of fresh cut fruits, with cream and cognac, is not bad, but the melon aux Pineaux is just cantaloupe and not noticeably transformed by the fortified wine of the title.

A couple of hard-working young men work the floor here. One of them is serious and a little dour. The other, who wears denim overalls and a happy smile, is a true restaurant type—he is French and he loves the food he serves.

★★ EL GAUCHO

93 MacDougal Street (near Bleecker Street)
DINNER.
Reservations, 260-5350.
Credit cards: AE, MC, V.
Medium-priced.

El Gaucho is the closest thing to a one-dish restaurant in town. The menu is longer than one dish, of course, but no one seems to come here for anything but the mixed grill. It is not just that the dish is good to eat, though it is certainly that. It is also, you should pardon the expression, fun. The popular production is delivered to your table as a pyramid of grilled meats and variety meats and sausages that are heaped up on a hibachi within which coals are glowing. Orders for two or more consist simply of greater mounds. You spear the item you want, place it on the plate before you and eat. It is non-U to snap up the choicest items for yourself, leaving the kidneys for your companions. When lots of tables are occupied, the room is filled with the blue haze of charcoal smoke and the delicious scent of charred meats.

The pyramid consists of thin slices of sweetbread, browned and a little fatty and crisp; a firm, salty sausage of smoky and spicy meat, speckled with fat and touched with charcoal black; a hefty and moist blood sausage, the color of purple wine and the texture of firm and meaty pudding—many consider this the star of the show, and some customers ask that extra blood sausages be added to their orders (for a fee); kidneys that are hard and clean, the crunchiest items on the stove; and red meat, slabs of short-rib steak and skirt steak, the kinds of blood-rich, fibrous and tasty beef that can stand up to this strong competition. The steaks are perfectly grilled, lightly tender and rare. If you want them cooked further than that, you simply leave them over the coals. The meats are mingled with strands of sweet and sour red peppers. This dish and a bottle of heavy red wine from Argentina or Spain may be all you need.

But there is more. You may begin with matambre, marinated flank steak wrapped around vegetables, hard-boiled eggs and fiery relish, poached in stock, cooled, and served in thin cross-sectional slices. The eggplant escabèche is a lovely enrichment of that vegetable, served in big, tender slices. The meat pie is a nice hot little pastry filled with steamy, spiced ground meat. If you do not go for the mixed grill, the club steaks and shell steaks are of good beef, excellently prepared. They are served with French fries that are okay, but not the last word in crispness or potato flavor. The Spanish-speaking customers, who make up a good portion of this establishment's clientele, order them separately and munch on them as an appetizer while they wait for their mixed grills.

The flan is the usual thing, but it is lovely if you order it with butterscotch sauce. Something called "sweet potatoes marmalade" is called candy by your waiter—it is a cool, gelatinous sweet that goes well with the side of salty white cheese you may have with it.

El Gaucho is mostly brick and wood, illuminated by hanging yellow lanterns and adorned with pampas-cowboy paraphernalia—wagon wheels, stirrups, a venerable yoke. A fireplace (rarely in use) is off in one corner, a stamped-tin ceiling in disrepair is over your head, a red-and-purple-neon sign glows garishly in the window. The waiters vary from sweet to courtly. Most of them are from very far south of the border. This is a late restaurant, with most of the customers arriving after nine.

★ LA GAULOISE

502 Sixth Avenue (near 13th Street)
LUNCH AND DINNER.
Reservations, 691-1363.
Credit cards: AE, CB, DC, MC, V.
Expensive.

Everyone who lives in Greenwich Village has been to Paris, and as La Gauloise has the unmistakable look of a busy Paris café, middle-aged, middle-class Villagers, nostalgic for the post-collegiate, pre-professional, pre-parental days of their carefree European swings, come here to relive. Many dress themselves not so much the way they dressed then, but in the manner of the subjects of early-twentieth-century French paintings. They come in tweed jackets, orange shirts, full beards, flowing robelike dresses, neckerchiefs, insolent lipstick. But don't worry, Greenwich Village is not what it was, and the local middlemen and storekeepers and dentists and professors of business administration come too. The place they have all made popular is a long spacious room, a little marble-topped bar at the front, huge mirrors in massive dark-wood frames occupying most of the ivory-colored walls, a tin ceiling and a wood floor. There is white linen on the tables, slender vases with a flower or two on the linen. The hard surfaces on all six sides make this a noisy box, and if you get stuck near loudmouths you are in for not only boredom but pain.

There is more of Paris here than just the look, at least more of what Paris is reputed to be. For with its popularity La Gauloise has adopted certain of the discourtesies that it takes as attaching naturally to success. You call at 7:30 for an 8:30 reservation, which is accepted. You arrive on time and it is made plain to you that reservations made tardily cannot be honored promptly. Or you arrive without a reservation at all, when the restaurant is emptying out after the dinner hour, and you are shown to a discommodious table. You ask for a better one, and you are informed that the dining room is all booked up, that you are fortunate to be seated at all without a reservation. (A dozen tables remain empty for the rest of the evening.) Your greatest temerity is to be a woman and to arrive with yet another woman, rather than with a man. Such monosexual parties are routinely seated at tables near the kitchen or in direct line of the center-aisle traffic, rather than in the snugger spots in corners or along the walls on the black banquette that runs the perimeter of the room. But if you get a comfortable table, this is a comfortable room.

Most of the food is good, but almost none of it is flawless. The pâté is strong and hearty, and it has a rich, livery core, but it is served at icebox temperature. The oysters are fresh, but they would seem even fresher if they had not been opened in advance; and the sauce mignonette with which they are served is sour rather than tart. A green-bean salad in a light vinaigrette is one of the best of the cold first courses. The hot appetizer called friture de truites consists of little chunks of deep-fried trout garnished with a thick mustard sauce that is essential to the perfectly crisped but tasteless fish. Trout alive it was not recently. The snails are OK, but they are not those big plump ones—and the standard snail butter is salted to the point at which the salt obscures the garlic. Happily, there is saucisson chaud, thick slices of hefty and spicy sausage, rimmed with flaky pastry, garnished with firm, hot, oiled potatoes and strong mustard—splendid coarse food.

But for the bit of grit that always seems to turn up in this establishment's scallops, the coquille St. Jacques à la nage is a good plate, a buttery and briny seafood broth abundantly populated with big scallops and strands of crisp vegetable and scallion greens. On Fridays there is bouillabaisse, which arrives as a craggy landscape of projecting shells and carapaces of seafood items that are knee-deep in yet another seafood broth. Mussels, scallops, clams, whiting, snapper, all are fresh (the scallops and mussels a little sandy), but the soup lacks the saffron fragrance suggested by the name, and to give it character you fortify it heavily with the thick red garlic sauce that comes with the dish. The grilled chicken is blackened outside, and on occasion, not quite cooked to the bone—still, this is a pretty tasty bird. Like many of the grilled dishes here, it is accompanied by French fries that are apparently obtained from Blimpies a couple of blocks to the south. Good sweetbreads: a hot and sticky stew with mushrooms and crisp carrots in the gravylike sauce, a garnish of good rice. Not-so-good cassoulet (on Sundays): the lamb and fowl and sausage are hearty, but the beans are soft, so the dish lacks some of its essential solidity. The grilled steak is not bad, the Béarnaise a little too sour for the beef. Much better is the veal paillard, the slight flavor of charring lovely on this buttery meat, a dollop of parsleyed butter the perfect sauce.

The goat cheese is superb, not one of the gamiest chèvres, but a firm and smooth one, graced with strong black Mediterranean olives. There is Brie, but though it is properly ripened, it lacks flavor.

The oeufs à la neige are white and light, the vanilla sauce polished, the sharp strands of candied grapefruit rind a pleasant texture and taste with the otherwise gentle dish. The profiterolles are the usual thing—light little chou pastries with decent ice cream and chocolate. The best of the sweets is the marquise au chocolat: a block of solid chocolate framed in a light sponge cake, buried in a chocolate custard sauce and sprinkled with crisp almonds.

★ GIBBON

24 East 80th Street
LUNCH, MONDAY TO FRIDAY; DINNER, MONDAY TO SATURDAY. CLOSED SUNDAY.
Reservations, 861-4001.
Credit cards: AE, CB, DC, MC, V.
Very expensive.

You probably would not have guessed that Japanese and French food can be successfully integrated. The unlikely feat is managed quite well here. This is not, mind you, something like Parisians taking up raw fish, or Japanese cooks adding sweet pastries to their repertoire. This restaurant prepares dishes in which characteristics of the two cookeries are blended. (The trick is not, however, tried throughout the menu.) That ecumenical spirit is carried even further—the waiters are unmistakably American, and the prices are decidedly OPEC.

Although the cooking is binational, the management is clearly from the East. Your host is a grim, trim samurai, with hard-edged hair, a parenthetical black mustache, a double-breasted suit—the unvented jacket reaches to his fingertips and fits like a glove —and the carriage and demeanor of the fellow who leads you to the other place when you are denied entrance to Heaven.

You enter to a softly lit room with walls of mustard-colored brick or putty-colored linen. Opposite the bar on your left is the fireplace, complete with fire when the weather is wintry. Low benches along the nearby walls, fitted with thin, spartan cushions, surround small tables at which you may sip a drink while waiting. At the back, several tables are separated into groups by partitions of stout bamboo poles and tied thatching. Eastern and Western art hangs on the walls, much of it representational—specifically of the monkey that gives this place its name. These rooms are quiet, intimate. Upstairs is another matter, the grand parlor floor when this brownstone was a residence. The ceiling is high, the gauze-draped front windows are huge, the rather brightly lit room is both somber and grand. You sit on a dark tufted banquette or on hefty armchairs that are studded with big brass upholstery nails. Solemn Japanese art, including a bleak four-part screen that almost covers one wall, adds portent to any occasion.

Though much of the commerce here is derived from stiff locals—headmistress types, pear-shaped bankers and other seeming asexuals who drink martinis but fail to unbend —the larger tables on the upper floor sometimes accommodate jovial parties that warm this place up. The parties, often as not, are made up of museum and/or gallery people, for Gibbon is apparently where the Upper East Side's art crowd heads to celebrate the historic milestones in twentieth-century culture—glittering openings, ravishing exhibits —that are marked in this neighborhood several hundred times each year. A not uncommon party of four at Gibbon consists of two trustees, a curator and a kook. And these days, you will note, artists eat no more hungrily than anyone else.

They eat cucumber stuffed with lobster, tablets carved from the crisp vegetable, standing like monuments, forming tubes that are filled with tender lobster meat that has been moistened with a delicate, lemony and vaguely sweet dressing. If this restaurant has one flaw more serious than another, it is that once in a while it serves fish that is less than perfectly fresh. When the fish is, moreover, raw, few will essay a second bite. On occasion the sashimi appetizer will be impeccable, but once in a while one fish or another will have noticeably lost its bloom. Happily, the special whitefish sashimi, called usuzukuri, seems always to be fresh, the translucent slivers of pale and tender meat arranged like the petals of a flower around an almost violent radish dip—you soften the impact by moistening the morsels with an earthy soy sauce. Shrimp, lotus root and strawberry vinaigrette may strike you as unlikely, but the fruity dressing makes a remarkable unity of the ingredients. The hot mussels are tender and delicate, almost bland, for they pick up little flavor from the lightly garlicked bean paste they are steamed in—a simple but good dish. Just as good is tataki, a charred disc of very rare filet mignon cut into slivers, garnished with crisp broccoli and shredded radish, and served with a dark sauce that is a little oily, very nut-flavored.

You may get lucky, but otherwise your sakura-mushi (a roulade of salmon and green noodles) is made with salmon of a certain age; a clear black sauce that is loaded with ginger manages, remarkably, to neutralize the fishiness. You wish it were not necessary. No problems with the prawns à la Kyoto: big shrimp in an enriched soy sauce that has been sweetened, in the French manner, with sautéed shallots. Slices of rare breast of duck are mingled with zucchini and water chestnuts and wild mushrooms in a tangy ginger sauce—sweet meat, and the flavors of the individual vegetables stand out. The roast veal with watercress sauce is almost pure French, the buttery meat moistened with a winy and salty sauce that is thick with chopped watercress. But lamb kocho, which is roasted very much like any rack of lamb, is served with pan juices that are given a strong Japanese flavor by the addition of soy sauce—a dramatically successful dish. Almost, in fact, as successful as negima, asparagus and scallions rolled in juicy thin slices of rare beef. The meat is moist and tender, the vegetables are crisp, all in a clear, lightly salted broth.

The banana ice cream tastes almost eerily like pure banana in a creamy form. The chocolate mousse is pretty standard, the lemon mousse pretty gelatinous. And the chocolate cake is heavily floured for today's taste, though there is no denying the thick coffee-flavored icing on top.

You are served chopsticks, but they are the splintery softwood kind that come joined together at the fat end. You can bring your own. Or eat with a knife and fork.

★ GINGER MAN

51 West 64th Street
LUNCH AND DINNER.
Reservations, 724-7272.
Credit cards: AE, CB, DC, MC, V.
Medium-priced.

One of New York's earliest simulations of the style of the British pub, the Ginger Man, by virtue of its clubroom comforts and barroom ease, has heretofore always managed to transcend its mostly mediocre and often pretentious food. These days the food is better—and simpler—than before. And though the restaurant has expanded in three directions since its inception in the mid-sixties—by the addition of inner rooms and an enclosed sidewalk café—the barroom-dining room that was once the whole of the place still sets its tone. The bar is massive, with great arched mirrors behind it. The floor is of barbershop tile, the tufted banquette of black leather. The tables are covered with white linen and surrounded by plain side chairs. The dark wooden walls are hung with framed paintings and prints and posters, side by side, one above the other, dozens of them all told, as if the stuff had been accumulated over the decades, each successive piece added wherever room could be found. It all seems to make nostalgic reference to the days when casual eating places did not look like a roped-off area on Bloomingdale's fifth floor. The Ginger Man's other rooms are a little off-key—simpler, but without the plain solidity and character of the barroom.

The dining rooms are patrolled by white-aproned waiters—plus a few waitresses—some of whom have grown older and larger along with the place. A number of them have even developed a level of semiprofessional competence. Still, when one of the big Lincoln Center halls empties out, this restaurant fills in a trice, and, with everyone wanting attention at once, the service can be slow. The Ginger Man does not draw the food-conscious set. You may find it something of a pleasure to mingle with this cosmopolitan crowd, for they seem to eat—and drink—not for its own sake, but to fuel themselves for the business of their lives. You hear lots of European accents here. Most of the talk is about the era's principal cultural preoccupations—art and money. Players from the pit and soloists from the stage are to be seen. James Levine himself has put in an appearance, sans baton.

As he has loftier things on his mind, he probably overlooks the fact that the shrimp in the shrimp cocktail are well cooked but poorly selected—they taste principally of iodine. If he cares at all, he will start with a Caesar salad, a straightforward combination of fresh romaine lettuce, crunchy croutons, strong ground cheese and much garlic in the good dressing; or with the salad of endive, arugula and walnuts, the nuts a nice contrast to the greens, slices of orange an unlisted pleasant surprise, the dressing light and creamy. A big mound of mussels, in their shells, is served in a briny broth that is flavored with white wine, smoothed with cream, sweetened a little with shallots— but the mollusks themselves are sometimes a little overcooked. These days almost everybody starts with potato skins, a recent Manhattan Island rage here rendered in one of its best versions. The semiellipsoidal shells are lightly greased, baked to an almost hard crispness, served with thick, cool sour cream.

The printed menu changes from time to time, the blackboard specials from day to day, so not everything described is always on hand. Sometimes there is sautéed red snapper, the fresh, browned fish served in a buttery sauce that is thick with parsley and scallions. Often there are bay scallops—they are bathed in a pale, lightly garlicked sauce, and the fennel leaves that are mingled with the rich little morsels are a striking note in the simple dish. The duckling is roasted until its skin is crisp and glistening, but there is plenty of moisture in the meat itself—sometimes it is served in a deep-brown tangerine sauce and with tangerine sections, their slight acidity a very nice foil to the fatty bird. The steaks are of decent—but not the best—beef. They are sometimes a little chewy, usually accurately prepared, always of good flavor. The lamb chops, prepared as a rack, share that description—the lemon-and-garlic-flavored pan sauce with which they are moistened hardly affects the flavor of the strong meat. Happily, the steak tartare is of beef recently ground. But for lack of sufficient oil in its powerfully seasoned preparation, it is without the richness one expects in this dish, a condition you may alleviate by adding oil on your own until the red meat shines.

After 10 P.M. a supper menu is also available. It lists the kind of food most people think of when they think of this place: huge omelets, well formed, well sealed, steamy and moist inside, the simplest ones—plain, or with fines herbes—the best; nice little hamburgers on seeded rolls; a steak sandwich that consists of a small steak about as good as the big one—it is served sliced, on toasted rye bread that is moistened by the blood of the beef.

The so-called ice-cream sandwich is chocolate ice cream in a nut crust, adorned with real whipped cream. The apple crisp with ginger ice cream consists of cooked apple, sugary brown crumbs, and the oddly flavored cream. The cassis sherbet is icy, dark pink, refreshing.

★★GIN RAY

148 East 50th Street
LUNCH AND DINNER. CLOSED SATURDAY AND SUNDAY.
Reservations, 759-7454.
Credit cards: AE, CB, DC, MC, V.
Medium-priced.

To Western sensibilities the Japanese geisha custom is virtually incomprehensible. The purpose of the custom is the brief, innocent distraction of men—in these times, mostly businessmen—from their formalities and responsibilities. The market for this form of diversion is great in New York, where Japanese businessmen now outnumber the combined fire and police forces. And just as empire builders of times past brought their ways to sometimes inhospitable lands, so the Japanese have brought the geisha to New York, where she will probably be mistaken for a naughty girl.

As is common in Japan, the setting for this intimate entertainment is a restaurant, in this instance an area of one that is separate from the regular dining room. So if, of an evening, instead of going to your right when you enter Gin Ray, you head left— as Westerners almost never do—you will find yourself in an exotic setting, albeit one into which Americanisms have been absorbed. The room is dark, long and narrow, low-ceilinged, metallic and hard-edged. At the near end is a massive, octagonal stainless-steel bar, at the other end of the tunnel-like room a bandstand, between the two ends tables and chairs. At around 9:30 three Japanese players—a drummer, a pianist and an electric-guitarist—mount the stand and proceed to destroy American jazz. The geishas, at a group of tables to one side of the bandstand, wait for customers to come. When the gentlemen arrive—usually in twos and threes—they are led to tables on the opposite side of the room, whereupon a number of the beautifully robed young women walk across to join them. Usually there is drinking, smoking, sometimes dancing. When the men leave they are walked to the front door by their paid companions. Invariably they look much happier than when they arrived. There must be something to it.

The restaurant proper is an improbable midnight blue and steel Deco creation, with carpeting on the floor and wood-framed rice-paper lanterns on the ceiling. Up front the long trim sushi bar is manned by three deft gentlemen in white, and fitted out with small built-in refrigerated display cases through a glass wall of which you may inspect the seafoods served at this counter. The tuna is firm, looks like raw beef, is smooth as velvet, sweet as spring water. The shrimp are snowy and crisp, flecked with red, of strong, utterly clean flavor. The abalone, a rather hideous-looking, seemingly moss-covered object, appears to glisten with a blue-green iridescence when it is sliced, has a strong, sea-gamy flavor. The octopus is a little rubbery, but not tough, mild. You may have these things straight, as sashimi, combined with vinegared rice and, in some instances, with seaweed, as sushi. They are served with vibrantly fresh ginger, strong mustard, vinegar, seaweed (which Japanese customers get automatically, and which other customers must request). All the seafood is impeccably fresh. While you struggle to manipulate an uncertain structure of rice and fish with your chopsticks, Japanese men at the counter pick the morsels up with their fingers. Some of them accompany these repasts with both Scotch highballs and sake.

At the white-linened tables in the dining room at the back, where you are waited on by young Japanese women in kimonos, you may begin your dinner with namaniku-sashimi, a striking dish of thin-sliced raw beef served in a soy sauce broth with strands of strong scallion and dried radish. Or with gyu-karashiae, cool and fresh spinach and thin slices of barely cooked beef, all in a fiery mustard—very dramatic and rousing. The kikkonasu is eggplant that has been broiled until it is a steaming hot mush—it is salty, dotted with morsels of chicken, served within a blackened perimeter of eggplant skin. The fresh, deep-fried oysters, called kaki-furai, are in a dry, crisped batter that actually seems to lighten them—they are served with a weighty soy sauce and with a good, mildly violent mustard.

Order udon-suki, and a "Portable Rangette" is placed on your table and plugged into a nearby outlet. Within it water boils. Next you are delivered a huge, deep platter of shrimp and carrots, duck meat and roots, scallions and cabbage, scallops, mushrooms, watercress, noodles, all beautifully mounded up—you add the duck meat to the water early, with the vegetables, to flavor the stock. After a while you cook the seafood and eat. The noodles are cooked last, and only very briefly. That appliance serves also for the preparation of shabu-shabu, in which the broth is prepared largely with vegetables, and in which you then cook very thin slices of beef for just a few seconds before dipping them in their vinegar sauce to make them tangy. If you prefer not to do your own cooking, try negimaki, in which sheets of beef have been rolled around scallions, broiled, cut into short lengths, and served in a blood sauce—there is much fat in this meat, which makes for a rich, weighty dish. The deep-fried salmon is perfectly prepared, the moist pink meat flaky within its light crust.

The broths, salad and ice cream (or sherbet), to which you are entitled if you order a main course, are simple and unimpeachable. The service at the tables is sweet, but at the sushi bar you may have trouble getting all your questions answered.

★★★ GLOUCESTER HOUSE

37 East 50th Street
LUNCH AND DINNER.
Reservations, 755-7394.
Credit cards: AE, CB, DC, MC, V.
Very expensive.

Gloucester House has a scrubbed quality, like the deck of a well-kept ship. It is spare, sexless. Though it looks down on its competitors from the highest-priced position of any fish house in town, it is home to only certain kinds of millionaires: those who worked so hard getting to the top that there was no time to develop a taste for luxury, and those from families of longstanding wealth, among whom the display thereof was abandoned within fifty years of the start of the Industrial Revolution. You see no playboys here.

The unlinened tables on the main floor are of raw hardwood, seemingly bleached by regular scouring. You sit on benchlike banquettes of painted wood—the seats are fitted with thin cushions—or on ample wooden armchairs. There is a balcony along two sides of the room, and up here there are dark polished surfaces on the tables. A handful of nautical paintings and a display of model ships do no more to offset the Spartan aspect of the upstairs part of the place than this really exciting display of sailor's knots does to make the downstairs feel like a playpen. And yet Gloucester House is not uninviting. It is spacious, open, and its ivory-trimmed Colonial-blue walls are lofty, extending to a ceiling from which hang two airy wooden chandeliers, glowing lamps at the ends of their long, graceful branches.

Males are required to wear jackets and ties. Naturally this requirement is not mentioned to you when you reserve. It is assumed that those with the sense to wish to eat here normally wear jackets and ties. If you arrive in an open collar, you are supplied with a clean ascot. The rule, however, does not ensure that all who come here will dress in the spirit of the place. When the eminent journalist and sage Victor Ziegel, after donning the ascot with which he was required to clothe his neck, got through seven courses at Gloucester House in under one hour, he became the first competitor to break the sixty-minute barrier while wearing no socks.

If you are not known here, and your party is incomplete, you will be asked to wait at the bar. If you demur, the host will start to lead you to a table upstairs. When you object again, he will aim you at an uncomfortable table at the first landing of the stairs. Eventually you get what you want. One good reason for avoiding the balcony: a waiter up there who makes speeches, e.g., "From Block Island today, we have the summertime swordfish, which is so much more succulent than the winter variety, and which you may have in a number of preparations, including one very unique preparation that is a personal favorite of my own, consisting of . . ." He goes on that way for about ten minutes (or until your throbbing becomes violent), but lacks the sense, as do all the waiters, to tell you in advance which dishes are "out."

Fortunately, just about whatever is not out is good. Good, for example, is the cold half-lobster in its shell, served with thick mayonnaise and garnished with crisp celery and tomatoes. The perfectly cooked little crustacean is sweet and tender. Good too are the Belon oysters from Maine, which are small, extremely tender, almost soft, their delicate flavor a subtle mixture of fruit and brine. You may have your oysters roasted, which is to say heated in their half-shells with just a little butter added. This intensifies their flavor and converts their juice into a briny hot broth. The melted butter served with this dish is superfluous. Or you may have your oysters as oyster stew, in which the warm and tender mollusks arrive submerged in a spicy, oceanic cream. Gloucester House serves good roasted shrimp, fresh-tasting and crunchy, in a delicately garlic-flavored butter. Perhaps the best of all the appetizers is the crabmeat wrapped in bacon, four tiny morsels of the mild white seafood encased in glistening and smoky hot meat. Of course there is New England chowder—it is laden with firm potatoes, and its strong clam flavor is a function of the copious broth with which the soup is made.

You will note, upon inspection of the menu, that the lobsters served here are identified either as medium or large. When you receive your "medium" lobster, you will understand at once why nothing could be found to fill the bill of "small." This lobster must have been caught with a mosquito net, for he could have slipped the bars of any trap. But when you slip into your reading glasses and commence to eat, your dismay is instantly magnified, for what you are not getting enough of is a perfectly broiled lobster, the meat so rich it seems buttery, its flavor vivid enough to make you heady. The price, by the way, is $29.50, which includes a lobster bib of softest linen. Though the place is stingy with its lobster, it is lavishly munificent with its crabmeat Newburg, the great mound of fresh crab powerfully intensified by its winy sauce. Or you can have your pearly crabmeat mingled with slivers of salty and smoky Smithfield ham—lovely food, dominated by the meat. Sometimes the house has baby frogs' legs. When sautéed, they are browned, delicate, a little dry—you sprinkle them with lemon and eat them bones and all. Nowhere is more careful attention given to the broiling of fish, all of which is utterly fresh. The skin of the whole trout is lightly blackened, and the meat is rich and flaky. The snapper is snowy, glistening with moisture within its browned surface. The crisp striped bass is juicy and delicately fibrous. But perfection is elusive —a swordfish steak is a little drier than you dreamed it would be.

You do not know the possibilities of French-fried onion rings until you have them here—the rings of onion are dark and sweet, as if sautéed separately before being lightly battered and fried. And the potatoes au gratin—a serving of which comes in a ramekin about the size of a small petri dish—is yet more sadism, for the buttery potatoes are crusted with just a touch of a cheese that has an almost brandylike strength. The broiled eggplant can be a little greasy, the French-fried zucchini chips crisp, but often rather tasteless.

The pecan pie has a rare intensity of nut flavor. It is served with thick and unsweetened whipped cream. The apple pie is lovely, the fruit spicy, sugared, and somewhat caramelized under its glazed crust. A very smooth strawberry mousse is powerfully flavored of the fresh berry, though it is perhaps a little gelatinous. The creamy and light raspberry mousse is pleasantly gritty with the seeds of the fresh fruit. If you want your raspberries straight, you get a wineglass filled with the firm, plump fruit—which you may sprinkle with confectioner's sugar—and a bowl of that good whipped cream. The New England dessert called blueberry slump is served, the juice of the hot stewed berries soaked into a chunk of one of this restaurant's fluffy hot biscuits. The solid and strong American Cheddar and English Double Gloucester are better than the French Brie or Roquefort.

Wine is kept cold in a cooler that is fashioned from a small, ovoid, copper-lined barrel attached to four legs.

★★ LA GOULUE

28 East 70th Street
LUNCH AND DINNER. CLOSED SUNDAY.
Reservations, 988–8169.
Credit cards: AE, DC, MC, V.
Very expensive.

La Goulue is an effort to replicate, with nothing less than movie-set realism, a bit of old Paris. Visually the performance is impeccable; and, much delayed blessing, the food these days is so consistently above reproach (albeit uninspired) that anyone wishing to soak in these lovely quarters may do so without fear of distaste.

Under a deep-brown tin ceiling, somber notes make a pretty tune. The walls are paneled in dark wood and mirrors, the silver backs peeling and flaking here and there, as if this really were a French restaurant that has survived since the turn of the century. The room is rimmed with high-backed banquettes the color of caramel, above which a thin brass railing gleams from bracket to bracket, pointlessly and beautifully. Light is cast from Art Nouveau brass sconces on the many-too-many little tables that are covered with snowy linen and set with simple china. One rose per table, in tall, slender glass vases. The first room includes a little zinc-topped bar, a few cocktail tables, and a handful of eating tables for two along the wall, for those who are without reservations, or just want dessert, or want to avoid the slight bustle of the dining rooms proper. The dark colors of the place, with just the brightness of the linen and the flowers, mirrors seen from an angle, the waiters in black and white, the almost invariable elegance of the crowd—gents in dark suits, ladies in simple little numbers—make for a scene of almost breath-taking respectability, not to say taste. We have here an admixture of high fashion and the senior partners of some very old law firms. It is true that excessive jewelry has been seen at the early end of the dinner hour and a bit of tipsy youth as midnight approaches. But the place takes no notice, remains its proper self withal.

La Goulue is getting old now, and it has settled down. The once hectic service is calm and available even at the busiest times, the waiters are confident and knowing, even pleasant, and everything is so utterly under control that when the host's pals arrive, he joins them for a drink in the front room, they in their evening-out clothes hardly distinguishable from him in his tux. What could be more civilized?

Well, the food could be more civilized. Though one could argue that the Assiette de Crudités is *too* civilized—four raw vegetables moistened with very nice vinaigrette, a slice of melon placed away from the dressing. As mama said, this you can have at home, though mama's ingredients were not invariably so crisp and fresh. Considerably less perfection with a bit more excitement is available in the Terrine de Canard, which is loudly livery, short on the flavor of duck meat, moist and spicy, served, happily, with pungent little cornichons. A good version of your standard snails. A bland one of onion soup.

The bass that is listed on the menu seems to be a symbol for a fish of the day; it is often not to be had, another fish available in its place. Sometimes it is poached salmon —an utterly fresh slice of the pink fish, unfortunately cooked a bit too long, so that the meat has lost its slight natural oiliness. It comes with a smooth hollandaise that has strong touches of spice and acid. Nice food. The Canard à l'Orange is the basic familiar item, very darkly roasted, garnished with slices of fruit, moistened with a tasty if far from deep sauce. The lamb here is served oddly. Called Medaillons de Selle d'Agneau, the dish consists of three substantial eyes of meat carved from their ribs, after the short rack was roasted in a dressing of bread crumbs that were oiled and flavored with garlic and herbs—good strong meat, but the dressing is somehow not integrated into the dish, perhaps because its flavors have not permeated. The Côte de Veau aux Morilles consists of a couple of eyes of veal chop, perfectly sautéed, so that the tender meat is lightly browned; but the creamy sauce of wild mushrooms lacks sparkle. Ask the waiter to substitute French fries and grilled tomatoes for whatever would otherwise come with your main course—they are the best vegetables in the house.

Good ripe Brie, at room temperature, served with excellent French bread. The Bombe Praline is a delicious sweet of little more than layers of almond paste and coffee ice cream. Good fruit tarts, in the simplest French manner, barely cooked fruit and flaky pastry.

★★★★ LA GRENOUILLE

3 East 52nd Street
LUNCH AND DINNER. CLOSED SUNDAY.
Reservations, PL 2–1495.
Credit cards: AE, DC.
Very expensive.

When Charles Masson died there was speculation as to the future of the famous restaurant he had built up. Surely his was the principal responsibility for the creation of this marvelous establishment. But in the care of his survivor, Gisèle Masson, it is today better than ever. Her method is simple: she is everywhere, watching, and setting an example of concern for detail that her employees follow. She is elegant and always unobtrusive, though the sometimes boorish crowd that mobs this place on weekend nights occasionally wears down her graciousness—leaving only a sturdy calm. On those occasions her maître, a mechanical little functionary who looks you directly over the right shoulder when you address him, has been known to hold tables near the front of the room while customers with reservations that were not honored on time are made to wait for something to open up in the back. This is an unpleasant fact of life for which Madame may well be ashamed. She gives no such sign. But Monday through Thursday the place is populated by ladies and gents who have just dropped in for a casual hundred-dollar dinner, little attention is paid to segregating money-come-latelies from the friends of the house, and the place is just one big happy family.

La Grenouille does something you want it to do—it dazzles, literally. You enter to a small room with a tiny, well-polished bar, a stunner on a perch behind the cash register, yet another behind the little counter in the hatcheck room. Just to the right of the entrance door is the great array of hors d'oeuvres and desserts, and to your left the dining room, with dozens of glowing sconces reflected in tall, broad mirrors, making the place shimmer. There are little lamps, like those on the walls, on all the tables along the rim of the room. And on every table, and in every corner, brilliantly colored flowers, thousands of them in all, so many that they are like part of the crowd. The expanses of the walls are painted a pale pea-green, and they are hung with scenic oils chosen for their predominance of darker greens—all that seems to recede, and everything about the place directs your attention to what glitters around you at table level.

Perhaps everyone who works here, with the exception of that maître, is a saint, or perhaps it is the effect of Madame's almost constant circulation in the aisles, but once you are seated, whether at the front, or back near the kitchen, you are treated like the prince you are—or should be. A waiter's jaw has been seen to drop like a weight when an empty water glass was pointed out to him. And the captains do not go off in search of a busboy to get you some bread when they are free to give it to you themselves. Madame's inquiries as to whether everything is all right are so warm that you fear that some of this Saturday-night crowd's metal-and-plastic hair and clothing will melt in her glow.

So you eat. From the assortment of hors d'oeuvres you select what you wish: an extraordinary céleri rémoulade, in which the crisp strands of perfumed root are served in a sparkling, lemony dressing—it is almost a crime to eat this dish here, for once you do, it will taste right almost nowhere else; plump shrimp that seem to burst when you bite into them, in what must be called Russian dressing, though this is a mayonnaise that was made pink and seasoned the day you eat it; cool bass in more of that creamy mayonnaise, this batch flavored with fresh herbs and a rather heavy dose of salt; slivers of cucumber in a dressing that is little more than vibrant white vinegar; pungent pâté de campagne; slivered avocado, firm and nutty, in a polished, mustard-thickened vinaigrette.

You order a Truite Fumée and your captain displays the smoked fish to you on a silver platter. You nod. Off he goes to filet it, returning it to you with a pitcher of Sauce Raifort. The fish itself is perhaps no better than good smoked trout anywhere, but this horseradish-spiked whipped cream is at once airy and creamy and sharp.

Les Little Necks Corsini are served here by the hundreds every night, tiny clams in their shells, awash in melted butter that has been strengthened with good, sharp salt and made sweet and a little crunchy with coarsely chopped parsley—the clams are delicately garlicked, and though they are hot, they are impeccably tender. They have the sweetness of the clams of the day.

The Billi Bi aux Paillettes commands a premium, which seems larky where the dinner prix fixe is $42.50, but whim will have its way. This is amazing soup, especially in that the strong flavor of the mussels in this thick and creamy broth is sharpened with brandy—lots of it, as much as such a soup could take without being made into a silly vehicle for a stiff drink—but it does not go over the edge. You have downed your cup and consumed the mussels you found at the bottom. Presently your captain blessedly shows up with a silver pot that holds yet another cup, and with his ladle he restores your delirious contentment.

How they get Sole Anglaise from Angleterre to East 52nd Street in this buttery condition should not concern you, since you are paying for whatever method they use. They do it, and they serve it as La Sole Anglaise des Gourmets, filets of the supple, gentle fish concealing a duxelles, under a white sauce that may give gilding the lily a good name. That duxelles, a hash of minced sautéed mushrooms, is of such concentrated mushroom flavor as to seem like the good earth itself. They may well have a special source for every special ingredient, for Les Grenouilles Provençale are made from the tiniest legs of the littlest frogs. They are lightly breaded and sautéed in a trice in garlic and butter; they are juicy and sharp and a little crisp, and they are graced with tomatoes that were cooked down with herbs until the resulting paste is like a dozen vine-ripened beauties concentrated into the volume of one.

La Poularde Poêlée à l'Estragon is a simple dish, a chicken roasted in a covered pot, its meat moist, its skin salty and a little crisp, served with a dark tarragon sauce that bristles with branches of the fresh herb; it is so thick with leaves of the herb that when you spoon the sauce over the bird, a green sediment is left on the meat—the scent of tarragon that rises from this dish is dizzying, the wild flavor of the dish almost shocking in its intensity. La Grenouille has always done wonders with chicken.

Surprisingly they list it as a specialty, for Le Steak au Poivre à la Fine does not seem like their kind of thing, steak studded with coarsely ground peppercorns being, simply, coarse. But if elegance can be made of this rather obvious invention, this is how it is done, with a brandied sauce of such rarefied headiness that the brusqueness of the spiced meat is overcome by the liquor. It is garnished, perfectly, with a small head of celery that has been braised apparently forever, until it is gentle, but somehow with no loss of strength.

La Grenouille makes dessert soufflés its own way, which is to say without egg yolks.

The results are odd creations in which the browned tops have the flavor of meringues, the flavored centers the airiness and spirit of light mousses. The marvelous soufflé of raspberries is shot through with bits of berries, and it is moistened with a hot raspberry sauce—a wondrous, light dessert. Good fruit tarts; a chocolate cake in which the layers of dark moist cake alternate with layers of good mocha cream; the chocolate mousse is very rich without being at all insipid, though it is served with a crème Anglaise that is on occasion watery and dull. You are brought a fanciful plate of petits fours, in which the assorted cookies are laid out in the shape of a lobster. There aren't ten restaurants in New York where the best dessert is as lively as this little throwaway.

This place has far from the most extensive wine list in town.

★ GROTTA AZZURRA

387 Broome Street (near Mulberry Street)
LUNCH AND DINNER. CLOSED MONDAY.
No reservations (CA 6-9283).
No credit cards.
Wine and beer.
Medium-priced.

In its heyday the Grotta Azzurra sported a line of waiting customers that extended from the front door of the subterranean restaurant, up the outdoor stairway to Broome Street, across the sidewalk (under the blue canopy) to the curb, and sometimes farther. Even in foul weather the devoted clientele waited, grimly. They brightened only when departing customers clawed their way through the crammed vestibule at the bottom of the stairs to drag their stuffed tummies up the steep flight, making everyone on line one party closer to seats at a table.

D'Grotta, as its devotees call it, is still a busy place, but the loyalty of old-time regulars has given way to the more relaxed allegiance of today's fans: except on weekends the waiting line rarely extends more than a few steps up. But the venerable restaurant is nevertheless a thriving survivor, one of the last of its kind. Within its garish confines may be found a re-creation of the teeming, hard-edged animal jollity that was once a real part of Little Italy, when it was a neighborhood instead of a tourist attraction.

The famous hole in the ground is small, low-ceilinged, brightly lit, gaudy and noisy. The walls of phony brick are adorned with murals of Old Italy in primary Mediterranean colors. The ceiling glitters, its rough, pale-blue plaster seemingly sprinkled with a million bits of rhinestone. There are great mounted fish on the walls, pics of celebs (R. Graziano shaking with R. Nixon), paneled mirrors and papal plaques, plastic flowers and an ancient, faded hand-colored photo of the couple who founded this place. Through a semicircular hole in the back wall you may watch the stolid cooks at nonstop labor in their brightly lighted steambox. The closely packed tables stand on a floor of barbershop tiles. The waiters must thread their way through them like cats through a thicket. These gentlemen—who are in black and white, with clip-on bow ties—perform their tasks with great shows of bravura suavity, as if leading you to a table or bringing you a plate of food were as miraculous as producing an elephant out of a top hat.

Garlic is used at Grotta Azzurra the way sand is used at the beach. The steamed clams and steamed mussels are loaded with it, big mounds of immaculately fresh mollusks, in their shells, served in a powerful red broth that is studded with slivers of garlic. Unfortunately, the clams are sometimes cooked too long, which toughens them. Pass up the pallid stuffed mushrooms and opt instead for the spedini alla romana, a huge repeating sandwich of bread and hot, pully cheese, the whole thing battered and deep-fried so that it is a crusty block, served moistened with a sauce that is touched with anchovies. The dish is like perfect junk food—utterly satisfying, and with no redeeming finesse.

Much pasta eaten here. The gnocchi are a red-letter item, but they are often claylike. You are far better off with the manicotti: spiced cheese, hot and soft, wrapped in envelopes of pasta, browned in an elemental and chunky tomato sauce—a solid plate of food. The spaghetti with garlic, oil and anchovies is at once mellifluous and sharp, the vibrant sauce startling against the firm noodles. The spaghetti Sicilian style is even richer, the noodles baked with eggplant, strong cheese and the house red sauce, served brown and bubbling.

You can get juicy, crusty chicken that is broiled with garlic, vinegar and olive oil; rich calves' brains that are further enriched by a sauce of little more than butter and parsley; whiting, Grotta Azzurra style, a whole fresh fish, poached to the perfect point, adorned with clams and mussels in their shells, and with chunks of squid and crisp shrimp.

But the quintessential Grotta Azzurra dinner (after your pasta) is the chicken, steak and sausage contadino (which is offered only in an immense $21 serving suitable for three or four people) with frittomisto (a similarly immense platter of deep-fried vegetables), which is the contadino's perfect garnish. The contadino consists of chunks of beef, bird and sausage, sautéed until crusty, mingled with slabs of roasted red peppers, oily and sweet, and with roasted potatoes, sautéed mushrooms and chunks of garlic, the whole mix made fragrant with fresh herbs. Fresh vegetables, crisp in their deep-fried crusts, make up most of the frittomisto, but cheese, brains and potato croquettes are among the unexpected contents of the amorphous morsels.

Cheese cake is the only dessert to have. These days it is spectacular, at once solid and fluffy, prettily sugared and lightly studded with candied fruit.

The crowd voyages here from Queens, Brooklyn and around the corner, clothed in denim or acetate, sharkskin or suede, and they are bejeweled with chains or cufflinks, high-school rings, costume jewelry, digital watches. The younger patrons are trim, the older ones wide, as if years of eating here gradually fatten them up. Members of all generations remove their jackets and roll up their sleeves. Sometimes there is an accordion player, and she does the best she can. "Happy Birthday" is sung at least twice a night, and you are expected to join in. Cigar smoking is encouraged.

Beer and wine are the only alcohol available.

★★HOEXTER'S MARKET

1442 Third Avenue (near 82nd Street)
DINNER.
Reservations, 472-9322.
Credit cards: AE, CB, DC, MC, V.
Expensive.

What distinguishes the crowd at this bar from the crowd at most of the other restaurant/saloons along Third Avenue is that many, before they come here from the office, go home and change first. This is a more costumed, more exhibitionistic, sexier set, people for whom public boozing is celebratory, a kind of party rather than an empty ritual performed for the attendant human proximity. Of course, desperately unattached swingers *(soi-disant)* do come here directly from their desks, but even when that depressing group predominates, you can easily overlook them amid the others, with their cowboy hats, exaggerated hair, peekaboo chests, translucent blouses with suspenders for modesty, wet-look pants, pointed boots. You see ladies here who look a little like birthday cakes, gents who look a lot like spacemen.

The barroom is dark. Track lights play softly on the walls and on the back bar, which is of elaborately carved wood and cut-glass mirrors. Factory lights hang low and glow dim over the bar itself. At the back of this room a big round table accommodates big happy parties who like to eat blind. A flashlight is brought for those who cannot otherwise read the menu. The dining room proper has walls of brick or of tan carpeting. The track lights are brighter back here, but they are aimed at the walls and a few dramatic prints thereon, so that people across the room are seen as silhouettes. If you could see them in greater detail, you would discern that they are not exactly the bar crowd. For in exchange for some of the best food on this strip Hoexter's specifies some of the most exacting prices, more than most of the bar customers will go for, but no trouble at all for the shrinks, surgeons, apartment-house administrators, fur merchants and their spouses, who, somewhat incongruously, have taken a shine to this snappy joint.

They like the superbly fresh oysters with their powerful horseradish sauce. They like the thin-sliced red, raw, juicy beef, with a vibrant, high and hot green-pepper sauce. The celery root and crabmeat ravigotte—served together—are fresh and crisp, sweet and peppery. The plump little snails come in a creamy tomato sauce that is touched with garlic. And the chicken pâté is tasteless, gelatinous.

The odd name of this restaurant traces to a butcher shop of the same title that was once on these premises. The butcher shop moved, but its excellent meat is still here. Hoexter's steak is the best in the neighborhood, at once beefy and tender, fibrous and juicy, impeccably cooked. The veal rivals it; the meat of the big plump chop is seared, browned, moist. The crisp roast duck is served in a polished sauce that is winy and sweet. And the fish of the day seems always to be fresh. A couple of odd but imaginative chicken dishes: chicken with lobster sauce—the sauce is rich, and a nutlike vegetable hash that garnishes the chicken is flavorful, but the chicken is too pallid for the dish to succeed; and a warm chicken salad with foie gras and walnuts, all in a hot vinaigrette, which has the same problem.

The chocolate cake is almost gross in its fudgelike thickness, but it is an admirable excess. The cappuccino mousse pie—a velvety mousse on a black crust that seems made of crushed coffee—is served with a giant dollop of rich whipped cream. The white chocolate mousse cake and the almond pot de crème are, by comparison, timid sweets.

★★HOME VILLAGE

20 Mott Street (near Park Street)
LUNCH AND DINNER.
Reservations, 964-0381.
No credit cards.
No liquor.
Inexpensive.

If you are longing for some duck feet, or deep-fried pig intestine, or perhaps a steaming platter of boiled tripe, this is the place. All the things you used to think were thrown away have, all these years, been grabbed up by the Hakka, a group of Chinese who, presumably as the result of an enforced status on the wrong side of the poverty line, have built a cookery of other peoples' culls. These odd elements figure in only a small portion of this restaurant's extensive menu, but they get all the talk.

Home Village is a brightly lit, two-story noise box, with lots of big tables for the big Chinese-family gatherings—complete with bottles of Dewar's and/or Harvey's Bristol Cream—that provide much of its commerce. Varnished knotty pine, bamboo, floral wallpaper, red-and-gold carved paneling, ceiling lanterns as big across as kettle drums. Downstairs, at the back, there is an icebox with a glass door—inside, cans of 7-Up, Coke, Tab. Upstairs, at the front, the cashier's station—the cashier keeps an eye on a small black-and-white TV when he is not cashiering. In the background there is music —have you heard "Oh! Susannah," loud, in Chinese? To clear a table just vacated by, say, a dozen celebrants, a plastic tub is placed at the table's center, and into it the dishes are clangorously flung. Two tubs going at once is really something.

The menu lists 183 items. Among them: baked chicken with salt, an extraordinary bird, pale and glistening, its moist meat (which tastes the way chickens tasted before they started assembling them in factories) imbued with the flavor of chicken fat—the bird is served with a dark, oily sauce, and with a powdery woodsy zest. The roasted duck, Cantonese style, is served sliced through, like a loaf of French bread. Its skin has a smooth, browned surface, as if it were shellacked, and its meat, which is extremely tender, is of intense duck flavor—the accompanying dark sauce is salty and sweet. The braised seafood in bird's nest is not in a real nest, but in a simulation thereof that is fashioned of crisped strands of taro root, a tuber much used in Hakka cooking. The nest tastes like a salted crunchy you might nibble with beer. And it is filled to the rim with sweet shrimps, chunks of sea cucumber, shafts of octopus (delicately rubbery, ocean-flavored), plump scallops, pale and tender squid and—of striking color in this pale setting—florets of crisp green broccoli. The baked prawns are huge, served in their shells, within which the mildly spiced sweet white meat is dry on the surface, juicy near the center—the edible shells become almost powdery in the baking. There is a good dish here of braised oysters and barbecued pork, the oysters hot tender morsels of slightly briny seafood in among chunks of fibrous and crusted meat that is salty, smoky, strong. The disparate elements are in a brown sauce to which scallion greens, strong scallion whites, and much fresh ginger have been added. Dozens of slivers of beef (medium rare) are the bulk of the dish called beef with satay sauce. The listing on the menu is asterisked, which means that it is supposed to be hot and spicy, but in fact the food is dominated by chunks of the rather sweet red pepper that, with onions and a sturdy brown broth, make up the sauce of the title.

Among the dishes the menu specifically identifies as Hakka is one called abalone with bone marrows and boneless duck feet. The disc-shaped meats of the abalone are good, as if of a naturally smoky seafood; the bone marrows are pale, soft, bland, rich; and the duck feet are cartilaginous and resilient, and probably not immediately accessible to the untutored palate. The dish also includes tiny whole bird eggs, baby corn of strong flavor and crisp, sweet, brilliant-green snow peas, all in a sauce that is touched with ginger. The deep-fried pig intestine consists of shafts of tubular gut about as long as your little finger, longitudinally bifurcated. The convex surfaces are dark red, as if painted. The inner concave surfaces are the color of the pale fat of which they consist. Few foods available to you are of an elemental animality to equal these musky morsels. Your waiter tries to steer you away from stewed pork with taro. He points at his stomach to indicate the section of hog from which the meat is carved. Do not be scared off. Though there is much fat on this pork, it is easily separated from the dark and exceptionally succulent meat, the big slices of which are served with chunks of dark taro cut to the same size and shape as the pork, so that when the dish is presented you cannot visually distinguish the tuber from the tummy. Taro has the texture of a firm turnip, and a flavor much like that of a sweetened yam. The meat and the root are served on leaves of Chinese cabbage, which wilt a little, but retain much of their crispness and all their sharp flavor.

The so-called fried rice chef's special seems like a dish aimed at tourists. The stuff comes in a deep glass plate that is about a foot across. Half the contents are red, the other half white, like two flavors of ice cream in a paper cup. The red side is sweet and sour, the white thick and bland. Shrimp and chicken are part of the stew-like mushes, under which there is a layer of yellow rice. For starch you are better off with pan-fried noodles with chicken and shrimp—some of the noodles are crisp, some are limp, and the shrimp and chicken are fine, as are the morsels of broccoli that add color and crunchiness to the dish.

Tea is gratis. Beer may be obtained in the grocery store that is across Mott Street and a few doors south.

★ L'HOSTARIA DEL BONGUSTAIO

75 East 55th Street
LUNCH, MONDAY TO FRIDAY; DINNER, MONDAY TO SATURDAY. CLOSED SUNDAY.
Reservations, 751-3530.
Credit cards: AE, MC, V.
Very expensive.

You enter to red tiles on the anteroom floor, and low plaster archways through which you see or proceed to the little dining areas that make up this small, posh place. The intended look is of a house in the Italian subtropics, airy and summery and sheltered from the sun. And the plaster walls—ivory-colored or pale Venetian pink—the leafy cloth on the upholstered chairs, the pale linen, the decorative pottery of soft earth colors and the abundant light manage to suggest that this luxurious spot, though it is merely a ground-floor store in a big-city building, is a low stucco house with an orange roof, the thick walls of which keep the interior cool in even the hottest months. It is not surprising, therefore, that the place is frequented by prosperous Italians, the gentlemen tailored and tonsured, manicured and tanned, their ladies besilked and demure, their occasional children angelic to behold. When you are among lots of them in this setting, you feel like a tourist in a better world.

Presently, however, you are wishing for a waiter from the old country, which is to say New York, one who speaks English well enough to talk to Americans who have no Italian; one with the sense to tell you in advance which items on the printed menu are not available when you are about to spend ten minutes of study; one who knows when to go away and when to come back; one who does not let you in on the secret of what part of Italy he is from, unless you make it clear you are dying to know. This same staff does not so presume when they are dealing with the aristocratic Italians, with whom they seem to share a commonality of understanding as to class.

But the food is the same for all. The seafood salad is cold and briny, crisp with onions and celery, the shrimp, however, slightly medicinal. The salad of mushrooms and celery is fresh, the mushrooms smooth and creamy white, the celery crunchy, the tart dressing fortified with grated cheese. You can have strong prosciutto, rimmed with fat, with ripe figs, their grainy and juicy pulp bursting from the leathery but tender skins.

Presumably the inaccuracies of the menu devolve from a degree of ambition in its conception that could not be matched in the reality. But when the name and description of the dish do not match the item it calls forth, your waiter makes no effort to forewarn you of the fact. So trenette (just like linguine) with pesto and potatoes turns out to be the green noodle with pesto sauce, the sauce powerfully garlicked, the noodles firm and tender, the potato lost somewhere in the translation. Still, this is a good dish. Even better is the paglia e fieno al funghi porcini, in which the green and white noodles and the wild mushrooms are served in a creamy sauce that is thick with ground walnuts. The pasta with five cheeses is profoundly cheesy, and would, you may be certain, be equally so with four—this is a showpiece of complexity first, good food only in passing. Avoid assiduously the fettuccine with Scottish salmon, a marriage made in Zabar's.

Lots of risotto (rice) on the menu, and nobody warns you that the risotto verde—described as with spinach and leeks—is without leeks. Good food nevertheless, the grainy rice and fresh spinach achieving a kind of high intensity of spinach flavor when you potentiate the dish with the strong cheese that is supplied. You can also get risotto with strawberries (not a dessert)—the puréed berries are not sweetened, and the fruit and grain are made into a solid and earthy porridge in which the flavor of the strawberries is like a touch of fruity wine.

If the perfect broiling of the red snapper does not offset the imperfect freshness thereof, opt instead for the deep-fried squid and shrimp, in which the crunchy shrimp are in contrast to the slightly chewy and astringent slivers of squid—the mingled seafoods are superbly crisped in their deep-frying, and when you squeeze on the lemon they come to bright life. Some good chicken dishes, including pollo all'aceto, in which the boned morsels of nicely browned bird are flavored with rosemary and moistened with a mildly tart vinegar sauce; and pollo in potacchio, in which the chicken is served in an oily tomato sauce that is at once peasanty, even heavy, and fragrant with herbs. The menu asserts that scaloppine of veal will be prepared any way you want it, but fails to mention that exceptions are made of those preparations with which the kitchen is unfamiliar. The veal is good, and the spicy pizzaiola sauce you may select is tart and lively, thick with little chunks of tomato. Some good vegetables: fresh peas mingled with slivers of strong ham, or in a solid tomato sauce; deep-fried zucchini, crisp and light, which arrives without the basil the menu promises. The white beans are dull. And among the salads the red radicchio, which comes with arugula, is as fresh and crisp as if just torn from the ground—it is dressed with a tangy vinaigrette.

Sharp Parmesan cheese, creamy (if somewhat bland) Fontina, soft and nutty Taleggio, pungent Gorgonzola—all the cheeses here are good. The place has served up perfect raspberries—tart and bursting with sweet juice—in thick whipped cream. The cheese cake is sugary and light—misplaced delicacy.

★★ HUBERTS

102 East 22nd Street
LUNCH, MONDAY TO FRIDAY; DINNER, MONDAY TO SATURDAY. CLOSED SUNDAY.
Reservations, 673-3711.
Credit cards: AE.
Very expensive.

"Oo-bears" is the pronunciation you get when you telephone the place, though the title derives from the surname of a perfectly native proprietor. You arrive and observe that the lady ahead of you is kissed on both cheeks (in a barely contactual at-arms-length embrace) by the birdlike hostess, her gentleman on one. You note that the young woman who emerges from a back room to take your coat is demurely clothed from shoulder to ankle, and that her eyes are to the ground, as if she were taking up the collection. You are led to your table by a short-tonsured and seemingly neutered young maleoid who, like most of the well-scrubbed staff, will, when his work program here is completed, return to his post at the Salvation Army. Huberts has a bad case of the paralyzing solemnities, but, fortunately, booze is served, and the staid crowd this place lures from behind the stone walls of Gramercy Park redoubts is so at home in this proper place that they tipple as if they were enjoying the privacy of their own drawing rooms. After a few marts, they do make enough noise to drown out the Army major, who whispers the specials of the day to you and answers questions about the menu.

The room is softly lit. Its uncurtained windows have small windowpanes, as in Colonial houses. The fireplace is without a roaring blaze. The pale walls are hung with small engravings. The floor is of plain wood. A seemingly misplaced large, curved bar is, of course, left over from the previous restaurant. (Serious drinkers have not yet made it a repair.) Your host and hostess sometimes stand with their backs to it and look out over their restaurant. Their radiant contentment is that of the headmaster and headmistress gazing over the bowed heads of good children at their studies. They maintain a certain distance. If anything needs prompt attention on the dining-room floor, they know where to go to find someone to do the job.

Considering all of which, you may be astonished to learn that the food is far from bloodless. There is, for example, plenty of garlic in the homemade white cheese with fresh herbs. This is something like flavored Boursault, but with a light and fluffy quality of being just made, and certainly never packaged—you may spread the strong and fragrant stuff on the good hard crusts that are served with it. Crisp, sweet shrimp and fresh local oysters are served hot in a smooth cream sauce that is flavored with coriander leaves—very stunning, this dish, for how well the disparate elements add up. No pasta appetizers on the menu, but the beloved noodle is regularly offered—sometimes with a thick white sauce in which an assortment of sautéed wild mushrooms (cèpes and chanterelles and the like) are mingled with slivers of good, strong bacon. The rabbit pâté is rimmed with fat, dotted with hazelnuts, and it is moist and meaty and pungently seasoned, lovely with the garlic-flavored crusts that accompany the heady meat. But the duck livers seem warmed rather than sautéed—you wish the chunks of rare organ meat were browned and crusted, to offset their heaviness. The herbed wine sauce that moistens them is fine.

Two uncracked lobster claws flank the meat of the tail upon a field of green and white pasta, all in a chunky tomato sauce—the lobster is well-cooked, firm and juicy, but the sauce is almost harshly acidic, and the lobster and its elaborate setting seem to be at odds. There are no such difficulties with the so-called salmon jordan. The perfectly poached pink fish, stuffed with a light mousse of sole, is coated with an intense, velvety, mahogany-colored red-wine sauce (a Jordan cabernet, no less, is used) and adorned with minced scallion greens that are like zesty grace notes to the rich seafood. Muscovy ducks are the rage all over town. This place roasts them rare and serves slices of the glistening red meat in a sauce that is nutted and sweet-spiced. Slices of brandied Seckel pear adorn the bird, and the texture of the hot fruit is lovely with the firm meat, as are the strong beet purée and gentle nockerl that garnish it. Tenderloin of pork can be pale and pallid meat, but here the powerful flavor of fresh ginger in the creamy sauce and the subtleness and smokiness of shiitake mushrooms make this a striking dish. The rack of lamb comes rarer than you ordered it. The meat is strong, but its flavor is not distinctively that of lamb, and the so-called rosemary crust has little flavor of its own and imparts none to the meat.

On a thin, brown and crumbly crust, a shallow layer of light, creamy custard, upon which slivers of tangy quince—a superb fruit tart. Between layers of chocolate-flavored, nutted meringue, a couple of deep layers of Grand Marnier ice cream, the whole served under strong chocolate syrup and crunchy hazelnuts—a very good frozen Grand Marnier soufflé. Alternated with three layers of the light sponge cake called genoise, much almond-flavored whipped cream, slivered almonds over the top—a very nice layer cake. The chocolate fudge cake is of powerful flavor, but rather heavy—the terrific whipped cream served with it leavens the weight somewhat. The maple sugar ice cream, with walnuts and maple syrup, is a swell sundae.

When you telephone to reserve, be sure to specify that you do not want any of those tables just inside the door, for they are very much in the traffic.

★ HUNAM

845 Second Avenue (near 45th Street)
LUNCH, MONDAY TO FRIDAY; DINNER, DAILY.
Reservations, MU 7-7471.
Credit cards: AE, CB, DC.
Medium-priced.

From the day of its opening, when this place introduced the cooking of Hunan province to the citizens of New York, it has been serving some of the best Chinese food in New York—along with some of the most mundane. Hunam is crowded, low-ceilinged, noisy. It was once a snotty place, and some of the higher-ups can still be surly, but the waiters nowadays are pleasant and helpful, even though their rudimentary English cannot always cope with the task of describing complex dishes.

Dishes to eat: turnip cake—golden fritter balls that are fluffy and firm, lightly oiled and solid, garlicky and spicy, tasting vaguely of seafood and only mildly of turnip, wondrous when they are dipped into the vibrant dark-brown sauce they are served with; hacked chicken—the familiar dish, but served here in a better than average version, broad strips of cool white meat with, spooned over them, a peanut sauce that is thick and hot, the dish garnished with sprigs of wildly fragrant Chinese parsley; spicy crisp whole sea bass—an enormous crusty beast that, within its deep-fry shell, is snowy and flaky and fresh, the entire production moistened with a sweet vegetable sauce that is shot through with greens and onions and suffused with a spicy, fiery heat; shredded lamb tripe—cartilaginous but tender strands of tripe in a peppery sauce that is laced with coriander leaves; duck with smoked flavor—large sections of the bird, the skin black and parchmentlike, the meat moist, the whole dish like fibrous, tender and oiled smoke; sliced leg of lamb—minuscule cutlets of the meat in hot oil and strands of scallion green and discs of scallion white, mingled with smoky mushrooms, a dish that is so utterly satisfying that to eat it any way but greedily is self-punishment; Hunam beef—slivers of tender meat, medium rare, with a few strands of scallion, in a dark and oily and garlic-flavored sauce that is studded with the red peppers that are the basis of this cuisine's hotness, the mound of sauced meat garnished with a clump of crisp watercress; eggplant family style—big chunks of the roasted vegetable, the soft oily pulp still attached to the blackened skin, the mound of eggplant spread with shredded vegetables and strands of bright ginger.

Dishes of less interest: corned pork—cold slabs of meat that are indistinguishable from canned corned beef; Lake Tung Ting shrimp and fillet of sea bass with shrimp roe sauce—a couple of compendia bound together in pale oil, decent ingredients that seem, in each instance, to cancel one another out to yield nothing, which, admittedly, is quite a trick; bamboo steamer's spareribs—tomato-red ribs in what seems like a honeyed breading, oddly spiced, so that what you consume now causes your lips to swell later.

Dishes to avoid: stuffed honey crisp bananas—a leaden item in an armor crust, sprinkled with red sugar (no longer served with honey).

The house will prepare the hot dishes with less than the usual spice if you wish, but the amount they normally use seems right once you get accustomed.

Sometimes you have to refuse here: you ask for a Perrier and you get a glass of ice cubes and bar-hose fizz. And certain dishes appear to be impossible to get unless you are Chinese; insisting helps not at all. One waiter here has developed the impression that Occidentals will not eat duck served on the bone.

★★INDIA PAVILION

325 East 54th Street
LUNCH, MONDAY TO FRIDAY; DINNER, DAILY.
Reservations, 223–9740.
Credit cards: AE, MC, V.
No liquor.
Inexpensive.

This little cave is a bit ramshackle, but that is obscured by the gay cheer of the young people who often crowd it from end to end of its long narrow dining room. The ceiling is low, almost everyone sits at one of the long row of small tables; for larger parties there are a couple of booths and two large tables at the rear, on a platform. The cursory decorations include carved wooden screens, a hammered brass medallion, an Indian stringed instument mounted on the wall. During the days of intense cold a space heater glowed from a cranny at the rear. The menus have been heavily emended by hand, but they still sport some of the lowest prices for good food anywhere in midtown Manhattan. You bring your own alcohol, too, so eating here is like putting aside a little something for your dotage. Many domestic jugs and imported magnums are in evidence —this food creates thirst.

The greeting and much of the serving are performed by a stocky, swarthy Indian whose smile makes of his face a dark sun and whose accent makes of the English language a melody played on a golden horn. Sometimes he is assisted by a lady, a compatriot of ample substance, in a snug coverall. They are a casual two, to be sure, friendly and smiling, but they take their work, as they say, to heart, which gives them and the place dignity.

Begin your dinner here with the India Fried Shrimp, small crunchy shrimp in a thick, dark sauce that is at once hot and sweet. Do not make the error of drinking beer with this kind of food, for these sauces are laced with vegetables and sweet spices, and wines of all kinds are fine with them, beer all wrong. Another good way to start is with the Assorted Hors d'Oeuvres, a collection of fruit and vegetable turnovers and fritters, battered, deep-fried—gentle food, each of the items distinctive of its principal component: chickpeas and green peas, bananas and potatoes, eggplant and whatever. They are served with a heavy sauce that is like a thick plum preserve. The Mulligatawny is like a heavy split-pea soup laced with a leafy vegetable, and you wish it were much hotter, for it is a little leaden at this tepid temperature.

Your Chicken Tandoori is the familiar dramatic thing, red and black, spicy and moist, the lightly burnt edges of the rather huge half-bird like a built-in zest. The dish is not made from a great chicken—it is probably frozen—but the preparation yields a sturdy plate of food. A Mrs. Kalayaniwalla, the menu informs you, is a winner of many prizes for cooking in India, and you are informed further that she has released her secret recipe for Moghali Badami Duck to our own India Pavilion. This is a spiced roasted duck, moist and crisp, almost crackling, and it is served with a vividly contrasting sauce that is as grainy as cereal, slightly sweetened, and made high by a heavy dose of coriander leaves—this is a long way from the underspiced spicy food you get in most Indian restaurants.

Those curries and vindaloos are served here, too, and according to yet another pronouncement on the menu, "Our curries are medium spiced. Hot sauce served on request." Don't make the request, for one man's medium is another's massacre, and a searingly hot sauce that is but a dash of salt to an Indian is probably the obliteration of all flavor to your unaccustomed palate. If you like the aroma of lamb, cooking, you will probably like the Lamb Curry here, for the aroma of lamb on the fire is principally that of lamb fat, and this spicy stew is like a distillate of that flavor, gamy and rich, perfumed with coriander. The Beef Vindaloo is yet another powerful stew, filled with huge chunks of fibrous beef, the thick and spicy sauce suggesting oils and vegetables. These things come with fluffy, buttery rice, mysteriously tasty, though the saffron with which it is allegedly made is difficult to detect. Of the breads, the paratha lacks the richness of the best versions, but the puri, that airy pillow of glistening, glazed dough, is superbly delicate next to this substantial food. The pickles, chutneys and yogurt are fine, the usual thing. The dahl, the tradional purée of lentils, is tastier than most because it is mingled with those fragrant coriander leaves. Sometimes you think they do things just for laughs, and as you sample an unheralded garnish of spicy raw onions, you realize you are being watched by your host. "Onions too hot for you, sir?" He seems to sing the question, smiling a little like a prankster. You need something to quiet those onions: "May I have a little more rice?" "By all means! Lot more!"

Splendid Bakhlawa, a flaky top, center of crunchy honeyed nuts, a bottom crust of browned and honey-soaked pastry. The two other Eastern desserts will strike you perhaps as interesting. There is ice cream and, surprisingly, awful tea.

The slightly mournful strains of Indian music make a background of soft sound. When things are slow a sinister chap in sweater, scarf and apron seems to make several extra trips from the kitchen through the dining room to the facilities. Sometimes the lights go off when a novice customer brushes the light switch while hanging his coat in the self-service coat room.

★★LE JACQUES COEUR

448 East 79th Street
DINNER. CLOSED MONDAY.
Reservations, 249-4920.
Credit cards: AE, CB, DC, MC, V.
Expensive.

As much as can be made of one half of a railway car has here been made. Past the little bar at the front, and you are in what amounts to a good-size smoking section, along the sides of which burnt-orange banquettes have been installed. Before them small tables have been placed, on the aisle sides of which stand handsome armchairs of walnut-colored bentwood and pale cane. That aisle—where chairs are back to back —is no more than one slender body wide. Only the svelte work this floor. And yet, once you are seated, conditions that in less pleasant surroundings would seem crowded, are here snug. Along one side of the room an ivory-colored wall is hung with pottery and prints. The wall across the way is faced with tinted, mirrored glass. The low ceiling has been sprayed with that furry stuff that soaks up sound, and the floor is carpeted. Even when the place is packed—as it often is—it is not noisy. And it usually gets a civilized crowd.

One of the slims is your hostess. She usually greets you, explains the menu—in, remarkably for these days, the manner of an informed human addressing an inquiring one—and takes your order. To eat at Le Jacques Coeur is to experience the startling sensation of finding yourself in competent hands.

Not only in the dining room, but, as it develops, in the kitchen as well. The kitchen hands prepare the likes of a pâté en croûte in which the gamy forcemeat is encased in a flaky pastry. At its center is a core of rich foie gras, it is dotted with pistachios, and it is garnished with a cool jelly that is actually situated in a little inner pastry compartment all its own. You will like that meat pâté, but the fish pâté will astonish you, for unlike almost all dishes of that category around town, this one has flavor—of fresh, clear bass, spiced and sweetened and intensified by green peppercorns, shallots and truffles. The restaurant's snails are fine—the butter literally thick with parsley. The smoked salmon, though without special merit, is unexceptionable.

A hot slab of grilled striped bass is fresh and browned and moist, and it is served with a Béarnaise sauce that is striking for seasoning that is strong but not excessive, and for the freshness of its abundant tarragon. The house makes a specialty of pigeon, serving the roasted half-birds packed with a moist stuffing of wild rice that has been mixed with fresh spinach. The meat of the pigeon is dark and rich—vaguely like chocolate—and the reddened sauce that moistens the dish is based on a sturdy stock. Game of the season is usually on hand, including, on occasion, wild rabbit that has been stewed until the fibrous meat is tender and falling from its bones. There are mushrooms and onions along with the juicy meat, all in a polished and winy sauce. The Jack of Hearts is not, however, invariably a winning card. You order a steak au poivre vert, and you are pleased to discover that the sauce is not the usual thing—it is creamy, mustard augments the spice of the pepper, and the two seasonings blend well in the rich base. But the steak itself is almost inedibly tough. A salad, in which fresh greens have been dressed with salty Roquefort mashed into olive oil, is recommended to partially compensate.

The tarte Tatin is hot, the slices of apple dark and caramelized, and the crème fraîche that is spooned on is smooth. That same cream may be had with raspberries that are something less than impeccable. Those berries are also converted into a raspberry mousse—it is more than a degree too gelatinous. The winner is the distinctive floating island, in which the island is a muffin-shaped almond dumpling—sweet and nutty— that is served in a cool and thick custard.

Late in the evening, when the place has partially emptied out, it is sometimes possible for couples to sit side-by-side on a banquette, and to have two small tables converted into one large one.

★★JANE STREET SEAFOOD CAFÉ

31 Eighth Avenue (at Jane Street)
DINNER.
No reservations (243-9237).
Credit cards: AE, MC, V.
Medium-priced.

This place has something of New England about it, or, anyway, elements that go to make up a romantic imagining of a snug tavern—complete with fireplace—in an old fishing village by the sea. The curtains that hang over the two small front windows are tied to the side. The floor is of old wood, the walls of brick or pale plaster. The ceiling is low. There are candles on the bare wooden tables. The café is not, however, pure nineteenth century. A four-bladed fan depends from the ceiling. Electric fans that swivel are mounted on the walls. (When needed, there is even air conditioning.) And it is mostly modern art that hangs here and there. Certainly the fish is timely. For of the seafood restaurants that have sprung up around town in recent years, in response to the fashion away from red meat to white, none serves fresher seafood than this one. Your ever-present shirt-sleeved host remains in the background while keeping his eye on everything. This has the splendid effect of bringing out the best in his waiters and waitresses, who treat you with a courtesy that thrives on the extra appreciation it receives from the boss. The folks they are treating so well are a Greenwich Village crowd (cabs do not draw up), all the classes, from those in sneakers to those in pin-striped suits.

They sit down to some of the best bread in New York, crusty and resilient and profoundly grainy, and to a bowl of coleslaw that is of coarsely chopped cabbage so crisp you will conclude that its creamy dressing, sharpened with celery seeds, was just added—the bowl is refilled as promptly as it is emptied. You will have very likely emptied it again by the time you have ordered and received your steamed mussels. Two dozen of them, and the deep bowl in which they are mounded up, arrive encased in a clear plastic wrapper. The film is removed when the dish is before you, and you are at once engulfed in the fragrances of garlic, wine, herbs and the fresh hot mollusks. The mussels stand in an inch of broth at the center of which you will find a slice of wine-soaked bread. The steamed littlenecks are just as good, though you get only a dozen and a half, and no polyethylene. Though they are hot, they are tender, which means that their steaming was carefully kept brief, and they are served with a little dish of garlicky and buttery brine, into which you dip them. The deep-fried oysters and deep-fried soft-shell clams are fresh, tender, lightly battered, and delicately crisped, and you may enliven them with a tangy and creamy tartar sauce—but good as they are, they have little seafood character. The baked clams are made with chopped clams, a manner of preparation that is yet to be justified—the dish is little more than a vaguely oceanic breading. The Manhattan clam chowder is fine, the lobster bisque rather special for its creaminess and for the intensity of its lobster-meat flavor.

There is an everyday menu (photocopied and supplied to you in a clear vinyl holder) and a listing of specials of the day (handwritten on a five-by-eight ruled card). It is from the former that you will choose the fluffy broiled fillet of gray sole—it is fresh and moist, and it is sprinkled with paprika, so you can differentiate the white meat from its white plate. But the index card is the source of the most interesting main courses: an inch-thick swordfish steak that is intensified by its enrichment with butter and its flavoring of wine and herbs; snowy, flaky red snapper surmounted by thick, crunchy strands of sautéed potato and by sautéed onion that retains much of its bite; fried whole smelts, crisp and light, which you dip in tartar sauce and eat from head to tail. Fresh flounder is served whole, carefully broiled. The bluefish has all its natural oiliness and strong flavor. The so-called broiled lobster is really steamed and then broiled—a poorly conceived method that dilutes the lobster's natural juice by steaming, while failing to add the special charring flavor that broiling all the way imparts. But the lobster is fresh, and you can have yours just steamed. Once in a rare while you will detect the flavor of butter that has been kept around the kitchen too long. It is excellent butter from your table, however, that you insert in perfect baked potatoes.

The walnut pie is all hot, spicy nuts and cool whipped cream. When the pumpkin pie has been refrigerated, it is a little clammy. The key-lime pie has a clear citrus flavor and a good graham-cracker crust, but it is more gelatinous than you want it. A rich and sticky chocolate mousse is tinctured with amaretto liqueur—not a bad note.

People stand in line to get in here at the peak of the dinner hour on weekend nights.

• J. G. MELON

1291 Third Avenue (at 74th Street)
LUNCH AND DINNER.
No reservations (650-1310).
No credit cards.
Inexpensive.

This place is adorned, if that is the correct word, with melons. There is a neon melon and a melon clock. There are melon paintings—a surreal melon in a de Chirico wasteland, a painted balloon melon pulling upward on a painted string, an endless slice of watermelon cut off at the ends only by the picture frame. There are melon photographs, models of melons, a melon bas-relief, a papier-mâché melon. Contrary to what you might expect, the effect is meloncholia. Midweek cocktail time, and the bar is lined with losers drinking and smoking their lives away, truculently pretending they have the world by the olives in their martinis. Sad and lonely women at the bar giggle deliriously as soon as someone recognizes them. On occasion these folks' affected camaraderie is so well rendered that the place takes on a beery jollity. Melon's is not, however, what it was. It used to be atmospheric. But one of those smoke-eaters has been attached to the ceiling, and these days there is an unreal clarity in the Melon air, as in a color transparency from which the haze has been filtered out.

Here no one tends bar. Instead one woiks behighnastick. Leave the stick-tender a tip, and he does not say thank you. He says, "God love ya, m' darlin'." The place is ramshackle and cozy, popular and insular. Anybody may walk in, have a drink, something to eat, be treated all right. But to the crowds that overflow this place, it is knowing the bartenders, the waiters and waitresses, the host and half the other customers by name that is the lure. Many come here straight from the office and do not leave until bedtime.

Melon's is a barroom with a handful of tables, a closet-size kitchen built in, ten tables more at the back. The tables are covered with green-and-white gingham, equipped with a sheaf of paper napkins and a bottle of Heinz ketchup. The menu is painted on a slate on the wall. The food is what you expect.

The chili, peculiarly, tastes of commercial pre-ground black pepper, and it is adorned with onions that, chopped in advance, are devoid of strength. Still, the beans are firm, the concoction sturdy, and it will handle your hunger. The spinach salad is a bowl of wet food. Beef is probably brought in already ground, and it is bloodless by the time it is converted into burgers or chopped steaks. The unchopped steaks are a good bet—they are of decent, tender meat, accurately broiled, though the potatoes you get with them are those corrugated-looking frozen things that do dishonor to the name of pulp. The omelets are not really omelets, for instead of being turned in a pan, they are cooked—or overcooked—on a grill and then folded, so the inside is as dry as the outside. A surprise winner is the chicken salad—a big dollop of tasty chunks of chicken and crisp celery in a mayonnaise dressing, garnished with slightly tired raw vegetables and a hard-cooked egg. The desserts—including a lemon mousse pie that tastes like a lollipop—are uninspired.

• JIM McMULLEN

1341 Third Avenue (near 77th Street)
LUNCH AND DINNER.
No reservations (861-4700).
No credit cards.
Medium-priced.

Ordinarily only dumb animals en route to the last roundup find themselves in a situation like Jim McMullen at dinner hour. Maybe it is the herd instinct that draws crowds to this place. More likely it is the low prices, the nonthreatening, institutional-food neutrality of the menu, the placeless, motel vacuity of the banal décor. The three things you least expect to encounter at Jim McMullen are a strong flavor, a divergent opinion and a teetotaler. The epidemic here is culturally induced narcosis, maintained by the juice that flows over the bar in tank-car quantities every night. To keep up with the demand, a McMullen bartender does about a marathon per shift, in short sprints.

You enter to the bar, on your left, to pipe coatracks in the aisle on your right, attended by two young women. They work the racks doggedly, extracting and inserting coats like two souls doomed to eternal shopping. Their station is in the direct path of heavy two-way traffic, and by the end of the night, if they are not black and blue, they are pale and trembling.

You elbow your way to the far end of the bar, submit your name to a gent who maintains a little list (no reservations accepted), mingle with the crowd—in the manner of the pork mingling with the beans—have a drink if the currents carry you to within signaling distance of a bartender, and wait for your name to be bellowed. An hour's wait is not unusual, so you have plenty of time to study the crowd. The place attracts Al Haig lookalikes, Clark Kent lookalikes and Robert Redford lookalikes *manqués.* The ladies you will recognize from advertisements in this morning's *Times.* Early in the evening much of the clientele is sedate, even elderly, but by midnight a bit of sleazy sexiness in the women creeps in, truculence in the young men.

Eventually you are led to one of three dining rooms—they are not individually named, but for easy identification they may be referred to as Brick 'n' Plaque, Windows on the Backyard, and Cave à Vin Ordinaire. The tables are set with white linen over red, the aisles are patrolled by innumerable young men and women in Paul Stuart inspirations, and you are waited on by waiters and waitresses in blue oxford-cloth shirts and chino pants or skirts.

As you have waited for your table, so your clams have waited for you. Opened in advance, they are up to their eyebrows in melted ice, devoid of their original sparkle. The cocktail sauce is indispensable. The tomatoes in the tomato-and-onion salad are cold enough to hurt your teeth, but at least the onions have strength. When you opt for the tomatoes and mozzarella, it is like eating ice and wax. The big winner among the first courses is the melon and prosciutto—the ham has flavor, and the fruit is ripe.

For an ulcerated gastrointestinal tract, the chicken pot pie: under its glorious golden brown crust it consists of flour-thickened milk within which you will differentiate the vegetables, by their hardness, from the chicken's blandness. The fish—halibut or salmon or snapper—is fresh, and usually carefully broiled, but low on flavor, a condition that often results from extended cold storage. You get lamb chops of rather mild meat, cooked rarer than ordered, most of the flavor from the charring—the dish is graced with a jigger of cold green jelly. And the steak tartare is little more than spiced raw beef; the succulence of the dish—a function of juicy meat enriched by oil and egg yolk—is missing.

McMullen's apple pie is famous for its four-inch height at the center, and for innards so constructed, of layer upon layer of thick apple slices, that the cross section revealed where the pie is sliced looks like a cleverly constructed wall of flat stones. Unfortunately the tartness of the crisp fruit is obscured by excesses of sugar and cinnamon; and the top crust of the pie—really a browned custard—simply adds to the vapidity. The chocolate mousse is ordinary, the cheese cake a dull excess. And the hot fudge sundae —which, working from the top, consists of a maraschino cherry, mechanically produced whipped cream, a brown syrup that is more chocolate than fudge, and pretty good ice cream, all in a giant goblet—fails to offset its mediocrity by its size.

★ JOANNA

18 East 18th Street
LUNCH AND DINNER.
Reservations, 675-7900.
Credit cards: AE.
Expensive.

This restaurant/café is big, a long curved bar at one side, an acre of white-linened tables across the aisle. The two-story-high avocado-colored walls are dominated by gigantic mirrors and by huge photo enlargements of vivid color close-ups of the private parts of pretty flowers—petals, stamens, pistils, *everything*. From these murals we learn that when flowers are made as big as elephants, though they lose the visual qualities of flowers, they do not take on those of elephants.

Joanna is convivially spacious, hectic and airy as a three-ring circus at the Garden. And during the late hours it is as busy as Hell since the Fall. This is rejuvenated commercial space, à la SoHo, with fluted support columns rising through the room. A dark-red banquette cuts around and across the spread of tables. Along its path, tall lampposts are surmounted by spherical white lights. Soft rock beats in the background, but you hardly hear it. Everyone on Manhattan Island—from intellectual artisans to intellectual stockbrokers, the young on college allowances and the retired on social security—is apparently bent on trying this place at least once. They arrive in L. L. Bean flannel shirts, Paul Stuart flannel blazers, sleek fur coats and ratty ones, leg warmers, pea jackets, raccoon tricorns. But do not forget that, appearances notwithstanding, bohemia is dead. Even the weirdly dressed are clean as a marine. And that gentleman at the bar, in jeans in which it is possible only to stand, and the daubed lady, whose papillary modesty has been entrusted to a loosely knitted vest fastened by a single gold thread, are trying, simply, to do what is expected of them.

The menu is as motley as the crowd and twice as cute. Most entries flourish indefinite articles, e.g., "A Lightened Minestrone," "An Omelet Fines Herbs" (sic), "A Steak for Big Eaters," "A Grilled Fish." A fine kettle of bushwa. Still, if you choose well, you eat well.

Choose the Cotuit oysters, which are icy, firm and tangy, served with lemon only, and there is nothing else they need. The cold mussels do not rival the Cotuits, but they are good, their tarragon-flavored mayonnaise obvious and absurdly salty, but fine if used sparingly on these fresh mollusks. Joanna's gravlax is tender and tasty and perfumed, but the cured salmon seems to have lost most of its fish flavor, and the sweet mustard-and-dill sauce (served with it in the hollowed-out rind of half a lemon) obscures what little is left—good food, but you can tell it is salmon only by its color. Eschew the "Mosaic of Eel & Green Herbs," which is actually a block of grass veined with indeterminate protein.

The green tortellini with sauce provençale look and taste as if their garish hue were achieved by a badly misjudged spin of the TV color-balance selector. They taste of nothing in particular (which is exactly what they are stuffed with), and their red sauce aims for a cheap thrill, instead of flavor, with some harsh spices. But you cannot generalize about the pasta, for the white noodles with cabbage, string beans and cream are neither discolored nor otherwise vulgarly adulterated. The noodles are eggy, the beans green by nature and of fresh flavor, the strands of cabbage a nice smooth textural note, the cream sauce thick—satisfying food.

There are simple dishes, like the sandwich of Black Forest ham and Brie on pumpernickel: an inch of smoky red meat, ripe cheese, much strong mustard applied to the crusty bread; and there are coarse dishes, like the roast-beef hash: fibrous chunks of meat and firm potatoes, the great Frisbee-size pancake veined with spinach, crusted, powerfully peppered, adorned with a glistening poached egg and parsley; and dishes like those Mama left out for you when you were coming home for dinner after dark because you worked as an errand boy after school, such as the room-temperature half roasted chicken, Mama's masterpiece here moistened with a touch of lemony dressing; and dishes you can eat without a knife, like steak tartare, which comes in a serving the size of a stack of pancakes—you are shown the ingredients (the meat is recently ground), asked which of them you want included, which excluded, and you are then at the mercy of your waiter, who does a good job of dressing and seasoning, though on occasion he adds Worcestershire sauce to beef the way other people add soda to Scotch; and dishes to hold you through cocktail time tomorrow, such as choucroute, a daunting mound of rather sour kraut, studded with hard black juniper berries, surrounded by and covered over with steaming blood sausage—purple, soft and rich —assorted wursts, a slab of ham, and boiled new potatoes; and Third Avenue restaurant/saloon dishes, among them veal paillard, enough to form two layers on a big plate, the pale meat lightly browned, a dollop of loudly garlicked herb butter melting thereon. None of these dishes is memorable, none of them is seriously flawed. A couple of items to skip: the fried potatoes (leaden) and the fried zucchini (leaden).

Sometimes there is an interesting pear tart, crisp leaves of the sliced fruit, on apple sauce, on a nicely browned pastry. The house makes much of its chocolate desserts, of which the chocolate pound cake is claylike, the chocolate pecan pie swell—the nut-and-chocolate surface of the pie has been baked until it is chewy, like a sharp nut candy. Whipped cream is offered with all these desserts, and it is the real thing.

★ JOE ALLEN

326 West 46th Street
LUNCH AND DINNER.
Reservations, 581-6464.
Credit cards: MC, V.
Medium-priced.

Perfect figures and imperfect dispositions set apart the young waiters and waitresses at Joe Allen, the theatrical hangout. They are on duty here because they are not onstage elsewhere, and the noble struggle to the top of the theatrical heap does not always seem so noble when waiting on table is part of the course. Many of the strugglers here sublimate their impatience for success (bad) into exasperation with their customers (OK). But their moods are sweeter between the hours of curtain up and curtain down, for then the city and suburban interlopers on theatrical nights out are safely encaged in darkened auditoriums, and half the people who walk in are, like the help, between jobs. Everyone knows everyone. There is much greeting and kissing between the staff and the paying guests, much broad gesturing, even a good bit of that sly smiling and one-eyebrow flirting that would get lost onstage but could easily be picked up by movie and television cameras.

Self-display is the name of the theatrical game, and in this place you are not surrounded by people so much as you are by types: muscular choirboys and nubile ingénues, soubrettes and Earth Mothers, tweeded and bearded country gentlemen, husky street boys in leather and brass. Pity the poor producers, who, among these, their hirelings, look like mere men of the world. And pity mere men of the world, who look like mice.

Joe Allen is your standard restaurant-saloon—an entrance room with a big bar and a handful of tables, another room with tables and chairs, red-and-white-checked tablecloths, blackboard menus and a hectic little kitchen visible at the back. There is much brick and wood. You walk on wood floors. Theatrical posters and photos adorn the walls, and a skylight over the rear of the dining room illuminates a few tables when there is light in the sky. The rest of the place is lit by old-fashioned lamps that hang from the plaster ceiling.

Here you eat black-bean soup, which is thick, peppery, fragrant with clove and adorned with a slice of lemon, and it is good. Or you eat the shrimp cocktail (with the usual cocktail sauce) and discover that the house obtains pretty decent shrimp for these days. A dazzling variety of salads are served in great wooden bowls, and they are made with, variously, good greens, fresh cheeses and vegetables and meats, crunchy croutons, hard-boiled eggs that seem new, dressings that are sprightly. Once in a while this or that ingredient may be tired, and canned artichoke hearts always are.

The steaks are unimpeachable, the chopped steaks juicy, the fish fresh—albeit usually overdone. It is well to avoid dishes that are cooked in advance—the barbecued chicken and ribs are often dried out, and they are not rescued by their sweetish sauce. Omelets, of course, are made to your order, and they are usually well turned, slightly browned. You can get them only at lunch.

Beer goes well with most of this food, and the draft beer arrives lively, with a creamy, long-lasting head.

Something called a hot-fudge éclair is really an ice cream éclair with a good, thick, hot, almost black sauce. The carrot cake is moist, sweet and spicy, the chocolate brownie cake rich and generously nutted. Avoid the tapioca, which is gelatinous and icky.

★ JOE & ROSE

745 Third Avenue (near 46th Street)
LUNCH, MONDAY TO FRIDAY; DINNER, MONDAY TO SATURDAY. CLOSED SUNDAY.
Reservations, 355-8874.
Credit cards: AE, DC.
Very expensive.

On the fringe of Steak Row, and only a slight variation on the meat-and-potatoes theme, Joe & Rose is less self-consciously he-man than some of its lusty competitors. The restaurant has, however, established its manhood. For this is one of those places that kept going while all else about it was being razed. There are photographs in the barroom of Joe & Rose going about its business during the demolition of every other building on its block, and then during construction of the skyscraper that today surrounds and dwarfs the plucky holdout. The place must once have had its own construction programs, for it gives evidence of having accreted, room by room, during a long history. The rooms are painted the color of coffee (regular), there is harmless art on the walls and photographic portraits of departed members of the family that still runs this place. The walls of the back room are muraled with whimsical townscapes —rooftops and turrets, treetops and spires—and from back here you may see, through an open portal, directly into the gleaming kitchen, wherein, on occasion, a venerable matriarch, silver-haired and all in white, sits and stares out.

The waiters wear limp linen jackets. Some of them look up over their Franklin glasses at you, down through them at their order pads. The customers are neat and straight. Many of them give every sign of having eaten in this place for decades, with the same mates—you see ritual dinners endured in perfect silence. Yes, jollier folk come too, as well as certain groups among whom the eldest male members wear expressions which suggest that all their facial nerves have been severed. At lunchtime Joe & Rose is just a busy midtown eatery.

As a steak-and-chop house, the place is reliable. As an Italian restaurant it is of interest principally as a living record of the mostly redded food that went as Italian cooking in the days when Joe and Rose were young. The local bluepoint oysters and cherrystone clams are fresh, served with a strong, standard cocktail sauce and accompanying Tabasco and horseradish, with which you may fortify it to your taste. For no less than $9 you get an admittedly copious spread of strong, smoky prosciutto over lots of ripe melon. The idea of preparing a pasta sauce when it is ordered is unthinkable in kitchens of this kind, so you will avoid the clam sauce, which was assembled at about the time they started taking the chairs down off the tables. But the manicotti is fine —in this version the big tubes of hot and creamy ricotta cheese are overlaid with slices of mozzarella cheese that become brown and pully when the dish, in its strong meat sauce, is baked onto its plate.

Two gigantic sides of broiled bass—fresh, floured, browned—are a little low on seafood sparkle, but not bad if what you want is dinner and enough to take home for tomorrow's lunch. You get about as many broiled scallops as are required to conceal a large dinner plate—these are breaded and browned, too, and if they suffer a little from their abundance of butter, generous use of lemon brings them to life. All the seafood dishes are served with a thick tartar sauce that is bright, creamy, tart. The broiled chicken is a bland bird, but it is well made, cooked through but still moist, lightly charred. Eschew the veal and peppers and the scaloppine dishes—they suffer severely from automatic comparisons with better versions all over town.

All of which is probably beside the point, for at Joe & Rose it is red meat you seek. The sirloins and filets mignons are big, fibrous but tender, blood-juicy within their seared crusts, accurately prepared most of the time. The huge lamb chops are just as good, and they have vivid, strong lamb flavor. You will, of course, wish to supplement your surfeit of meat with an excess of potatoes. The chunky hash browns are salted and a little greasy, peppery, crisped at the edges. The lyonnaise potatoes are much like those, but with slippery strands of sautéed onion in among the hefty slices of tuber.

The strudel, rumcake, and cheese cake are of no distinction. There are ice cream items.

No wine list is printed up, but bottles of all (Italian) kinds are on display. One waiter recommends a barolo to one of his clients, quoting a price of $25. One of his colleagues passes by, overhears, argues that the correct price is $17.50. A third chances on the scene and says that the gattinara is better anyway. A conference ensues. The man orders chianti.

★★ JOE'S

79 MacDougal Street (near Bleecker Street)
LUNCH AND DINNER. CLOSED TUESDAY.
Reservations, 473–8834.
Credit cards: AE, MC, V.
Medium-priced.

Joe's has always been one of the best of the old-style Italian restaurants in Greenwich Village: a little out of the way; a little more expensive and more elegantly appointed than most of its competitors; not frequented by the Bohemian side of Village society, rather by the stolid types whose supposed affiliations were whispered about; and serving food that went well beyond the narrow range of red sauces over noodles and veal that made up the bulk of what was served in the places with the checkered tablecloths and candles in Chianti bottles.

In the old days the riffraff stayed away; perhaps they still do; but now it is difficult to tell—it is fashionable to dress like riffraff no matter what your status, and these T-shirted and dungareed neighbors may pay their checks and pull away in a chauffeured limousine that is just like the one waiting for those obviously moneyed advertising types making all the noise. There are still a few seeming-underground potentates around—they are very stiff, apparently offended by the relaxation of standards.

You ask for the fried zucchini as soon as you sit down. This establishes you as one who knows his way around the customs and secrets of this place and, in addition, provides you with some excellent fried zucchini! It is traditionally munched, in this restaurant, during perusal of the menu, on which, by the way, you will not find said fried zucchini. (Think of the insular types—there must be such—who have been eating here for decades and have never had the famous zucchini.) The stuff comes wrapped in a napkin—the thin strands of the vegetable have been lightly breaded and deep-fried in extremely hot oil, so that the breading is extremely crisp, the strong-tasting squash barely cooked. You eat it with your fingers.

Meanwhile you have ordered your dinner, beginning, probably, with the quite remarkable stuffed mushrooms. These stuffed mushrooms are unlike any other stuffed mushrooms in town—no oiled, herbed breading; no minced mushroom stems; just cheese—ricotta and something much louder on top, the mushrooms themselves sautéed until dark, the cheese lightly browned. One order consists of four such mushrooms, which seems paltry, but they are worth more than the price. There are excellent baked clams, juicy, tender, the breading delicately browned. And you can have one of the clams and one of the mushrooms as part of the pretty good hot antipasto, which also includes some thoroughly sautéed eggplant and a huge shrimp. What distinguishes this hot antipasto from all others is its red sauce—it is studded with huge capers and loud olives.

Nowadays when you order the Home Made Egg Noodles, Carbonara Sauce, you are getting green noodles. True, green noodles are made with eggs, but one does not think of something called an egg noodle as being green. Hues aside, the food is delicious. The noodles clearly *are* made on the premises; they retain the flavor of spinach, and they are served in a thick, creamy egg-and-cheese sauce that has been mixed with slivers of smoky ham. The same noodles can be had in a very meaty meat sauce—spicy and oily —to which fresh mushrooms have been added. For something more primitively red, there is a sharp and acidic tomato sauce on the manicotti—the pasta is thin, tender and firm, and the filling is a simple one of steaming ricotta cheese.

Chicken Livers Cacciatore: soft, succulent livers; crisp mushrooms; a bright tomato sauce; a garnish of one potato croquette, fluffy, spicy and perfectly browned. Chicken Scarpariello: chunks of chicken on short lengths of bone, sautéed until browned, with chunks of garlic, big slices of mushroom and herbs. Veal Francese: good veal, if not the best, in a smooth and lemony sauce with slices of ham in the sauce, a nice variant; all in all, one of the best versions of this dish around. The stuffed veal cutlet, a sometime daily special, is good, but basically no more than a run-of-New York veal Parmigiana.

Good vegetables, including sautéed escarole that is dry, fibrous, salty, and mingled with the chunks of sautéed garlic that contribute to its potent flavor. Good salads, including, when available, very fresh and crisp arugula, in a clear, strong and salty vinegar dressing.

Joe's serves one of the best cheese cakes in New York. It is wildly excessive, very wet, intensely sweet, heavy and thickly studded with candied fruit. And an excellent zabaglione, hot and thick, and strongly flavored with good Marsala wine.

Joe's is a brightly lit, clean, comfortable place. The immaculate kitchen is visible through a portal at the rear of the front room. The waiters are at once casual and quick.

★★KITCHO

22 West 46th Street
LUNCH, MONDAY TO FRIDAY; DINNER, SUNDAY TO FRIDAY. CLOSED SATURDAY.
Reservations, 575–8880.
Credit cards: AE, DC.
Medium-priced.

The fancier of New York's Japanese restaurants are supported, principally, by the thousands of youngish Japanese male executives who work for Japanese companies in New York. These restaurants are their social centers, they come here in groups, dressed, almost uniformly, in dark worsted suits, white shirts and ties. They talk business, golf and baseball. They stack their attaché cases on empty chairs. Americans come to these places too, and they sit around and talk about Japanese food.

Past the elevator leading to the upper floors of the modern office building that houses this sleek establishment, to the little bar lined with Japanese men sipping beers and Bloody Marys and, often as not, watching baseball on the color TV. Farther back, rows of nifty black-topped tables under spherical paper lanterns that hang from the ceiling; farther back still, a square dining room similarly furnished, but with a hint of a Japanese interior in the otherwise smooth, Western-modern rooms—rice-paper panels and a wall of wooden slats. Everything in the place is tasteful, if a little sterile, right down to the handsome stoneware ashtrays and tiny vases for the flowers on each table.

The waitresses here are motherly, which is good and bad. Unless you are Japanese, they try to steer you away from what Occidentals before you have not enjoyed, and efforts to learn the ins and outs of the Japanese-language menu that is printed on the back of the regular menu lead almost invariably to the allegation that all those things are really the same as the English-language items. Nevertheless, there is plenty of good food here, none that is bad.

As in most Japanese restaurants that do not specialize in raw-fish dishes, the sushi and sashimi lack the sparkle of what you get at the places with the busy sushi bars—the fish is perfectly fresh, you understand, and the mustard and the vinegared rice that fortify the sushi are lively, but the fish lacks a certain sprightliness.

So begin your dinner with Sunomono, a Japanese salad of crabmeat and cucumber —the seafood and the crisp, thin slivers of cucumber are flavored with a gentle vinegar and a little ginger, which combine to make the dish sing. Red caviar and horseradish, called Suzuko, may strike you as unlikely, and the caviar is in no way extraordinary, but the horseradish is—instead of the hotness you expect, you get the powerful and earthy flavor of a root just pulled out of the ground; it makes a dramatic contrast to the fish eggs. In Japan, warm clams are served with paper-thin rounds of lime; what seems to be a variant of that dish, designed for American taste, is served here as Yaki Hama. The clams are broiled until they are warm but not colored; they are surmounted with thin circles of lemon or lime, and they are served with a cousin, several times removed, of cocktail sauce—a garlicked tomato purée that seems more Italian than either Japanese or American. Odd but good.

The shrimp tempura cannot be recommended—the shrimp are not fresh, and these days you almost have to expect that, but they have the loud taste of iodine; and the tempura batter here is a little thick or the frying oil is insufficiently hot, for the crust is heavy and barely crisp. The Yaki-Tori is described on the menu as "Broiled Chicken and Scallion, Skewered," but the chunks of chicken are alternated on the little wooden skewers with slices of ordinary onion instead, which tames this dish. The meat and onions are dipped in sweetened sake and soy sauce before they are broiled, which sweetens and spices the chicken, and it is no contrast at all against the onions, which become sweet anyway when cooked. Shio-Yaki is broiled, salted fish—you can have it made of mackerel (a little loud) or salmon (rich); the fish is fresh, it is perfectly broiled, moist and flaky, and if you moisten the horseradish garnish with a bit of soy sauce, it makes a perfect condiment.

To-Banyaki is the solid climax to most of the dinners here, especially substantial if you have the version made with pork. This is a steaming stew that arrives in a deep ceramic pot with a close-fitting lid. The slabs of tender meat are rimmed with fat, there are chunks of soft bean curd and slices of crisp squash alongside, all in a meaty broth that is heavily flavored with sesame. For all its solidity, there is no heaviness to this stout food.

Beer is the best drink here. Unfortunately, the house does not sell Kirin, and the Sapporo that they push is a little dull in comparison.

★ K.O.'s

99 Bank Street (at Greenwich Street)
DINNER. CLOSED MONDAY.
Reservations, 243-0561.
Credit cards: AE, MC, V.
Expensive.

If you are going to run a steakhouse in the old steakhouse style in the 1980s, you do not, of course, have to replicate the past. You may, if you wish, reinterpret the concept in, as they say, contemporary terms. That, unfortunately, is not exactly what K.O.'s has managed. They have modified the old he-man style not by way of some new he-man style, but, rather, with what used to be called a woman's touch. Pastel linen in a steakhouse? Dove gray, no less? Flowers? Even the barbershop-tile floor is gray. Who ever heard of a gray barbershop? For some reason the lower halves of the great foursquare windows that, between massive maroon columns, occupy most of two sides of this corner store have been hung with pleated gauze curtains, presumably to shield your eyes from the hard-edged cityscape without. The banquette along the 12th Street side of the store is perhaps the most misplaced note of all, done up, as it is, with plump cushions, all in a lovely nubbly tweedy plaid, as if the place were hoping for a spread in *House & Garden*. Oh, yes, the manly side of things—wood and brass and straight lines, waiters in long white aprons, old meat market photos, a couple of walls of some sort of corrugated, galvanized construction material that would be just the thing if you wanted to toss up a fast shack. Withal, the place is not ugly or uncomfortable, just thin on character. And, of course, real he-men do not care about the appointments nohow anyway. They come to eat the food.

The shrimp cocktail has disappeared from many menus around town, gone up to $2 per shrimp in some of the uptown steak places. K.O.'s finesses the situation with rock shrimp, which, the waiters are trained to assure you, taste just like lobster. They do not. They are rather dull, but you get lots of them for your $3.95, and each order comes with a set of instructions, delivered by your waiter, on how to shell them—you figure out how to dip them in the melted butter yourself. For a mere dollar more, however, you may have some sublime smoked salmon, served, when the carving is going right, in a single huge pink slice. This is superb salmon, moist but not oily, sharp but not salty, served with good olive oil, which enriches it perfectly. The stuffed artichoke is over-cooked, the zucchini frittata—akin to a quiche—has too obviously been reheated. A patty of mozzarella cheese, breaded and fried until it is hot and pully and crisp, is this establishment's rather restrained, even elegant, version of Mozzarella in carrozza—it comes with a little pitcher of thick, salty anchovy sauce.

Because this place is owned by meat wholesalers, commentators have felt safe to declare its beef first rate. You have had better, but this will eminently serve. They call the basic article a "New York Strip Steak," but it is a sirloin to the rest of you. It is seared, blood-juicy, tender if not velvety, accurately done. You wish the grilled tomato with which it is graced were not cold. Nothing is done to beef up the flavor of the filet mignon—it is every bit as well made as the strip steak, but delicate to the point of blandness. To some beef specialists ground beef is the ultimate beef. It may be said in favor of K.O.'s chopped steak that it is of meat just ground, and not ground too fine, which means that it has a nubbly texture and holds much of its blood within its crusty surface. But chopped beef should be the tastiest beef, for tough-but-flavorful cuts can go into it. This one lacks much of the animal minerality of chopped beef at its best. The loin lamb chops and veal chops are unexceptional, the duckling well roasted but of scant flavor—its orange sauce, which, happily, is served on the side and not on the duck, is a couple of steps too close to candy. The contents of a giant baked potato are removed from the skin, mashed and seasoned, put back, browned—the item has the quality of very nice browned mashed potatoes. The home-fried potatoes are prepared with skins on, a nice note, and they are mingled with slivers of sautéed and blackened onions—they are fine, but lack some of the sinful greasy crustiness you probably look for in this dish. The sweet-spiced creamed spinach is not puréed, has texture as well as the flavor of the fresh leaf.

The chocolate cake is polished and concentrated, almost spicy in its chocolate strength, the best dessert in the place. The crème brûlée is heavy, the banana cream pie heavier. The apple tart will put you in mind of apple sauce. The whipped cream that accompanies some of these items is fashioned of real cream, but it is spewn from a machine, so it is airy but lacking in butter-fattiness.

★ LAUGHING MOUNTAIN BAR & GRILL

148 Chambers Street (near West Broadway)
LUNCH AND DINNER.
Reservations, 233-4434.
Credit cards: AE, DC, MC, V.
Medium-priced.

This one is like a kid's room, big walls of deep blue, deep green, red up front near the bar, a little lemon yellow, painted-on nonsupporting pillars of dead white. The banquettes along the side walls of the main dining room are more like benches, fashioned, as they are, of wooden boards, which are softened a little by long cushions on the seats. The chairs are director's chairs, canvas and chrome. There is a small back room, under a skylight, all green, its foursquare, high-backed wooden booths inspired by the architecture of bunk beds. Throughout the place the table tops are of marble, from which it is *so* easy to wash away the finger paints. All this playfulness requires children—or adults—playing, for the garish room is not inviting until it is filled with people. And though it often is at lunchtime, things have been slow at dinner. But this is, you must remember, a beachhead in Tribeca, New York's next SoHo, many believe. If they are right, Laughing Mountain will laugh later.

Meantime the food is good, perhaps the least of it the appetizer of endive with anchovy dressing, the crisp raw leaves of endive arranged like the petals of a daisy around a pool of creamy, pink, vaguely seasoned dressing—but this is really no more than a small salad, not tossed. Much more interesting is the asparagus in puff pastry, strands of the fresh vegetable, thin and firm and tender, moistened with a light hollandaise, and served up between two slices of flaky pastry. The entire production looks a lot like an asparagus sandwich, though its warm, dripping sauce rules out picking it up. You can get grilled bay scallops, tiny and tender, their flavor vivid, served in a pool of butter that is lightly garlicked. Or you may begin with a half-order of pasta, what Laughing Mountain calls linguine, and what you call fettuccine and what everybody calls green—the fresh noodles are smooth and firm, and the clams and shrimp and asparagus are vivid in the polished cream sauce. Prices are not notably high at Laughing Mountain, but the salads are especially inexpensive. The one composed of tiny, sharp, black Mediterranean olives, strong and creamy Gorgonzola cheese and cherry tomatoes, all mingled with fresh greens in an oily dressing, at a piddling $4.50, is copious enough to make a good first course for two or three.

The grilled red snapper is fresh and flaky, its exterior darkened and crusty, adorned with a green swath of herb butter that, though it is nice enough, really seems to have developed no connection to the fish. Large, thin slices of eggplant are formed into a roulade with mozzarella cheese, Gruyère and Parmesan, baked until the cheese is gooey and loud, and served in a sauce that is more like an herbed vegetable stew—of carrots, tomatoes, zucchini, celery and more—in a red broth. This is a little like college food, but it is satisfying. A slightly goofy-sounding chicken dish—the sautéed white meat is served in a hazelnut sauce under pear purée—is better than you have any right to expect: the chicken is moist; the sauce has a subtle hazelnut flavor that is made earthy by the strong grain flavor of the good flour with which it is thickened; and the fruitiness of the purée—and of the slices of cool pear that garnish the chicken—is a well-placed note against the meat and the sturdy sauce. LM serves some perfectly decent roast duck, but its so-called hoisin sauce lacks the intensity of sauces that go by that name in Chinese restaurants. The grilled steak is all right, though this is rather bland beef. Much better is the rack of lamb, which is strong, seasoned with mustard, moistened with a slightly sweet sauce that is redolent of rosemary.

The best of the desserts is a raspberry roll that consists of little more than white cake, berries—the slight grittiness of the seeds lovely against the soft cake—and fluffy whipped cream. The warm apple pie has a bit of lemon in it and a little cinnamon, more of that whipped cream on top. Avoid the banana cheese cake, which is cold, thick, utterly devoid of breed. The chocolate cake, with its white layer of ricotta cheese through the center, is refrigerator cold—the cheese seems to have no impact on its flavor, and the dessert will remind you of something you found waiting for you in the icebox, and which you washed down with a glass of milk before going out to play.

Only an expert can distinguish for sure the Tribeca crowd from the SoHo crowd. The former is perhaps a little less artsy, somewhat younger, not yet mingled with so many middle-class formerly marrieds starting new lives in lofts. Tribeca is the frontier, and until it is settled it is not entirely safe for uptownies.

The menu is changed every couple of months, so what you find available may not be what you set out for.

★★ LE LAVANDOU

134 East 61st Street
LUNCH AND DINNER. CLOSED SUNDAY.
Reservations, 838-7987.
Credit cards: AE.
Very expensive.

What sets this place apart from the fancy French restaurants with which it is generally mentioned in one breath, is that it has never been quite chichi. Opened in the mid-1970s, and popular almost from the first, the restaurant's appeal has been almost solely its food. Famous faces are not regularly alleged to have been seen at Le Lavandou by gossip columnists. The place has never been quite expensive enough to attract those who are happy only when paying top dollar. And so, of course, the camp followers have no one to follow here. To this day the crowd is composed of tasteful people who come merely to enjoy their repast and one another's company. The grim ritual dinners you see acted out at, say, La Caravelle, are never endured here. The restaurant is full of talk and contentment. And if the food is not quite what it once was—perhaps because Jean Jacques Rachou now divides his proprietorship between this place and La Côte Basque—the spirit remains, and it is difficult to have less than a pleasant time in this comfortable place.

Le Lavandou has never looked better. The ivory-colored walls have been adorned —between panels of latticework—with light, Dufy-like murals of coastal scenes in southern France. The ocean is rendered in all of them in a vivid cerulean blue, a cool note in this room's golden light. That sunshine is cast by little shaded lamps on brass sconces, and by more of them on the three chandeliers that hang over the center-aisle tables. A banquette of deep burgundy rims the room. Walls of paned mirror at the front and back add a touch of glitter to the pretty place. And the service is good—nowhere in New York is it better.

But no matter how graciously it is served, it is distressing to order an assiette de pâtés et terrines and be delivered two substantial slices of but one pâté. Nice pâté, pink and fatty and shot through with strong ham, but not the more interesting dish billed. Then there is le panache de caviar à la sauce aux herbes et vodka—cucumber chips and a little dollop each of red and black caviar from California; if the latter substances were not entitled to the name caviar, no one would eat them. The vodka, which seems to have been added directly to the roe, and the herbed mayonnaise do not help.

Happily, you can do much, much better. The cassolette de morilles et homard, for example: a little copper pan filled with juicy lobster meat, wild mushrooms, and a dark-pink lobster sauce that has the sweetness and richness and depth of some oceanic essence. In a little pot (complete with lid) formed out of flaky pastry, you are served the vol au vent of scallops and leeks—the scallops are tiny, light as air, ever so slightly briny, surmounted by strands of leek; the whole dish is moistened with a pale sauce, light and creamy. The gentleman at the next table orders some snails, and as they are delivered, noses at all the tables round about are raised in appreciation of the strong garlic. So you, too, order snails. Unfortunately, yours were ordered just after the pungent root went out of style, and they arrive in a hot butter flavored with Pernod and little else.

Wonderful paupiettes of grey sole—big dumplings, light and peppery and strongly flavored of the fresh fish, under slivers of warm kiwi—are served on sweet-spiced spinach. La suprême de volaille Jean Jacques consists of the boned white meat of chicken formed into a log around a forcemeat of pigeon. It is served in cross-sectional slices, and the pale meat and its salty, spicy, slightly gamy stuffing are moistened with a tarragon-flavored white-wine sauce—a lovely dish. The rack of lamb is perfect, though the thyme with which it is ostensibly flavored is not evident either in the meat or in its roasting-pan juice. The sweetbreads are plump, crusted, served in a sturdy sauce with onions and strong mushrooms—solid food. But if it is solidity you want, Le Lavandou's cassoulet is the Rock of Gibraltar. The serving is abundant, the beans are firm, but without a touch of hardness, the sauce is thick, its flavor intensified by the regular turning under of the crust that forms across the top of the cooking pot. One of the sausages is fatty and rich, the other spicy and fragrant of fennel. The lamb is gamy. The duck is good, but no longer recognizable as duck, for it has taken on the many other flavors of the complex dish.

Soufflés are made only for two, and they are better than the usual—light, none of that heavy wetness at the center. There is sometimes available an apricot soufflé—it is moistened with an apricot sauce, of brandylike intensity, that is studded with bits of the fruit. The lemon sherbet is sweet and a little astringent. The chocolate mousse is thick, cocoalike, sticky. And the strawberry tart is made with plump ripe berries and a pastry that has within it a layer of nut paste, all under a thin glaze that is still liquid when served.

★ LAVIN'S

25 West 39th Street
LUNCH AND DINNER. CLOSED SATURDAY AND SUNDAY.
Reservations, 921-1288.
Credit cards: AE, CB, DC, MC, V.
Medium-priced.

You probably did not know that for decades there was in New York a body known as the Engineers Club. Surely you were unaware that their 39th Street headquarters housed a so-called Grill Room. The club is now defunct, and the Grill Room has been turned into a public eating place. Nobody knows whether nostalgic engineers ever drop in.

It must have been a swell club in its day, for the spiffed-up dining room, long, wide and handsome, reveals old oak-paneled walls, now refinished to a chestnut glow, under a high ceiling. The place is furnished with long rows of tables and chairs, much the way restaurants were in simpler times. But all is laid out on dark-mauve carpeting that has a cushy sheen, and the lights are soft and indirect, so the old place has a modern glow.

At the front a square travertine-topped bar has been installed, and at lunchtime people from local stores and offices who fail to get a table in this busy place have napkins spread for them on the marble counter and lunch there. This is a commercial neighborhood, and though there is dinner action, much of the evening's commerce is in liquids, at the bar. Young women from Lord & Taylor or from Consolidated Crank & Joint undo the topmost button or two of their blouses on their way over here, and sip their first drink slowly until they are proffered another by, say, the young, ambitious and clean-cut Assistant Manager of Billing Processing Services. They are titillated to discover that he gets a little unbuttoned himself after an extra dry mart and some encouragement.

In what is rapidly becoming the manner of this day, the menu betrays no specific culinary bent, but offers an assortment of mostly popular dishes from the cooking of many nations. Such selections always include pasta, and the soft noodle is one of this establishment's strong points. The tortellini, for example, filled with ham and chicken and veal, are sweet-spiced, and served in a buttery sauce of strong Parmesan cheese that is browned just before the pasta is served. And the linguini primavera (a dish that has become an overnight old favorite in New York) is one of the few versions in town in which the vegetables—including red peppers, string beans, carrots and broccoli—are an integrated part of the garlicky dish while retaining their crispness and individuality.

The place offers lots of cold dishes, among them a platter of smoked chicken and duck, served with cool and crunchy snow peas and a purple, thick hoisin sauce that is salty, tart and fruity. The duck is sweet and smoky, the chicken dry and smoky; the rice salad, which also garnishes the meats, is brightly flavored with strong dill. Pass up the market salad, which, for all the freshness of its vegetables and greens, and despite the chunks of smoked duck that are nuggets of lovely flavor therein, just fails to add up.

The fish of the day is usually fresh, but a perfectly cooked swordfish steak has been served that could have done with around twenty-four hours of additional youth. The scallops provençale are splendid, the deep-browned meat of the mollusks in a hefty tomato sauce that is loud with garlic and thick with capers and strong black olives. The tender medallions of pork are medium-rare (they won't kill you), in their lightly garlicked parsley butter—this is rich meat, but its sweet flavor has not been brought out. The lamb riblets consist of sturdy bones, much succulent fat, and specks of blackened meat—good food, but dismaying. The steak is not first-class meat (albeit described as "prime"), and the dollop of wine-flavored butter with which it is adorned melts down to a greasy sauce. Straw potatoes accompany many of the hot dishes (and may be ordered separately)—they are thin, crisp, tasty.

The fruit and cheese is expensive, but the fruits are fresh, the cheeses ripe and well chosen, including some very decent Brie. Something called apple crisp is a hot, crusted, sweet and cinnamoned pielike affair served in individual ramekins. The crème brûlée has a lovely, caramelized glaze over its custard—but that custard, though sometimes creamy, is sometimes coagulated.

★ LELLO

65 East 54th Street
LUNCH, MONDAY TO FRIDAY; DINNER, MONDAY TO SATURDAY. CLOSED SUNDAY.
Reservations, 751-1555.
Credit cards: AE, CB, DC, MC, V.
Very expensive.

Pity the poor philanderer. He deduces from the looks of this chic, jewel-like establishment that it is a worldly spot. Having thus misguided himself, he entertains a close friend at Lello one evening, a close wife an evening or two later, on which latter occasion he is demonstratively greeted with "Good evening, Mr. A, so nice to have you back so soon. You must have enjoyed your dinner the other night to visit us again right away," &c, &c. The spiel lasts less than a minute, but it seems never to end.

As Mr. A's previous Lello dinner was excluded from accounts of his movements, Mrs. A sensibly concludes that lubricious facts have been concealed. Dinner takes place in glacial silence—prelude to contemptuous, hissed rebukes later—and a solitary night is spent on the living-room couch. Moral: adultery is wrong if you lack a spare bedroom.

What good is a public place if you get no privacy there? You might just as well stay home. Especially in a restaurant like Lello—where the cushy surroundings, low lights and suave staff suggest not only discretion but intimacy and secrecy—you quite reasonably expect that your waiter will not, for example, ask after your kiddies even if you ask after his. There was a time when New York's worldlier restaurants would treat a habitué as anonymously as they would a visiting prairie boob—and you did not have to wink to arrange it. Manners and their uses have been lost in that mindless democracy that is not only of classes, but of roles.

If mitigating circumstances are sought for the restaurant's failures of tact, a few may be found in the establishment's clientele. For with all the restraint that seems to have been built into the place, the customers that come bring none. The gentlemen drink quite enough, tell their bad jokes loudly. A few snap their fingers when they want another highball. The ladies have their hair done daily, their omphalic necklines are habitual, no longer seductive in fact or intention. And everyone is easily distracted by the purely ritualistic "finishing" of dishes over a burner on the serving cart that is wheeled through the aisles. Some shriek a little when something is, as they would put it, flambéed. The situation is worst on weekend nights. The captains suffer it well.

As will you the carpaccio—the raw beef is perhaps sliced a while in advance, for it lacks the blood-juiciness of the just-cut article, but this is good sweet raw beef, and the green sauce with which it is served is tart and thick and fragrant. You create a marvelous morsel when you wrap a dollop of the sauce—with some of the capers and chopped onions that garnish the dish—in one of the slices of red meat, and moisten the whole with a squeeze of lemon.

Tucked away at the bottom of the right-hand column of pasta dishes is a non-pasta dish, risotto alla certosina. Many Italian restaurants list risotto dishes—the various special rice preparations of northern Italy—but many Italian chefs refuse to make them except under pressure, for it entails a break in kitchen routine. You may be refused it here if you lack leverage, but threatening to leave should be all it takes, and worth it. The rice is hot and mealy and comforting, like a homey cereal, and the green peas and crunchy chopped shrimp with which it is mingled are startling—pink and green against the light-brown rice, the sweet flavor of the vegetable and the slight tang of the oceanic seafood against the warmth of the earthy grain. A sauce that is a little winy, a little peppery, polished with oil, moistens the dish, and you may fortify it with the good grated cheese available here.

Among the noodles, the dish to have may be the linguine ai frutti di mare—the linguine, like all pasta here, is carefully cooked, firm but tender, and the exceptional creamy sauce—studded with mussels and shrimp and chunks of lobster meat—is reddened and made fragrant with saffron. The tortellini bolognese, though served in a satisfying meaty sauce that is at once rich and acidic, lack a well-flavored meat filling and seem simply like lumpy carriers for the bolognese. And the spaghettini primavera, though prepared with fresh vegetables—carrots, peas, zucchini, broccoli, and more—in a creamy sauce that is touched with tomato, is more a collection of vegetables than a finished dish.

Very nice snapper, the snowy and flaky fish sealed within a brown crust, moistened with a perfumed tomato sauce, garnished with a couple of fresh clams and a couple of rather sandy mussels. Further mussel troubles may await you in the so-called zuppa di pesce, in at least one serving of which the mussels were not only gritty but rank. Despite its title, this is a soupless dish, the lobster, shrimp, squid, clams and fish heated in a marinara sauce until the moisture is cooked off, leaving a seafood assortment that is touched with spicy tomato—on request additional sauce will be spooned over the rather dry seafood. Duck is listed as a specialty, which is probably a reference to the fact that the bird is flamed to the dining-room ceiling before it is served. The bird is moist, crisp, garnished with apples and oranges, but the viscous sauce, flavored with the sweet orange liqueur which was the fuel of its conflagration, is obvious and over-powering. A huge veal chop is butterflied, stuffed with ham and mild cheese, breaded, browned, moistened with a tomato-and-mushroom sauce that is enriched a little when the melted cheese oozes into it—a good dish. You may have either steak or veal in the manner described as "vesuviana." The scallops of veal are nicely browned, and the steak is of tasty, tender meat, albeit inaccurately grilled. The sauce in either instance is thick, nubbly, subtly garlicked, sturdy.

In consideration of what the sweet desserts are like, you are fortunate that Lello has on hand some of the best cheese available in any Italian restaurant in town. Included is hard, aged Parmesan, the miraculous substance that manages to be at once sharp, a little sweet, brandylike, solid but never heavy, revivifying at the end of a substantial meal, perfect with old Italian wine. Other good cheeses, including provolone and romano, are available as well. Such items as the chocolate mousse cake, Grand Marnier cake, and crème de cassis cake are light, fresh, moist, sweet—and insipid. There are berries—you should inspect them before ordering, for on occasion they are not ripe—and they are served with perfect, albeit sugared, whipped cream.

★ LION'S HEAD

59 Christopher Street (near Sheridan Square)
LUNCH, SATURDAY AND SUNDAY; DINNER, DAILY.
Reservations, 929–0670.
Credit cards: AE, CB, DC, MC, V.
Medium-priced.

The Lion's Head is known as a journalists' and writers' bar, but all Greenwich Village frequents this place on Christopher Street—NYU professors and NYU students, bartenders and bar owners, bookstore operators and boutique proprietors, the last looking very un-boutique in their sneakers and sweat socks. In this place, if the jacket matches the pants, both are blue denim. Tweed caps are worn, pipes are thoughtfully puffed, exchanges may well be terse. (Many of the regulars, it seems, sense an obligation to maintain the establishment's pub tone.)

In the big brick-and-wood barroom the dust jackets on the wall include *Get Along With Your Stomach* and *Seizing Our Bodies*. By and large, if you seize your body and take it into the spacious, informal and comfortable back room and feed it there, you will get along very well with your stomach. The waitresses are in civvies. They sit down when they have nothing to do; they lean on your table when they answer questions. Such is this subculture.

Once the Lion's Head was a hamburger place, which was consistent with its beer-and-tobacco clientele. The burgers are still good, but the place essays an ambitious menu now, and it includes superb Irish smoked salmon; a tender squid appetizer in a bright, lemony vinaigrette; snails that are rather coarsely seasoned and excessively buttered, but plump and tender and good; quiche Lorraine that is remarkably fluffy for a restaurant quiche; and a pretty good pâté that is overly flavored with sweet spices and unnecessarily fancied up with nuts. The fish of the day is fresh, the chopped steak gigantic, the shepherd's pie a bargain, the shell steak accurately grilled and delicately flavored with garlic butter. Most of the rest of the menu is well prepared. The apple pie and chocolate cake are low on finesse and high on flavor.

The wine list is banal, but the big selection of ales and beers available on tap are at least a one-credit course in guzzling.

★★ LA LOUISIANA

132 Lexington Avenue (near 29th Street)
DINNER. CLOSED SUNDAY.
Reservations, 686-3959.
No credit cards.
Medium-priced.

Some have insisted that La Louisiana's claim to New Orleans cuisine is spurious. Purists, of course, are capable of approving food only if a textbook somewhere certifies it as correct. (Don't bother them with delicious.) The food at La Louisiana has life, sparkle, individuality. Even if it is the only food of its kind, it is for real.

This is a long, narrow store, painted pink. On your right as you enter there is a little bar, beyond that a row of tables down each side, the aisle between them about one fat man wide. The bar is the focus of activity, and at least on occasion everyone—waiter, waitress, hostess or chef—gets behind it to mix a drink, answer the phone, and while at one or both of those, greet entering customers. The staff is very much a team, and when all other hands are at work, someone in kitchen whites will emerge from the back to serve just-ready food to waiting customers. Your hostess is a comely Oriental who seems to own the place. She is always about, overseeing, sometimes sitting down with customers she knows well. And sometimes, when things are quiet, she and her chef sit at the bar and make goo-goo eyes at each other. Withal this is a well-run place, the intensity of activity does not impinge. Your allotted space is as tranquil or as hectic as you, not the house, make it. And the under-forty crowd that crowds La Louisiana makes a happy but less than boisterous din.

They are happy about their crudité de boeuf—thin slices of tender raw meat served with a fiery mustard sauce that flares the nostrils and dilates the pupils. The smoked chicken is all white meat, a great slab of it, quite salty, and suffused with the fragrance of burnt wood—it comes with a mild and creamy horseradish sauce and a vividly hot pepper sauce. The so-called scallops Rockefeller are a simple dish of sweet seafood in fresh greens, the alleged Pernod therein applied with an abundance of restraint—still, this is lovely food. As is the boudin, a sausage that is gentle despite its sharp spiciness, a little rich, soft and homey food—you get a thick mayo with it that may well seem superfluous. Always there is a gumbo—the meat or seafood added varies from day to day; this is stout soup, thick and slightly hard, densely populated with green and red peppers, served with a dish of fragrant rice that has a grainy flavor—you may, if you wish, spoon the rice into the soup. Even better is the sometimes available crawfish bisque, an almost syrupy tomato-based soup, smooth as honey, cut through with a strong and vivid seafood freshness.

Your waitress, to her credit, is slightly discomposed when you ask her to explain how, exactly, you feed grain to a catfish. (The menu refers to "grain fed Louisiana catfish.") She mumbles something. You do not press your inquiry. This is delicate fish, boned and breaded and fried golden-brown, the three fillets steamy within their crusts, served with a tartar sauce that is tart and thick. The breast of chicken "jolie blonde," as the menu has it, is nicely sautéed, browned and tender, and the warm and lemoned white seedless grapes with which it is surmounted are firm and fruity—but the grapes and bird do not quite add up to a dish.

The red-meat dishes are all good: superb calf's liver, with an extremely deep, blood-rich flavor, the soft meat sprinkled with little chunks of slab bacon, the sharpness of them perfect against the organ meat; beef paillard, tasty meat that is made very tender when it is pounded to cutlet thickness, then sautéed until it is crisped, and served— if you want it that way—with what the house calls sauce diablo, a plum-colored paste that serves something of the purpose of mustard on a hamburger. The surprise is the southern fried steak, beef that is breaded but not thereby made leaden, with some more of that purple sauce. The big winner is the pork, scallops of the sweet meat, the thin slices crisped and browned and glistening, served in a caramelized, reddish-brown sauce, and with hard crusts of toasted bread.

The pecan pie is too much the usual thing, though the cornstarch filler is less in evidence than usual. The fruit pies (which vary from day to day) are better: one day a filling of cinnamoned plums, the fruit cooked down to a sweet, tart—even slightly bitter—intensity; another day a nubbly blueberry goo, sugary and thick, though far from the original fruit. You will do well if you settle for the splendid cookies and mint-flavored brownies, which are very nice with this establishment's good coffee.

★★★★ LUTÈCE

249 East 50th Street
LUNCH, TUESDAY TO FRIDAY; DINNER, MONDAY TO SATURDAY. CLOSED SUNDAY.
Reservations essential, PL 2-2225.
Credit cards: AE, DC.
Very expensive.

During the first decade or so of its existence, the kitchen at Lutèce turned out the best restaurant food obtainable in New York. At the same time, certain members of the dining-room staff, with the encouragement of one of this establishment's proprietors, did what they could to keep people from enjoying it. M. Surmain's contempt for all but a rich and/or famous few was given by analysts of the parvenu mind as the key to the intense demand that obtained for the privilege of eating in this place; other analysts of minds, while not necessarily quarreling with that theory, held that the underlying purpose of Surmain's pompous hauteur was to obscure his bourgeois beginnings. Surmain's motives, always a boring subject, are now an irrelevant issue, for, happily, he divorced himself from his baby a few years ago, leaving Lutèce entirely in the more capable hands of his former partner, André Soltner, who has always been its chef. Perhaps snobbery was the lure that drew them in when this place was getting started. Still, arrogance departed right behind Surmain, and the customers have not. Today Lutèce is the most charming and relaxed of New York's famous restaurants. Anyone who is uncomfortable here is uncomfortable.

You are greeted by Madame. Her attitude toward her customers is—get this—that of one human being to another. A little better, even, for she is all concern for your wishes. Unknown customers, for example, are asked whether they would like to sit upstairs or down, and then they are led to the best open table on the floor they choose. If they prefer another table, and that one is free, it is theirs.

But all that is a bit previous, for first you will want a drink in the little front room, four tiny tables and a miniature zinc bar, behind which there is a barman who seems to enjoy his work. He polishes glasses until they are crystalline and stirs cocktails until they are icy, ever serious when at work, smiling a French elf's smile when exchanging small talk with the customers. Though there is hardly room for them, you sit in ample wicker chairs while you sip your drinks and stare about you. The walls are innocently adorned with a mural of Paris, a street sign from the same city (Place de Furstenberg, 6° Arr.), *Holiday* magazine awards and a letter of tribute from the *Mobil Guide*. Those publications, displayed in this place, are getting the better of the bargain. Off this room coats are checked, in a wee closet, and bills are processed, at a minute cashier's counter; and the crowds—of customers around the *vestiaire* and of waiters around the little desk —make for an occasional congestion that would infuriate anywhere else: at Lutèce everyone is so relentlessly civilized that the principal delays result from everyone's eagerness to defer to everyone else.

You may eat upstairs, where a couple of small, comfortable and comparatively formal rooms accommodate a handful of tables each. But if you want the feeling of being where this restaurant is, eat on the ground floor, in the famous "garden."

You are led through a narrow corridor (past a reclining nude smoked salmon) to, first, the antegarden, a small, cozy room with a table in each corner, grotesque paper of cavorting fern fronds on the walls and a view through glass paneling and a glass door of the garden proper, a fantasy candyland of outdoors elegance, pink stucco walls behind snowy latticework, columns of whitewashed brick supporting palms in great brass pots. You walk on flagstones and look up to a vaulted glass ceiling lined with pale-green blinds—by day the sun shines through. The tables are in two rows, surrounded by deep wicker chairs and set with white linen and china, glinting silver, gleaming crystal.

M. Soltner is a restless cook, so it is wise to discuss with your captain the chef's whims of the day, which are in addition to the menu listings and frequently of special interest. Failure to do so may lead, for example, to your humbly ordering Foie Gras en Brioche, only to then have your captain point out that it is foolish to have your foie gras in bread, when only this morning the chef packed the stuff into quails. The little birds (they are about the size of a fist) have been boned (but for their legs), roasted, stuffed with the foie gras, coated with aspic and cooled. Your quail is bisected on a carving board near your table and served to you, a couple of eccentric doughnuts of pink bird meat, a leg protruding from each, a bull's-eye of the buttery concentrate of liver at each center. This is, of course, a visual conceit, the flesh of the quail playing the part of the brioche bread, the dark jelly that of the crust, the foie gras doing a terrific imitation of itself. A few white grapes garnish the little masterpiece.

Remarkable hot first courses, including this establishment's famous snails, styled as Timbales d'Escargots à la Chablisienne. They are not served in snail shells, but in eyecup-size ceramic pots, the tender morsels submerged in a liquid butter that is winy and powerfully scented with fresh herbs. Equally deserving of all the syllables are Pélerines à la Méridionale, bay scallops that are the size of sea scallops, sautéed until they are lightly browned, but not a second too long, so that all their sweet richness is retained, no toughness added. Though you get about a dozen of them, they are so fluffy and airy that they are not excessive; they are served in a sauce of such profundity and fulfillment that it controls your entire attention—a dark and oily concentrate of tomatoes, garlic and mushrooms that is poured over the shellfish and over a crust of toasted bread as well—which supplies a crusty texture that rounds out the otherwise supple dish. The Truite Fraîche à l'Oseille is a gentle dish—a skinned trout, separated from its outer bones but still attached to the central ones along the spine, in a pool of buttery sauce made colorful and tasty with chopped sorrel and parsley and strands of carrot. The trout is firm and sweet and moist. The scent of a wild perfume seems to rise from its plate.

It is called Cassolette de Crabe "Vieille France," but this main dish is made with the best American crabmeat fished from the water. This is a stewlike dish, arriving in a little pot under a pastry top. When that crust is inverted onto your plate and the contents of the pot spooned over it, a vivid aroma of crayfish shell and wild mushrooms permeates the air. The crabmeat is almost unbelievably delicate and sweet, the light-brown sauce at once clear and deep, the copper-colored flaky pastry something you toy with to prolong the remarkable experience. The Poussin Basquaise is a whole young chicken, browned and moist, in an earthy sauce that is studded with wild mushrooms; artichoke hearts—fresh, firm, delicately acidic; and nuggets of tomato—cooked down until they have reached an extreme intensity of concentrated tomato flavor.

When local venison is available, this establishment prepares it as if it were beef—the meat grilled, moistened with a polished wine sauce that has a few mushrooms in it and served with salty noodles that make an excellent foil for the sweet, tender meat. Technically this is game meat, but there is nothing gamy about it or its preparation: classical cooking applied to a slightly unfamiliar meat, and the results are perfect. All is not heaven, though little approaches the mundane. What does is Délice de Veau aux Girolles, which turns out to be that most indelicate of dishes, veal Cordon Bleu, in a house variant that includes the crinkly mushrooms called chanterelles. The crust around the veal, ham and cheese is deeply browned, and the meat and cheese within form a hefty sandwich, lightened and sharpened a bit by lemon. But even the vaguely wild flavor of the mushrooms fails to ennoble this earthbound item. Good vegetables, including spinach that seems to have its natural flavor greatly magnified; morels that are at once cartilaginous and tender, in a creamy brandied sauce.

If you are one of those in whom abundant eating begets further gluttony, you may want cheese before your dessert. The bread here is crusty and strong, and the selection of cheeses, though conventional—Brie, Roquefort, Pont l'Evêque, etc.—is remarkable for its consistently high quality. If, however, your hunger has been oversated, you may proceed at once to mere sweets. Did you know that there is such a thing as *marc* of Gewürztraminer? There wasn't until only a few years back. Now that it is here, of course, it may be toyed with, and at this establishment it has been discovered that this cousin of brandy makes a head-clearing sherbet; has in it more than a hint of the Alsatian grapes of which the eau-de-vie was made. Half the customers have the "Soufflé Glacé" aux Framboises, and toward the end of the dinner hour white ceramic pots of the deep-pink sweet are dispensed with rapid regularity. This extraordinary dessert consists of cool layers of raspberry-flavored frozen cream and crumbly cake, over which fresh raspberries are poured, in a raspberry sauce that is so strongly flavored of the fruit that it is almost a liquor. This place manages to serve you berries out of season that seem just off the bush. While everyone is competing to caramelize the apples in their tartes Tatin to the color of deeply stained mahogany, Lutèce, these days, is giving the apples a light treatment, so that they retain a good bit of the flavor of the fruit. Naturally, they start with tasty apples, and the result is sweet, slightly acidic fruit on crumbly, deeply browned pastry.

The captains are all courtesy, their jobs so well in hand they seem free to discuss the menu with you endlessly. The waiters are simple seriousness, the occasional awkwardnesses of these young Frenchmen actually charming.

There is a wine book with runs of great wines, prices into the hundreds of dollars. Most people order from the secondary list of around two dozen still wines at prices of

$14 to $24. No other restaurant of this class makes so extensive an offering of good wines at these prices. Lunch reservations can usually be had on a couple of days' notice, as can weekday dinner reservations. Weekend evenings, however, are usually booked a week or two in advance.

★★★ MADAME ROMAINE DE LYON

32 East 61st Street
LUNCH.
Reservations accepted for five or more, 758–2422.
No credit cards.
Beer and wine.
Medium-priced.

Hatpin handicapping is a race track system for the selection of horses. One purchases a program of the day's races, and without opening the booklet, pierces it at an arbitrary point on the front cover, through to the back cover, with a hatpin. The hatpin is removed, returned to its hat, and the program opened. The selections for the day's races are the horses whose allotted spaces on each page are perforated.

This system is indispensable at Madame Romaine de Lyon. It's impossible to decide that one omelette is preferable to 519 others, and as the 520 omelettes offered here are listed on 16 pages, a hatpin reduces the problem by 97 percent, from 520 to 16. The patron is still faced with a dilemma, but one of human proportions.

A selection of 520 omelettes is such a wonderful gimmick that a restaurant could succeed even if the omelettes were bad. Madame Romaine produces omelettes that are the equal of the best on earth. Not only are the eggs fresh, the butter sweet, the pan hot, the preparation rapid, and the delivery instantaneous (omelettes go bad in just a few minutes), but the ingredients—the beef, brains, mushrooms, chicken livers, etc.— are pre-cooked superbly: the beef is sautéed, the brains marinated, the bacon fried (but not to a crisp) by an expert who could have stopped right there and still delivered an excellent dish.

There is a palpable pleasure in simply reviewing the names and ingredients of some of these fabulous concoctions: Rochambeau (spinach, sausages, mushrooms, cheese); Jourdan (caviar, ham, bacon, onions, mushrooms, cheese); Maxim's (beef, foie gras, mushrooms, spinach, tomatoes, walnuts, Courvoisier sauce); Suprême (chestnuts, chocolate sauce).

No main courses except omelettes are served, but brioches, croissants and rolls are available, as well as a salad of good greens and a light, refreshing dressing. Desserts are a huge assortment of pastries, a chocolate mousse of the heavy, black, you-can't-be-hungry-after-this variety, and a macédoine of fruits which the menu happily defines as "all kinds of fruits mixed."

Assuming that the hours are lengthened, and that one eats three meals a day here, seven days a week, it would require twenty-four weeks, five days and a breakfast to consume one of each omelette.

★★★ LE MADRIGAL

216 East 53rd Street
LUNCH, MONDAY TO FRIDAY; DINNER, MONDAY TO SATURDAY. CLOSED SUNDAY.
Reservations, 355-0322.
Credit cards: AE, CB, DC, MC, V.
Very expensive.

Nobody goes to Le Madrigal anymore. Oh, yes, crowds fill it at lunchtime, but they are largely composed of those who spend corporate money here to prove that they are as powerful as their titles suggest. If your self-importance needs a little reinforcement, Le Madrigal does the job. And surely no target of executive piracy, no purchasing agent, no friend of a friend in Washington will find fault with this impeccable place as a setting for persuasion. Which is the point. Le Madrigal has become respectable. The wild young beauty of ten years ago has settled into demure middle age. The restaurant is as pretty as ever, but at the dinner hour you look around at these couples —who appear to have been designed for each other in the workrooms of Saks Fifth Avenue—and find it hard to believe that not long ago the specialty of the house was adultery. There was particular emphasis on summer romance behind the backs of wives in the Hamptons (though during the rest of the year as well, this was a place where everybody was careful to recognize nobody). If it was said that so-and-so was seen at Le Madrigal with so-and-so, there was nothing more to say. Columnists said it about lots of people, and lots of people came to see what the gossip was about. Every table was taken.

These days, of an evening, the place is rarely more than two-thirds full. Apparently no one thinks of coming here with anything but a spouse, a business associate (for some paralyzingly earnest business talk), or, at the very gayest, a close friend of the opposite gender for whom one sets only the most honorable plans. In at least one regard, this is difficult to explain, for your gargoyley host still greets you with an expectant leer of such insinuation as to strike you guilty for being strictly on the legit. But when considered with respect to the menu, the slightly stodgy current condition of this establishment makes sense, for this is fancy food old-style, with nary a strawberry on your littleneck clams. And the appointments, though lovely as ever, are fussily dainty by the snappy standards of today's most fashionable trysting places.

Le Madrigal is long and slender, low-ceilinged, carpeted, aglow with soft ivory light. Down its sides run cushy banquettes, old-rose in color, velvety in sheen. Before them are capacious tables adorned with a few colorful flowers, and glass lamps with fluted gauze shades; above them, on the pale walls, murals of eighteenth-century France when, to judge by these spacious and peaceful paintings, the citizens wandered around in Directoire costumes, were gracious and mannerly to one another when they met in the open squares of their prosperous towns and all was well with the picturesque world. Appended to the back of the restaurant is a small, dimly lit so-called garden room. Its deep-green walls are covered with green latticework. Through its mostly glass back wall you look out on illuminated foliage. Long pink tapers stand on each of its tightly assembled little tables. This used to be the location of choice for those who were in hiding, but nowadays it is often in disuse at dinner. Who, after all, wants to hide where no one will seek?

Of course you may come here simply to eat, among other things Le Madrigal's recently discovered Scottish smoked trout. This is presumably a salmon trout, for the meat of the rarity is bright pink. It is also smoky, tender, a little salty, not at all oily, of clear fish flavor—you are served it with capers and lemon, and you put it away in a trice. Or you may begin with crabmeat Madrigal, a great mound of flakes and chunks of the pearliest sweet seafood, in a Russian dressing that is fragrant with fresh herbs. When you enter this restaurant you pass by a display of salads, dressed vegetables and other appetizers, from which you may choose a selection for a plate of hors d'oeuvres variés. Choose—to mention some of the better items—cool, deep-purple beets, sweet as sugar, crunchy, coated with butter; celeriac, long strands of the fresh, crisp root, in a cold, tart sauce; ripe avocado in good mayonnaise; dark ham, fibrous and strong, wrapped around a slice of ripe pear; crisp cucumber salad. There are a dozen items to choose from. What the menu refers to as "les trois terrines" includes a truffle-studded duck pâté with a core of foie gras, and a vivid flavor of seasoned duck meat; a country pâté that is rather excessively salty and coarse; and jambon persillé, much ham—in little cubes—suspended in jellied broth, the flavors of smoky meat, strong stock and garlic making a strikingly earthy dish in this elegant place. The crêpe de fruit de mer is yet another bistro item, a browned pancake wrapped around a mass of scallops, crisp little shrimp, crabmeat and chunks of fresh mushroom, all in a rich, almost heavy sauce —an item for a winter night.

Some swell Dover sole—the four filleted quarters of the fish—is arranged around rich little scallops and shrimp, which are moistened with a creamy wine sauce. Those shrimp, however, are medicinal, loud with iodine. You arrange them in a little row along the edge of your plate and proceed with the balance. You are shown your duck. Its lightly blackened hide leads you to suspect it is overdone, but within that crisp skin is a cleverly roasted bird, utterly moist, but not fatty. Chunks of hot apple are served on the dark meat, and a sauce that is studded with green peppercorns is all around it —a terrific dish. Thick slabs from the tenderloin of veal (firm, buttery, juicy meat) are served in a creamy, slightly brandied sauce, an abundance of woodsy morels therein —an old-fashioned dish perfectly prepared. A deep-mahogany sauce coats the sweet-breads—the organ meat is tender and flaky, its sturdy sauce winy, spicy, thick with minuscule chanterelles. The filet au poivre is a steak the size of a middleweight's fist, and though its top and bottom surfaces are heavily coated with green peppercorns, they do not—because of the meat's thickness—overpower the tender, blood-juicy beef. The steak is moistened with a pink sauce that is bright with brandy.

Your captain patiently cores, peels, and slices a ripe pear, which he serves to you with your cheese. The Pyramide is strong, one of the goatiest of all chèvres. The Beaumont is supple and nutty. But some of the cheeses you are shown are obviously tired, as your captain apologetically acknowledges. Little cheese is sold here—which is no excuse—for this crowd does not know from fromage. Making soufflés is such old hat in these old-line places that perfection is routine. They arrive monumentally risen above the rims of their china pots, their deep-brown top crusts aglow with white sugar. The interior of the raspberry soufflé is deep pink, and it is suffused with berry flavor. Over it is poured a hot, liquor-like raspberry syrup. An exceptional St. Honoré—light pastry, velvety custard, and airy whipped cream—is adorned with peeled orange sections, juicy and tart, ripe raspberries, glistening green slices of sweet kiwi. On occasion the cake of the day consists of a log of chestnut mousse studded with chopped chestnuts, the whole wrapped in a pale and sugary chocolate icing. A slice of it is served you in a pool of crème Anglaise—a marvelous sweet. If none of those is enough, this establishment's petits fours are among the crispest in town, as if just from the oven—when you have dispatched your first allotment, one of this restaurant's exceptionally sweet waiters or captains delivers another plate.

★ LA MAISON JAPONAISE

334 Lexington Avenue (at 39th Street)
LUNCH, MONDAY TO FRIDAY; DINNER, DAILY.
Reservations, 682-7375.
Credit cards: AE, CB, DC, MC, V.
Medium-priced.

Of the New York restaurants that, in recent years, have brought together Oriental and French cooking, this one is the least daring, for in few of the dishes are characteristics of Japanese and French cookery integrated. By and large the food—particularly the hot food—is one thing or the other. But the menu is so chosen that none of the food seems to be inappropriate before or after any of the other food. It may just be that Japanese cooking and French cooking are compatible. It may just be that all kinds of cooking are compatible.

La Maison is two floors of plain-looking restaurant. The long, pale street-level room is fitted out with good-size maroon-linened tables along each long wall. Copper utensils adorn the back wall, flora the front window. You avoid tables near the front of the store, because small crowds congregate there—waiting around to eat—when the restaurant is busy. The upstairs room is square, high-ceilinged, charcoal gray. Beige muslin curtains cover the large windows. A charcoal-colored banquette rims the room. The butcher-block tables are unclothed. Upstairs is a little more commodious than the heavily trafficked downstairs.

You do well to start with the mushroom and endive salad, the named ingredients utterly fresh and crisp, their soy-sauce dressing tart and tangy, the entire little item vibrant and stimulating. Three small meat dumplings—shumai—are pink and moist, studded with bits of vegetable, wrapped in silken noodle casings, garnished with fiery mustard. Of the two Cheddar cheese quiches, ham or spinach, the former suffers from its pallid meat; the latter is fine if you get it when it is fresh and fluffy. The cream of avocado is a cold soup the presence of avocado in which is subject to reasonable difference of opinion.

Japanese and French they can usually do, but skip the filet of sole Chinoise, the dull fish in a treacly version of a sweet Chinese ginger sauce. Have the yosenabe instead (which the house characterizes as "bouillabaisse Japonaise"), an iron kettle of hot broth, spiked with soy sauce and sake, in which crisp vegetables and a variety of seafood have been simmered gently—the scallions and watercress, clear noodles, shrimps and fish and clams are all fresh and of clear flavor. The kakiage tempura—great slabs of deep-fried seafood and vegetables—is delicately browned, light, crisp, its airy crust the perfect carrier for the pungent soy sauce in which you dip it. A house oddity given as "cold ginger chicken salad," made up of lots of white meat and four garnishes—sprouts, tomatoes, lettuce, watercress—is served with a pitcher of slightly sweet, strongly gingered sesame sauce. You can get a more than decent boeuf bourguignonne here—it has just the slightest touch of the flavor of charred wine, which is characteristic of this dish

168

at its best. The sauce of the pork curry, though seemingly of commercial curry powder, is a first-class version of that second-class thing—the pork itself is well stewed, moist and tender. You may have the bourguignonne or the curry with rice or, much better, with some good, eggy noodles.

Mt. Fuji is vanilla ice cream, hot fudge, dried coconut and green crème de menthe —it looks frightening in its huge wineglass, but tastes fine. The brandy Alexander pie is loaded with spirits, buried in fluffy whipped cream, utterly without breed, very good to eat. The mousse is little more than chocolate pudding. The crème caramel is gooey.

★ MALAGA

406 East 73rd Street
LUNCH AND DINNER.
Reservations, 737-7659.
Credit cards: AE, CB, DC, MC, V.
Medium-priced.

Bullfight posters, unspeakable oils, framed moments (on linen) in the life of Don Quixote, red lights on the gaudy chandeliers, sexy Spanish ladies painted onto the big barrel-bottoms that are mounted on the wall behind the little bar (just under the wine baskets that hang from the tiled, sloped mock roof); not to mention the black-and-white television set that is occasionally turned on, nor the tall gray Model-T air-conditioning monster, the coats that are on display on the attended plain pipe rack just inside the front door; never mind the crowds that come, young marrieds escaping the kitchen on weekday and weekend nights, whole families escaping it on Sundays, slummers in suits and ties and perms any old time. It is remarkable how so much paraphernalia and activity can fail to make a place look other than gaunt and spare. That, of course, is the front room. The back room lacks even the paraphernalia, except for its own unspeakable oils and monster.

On the Upper East Side, Malaga is the only establishment of its exact type, sporting the standard menu that was set as New York's version of Spanish cooking as long ago as the 1930s and 1940s, in the couple of dozen Spanish restaurants that were then around town. The type has not died out, but now most such places are downtown, and Malaga has itself a little monopoly here. Perhaps for that reason the place does not try too hard. This is a decent restaurant, but you love it more when you know it better, for some of the food is good, and some is not.

Not the Spanish ham and olives, for the ham is coarse, even coarsely sliced, though the green olives are strong and sharp. Far better are the cold Malaga mussels, sweet and fresh in their shells, spread with a bright dressing of chopped tomato and onion and parsley. This place makes a good salpicon and sells it in a $5 serving big enough for two—it is a cool chopped salad of crabmeat, hard-cooked eggs and greens, the strong parsley called cilantro, chopped tomatoes, all in a sharp and refreshing dressing.

You can get lots of hot crunchy shrimp in a bubbling sauce of oil and garlic; a small beach of chorizos, discs of Spanish sausage, that are grilled until they are crusty; a garlic soup that is red with red pepper, thick with chunks of bread and with egg that is cooked in the broth—the soup is homey, but not tasty.

Main courses arrive on a cart in big iron pots, and a huge platter of good red-peppered rice is served with all of them. But the egg sauce that is served on the mixed seafood (mariscada) is thin, hardly eggy at all. And the paella—the biggest pot on the wagon—contains a lobster that is little more than an empty shell, and a lot of other ingredients that are mostly overcooked. Choose instead the crabmeat in green sauce, for it has texture and resilience, and its sauce is fragrant with abundant parsley. Or the shrimp diablo, those good shrimp again, very crisp, in a spicy sauce that is thick with green peppers. The veal extramena is of tender little morsels of meat, but its sauce, allegedly of onions, sausage and peppers, is notable mainly for its good garlic intensity. Eschew the pork with almond sauce—which is flat-out of no interest—in favor of the chicken villaroy, the two halves of a breast of chicken, artfully prepared, coated with béchamel, breaded and crisped. Remarkably, the dish is light.

As everyone knows, the desserts in Spanish restaurants vary not at all from restaurant to restaurant, only a little from dessert to dessert. Malaga has added a standard New York cheese cake to the standard list, and it is not bad if you like that kind of thing. The best of the Spanish desserts is the guava with cream cheese—the fruit is candied but seems brandied, for it is sweet and sharp, and the block of cheese that comes with it is solid. The dish arrives with a couple of saltines standing in it, like a couple of sails.

★★MANHATTAN MARKET

1016 Second Avenue (near 54th Street)
LUNCH, SUNDAY TO FRIDAY; DINNER, MONDAY TO SATURDAY.
Reservations, 752-1400.
Credit cards: AE, MC, V.
Medium-priced.

The Market's handsome furnishings are almost lost in the overwhelming, anonymous blankness of its modernity. You enter to a long narrow barroom, its old floor of white barbershop tiles, the massive bar that runs the length of the room surfaced with mottled stone of earth colors, soft polish and utter solidity. Behind the bar a triptych of mirrors is set in a carved frame of stained oak, to which are attached old sculpted sconces. The ceiling of this front room is a couple of stories overhead, and from it hang three great lights—relics, it is reported, of an old railroad station—of etched white glass in brass fittings. Withal, the sleek slate-gray angularity of everything else about this room makes its contents seem misplaced. And the bar attracts a sleazy "singles" crowd —bare shoulders and padded shoulders, much talk and considerable ennui—which is the final undoing of the room's charms.

Further back is the dining room proper, a square charcoal block of a place, hung with big black-and-white enlargements of New York after dark, bridges and skylines, conventional, adoring photographs of the beloved, bejeweled night world. Rows of linened tables are surrounded by bentwood armchairs of blond tubing and pale cane, and even these seem subminiaturized in the banal rectilinearity of these gunmetal walls. Only the back of the dining room provides relief. The rear is a glass-enclosed extension looking out on a plot of urban landscaping, and this proximity to a nongeometric world colored other than gray is like a bit of the countryside next to this posh jail.

Waiters and waitresses in casual black-and-whites, with over-the-head aprons, attend to your wants cheerfully and briskly, comportment that contrasts with that of the customers, who are almost unanimous in their flaunting of expansive informality—they lean way back in chairs that are pushed way back from their tables, cigars and cigarettes held at bent-arm's length sending up smoke signals of luxurious ease.

So smoked salmon mousse suggests itself, and the pully, almost sticky mousse, powerfully flavored with fresh dill, has lightness as well as a vivid flavor that is strong without being fishy; the garnish of cool snow peas is crisp in its mustard dressing. But the calamari vinaigrette is leaden, a mound of mildly rubbery gray matter that is neither livened nor lightened by its dressing—squeezing on lemon helps only a little. You can get something akin to Manhattan Market's duck terrine almost anywhere, though there is no denying the pleasant herb-and-garlic-and-peppercorn flavor of this one, and the crunchiness of its nuts. But where else can you obtain what the menu unblushingly refers to as a "mosaic" of fresh vegetables? Unfortunately, it is not a work of art, more like a vegetable strudel, a serving consisting of a couple of slices from a refrigerated loaf, the pastry sweet-spiced, not quite right with cold vegetables, but an interesting essay.

Each day a couple of pasta dishes are offered, including, sometimes, spinach fettuccine primavera, a grand assortment of vegetables—mushrooms and zucchini, squash and carrots, and others as well—in a chunky tomato sauce, over noodles that are sometimes, unfortunately, a little coarse, lacking the mellifluousness of pasta at its best. The second dish is always a seafood item, fish and/or shellfish in sauces of various hues —the seafood is always fresh, the sauces well-made, but the pasta itself is not invariably just right.

When the fish of the day is Cohoes salmon, have it. This is a small fish (each one just right for a medium-size human), prepared with the body laterally bifurcated—the head and tail remain intact and attached—so that the pink flesh may be exposed to the broiler. The salmon is just out of the water, its rich and polished sauce lovely against the moist and flaky fish. You have sound reason to expect that something styled "pecan-breaded chicken breasts with mustard sauce" is too gimmicky to be good food. In fact, the nut-crusted chicken is light, the flavor of the pecans just what today's tasteless chicken can use, the thick mustard sauce a dramatic foil to the coarse-ground nuts and the tender white meat. The big pork chop is only a little overcooked (an achievement in this city of pork phobics), so that it retains much of its sweetness and moisture—both of which are supplemented by the stewed black currants spread across the eye of the chop. The calf's liver is artfully grilled, though its sauce, of currants and sherry vinegar, seems a bit candied for this blood-rich meat. Roast leg of lamb is sometimes offered, and the meat is carefully roasted, served rather rare, and it has a strong and gamy flavor. Some of the main courses are served with what the Market has rechristened "potato shavings." These are potato chips, warm ones, crisp, just a little oily, touched with salt. You can get them à la carte.

The salad of three greens is mingled with nuts, dressed with walnut oil, garnished with a substantial helping of good goat cheese—the greens are mostly crisp, and there are enough of them for two.

Something painfully titled "chocolate sweetness cake" is made without flour, has the vibrant flavor and aroma of chocolate just cooked, is light, is buried under good whipped cream. The orange poppy-seed cake is something special, a solid breadlike cake with the nubbly texture of nut cakes, peppered through with poppy seeds, subtly flavored with orange rind, garnished with whipped cream that is studded with strawberries—a splendid dessert.

• MARCHI'S

251 East 31st Street
DINNER, MONDAY TO SATURDAY. CLOSED SUNDAY.
Reservations, Monday to Thursday, 679-2494.
Credit cards: AE.
Medium-priced.

Marchi's has been on East 31st Street for almost half a century, and it will probably outlast our way of life. It has already outlived its own best years. Marchi's serves a single fixed meal to all comers, the same dishes day after day. This is comfort for those who are intimidated by menus and by the minor human manipulations required in restaurants. The place would be fine if it were still serving—as one easily imagines it once did—rustic greenhorns in the big city. But this is no longer a simulation of Mamma's kitchen. The only excuse for this place is its former perfection—it never produced great dinners, but it did serve flawless ones.

The old place has several rooms now, simply laid out, carpeted, paintings on the walls, linen on the tables, all solid and homey. The current version of the fixed dinner begins with an antipasto of crisp celery, the kinds of tomatoes you find in cellophane-wrapped boxes in supermarkets, unscraped radishes, mild Genoa salami, and ripe melon, with a dry salad, desperate for oil, of tuna, olives, capers, red cabbage and celery. The climax of your dinner arrives early, a lasagne of tender noodles in a profound meat sauce that seems to have been cooked down for an age to the essence of its ingredients. Then comes the deep-fried fish, fresh but bland, its lemon indispensable, served with crisp beets and leathery string beans, both lightly dressed. These are followed by nicely roasted chicken that suffers from being chicken of our time, roast beef that simply suffers, sautéed mushrooms that are sodden with oil, and a fine little mixed green salad. Dessert consists of strong cheese, a hot and steamy deep-fried lemon fritter, a bowl of warehouse-ripened fruit, and a house-of-cards structure of crostoli—crisp, deep-fried dough that is sprinkled with sugar, a nice item to toy with while you finish your coffee.

There has always been something regimental about Marchi's. Jackets are required; your waiter commands you to move your eyeglasses to make room for your fish; the busboys work with their eyes lowered, as if they were indentured and scared.

★ MAXWELL'S PLUM

1181 First Avenue (at 64th Street)
LUNCH AND DINNER.
Reservations, 628-2100.
Credit cards: AE, CB, DC, MC, V.
Expensive.

At Maxwell's Plum you may, if you wish, order a balloon. Many people do. The balloons are inflated with lighter-than-air gas, and they are fastened with strings. Grown patrons may be seen eating one-hand food (e.g., black bean soup, fillet of sole, chocolate mousse) with one hand, while clutching the loose end of a balloon string with the other. The balloons bob about in the breezes just a few feet above their heads.

Sometimes, however, a diner becomes so engrossed in what he is eating that he unthinkingly releases his string. If he is eating in the Café (the huge, enclosed, L-shaped sidewalk café that is wrapped around two sides of this mammoth corner restaurant), the balloon drifts upward to nuzzle a plaster animal, hundreds of which are hung just below the striped awning that is the café ceiling. The animals include elephants, rhinoceri, hippopotami, tigers and lions, zebras and leopards, not to mention gorillas, and many, many more. No snakes. The animals, when they are not necking with balloons, are cavorting among the hanging plants and stained-glass lamps (the size of kettle drums) that make up their natural environment; or else they are looking out the café's picture windows, which afford a view that, from this setting, is serene—First Avenue traffic fighting its way north.

Though inelegantly referred to as the Back Room, the back room is the more poshly intended of the two eating areas. You may also have a balloon back here. But don't release it, for if you do, the poor thing has little to cuddle up to but a glowing, floral fantasy stained-glass ceiling the size of a tennis court (singles). There are, it is true, pink pointillist nudes all over the walls, languidly intertwined, but struggle as a balloon may to fasten on one of these, the laws of physics carry it to the cold comfort of hot glass.

Nary a square inch of this establishment is without ornament. There are carved, coppered ceilings, medallioned beams, bejeweled columns down the sides of which water flows, making their golden colors shimmer. But the centerpiece of the place is right at its center—the huge horseshoe counter that, through much such use, is a singles bar. It was while making his approach to this famous fixture that the now never-to-be-forgotten young man, addressing his male companion, uttered his immortal line, viz, "If we can't make out here, we might as well give up."

The unattached come to this place and regard one another with the frank appraisal of a cop regarding a corpse. The types around the bar are nervous or suave, hyper or cool. But they are losers, one and all, for with all their flashing of skin and swagger, they reek of depression—pathetic hysterics who exist only when spoken to. You may be interested to learn that some young ladies still giggle insanely when addressed by strangers; that others, even in singles-bar circumstances, chill forward young men with looks of transcendent indifference. You do not see any balloons at the bar.

Some idiot once awarded this place four stars (out of a possible four). That was the result, rather than the source, of a well-orchestrated reputation. For a while the Plum was taken seriously enough for everyone in New York with any taste at all to have tried it and fled it, which accounts for the uniform inelegance of the considerable numbers who remain to fill it—mustachioed to the ear, low-cut and highly scented, spit-curled and painted purple, obese or emaciated. But Maxwell's is not a bad restaurant. It just cannot prepare food that is anywhere near as good as everything else about it is silly. Few places can. But this social scene should not be missed, and you need not eat badly to catch it.

Maxwell's menu is international (stopping short at the Orient) and extensive, reaching not only to the edges of Western civilization, but a little outside them, to Florida, from whence the Plum imports Florida stone crabs, a marvelous delicacy native to that state's coastal waters. You are served a handful of the beasts' hefty claws, their flamingo-pink-and-black shells partly cracked, in a great silver dish of crushed ice—with nutcrackers, a garnish of fresh garden salad, a half-lemon (elegantly wrapped in cheesecloth, to prevent passage of the seeds with the juice), and a mustard-mayonnaise sauce that is lovely with the sweet, nutlike flavor of the juicy crabmeat. The crabs are not quite the equal of the just-fished article you get at the famous Joe's Stone Crab in Miami Beach, but this beats going to Miami to get them. The shrimp-and-avocado guacamole is a letdown, the shrimp devoid of crispness, the avocado apparently the tasteless Florida variety. And the raw paillard of beef is apparently pounded in advance to thin pancake-size discs and stored somewhere, so that the meat is dry, and arcs of brown adorn it where one disc overlapped another—the tart green-pepper sauce that accompanies this dish is not only good to eat, but indispensable. You get pretty good garlic sausage here—three hefty slabs of glistening, fatted and spiced warm meat, accompanied by hot potato salad—a sturdy first course. And there is a black bean soup that is grainy, thick and deep, though the minced onions that come with it are chopped early, and lack bite.

Oddly for a non-Italian restaurant, this one prepares decent pasta. It is perhaps pretentious that they mingle white and green noodles and call them, in the Italian way, straw and hay, for the individual flavors of the two noodles are not distinct enough to make the magic of that combination; but the cream sauce, with mild sausages and an abundance of fresh, sweet peas, has a gentle warmth to it, and the dish can be fortified and transformed with strong ground cheese and fresh pepper.

You may make a steakhouse of this place, for the steaks are fine; the roast beef is the size of New York State, thick as Mount Marcy, very tender and fairly tasty, though the Yorkshire pudding is far from the true suet-flavored article; and the broiled lobster is bigger than its plate and is served fresh and sweet, broiled to a very fair accuracy (maybe a little overcooked) and accented with the flavor of charred shell.

But the exotic is more the style of this place, as exemplified by roast wild boar. If you expect something gamy and loud from a dish with so ferocious a name, relax, for the slivers of meat are sweet and tender, not unlike venison, and the crisp gingered apples and sweetened sour lingonberries that are served with it make nice foils to the rich meat. But the boar is spread with a thick and excessively tarragoned sauce Béarnaise, which adds nothing to the dish but its presence.

A nicely brandied orange sauce studded with raisins cannot quite redeem this slightly dried-out roast duckling Normande. But the lime-grilled chicken is a successful and amusing dish. The little chunks of bird—which arrive surmounted by circular slivers of raw lime—are deeply browned and heavily flavored with citrus—fun food. You get terrific sweetbreads here, the slabs of pale, tender and very rich meat in a sherry vinegar sauce that is clear, polished, and winy. A dish of such unabashed excess does wonders for your gluttony.

Attention to the niceties of sautéing or grilling or poaching fish is something for which this kitchen may not be geared, so your salmon may be overcooked. Moreover, it may be frozen, for, though it has not gone bad, it lacks almost any of the flavor of the fresh fish.

There is a nice little salad of crunchy limestone lettuce and Stilton cheese, served in a tart dressing. But the platter of cheeses is straight from the icebox, and they are cold and flat. The sweet desserts, however, are good, if lacking in subtlety. There is a tarte Tatin of caramelized apples on a browned pastry; banana fritters of soft, sweet, ripe fruit in a crackling crust, served with a warm, syrupy cinnamon sauce; and, the big winner, a chocolate soufflé that is made for one in little white ramekins—well-risen and fluffy, it is sharp with the flavor of strong chocolate, and it is enriched when served with melted chocolate and whipped cream. Such concoctions as sherbets with fresh fruit and banana splits may be right if you are in a larky way, but be warned that there is nothing special about Maxwell's productions of this kind of thing—they are just soda fountain stuff, and if you do not eat them right up they become puddles.

Your host is imperious even though he shuffles; your captain introduces himself by name (Ronny, Jimmy, whatever); and your neighbor asks where you have your hair cut. It is all part of the show. And if you want to take flash Polaroid snapshots, no one will stop you.

★ McFEELY'S

565 West 23rd Street
LUNCH, SUNDAY; DINNER, DAILY.
Reservations, 929-4432.
Credit cards: AE, MC, V.
Medium-priced.

In the days when voyagers from Manhattan reached the outside world by water routes, there was life at the edges of the island, not just cargo. Travelers to such romantic lands as Weehawken, Hoboken and Jersey City departed by ferry from the great terminal at the foot of West 23rd Street. If they got to the pier with time to spare, they maybe had a drink in the tavern on the corner of 23rd and Eleventh Avenue. That was long ago. Though the ferries have not been restored, and are not about to be, the corner tavern has. This is not, of course, an act of landmark preservation. It is a commercial acknowledgment that Chelsea—the main crosstown street of which, West 23rd, was the city's Great White Way a century ago—is rousing itself from decades of drowsy anonymity. Instead of Cavanaugh's or Petipas or Guffanti's, three famous restaurants that thrived around here for half a century when Chelsea was Chelsea, there is today McFeely's, which seems embarked on a quite long run of its own. The place has a little bit of almost everything that makes for success these days. It is casual— you may come either as you are or as you were. It is eclectic—the menu reflects not only the mixed heritage of this neighborhood, but of half the popular restaurants in town. And its overriding theme derives from this day's seemingly ubiquitous *nostalgie de la fin de siècle*—the establishment styles itself a "Victorian saloon."

There is a bar in the big front room shaped like a racetrack cut in half the long way, and only a little smaller than that. Behind the bar, ancient mirrors, stained glass and much wood that was carved long ago and scraped clean recently. The old refrigerator compartments have glass fronts and brass handles. On one glass door the words "Trommer's White Label Beer" were applied, in gold leaf, long before the Second World War put local beers with German names out of business. The floor is paved with barbershop tiles. Brass-and-cut-glass chandeliers hang from a back-painted glass ceiling, the intricate decay of which has been lovingly preserved. A couple of four-bladed ceiling fans turn slowly or not at all. The walls are of wood paneling. Big windows look out on the street. An old upright, its front to a corner, looks out over the room, a hefty loudspeaker mounted, frighteningly, on its back. When no one is diddling the keys, taped honkytonk—the whistle-and-bang sounds of trumpets and clarinets and ukeleles and snare drums—is pumped into the air. A dozen or so green-linened tables are distributed around the room. At these you may have first courses, salads, burgers, desserts, coffee.

But if dinner is what you want, you must repair to the back room, which has more space than the barroom, and much less noise. This room is more like the Palm Court than the Palm Court, long-leafed tropical trees all about, much space between the many tables, more of those chandeliers and languid ceiling fans, and, framed by walnut-colored wood paneling, deep emerald-green walls hung with neatly framed prints. There is more airy, relaxed spaciousness back here than the financial demands of Manhattan real estate permit anywhere near the center of town. This is a frontier tavern.

The restaurant gets young people who moved to Chelsea for the rare combination of less-than-insupportable rents and an overland route to a New York office. And it gets older folk who have lived patiently in London Terrace—some of them since 1930, when the huge apartment building first went up—waiting several recent decades for a decent eating place within walking distance. They mingle here with the young without friction, and eat from the same menu.

But they do not eat from the same menu all the time, for the listings are changed every week or two. On occasion there is smoked trout, very much that slightly oily, slightly smoky fish you get all over town, and every bit as good, though the horseradish sauce here is pallid and watery. You get fresh asparagus, carefully cooked and crisp, but unfortunately not peeled, so the bigger spears are fibrous—they are moistened with a sour vinaigrette that is thick with herbs and minced onions. The white bean salad is abundant and crunchy, but only mildly seasoned. A couple of surprise winners: deep-fried mushrooms, fresh and crunchy, lightly battered and crisped, which you bring to life with lemon and/or with the sparkling tartar sauce that garnishes the dish; and, unlikely as it may seem, ratatouille quiche, reheated of course, but the smooth custard, spicy vegetables and dark crust make an elegant little pizza.

The bluefish is fresh, and sometimes it is served with good bacon, which makes the dish smoky, and with a vaguely dilled sour-cream sauce, which makes it moist. Some-thing given as "honeysuckle shrimp," and described as "broiled with honey, sherry, garlic and butter," is only so indistinctly touched with those flavorings that if you squeeze on lemon you end up with an entirely new dish called "lemon shrimp on rice" —not bad for an accident. Apparently someone who takes the menu more seriously than whoever cooks the shrimp is responsible for the chicken breast, which is "mari-nated in dark beer . . . served with a light lemon-cream sauce." This item has plenty of everything billed, and the sautéed white meat is good in the somewhat indelicate collection of flavors. You get fine liver, the slivered green apples and the cider sauce pleasantly tart against the rich meat. But the steak au poivre, though of decent meat and a sauce of brandy, mustard and cream, is simply outnumbered by the peppercorns that make up its armor.

Chewy layers of meringue and creamy ones of mocha make up the very good dacquoise—the dessert does not need its chocolate icing at all. The so-called chocolate diablo cake is like a super brownie, with a strong cocoa flavor, good ground nuts throughout, polished icing. Sour cream apple pie is just like regular apple pie, but a little creamy. The strawberries are ripe, their whipped cream is real.

There are several big round tables in the dining room that can accommodate groups of eight or more.

★★ IL MENESTRELLO

14 East 52nd Street
LUNCH AND DINNER. CLOSED SUNDAY.
Reservations, 421–7588.
Credit cards: AE, DC, MC, V.
Very expensive.

A disregard for appearances suggests preoccupation with higher considerations. Il Menestrello, which has supplanted the slightly mourned Le Mistral, has taken on the French appointments of its predecessor, changing hardly a stick, even though the new establishment is of thoroughly Italian persuasion. "What does it matter what we look like," these Italians ask, in effect, "as long as we run a good place?"

And, after a slow start of too many months' duration, this *is* a good place, one of midtown's more reliable Italian restaurants, on a level with San Marco and the 50th Street Giambelli when those places are on their better behavior. Il Menestrello, however, is more relaxed than most of the big-deal Italian restaurants in its neighborhood; and things could hardly be otherwise in so wacky a setting, for at Il Menestrello such mouthfuls as "ravioli al sugo di carne alla Romana" and "spigola con funghi e salza di pomidoro" are swallowed in dining rooms that are dominated by murals of sunlit southern France, painted tricolors flapping in the breeze over the sea and sands around Cannes and Nice.

Italianate touches have been added, however. There has been a dramatic general darkening of the room, with brighter light focused on the high points, so that the rough plaster walls (the color of old ivory) and the dark-brown ceiling beams are now somber and heavy, the crimson velvet banquettes brilliant, almost gaudy in this setting. And to the scenes of the Riviera that Jean Pagès painted on these walls more than a decade ago have been added a few five-and-dime oils in ornate frames, including one of a boy and his guitar, the former singing, for *menestrello* means "minstrel."

All of which adds up to the slightly tasteless but comfortable posh that is the quintessential quality of New York's more ambitious Italian restaurants. Angelo's and Alfredo, Benito's and Barbetta, Forlini's and Orsini's, all are innocent eyesores with the position in New York restaurant design held in architecture by Miami Beach hotels.

In such a setting it is startling to encounter purity and simplicity. Yet for the price of one fin you may begin your dinner with food of almost chaste refinement. The dish is called insalata di funghi freschi; it consists, principally, of fresh fragrant mushrooms, pale as cream, sliced to parchment thinness and dressed copiously in a gentle vinaigrette, so that each pearly sliver is rich with seasoned oil; the mushrooms are mingled with chopped celery, hard and crackling, an inspired counterpoint.

Bresaola is the salted dried beef of Italy, served here in thin slices the size of playing cards, the mahogany-colored meat fibrous and a little gamy, moistened with a cool, lemoned mixture of oil and parsley. This is loud meat, with a flavor that can seem "off" if you are unaccustomed, but if you can accept it, it makes a stimulating first course.

What usually goes by the name "spiedino" in this city consists of small squares of ham, mozzarella cheese and bread in a four- or five-inch repeated series, assembled on a skewer, battered, deep-fried and served with anchovy sauce. Il Menestrello's version, though made with tasty ham and decent enough cheese, and though served in a well-browned and airy crust, is heavily weighted toward bread, which makes it somewhat leaden. But it is the sharp and salty flavor of the hot and oily anchovy sauce against the crusty sandwich that makes this dish what it is, even in this heavy rendering.

This place bakes clams several ways—it uses fresh clams and flavors them strongly and well, but the baking is often too long, which toughens them. The raw clams are sparkling.

Sturdy broths and soups are served in broad soup plates. The zuppa di spinaci is a deep-yellow chicken broth, hot and fatty, replete with fresh spinach. Even sturdier is the minestra di fagioli con pasta (which usually goes by some variant of the name "pasta fazole"), the bean-and-pasta soup that is served here in an extremely solid version, with only limited space for the thickened broth in the interstices between the firm beans, pasta shells and chunks of ham. Just before serving, the copious plate is strewn with parsley, which livens the earthy stuff, and if you wish, strong Parmesan cheese is grated on at the table.

Spaghetti carbonara is prepared, for your amusement, beside your table. Onions and ham are sautéed in oil and butter, then simmered in consommé thickened with egg yolk, fortified with Parmesan cheese and tossed with the just-cooked spaghetti in a hot pan —pungent food. The spaghetti bolognese is tame, as if the ground meat should have been further browned early in its preparation. The tortellini alla panna, though very much a careful rendering of the chicken-and-cheese-filled pasta tubes in cream sauce, is little more than richness and texture, the flavor of the stuffing vague. But the capelli d'angelo Il Menestrello is a winner, about five miles of ultra-svelte spaghettini slithering about in a tomato sauce that is given a sweet, oceanic perfume of crabmeat.

Forty-five main courses are listed, and pickings among them are slim—nothing outright distasteful, you understand, but none inspires amaze. The deep-fried squid are tender, crisp and tasteless. If you squeeze on lots of lemon, they taste like lemon. You take it that filetti di dentice Fiorentina is a dish of Florentine boned teeth, and you are disappointed to get slabs of snapper on a field of spinach, adorned with pale-yellow puddles of gooey sauce. It looks like an abstract by an untalented child and tastes only a little better. The shrimp dishes are no worse than the shrimp available in this city these days. You can get fine seafood here if you order a simple striped-bass preparation.

Inquire about the veal-chop preparations, and your waiter suggests you have it in a paper bag (not listed). It often arrives in a puffed-up enclosure of aluminum foil, the size of a baby's pillow, within which are steam and a big chop, juicy and tender, with a simple mushroom sauce—very good food. What you call chicken scarpariello they call spezzatino di pollo del contadino. These sautéed chunks of boned chicken are rather heavily oiled, and though there is garlic in the dish, the chicken is heavy and lacks vibrance. Splendid fried brains are available, the smooth gray meat gentle and hot, lightly crusted and sprinkled with capers and their juice. Or you can have huge chunks of spicy Italian sausage in a slightly sweet tomato sauce that is thick with sautéed onions and peppers—something to put aside for winter.

For relief there is a cool salad of green beans and beets. For dessert there are the usual excesses: strong-and-wet rum cake under several inches of meringue; ponderous cheese cake; zabaglione that varies in Marsala content, temperature and foaminess with the enthusiasm of your waiter.

The crowd crowds in, cigarettes hanging from every other lip. No tailored lawyers, media sophisticates or high-fashion style setters are to be seen. Middlemen, salesmen, visiting buyers and their temporary companions all are comfortably assembled around the commodious tables. Drinks, too much food, and wine and cigars are preludes to closing the deal. "What Ah want for Dallas," a Texas retailer announces over his spumoni, "is a hip [pause], updated [pause], short-sleeve [long pause] safari shirt." His hosts take furious notes.

★★ LA MÉTAIRIE

189 West 10th Street
DINNER. CLOSED MONDAY.
Reservations, 989-0343.
No credit cards.
Wine.
Expensive.

Though the room is tiny (seven tables) and the menu extremely limited, you can eat once a week in this place for a year and not repeat yourself. Apparently, the young, Brooklyn-accented New Yorker who is the chef—for the Frenchman who owns this place—is free to buy what she wishes and cook it according to her well-educated whim.

The restaurant is French rustic—to just this side of self-satire. There are cooing doves in the birdcage. The unlinened tabletops are of thick, rough-hewn planks of wood (their polyurethane sealant gives them away). Crude culinary implements and pottery adorn the scarred-plaster walls. You walk on an old wooden floor, and you sink into narrow, straight-backed chairs that have cushions on their sagging seats. Nor is that the only minor discomfort, for when you entered the restaurant, you did so through a door that opens only inward, the arc of its swing overlapping that of a Dutch door just beyond it, which swings either way. If the half-door is opened out just as you are coming in, staff assistance is required to adjudicate the confusion. Then there are the waitresses, who are not at home in the restaurant business, and seem permanently resentful at having been chosen by God to deal with the public. You are informed, for example, that you are a few minutes early in a manner that would be suitable if you were a few hours late. They do relax when they get to know you (or when they are flirted with), but they have never learned to talk to customers about the food other than in the manner of a schoolboy, with games on his mind, reciting aloud in class.

However, once your order is taken, and you have adjusted to the cramped seating, eating here is pleasant. The tiny crowd is mannerly, and the imaginative but never sensationalistic food is good.

From a little blackboard menu you choose the salade Jeannette. That is not a dish but a category. It means different things at different times. Sometimes it refers to slivers of fresh ham and slices of chestnut, sautéed until crisp, served on alfalfa sprouts with green mayonnaise and strong black olives. Another salade is of cool spaghetti and strands of delicate smoked salmon in a tangy dressing, garnished with florets of crunchy broccoli in an herbed green sauce that is dotted with capers. The ingredients come together so naturally in most of these improvisations that they seem rather like traditional combinations you simply have not encountered before. The assiette Métairie is also a category rather than a dish. Of the items that have been served under that heading: hot clams and mussels, with leeks and green peppers, served on melted smoked mozzarella cheese—the liquids of the seafood and vegetables combine with the cheese to form a thick, buttery liquid, so the dish is like an extremely flavorful seafood-and-vegetable stew. In a variant of that, fresh mushrooms are substituted for the shellfish. But another assiette is no relation at all—calf's liver, coated with bread crumbs and mustard, grilled until crisp but still rare, brought to you on a mound of shredded celery root, with cold roasted red peppers (very strong and sweet), sprouts and watercress, all looking very pretty around the centerpiece. Soups and assorted charcuterie are also on the menu. They are fine, but those experimental numbers are the things to try.

The main courses are more conventional: salmon, fresh as fresh air, in a buttery tarragon sauce; tuna in a deep-brown sauce—smooth, almost syrupy—of the red wine the fish was cooked in; a well-chosen chicken, moist and of good flavor, its skin crisp, in an enriched wine sauce laden with fresh mushrooms. The lamb stew is of shoulder meat (you will recall that your waitress pointed at her own shoulder to make that clear) still on the bone, strong and tender and juicy, surrounded on its plate by a couple of dozen artichoke leaves, the slight bitterness of which is good against the fat-flavored meat. Thin slices of leg of lamb are sautéed and served—with white beans—in a thick brown sauce, the tomato flavoring of which gives the dish an Italian cast.

Good cheese is always on hand. The salads are of fresh, crisp greens, to which your chef will sometimes do unexpected things—she has been known to march into the dining room and sprinkle ground macadamia nuts on every salad in sight. The very nicely caramelized tarte Tatin is of good apples; it is flamed, and its syrup would be much better if the help learned to tip the plate back and forth to burn off all the brandy. The chocolate mousse cake is a little heavy, but powerful. The quince purée could as well be applesauce. When the quince is served whole, however, under almond purée, that is rather nifty.

• MICHAEL PHILLIPS

994 First Avenue (near 54th Street)
LUNCH AND DINNER.
Reservations, 888-0018.
Credit cards: AE, CB, DC, MC, V.
Expensive.

Yes, children, there *is* a Michael Phillips, and he used to work at Manhattan Market, an estimable eating place one avenue west of this one. Michael learned as much as he could while he was at the Market, and then he opened a place of his own. In publishing this much education would be called plagiarism. Oh, sure, everybody has to make a living, all's fair and imitation is, after all, the sincerest form of modesty. But what makes this knockoff embarrassing is that the fellow put his very own name on it. He thought no one would notice, that he would get away with it. And he did. The place is doing business. There have always been those who liked the movie better.

What was most clearly borrowed was a certain intended look of grand, rather cold starkness that, in the fitting out, is meant to be relieved a little by the contrasting warmth of the appointments. To a degree this has been achieved. The restaurant is a rather dark box, its lofty walls a handsome blue-gray. Along one side an old bar of carved oak, mirrored behind, glows in its light. At the front a wall of French doors looks out on the world—they are opened a little when the weather is nice, and the sounds of First Avenue and its traffic trickle in. Massive pillars faced with dark mirror rise through the room—almost invisibly when the lights are down—and they add a glitzy note to the hard-edged place. The floor is carpeted dark blue, and the room is furnished with rows of pink-linened tables. Planters of greenery break up the space a little. All that would have been fine, a straightforward lift. But you get the impression that Michael wanted to surpass. And so there are these rather grotesque surreal prints on the walls—happily, only a handful; and stained-glass windows that have been installed, with back light, over the bar—since they were in their first life intended for vertical installation and have tops and bottoms, there is no way to place them in a ceiling without their seeming cockeyed; and finally there is—well, what is it?—a kind of fountain, or waterfall, or liquid screen against the back wall, consisting of perhaps a hundred micturitional streams, which flow continually, so that suggestible customers seated within the orbit of their sound spend the greater portion of their time here seeking out the facilities.

Between trips they discover that, though some of the dishes are successful, the cooking betrays the very same desperate search for the unusual that culminated in that shower curtain. A crabmeat and grapefruit salad is an example that is sometimes offered —the crabmeat is mingled with slivered almonds and a few greens, moistened with a mildly lemoned dressing, and surrounded by grapefuit sections. The dish suffers more for its preserved (rather than fresh) crabmeat, and its canned grapefruit, than it does for the pretentiousness of its conception. But the place turns out nice snails and serves them with chunks of tomato and mushroom in a sauce that is thick and creamy. And they serve tender hot oysters, five of them, in their shells, moistened by a pale and winy sauce—for some reason they arrive on a small beach of table salt.

Every day Michael Phillips struggles anew to come up with a dramatically different pasta dish: they have dressed some perfectly nice tortellini with strands of salami, mushrooms, a thin sauce of cream and wine—tasty but silly; and they have chosen for their red fusilli (corkscrew-shaped pasta prepared with tomato sauce) a garlic-flavored cream sauce—the tomato in the pasta is discernible only by its color, for the garlic in the sauce completely overwhelms the dish. The experiments continue.

Trial-and-error has also produced Dover sole with strawberry butter, a perfectly executed idea the arrival of whose time, however, you should not hold your breath in the expectation of. The scallops are good—tiny, just lightly browned, in a film of butter that the help is trained to refer to as beurre blanc. Your waitress, with a face straight enough to suggest a capacity for shrugging off torture, informs you that the evening's special is "pheasant roasted in a baked potato." You are delivered two quarters of the bird. The breast is lodged between the larger part of the hollowed shell of a baked potato (which is filled with wild mushrooms and garlic cloves), and the smaller part (which sits upon it like a cap several sizes too small); the leg is beside it (and, presumably, beside itself) looking on. The duck, by comparison, gets off easy, the sliced meat—juicy, rimmed with fat—is served in a dark, slightly sweetened sauce that is mildly sharpened with grapefruit and grapefruit rind. Two slices of sautéed veal are upon, respectively, a duxelles of mushrooms and a mound of spinach; in the same order, they are under a dark sauce and a cream sauce that is hot with pink peppercorns: the slices of veal are too thick to be successfully cooked by this light sautéing, and the dark sauce is of no note; but the peppercorn/spinach half of the act tastes fine, and you can probably arrange for a double order of that only. The rack of lamp is fine, though the billed mustard is remote.

A circular Belgian waffle is warm, just made, sports a dollop of melting vanilla ice cream on each quadrant, and a surrounding pool of strawberry purée—very good. The chocolate mousse pie is cold, and has the kind of depth of chocolate flavor you find in strong Italian ice cream—the pie is good with Michael Phillips's very nice whipped cream. As is the hot apple tart on its crunchy, nutlike crust. Sherbets and fruits are offered, including, on seasonal occasion, blackberries with strong chocolate sherbet that is almost as dark as the fruit, and more of that good strawberry purée.

Michael Phillips gets a good bit of what is known in the trade as the bridge-and-tunnel crowd. Sometimes they are noisy.

The help is well-meaning but often a little out of it. One youngster, when asked why she did not enumerate the many dishes that were "out" when she brought the menus, answers that she just hoped you would not order them.

○ MR. CHOW

324 East 57th Street
LUNCH, MONDAY TO FRIDAY; DINNER, DAILY.
Reservations, 751-9030.
Credit cards: AE, DC, MC, V.
Medium-priced.

Every appointment in Mr. Chow gleams, with the exception of the cluster of battened green junk sails that hang from the center of the ceiling as, presumably, a sculpture. You enter through carved glass doors. You descend a brass-balustraded stairway to the dining room proper. The floor is of marble blocks. The walls are covered with tinted mirror or lustrous paint—cream-colored or black—that has the glint and sheen of nail polish. Illumination emanates from large, fan-shaped tortoise-shell sconces that are supported by polished silver brackets. The room is rimmed by a shiny black banquette, and the chairs that face it, across the wee, cheek-to-cheek tables, are of Chinese inspiration—legs and backs of dark-brown enameled rods constructed around circular upholstered seats. And though the linen on your table does not itself gleam, it glows, for, under the tablecloths, the center of each table top is a rectangular panel of glass, through which an electric light, built into the underside, shines. The cool customers who come here try not to giggle about it too much, and by the third or fourth visit they begin to take it for granted.

It is possible that Orientals have been on these premises, but no one has stepped forward to testify to having seen one. The host/captains are a matched set of six-foot, dark-haired, crew-cut dandies. They drift about like sleepwalkers on roller skates. Their politeness is schooled, right down to the five-degree angle at which they tilt their heads when directing a sad smile at an eager client. You get the impression that if someone turned up their power they would swiftly kill. The waiters, recruited from New York's French restaurants, call customers "madame," or "monsieur," and betray, generally, such contempt for this clientele that you are hard put not to admire them for the judgments they automatically make of anyone who would eat in this place. But they are too hasty, for this is a decent enough crowd. What is most notable about them is that they look just like the restaurant. Side-by-side ladies, one in a black dress with black spaghetti straps to show off her pearly skin, her companion in something pale, with pale spaghetti straps, to accentuate the beautifully bronzed tegument she has just brought back from a subtropical shore, both of them with gold around their necks, no one should doubt for a moment the financial resourcefulness of the husbands across the table, who are all dressed up in tonsured mustaches, double-knit suits and Italian shoes. In Mr. Chow they have struck a home.

In the era between the wars, New York was home to as many Chinese restaurants, probably, as it is today. But in those times, when eating had not yet become the fad of fashion, all Chinese restaurants were alike, and every neighborhood had one. Once a week, or whatever, you would "eat Chinks," as it was delicately put. "Let's eat Chinks tonight" was how an expedition to the local bamboo-and-Formica rice emporium was initiated. If two such restaurants were within walking distance, you chose the nearer one, because it was closer. Chicken chow mein was a popular dish. You sprinkled it with hard noodles. You ate it with a fork. You washed it down with tepid tea, or if you were flush, with Pepsi-Cola or Mission Orange. Coffee was another possibility. Whatever you ate, all the food tasted the same. That the nation China was divided into provinces, that many of the provinces had, over the centuries, developed distinctive styles of cooking, and that in certain great cities of China these styles had been amalgamated and refined into elegant cosmopolitan arts, were matters of as much importance to New Yorkers as the standings of the teams in the Bolivian Soccer League. If, after eating Chinks, your stomach was upset for a couple of days, well, it was all part of growing up.

Then came the cultural revolution (ours, not theirs). Eating was part of gracious living. Chinese restaurants sprinted to keep up, get ahead. They started referring to their merchandise as "cuisine." They reprinted their menus, deleting chow mein, chop suey. They discontinued the use of canned chicken broth in wonton soup. Then they discontinued wonton soup. The old order was giving way. Everything was changing. *A real danger existed that the historic Chinese cookery of New York's Depression years would vanish forever.*

Comes to the rescue Mr. Chow. In disguise yet, all dressed up as today. But there is no mistaking the food, no matter what fancy names (including learned borrowings from the Romance languages) they call it by. You cannot fool the experts. And the experts are here. The very boys and girls who made jokes about flied lice, and crossed their eyes and sprang their upper incisors to laugh about it, have grown up and made it big. But their loyalty to the old values is undiminished. Oh, sure, these days they swill Pouilly-Fuissé with their egg rolls, instead of 7-Up, maybe even a Napa Valley cabernet with the beef and oyster sauce, cognac with the cappuccino. But they give themselves away. None of them uses chopsticks, and everyone pouts when the lichees come without fortune cookies.

Then there is the menu, the physical thing, bound in boards that are upholstered in tooled leather and grosgrain, the pages of the unwieldy book screwed together by brass bolts. Most of the dishes on the two-page listing at the front of the book are described on one of two sides of around thirty separate one-third pages at the back. Getting information out of this document is like searching through a scrapbook of newspaper clippings that is coming unglued. Then there are the contents. Eppis essen yclept aubergine en croûte is explicated as "Aubergine stuffed with goodies, dipped in light batter and deep fried. It tastes like fried oyster." It tastes like fried bubble gum.

The fried dumplings (listed under "pasta") are leaden and greasy, precisely what you got in the most exhausted neighborhood dive in Washington Heights in 1941. The squab with lettuce is made with chicken—you wrap the pebbly amalgam in a leaf of iceberg lettuce, dip it in a viscous and insipid plum sauce, and eat the package with your fingers. Then you wash your hands of it in finger bowls that have pink petals floating in the water. The shark's-fin soup tastes like the chicken broth they stopped using in the wonton soup, albeit it is colored red. Korean meat is a decent first course —thin and tender pork, much fat around the edges, served tepid, in a spicy garlicked liquid, with pickled cucumbers.

The nine seasons prawn is simply not for this or any other season; the gambler's duck is one of those quasi-Peking duck preparations, here prepared with oodles of fat under the skin of the bird and with scallions that were shredded with the dawn, so that they are tired by dinner time. What you used to call roast pork they call char sieu pork. It was better as roast pork, for this version is at once coarse and sugary. The beef with scallion greens is edible principally because its excess of salt conceals whatever characteristics it possesses.

The French pastries are tolerable, the oranges in Grand Marnier would not intoxicate a ladybug, and the lichees come from a can. You can get ice cream, which is served, of course, with amaretti. Those Frankenstein hosts see to it that you leave pronto when the place is busy—they clear your table of everything, including water glasses, before you have asked for your check.

★★ MITALI

334 East 6th Street
LUNCH, SATURDAY AND SUNDAY; DINNER, DAILY.
Reservations, 533-2508.
Credit cards: AE, MC, V.
Inexpensive.

Where once (decades ago) Chinese laundries, kosher butcher shops and Italian ice stores struggled grimly side by side in twelve-foot-wide storefronts, there is today, like a single file of lost, searching pilgrims, a row of no fewer than nine Indian restaurants. This anomalous concentration is situated on East 6th Street between First and Second avenues (more specifically on the eastern end of the southern side of the block), enterprises that seem to cling together while they compete, like a miserable family.

The head of the family (these days, anyway) is Mitali, which has experienced sufficient success in recent years to move from one position on the chain to larger quarters a few doors west, and to fit out the new premises in a manner appropriate to the master dining room. Owing to heavy curtains, the interior of Mitali may not be seen from the street, so when you enter, from the gray wreckage strewn with garish waste that is this part of town, you may be startled to find yourself in a dark, posh, womblike place, its walls sheathed in deep-red velvet, its white-linened tables aglow in the light of the tiny white candles that burn thereon. Bejeweled Indian cloths are spread across the low ceilings. The two small rooms are filled with the gentle, mournful plinking of recorded Indian music. The swarthy, black-haired waiters wear white jackets and bow ties. But the prices are low, this is East 6th Street no matter how you furnish your store, and the patrons are very much of the neighborhood. If, on the streets, you see young people in stockings of two different primary colors, hair of three, others in mixed tatters and hip-high fishing boots, Mitali is a filter that separates out the most extreme ists—inside, you get clear-eyed girls, in gauze raiment and pigtails, who smoke between courses; boys who eat with one hand and hold their hair out of their food with the other. But the neighborhood is changing (perhaps the denizens are growing up and becoming fuddy-duddies), for there is a germ of a comfort-loving middle class here now, young unmarrieds mainly, and of the restaurants on the row, theirs is Mitali.

They come here for what the menu styles "Fresh Shrimp," crisp chunks of the little crustaceans in a thick spicy sweet-and-sour gravy that is studded with bits of lemon —the dish is served under a single poori, the light, flaky, almost powdery, balloonlike Indian bread. And they come here for Dacca liver, a sparkling chicken-liver paste, herbed and seasoned, mingled with orange rind and vegetables. And they order vegetable pakora and banana pakora, light fritters, the former mildly spiced and crisp and just about weightless, the latter almost creamy with their filling of hot, soft fruit. There is an odd first course called sheek kebab, sausage-shaped logs of spiced ground meat that are cooked in a fire and served cut into discs—the meat is dry, almost hard, but you squeeze lemon onto the morsels and sprinkle them with chopped onions, which brings the meat to life. And there is a soup called kanjeevaram, a thick, red, satisfying cabbage soup that is flavored with tomatoes and sharp spices and studded with hefty chunks of cabbage.

It is possible that your notion of freshness, in fish, does not correspond to that of a subcontinental. Or perhaps this low-priced restaurant cannot afford to throw anything away. Anyway, eschew dishes made of animals that had fins. Opt instead for the seafood kurma made with oysters, a creamy pink sauce that is crisp with almonds, gently chewy of the minced oysters—the food is extremely spicy, but the oysters moderate the intensity with a mild seafood sweetness. Crabmeat pathia is a hot mush, deeply oiled, yet not oily, laced with onions, and served with a warm souplike preparation of lentils, which leavens the fiery spiciness of the crabmeat.

Something called malai lamb is a stewlike mixture of strong meat, in substantial chunks, mingled with bits of coconut in a thick sauce that is powerfully spiced without being hot. Even better is the intricately textured lamb biryani—sautéed meat fragrantly herbed, its spiciness almost dazzlingly complex, mixed with firm rice. The item given (with a typographic crypticalism common on this menu) as "culf liver" would be lovely if it were more rapidly sautéed, for the garlic and ginger seasoning is fine, but the strands of liver are a little leaden and a little tough. You are much better off with kati chicken, in which the fibrous but tender meat of the bird, profoundly flavored with the oil and spices of its marinade, is mingled with strong spinach that is at once earthy and loud—a striking dish. There is more of that spinach in shaag ponir, a homey dish of fried cheese and the fresh, leafy green.

A violent onion garnish and a gentle tamarind sauce are supplied, in little steel pitchers, for those who wish to tinker with their food. Decent rice, in abundance, is served to one and all. The breads are good; the one called mughli paratha—buttery wheat bread, stuffed with meat, eggs and vegetables—converts a normal meal into one of postgraduate gluttony.

The Indian desserts are difficult to appreciate. There is ice cream. The gentle yogurt drink called lassi may be the best conclusion to your dinner.

• IL MONELLO

1460 Second Avenue (near 76th Street)
LUNCH AND DINNER. CLOSED SUNDAY.
Reservations, 535-9310.
Credit cards: AE, CB, DC, MC, V.
Expensive.

The people who run this place have started up other restaurants as well. Their pattern has been to move into quarters vacated by failed eating places, accept the fittings exactly as they find them, serve good food and make lots of money, all without recourse to architects or designers or decorators. It began with this place, which was Villa Doria before it became Il Monello in the mid-seventies, with only the name and the food changed. But eventually money and success went to the management's heads, they redecorated, and the ugliness that was Villa Doria was replaced by Il Monello's own. "Il Monello" is "The Street Urchin," so several of the many five-and-ten-cent oils (which hang on walls of alternate panels of worm-eaten and smooth mustard-colored wood) are of angelic young boys in ragged duds. And each and every one of these genuine oil paintings comes with its own attached, individually controlled electrical light fixture for superior viewability. The banquettes that rim the restaurant are of multicolored plastic that halfheartedly simulates a tapestry weave. Assorted chandeliers drip crystal or ooze warmth. The ceiling is of sprayed-on gray foam. Thin silver vases of exotic flowers stand on the white-linened tables. And the people who come here are very much a part of the place—successful professionals and their well-kept wives. Fifty-dollar silk neckties and hundred-dollar permanent waves are standard. It is not a jolly crowd, but it is not a worried one either. Nor an astute one, for the restaurant they learned to love in its early years, though it is still of some merit, is not what it was. Love, however, is a fixation, and so it is not susceptible to facts that would temper more dispassionate judgment. Accordingly those neckties and perms literally stand in line to eat here.

Then they sit down to spiedino alla romana, squares of bread, ham and cheese that have been impaled on a skewer, fried, and then served in an anchovy sauce. The solid ingredients are rather leaden, but the dark and almost overpowering sauce is so thick and strong and deep as to redeem the dish. The crostini di polenta is another matter, blocks of browned cornmeal in a rather gentle meat sauce onto which your waiter grates a bit of mild cheese—a satisfying dish, but not a striking one.

The captains here, some of them, are fond of themselves, strut a little, narrow their eyes in sharp evaluation as they listen to and judge your selections. They parade their suave expertise. Watch this one prepare your capelli d'angelo primavera over a burner on the sidestand. As he measures out the ingredients his features betray a veritable transport of concentration. He adds just the tiniest bit more of this, just a pinch more of that. He stirs, managing to make the act as serious as a tea ceremony. He adjusts the flame to within a micrometer of the ideal height. Then he goes away while the stuff is bubbling. He returns whenever he happens to get a chance. If his chance is a lucky one, your pasta is good—fresh vegetables, slivers of ham and a creamy tomato sauce, all mingled with tender noodles. The white clam sauce is pallid, low on garlic and lacking even brininess. And the green and white noodles, with cream sauce and ham, are absurdly salty, and your waiter's suggested addition of cheese to this heavy sauce would only make it more so. But the linguine matriciana sports a tangy red sauce that is leavened a little with cheese—ham sharpens the dish, and onions sweeten it.

Il Monello has been known to cook perfectly good snapper down to a mush. But the crosta cei marinara—a kind of shellfish stew in a powerful red sauce—does much justice to its clams, mussels, shrimp and tiny lobster. The Italian sausages are coarse rather than strong, and their vibrant sauce pizzaiola—thick with peppers and chunks of garlic —does not offset their harshness. The chicken cacciatora, in a winy red sauce that is dominated by rosemary, is decent food of absolutely no class. Good veal is made into good saltimbocca—the tender scallops of pale meat overlaid with strong ham, the two moistened with a gentle sauce that is lightly flavored with sage. But that same veal is made into an absurdity called bocconcini di vitello—your captain mentions garlic and shallots and herbs, but the thing really tastes like candy. A la carte vegetables: string-beans that have been on the steam table since yesterday; sautéed quartered artichokes that have not been properly trimmed—at the base or top—of inedible fibrous material; pretty good sautéed fresh spinach, cooked with garlic. You cannot count on the greens in your salad to be fresh.

Cheeses are not listed, but they are available: you are served so gigantic a slab of Gorgonzola that you figure they are trying to get rid of it rapidly before it gets even older; the Parmesan, on the other hand, is good cheese, though it is not the aged best. Il Monello's zuppa inglese is the usual rum-flavored fluff. The berries are not perfectly chosen—underripe strawberries one day, overripe raspberries the next—but the cool zabaglione that is poured over them is winy and not too sweet. The cheese cake is the best dessert, studded with candied fruits, heavy with moisture, lemoned, sugary, the genuine Italian article.

If you are unknown here you will probably be shown to Coventry, an ill-ventilated back room. Simply demur, and you will be taken to a table in the front.

★★★ MON PARIS

111 East 29th Street
LUNCH, MONDAY TO FRIDAY; DINNER, MONDAY TO SATURDAY. CLOSED SUNDAY.
Reservations, 683–4255.
Credit cards: AE, MC, V.
Expensive.

Crimson fleurs-de-lis of velvety flocking adorn the walls; carpeting cushions the floor; there are street lanterns, framed travel posters, jolly art; chandeliers that are bouquets of little red lampshades shine down on tables snowy with stiff white linen. The waiters serving you are in scarlet doublets; their boss, ever-present and watchful, mindful that they do it well, is portly and contented in his snug, too long jacket. He is a kind of burghermaster among the self-made middlemen spending their money here. The rather obvious posh of the institution he presides over fulfills the early dreams of the jobbers, head bookkeepers, salesmen and bejeweled housewives who compose the couples, and clusters of couples, that fill this place.

No one here was born with a three-bedroom apartment and a terrace in his mouth;

there is nary a prep-school diploma or B-School master's in the house. They are all perfectly well off, you understand, but their pleasures are not quite taken for granted, and while they betray considerable satisfaction in the comfort and solid food they find here, and visit with each other heartily about such subjects as making connections between Acapulco and San Juan during what is known as the height of the season, their preoccupation with the wherewithal to prosper again another day is rarely more than just under the skin of their conversations. A cocktail or two, a little time with the menu, two minutes with the waiters—hardly have the crevettes Provençale arrived when talk among the men switches to market conditions, among the ladies to supermarket conditions and the chances of getting Himself to spring again for a fortnight on the sunny sands.

You, however, will give all your attention to those shrimp Provençale; plump, crunchy and sweet, they are moistened with a garlicked sauce that is red, tart and heavy, glistening with oil, thick with little chunks of tomato, prettied with a liberal sprinkling of fresh, fragrant parsley. The escargots de Bourgogne are equally blunt, served in New York's most forthright snail butter, so nubbly with bits of minced garlic that it has the texture of cereal, and so pungent of garlic flavor that the abundance of parsley can be detected only by its vivid green color.

Cooler beginnings include smoked trout with a sauce Raifort that is made with plenty of horseradish and little finesse, and the Terrine de Canard, heavy with duck meat and liver, salty and thickly fatted, very good with the crusty bread served here and some cold white wine.

It is a sign of the familiarity of the customers with the peculiarities of the house that about half the tables order a dish that is never listed on the menu—a profound lobster bisque that seems to crackle with the essence of lobster shell. It is deep and winy soup.

The secret of the bisque, of course, is the availability of lobster shells, and they are in abundant supply here because of the popularity of Le Homard sauté à l'Armoricaine. This is not a dish for lobster purists, being several removes from the elemental thing you dip in butter. The crustacean arrives in hefty chunks—meat and shell—that are piled to the rim of a deep bowl. The bowl is filled with a spicy, dark-brown broth that is heavily tomatoed, lively of wine. Blatant food. The frogs' legs are subtle by comparison, though the nicely crusted, tender thighs are liberally sprinkled with sautéed minced garlic and moistened with a strong tomato sauce.

Jump not quickly to conclusions, for many dishes here lack even a hint of tomato, among them brains in black butter, a good version, tender, smooth and a little tart, crusted and browned, moistened with a carefully burned butter that is studded with sour capers. The Poulet au Vin Rouge is the standard thing, the chicken well browned before it is simmered in wine and stock. The bird is a good one, with the clear— nowadays rare—flavor of fresh chicken; and its cooking liquid has an earthy taste that is imparted by the fresh mushrooms that are part of the stew. A more interesting dish, and not just for its rarity hereabouts, is Le Pigeon Grillé Maître d'Hôtel. The entire little bird, spread open, is herbed and buttered, and broiled until its skin is almost blackened, its dark meat, hot and moist, at a peak of high, sweet flavor. Splendid lamb chops are available here, as well as good steaks—they are of tasty and tender meat, accurately prepared and handsomely crusted. The accompanying vegetables for all of these are a bit sad, but many of the main courses come with puffed potatoes, tiny golden balloons that you can have with any main course if you so command. A crisp salad of fresh greens in a lively vinaigrette comes with your dinner.

Sometimes the cheeses are fine, sometimes not. You may send for them, look at them and judge for yourself. The remainder of the printed dessert list is boring—mousse, peach Melba, coupe aux marrons, commercial pastries, etc. Regular customers, as soon as they arrive, order the unlisted soufflés, and late in the evening these flow from the kitchen by the dozen, their browned tops high above their white ceramic pots. They are not the greatest soufflés in town, but they are fine—though the Grand Marnier is a little heavier than the ideal, and one wishes the accompanying crème Anglaise were not cool; the chocolate soufflé would be more exciting if its flavor were more intense.

★★ IL MULINO

86 West 3rd Street
LUNCH, TUESDAY TO FRIDAY; DINNER, TUESDAY TO SUNDAY. CLOSED MONDAY.
Reservations, 673-3783.
Credit cards: AE.
Expensive.

The place is in the middle of Greenwich Village nowhere, on one of the community's more desolate blocks, but it was discovered early in its recent youth and was promptly occupied by a corps of obsessional admirers, in large part locals. (It remains little known beyond the borders of its natural market—those who, on weekend nights, come to Manhattan from across the waters do not come here.) With respect to its neighborhood and its somewhat earthy clientele, the posh of the place is anomalous, if not weird. You are made to feel utterly at home by cordial gentlemen in no less than white tie. Captains stir sauces and pasta over burners on side stands. But except for a few appearances, there is nothing very fancy about the place, except for some very fancy food.

You enter to a spacious barroom, separated by a "wall" of potted palms from a good-size dining room in which around fifteen large tables with snowy linen stand on cushy carpeting. The high-ceilinged room is all glazed brick, gray wallpaper, soft light. On one wall there is a big, bold drawing of an old mill—hence, "Il Mulino."

When you are seated you are given a micro-antipasto on which to nibble while you consider the menu, and, presently, you commission an order of carpaccio. It would be well if the raw beef were not quite so cold, but you cannot quarrel with its green sauce, which is herbed, touched with mustard, tart and tangy. Or you get some prosciutto and —when available—raw figs, the seeded pulp of the ripe fruit lovely against the gamy meat. It is a rare Italian restaurant that serves decent stuffed mushrooms. This is one. You get five of them, they seem just made, strong seasoning in their cheese stuffing, parsley strewn over them and over the tomato broth in which they stand.

Mulino's carbonara is sexy—anyway, overwhelmingly assertive. It is eggy, strongly peppered, weighted with an abundance of Italian bacon, served to you on carefully cooked thin spaghetti. Even thinner spaghetti is served "all'arrabbiata," which denotes a red sauce—studded with olives and tart capers—that is like a fiery red oil. In contrast to that is the sauce Il Mulino, which is offered on thin spaghetti or, on occasion, on heavy pasta squares—this red sauce is creamy and thick, and it is densely populated with ham, wild mushrooms and sweet peas, which give it a dazzlingly complex character.

The bass brodetto is juicy, surrounded in its pool of piping-hot broth by fresh clams and mussels. More of those tender clams in the clams Posillipo—littlenecks are mounded up, in their bowl, over a powerfully garlic-flavored red broth. The saltimbocca is plain, direct—buttery veal, sturdy ham, sage, a simple sauce. In fact, all the scaloppine dishes have strong character, as does the giant veal chop, which, with its pully cheese, wild mushrooms and pungent sauce, approaches the substantiality of a force of nature. For pure strength, however, it is overshadowed by the filetto di manzo alla romana, in which the good, bloody red beef is put forth in a strident, sour caper sauce, to which, on occasion, hearts of artichoke are added.

Good Italian cheese. The cold zabaglione is loaded with Marsala, enriched with whipped cream, crunchy with ground amaretti. You may have yours hot. Either way, you may have it over ripe berries.

• NADIA'S

994 Second Avenue (near 52nd Street)
LUNCH, MONDAY TO FRIDAY; DINNER, MONDAY TO SATURDAY. CLOSED SUNDAY.
Reservations, 888-6300.
Credit cards: AE, CB, DC, MC, V.
Very expensive.

Yes, there is a flesh-and-blood Nadia. And on occasion she is your hostess. Nadia is a little on the monumental side, ten or eleven stone of unruffled flesh on the medium frame of a contented lady. She is draped in layers of black chiffon, a furlong of pearls is wound many times around her neck and hangs to her waist. There are rhinestones in her jet-black hair. A particolor of paints and powders has been lovingly applied to the unwrinkled luxurance of her features. Nadia is perfectly cordial to you, but her real pleasure is greeting, and sitting with, her friends. They include gentlemen who, if white-on-white shirts were still sold, would be wearing them. Instead they wear black cashmere turtlenecks under their black suits. If there is a shirt with a necktie, the four-in-hand is held in place by a jeweled stickpin or a gold clip. You see guys here with rugs, cigars and Oriental girls they do not know well; and, a specialty of the house, gentlemen who were old when their female companions were born. These girls dress for the occasion, but they have no way of disguising their punk haircuts. Their escorts are not thinking about haircuts. Says one senior citizen to his young friend, "A man takes care of himself [significant pause], but a woman has to think of her future." With this, he pokes a hirsute, liver-spotted finger at her peachy complexion, and goes on to explain that he likes to spend his money freely because he knows he will not live forever. She seems to be going for it.

This Italian restaurant is as overdecorated—if you can imagine such a thing—as an overdecorated Italian restaurant. The stools at the front bar (as are the chairs throughout the restaurant) are of black-enameled wood and lavender plastic. Opposite the bar the wall is festooned with a score of track-lighted oils, part of a carload lot from Artland. In the dining room proper, floral wallpaper is framed in brown moldings, sconces that drip crystal share wall space with more of those paintings, including one of an ancient guitarist in a Santa Claus hat. The linen is pink, the carpeting is red, an immense crystal chandelier hangs from the maroon ceiling.

Your order is taken by the captain, a gentleman who is second in eminence only to

Nadia herself. His dress shirt has a ruffled front and ruffled cuffs. He is a little ruffled himself. His hair is arranged in wild disarray. If you call to him unexpectedly, he may spin in place, quickly, alternately clockwise and counterclockwise, like a compass needle in a magnet factory. When he addresses you it is an oration for the benefit of the whole house.

But he will probably not tell you that if this restaurant is of culinary interest at all, it is for one or two dishes you do not find everywhere (none of them among the appetizers)—for example, tonnarelli alla gorgonzola, which turns out to be spaghetti in a sauce that has the singular, salty, head-clearing strength of the ripe cheese. Nadia's version of puttanesca sauce suffers from its canned olives and the almost undetectability of its fish; still, the creamy red sauce is pungent and pleasantly acidic on the pasta. Eschew the risotto pescatore, which is just an ordinary seafood sauce on ordinary rice.

The scaloppine pizzaiola is good veal, but the tomato sauce lacks the peppers the name leads you to expect. The chicken scarpariello is browned a little, lemoned a little, of interest a little. But the bass marechiara is fresh, and it is adorned with clams and mussels, and it is served in a hot tomato-flavored broth. The scampi alla lombarda—crunchy shrimp in a tomato sauce that has been touched with anchovies and capers—would be fine if these were not today's slightly off-tasting shrimp.

Often there are good cheeses—sharp and spiky Parmesan, strong Gorgonzola in its uncooked form. Avoid the blueberry cheese cake, which is blueberry jelly on cream-cheese cake. The Italian cheese cake is moist, bright, lemony, studded with spiced fruit—very good.

• NICOLA'S

146 East 84th Street
DINNER.
Reservations, 249-9850.
No credit cards.
Medium-priced.

Nicola's is an athletes' restaurant in which the athletes are writers. Also publishers, editors, agents and groupies. Edward Jay ("Eddie") Epstein and Clay ("Clay") Felker, for example, seated together, competing in flatness of expression and casualness of seated slouch. Just a couple of killers, you understand, between assignments.

The greats are, of course, honored in the usual way, by mementos on the walls—book jackets and photos of David Halberstam, Gay Talese, Mario Puzo, Peter Maas, George Plimpton and lots, lots more. No one knows what this place has against literature. These guys write hardball, and for keeps. All of them are in the record books: biggest advance for an illiterate work by a minor leaguer, most pornography sold through supermarkets by a rookie, for two. Irwin Shaw's presence in this company is that of Tolstoy among the goats.

If you expect nothing else in a place like this, you expect a good bar. But the bartender serves up a glass of wine in a puddle of wine (the bar itself is just one great big coaster), mixes slightly tepid martinis, would not offer a fresh beer glass at the twentieth round unless asked. Then again he is a busy man, much of his time taken up vacating of prandial detritus the interstices between his molars, the tool of these excavations the chewed-flat end of a short straw. When he is concentrating on dental hygiene, he is just about doubled over.

Maple-stained knotty-pine walls, blue-and-white gingham showing under the white linen tablecloths, green carpeting (the playing field), a big color TV at the street end of the long bar. The wagon-wheel chandeliers and rococo beer tankards are leftovers from the days when this was a neighborhood German tavern. If the jukebox (Bunny Berrigan, the Ink Spots) is not playing, the radio is (news on the hour).

You arrive early in the evening, and it is as if the refuse collector has entered the operating room. A clutch of waiters turns from their preoccupation with one another to stare with outrage at the interlopers. You are led to a remote table in the back room, where you immediately establish yourself as a deviate by asking for the wine list. You are patiently informed that there is no such thing, but that the house does store, for occasional nonmembers such as yourself, wine of two colors, red and white, so pick a color. You toss a coin, announce a color and the waiter rattles off a few names. You inquire about details, and, distressed at the prospect of perhaps further questions, the waiter departs, returns with a bottle and stares at the ceiling while you consider the label and get your answers for yourself. If you want to taste something really gruesome, try a bottle of Fazi Battaglia Verdicchio sometime.

The proprietor, a nervous weasel with large hair, who sometimes asks you if everything is OK in the manner of a schoolchild who cannot wait to be dismissed, was once an underling at Elaine's, the terrible media restaurant on Second Avenue. At his former employer's, customers in the know order the unlisted squid salad, just about the only good food in the place. Here the words "squid salad" are printed right on the menu, but the dish itself is nowhere, mostly mussels rather than squid, a little moldy on those occasions when you are getting yesterday's batch, lacking seafood quality. The so-called mussels dijonnaise are ice cold, a little tough, in a mustardy mayonnaise. The allegedly fresh roasted peppers are icebox stale. And the stuffed mushrooms, under a layer of melted cheese, are OK in a coarse way, but too obviously reheated too long after the original preparation.

But there is some decent food: the raw clams are fresh; the cannelloni are stuffed with a tasty forcemeat, spread with some more of that acceptable melted cheese, served in a bright tomato sauce; the linguine with white clam sauce, though rather high on salt and low on garlic, is made with perfectly good clams, and if you hit the kitchen at the right moment, the pasta will not have been waiting too long for you in its water.

The steaks may be tough, but they are seared, accurately cooked, cut from good beef that simply needs more aging. The sautéed lobster is a huge platter with chunks of tender lobster in a shell at the center, clams and mussels all around, everything up to the water line in a red, winy broth—all is well but for the clams, which have been cooked until they are leathery. The fish of the day is fresh, if often a little overcooked, and the scaloppine dishes—the standard ones are on the menu—are of pale and tender veal, though their sauces vary from the obvious to the exaggerated.

For dessert there is cheese cake, which is thick and sour, with a layer of crushed canned pineapple between the cake and its crust. Pretty dreadful.

The place fills late. If you do much reading, you are sure to spot a face or two that you have seen on dust jackets.

★★★ IL NIDO

251 East 53rd Street
LUNCH AND DINNER. CLOSED SUNDAY.
Reservations, 753-8450.
Credit cards: AE, CB, DC, MC, V.
Very expensive.

Once upon a time these rooms were home to an earlier fancy eating place, Hermitage. The restaurateurs currently in occupancy do not confuse house pride with nationalism. They are content to do their Italian thing amid the very things left behind by French predecessors. The dark timbers crisscrossed on these ivory walls of rough plaster are the same ones as before, as are the dark-brown banquettes, the black-enameled side chairs. Here and there, beveled mirrors, like windows in pale frames, are a touch of glitter in the dusky surroundings. The lights have been lowered a bit, which adds Italian drama to the French elegance. And surely these lush exotic flowers reflect the preference of the current owners and would not have been found here in the old days. The people who operate Il Nido have been in on a number of other restaurants around town. They have never dumped tons of money into substituting new appointments for old. They simply move in, tidy up, sell good food and make frequent deliveries to the bank.

This is a busy place; the press has been kind to it. Even when the guests are seated, the aisles swarm—with waiters in white and captains in black and white, tending dessert carts and sidestands (which are equipped with burners that occasionally foul the air), all of which is in contrast with the cool clientele, moneyed and unhurried, that contentedly fill this place. For some reason they even fill it late. There seems to be an extra crowd, at around 10 P.M., of well-bred diners who keep Spanish hours—they come fresh and hungry, as if from a siesta and shower.

Rather than shock the recently sleeping tummy, they start out easy, with insalata di funghi freschi, creamy slivers of fresh mushroom mingled with fresh celery, in a sparkling dressing. If they were up before sundown, and have had a drink or two, they may go so far as bresaola, the gamy, air-dried beef of Italy, served in thin oxblood slices, pleasantly rank, peppery, moistened with a lemony dressing—wondrous simple food. The spiedino alla romana is the familiar multidecker sandwich of bread, cheese, ham, skewered and deep-fried, the massive solidity moistened with an anchovy sauce that is sharp and salty. Then there is the crostini di polenta, a peasanty dish of fried cornmeal on bread, buried in a hot and meaty mushroom sauce.

Say hello to the sixteen-dollar noodle, capelli d'angelo grenzeola, a mound of thin pasta, firm and tender and slippery, mingled with an oiled red sauce that is touched —rather restrainedly—with sweet crabmeat. Those same noodles are served primavera, this version of the popular dish dominated by sweet fresh peas and discs of asparagus, in a creamy sauce that is fortified by a strong cheese grated onto the noodles—with a little Mouli rotary grater—at your table. For something even sturdier, the tortellini a quattro formaggi, pasta packages filled with a meat stuffing that is redolent of just-ground nutmeg, in a strong and viscous cheese sauce.

Among the mixed-seafood dishes served in Italian restaurants around town, you will not find one to surpass the production that this place sells as crostacei marinara. Its red base is an elemental sauce that is thick with chunks of tomato. The seafood comes in a great bowl, and it includes half of a substantial lobster; lots of the good shrimp this place somewhere obtains; and an abundance of little clams and mussels, all of them tender and sweet and fresh. The sauce is powerfully seasoned with saffron, in addition to the garlic you expect, and when you have dispatched the seafood, the remaining sauce is like a pungent soup that you will probably consume by soaking it up with bread. You get a remarkable shrimp dish here called scampi salsa milanese, stunning in that the clear flavor of the shrimp is vivid despite the intensity of the anchovy and caper sauce with which you moisten them. A sturdy chicken dish goes as pollo toscana, sautéed chunks of chicken and chicken liver, laid over eggplant that is rich with oil, all in a creamy tomato sauce, the whole topped with strong melted cheese. The veal chops are fat, juicy, their surfaces browned in a crosshatched pattern by the grill. But the chop prepared as costoletta milanese—sliced thin, breaded—requires plenty of lemon to bring it to life. Good brains—fluffy, almost airy, in a thin crust that is light and lemoned. And the paillard of beef is just about impeccable—the huge expanse of red meat pounded thin, browned on the hot grill, juicy pink inside, even livelier when lemoned.

Among the good salads is a rare one of string beans and sliced mushrooms, with slabs of beet and tomato, in a strong vinaigrette. That salad, with or without some of this restaurant's pungent Parmesan cheese, is probably the best way to conclude one of the rather solid dinners you get here. If you are still game, the layer cakes are fresh, rich sweets; the chocolate mousse is as good as any in an Italian restaurant in New York, intense, light, sticky, served with real whipped cream. Avoid the cheese cake, which is the worst sugared cream cheese.

★★NIRVANA

30 Central Park South (near Sixth Avenue)
LUNCH AND DINNER.
Reservations, 752–0270.
Credit cards: AE, CB, DC, MC, V.
Medium-priced.

You are greeted by a dark-haired, sari-clad young woman with a rose behind her ear, a spot on her brow, a diamond on her nostril and a very throaty delivery. This vision is not the result of light-headedness after your fourteen-floor voyage to this aerie overlooking Central Park and points north, for of all the Indian restaurants in New York, Nirvana lays on the subcontinental schmaltz with the heaviest hand, and your hostess, born to it though she may be, plays the part of her exoticism with operatic breadth. Even her gleaming eyes and sparkling teeth seem to be acts of volitional electricity here in these dim rooms.

Professional basketball players and other lengthies must, from the moment they disembark from the elevator, take care not to brush their heads against the garish, bejeweled cloths that billow down as low ceilings in all the rooms of this place. The reds and blacks, gold and turquoise are repeated in wall hangings that surround the gilt-framed Indian art. If you want a choice table, you may have to wait in the anteroom, among wicker chairs, a couple of private tables hidden behind carved screens, and a short bar, behind which a comely Occidental lass is getting the old colonial treatment in repayment for British transgressions. She must sprint through her shift like an Olympic potato racer, taking orders at the tables, mixing drinks at her station, delivering them back to the tables all while making the most of casual conversation from entranced observers at the bar. She stirs a mean martini, however—Bombay gin, of course.

What you were waiting for at the bar was a table with a view in the oblong main dining room, one lengthy wall of which consists of picture windows that look out on Manhattan's great rectangle of trees, traffic and assault. From up here all you can see are the first two, and the auto lights look very pretty carving their way through the jungle. You are attended to by gentle young men in gauze shirts that hang loosely over their trousers. They are solicitous, which does not entirely offset their rudimentary English. Have your waiter bring you another martini or beer, for the wine list here is ludicrous, as to price, and of abysmal quality, especially the inexpensive bottles.

A shrewd menu, with all the conventional dishes that will satisfy the once-a-year sampler of Indian food, and a goodly number of rarities for sophisticates. If you choose the complete-dinner plan, you will begin with Assorted Appetizers, which consists of nothing new, but much that is well-made, including the sweet and spicy onion fritters called Piazi; a stuffed puri, called Dal Puri, in which the light bread is filled with a solid and steamy mash of chickpeas; and Singara, a thin whole-wheat bread filled with curried vegetables that are mild enough to be fairly called bland. But if you eschew the prix fixe for more adventurous essays, you may precede or surround your main courses with such obscurities as Anda Bhaji, a lightly oiled mix of eggs and vegetables, stir-cooked until it is almost pebbly, flavored with green peppers, onions and herbs—the solid substance of the ingredients notwithstanding, the dish is light; or with Bagon Bharta, baked eggplant that has been mashed with onions, peppers and fragrant coriander leaves—this, on the other hand, is not light at all, but solid and oily and extremely satisfying in that way; or with Mach Bhaja, fried fish with a deep-brown exterior that is like a filament of sweet spices—this is fresh-water fish, and the pale meat seems especially delicate next to its tasty crust.

Nirvana doesn't manage to obtain better shrimp than most of its restaurant competitors these days, so you would do well to pass up the shrimp curry. And though you may be inclined to leap at a goat-meat curry, for no other reason than its rarity in New York restaurants, this sturdy stew betrays none of the particular character of kid. Do not therefore abandon the whole idea of trying the rarities, for the curry of lamb brains is one of the best dishes available in any Indian restaurant in New York, a rich and solid stew that is powerfully herbed and fragrant of sweet spices. And if you sensibly wish to by-pass lamb because it is so much the usual thing, pause at least briefly at the special lamb curry made with spinach—the green vegetable gives the dish a wild and intensely grassy flavor. Good chutneys are available, strong or sweet, and the rice that accompanies your meal is light, buttery and flavored invariably with saffron and with different spices as well, which vary from day to day—cloves give this rice a particularly heady quality. The breads here are good—the puri is the size of a soccer ball, but much lighter, and the parata is browned and buttery, with the strong clear taste of whole wheat.

Much of the brief dessert menu is often unavailable. The rice pudding is pleasantly musty, studded with nuts and raisins. The ice cream the menu refers to as "celestial" is mundane. On occasion the tea is sour, as if it has steeped long past its bedtime.

As the evening wears on, the recorded background music gives way to a sitar player and a gentleman who taps lightly on little drums. They do their thing from comfortable positions on the floor.

★ NISHI

325 Amsterdam Avenue (near 76th Street)
DINNER.
Reservations for three or more, 799-0117.
No credit cards.
Medium-priced.

Black enamel or black glass covers the walls. The air is crisscrossed by beams of light from spotlights hung below the black ceiling. The two small rooms that make up this establishment are rimmed by a banquette that is upholstered with the same red carpeting that covers the floor. The small tables are linened with mauve napkins that do not quite cover the black tops. In the entrance room a five-stool sushi bar cuts across one corner. The silk of a brilliantly colored spotlighted kimono glistens on one wall. Illuminated bursts of flowers glow here and there. Rice paper and bamboo, you understand, are not present. Though your place is set with steel flatware, chopsticks are available, the splintery kind that are attached at one end and come packaged in paper sheafs—they are carried around in pockets of the change aprons that the muscular young waiters here, many of whom are Occidental, wear just below their tight-fitting red-and-white NISHI T-shirts.

Then there is the crowd: punk hair, polo shirts with animal emblems, jeans and painter's pants, swank suits over open-at-the-neck shirts, flimsy blouses and wrap-around skirts. Guys and girls with motorcycle helmets tucked under their arms park at the tiny bar and have raw fish and Sapporo beer. West Side daters come here, for even as in the olden days, young gents impress young ladies with their knowledge of singular, out-of-the-way spots. One such dude, who has managed to exchange a few words of Japanese with his waiter, is flaunting rather shamelessly his intimate knowledge of the culture of Japan. His lady friend is eating it up. His summation, for example, of Japanese drama: "Better than Shakespeare. Believe me, *better* than Shakespeare." She nods, agape.

To the Western tastebud, the finer distinctions among grades of raw seafood—this tuna is paler and richer than that one, that squid is younger and more velvety than this, &c.—are close to undetectable. It is enough to note that here the tuna and squid, the mackerel and sea trout, the fluke and bass are all fresh. They are served prettily, garnished with sharp pickled ginger, violent green mustard, dark and pungent soy sauce. You can get them straight, as sashimi, or combined with vinegared rice and seaweed, as sushi; or as both, in the big sushi-sashimi combo, an encyclopedic assemblage that is more than a general introduction to the subject.

If your taste for the exotic is limited, and you would rather just dabble, have an appetizer of raw octopus, rather chewy slabs of the resilient meat, cut from the tentacles of a big fellow (each slice the diameter of a silver dollar), and served in a slightly sweetened vinegar, with sesame seeds and a few shredded vegetables—this is subtle food, in which the vague ocean flavor and the crispness of the seeds and vegetables seem somehow to exist side by side, but on different planes. Considerably more exotic is the seaweed vinaigrette—dark green seaweed, pale green seaweed, red seaweed, all mounded up over beansprouts—the vibrant sea-gaminess probably takes an early start in life to learn to like, but this serving of it has the unmistakable, albeit rank, flavor of the genuine article in an unadulterated state.

Something given as "conch barbeque" arrives in a conch shell surrounded, on its plate, by blue flames. Presently the fire goes out, and you fish the slivers of mildly spiced, tender, fresh conch meat from out of the shell, wherein the mound of them is knee deep in a mild broth. Or you may begin with the eggplant and miso sauce—four substantial slabs of the soft and succulent vegetable, warm and oily and rimmed with purple skin, covered with a spicy red sauce of fermented soybean, all under a cloud of cured bonito shavings, which, despite their near insubstantiality, make the otherwise oily dish light. A few items on this menu seem more Chinese than Japanese, including the hot dumplings—these are light little morsels, and though the ones made with pork seem always to be fresh-tasting, strong and subtle at the same time, those of shrimp or crabmeat sometimes suffer from second-rate seafood.

The menu lists a poached fish of the day. As far as anyone has been able to determine, that fish is always porgy, and it is always the best available main course on the menu. The whole fish is perfectly poached, moist and flaky, served up in a dark soy-sauce broth, strewn with slivers of ginger—a perfect dish. Nishi's vegetable tempura is not light, is in fact greasy, and its seafood tempura is really that vegetable tempura plus a few poorly chosen shrimp and some indeterminate fish. Something called apricot chicken casserole consists of sections of moist chicken and raisins in a warm and fruity sauce—harmless food. The pork cutlets are coated with beautifully crisped batter, which soaks up the dark soy sauce like a sponge, turning the slightly dry meat into very juicy stuff. The beef teriyaki is tasty but bloodless.

Little serious effort is made to disguise the non-Japanese nature of the desserts. The mandarin yogurt chiffon pie is pale yellow, citrus-flavored, studded with bits of mandarin orange, covered with yogurt—good, but too gelatinous. The fresh pineapple is fine, the fresh strawberries not invariably at the peak of their ripeness. But half the place seems to go for the "Hot Fuji," in which a huge ball of vanilla ice cream stands, like a volcanic island, in a sea of hot, steaming fudge—a very good sundae, served in a giant wineglass, that is frequently shared by three or four eaters.

★★ODEON

145 West Broadway (at Thomas Street)
LUNCH, SUNDAY TO FRIDAY; DINNER, DAILY.
Reservations, 233-0507.
Credit cards: AE, MC, V.
Expensive.

In ancient Greece and Rome an odeon was a small theater in which were held musical and dramaturgic competitions, prizes awarded to the winners. At this Odeon the music is provided by a tape deck, which competes only with the noise of the crowd. And if dramas are here enacted, it is secretly, within the bosoms and souls of the players. For to judge by the facial expressions in evidence, the range of emotion of this clientele extends only from painless boredom to contented passivity.

Competition, however, there is. Take for instance this prize-winning lady in a gentleman's vintage shirt of gossamer silk, its tails down to mid-thigh, which she wears over lacy bloomers that are tied at the calf with blue ribbons; her black, patent-leather high-button shoes are equipped with five-inch heels, the points of which could easily pass through the eye of a needle. Certainly she is competing with this other, the one in saddle shoes, black net pantyhose, plaid Bermuda shorts and a purple cashmere sweater, the gaping V of which barely frames a bivalvular cornucopia that threatens to burst, and pour forth the full endless measure of its pent-up ennui.

The men, however, compete at the office, so most of them come here in everyday raiment. It is not unusual to find a professional chap in a navy-blue suit escorting a nymphet in crow-black, hatchet-chopped punk hair—the brilliantly colored glistening sheath she wears is unblemished in its smoothness by any telltale sign of scanties. Ambiguity, too, is part of this style, and it is impossible to determine from a posterior view which gender accommodates this fedora and the pigtail that hangs below it. A front look helps only a little. For duds Friday is the best night.

The premises housed a cafeteria for a long time, one that sported the sleek lines and smooth surfaces of Deco Econo, an architectural style of the period between the wars, via which, you will recall, every apartment-house lobby on the Grand Concourse was fitted out with a little bit of Rockefeller Center. Much of the cafeteria and much of its historic style have been retained by this up-to-date place, and they are like faint reverberations of the past.

Not surprisingly, Odeon is about as big as a medium-size cafeteria. On a terrazzo floor—in the old days mopped three times daily, between meals—the white-linened tables are set with inverted tumblers rather than goblets, and with water pitchers that you yourself may fill at spigots affixed to one of the pillars that rise through the height of this two-story room. That pillar also accommodates stainless-steel shelves, bottles of mustard and ketchup thereon, and a magazine rack, complete with literature, a reminder, if not a relic, of the days when a 5c. cup of coffee, a 3c. daily and a warm cafeteria were the foundations of a calm afternoon out of the weather. Perhaps you sat in one of these very chairs of pastel plastic and chrome tubing—they were high style then. Where the hot table was, the bar is now, mirrors on the wall behind it. The windows that look out on Thomas Street and on West Broadway are hung with old-time venetian blinds of flat wooden slats, enameled white, and broad tapes. The place is illuminated by big white globes that hang from the ceiling and shine softly. And the Odeon air is filled with period music of the twenties and thirties—"Harlem on My Mind," "If I Had a Talking Picture of You," "There'll Be Some Changes Made," &c. —much of it in the voices, both worldly and plaintive, of the lady singers of those days, or in the mellifluous baritone of the crooners.

You are attended to by capable young people in white aprons, white shirts and neckties. The food they deliver is pretty nifty. For example, a so-called "salad" of ham and green beans: large thin slices of smoky ham, scrunched into a rippling circle of the red meat, around crisp beans and mushrooms, which are moistened with a delicate dressing that is little more than seasoned oil. Even better is the salad of chicory and chicken, the slices of gentle white meat arranged on a great mound of fresh sharp greens, the whole dressed with a slightly tart vinaigrette and adorned with cracklings. You get good smoked salmon here, accompanied by a half-lemon so carved as to give it teeth, and by warm toast—sans crust—served hot and wrapped in linen. And you get good smoked chicken, the not-too-smoky white meat served with slivered mushrooms and a powerfully herbed mayonnaise.

The terrine of chicken livers is red and spicy, rimmed with pale fat, but it is rather aggressively salted, fatted almost to the point of greasiness; the Pommery mustard served with it seems to cut the wrong way, and the bread that such food demands is chronically stale at Odeon. Splendid snails, sweet and tender, are served in a kind of sandwich, the little morsels between two oblongs of hot brioche pastry, the upper one prettily glazed, all in a buttery sauce that is sweet with shallots, green and fragrant with parsley. The poached oysters are not good when they have passed retirement age.

Duck two ways: a ragout consisting of three substantial chunks of bird, rich meat and glistening skin, ranked alongside a mound of spiced green noodles, a polished red-peppery sauce over the meat—a modern essay on old-fashioned *Mitteleuropäisch* cooking; and sliced breast of duckling, the meat warm but barely cooked, red as rare beef, graced with woodsy wild mushrooms, and moistened with a sauce much like the one on the ragout—good food, but the near rawness of the duck is an effect without a purpose. The steak is of good, tender beef, crusty and moist and accurately cooked, its butter strongly flavored with fresh herbs. And the rack of lamb—of minuscule baby chops—has been coated with herbs and roasted with whole cloves of garlic, which yields an earthy pan juice for the delicate but tasty little ribs. The meat of your lobster has been removed from its shell and arranged on your plate in the shape of a lobster, the head and tail in place. The meat is gentle and sweet, mingled with leeks, in a buttery and lightly lemoned sauce that is flavored with parsley and chives. Poached baby halibut is an occasional fish of the day, fresh and firm and fibrous and juicy, its creamy sauce vibrant with chives—the bit of black caviar atop the fish is an irrelevance.

Among the desserts there is an icy combination of intensely flavored sherbets—coffee and bitter chocolate; a warm apple tart that is cinnamoned, moistened with apricot sauce, adorned with a great dollop of whipped cream; cold poached pear on pastry, with ice cream and warm chocolate sauce—an adult's sundae on a plate; and a chocolate cake that is striking for being cool, light, refreshing, despite the pungency of its chocolate flavor.

★★ OENOPHILIA

473 Columbus Avenue (near 83rd Street)
LUNCH, SUNDAY; DINNER, DAILY.
Reservations, 580-8127.
Credit cards: AE, CB, DC, MC, V.
Medium-priced.

The classification of New York's middle class is best organized by where the members summer. The crowd at Oenophilia are Fire Island straights. Hamptonists do not come here, never mind the Martha's Vineyard set. The folk here make up a milieu in which one is more thrilled to meet a prize-winning art director than a Knopf novelist. And in which one may happily skip either of those to go sailing with a marriageable shrink.

These people do not compose a society of manners. Their obsessions with financial well-being and family formation are so pervasive that they have lost sight of the formal graces potentially attendant thereto. Accordingly their affection for this establishment, which is as easygoing as a picnic on the sands of Ocean Beach. "Be right with you," says your host airily when he eventually notices you wandering around in search of an official. He is not rude, you understand; in fact, he is cordial. He is just relaxed, as if by a drug. And the waiters recite their speedy—and hopelessly unmemorizable—two-minute spiel of the specials of the evening in an inflection so conversational that if you were to guess at its content from its cadence alone, you would sensibly conclude that the subject was anecdotal, even jocular.

The subjects among the diners, however, are unmistakable:

"One minute he loves me. The next minute he's back with his wife. I don't know what to think anymore. If he knew about Norman he would probably kill me."

"If the stock market is going up or down—or if a single stock is going up or down—people don't always know why."

"The thing about a business, to me, is that it's basically no good unless you can be an absentee owner."

You enter a large room. Track lights on the high ceiling cast a glow on the ivory walls, which are adorned with oil paintings by real painters, mirrors and old engravings, which hang at various degrees from plumb. For some reason hefty ropes attached to a ceiling pulley extend down and aslant to a floor-level planter. Potted palms and hat-and-coat racks stand about. Most of the tables, which are set with pale-pink linen, are away from the walls, which makes the room seem vaguely untidy. The two smaller rooms at the back (reached by a corridor that is furnished with a bench on which you may park until a table comes ready) are snugger, but they can be noisy when wine has amplified the volume of what should assuredly be private conversation. "It is a given," bellows one idiot to his companion eighteen inches away, "that these bodies of ours have survived these thousands of years because of the happiness-pleasure syndrome."

Still, you eat well in this place. You may start with the pâté verte, a smooth slab of veal and chicken and chicken liver ground together, veined with spinach, and made heady with brandy, its slight heaviness perfectly offset by the sharp mustard it is garnished with. Or you may begin with the hot scallop mousse, one of the few seafood mousses in town that, owing to a happy scantity of gelatin in its composition, is not gluey. It has a bright seafood flavor, it is light, studded with unexpected chunks of carrot and broccoli, and it is moistened with a polished Mornay sauce—a superb dish. They serve snails in one of those special snail plates with six dents, and the departures from the standard preparation are the addition of sesame seeds to the shallot butter (undetectable) and a film of melted Parmesan cheese over the plate of food (unmistakable). The snails are big and plump, the butter is sweet and mildly garlicked, freshened with parsley, and the browned cheese adds a strong, crusty note. Splendid fettuccine is served as a first course, the firm eggy noodles in a thick cream sauce that is fortified with Parmesan cheese, studded with bits of pungent ham, and spiced with fresh nutmeg—a plate of very rich food in which the sharpness of the meat and the fragrance of the spice seem to leaven the weightiness of the noodles and their sauce.

Your waiter, who has a comment for every dish on and off the menu, pushes the swordfish (a frequent fish of the day). "Very popular," says he. You ask if that means it is good. "It's reeeeal good," he intones quietly, intimately, leaning forward as he does so, as if you have become his special favorite. The serving is dismayingly slim, but the fish is fresh, it is enriched and made especially moist by the garlicked olive oil in which it has been marinated. The strands of fresh ginger under which it is baked are revivifying (whether you need that or not), and the cool cucumber sauce that is served with it is a judiciously chosen foil to the hot fish. A couple of crisp quail are stuffed with brandied apricots and served in a purple sauce that is flavored with cardamom. The apricots are lovely, but the sauce seems bitter rather than seasoned, the exotic spice misplaced. Each day there is a veal scaloppine of the day, and sometimes the nicely sautéed slivers of pale meat are served in a peppered plum sauce, slices of fruit in among the slivers of veal, the fruit-and-spice sauce lively, if a little obvious. The lamb chops, roasted with garlic and served in a peppery wine sauce, are perfectly prepared, but the meat is pallid. The potatoes or rice or vegetables that accompany the main courses are always well made.

The pal of a waiter winks at you and makes certain the boss is not around when he lets you know, strictly between him and you, that the chocolate-mousse cake is just so-so. So you order it, and you get what every chocolate freak fantasizes about: three forms of chocolate—dark cake, rich and sticky and silken mousse, and velvety black icing—all on one plate at the mercy of one fork.

Something called vicarage pie consists of sweetened and cinnamoned ground walnuts under thin-sliced apples on an old-fashioned crust, the whole served under a dollop of excellent whipped cream that is strewn with slivered almonds. More of that whipped cream is heaped on the tarte au beurre, the dark, liquorlike, raisin-studded bittersweetness of which is vaguely like mincemeat. The strawberry-raspberry mousse fills a large wineglass, is fresh and sweet and icy, but has lost a little too much of the flavor of the fruit—it is topped with yet more of that rich and fluffy whipped cream, which just about rescues it.

• O'NEALS' BALOON

48 West 63rd Street
LUNCH AND DINNER.
Reservations accepted for three or more, 399-2353.
Credit cards: AE, CB, DC, MC, V.
Medium-priced.

O'Neals' Baloon is big and brassy, many-leveled, of many compartments, sprawling. It is as colorful as a midway, tacky as a waterfront coffee shop, convivial as a Main Street saloon (its bar is populous with operators of libidinal intent). The waiters and waitresses are actors and actresses and dancers, *manqués* or unemployed, and one bartender wears an illustrated T-shirt, a Rip Van Winkle beard and a pencil behind his ear. The place is illuminated by at least a dozen different kinds of lights and lamps, adorned with posters and murals, and it is naked—a glance upward reveals its vitals, the ceiling crisscrossed with pipes, ducts and conduits.

The service is whimsical as to when, in-passing as to how, as social as a family gathering. In exchange for a demonstration of how to lever a cork from a bottle of wine, your waitress suggests that you "stay away from the shrimp tonight, honey, they're loud." And when she arrives with your main courses, having neglected to remove the previous plates, it is just understood that you will help out by transferring the used dishes to a table nearby.

Chili, with onions and sour cream, is the best first course, thick and spicy. The fried chicken and the fish and chips are both admirably deep-fried, so that they are crisp and moist—but the former is of contemporary chicken, the latter probably of frozen fish, and both have but a hint of flavor. The same chicken is the bulk of the chicken salad (which is stuffed into a tomato), but there is a huge garnish of lovely, crisp cole slaw with this dish. The chopped steak and burgers are tasty, the sirloin steak mealy. Ketchup can rescue the French fries, but there is no cure for those greasy onion rings.

For a small extra charge you can have terrific whipped cream on your chocolate mousse pie (tastes like good chocolate ice cream) or on your lemon mousse pie (much like lemon chiffon pie) or on carrot cake (moist, nutty and loaded with sweet spices). The apple pie is icy, the pecan pie the usual layer of nuts on congealed corn syrup.

• OREN AND ARETSKY

1497 Third Avenue (near 84th Street)
LUNCH, SUNDAY; DINNER, DAILY.
Reservations, 734-8822.
Credit cards: AE.
Expensive.

Oren and Aretsky (the owners, not their establishment) are an act in search of material. Their roles are contemporary, but the product of a tradition that extends back at least as far as Laurel and Hardy. Oren is small, wiry, leather-tan. His business is urgent. His hand is gripping his three-inch-wide leather belt. He is calm, but also serious and alert. Addressed by a subordinate, he listens with the grim intensity of the bloodied lance corporal (senior survivor of the sneak massacre) receiving word from a trusted native scout that ten million enemy troops are hard upon his weakened flank. You know he is going to pull this one out. Hardy—er, Aretsky—is not so sure. Of anything. He never comes to work unless his beard and hair have just been repainted —on his large, pale, ovoid head—with a freshly dipped black brush. He fingers his necktie constantly, like a man without a memory who must repeatedly reassure himself that he put it on. Aretsky has been known to commence rising before he has quite completed sitting. And as he circulates among the tables, making nice to the customers, he smiles the smile of one who fears that at any moment a look of horror may be more appropriate.

There is a big television set high up over the bar, and when a hockey game is being broadcast, the set is turned on. This is a players' and fans' hangout. Lots of the gents present are so tall that you automatically look down to see if they are wearing their skates. They could, if they wished, look at the TV without craning their necks; but mostly they look down instead, at the adoring young women who come here seeking attention. The girls nibble salties, make one drink last until they are noticed, and smile as fast as a left wing can say—uh, excuse me.

Oren and Aretsky is a barroom and a back room: up front, turn-of-the-century light fixtures, a handsome old bar, horticultural prints, low light, very audible background music; in back, much of the same, with windows that look out on a fenced-in area where food and drink are served when the weather is fine.

Even the worst weather, however, surpasses the food: formerly frozen, latterly soggy crab claws; so-called "Escargots aux Cognac," which are leathery little bodies in a cup of tepid soup; OK smoked trout with watery horseradish sauce; steamed mussels that were apparently machine-washed rather than cooked; and a pâté that could be improved by the addition of anything.

Oren and Aretsky, when it manages a decent veal chop with sauce Béarnaise, serves French fries and a bottle of ketchup at the same time. Béarnaise and ketchup, however, are a better combination than stewed liver and greasy onions. The properly prepared steak is of nowhere beef. The correctly broiled chicken is a tasteless bird. Your best bet is the fish of the day, which is fresh and judiciously cooked.

Do not take any chances; have the terrific brownie for dessert. It is crunchy, it has an intensity of cocoa flavor and it is even better with the good Bassett's ice cream and hot fudge. Do not be deflected by the Toblerone mousse (sugar pudding) or the cheese cake (ice pudding).

Reservations are accepted for three or more. But you will not necessarily be promptly seated if you arrive on time. And friends of the house—even without reservations—may be given preference.

★★OYSTER BAR & RESTAURANT

Grand Central Station, lower level
LUNCH AND DINNER. CLOSED SATURDAY AND SUNDAY.
Reservations, 599-1000.
Credit cards: AE, CB, DC, MC, V.
Medium-priced.

If you think you know from fresh, you should have some fish at the Oyster Bar. After a few months of casual seafood, chosen from French menus, or Italian ones, or whatever, come to the Oyster Bar to brush up on freshness basics. This is not the only New York fish restaurant at which the fish is fresh every time. There are a few others (at a couple of which there is perhaps more finesse in the kitchen than here). But no one else offers thirty or so varieties of fish and shellfish in just-caught condition every day. (The Oyster Bar even prepares the stuff lots of different ways.) In seafood, freshness may not be all, but you cannot make really good seafood dishes without it.

In the mid-1970s this place was taken over by new interests, after an extended moribundity that had just climaxed in a muffled whimper. But, though there had been a demise, there had been no decay, for this place had been built—more than fifty years before—as an integral part of Grand Central Station, which is to say it would take a wrecking ball to make it crumble even a little. Spiffed up, the place at once revealed its ancient grandeur, quite unspoiled. And you can see it now. The main room, entered from the lower level, is at least a short block long. Under a lofty vaulted ceiling of glinting sand-colored tiles, and walls of maple-stained wainscoting with old marble at the base, there is an acre of tables at one end, a furlong of white countertop, in a repeating S, at the other. You walk on red tiles, you sit in armchairs, or on the banquettes that are along the edge of the room here and there. Or you eat in the saloon, a separate department at the east end, accessible via a flight of steps down from the entranceway near the low end of the ramp at 42nd Street and Vanderbilt. It is not only the stairway access to the saloon that makes it seem subterranean. The room is window-less and clubby-looking, like a speakeasy or a cavernous den. The walls of wood stripping are hung with nautical prints, ships' models behind glass, mountings of big game fish, varnished and glistening. A bar runs along two sides of the room—fifty may water easily along its length. Several dozen gingham-topped tables take up most of the floor. At the late end of mealtimes, when the big main room is sparsely populated, this room may be two-thirds full and cheery. When busy, either room provides enough noise to distract you.

Clams and oysters are sold by the piece. You can come here, order one of each listed oyster, plus a littleneck and cherrystone, and go home sated. On a good day there are as many as ten varieties of oyster available, and if you order an assortment, your waiter (in the main room) or your waitress (in the saloon) will tell you which is the Chincoteague, which is the Malpeque, &c. You will find that the little Belon oysters are as sweet as melon, the Chincoteagues briny and strong, the Cotuits a complexity of fruit and oil and the ocean. By late in the evening the more exotic varieties usually run out, so if you want to sample those Belons or Box oysters, you are more likely to find what you want at lunchtime, or before 7:30 at dinner.

This place has taken to smoking fish (no, not a new fad), and it does a delicate job of it. You get smoked sturgeon, thin slices spread across a big plate, light, ever so slightly soapy (which smoked sturgeon can be ever so excessively), the smokiness at once restrained and vivid—the horseradish sauce that garnishes the pale meat is sharp, even though it is mostly whipped cream. The smoked salmon is pale, moist without being oily, so tender it is almost fugitive—capers and chopped onions are served with the pink fish, but they should be used with restraint or they will obscure the salmon. The Point Judith herring these days is not much more than ordinary pickled herring. The clams Cassino are plump cherrystones, not buried in breading, just touched with it, and with a bit of bacon—the big clam shells are standing in a film of herbed butter, and the warm clams have a strong and tangy flavor. If you are lucky enough to come when she-crab soup is on the menu, do not pass it up. This is the famous Carolina soup, here made with Maryland crabs, presumably the female of the species, and the resulting bowl is a thick, buttery, subtly spiced and steamy richness that is dense with sweet white crabmeat.

The impeccable freshness of the ingredients is not, however, invariably matched by their preparation. Lotte is a fish that swims all over the Atlantic. It has never been popular in New York because it is (1) ugly to look upon when whole and (2) rather obscure of flavor when cut up and cooked. Here it is served in hefty chunks that the menu refers to as "tournedos," their surfaces handsomely browned, with a sauce Béarnaise that is presumably intended to compensate for the slightness of the flavor of the fish. The sauce, however, is as green as grass, as sweet and thick as molasses. The fish is pretty good if you substitute lemon for the sauce. That Béarnaise is particularly hard to understand in light of the pretty good hollandaise that comes with the carefully broiled, fresh and flaky bass. There is broiled halibut steak, and it falls into tender flakes that are velvety and snowy. In season there is shad and/or shad roe. The fish is floured and browned, the white meat sealed in the buttery crust. But the roe is probably parboiled before its final preparation, and it is a little dry, more like grit—less like caviar—than this dish at its best.

The shellfish stews are homey, big chunks of sea scallop, for example, in a hot and buttery cream broth that is red and spicy with fragrant paprika—the soup is a little briny from the juice of the scallops. The Pacific Coast's renowned Dungeness crab is sometimes available. They must fly it in on a Concorde, for the big crustacean seems to be as fresh as the local items. You get one crab to a serving, it is bright red, cold, it entirely occupies a long platter, and it is garnished with strong, mustard-flavored mayonnaise. There is abundant meat in one of these beasts if you know where it is stored, and have the patience to dig it out. A Dungeness crab is about twice the work of a lobster, but this is sweet seafood and worth the bother.

Steaks and chickens are available for inlanders; mixed seafood dishes, complex stews, seafood omelets; shore dinners after 5 P.M.; and live lobsters—you can pick yours out.

Most of the desserts are old-fashioned American items: a cool, custardy banana-cream pie, intensely banana-flavored, touched with slivered almonds; rice pudding, a frothy, cinnamoned, raisin-studded sweet, obvious but good; a whole-wheat apple pie, on occasion, the grainy crust around nuggets of tart apple, only lightly sugared; blueberry pie, a deep-purple filling of the jellied little fruits filling the lard crust to plumpness—too bad it is served so cold.

A new menu is printed daily, prices written in next to those regular dishes that are available that day; a dozen or so special dishes of the day written in as well.

By now everyone knows that the Oyster Bar serves nothing but American wine, almost 100 different bottles from four states.

★★ PALACE

420 East 59th Street
LUNCH, MONDAY TO FRIDAY; DINNER, MONDAY TO SATURDAY. CLOSED SUNDAY.
Reservations, 355-5150.
Credit cards: AE, CB, DC, MC, V.
Very expensive.

The quintessential Palace party is thrown by the rich uncle. He reserves the large table that, though it occupies the center of the dining room, is somewhat set apart from the rest of the place by the broadly portaled inner walls that surround it. Uncle arrives early—all six feet, and all 300 pounds of him—and stands where his guests must receive his hearty greetings before they are seated. Despite the counterbalancing weight of the one-inch by eight-inch cigar that protrudes—yes, even before dinner—from his teeth, he must stand back on his heels to place his center of gravity plumb to his feet. Now the guests come, in ones and twos, and each grateful arrival receives attention. Ladies and gentlemen of uncle's own generation are, respectively, kissed on the cheek or pounded on the back. A nephew, when his arm is pumped, is gripped by both the hand and wrist. Best loved are the nieces. They are held in extended, clutching embraces. Especially drawn-out is the affection granted the comely young thing whose impending holy wedlock this gathering honors. Her young man looks on.

Perhaps you have been under the impression that the crowd in this famously expensive restaurant consists of jaded couples who, at loose ends of an evening, and unable to think of anything better to do, drop in on the Palace for casual $300 dinners and attendant small talk. Hardly. No one in the place, in fact, forgets for a minute that he is spending money as fast as he can eat. Of course some very offhand demeanor is on display, but it is somehow unconvincing. Consider, for example, these two gents smoking and sipping brandy after dinner. Each is so far back in his armchair, in the effort to look more at home in this place than the other, that when one of them turns to his erect wife, he finds himself in precisely the relationship of a client to his dental hygienist.

The Palace is a big square room, that smaller room at its center. The place is papered with flocked gold, curtained with pleated gauze, draped and valanced with heavy silk. Carpeting covers the floor—the intricate floral convolutions of its pattern are the kind of thing that is chosen because it does not show the dirt. Gilded sconces and elaborately framed mirrors hang on the walls, between them oil paintings. When the Palace was new the art looked like Artland remainders. That stuff has since been replaced by oils that, if they are far from art, are at least painterly, actually decorative, especially those that are not askew. You sit—in stuffed chairs that look like something out of the Bettmann Archive—before huge tables on which the gold-edged service plates glint in light that has been refracted by cut-crystal stem glasses, three of which stand at each place. You will find a tall candle, fresh flowers, and sweet butter in, respectively, a sterling silver candlestick, a sterling silver vase, and a sterling silver miniature bathtub with a swiveled lid.

Your host leads you to your table and introduces you to your waiter, who, because you are a stranger to the management, and because the restaurant is nearly full on this weekend evening, will take care of you instead of a captain. "Alex," he says, "this is Monsieur Nomerroné. Monsieur Nomerroné, this is Alex, who will be taking care of you this evening." The principal difference between the waiters and the captains is that the captains, when they talk to you, are not continually distracted by the search for a place to stash their hands. The style here is for the menu selections from the first three courses to be described to you in stages. You are expected to choose your first dish before you know about those from which you will choose your second, and so on. Since you cannot be certain of what you will want first if you do not know what will follow, chaos is the invariable consequence. Yet staff assistance is essential, for many of the dishes have names like "La Paquette Henri Duvernoid façon Michel Fitoussi." The waiters and captains invariably attempt to delimit the process by skipping over dishes that require intricate explication. Still, when finally you work something out, the food —which, at dinner, consists of two first courses, a main course, salad, a series of sweets, and coffee—is almost always good to eat.

Take for example the salade de homard du Palace, chunks of tender lobster meat and fresh, firm artichoke hearts in a light walnut-oil dressing; or take the délice de crabe de Maryland tout-Paris, a mound of impeccable crabmeat set between two pools of cool sauce—a pale, spicy, light mayonnaise, and a green and grassy herb sauce. One of the first courses survives from this establishment's original menu—roulade de saumon d'Ecosse fourrée au caviar. It consists of Scottish smoked salmon wrapped around whipped cream and black caviar, the whole served up in a boat made of flaky pastry —a superb morsel, at once light and of strong flavor. You get pretty good raw beef (it is not without gristle) that is utterly redeemed by the substance with which it is spread —a thick, tart, salty, mustard-flavored sauce that is greened with parsley, dotted with capers.

Visualize, if you will, a large white napkin so cleverly folded that its four corners are formed into four linen bassinets, in each of which you find a warmed oyster on a half shell. Each mollusk has for company a little lobster dumpling, the core of which consists of uncooked lobster roe, and, sometimes, a sea urchin as well. The noon and six o'clock oysters are adorned by black caviar, three o'clock and nine o'clock by red. The oysters are fine; that the quenelles are of lobster you take on faith, for they have little flavor; the caviar is a pointless conceit; and, anyway, the sea urchins (which look like samples of wet mattress stuffing) are of such strident fishiness as to drown out anything served with them. M. Fitoussi, the gawky young chef and proprietor, some-times comes out of his kitchen and wanders among the tables in a dirty apron. He boasts that the dish is "Exclusive with me." $10 extra.

Each dish is delivered to the dining room on a tray that is adorned with a fanciful figurine or model, fashioned of foodstuffs—statuettes sculpted of lamb fat, a tower of pasta, etc. A three-masted ship, the rigging of which is of deep-fried bread, sails in escorting one of the specialties of the house, which is right beside it, concealed under a silver dome that is the size of a prizewinning watermelon. The tray is presented to you. The dome is lifted. And *voilà*—a sausage, caught napping, on its side and curled up. It is transferred, still asleep, to the place before you, and you discover that the meat with which it is filled is pale and juicy and powerfully spiced, and that it has been reclining on a sheet of cool sauce, which is flavored with puréed watercress and adorned with whole leaves. A small dollop of extremely thin pasta (cheveux d'anges), very tender, but not soft, may be had in an enriched tomato sauce that is fragrant with fresh basil. There are ravioli stuffed with ground sweetbread in a thick, stout, sherry-flavored sauce that is redolent of sweet spices. The mussel soup is a hot cream threaded with vegetables, touched with saffron and occupied, at the bottom of the little bowl, by two fresh mussels out of their shells—very good.

You order St. Jacques au poivre vert, and the amateur who is waiting on you neglects to point out that scallops are now prepared otherwise, with cèpes, in brown sauce—splendid food, woodsy and oceanic, but you may find it distracting at first to look for flavors that are not present. The veal chop is huge, browned, moist, served already cut into tender slices of buttery meat, in a light and very sweet cream sauce that is laced with fresh mushrooms—delicious, but the tarragon the menu leads you to expect may require an assist from your imagination. A fine Béarnaise sauce, smoky and rich and light, cannot make the decent steak into anything more than that. Game is offered when it is in season, including, on occasion, partridge, which is served carved away from its bones, the crisp skin and fibrous but tender meat moistened with a pale sauce that has a touch of fruitiness. The main courses are garnished with artichoke hearts stuffed with an earthy duxelles; feathery pommes soufflées; bundles of matchstick vegetables tied up by strings fashioned of scallion greens.

Salad is included, and the Palace sometimes obtains fresh hearts of palm—the discs of the crunchy but pallid rarity fall into rings; they are served, with greens, in a sprightly lemon dressing. For an extra $5 you may sample the cheese tray—the cheeses are in good shape, but they are accompanied by unripe pears, half-white strawberries and cooking apples.

The white chocolate mousse is fluffy, and it arrives in a pool of intense strawberry purée. The coffee ice cream is pungent, as if made with espresso beans ground directly into the cream—it is served in a caramel sauce, and it is decorated with good whipped cream. The apple tart is dull and doughy, but the chocolate mousse cake is dark, sticky, studded with bits of crisp macaroon, and enriched with leaves of pure dark chocolate.

The prix fixe these days is $70. A 20 percent service charge is added. The place can be depressing early in the week, when it is sometimes close to empty. You may want to visit the Palace once in a lifetime, but it is not a once-in-a-lifetime experience.

★ PALM and PALM TOO

837 Second Avenue (near 45th Street); 840 Second Avenue (near 45th Street)
LUNCH, MONDAY TO FRIDAY; DINNER, MONDAY TO SATURDAY. CLOSED SUNDAY.
**Reservations for lunch, or for four or more at dinner at Palm Too, 687-2953 and
697-5198.**
Credit cards: AE, CB, DC, MC, V.
Very expensive.

The classes of people that yearn to be accepted in men's locker rooms are two: men and women. Men have never had much trouble getting in, but, until recently, women have not even tried. Instead, women went (or, much more often, were taken) to the Palm, which has all the strident camaraderie of the real thing, and none of the inconvenient undress. At the Palm a woman can permit herself to be titillated to breathless excitement by the sounds and press of male animals, all the while smiling sweetly. And, of course, those male animals are never so swaggeringly confident—and irresistibly desirable—as when they are surrounded by their brothers in bravado.

What happens, see, is a bunch of the guys grab a bunch of the gals and take 'em to the Palm, where the guys proceed to ignore the little things for the rest of the evening, preferring instead to exchange tales of how they changed the world in their day, any number of times, with just a few well-placed words here, a few others there. By the end of the evening the little ladies think they are at the center of the universe.

No one loves the locker room on Second Avenue more than women reporters. Their love is like the competitive devotion of abject groupies for an aloof star. "I love you more." "No, *I* love you more." Ultimately, of course, there must be a top Palmiste, a *prima buffa,* and so a deciding bout has been arranged. But this heavyweight championship, so to speak, threatens fistfuls of hair, shredded Lastex all over the ground, unless rigid restraints are imposed—for in one corner stands none other than the imponderable Lulu Waldorf, opposite her the voracious Yumyum Plentee. In the heat of their carnivorous lusts the contestants tug at their chains. And as the winches are slowly turned, the opponents move, step by tiny step, to the laden table at center ring, fall into their respective battle chairs and begin putting it away, the first to cry "Enough!" the loser.

Waldorf opens with a crabmeat cocktail, taking it as delivered, with spicy ketchup dumped all over the lovely pink-flecked and ocean-sweet white meat. Plentee counters with a crisp green salad that is garnished with good red tomatoes, served in a Roquefort dressing that is vibrant with the strong flavor of the veined cheese. Then Lulu forces her way through a limp first course of overcooked cold string beans sprinkled with minced onions that may have been strong and crisp when they were chopped hours before. Yumyum moves ahead on points as she dispatches an order of sliced tomatoes and onions, the alternating red and white slabs firm and tasty in their tart oil-and-vinegar dressing. Lulu tries to get even with clams posillipo, a mound of hot mollusks, in their shells, in a plate of red broth that is at once garlicky and briny, but she must overlook the fact—and easily does—that these fresh cherrystones have been toughened and ruined by overcooking. Neither contender takes critical note when spaghetti is ordered thirty seconds into round nine and arrives fifteen seconds later—it has been

208

waiting in hot water, and it is limp and soft, though its white clam sauce is bright and fragrant with garlic and parsley.

Round fourteen is a holding action involving some striped bass that should have lived longer or been cooked sooner, the closely matched contestants manifesting equivalent contentment as they chew through the nicely broiled but slightly loud white meat. Their thoughts, of course, are on round twenty, lobster, the Palm's $30 masterpiece, broiling being the ultimate method of lobster preparation, its execution at the Palm artful, so that the tender meat, cooked only in its own liquid, is a concentration of sea flavor accented with the scent of the blackened shell. The lobsters are not invariably done to the perfect point, but the proper broiling of a lobster is an exacting task, and the Palm does it as well as any place in town.

The object, however, is steak, and if the Palm makes steak these days with remarkable consistency and accuracy—both sirloins and filets mignons—tender and crusted as the meat may be, these steaks lack the mineral blood-sweetness of broiled beef at its best. These are good steaks, no doubt of it, but their reputation is part fact and part legend. Lulu and Yumyum, who are both believers and spreaders of the legend, get through their pounds of rare prime with tears of happiness dripping onto their plates. Now Ms. Plentee, the sheen around her mouth spreading toward her cheeks, her eyes hot and bright, attacks a rib of roast beef, unawed by its immensity, tolerant of the absence of silkiness in the tender meat, mindless of the pseudo-"jus" with which it is moistened, a brownish liquid with the metallic flavor of a reconstituted bouillon cube. But Mme. Waldorf fights back with Steak à la Stone, sliced sirloin spread across sautéed onions and pimentos on toast, an oleaginous creation that would benefit from crustier edges to the beef against the pinguid and pallid vegetables—an odd dish.

In round twenty-five Yumyum declares all-out love by commissioning an order of Beef à la Dutch, a mound of food the size and shape of half a football cut the long way, consisting of chunks of stew meat, with sautéed mushrooms, onions and green peppers, in a tomato-flecked wine gravy, a couple of pints of the meat and vegetables mounded up over a hillock of wide noodles. Beef à la Dutch is the first and last word, and all those in between, in solidity, and Yumyum never looks up until her fork is scraping china.

Round thirty is a breather for both sides, three double lamb chops apiece, just about as good as lamb chops get, the lovely lamb-fat blackened and crisped, the charred bits of meat on the bones like zest for the tender pink eyes of the chops.

Throughout, the combatants have been mortaring up the interstices between meat and seafood with the Palm's remarkable hashed brown potatoes, giant pancakes darkened to the color of mahogany, the slightly grease-moistened spuds inside pale and firm; and with fried onions, about a kilo of them, slivered, and deep-fried until they are crinkly and copper-colored; and with the somewhat more incomprehensibly beloved cottage-fried potatoes, deep-fried discs that are sometimes crisp, sometimes hard, virtually devoid of potato flavor, admirable only for the fact that the noise of chewing them may be audible above the din of the restaurant.

There is no point in actually eating the cheese cake, when you can just as easily spread it directly on the surface of your body, but Lulu and Yumyum each dispatch a portion the size of a mastodon's fist, even though the stuff is nothing more than sweetened cream cheese with a touch of lemon. The Palm gets pretty good strawberries, and neither Waldorf nor Plentee is offended by the sugared, machine-made "whipped cream" that comes with the ripe fruit.

The fight goes on, and at this writing neither gladiator has shown signs of leaving the table. Greater love hath no man than the Palm.

The Palm consists of two long narrow stores, connected at the back, with an additional room upstairs. Each level has its own noisy kitchen at the rear. The restaurant's annex, Palm Too (joke), is directly across the street, with a noisy kitchen of its own. Reservations are required at lunch, refused at dinner, at which time you must show up and wait, at the tiny bars or in the aisles. Tables are sometimes promptly available very early or very late. No one at either restaurant maintains a list for the purpose of seating customers in the order of their arrival, and customers known to the management are given preference.

As everyone knows, the walls are covered with cartoons, some of them decades old, many of them recently added. There are even cartoons on the ceiling, and of course there is sawdust on the floor. The waiters—bored oldtimers at the Palm, somewhat more enthusiastic young men at Palm Too—recite a mere fraction of what food is available (customers are not handed a printed menu); when prodded they mention one or two items more. Many of the dishes that Lulu and Yumyum enjoy so much are almost never served to the general public, because the public is not told of their existence. Typed-up menus do exist—one is posted at the back of the Palm's upstairs room, another is at the front of Palm Too. The wine list (actually printed up at Palm Too) is brief and banal. Beer is an important item with this kind of food, but the glasses you get are so unclean or soapy that the bottled Heineken or Budweiser goes flat at once.

The crowd is mostly suited businessmen and journalists and their decorative girl friends, plus a number of working women. "Happy Birthday" is heard once or twice a night, and it is answered with the kind of cheering and applause usually reserved for a tie-breaking, last-minute Ranger goal before a packed Madison Square Garden crowd. Often you must pause in your conversation to make way for the conversation at the next table: "OH, MY GOD. LOOK WHO'S HERE. I DON'T BUHLIEVE DIS. CHARLIE BABY." This is especially disruptive when half-a-dozen guests arrive, one at a time, each to that kind of greeting.

★ PAMIR

1423 Second Avenue (near 74th Street)
DINNER.
Reservations, 734-3791.
Credit cards: MC, V.
Medium-priced.

For lack of trying, if for no other reason, Afghan restaurants have never made it big in New York. The food is fine. The big surprise has to do with what may be learned, on the basis of visits to Pamir, of Afghan interior design.

You will be astonished to discover, for example, that apparently because Afghanistan is a landlocked nation, Afghans express, through their choice of furnishings, a yearning for the ocean. How else to explain the captain's chairs that surround the tables, and the ship's lanterns that stand on them and glow dimly, as if seen through a fog at sea. Except for the Afghan travel posters and the brilliantly colored, presumably Afghan, rugs that hang on the walls, the remaining features of this place are harder to explain: ersatz Tiffany lamps, a few of them fringed; dark walls of glazed brick or wood stained almost black; the stools of iron and red-plastic upholstery that stand at the little bar at the front; the massive overhead rafters, which in this darkness go unnoticed. The daisies on the tables strike yet another seemingly incongruous note, but then again, perhaps the daisy is the national flower of Afghanistan. To the inexpert ear the background music will sound exactly like the sounds to which Near Eastern dancers undulate their navels. The restaurant is staffed by gentlemen who seem somewhat awkward in their Occidental clothing. But they are cordial, and you are made to feel at home in these comfortable, albeit somewhat perplexing, surroundings.

The hot first courses called bulanee gandana and bulanee kachalou are large, flat two-layer pastries in the shape of isosceles triangles: the former is filled with sautéed scallions, herbed and highly seasoned and a little oily; the latter is filled with a peppery blend of potatoes and ground beef. Both are garnished with cool yogurt, and both are stimulating and satisfying. Then there is aushak, a dumplinglike pastry filled with seasoned scallions and topped with a sauce of yogurt and ground meat that is seasoned, unfortunately, with dried mint. The dish called sambosa goushti is filled with a spicy mixture of meat and chickpeas, and it is served with a green sauce that is perfumed with the strong parsley called cilantro.

Lots of lamb: sabsi-chalaw, for example, spicy chunks of good meat in a thick and lightly garlicked spinach sauce; and quabilli palaw, a great mound of brown rice, crisscrossed with strands of carrot, studded with juicy raisins and almonds and pistachios, under all of which is concealed yet more of this establishment's tasty lamb. Lots of skewered dishes: that lamb again, or chicken white meat, or spicy and crusty beef meatballs, or whole rib lamb chops, all of them marinated and then broiled with tomatoes and onions and green peppers; the meats are tender, mildly and pleasantly flavored and oiled by their marinade, and the vegetables are charred black at their edges. You can starve a little here on one of the vegetarian main courses. The slightly tart eggplant stew—with tomatoes and onions—called chalaw badenjan, under its yogurt topping, will probably leave you feeling protein-deprived, even if you dispatch the entire mound of spiced white rice with which it is served.

Of the two desserts, have the firnee, a cool, gentle, milky and nutted rice pudding; and eschew the baghlawa, which is a refrigerated and slightly heavy pastry, with nuts and honey, that usually goes by a different spelling in New York's lesser Near Eastern restaurants.

★ PANTHEON

689 Eighth Avenue (near 43rd Street)
LUNCH AND DINNER. CLOSED SUNDAY.
Reservations, 664-8294.
Credit cards: AE, DC, MC, V.
Inexpensive.

There is an old-world primness and innocence about the Pantheon, the venerable Greek restaurant on Eighth Avenue. You are greeted politely. You hang your coat on a simple rack and walk across a floor of neat terrazzo squares to tidily linened tables that stand in rows. The walls are hung with tall, rectangular mirrors and, between those, slightly hilarious paintings. When your waiter comes to take your order, there is a napkin draped over his forearm; what he says is civil and to the point, and the dishes that he and you discuss are, by midtown standards, cheap. Pantheon is not a great restaurant, but it is so utterly free of hokum, so devoid of pretension, so essentially a restaurant and nothing else, that eating here is a primal New York memory of the way things were when eating out at its best was sustenance in comfort rather than a theatrical thrill.

Conventional is the name of the menu: the inevitable tarama appetizer, a cool, freshly prepared lemony paste of red caviar and moistened bread; logs of cold rice, flavored with sweet spices and wrapped in parchment-like grape leaves that are shiny with lemon and oil; a pungently aromatic pie of strong feta cheese and spinach on a pale, flaky pastry. Among the few oddities is a startling cold dish of crisp, buttered beets garnished with powerfully garlicked mashed potatoes.

There is safety here in roasts, the roast chicken homey and moist within its crisped skin, the roast pork tender and pleasantly fibrous, albeit sometimes a bit dry away from the bone. The barbecued baby lamb is exceedingly rich, the delicate meat protectively wrapped in thick layers of gentle fat. Naturally there is shish kebab, but though it is carefully broiled, the meat has been marinated until all its natural juiciness is gone, which will displease the standard local palate. There is good fish, especially a broiled snapper that has a beautifully crisped skin around the perfectly fresh white meat. The moussaka is for the tourists. And, like all Greek restaurants, this one has no capacity for dealing with veal.

Sweet, sweet desserts, most of them honeyed or nutted or loaded with rich custard —no finesse, but they are all decent. Only Greek wines are available, and to like most of them takes learning. Background recorded bouzouki music.

• EL PARADOR CAFÉ

325 East 34th Street
DINNER. CLOSED SUNDAY.
No reservations (679–6812).
No credit cards.
Medium-priced.

Its proponents claim that what distinguishes El Parador from the myriad of mediocre Mexican restaurants that are beginning to line Manhattan's avenues in the middle-income neighborhoods is not the food based on the tortilla—no, the tacos, tamales and tostadas at El Parador, they admit, are just junk food, sound excuses for an evening of beer drinking. It is, they claim, the more pretentious specialties that make this quite pretentious establishment. It is true, they are better than the junk food.

El Parador is a busy restaurant, but it is not the mob scene it once was. Nevertheless, when you arrive and there are tables empty and ready (and they cannot be ready for anyone in particular, because the house does not accept reservations), you are told that there will be a wait at the bar, you are assured that it will not exceed thirty minutes, and the scene has been set—here on 'way-East 34th Street, what can you head for and be sure to be seated in much less than thirty minutes? So you hit the bar, order the two drinks the whole charade is designed to sell, and as soon as that transaction is completed you are seated at one of the several available tables. And your host is so gracious! Shame, *shame,* Señor Jacott. Just to sell a couple of your excellent Margaritas? You are led to your table by a waiter carrying your barely sipped drinks, lambs from the slaughter.

Ceviche is a marvelous dish of raw fish that has been "cooked" by marination in lemon or lime juice and any of several other ingredients, depending on which Latin country is the source of the recipe. If we may take it that the seviche at El Parador is typical of the Mexican method of preparing this dish, then we may conclude that Peruvians, Bolivians, Cubans, etc., enjoy it more. They start out with a nice fish here —red snapper—and they marinate it in lemon juice, but somehow some of the fish becomes chewy in the process. Then they garnish it with a couple of slices of avocado whose quite brown, loud overripeness could not have been concealed in a guacamole, and serve it on a pile of shredded iceberg lettuce that becomes limp in the drained-off marinade from the fish. The production is strewn with fresh peas. Unusual. The latest sampling of guacamole at El Parador is superior to the bland stuff this restaurant used to serve—it is garlicky and sharp, almost winy, and it would be first rate if it were not served at refrigerator temperature.

You were warned when seated that your Chicken a El Parador would take thirty minutes. You should have been warned twice. Eventually it arrives, a giant serving of crusty, garlicked fried chicken, garnished with a huge poached onion and a scattering of fresh peas. This is good fried chicken, albeit a bit heavy, but its reputation is not on its merit, but on its comparison with most Mexican food in New York. It may be the best dish in the place, but that is not a particularly exalted position. There is a pretty fair dish of shrimp in green sauce served here—good shrimp in a sauce that has a loud, clear flavor of fresh parsley. Unfortunately, the sauce is watery and if you spoon it over the excellent rice that is served with the main courses, you ruin the rice.

Slightly better than average Mexican-restaurant desserts, including nice guava shells, grainy and tart, with a creamy cheese and crisp saltine crackers—homey but good.

El Parador is a dim, sexy place, but avoid the downstairs room—Grand Rapids brick and ornate mirrors, and every time the kitchen door opens, the glaring white light jars.

★★★ PARIOLI, ROMANISSIMO

1466 First Avenue (near 76th Street)
DINNER, TUESDAY TO SATURDAY. CLOSED SUNDAY AND MONDAY.
Reservations required, 288–2391.
Credit cards: AE, CB, DC.
Very expensive.

This is a dark little den through which waiters wander by the seeming dozen. They are dark-haired, immaculately tonsured and handsome, and they are suited up in formal blacks, their shirt fronts and ties stiff and snowy. There is something religious about their uniform look and courtliness, but when they unbend and hover over your uttered wishes and over the tasks of carrying them out, it is the soma that is being nourished, not the soul. And very well, too—Parioli manages to serve some of the best Italian food in New York.

In the hierarchy of the priesthood of pleasure everything is upside down: the captain of the waiters is distinguished from his fellows by the rakish cut of his suit and by the broad wings and gay color of his bow tie; and your host, who carries out many captainly functions—discussing the menu with you and announcing and pushing special unlisted selections of the day—is resplendent in mufti and luxuriant hair. The moral is, When you make it to the top you can relax. And folk who have made it sufficiently high up the economic ladder to be seen in this steep place are very much at home here. Parioli, Romanissimo, is kept busy by a small but devout following of prosperous Upper East Side New Yorkers: the professionals come early in the evening, and the place is medically and legally sober for a few hours; then come the creatives, sporting their stylish hair and duds, chairs are pushed a few inches farther from the tables, and the sounds of gay but restrained cheer that filled the room at eight are replaced by a slightly cacophonous din—this room can be noisy.

You enter through a handsome wrought-iron street door to a tiny vestibule, wherein strays are rejected by the snooty sign: "By Reservation Only." Having arranged ahead, you proceed, into a longish room which, by a separated, two-steps-up level on the right, a turn to the left at the back, and wrought-iron partitions here and there, is divided into intimate sections. That raised level is given a light garden treatment—a few potted plants, the suggestion of an awning, metal chairs painted white—while the rest of the place, unblushingly unrealistic about the absence of a separating wall, suggests the interior of the parent house—gold wallpaper, racks of wine, framed mirrors, in one corner a spectacular arrangement of cut flowers, the single bright note in this dim fairyland. Parioli is something of a jumble, but the soft light calms it.

This is one of those establishments that are famous for their secrets, where frequenters push aside the proffered menu and ask about the day's unlisted items. This is most useful in selecting first courses, for though the various stuffed clams, scampi and prosciutto are unimpeachable, an occasional specialty like the Vitello Tonnato borders on the amazing—cutlets of cool veal, pale and tender, under a tuna mayonnaise that is at once creamy and light, sharpened with lemon.

While the rage among New York's food freaks is making one's own pasta on one's own little pasta machine or, at the very least, buying fresh pasta at one of the several outlets around town where it is manufactured each day for prompt sale, this place, bound to a more old-fashioned snobbism, imports its macaroni, dried, from Italy. It is difficult to believe that anyone's spaghetti in clam sauce could surpass this one, no matter what the provenance of the noodle. The spaghetti is extremely thin—vermicelli, actually—boiled to that perfect point at which it has lost all hardness without showing even a trace of mushiness; and it is served in a briny broth redolent of garlic and studded with an abundance of minced fresh clams that are as firm and tender as littlenecks two minutes out of the sea. The dish comes adorned with a couple of whole clams still in their shells and a small cloudburst of fresh parsley. By comparison the Tortellini Bolognese should not be asked to suffer, for these are nice enough little crescents of pasta wrapped around ground meat; and the sauce, a nubbly thickness of ground beef, mingled with oil, spices and chunks of tomato, is totally satisfying, if far from elegant.

The most expensive seafood dish on the menu, Pescatora alla Veneziana, can be the most disappointing item in the house. This is stew, principally of shellfish and squid, in a brothlike sauce made fiery with fresh red pepper. But the circlets of squid are tough, the mussels limp, the flavors of the shrimp and clams obscure in this setting; what is worst is the slice of fish at the center of the abundant mound—it is cooked beyond any flavor or texture other than that of wet cotton wool.

The same kitchen produces Piccata di Vitello al Limone, probably the best version of veal in a lemon sauce available in New York. The meat is buttery, the sauce creamy and sparkling with the vibrance of fresh lemon. The Suprema di Pollo al Cognac is a sautéed chicken breast inundated in sautéed fresh mushrooms and a cream sauce that is thick and lightly brandied—rich, smooth, polished food. Rare for New York's Italian restaurants, even the steaks are good, not to mention joyously labeled. Try, for example, the Lombatina di Manzo alla Toscanini, a section of filet mignon about the size of your fist, tender, accurately cooked, and served in a sauce of wine and green peppers that livens the meat. It is true of almost all the sauces here that they have character and individuality and that they brighten the meats they adorn—these are sauces with a function beyond fanciness. Good vegetables and salads, including Spinaci all'Aglio e Olio, a remarkable spinach dish in which the leaves of the vegetable retain their texture even though they are utterly imbued with the smoothness of oil and the strong scent and flavor of abundant garlic. Perfect greens—sharp, sweet, crisp endive and fragrant arugula—in a dressing that will wake you up.

The zabaglione is ceremoniously prepared in a copper pot at a serving stand near your table and it is not bad—frothy and winy. And there are perfectly fine cheeses with fruit. But the facts are that you must have the chocolate cake or the cheese cake. The chocolate is airy and moist, and it has a flavor that will remind you of the aroma of real cocoa when a fresh package is just opened—the thick whipped cream on top verges on light butter. The cheese cake is something else—a velvety and sweetened richness of ricotta cheese, sparkling with chunks of fruit, the blackened exterior of the cake making for a delicately bitter accent. A minor wonder.

★★ LE PARIS BISTRO

48 Barrow Street (near Bedford Street)
DINNER.
Reservations, 989-5460.
Credit cards: AE, CB, DC, MC, V.
Medium-priced.

The garden of Le Paris Bistro is prettiest when there is still light in the sky, when the rows of white-linened tables, pyramid-folded napkins thereon, give off a garden-party glow against the grassy-green carpeting. Boxes around the sides hold greenery, and overhead there are rafters to support the roll-down ceiling that protects this place in cold or wet weather. If you cannot get a table in the garden, the front room is your basic Village den, with a bar, brick walls, low ceilings, all the comforts of home plus waiters.

The garden and the front room are connected by a passage through the kitchen, which, despite the distraction of trespassing customers, turns out some fine products. These are the best: moules ravigote—fresh mussels, in their shells, covered with a mayonnaise sauce that is sharpened with a bit of mustard; strong sausage in a flaky pastry—warm, spicy, and served with a good sharp mustard; snails in a garlic butter that makes no pretense of subtlety. The daily seafood specials are always fresh—sometimes soft-shell crabs that are lightly anise-flavored from being flamed in Pernod. Buttery veal, browned and covered with sautéed mushrooms and a creamy wine sauce, goes by the name of escalope de veau à la Savoyarde—it is a simple, rich and elegant dish. Good steaks, au poivre or in mustard sauce. And, for dessert, particularly rich tarts, made with fresh fruit and lots of custard, and a pecan pie that is little more than crisp nuts and browned crust.

★★ PARIS COMMUNE

411 Bleecker Street (near Bank Street)
LUNCH AND DINNER. CLOSED MONDAY.
Reservations, 929-0509.
Credit cards: AE, MC, V.
Medium-priced.

On occasion the only female in the place is the waitress. On looking around, one might reasonably judge that when the way to Moscow was barred, the men's half of the Olympic team came here instead. On the ton or two of humanity displayed during the dinner hour, there is nary a kilo of superfluous fat, nowhere a fold of limp skin. Every strand of everyone's impeccably tonsured hair follows faithfully its assigned curve, every inch of skin glows with cleanliness. Muscular shoulders bulge around the straps of pastel athletic shirts. Each pair of jeans fits like the pelt on a racehorse. Michelangelo himself carved in marble the taut convolutions of these arched, thonged feet.

The Paris Commune is yet another of Greenwich Village's innumerable semiamateur (or semiprofessional) eating places, this one put together with an extraordinary degree of simplicity and charm, considering that on close inspection the place resembles nothing so much as a small and immaculately refurbished warehouse. The storefront's colors are gray (the wainscoting along the lower walls) and faded tan (the stamped tin) and brick. The floor is of ancient, pockmarked wood. The seats of the simple chairs are upholstered in mattress ticking. And at each place on the unclothed, dark-stained wooden tables, the dinner napkin is actually a small towel of coarse cloth. Your wineglass is a tumbler, your water glass a larger one. Second-hand factory lamps (their inner enamel surfaces are chipped) hang low and glow dim. The place is not without its touches of elegance: the fireplace near the front—which is surrounded by a table, a bench and a couple of chairs, where you may have to wait for the next available table —sports a couple of long tapers on its mantel. And above the gauze curtains that hang over the lower part of the front windows you may, during daylight hours, see out to the greenery of the little park across Bleecker Street.

You select your dinner from a blackboard menu, which is revised regularly, and the very good dishes it has listed include a peppery lentil salad garnished with slices of tomato that are lightly dressed with oil, the elements adorned with a crisp sprig of fresh mint; mussels and curry mayonnaise, a semicircle of poached mussels, fresh and in their shells, arranged on a leaf of red cabbage, a dollop of the rich, spiced mayonnaise at the center—impeccable food; a ceviche of bay scallops, the citrus-marinated morsels of fresh shellfish bright and tart and spicy, mingled with minced sweet peppers; and a dish the house styles "summer pasta"—cool spaghetti, lightly oiled so that the strands do not stick together, topped with a gardeny dressing of minced tomatoes and fresh basil. And sometimes the pasta is hot, such as a cheese ravioli with a grain filling, served with a simple tomato sauce and fresh spinach, the entire dish heavily doused with, and fortified by, strong Parmesan cheese.

216

The Paris Commune, sensibly, serves those varieties of fish that are local, good-tasting, relatively unpopular and, therefore, relatively inexpensive. Tilefish, for one, browned in grapefruit butter, the white meat flaky and tender; the thin reddish-brown crust and the strands of browned grapefruit rind are sharp zests to the fresh fish. Lotte (angle fish), for another, also fresh, garnished with ginger-flavored mustard, and moistened with a cream sauce that is flavored with herbs. At times either liver or veal—excellent meats, carefully sautéed—is served with slices of sautéed apple and a lightly brandied sauce. A single thick slab of sweetbread, rich and sticky, is contrasted with pine nuts in its dark sauce, and spears of fresh asparagus. The very decent sirloin steak, accurately cooked, is salty and crusty and rubbed with sage for a touch of exotic flavor.

Rich chocolate cake, studded with bits of whole chocolate, is wrapped as a roulade around thick whipped cream (sometimes the same components are served in a different layout). The Paris Commune is under the notion that deep-dish apple pie is everyday apple pie in a deep dish. That aside, this is fine, elemental pie, a lard crust and chunks of tart apple, with a dollop of this restaurant's excellent whipped cream. The blueberry tart, though made with fresh berries, is cold, on coagulated custard, and no pastry crust can seem quite right at icebox temperature.

★ PARMA

1404 Third Avenue (near 80th Street)
DINNER.
Reservations, 535-3520.
Credit cards: AE.
Medium-priced.

Six physicians at a large round table look quite ill as they consume much too much pasta while discussing the poor progress of an associate's malpractice trial; a couple of tanned gents in sharkskin suits and silver neckties stand at the bar bartering apartment buildings for air rights; ladies of the office come here in pairs and trios to wryly discuss office politics and their love-lives over martinis and spaghetti. When they come here with men they are out of their era—the girls ask timid questions and the guys have all the answers; girls of even longer ago, who have, as they would put it, if they were speaking of themselves in the third person, "buried their hubbies," play out their twilights in endless small talk, enjoying what would be the last laugh, but for the fact that they do not wish to crack their make-up: such is Parma, the restaurant the Upper East Side needed since World War II, and which it embraced the moment it appeared in the spring of '78, the kind of place that does not even call its cuisine "cuisine," much less "Northern Italian cuisine," where there is a pay phone by the front door, travel posters and coat hooks on the wood-paneled walls, rows of tables and simple chairs, waiters in white shirts and black ties, a brass rail in front of the bar, a burly, silver-haired ex-cop (or a superb character actor) behind it. There is a framed American flag, and a sign announcing that no checks are accepted. In a place like this you know where you stand.

The mussels al vino bianco are abundant and fresh, mounded up over a hot broth flavored with garlic and wine. The seafood salad, squid and mussels and shrimp, with a touch of celery, has a lifeless dressing and no garlic, but adding lemon almost brings it to life. The mushroom salad, slivers of the fresh fungus mingled with still more celery in a simple vinaigrette, is crisp and lively, the mushrooms having soaked up the lightly applied dressing without losing their crunchiness.

Fresh pasta is a refinement that has not reached Parma, but they do not do bad with the packaged stuff, sometimes undercooking it just a little, occasionally going a bit too far: the sauce amatriciana is a hefty red mixture, though the smokiness of ham and the sweetness of sautéed onions you expect in sauces of that title are present only as remotenesses; occasionally there is green lasagna with a polished stuffing of melted ricotta, a rich and creamy sauce, browned cheese across the top; and sometimes there is spaghetti mimosa, the pasta served in a red sauce that is fortified with sautéed eggplant and crisp vegetables, the dish topped with grated hardcooked eggs—a good dish, but for all its vegetables it lacks the intended garden freshness.

The fish of the day—often bluefish or bass or both—are fresh, but the sauces, such as a creamy red one with peas and anchovies, seem unrelated, rather than part of the dish. You get a splendid big plain veal chop here, served, as in the old days in places like this, with a couple of slices of lemon, nothing else on the plate. The scaloppine dishes are of good veal more or less obscured by inappropriately zealous preparation. But the chicken scarpara (scarpariello everywhere else) is fine, crusty and pungently garlicked chunks of chicken, on the bone, a bit of salty sauce on the plate. The warm green beans that sometimes accompany some of these dishes are quite green and quite tough.

The closest you can come to cheese is an item listed as an appetizer—insalata caprese: slabs of powerful red onion, slices of smoked mozzarella, and discs of tomato, all in a tangy vinaigrette that is nearly ruined by dried herbs. Even with a head cold you will be roused by the flavors and strengths of this food, and without one you will be roused by an order of it at the next table.

The strawberry tart is dreadful, but then again, you know that this is not a place in which to order a strawberry tart. The cheese cake is light and moist, a lemony exaggeration of sugar and richness. To many, that is perfection.

Red corvo wine is listed, and if you remember to order it with an ice bucket when you sit down, it will be chilled by the time you have dispatched your vodka whatevers and are ready to embark on your first course. Often on weekends, and sometimes on other unpredictable evenings, the restaurant is booked up well in advance. At other times you can just saunter in and be seated.

★★LA PETITE FERME

973 Lexington Avenue (near 70th Street)
LUNCH AND DINNER. CLOSED SUNDAY.
Reservations, 249-3272.
Credit cards: AE, CB, DC, MC, V.
Very expensive.

When the first Ferme showed up in New York, down in Greenwich Village more than a decade ago, it caused a sensation that, seen from the vantage of today, was of an appealing innocence. The town was all atwitter over a place that was so quaint and cute and sweet and charming, and above all so wee. Today, of course, a farmhouse setting, right down to the cooing doves, is just one of a thousand fantasies that, rendered to a fare-thee-well, are now the very stuff of New York eating out. (The nuts-and-bolts restaurants of yesteryear are relegated to the status of mess hall in the eyes of some.) But there was more to the humble cottage on West Tenth Street than its suggestion of the pastoral hearth, for the food was—how you say—très simple. It is never noted, but La Petite Ferme was New York's initial encounter with a variation on French cooking that was, starting then, becoming a principal theme, the characteristics of which were elementality, dramatic clarity, lightness. For New Yorkers to whom, theretofore, French cooking was either haute cuisine (all those fancy sauces) or country cooking (sticks to your ribs), the new food was not a surprise so much as it was a revelation. Even to a relatively imperceptive palate it was clear that this cooking was nothing new, but simply certain elements of French cooking undisguised by any other elements of French cooking. It was, therefore, a cookery immediately accessible to folks brought up on meat and potatoes. M. Chevillot (such was the proprietor's name) offered the shortest menu in town in a twenty-one-chair restaurant. The traffic heading south on Seventh Avenue, bent for his place, clogged the thoroughfare with so many limousines that the scene was often mistaken for the solemn delivery of a higher-up in the underground economy to his last resting place in Brooklyn. It was not just that Chevillot was establishing a trend. He was also preparing impeccable food.

When the Ferme was moved to a site uptown more proximate to its trade, the enterprise left behind much besides its minuscularity (retaining, nonetheless, the "La Petite"). The present quarters are big enough for a middling plantation, and they only hint at the rusticity of the original place. The walls are plain white plaster, the motifs stenciled thereon (of natural dyes pressed from the products of the soil, one assumes) presumably primitive embellishments applied to the stucco when the farmhouse was new. The tables are bare and rough-hewn (though the wood is sealed to a contemporary luster). You sit on chairs of sticks and twine that have little pillows on the seats. Along the wall, the flat cushions on the built-in bench/banquette are hardly more than a gesture to the plight of a thin man's bones. Your napkin is a plaid dishcloth. Through the wood-framed windows on the small back wall you see tiny lights on the branches of a small tree. Inside, the light is low, supplemented by the steady flame of the hefty, white columnar candles on each table. Its quasiprimitiveness notwithstanding, this is not an uncomfortable place. Among its virtues are some big round tables, which hold six easily, more with not much difficulty, and so the prosperous Upper East Siders that frequent this restaurant are sometimes on hand in two or three well-behaved generations.

Your wine list is about five pounds of slate (within a wood frame), with chicken scratchings (white wines scratched on one side, red on the other). You don your glasses, squint, and perceive that a couple of Burgundies and a California pinot noir are listed under the Bordeaux. Your menu is another slate, with far fewer entries than on the wine list, for La Petite's bill of fare was not lengthened at all with the move to larger quarters. What few puzzlements the listing may present you with are resolved by your waitress. She stands at tableside, the slate before her and facing you. It is held in place by her hands on its upper corners. Her recitation of its contents and her explication thereof lack only the rubber-tipped wooden pointer. She is at once the school teacher making the original audio-visual presentation, and the student demonstrating that she has memorized her lesson (for she never once glances at the slate as her recitation proceeds from item to item down the list). You hope she has another way of addressing her friends.

The menu changes from time to time, but the splendid mussel appetizer has been a steady for more than ten years. In a wooden bowl, a couple of dozen mussels, in their shells, fresh and clean and cool and sweet, are mingled with a storm of seemingly just-chopped red onions and a vibrant vinaigrette. Often you are offered a first-course salad—the one of endive, lettuce and red lettuce, arugula and watercress, slivered fresh mushrooms, dill, is of immaculate ingredients in a spanking dressing—a rousing first course. For something considerably weightier, a crêpe filled with ham and cheese, the whole moistened with a pale and creamy sauce—nice cheese, hot and pully, but the ham is dull, the dish a little leaden.

Poaching is not the ideal treatment for a lobster—except here. Whatever ingredients there may be in the cooking liquid are exactly those that make the crustacean more than itself: the meat is juicy and sweet, resilient but tender, and it is moistened with a sauce—little more than butter—that subtly underscores the lobster's mildly oceanic flavor. Fresh tilefish is poached as nicely as that lobster—it is firm, barely flaky, and it is served in a vinegar sauce that is tart, sweet, polished. A splendid duck, of vivid flavor, its meat fatted but not fatty, its skin browned but not hardened, is moistened with a well-calculated green-peppercorn sauce that manages to be powerful without obscuring the bird. The entrecôte is something shy of the greatest American beef, but the steak is tender, accurately prepared, juicy within its crusted exterior—the Béarnaise with which it is served is as fluffy and fragrant a version of this sauce as you will find in town.

From among the eight or so cheeses offered, you will always be able to select several that are in perfect condition. You can get big ripe strawberries; a dark and sticky and not-too-sweet chocolate mousse; a lovely profiterole of cool custard in a fresh and eggy pastry under warm chocolate sauce. Something given as "succès" is a rich, cool dessert of meringue filled with an almond cream that is as light as whipped cream—the elegant sweet is spread with ground nuts.

★★ LE PETIT ROBERT

314 West 11th Street
DINNER. CLOSED MONDAY.
Reservations, 691-5311.
Credit cards: AE.
Expensive.

The place looks sunny on a dark winter night. An old two-room corner store has been coated a lustrous ivory: the plaster walls, the brick walls, the wooden walls, an old side door now in disuse, a few exposed pipes, anything a paintbrush could reach. Wooden banquettes run along two walls of the back room and one of the front. They are fitted with pale bolsters and strewn with brightly colored cushions of patterned velvet. A single good-size table stands near the center of the front room. The floor is covered with brown carpeting. There are flowers here and there. And the place gets the most civilized and engaging crowd in the Village, albeit including the occasional exhibitionist.

Order the goat-cheese soufflé, which is prettily browned and loftily risen over its little white pot. Its texture is cloudlike, its flavor sharp but not too goaty for the elegance of the dish. Sometimes it fails, and then it is soggy and soupy. Little Robert's mousse of chicken livers is a buttery meat paste—made slightly sweet by its admixture of port wine—sealed in a little ramekin under a layer of polished fat. His cucumbers in champagne vinegar are a big soup plate of pale-green discs in white vinegar that really seems to sparkle. A wonderful salad of fresh artichoke hearts and crisp pecans is moistened with a parsleyed dressing made with pungent olive oil. You can spend considerable money on very little food on the rare occasions when the house obtains tiny crayfish and serves them cool in their cooking broth—there is surely enough meat in each of these beasts for scientific-testing purposes, but as sustenance they dismay; the broth will remind you of those instances when you accidentally inhaled seawater. But then there is the remarkable mushroom soup, which somehow has a greater concentration of mushroom flavor than even the just-sprouted fungus right out of the ground.

When there is matelote, do not pass it up. The fish stew is made here in red wine. The ingredients vary, but squid, mackerel, cod have been used. They are all fresh, none overcooked, and the velvety red sauce that coats the seafood sets off its flavors with a sweet-spiced wininess. Other times there is a ragout of shellfish, the fresh oysters and clams, scallops and mussels served with hot endive in a thick cream that is alive with saffron. Roasted mallard duck is served in moist, somewhat rare slices in a simple reduction of the roasting juices and wine. This place converts stuffed cabbage into country elegance: The peasanty dish of ground meat wrapped in the heavy leaves—pot-roasted with vegetables and chunks of pork—is perfectly balanced between its solidity and its vivid meat and vegetable flavors. The thick slice of braised shoulder of veal is larded with pork fat, which keeps it moist and makes it sweet—its sauce is almost like honey, the morels in it fresh and crinkly. Robert makes a good steak, serves it with mushrooms in a buttery green-peppercorn sauce.

The apple tart is perfect, the thin-sliced fruit slightly crisped, caramelized, on a pastry that is virtually weightless. Chunks of caramelized hot pear are served—as pear feuilletée—between blocks of flaky pastry, the whole set in a crimson pool of raspberry purée and garnished with fluffy whipped cream. The pot de crème is a frothy custard, slivers of fresh ginger just under its surface. And the chocolate délice is a dark, moist cake coated with black icing, adorned with a sprig of fresh mint.

Perhaps you think you eat late. You should see them pile in here when you are leaving at around 10:30.

★★★ PHOENIX GARDEN

46 Bowery (in the arcade, near Elizabeth Street)
LUNCH AND DINNER. CLOSED MONDAY.
No reservations (962–8934).
No credit cards.
No liquor.
Inexpensive.

From the Bowery to Elizabeth Street a new street has been carved out, more storefronts for the commercially insatiable, retail-obsessed merchants of Chinatown. The arcade is a few years old now, and fully occupied. It's one of the places the locals go for pizza. There is a candy store that sells beer, for the patrons of the restaurants that don't. But the principal attractions along this chain of baubles are the Chinese restaurants, and no one can tell, just by appearances, which of these gilded boxes is worth looking into. This is the place.

The place looks like the inside of a refrigerator with the light on, all white polished surfaces, with here and there some hardware, ducks and chickens hanging at the front near the stainless-steel counter, a bustling little kitchen at the rear just beyond the stainless-steel coffee urns. The stainless-steel silverware is available on request; otherwise you get chopsticks.

Cantonese cooking has, of recent years, been looked down the turned-up nose upon. The foods of the provinces to the north and west have been the local favorites and fads. Your Chinese-restaurant goer doesn't merely utter the word "Cantonese," he expletes it, a one-word dismissal of a restaurant. There is an explanation, of course: hundreds of dreadful Cantonese restaurants in New York. But no, the Cantonese are not to China what the Dutch and Germans are to Europe, that is, plain ignorant about food; it is we, rather, who are ignorant (those of us who are not Cantonese), though admittedly at the hands of unscrupulous restaurateurs who have for years purveyed slop as Cantonese food, to the miseducation of the locals. At its best, Cantonese food is simple and subtle and light (rice provides the weight), emphasizing the basic ingredients and textures more than the flavorings and seasonings, a relationship that is reversed as you move away from Canton. Please, exception us not with exceptions to the rule.

Begin with "Pepper & Salty Shrimp (in shell)," which is not what it says, being peppery, not pepper, and thereby a good introduction to the English served here. These remarkable shrimp are either fresh or so carefully frozen that virtually no damage has been done to the sweet flavor and crisp texture. They arrive pink, bursting from their crackling shells, lightly spotted with bits of black pepper and moistened with an oil which is flecked with slivers of scallion and fresh ginger—everything conspires to emphasize the pristine flavor of the shrimp themselves.

Fried Fresh Milk with Crab Meat will strike you as yet another typo, and there are perhaps better translations of whatever the Chinese name for this dish might be, but as the dish is singular, it might as well go by this unique title. What arrives looks like a giant mound of moist white soufflé; dig around under it and you find crabmeat and crisp rice noodles. The meat is moist and firm; the noodles, included for texture, are crisp and slightly chewy; and the "soufflé" is glistening white, light and airy, and only faintly flavored with the slightly burnt taste of cooked milk. You may not like it, but that is merely culture shock.

Steam Flounder is not a new kind of flounder, but a steamed flounder. Now, you may say to yourself, "Steamed flounder, big deal." Well, first of all, this flounder is *fresh,* almost sugary in its sweetness, so fluffy it is difficult to hold it in chopsticks. It should be eaten alone because it arrives at a point of steamy perfection from which it deteriorates, since it continues to cook in its own heat. Quickly now, while the silvery fish is still somewhat hidden in the hot rising water vapor, push away the bony edges of the fish, pluck the moist, snowy meat from the spine and large central bones, and swallow it down. When it is all gone (in about two minutes), you can concentrate on the mushrooms and scallions you left behind in the broth the flounder was steamed in.

Fried Stuffed Bean Curd is, you guessed it, bean-curd sheet stuffed with bean curd, crinkly layers of the sheet around bricks of the soft and mealy bean paste, in a brown sauce that is oily and just vaguely fishy. This is a mother's-milk kind of dish, warm and satisfying, like buttered noodles, or bread and jam, or grits, and neither a fine nose nor tuned palate is needed to appreciate the simple oral pleasure of gumming it down.

Another good transition dish (we are heading toward birds and beasts) is Mixed Vegetables with Noodles, which is a party on a plate, here a carrot, orange and crisp and cut in the shape of a butterfly, and there one in the shape of a fish; ears of baby corn and brilliantly green snow peas; straw mushrooms and cloud ears, the mysteriously smoky fungi of your mysterious East; soft and buttery gingko nuts. The vegetables are not married, just joined in a gentle syrup, with rice noodles for a contrasting texture of dry crispness.

Head and all, here comes your Phoenix Special Roast Squab, much pushed by the waiters, advice that is much appreciated by first-time starters. The former bird arrives disjointed, skin browned but still soft, meat fibrous but still tender and moist, some of the little bones sufficiently crisped to be chewed down and appreciated for their salty oiliness. The bird is good as is, better when dipped in the seasoned salt that accompanies it, and utterly transformed when moistened with the lemon that is supplied. Enthusiasts eat the head.

Those birds hanging in the front window are not just for atmosphere. You can eat them. Recommended is the Roast Duck, listed under "Barbecue" on the menu. Your relentlessly sensible waiter (the one who insisted you eat your flounder in a trice) suggests most seriously that you have the duck as is, at room temperature, not reheated and dried out. Sure enough, it is profoundly succulent, not to be tampered with, served, in a way that seems French, over white beans that are in a bit of peppery gravy. To make one bite a little different from another, you dip it in the little dish of sweet ginger sauce.

You get your beer across the arcade.

★★ PIETRO'S

201 East 45th Street
LUNCH, MONDAY TO FRIDAY; DINNER, MONDAY TO SATURDAY. CLOSED SUNDAY.
Reservations, MU 2–9760.
No credit cards.
Very expensive.

Pietro's is busy and little-known. It thrives on the commerce of a small, addicted following. The peer of the best steak restaurants here on Steak Row or anywhere else in town, it is rarely mentioned when the talk turns, as it tediously often does among New York's restaurant freaks, to favorite steakhouses (when everyone gets down on the floor and wrestles over the Palm vs. Christ Cella vs. Peter Luger, et al., in an effort to establish who is tougher about what is tenderer).

Pietro's is a memory of New York. If you were out of town, unborn, or interred in the Bronx in the thirties and forties of this century, Pietro's is a glimpse from which you may extrapolate a city and an era, a time when a public eating place was a room with rows of tables. Atmosphere had not been devised. Menus were mostly in English. It was the waiter's function to find out what you wanted to eat and bring it to you. Your host was a supervisor, a hail-fellow only in passing, if at all. Conspicuous consumption had been invented, to be sure, but had recently suffered a grave setback— eating was too serious a business to be carried out ostentatiously. Something has changed all that, but hardly at all at Pietro's, a restaurant best defined by what it is an escape from: Section C of the *Times,* Lincoln Center for the Performing Arts, and universal psychotherapy. Pietro's gives us the simple life. Take one, please.

Up a flight of stairs to a tiny vestibule, where you present yourself to the man. He has a bundle of three-by-five slips in his jacket pocket (a unique reservation system). You announce yourself (very loudly and clearly in this din) and he leafs through the slips as if looking for the joker in a pack of cards. Tipplers at the bar, a dozen or so customers waiting for their assignments, hustling waiters sprinting through—this is a well-worn little room. And it gives directly, through large doorless portals, on two additional centers of dense activity.

To one side there are seven men in white in a garishly lit stainless-steel closet that is the kitchen. They have been working so long under the direct gaze of customers that all self-consciousness has gone. Julia Child has taught us that "When you are alone in the kitchen, no one can see you" as she retrieves a slippery chicken from the floor. Perhaps these fellows think they are looking out through one-way glass, but it is not exactly an oddity to observe one of them pinch a clump of clams from the top of a diner's plate of spaghetti and plop them into his mouth as he stares directly at (through?) you. Kitchen nibbling occurs all over town, you can be sure, but rarely in view of the audience.

Opposite the kitchen is the dining room, a dozen-and-a-half tables in a room that could not hold many more. The paint on the walls is fresh, the floor is polished, the paintings are undistracting. The choice tables are beside the curtained windows. This is where the action is, and this is where everyone wants to eat, but if a bit of calm is what you need, there is another dining room, like this one but smaller, another flight up. The food is the same, the noise is less, and reservations that may not be honored on time down below can usually be taken care of at once upstairs.

It is possible that Pietro's has the best serving staff in town. The waiters are at ease, polite, available and prompt. They ask for specifications you had not thought to specify. They understand what you say the first time you say it. They do not intrude, they do not visibly suffer, they seem to like their work even when they are carrying heavily laden trays of food up the stairs. They even look good—in old-fashioned crisp blue-linen jackets that are somehow much more professional than the quasi-formals or carefully designed casuals that are the rule in most of this city's spots.

The customers avoid chic as they skirt vulgarity. Very little denim, few pinky rings, and no Wildroot Cream Oil Charlie. Cigars and plaid suits; coiffed hair and knee-length skirts; tans. But they eat like starved children of the Depression who have struck it rich —you get enough food here to handle today's hunger and yesterday's as well, and these folks dispatch it casually. They may have hocked their jewels to come here, however, for the prices are impressive.

Appetizers appear on the menu in three categories. Under Antipasti we have your basic dollar-a-shrimp shrimp cocktail—five immense, snowy, pink-flecked crustaceans, sweet and crisp, so carefully removed from their shells that each of them is intact down to the last millimeter of its tail; and Clams Sauté, a singularity of the house, a handful of littlenecks, out of their shells, breaded, gently sautéed so that they are not toughened, served in a pool of butter, sprinkled with chives—the breading soaks up a lot of that butter, making for a richness that obscures the clear flavor of the clams, but a generous squeezing on of lemon brings them to life. The heading Spaghetti covers a few pastas of other shapes, but mostly the noodles are the thin strings of the title. The clam sauce, the chef's taste for it notwithstanding, is less than wonderful, despite fresh clams and much butter and parsley—the dish needs garlic or salt or pepper or thyme to bring it to life. And then there are the so-called Salads, including one called Broccoli, which is the best and sanest kind of item with which to preface Pietro's main courses: huge branches of the crunchy green, blanketed with broad lengths of roasted red pepper— a little sweet, a little sour and vaguely burnt—the whole wet with oil and lemon. A great dish.

But of course steak is the thing. You may have a large steak (sirloin) or a larger one (sirloin) or a double one (sirloin, not listed on the menu). They are of superb beef, tender without being mushy, juicy within their seared crusts, and cooked with uncommon accuracy. The thing to have is a friend with whom to share the double steak, for these are carved by the waiters into ten red discs with dark brown borders, served five discs to a plate. That kind of beef with a monster platter of thin and tangy French Fried Onions and/or a crusty hillock of Hash Brown Potatoes has been known to make grownups slowly shake their heads, as at a first encounter with Chapman's Homer.

You order Calf's Liver and your waiter asks whether you want slices of liver or a "liver steak." As the latter had never occurred to you, you opt for that, and you receive, exactly as you requested, a calf's liver. Or certainly most of it. When a portion of liver this large is cooked rare, its center may be too, shall we say, natural? But this is wondrous liver, tender and delicate, cross-hatched with dark stripes from the grill. It is served with sautéed onions that are made vividly sharp by the bits of blackened onion in among the tender oily strands; and with lengths of very good bacon.

Pietro's is also an Italian restaurant, and in this regard it is not unbeatable. The Veal Cacciatore is a wonderful stew, but the scaloppine dishes, though perfectly decent, are not much more; among them a Veal Française which, though of tender, pale veal, has a crust that is so eggy and browned that the dish tastes vaguely like an omelet. An item called House Special Chicken consists of chicken that has been sautéed with prosciutto and mushrooms—wonderful ham and terrific mushrooms, but the chicken itself is the too familiar, bland current product—the only meat in the place that is less than first quality. Those sautéed mushrooms are available as an à la carte vegetable—a mere $4 for a casserole dish of them, and they are profoundly garlicked, heavily salted and cooked until they are dark-brown and strong.

Blessedly the dessert menu is a cursory gesture in a direction no one takes here. The rum cake consists of well-rummed layers of white cake among layers of icing, pastry cream and chocolate custard—not worth bothering about. There are the usual Italian ice cream things.

Most everything that goes on here is on the up and up, but Pietro's is just being discovered for its potential as a secret rendezvous. That could change everything!

★★★ PINOCCHIO

170 East 81st Street
DINNER. CLOSED MONDAY.
Reservations, 650–1513.
Wine and beer.
No credit cards.
Medium-priced.

Father cooks, son and daughter work the dining room. There are but a dozen tables in this tiny place, and with a seemingly well-knit family attending to its limited requirements, it is not surprising that virtually nothing goes wrong.

The marble bust of a poet stands on the radiator; vaguely Italianate bas-reliefs hang on the bare-brick wall. The stamped-tin ceiling is of a lipstick red that would be garish if there were enough light in the place to get a good look at it. You are presented with a menu that is handwritten on a sheet of paper that is torn from a spiral-bound sketch pad. There is a pipe rack just inside the front door, whereon you hang your own coat. Most of the illumination is supplied by a chandelier of glass grape clusters, electric lights therein. Can such perfect innocence be for real? Is there a man with soul so free of pretension that his hero is Pinocchio? Who is so artless in his adoration that he names his livelihood after the nosy fellow, but sets up no greater altars to his paragon than a doll figure astride the partition between the dining room and the kitchen, another in each of the two front windows? Ask no further. There may be danger in finding out.

Despite the signs, this is not a bring-your-own-wine restaurant. You contemplate the reasonably priced wine list while eating butter on crusty warm bread. Be advised, in this place you do not get warm bread when you sit down, cold bread later. Whenever you get bread, it is warm bread. So butter up and prepare for a lengthy series of wonderful foods, almost all of them made from scratch in the little kitchen at the back of this homey place, of ingredients as fresh as you can get them.

Carpaccio, thin slices of raw beef spread all across a good-size plate, decorated with green stripes of a thick, crunchy and oily sauce of capers and onions and parsley. Cacciatorini, a half dozen hefty slices of sausage, fatty and garlicked, garnished with a sliver of marinated red pepper that is sour and sharp. Caponato, a collection of marinated vegetables, eggplant, zucchini, celery, garnished with pimento—one wishes the marinade had not been so sugary and that the eggplant had been given more time, for it is slightly leathery. Stuffed Mushrooms, filled with ham, spinach, mozzarella cheese that tastes, miraculously, like cheese, all these flavors conspiring, somehow, to make these fresh sautéed mushrooms doubly vivid. Stuffed Eggplant al'Olio, thin cutlets of white eggplant, marinated and sour, wrapped around an oiled breading that is salty and herbed—they are like tart crunchy sausages. Fettuccini Alfredo, powerfully eggy noodles, aswim in a sauce of eggs and cream; you add your own cheese from the bowl of the redolent stuff that is placed before you, and you grind on the fragrant pepper from a hefty columnar mill—the proportions hardly matter, these are superb ingredients.

This is an elemental Saltim Bocca—thin slices of pale, sautéed veal folded over thin slices of sharp, salty ham. A bit of garlic introduced somewhere along the way emphasizes both meats; you may squeeze on lemon, and that makes the dish sparkle. Boneless Chicken Marsala—cutlets of boned chicken and sautéed fresh mushrooms powerfully flavored with chunks of garlic and moistened with a bit of wine sauce—is, like most of the dishes here, simple and elemental and strong, but with none of the flavors hidden by any of the others. Fegato Veneziana—rapidly sautéed morsels of tender liver, browned yet moist, mingled with sautéed onions—is served in a substantial mound that tiny people have been known to dispatch in a twinkling.

A limited number of desserts, among them a hot and frothy zabaglione that could do with a bit more wine—if you wish, you can have it served on some pretty good strawberries. The Warm Brandy Cake is a fresh, nut-flavored spongy baba soaked in hot liquor. Good coffees, plain and fancy.

The tables at the front suffer a bit from the ventilation through the louvered front door, even more from gusts when the door is opened. The customers are couples and couples of couples, young and earnest mostly, and very content in this, their marvelous neighborhood joint. As the place empties out, the tape deck is turned on, and you are serenaded by Beniamino Gigli, Jussi Björling, Enrico Caruso, and such, which makes the face of the male offspring sparkle. "My father has a nice voice, too," he says.

○ P. J. CLARKE'S

915 Third Avenue (at 55th Street)
LUNCH AND DINNER.
Reservations, PL 9-1650.
No credit cards.
Medium-priced.

P. J. Clarke's, the durable gin mill, has always disdainfully gone its own way. When a skyscraper was to be built on its block, P. J.'s sneered at the fortune its property could have brought, and stayed put. In consequence there is a notch in the southwest corner of that tower where a column of offices might have been. Today, when restaurant-saloons—as well as many other forms of low-down high style—are the rage, when dandified taverns crowd East Side avenues like off-duty cabs, Clarke's does not even bother to compete with the upstarts. It proves its superiority to any of them by consistently packing its rooms with an eager clientele while feeding them the worst food the place has turned out in decades: spread across the bottoms of dog bowls, so-called tartar steaks that are brown and dry from long, warm storage; hamburgers that are at once burnt, cold and mealy, served on dreary diner rolls; salmon that should have been poached sooner or caught later; steaks so pallid they need salt and pepper the way a peanut-butter-and-jelly sandwich needs peanut butter and jelly; spinach salads that should be returned to the laundry for more starch; pumpkin pie that is ornamented with what seems like whipped cream fabricated from skim milk. Once in a while you get a plate of decent food: an appetizer of tasty ratatouille that is only partially undone by its icebox temperature; one sirloin that is better than the others; crusty home-fried potatoes; a fairly bright-flavored lime mousse. But then there is the draft beer, which seems the logical beverage for this cuisine. If the head has not vanished by the time your glass reaches you, you can stare it down in a twinkling; and if you order Beck's, you are just as likely to be served Heineken. With beer at $1.25 the glass, that is not a negligible liberty.

Though it has all kinds, Clarke's features white-haired, red-faced bartenders. They have been here forever, and they strut along their duckboards affecting the deportment of certified salt of this earth. Their exchanges with their chums across the bar consist principally of sardonic references to regular customers who happen not to be present and to managerial personnel who are out of earshot. Their wit is usually weather-related, treating, for example, of what part of an elephant's anatomy this cold snap could freeze off.

Then there is Frankie. (His title, if he has a title, is on the order of Reservations Pundit.) Something seems to have happened to Frankie. For years he paraded through this place like Ronald Reagan through a field of Mexicans, but these days he appears depressed. Think of it: Frankie is depressed. Well-heeled and well-oiled regulars press unearned money into his hand, and still he does not cheer up. He does not even try to throw his weight around anymore. All he does now is maintain his little list and point people to tables. Careful, boys. If this place becomes easy to deal with, no one will want to come here anymore.

The front room of P. J. Clarke's is a garishly lit broken-down saloon, with a weather-beaten bar, a hamburger counter, stained glass over the men's room, dusty flags of old Ireland and the USA over the disintegrating mirror above the back bar. The crowd includes advertising middle managers, their worshipful administrative assistants, huskies in porkpie hats, models of both genders, a bouncer in the shape of a whale, the dumpy and the dashing, all packed together as if this were the only game in town with oxygen. The back room (dining room) is dark, with checkered tablecloths on the tables, nameless framed objects on the walls, yet another dingy bar—this one for service to waiters only—and, visible to the eye, what looks like a small prison kitchen.

★ LA PLACE

21 East 62nd Street
LUNCH AND DINNER.
Reservations, 838-4248.
Credit cards: AE, CB, DC, MC, V.
Very expensive.

"Your ambience is exquisite," coos the dentist's wife to her dapper host. It is as if she were gurgling over his foie gras d'oie frais en gelée.

"And," says he, "I have just spent $3,000 on new china. We are going to have *all* new china."

"Ooh," says she, "new china."

"It will have a blue line," says he.

"Ooh," says she, "a blue line." She is so excited that it may be necessary to get her to someplace where an accident will not be an embarrassment. For that chat, in effect, has granted her the status, in this new purlieu, of an habituée, the urban equivalent of membership in a choosy country club. There is a good chance that pretty soon Mr. & Mrs. DDS will be eating off a few root canals' worth of blue-line china at home.

228

La Place was so shrewdly conceived that, even before folks of any importance had been reported seen in the place, the camp followers were pursuing them there, certain they would eventually come—just as if they had been given a tip on a stock well in advance of its upward move, and were confident of their sources. However, as everyone knows, where fools rush in angels prefer not to tread. La Place peaked too soon. It may well succeed, but it will never have a past.

When the weather is fine, there are a few tables out front on the sidewalk. Just inside is the bar and, along the opposite wall, a handful of tables—they are used mostly for drinks, but you may eat at them as well. Further back is the dining room proper, an intentional clutter, as of a busy, crowded little café. Encircled by the banquette of carved, navy-blue velvet, which rims the room, a couple of dozen white-linened tables. A big potted palm occupies the center of the floor, its branches leaning out in all directions. The walls are hung with mirrors of a dozen shapes—in frames of every degree of simplicity and elaborateness—and with, seemingly, a hundred examples of corny, turn-of-the-century mass-market art. Big bursts of flowers have been stuck where there is room. Every table sports a vase or bottle of colored or painted glass, flowers in each. The place looks like a family parlor with three or four generations of accumulated junk. Its constricted aisles are patrolled by young men in shirts and ties and long white aprons. Even when the restaurant is crowded, however, the noise is no more than a pleasant din, and the visual cacophony of the appointments is made tolerable by the low light.

You will perhaps deduce from its $9 price that Norwegian smoked salmon is something special, but, though it is tender, pleasantly oily and of vivid flavor, it lacks the subtlety of, say, Zabar's second best. And though you may suspect from its position on the menu—among the hors d'oeuvres—and from its title—"salade du jardin"—that said salad is something else, it is just a lettuce salad, albeit with a few scrapings of radish and carrot, and slivers of fresh mushroom, all in a decent vinaigrette. But the artichoke is just what you hope for—it is perfectly poached, firm but not hard, and it is served with a thick, tart dressing that sets it off nicely. Four shrimp, crunchy and of clear, sweet flavor, are brought to you arranged over a mound of mushrooms and crisp celery that is moistened with a lovely light dressing—a refreshing dish. Exceptional snails, large, plump and tender, are served mingled with a dozen or two midgetary chanterelles, all in a rich cream sauce that is strong with brandy. That foie gras d'oie frais en gelée is buttery stuff—it is about the size of a slice of bread from a canapé loaf—and it is rich, polished, and of strong flavor, but it lacks the elegance and breed that are needed to convert a little morsel into a big experience.

You get good grilled bass, crusted and moist, served up in a pool of creamy sauce that is suffused with the flavor of fresh fennel, and it is garnished with chunks of fennel root, deeply browned and buttery. A couple of dozen carefully sautéed scallops are served in a creamy sauce that is dotted with little chunks of tomato, freshened with parsley and dominated by a strong dose of fragrant saffron—a singular and utterly successful dish. The house does not obtain especially good chicken, but when it bones the breast and serves it encased in what seems like a perfectly crusted cheese soufflé, the bird is just about redeemed. Bits of foie gras and, it seems, dozens of impeccably fresh morels are mingled with chunks of sweetbread in a pink sauce that is at once salted, sweet, winy, woodsy with the flavor of those wild mushrooms. The lamb steak, however, is chewy, the abundance of thyme is its dark sauce rather obvious. But the liver is fine, though its gimmicky presentation may put you off, for after it is cut thin and rapidly grilled, it is served in a light sauce that is slightly sweet and a bit tart from the juice of the orange and grapefruit sections that are arranged upon it. All the main courses are served with an assortment of crisp vegetables.

Some cool Brie and mild goat cheese are garnished with fresh fruit, the entire little plate of food in sparkling condition. The fruit tarts are of thin, crumbly pastry, deep layers of creamy custard and, on occasion, slices of fresh orange across the top, a row of ripe raspberries along the edge. Something called gâteau La Place is a dull sweet—white cake, layers of rather gooey chocolate, whipped cream. You may have some superb vanilla ice cream with candied chestnuts. Sherbets, white chocolate mousse and good berries are usually available.

Your check, which is produced by a machine, prints out "merci" at every subtotal and total. The place is jolly when full. A young set sometimes takes over late of a weekend evening.

★★ IL PONTE VECCHIO

206 Thompson Street (near Bleecker Street)
DINNER.
Reservations, 473-9382.
No credit cards.
Medium-priced.

Asphalt-tile floors, light- and dark-tan walls (a random assortment of art and posters thereon), rows of tables occupied by locals in casual clothes—drinking, mostly, carafe wine and enjoying the low prices and good food. Those who are not eating are at the tight little bar in the front room, drinking, probably waiting for a table to open up. You will find little here but basics, and nothing to complain about.

You will find fresh raw clams that are tiny, sweet, cold. You may also have them as clams Posillipo, a massive mound of the steamed littlenecks in a hot red broth, herbed and oily. (You can have fresh mussels made the same way.) You will find shrimp oreganati, big sweet ones, albeit only three, in a strongly salted oil that is flavored with oregano and much lemon.

Everybody orders the unlisted linguine alla Johnny, the al dente noodles in a peppery red sauce that is thick with shrimp, fish, great chunks of plum tomato. The carbonara is creamy, sharpened with Italian bacon, made fragrant with fresh parsley. Amatriciana is this establishment's simplest red sauce—it is served on thin spaghetti, it is aggressively seasoned and it is superb when it is made thick with ground cheese. The manicotti is elemental, little more than ricotta cheese stuffed into pasta pillows and baked in tomato sauce—it arrives sizzling.

No bass on the menu, but it is usually present in the kitchen. You may have yours broiled, touched with thyme, moistened with a light, lively tomato sauce. The zuppa di pesce is a bristling platter of mussels, squid, shrimp, fish, all in a briny red broth. The place obtains chicken that tastes like chicken, converts it into chicken Ponte Vecchio—slices of boned white meat under red peppers in a pale wine sauce. The same good bird goes into the chicken cacciatore, in which the smooth and winy red sauce is thick with mushrooms, onion, garlic. When rabbit is available, the pale and tender meat is served in a sauce much like that one. The veal paillard is of veal pounded out to the size of a big platter and grilled until it is blackened a little but still moist—you bring it to lively life by squeezing on lemon. The veal francese is lightly crusted with its eggy batter, lemoned, parsleyed—a delicate dish. Indelicacy is the name of the veal chop. It is not listed, but is usually on hand—the house makes it many ways, but in all cases you get a chop the size of a club, juicy inside, charred outside, of an unmistakable sufficiency.

The provolone will open your eyes and clear your sinuses. The pleasantly wet Italian cheese cake is dotted with black raisins. The hot zabaglione is frothy, loaded with Marsala.

• POST HOUSE

28 East 63rd Street
LUNCH, MONDAY TO FRIDAY; DINNER, DAILY.
Reservations, 935-2888.
Credit cards: AE, CB, DC, MC, V.
Very expensive.

The Post House has a plain, spacious, well-lit solidity, which suggests the days when eating houses were busy rooms with tables, chairs and no nonsense. This rendition of the old days is aimed at masculine tastes. You enter to a long room with a long bar that you can pound your fist on to emphasize a point without causing a ripple in your drink. Farther along, down a few steps, is the big rambling dining room, with a hardwood floor and tall ivory walls, along the base of which wainscoting of polished wood is trimmed with a handsome chair rail of ornamental tile. The tufted red banquette is of the finest top-grain plastic leather. The chairs are commodious enough to accommodate a fat man. Though the name is Post House, there is nothing horsey about the adornments: a flagpole topped by an eagle on a ball (for some reason the flag of Italy is flown); ship hulls; olde American statuary; and assorted framed art, including, in a central position, a seriously intended oil of a very slightly draped lady seated alone on a rock in the woods, her finger to her cheek, puzzlement and impending distress plain on her face. Your principal amusement may be an impromptu game of Balloon, in which the object is to deduce the lady's probable thoughts, for a balloon caption. Example: "Soon it will be dark. Maybe he meant some other rock." Of course you will do much better.

The floor is managed by imperious young snots in Ivy League suits. They all but snap their fingers when they instruct you to wait or to follow. But most of the actual seating is handled by Leo, who is quite another matter. Bored of face, baggy of black suit, scuffed of brown shoes, ambling of gait. At 9 P.M. you ask for a larger table than the tiny one he offers, and, lying as naturally as you breathe, he assures you that the dozens of unoccupied ones you see are all reserved. They go unused until closing. Sometimes when Leo has nothing else to do, he proudly wheels a large live lobster through the dining room on a cart, as if he were its father. ("*Very* nice," say its admirers appraisingly as it goes by. In a pinch they could not distinguish a live lobster from a sheared chihuahua.) The waiters, however, are almost uniformly courteous and efficient.

Entrepreneurs who fought their way up to the Upper East Side come here, with wife. Also guys who part their hair half an inch off center, slick it down and look at you through slitted eyes. Groups of district managers in town for the big sales meeting (they have too much hair, and metallic threads run through the plaids of their sports jackets) are fed and watered here by a snappy exec from the home office—blue blazer, white shirt, striped tie, short hair, and all the answers.

The food is lovely to look at, not always to eat: stone crabs that left all their flavor in Florida; a lobster cocktail that is a lobster so tiny even a shark would throw it back —remarkably, it is a little tough, but tasty; a crabmeat cocktail of sweet, fresh white meat—like the little lobster, it comes with standard cocktail sauce. The steaks and chops are so big and so tender and beautifully seared that no one seems to notice their tastelessness; the roast beef is no better—worse, in fact, if you count in the peculiar, viscous horseradish sauce. The huge chopped steak is of beef that seems to have been crushed rather than ground—the accuracy of its cooking, like that of all the steaks and chops, is chancy. The main-course lobsters are gigantic, expensive and often good. If you want one broiled, you get it boiled and then broiled, a disastrous preparation. Boiled is better. The fish may well be frozen—it never tastes bad, but it lacks the clear flavor of fish just caught. Avoid the greasy onion rings in favor of the hashed brown potatoes, which are firm and crusty, studded with bits of sautéed green pepper and onion. The best dessert is the cheese cake—lemony, light and rich.

The Post House is a comfortable place, once you are seated, and the food, though disappointing, is never offensive. Popular.

★ PRIMAVERA

1570 First Avenue (near 81st Street)
DINNER.
Reservations, 861-8608.
Credit cards: AE, CB, DC, MC, V.
Very expensive.

You arrive ten minutes early for your reservation, and you are asked to wait at the bar. Unoccupied tables are all about. You ask why you must wait at the bar when there are unoccupied tables all about. It is explained that you must wait at the bar because you are ten minutes early for your reservation. No one has ever lived to tell what happens when you arrive ten minutes late.

But a taste for mindless authoritarianism is only one facet of the complex Mediterranean mentality, and at Primavera the trivial egos in charge flex themselves with these power plays only at the expense of strangers (invaders). For the many who have made this spot popular, and whose faces are familiar here, the mindless authoritarianism is dropped in favor of mindless unction. Elderly ladies may be seen wriggling involuntarily in their chairs as their pompadoured host describes for them, in heavily Italianate English, garnished with gentle caressings of the air that hangs before their very eyes, and by subtle but emphatic, minimally pelvic gestures of his double-breasted, custom-tailored torso, the ostensibly sublime dishes of which they will presently partake. Even the men love it. The waiters, however, happily, retain their dignity, and it is with them that you have most of your dealings.

Primavera has applied to itself the look of cozy intimacy, in the manner of the application of abundant rouge to the features of a venerable prostitute. The lights are low; the painted walls are of deep salmon pink, the one of brick glazed, as if coated

232

with simple syrup. The oil paintings were acquired, framed, in a one-dozen lot. There are potted palms, flowers on the tables, a solid-marble top on the little bar. The back of your chair may well be closer to the table behind you than to your own. You are in the midst of conversations you otherwise could never imagine:

"I don't understand you," says he.

"I'm a typical shicksa," says she, explaining herself.

"I don't want a typical shicksa," says he.

"What *do* you want?" asks she.

"I just want a *normal person.*"

Cuff links and tiepins on the gents, metallic threads through the intricately patterned plaids of their sportswear. The ladies are in silks and tortured hairdos. Tank watches are strapped to the wrists of both genders. On occasion the mixed drinks ordered by a party of six represent every color of the visible spectrum. Much of the conversation is about vacations past or planned. Says one hail fellow, to his pals heading west in the morning, "You get a good meal at the Hawaii Hilton."

And not a bad one here. The seafood salad is lemony, laced with slivers of garlic, seemingly just made of morsels of squid, shrimp, octopus and, unfortunately, rubbery conch, which is far from enough to undo the sparkle of the tart dish. If you do not mind dropping more than $7 for three shrimp (huge ones), the gamberi aromatici are sautéed with lemon and wine and abundantly parsleyed—the crunchy shrimp are lightly blackened here and there, which accentuates their sweet flavor. Even the stuffed mushrooms are not bad, the fresh caps filled with a slightly gamy meat stuffing, moistened with a polished, mildly sour tomato sauce.

The pasta is carefully cooked, but some of the sauces are better than others. The thin spaghetti with vegetables (spaghetti degli inamorati), for example, is made with canned artichoke hearts, the elimination of which will improve any dish—the zucchini and mushrooms and onions are fine, and the creamy tomato sauce is smooth and rich, but the dish lacks the garden freshness of this kind of thing at its best. But the pesto sauce, served on narrow noodles, though it is an oddly creamy version, is still fragrant and pungent of the basil and cheese. And the mixture of green noodles and white ones is served in a creamy sauce that is studded with salty ham and green peas—a nice dish, the ham a striking contrast to the rich weighty pasta and its weighty sauce; the peas, however, are so brilliantly green and so lacking in sweetness that they might just as well be frozen.

The sautéed bass marechiara is fresh, its creamy red sauce is smooth, but the mussels and clams that garnish the fish are respectively tasteless and tough. Much better is the gigantic broiled veal chop, extremely tender and juicy, artfully browned at the edges. And the scaloppine alla zingara is made up of a heady sauce of olives and mushrooms, ham and peas, and delicate slices of pale veal. The beef paillard is pounded thin, and it is cross-hatched with the black marks of the grill; but it may have lost some of its juiciness from overcooking, a condition that may be somewhat remedied by squeezing on the lemon that is supplied. On occasion the restaurant roasts baby goat. The rich, vaguely livery meat is pink and moist, its crust salty and charred; it tastes more like rabbit than anything else, and though the young meat is rimmed with fat, it is not marbled, so what you eat is lean.

Good arugula salad is available, the crisp and tasty greens just barely oiled and seasoned. Gorgonzola may also be had, the blue-veined cheese strong and creamy, as well as aged Parmesan, which is hard and flaky, its scent and strength like brandy. The sweet desserts—a coconut-flecked, rum-soaked and chocolate-striped zuppa inglese, and a hefty chocolate cake with dark icing, among them—are high on sugar and low on finesse.

★★RAGA

57 West 48th Street
LUNCH, MONDAY TO FRIDAY; DINNER, DAILY.
Reservations, 757-3450.
Credit cards: AE, CB, DC, MC, V.
Medium-priced.

Of the dozens of Indian and Pakistani restaurants in town, only a handful persuade you that the food they serve is something like the genuine article. Food does not have to be authentic to be good, but restaurateurs who pass one thing off as another are never interested in excellence, so each of the two qualities tends to be found where the other is. You may not care whether what you eat is authentic, only whether you like it. But good food that is also the product of a great tradition seems to resonate, to suggest more than itself, to provide not only a taste of something to eat, but of a culture. The food at Raga does that.

Raga is housed in a large room of great height, its spaciousness timbered with slender wooden columns that rise to crisscrossed matching beams on the ceiling. At ground level, low partitions—some of them planted with greenery—divide the dining area into groups of several tables and even into islands of only one—these latter are large tables usually given over to semi-private parties, most of them unanimously Indian.

Elaborately carved dark wood occupies most of one large wall, simulating a palatial facade. Elsewhere the walls are covered with raw silk and hung with Indian musical instruments—sitar, veena, rubab and dilruba are some of their names—many of them elaborately hand-painted. Sometimes during dinner a lad toots an Indian flute.

You walk on brilliantly striped carpeting of ivory and black, red and green and gold. You sit on chairs or banquettes that are upholstered in bright, heavy, nubbly cloth, at tables that are covered with beige linen. You choose your dinner from a large, handsomely printed menu illustrated with reproductions of some of the instruments that hang on the besilked walls. But with all its color, even splendor, Raga is softly lighted and subdued.

The captains are dressed in dark occidental suits, and they speak the meticulous music that is Indian-accented British English. The waiters, in bright-green shirts, seem to be picking up their English here, and they are sometimes hard to follow. Their courtesy, however, is genuine, the captains' sometimes condescending.

Whether condescendingly or politely, your captain will ask whether you want your food mild, medium or hot. And if you leave that to the preference of the chef, you will receive it hot—which takes getting used to. But it is worth an effort, for in many of these Indian dishes the fiery spice, when you learn to taste through it, is the medium that joins together the myriad flavors of Indian food.

Jingha chat is a cold appetizer, a mingling of shrimps, raw onions and chunks of pineapple, flavored, like much of the food here, with the heavy perfume of coriander leaves—a crisp, searing and invigorating dish, though the shrimps have little character of their own. A similar cold chicken appetizer is called murg ki chat, the slivers of reddened chicken, with onions and potatoes, in a stinging juice—when you squeeze on the lemon, the food seems to sing.

The mulligatawny is a thick and satisfying lentil purée with the flavor of grain, sweet spice and coconut, textured with shredded chicken and bits of vegetable. And the madras soup is a creamy burnt-orange tomato soup that is somehow vibrant without being spicy.

Among the hot appetizers there is an unfortunate crabmeat dish—crabs goa—that suffers from being made of crabmeat that arrived in town in a can or frozen box. The crabmeat is mingled and sautéed with many things, none of which can disguise the seafood's unnatural provenance or its imperfect separation from its shell. Oysters, however, are obtainable fresh in the big city, and Raga's oysters bombay is a dazzling, complex stewlike dish of plump mollusks among sweet onions and bits of meat, all in a red and spicy oil that is loud with fresh ginger.

But the really fabulous dishes here are some of the main courses: lobster malabar, tender chunks of lobster meat, their fresh flavor glistening through a fiery, mahogany-colored sauce that seems to shimmer with a hundred flavors; murg mumtaz, a chicken-and-chicken dish, cutlets of white meat wrapped around a chicken paste that is studded with dried fruits and whole cloves—the menu refers to a "mild aromatic gravy," but that gravy, shot through with slivers of incendiary green pepper, will fog your eyes from inside.

Gosht palak is one of those dishes that seem to enlarge your understanding of what food may be, even though its principal ingredients are simply lamb and spinach. In this dish they are combined into a weighty, almost black-colored solidity of meat and green leaves that is dominated by the flavors of lamb fat and sweet spice. Yet another of the lamb dishes, margisi kofta, is utterly surprising—ground lamb wrapped around hard-cooked eggs, the great lumps of stuffed meat bathed in a thick sauce that is fragrant of coriander and studded with little nuggets of spice.

The tandoori chicken, one-half of a lightly charred bird, is red and black and angry-looking, but the meat is moist, tender, and artfully and delicately spiced. The tandoori mixed grill is a tourist's dish of bits and pieces. Vegetables, lentils, grainy breads and fluffy rice dishes—there are a score of small items on the menu with which to garnish your food, and they are all well made.

But for the ice creams, which will seem fatty to the domestic palate, the desserts are refreshing: rasmalai, grainy nuggets of sweetened cheese, cold, strewn with chopped pistachios, served in a pool of cool milk; kulfi, an ice cream dish that is unlike the others, white cream flavored with mild spices, overlayed with hammered, ultra-thin silver (which you eat), garnished with carrots and syruped with honey.

The tea is disappointing, the wine list thin, beer not quite right with food made with sweet spices, as much of this menu is.

Raga is stylishly conceived, but the tone of the place is somewhat undone by the sweatshirt and sneaker crowd, which tumbles in here for tandoori chicken and white wine. Those big island tables offer the lure of quasi-isolation.

★★★ RAOUL'S

180 Prince Street (near Sullivan Street)
DINNER.
Reservations, 966-3518.
Credit cards: AE, MC, V.
Expensive.

SoHo is a little bitter about Raoul's. It seems that the neighborhood warmed to the place right from its start, made it popular and successful almost at once. But then, as is the way with out-of-the-way restaurants that serve first-class food (or get first-class notices), people from all over town heard about Raoul's and just about took it over. Uptownies downtown for a day of artsy slumming call ahead for a table at Raoul's, so that they can climax their cultural expedition by mingling with the natives at dinner. Often as not they find that they are mingling not with the hoped-for cannibals, but with their own Sutton Place or Riverside Drive neighbors.

The place bears no physical resemblance to any other restaurant in the neighborhood. It exemplifies none of the SoHo restaurant styles. But if any restaurant is the quintessence of SoHo, it is this one. SoHo is much art with few trappings, middle-class prosperity in Bohemian disguise, the lap of luxury in baggy pants. And Raoul's is simply a terrific French restaurant that charges midtown prices—and it is housed in an unmitigated old saloon.

It has everything: a stamped-tin ceiling and stamped-tin walls; a plain pipe rack for your coat and a red-and-white EXIT sign glowing over the front door for your escape, just like the signs that glare in darkened movie houses. The old bar—on your left as you enter—is mirrored behind, garishly lighted. A coffee machine stands on one end of it, right near the pay phone, and stools topped with red plastic stand all around it. Across from the bar, under old framed mirrors and casually stuck-up posters, is a black banquette that runs the length of the front room, six or eight commodious tables before it. This is perhaps the best place to eat, for with your back to the wall you can watch the action at the bar, which is populous with a youthful clientele in the variegated and colorful costumes that are the uniform in this part of town. The crimson vinyl seats are polished mostly by denim, but silks and sateens are common here, leather and tweeds not rare. You see parachute cloth and cashmere, sailcloth and seersucker and bleeding madras. You see illustrated and captioned T-shirts and stockings, baubulous jewelry, hair in two dozen colors and three hundred shapes, and many, many a striking hat that is really a thumbed nose. If you want to get even closer to the action, you may eat right *at* the bar, for crayoned on the mirror behind it are the foods (and prices) that are served at the counter. And if you are by yourself at the bar, you may direct your attention to the bartender, who is a bit of a show. He chats with his girl friends to the accompaniment of his own lithe and graceful gestures, sly smiles, dramatically timed puffs on his cigarette. He does not mind being the center of attention.

But the back room is apparently the room of choice (especially for visitors from the north). It fills first—not only the comfortable plastic booths along the sides, but even the tables down the center, which are so upon one another that they are virtually a common board. Wherever you sit, you are eating at tables that are covered with white

236

butcher-paper and equipped with diner-style glass sugar pourers. Unfortunately you must select the courses of your dinner from a timidly scratched-at slate that is brought to the table. In the dim light of the back room the slate is practically useless for the merely sighted. You have to be clairvoyant. But there is a larger menu mounted on the back wall, and from certain vantages that can be made out. When the place is crowded it has the hectic cheeriness of a superb party in a commodious apartment; when it is half full it is as relaxed as a perpetual café from which no one ever has to go home. The waiters and waitresses pick their way through the crowds and tables with, for the most part, smiling, slightly exhausted contentment. Raoul's is a comfortable place.

Fresh sweet crabmeat and slices of crisp mushroom make up the crabmeat salad, which is mounded up copiously on tender lettuce and dressed with a thick vinaigrette —the pink-flecked shafts of white meat are sweet and tender. Or you may begin with poached leeks or asparagus, the former cool and crisp in a thick, mustardy dressing, the latter hot, in a heavy but smooth and lemony hollandaise. A platter of *crudités* will set you back $4.50, but it will serve two, and the vegetables are all crisp; the centerpiece of the dish—sautéed mushrooms that have been cooled and then moistened with a garlicky tomato dressing—provides a bit of sauce for the shredded carrots and red cabbage, chunks of cauliflower, quarters of tomato, et al. There is good pâté that is splendid with sharp mustard and this establishment's crusty French bread. But the best of the first courses are the snails—they are fat and soft, mingled with mushrooms and served in a buttery, truffle-studded sauce that is strongly laced with cognac.

While the season is on Raoul's sometimes does soft-shell crabs, sautéing them in butter with slivered almonds, making a dish that is at once gentle, crisp, sweet, mildly oceanic. You can have snapper the same way, and the fish is utterly fresh, moist and flaky, cooked to the perfect point. On Sundays there is couscous, the North African dish that the French colonists ran off with even before they left. In Raoul's version a huge chunk of lamb, with an immense marrow bone, is served on a dune of semolina, with hot vegetables. Still more vegetables come in a separate deep plate that is filled with a meaty broth. In yet another dish you are served a thick red sauce that is spicy and fragrant with garlic. You fortify the broth with the sauce, moisten the lamb and grain with the broth, according to your taste. The dish stays with you.

The veal chop is as thick as a club sandwich, pale and tender, moistened with a dark sauce and mushrooms. The steaks are perfectly made. And there are good birds, including a pigeon, its meat dark and almost chocolatey in flavor, served on a deep dish of sweet peas that are mingled with sprigs of parsley and moistened with a meaty gravy that is studded with bacon. Or you may have a pheasant (prepared only for two)—this is a more delicate bird, roasted until its skin is crisp, served up on a great platter in a brown-stock sauce that is polished, mellifluous and winy. The place makes wonderful things of organ meats, including a stewlike dish of sweetbreads that comes in a deep ceramic pot—the sweetbreads are immersed in a thick liquid that is buttery but not fatty, sharpened with apple brandy.

At the rear of that center row of tables in the back room stands an ancient gas range on which are displayed the cakes you can have for dessert—a splendid French version of Black Forest cake, pale brown layers of cocoa-flavored cake, the smooth layer of white cream between studded with crunchy black cherries. There is chocolate cake, and it is dark, polished with black icing, livened with Grand Marnier. The cream puffs of the profiterole are almost airy, their chocolate sauce thick and warm. And sometimes the house prepares a strawberry mousse—it is served in champagne glasses filled to their tops, and it has the clear flavor of fresh, sweet fruit. Good coffee.

There are several decent bottles on the brief wine list. Big bottles of Perrier are available cold.

• RAVELLED SLEAVE

1387 Third Avenue (near 79th Street)
LUNCH, SATURDAY AND SUNDAY; DINNER, DAILY.
Reservations, 628-8814.
Credit cards: AE, CB, DC, MC, V.
Medium-priced.

The barside crowds in Third Avenue's restaurant/saloons consist in large measure of folks who progressed, from preparatory schools to Ivy League and Seven Sister colleges to these brass rails, with ontogenetic inevitability. But just as the lives of certain organisms are cut short only partway through maturation, leaving eternity with fossilized examples of arrested development, so the Ravelled Sleave is the repository of those who would have preferred to spend eternity at Princeton.

The guys may be lawyers and sales representatives and associate account executives and assistant product managers, but they still chug-a-lug their beer from the bottle, pointing the bottom at the ceiling as they suck the last drop. They wear blazers and striped ties and button-down shirts and crew cuts and expressions of jaded confidence, which come with the certain knowledge that if at first you don't succeed, you can always go to work for Dad. If they ever grow up, they will all look like John O'Hara. Their properly-brought-up female counterparts are not so proper that they do not come here, in twos and threes, and size up the eligibility of these young men with the same frank, resigned appraisal they would direct at a tawdry summer bungalow not near enough to the sea. That the young men seem bent on nothing in their lives so much as the assuagement of their thirst enters not into the evaluation. The girls are as uniformed as the boys. Even in this denim age, not a one of them is not in a skirt three hours after the office closed; not to mention earrings, silk scarfs, silk blouses, tailored jackets, bracelets, nail polish, heels and, over every shoulder, a leather bag on a long strap. It's getting to be a habit. And as between these genders, there is about as much sex in the air as in the last act of *Macbeth*.

Beyond the murky barroom, two dark dining rooms—one has a fireplace (with flames), the other a spinet (with pianist). Back here, a different crowd. They hardly bother to strain their eyes to read the menu in the dim lantern light. They come to these intimate rooms to talk, and the second-rate food is secondary. The dishes to avoid include a reheated quiche that is hot outside, cold inside; mushy deep-fried shrimp; pasta with vegetables, vulgarized with bacon; beef Stroganoff made with the kind of onions you find in Gibsons; something called veal Alice, which is coarse veal parmigiana on leathery eggplant. Instead of a first course, have the mussel-and-pasta salad—it is gratis with your main course, and it is solid and tangy and refreshing. Proceed to the fish of the day, which is fresh and not overcooked. Or to a steak, which is pallid but palatable.

The chocolate-chip rum cake is icy and icky. The hazelnut-praline bombe is icky and icy. The cheese cake is icky.

★ LE REFUGE

166 East 82nd Street
LUNCH AND DINNER. CLOSED SUNDAY.
Reservations, 861-4505.
No credit cards.
Expensive.

Here is the countryside without animals, a French farmhouse that looks like an English tearoom masquerading as a French farmhouse. The front room is timbered and wainscoted with roughened wood. Tapestries and murky oils fail to suggest the passage of time. The table tops are irregular, as if hewn by ax from raw pine, but they are smooth, and they glisten in their sealant. The chairs are meant to look as if they were whittled into shape. Instead of a linen napkin, you are provided with a plaid dishtowel that is intended to seem like a swatch of common cloth that would ordinarily be kept in a poor peasant's napkin ring from meal to meal for a week or two. In an open pantry, rows of mustards in crocks, preserves in jars, teas in cans, waters in bottles are on display, as are vinegars and oils, preserved pickles and peppercorns. It is as if, of an afternoon, ladies who drop by for trimmed sandwiches and lemonade will be tempted to take a little something home. Wine is on display as well, but it is available only for on-premises consumption. Since moving here from its original site a couple of blocks away, Le Refuge has added two back rooms (and dispensed with the harpist, whose playing was, in any event, almost inaudible when the restaurant was filled). The new rooms come off better. There is much brick, handsome pieces of side furniture, space. But that front room sets the tone, and Le Refuge gets the most uniformly straitlaced crowd in town. You get the impression that one thing they like about this place is its avoidance of the tawdriness of accepting credit cards. But the food, too, must be at least in part responsible for the conservative clientele, for the menu—a couple of slight oddities notwithstanding—is a reliquary of the kind of cooking by way of which New York was first made acquainted with French food. Which does not make the offerings bad. Most of them are good.

The fish pâté, for example, a pale slab of ground and seasoned fish sporting a circular, pink, salmon core. It is presented in a pool of sauce that is redolent of fresh dill. The fish itself is highly seasoned, and will put certain of you in mind of a restrained gefülte fish. Good mussels and fresh mushrooms in a thick sauce are served—as bouchée aux moules—in a cup-shaped pastry that is light and flaky. The almost harsh saltiness of the sauce just about obscures the good flavors of the other ingredients. More of those mushrooms are quartered, mingled with plump snails and served (in a little china pot, complete with cover) in a mild wine sauce that is little more than herbed and seasoned butter—you will find a few white raisins in the dish, like juicy afterthoughts. To sauté chicken livers with blueberries is about as deviationist an act as this restaurant commits (though they have had the item on the menu from the beginning). When the berries are not locally in season, the fruitiness of the sauce is slight—still, what sweetness there is is good against the rich organ meat. Of course there is pâté—happily it is pink; naturally it is fatted and strongly seasoned; unfortunately it is cold.

Some fresh poached salmon is covered with a beurre blanc that is artfully seasoned and thickened with bits of tomato. The bouillabaisse is a tame version. The broth, though of good seafood and saffron flavor, is watery, and the red garlic sauce with which you are meant to intensify it according to your taste, can as well be omitted or added complete, for it is flat—the fish and shellfish, however, are fine. You cannot tell from the title (cervelle de veau au câpres) that the preparation of brains does not involve the usual black butter. You learn the hard way that a cream sauce is excessive with this meat, though the misguided dish is perfectly prepared. The liver is floured and nicely sautéed—that its pleasant sauce is made with what the menu refers to as mint vinegar seems to be a fact of undetectable consequence. The big winner is the duck— rich meat, browned but supple skin, vivid flavor and those sweet little canned peas the French favor, which are the perfect foil to the stout bird. Resilient kale, buttered new potatoes, crisp parsnips are among the good vegetable garnishes served with the main courses.

Come on Monday, and the cheeses appear just bought. Near the end of the week they have been crazed by this into-and-out-of-the-icebox routine. The apple tart is simple and crisp, its light whipped cream slightly brandied. You get three flavors of sherbet, all in a bowl, but they are not especially sparkling. The chocolate mousse—either white or black—is nutted and rich. The almond mousse is like an airy marzipan, if you can imagine such a thing—it is served with a sugared sauce of sour berries. Lots of people have the apricot soufflé—it is no more expensive than the other desserts, and it seems always to be well made, the bit of lemon in it a nice note.

★★ LE RELAIS

712 Madison Avenue (near 63rd Street)
LUNCH AND DINNER.
Reservations, PL 1–5108.
Credit cards: AE.
Expensive.

From the first this restaurant has been besieged by every stripe of Upper East Side society. Each wants it for its own, or so it appears. The phone lines are jammed. The reservation book is an indecipherable, frantically scribbled wilderness. The tiny bar is restive with the impatient, waiting, Perrier-and-limes clutched in their hands like boarding passes for the last plane out.

All the excitement is about a little plot of France that has been planted on Manhattan Island. Nothing from the old country has been duplicated, you understand—nothing like the eerie second coming of P. J. Clarke's in Macy's basement, or one of those long-ago living rooms replicated in a contemporary museum.

It is, rather, the flavor that has been brought over, of a simpler time when, if a man made a restaurant, he would quite naturally decorate it and light it and keep it tidy the way he would a room in his house. You did not, in those days, have a decorator in. Le Relais seems so convincingly a surviving old eating place from the early part of this century that a displaced Frenchman, dining here bemused, rouses himself from his dream and announces that, for a moment, he thought he was having dinner in Paris, surrounded by American tourists.

The effect is achieved, in part, by the myriad framed objects that hang, among softly glowing sconces, on the pale, slightly glossy ivory walls: old prints and engravings, etchings and sets of wine labels, large mirrors that casually hang forward at the top (providing bored voyeurs with a slightly overhead view of this crowded and bustling place). They are like mementos and *objets d'art* and furnishings accumulated over a long family history, which makes the place feel like part of the past.

The floors are of wood, the banquettes of brown velvet. There are lots of tables for this not large room, and they are convivially assembled as close together as blades of grass. They are set with white linen and plain white china, and on each one there is a long-stemmed exotic flower in a slender glass vase. The façade of the restaurant consists of hinged doors of wood and etched glass, and when the weather is temperate these are folded back, so that diners at the very front tables can reach out their hands into Madison Avenue air.

The appeal of this establishment's simple charms is so strong that almost no group is willing to yield the place to any other. Investment bankers wearing school ties find themselves at tables adjacent to gentlemen wearing digital watches. The place attracts lawyers' lawyers and counselors to the disreputable, cosmetic surgeons to the slightly dissatisfied, hairdressers of bored women, bored women. Sun drinkers of every stamp come here, bronzed on East Hampton beaches and East Seventies terraces. There are shirts open to the navels of both genders. There are chiffon and sailcloth, sandals and golden slippers. A couple of brass-buttoned blazers are always on hand, as well as a good bit of denim. Topsiders have been seen, beads on boys, sunglasses high up on artfully coiffed and colored tresses. And the word has got around, even across the narrow waters, and many an eastbound Buick has carried seekers of chic through the Lincoln Tunnel to Le Relais. They, however, do not quite get it. They eat, look about them, stare at each other in shared, communal incomprehension, and leave, never to come back. New Jersey dentists.

Critics have found Le Relais boring. They reason that if one restaurant does a thing well for twenty years, that is fine. If another comes along and does the same thing well, that is "boring." New restaurants, you see, must be new in the way that a box of soap with a new ingredient is new—they must be *NEW*. It is a fixed rule that pursuers of what is novel in luxury are content with what is traditional in art. They demand of today's French restaurants *la nouvelle cuisine* (but they will sit still for nothing later than Brahms).

Not that the kitchen of Le Relais is a modern relic, for the dishes it turns out have a simplicity that is undoubtedly derived from the style of this day. But this is old-fashioned French cooking with an easy touch, rather than a revolutionary departure from the past, for with all its lightness, what you get here is unmistakably bistro food —and much of it is very good.

The brief menu changes from time to time, so that, regrettably, one menu's tarte aux poireaux, a fluffy quiche, browned, hot and steamy, shot through with leeks and perfumed with their flavor, is supplanted on a later one by a spinach tart that is almost leaden with a density of the leafy green vegetable. On occasion there is asparagus in a smooth, polished vinaigrette, made with velvety oil and good vinegar that you want to call tart rather than sour; unfortunately the vegetable is at icebox temperature, which is ruinous. A fish terrine suffers somewhat from the rubbery texture imparted to it by an excess of gelatin, but the clear flavors of fresh fish save the dish. Best of all, when it is listed, is the sorrel soup—cool and creamy, the characteristic flavor of the sorrel, at once earthy and metallic, vivid against the potato base of the smooth, pale-green purée.

Once in a while a serving of fish in this restaurant will be something less than perfectly fresh, but only rarely. And the fish seems to be always carefully cooked, not overdone, moist and flaky and tender. The place serves good snapper, browned, almost crusted, the meat slightly fibrous. And often there is bass, moistened with a sauce that is principally butter and slivers of cucumber that are limp but still a little crisp. And you get good salmon here, the glistening pink meat covered with a creamy watercress sauce. In season, soft-shell crabs are available all over town, but you will not find better ones than those you get here—these are tiny, three to a serving, lightly floured and sautéed in butter, so that the shells are crisp and flaky, the meat within soft, sweet and juicy.

There is red meat as well, including pink roast lamb that is dressed with a well-seasoned pan sauce, and there is thinly sliced liver, accurately grilled until it is browned outside and still rare within, the cutlets of juicy meat adorned with a light raisin sauce, the sweetness of the plump little fruits lovely against the light crust.

Simple desserts: large wineglasses filled with big ripe strawberries or with tender and powerfully perfumed raspberries; an odd lemon tart that is actually an almond-flavored lemon pudding, fluffy and browned, on a crumbly crust; and a rather airless though tasty milk-chocolate mousse buried under a huge mound of thick whipped cream.

A handful of wines are reasonably priced; several dozen are absurdly expensive—or so you surmise, for the wine list does not state vintage years, and evaluating is often impossible. But the food prices are low for a restaurant of this quality, in this neighborhood, enjoying this popularity in this high-priced year. Busy as the place is, you can often get a table without a reservation if you arrive after nine-thirty, which is, by the way, when the younger crowd shows up.

★★RENÉ PUJOL

321 West 51st Street
LUNCH, MONDAY TO FRIDAY; DINNER, MONDAY TO SATURDAY. CLOSED SUNDAY.
Reservations, 246–3023.
Credit cards: AE, CB, DC, MC, V.
Medium-priced.

Here on far-west 51st Street some of the densest French country kitsch in town may be waded through at the popular René Pujol: beamed ceilings and brick walls, copper pans and peasant crockery, a stuffed deer's head over the fireplace and an ancient grandfather clock that faithfully chimes the hours. No cliché has been left out, and Muzak has been left in. Withal, this is a comfortable place. West Side Gauls jaw in French at the gaudy bar up front. Some of them even eat here. Music teachers and social workers know this place, as do theatrical types who have not yet got their names in print. Lincoln Center people come here—many who may be heard from the pit, but few who have been seen onstage. An aspiring and youthful place, by and large, with lots of health and beards on view, and, though it is in the theater district, René Pujol does not empty just before curtain time, for this place serves its community much more than the town and country strays who periodically come around for theatrical rites.

The menu is no more inventive than the décor, which is perhaps just as well, for should you begin with one of its few oddities—"Les Little Necks aux Amandes"—you may leave at once with the wrong idea. These clams seem to have been stuffed with mashed potatoes and almonds. Try not to think about it. Think instead of the quiche Lorraine. Extremely rare for a restaurant quiche, it actually has some of the fluffiness and steaminess of the just-baked item and a deeply browned crust as well, and lots of strong and salty ham in the inch-thick custard filling. The snails are OK, powerfully garlicked and all that, but they lack character—they are strong rather than tasty.

You are not to be faulted if you long ago gave up ordering mushrooms à la Grecque, for it is a sorry item in most places. Here, however, the little champignons are marinated from a fresh start, and the perfume of their marinade is dominated by the sweet, spicy flavor and scent of coriander seeds. La Terrine du Chef is prepossessing for its design alone, each cross-sectional slice a mosaic of duck and spicy forcemeat, buttery foie gras and bits of black truffle, all bound in white fat, rimmed in darkened fat, and served with vibrant little pickles. You will see a side of smoked salmon on display just inside the door when you enter—order some, and thin slices of it are spread abundantly across a large plate. It is served with onions and capers, lemon and clear oil. Good food.

No effort is made to create a delicate dish out of the veal kidneys. These chunks of organ meat are gamy and cartilaginous, fat at their cores, and they are served in a mahogany-colored sauce that has the strength of blood and wine. For something else along that line, but nowhere near as far, there is boeuf bourguignon, a good stew of meat that is browned well and simmered long in its wine until the fibrous beef is succulent and tender.

Le Poulet au Calvados is a dish of sautéed chicken, with apples, in a white sauce that is flavored with apple brandy. On occasion the flour in this sauce is raw and obvious, but the dish is made with good birds, the skin browned artfully, the meat cooked until it is done, but still moist and tender; and the frankly creamy sauce is very satisfying in its simple way, especially when it is mingled with the rice that accompanies this chicken.

Good steaks, including a crusty steak au poivre that is peppery without obscuring the blood of the meat. The splendid racks of lamb are of tender young meat, each chop yielding up a plump morsel of pink juicy lamb and shreds of salty brown meat along the ribs; a bit of well-seasoned liquid from the roasting pan and an array of good fresh vegetables garnish the chops.

The quality of the cheese is a matter of chance. Usually there is a good cheese or two among those offered.

The house gets good berries, even out of season, and serves them with sugary whipped cream—what could be bad? They are a better choice than the merely decent pastries, tarts and fruit.

★★★ RESTAURANT RAPHAËL

33 West 54th Street
LUNCH AND DINNER. CLOSED SATURDAY AND SUNDAY.
Reservations, 582-8993.
Credit cards: AE, DC.
Very expensive.

Nobody is boisterous at Raphaël. You may arrive ready to fly, but the leanness of the place—its spare geometry and sober appointments—verges on the monastic, and you are immediately down to earth, albeit a rare earth.

The room is small, long and narrow, a brick wall facing a painted one, short dark beams overhead, a line of tables down each side, one line a long rank of tables-for-two alongside a dark banquette, the other a row of larger tables surrounded by straight-backed chairs. At the rear a glass wall gives onto a backyard that has been made a little cheerful with tables and chairs and a wooden fence—drinks are served here when the weather is fine. Inside there are, of course, items among the restaurant's appointments that are meant to warm the place up. But the fireplace gives off only an electric glow. The single burst of flowers, the touches of greenery, the crockery that hangs on a panel of one wall, all point out rather than relieve the starkness of the room. And as for the tidy brass sconces, with their pinpoint lights, and the formal, framed Renaissance portraits, with which they alternate on the brick wall, these are very much of a piece with the high seriousness that pervades Restaurant Raphaël.

To find the source of the cool taste that informs this room you will not look far, for your host is a trim gentleman in carefully tailored apparel, closely tonsured hair and metal-rimmed glasses. But the sober look of his establishment and his own orderly aspect belie his personal charm, though not at all the intense consideration that enters into the preparation of food in this carefully run establishment.

Ordinarily when a good restaurant opens in New York, it enlarges the city (by more than one new eating place, for it adds not only itself, but possibilities). But Raphaël seems to fall outside the city, to be something of a denial of it. You will never come here on a festive impulse, more likely on a pilgrimage. And when you enter the restaurant, nothing in your first impression of it engenders an overpowering content-ment. You do not remark to yourself, "Nice place." For the look of Restaurant Raphaël does not quite manage at either end of one restaurant continuum: it is not posh, and it is not jewel-like. It is merely correct.

But there is no denying the food, nor, by the way, the cordial service.

Many of the dishes here are very modern. Even the terrine de canard is modern, for though the slice of cool spiced fowl, pink and pistachio-nutted, is merely a perfect example of this meaty, fatted and fragrant first course, it is served with pickled straw-berries, no less, and in this instance—as so rarely in restaurants purveying the so-called nouvelle cuisine—this fruit garnish really belongs with its meat. The berries, at once tart and sweet, are like a bridge between the terrine and your wine. Raphaël serves impeccable raw salmon that has been lightly marinated; it is garnished with crusty little toasts that are spread with anchovy paste; and with artichoke hearts, impeccably poached, dressed in walnut oil. One of the three or four best snail dishes in New York may be had here, the slivers of meat from the plump snails seem to have enjoyed an exponential intensification of their gamy flavor, and they are served in a rosy tomato sauce, creamy and peppery and rich, that is both a harmony with them and a dramatic contrast. There is a remarkable lobster dish—le chou farci de homard au beurre de baies roses (it takes a wide menu to accommodate Raphaël's titles)—both homey and elegant, consisting of a great leaf of cabbage stuffed with lobster meat, mushrooms and slivers of crisp truffle, flavored with dill, and served in a mild, polished and slightly fruity sauce —wondrous.

Bass is steamed with seaweed here, and the process, you think to yourself, when you taste the fish without its sauce, robs the white meat of some of its oil; but the mellifluous crayfish butter that you spoon over the bass enriches and polishes the fish, entirely restoring its balance and potentiating its flavor. This restaurant even steams lamb—a rack—and though you may miss the crust that roasting or broiling yields, and the charred meat along the bones, this lamb has a naked quality, a pristine meatiness that seems more essentially lamb than any other preparation. The place makes marvelous sweetbreads, thin slices of roasted meat, served in a nubbly and peppery sauce, and garnished with artichoke hearts that are covered over with an Italian-seeming sauce of olives and tomato. And this restaurant's duck, despite a number of superficially similar dishes around town, remains singular. The meat is so carved from the bird that the thick slices seem to have been cut from the tenderloin of some huge beast. The edges of each disc are dark and crusty, the centers pink, slightly oily, tender, so that the sweet sauce that moistens the dish is almost superfluous. When Raphaël's vegetable garnishes are simple, they are perfect; when they are complex—a purée of something topped with a stewed apricot, for example—they may seem irrelevant, but never less than well made.

At the front of the restaurant there is an earthenware crock. In it there are chunks of goat cheese, the size of small lemons, marinating. The cheese—styled crottin de chavignol mariné à l'huile d'olive—is strong, hard and flaky and quite salty, flecked with little shafts of rosemary and other herbs, and coated with oil. It is splendid with the good crusty bread you get here and red wine.

The hot raspberry soufflé is frothy and browned—a tart, thick raspberry sauce is poured through a hole in the top when the dessert is served. The frozen rum-raisin soufflé is like a superb ice cream, garnished with slivers of strawberry and a slice of bright green kiwi. The pear sherbet is little more than a snowy froth of pear liquor, again garnished with strawberries. And if you think you know chocolate mousse, know that it becomes much more than itself when it is made with bitter chocolate, spread with a thick layer of ground hazelnuts and adorned with a dollop of rich whipped cream.

No tipping; a 20 percent charge is added to your bill, which is steep if you select a $100 bottle of wine.

★★EL RINCÓN DE ESPAÑA

226 Thompson Street (near Bleecker Street)
LUNCH, SATURDAY AND SUNDAY; DINNER, DAILY.
Reservations, 475-9891.
Credit cards: AE, CB, DC, MC, V.
Medium-priced.

A rickety wooden fence separates the small bar, and the handful of stools around it, from the dining area of this crowded, compact place. The bar is festooned with the accumulated paraphernalia of any neighborhood saloon (postcards from customers on vacation and photos of the staff and their families, plus, you should not forget this is a Spanish restaurant, a set of bull's horns from which depends a wineskin just like the ones in Hemingway novels). The predictable New York Spanish look of these quarters features black wrought-iron chandeliers, a timbered ceiling, walls of rough white plaster or red plaster or plaster "flagstones." The required bullfight art is in place. The main lights in the chandeliers are housed in perforated tin cans. Directly beneath them the illumination is strong. Elsewhere it is dim. At an hour between nine and ten a gentleman seated at the bar commences strumming a guitar and singing. It is impossible to generalize about his musicality because his identity varies from night to night, but none has been heard so far who was less than ardent. And as even a seasonal sniffle at the front of this little sound box causes alarms at the back, when one of these troubadours sings his heart out, everyone else must shout his lungs out simply to converse. Happily, what might be painful elsewhere is only slightly short of appropriate in this convivial spot. You are served by cordial Spanish waiters in red jackets and black hair, and you are surrounded by a crowd that does not really need musical assistance when it is in a boisterous mood.

The ham is referred to as "Spanish Mountain Ham," and the salty, smoky and chewy meat is served in thick slices with a great section of ripe melon. You order gambas à la plancha and you get eight sweet, crunchy shrimp—they have been sautéed in their shells, and they are served in a sherry sauce that is lemoned, ruddy with red pepper, loaded with garlic. A few dishes on the menu are identified as specialties of the chef, among them the mejillónes à la Carlos: A couple of dozen utterly fresh mussels stand in a deep pool of oiled and briny broth that is studded with chopped tomato and onion, formidably peppered, and flavored with fragrant herbs—like many appetizers here, this one is plenty for two or three.

The main courses enter the dining room in great covered pots, from which more than you think you can eat is spooned onto your plate, that much again left behind for your second helping. Codfish gallego consists of huge chunks of salty fish, slabs of potato, strands of green pepper and thick slices of onion, plus a hard-cooked egg, all in a garlic-flavored red sauce of oil and tomato. This restaurant's egg sauce is light, of strong egg flavor, liberally sherried and vividly alcoholic, and in the zarzuela de mariscada it is served over a copious assortment of fresh shellfish—mussels, clams, shrimp, lobster, scallops. Order the paella marinera and you get all those as well as sweet green peas —but this dish lacks the abundance of saffron that colors and flavors most paellas around town, so despite its good preparation, it may disappoint. There is plenty of wine in the green sauce, but the crabmeat on which it is served does not taste fresh. The big deep-sea winner is the octopus, upon the wondrous preparation of which this establishment's reputation is in large measure built. You get a huge mound of the pleasantly resilient but tender morsels, in a red oil that is flavored with an elegant—but potent —balance of garlic and herbs, onion and strong spices. If you come here only once, it is the dish to have.

The chicken has chicken flavor, and the pollo en cazuela is a splendid, stewlike dish in which the meat of the bird is buried in tomato, onion, green peppers, and much garlic. The hefty veal chop is broiled until it is perhaps a little dry. But the veal with Spanish sausage is fine—the slivers of pale meat are sautéed until crisp, and they are mingled with slices of strong sausage, plus onion and peppers, in a sauce that is at once tart and sweet.

The vanilla and caramel custards are indistinguishable from thousands of others. The guava jelly has the intensity of concentrated preserves, and its sweetness is good with the block of cream cheese that garnishes it.

★ RIO DE JANEIRO

41 West 57th Street
LUNCH AND DINNER.
Reservations, 935–1232.
Credit cards: AE, MC, V.
Medium-priced.

Rio de Janeiro seems like an innocent place, the softly lit and draperied cocktail-lounge posh of its barroom, the tropical-greenery wallpaper of its dining room, its wall-to-wall carpeting, and the white linen on the thirty or so fairly crowded tables providing New York's Brazilian community (and others) a little Saturday-night luxe six days a week. (When it is in fact Saturday night, the place is jammed, and half the crowd has been to the hairdresser Saturday afternoon.) As in all standard Brazilian restaurants, the waiters are as sweet as lovers, the busboys as diligent as surgeons, and the food as assertive as the blarings of a Latin band.

When you sit you are immediately granted a little plate of pungent broiled sausages and tiny black olives, to hold you while you read the extensive menu and consider the blackboard listings of lobster prices and fish availabilities. Then you may begin with clams in garlic sauce, or a pot of hot cherrystones in strong broth, strewn with red peppers, or with what the house calls seafood antipasto, a cold and stimulating salad of conch, shrimp and squid in a spicy liquid. The sturdy soups include the traditional caldo verde, a solid thickness of potatoes that is sharpened with the metallic edge of kale.

The lobsters are live, carefully cooked, and served in vibrant preparations, including lobster a baiana, in which the red beast lies in a peppery broth of beer, wine and tomato, under a mound of onions, peppers and olives—a sparkling dish.

Loin of pork a alentejana, a remarkable pork dish, is available—chunks of highly peppered meat mingled with hot cherrystones (in their shells), all in a salty, herbed and polished brown sauce. No simple steaks here—they come with eggs or ham or garlic or sausages or mushrooms or combinations thereof. The meat is ample, usually tender, and the flavorful adornments work well with the red beef. The sole bird on the menu is chicken a bossa vellha, a comparatively delicate affair of crusty and salty fried chicken that is livened with the flavors of garlic and red pepper.

Primitive desserts—the coconut custard actually a honeyed marmalade; the doce deleite caramelized milk that is served with a side of thick cream cheese. Of course there is flan, and it is well made. The Brazilian coffee will keep you going until breakfast.

★ LA RIPAILLE

605 Hudson Street (near 12th Street)
DINNER. CLOSED SUNDAY.
Reservations, 255-4406.
Credit cards: AE, MC, V.
Medium-priced.

Yet another small French farmhouse facing on the sidewalks of New York. The place is dark, has walls of rough plaster or scarred brick, a venerable clock, a bar that consists of a plank counter astride three old barrels, timbers and rafters, hurricane lamps and flickering candles, here a rusty garden tool, there a string of heads of garlic, at the back a kitchen that is visible over a swinging half-door. At certain tables you are expected to poise yourself on chairs that place you at barstool height, and which have seats that catch you well short of mid-thigh. Once in a while someone objects, and one of the young Frenchmen who run this place moves some furniture around. But a great many of the people who come here are on such good behavior that nothing can make them complain about anything. The restaurant appears to attract more than its share of computer-matched couples (someone must have awarded La Ripaille a Highly Recommended for dating), and they are determinedly cheerful about absolutely everything throughout the mechanical consumption of their ritual dinners, right down to the prearranged fifty-fifty division of the damage.

Still, they could do worse. The menu is brief, but you rarely get a dish of less than decent food. The country pâté, which a place like this cannot be itself without, is fine here, fatted, sweet-spiced, formidably seasoned, very good with the strong mustard and with the sour, crusty and resilient bread. The mousse of broccoli is a hot green muffin, very fluffy, of vivid vegetable flavor, under a steamy lemon-flavored butter. The snails —in a cream sauce that is thick with ground hazelnuts and flavored with orange rind —are a little misguided. But the fresh, very eggy fettuccine, in another rich cream sauce, this one pink with smoked salmon, is striking, seems not at all contrived despite its somewhat unlikely composition.

Some fresh trout, its skin crisp, is served under sprigs of dill—they are in lovely contrast to the good fish. The fricassée of lobster, in a simple sauce of little more than butter and basil, is perfectly made but fails to add up—you eat every bite of the dish wondering all the while why they went to all the trouble, when the lobster would have been better with just the simplest of attentions. The big winner is the sautéed chicken —excellent chicken flavor in the morsels of nicely browned bird, and the smooth tarragon sauce is fragrant of the herb. Utterly clean and very crisp kidneys are served with fresh mushrooms in a sharp and well-peppered mustard sauce—solid food.

The Brie is at room temperature. La Ripaille must sell a lot of it, for it seems always to be fresh. The black-and-white layer cake is less fortunate—it is too cold to be good. The striking crème caramel is orange flavored, and there are strands of sharp orange rind in the sweet sauce.

★★★ RUSSIAN TEA ROOM

150 West 57th Street
LUNCH AND DINNER.
Reservations, CO 5–0947.
Credit cards: AE, CB, DC, MC, V.
Expensive.

The Russian Tea Room, Carnegie Hall's West 57th Street neighbor, is the province of a low-ranking god who has been given the place as his small planet. But this deity is an undisciplined collector, his eyes bigger than his restaurant, and the glittering heterogeneity of things to eat, people, and objects that he has crammed into his little world would far exceed its physical limits were it not for his capacity to transcend physical bounds. The Russian Tea Room is possible in the same way that it is possible for all the angels in the universe to dance on a pin—by divine intervention.

Under a red canopy and through revolving doors you go, into the choice front room —theatrical posters and New York's smallest two-bartender bar, the saucy clash of lipstick-red banquettes against flamingo-pink table linen, the waiting line of the patiently waiting, the giant charcoal-and-ivory mural of a park café in a very civilized city somewhere long ago. Through this room the endless democracy flows—*grandes dames* in floor-length dresses, tomorrow's ingénue with last year's manager, musicians and musicians' mothers, opera freaks and lieder singers, children with their dates, drama critics with boring producers, rabbis with their wives, priests with other priests, purveyors of all culture, hustlers of all commodities, scribblers of all propaganda.

The deep-green walls of the big back room are hung with a hundred paintings and as many shining samovars; chandeliers and sconces glitter with golden tinsel; dark-red lanterns glow on the tables. Dozens of men in red or green bring and take away as they have for fifty years, and as they and their followers obviously will for fifty or a hundred more.

Remarkable food, like kholodetz—pickled calves' feet—cool blocks of firm jelly, textured with meat, garnished with whipped cream that is vibrant with powerful horseradish. Eggplant orientale, a rich, oily, tomatoed paste with a bit of garlic in it —you spread it on pumpernickel bread. The herring are firm and pungent, the smoked salmon pale and tender. And the caviar—four grades of the black are available—is superb.

The "cold" borscht is cool, polished, purple and creamy, its sweet beef flavor livened with slivers of seeded cucumber and lots of dill. The hot borscht is tart and salted, the dollop of cool sour cream lovely against the warm red broth and shredded beets.

The homiest foods are cotolette Pojarsky and luli kebab, the former veal-and-chicken patties, the latter lamb patties, the warm, spicy ground meats moistened with a pleasantly fatty and peppered mushroom sauce. And the most elegant main course is the blini with red caviar and sour cream, buckwheat pancakes that are browned, earthy and seemingly weightless. You soak them in melted butter, wrap them around the sour cream and pale amber-colored globules of salmon roe, and eat. The broiled lamb dishes —shaslik and lamb chops—are of tender and tasty meat, artfully charred. And such vegetarian oddities as mushrooms or eggplant au gratin are like thick vegetable stews, weighty with hot sour cream, served on rice.

A winy stew of prunes, pears and apples, in thick syrup, goes by the deceptive name of fruit compote. And the pastries, creams and custards that make up the fancy little desserts are all smooth and moist, polished and fresh and airy, their sweetness never excessive, the nuts and crusts and cakes browned, crisp and tender. Yes, tea comes in a glass.

Vodka and champagne are the drinks to drink. Vodka is ordered from the vodka menu.

★★ SABOR

20 Cornelia Street (near Bleecker Street)
DINNER.
Reservations, 243-9579.
Credit cards, AE, MC.
Medium-priced.

Though you have, very likely, never been to Cuba (and though in fact the only Cuban in this long, narrow store is one of the waiters), you will, probably, be persuaded at once, by the appearance of the place, and later by the food, of this establishment's Cuban "authenticity." Everybody is. Judging only by the food you get in New York's other Cuban restaurants, what differentiates Sabor's is only its superiority. The food is the genuine article, at least as genuine as it is anywhere else in town.

But in choosing its appearance, Sabor was guided not by the gaudy looks that are traditional in Manhattan's Cuban restaurants, but by the plain look of cafés and simple restaurants in Spain and in the old parts of the old cities of the Caribbean islands. The room is painted ivory and dark tan, the wooden floor is dark reddish-brown. The ceiling is of stamped tin, ceiling fans hang from it. There are straw baskets on the walls, green plants here and there in the dining room, as well as in the front window. There is a tiny service bar at the back, and when a Caribbean rum drink is being prepared in the blender, conversation at the rear of the restaurant halts, for Sabor—especially at the back—is something of a soundbox. You put a little noise in, you get a lot of noise out. Between frozen daiquiris, Latin music jangles from the speakers. When the place is busy, there is a bit of boisterousness from the sometimes loudly self-satisfied clientele, for it is easy to spend freely on lots of food and wine when prices are this low. Sabor is a jolly place, and though it is loud it never seems inappropriately so.

Your waiter (the chap with one earring), when you mention to him that your table is remarkably small, cheerfully agrees with you, as if you are exchanging pleasantries. When you ask if there is a wine list, he informs you that there is. Actually to see it requires a more pointed approach. He is perfectly nice, you understand, just a little out of it sometimes.

Sabor is never out of escabeche, a firm, cold, sour side of a small fish, surrounded by crisp vegetables—onions, celery, diced carrots, green peppers, salty green olives, capers—all in the tart pickling marinade. The marinated squid is cold, but spicy-hot, the circles of tender meat mingled with hot red peppers. And you can get shrimp (camarones picantes) prepared the same way—the house obtains very good shrimp, and if you eat them carelessly, your lips will burn for a while after. The hot appetizers include empanadas, triangular dumplings of browned pastry filled with ground sausage that is both fiery and a little leaden—earthy food; and frituras de malanga, fritters composed of garlic-flavored chunks of a Caribbean root vegetable—the flavor is not immediately distinctive, but lemon converts the nuggets into more-than-pleasant hot morsels. Sabor's gazpacho is more watery than oily.

For fancy fish, you order the poached red snapper, which reaches you whole, in a casserole dish, head and tail on, under a thick blanket of sauce that is green with parsley, winy, tart of its capers and lime juice, oily and garlicked. The snapper is fresh, perfectly cooked, moist and flaky. For humble fish, you opt for the bacalao à la Vizcaina, a weighty stew of salted codfish, heavy with potatoes, sharpened by capers and olives, served in a strong tomato sauce. For all its weight, the dish is not leaden. Sabor serves chicken in a so-called curried prune sauce, with whole prunes and mushrooms: these spices are not packaged curry powder, and they make the dish remind you a little of good Indian cooking; the chicken is stained dark from being cooked with the sweet fruit. There are more of those prunes in the pot roast of beef, but this *is* a heavy dish, the slabs of meat are a little dry despite a moist stuffing of sausage, fruits, capers and olives; even the dark and winy sauce does not quite redeem the tasty but ponderous meat. Ropa vieja is an odd component of Cuban cookery, which non-Cubans usually eat once. This is because the name means, and the dish often resembles, "old rope." The way this dish is usually prepared in New York's Cuban restaurants, the shredded meat is as resilient as hemp, resulting in a marathon for the jaw. Sabor's version, however, is by comparison a piece of cake, the mound of dark strands in an oily tomato sauce flavored with cloves and cinnamon—a striking dish. Pretty good black beans and rice are served with just about everything, but certain vegetables available à la carte are also of interest, among them yucca, another Caribbean root, this one white, hefty, with a texture like that of yams, served in a garlic-flavored oil—strong and primitive food.

The little individual key-lime pies are made on a very ordinary crust, and the pale-yellow chiffon reveals little citrus flavor—the superb whipped cream helps. The flan is something the precise likes of which you have tasted every one of the thousand times you have ordered flan. And the roulade of sponge cake and custard, wetted down with liqueur and orange juice, is an obvious sweet. The big winner is coco quemado, a hot, sweet, nutty coconut dessert, made with sherry, flavored with cinnamon, and served with more of that terrific whipped cream. If that does not suit, there is fresh pineapple on hand.

★★SALTA IN BOCCA

179 Madison Avenue (near 34th Street)
LUNCH AND DINNER. CLOSED SUNDAY.
Reservations, 684–1757.
Credit cards: AE, CB, DC, MC, V.
Expensive.

A collection of hideous paintings on the walls can make a restaurant seem honest, as if the stuff is hung there by a proprietor who thinks the customers expect such things, but whose mind is elsewhere—on the food, perhaps. The glum salmon-pink of these walls was obviously selected by a relative known for excellent taste; the red carpeting is the necessary gesture to luxe. (None of this is surprising, for Salta in Bocca is an enterprise of the owners of Il Monello, on Second Avenue in the East Seventies; and they, after all, when taking over the hideous Villa Doria, left every stick in place.) The effect of it all is to direct your attention to what is placed before you, which is mostly good, sometimes wonderful.

If it is your habit when trying new eating places to look around to see what the regular customers order, you will have no trouble reaching at least one conclusion here. It seems that half the tables sport steamy bowls of Vongole e Muscoli al Vino Bianco —fresh clams and mussels, in their shells, mounded up over a deep pool of vibrant buttery broth that is strongly scented of garlic and parsley. You transfer the empty shells to the plate provided and drink the hot soup with a spoon. Very good Spiedino Romano, a crusty deep-fried, multi-layered sandwich of bread, cheese and ham in a strong anchovy sauce that is livened with capers—juicy food, wonderful with cold white wine.

This establishment prepares some of the best Spaghetti Carbonara in New York— very thin noodles, firm and tender, sliding around among themselves in a rich sauce of butter, sautéed onions and strands of tangy ham, all thickened with egg yolk and colorful with fresh parsley. Do not add cheese; the dish is impeccable the way it is. The Cannelloni di Carne is struggling along several furlongs behind the front-running Carbonara—the ground, herbed meat within the pasta envelopes is dry and grainy, and the creamy tomato sauce, good as it is, cannot rescue the dish.

Cernia Livornese is snapper in the familiar Leghorn tomato sauce that is fortified with chopped olives and capers—this fish is, on occasion, a little overdone, and the sauce is a rather gentle version of this usually vibrant substance; but the dish is satisfactory nevertheless. The Pollo al Vino Bianco e Funghi is a nice little chicken dish, skinned breasts in a simple sauce of wine, mushrooms and onions.

But it is the veal that you should have. You would expect that the dish for which the restaurant is named, Salta in Bocca, would be the best in the house, and there is no denying the buttery tenderness of the veal, the stout flavor of the ham, the smoothness of the pale sauce they are served in, nor the freshness of the spinach garnish. But that is nothing next to the Costoletta alla Fiorentina, a butterflied veal chop that is stuffed with a fabulously rich mixture of ricotta cheese, spinach and bits of this establishment's excellent ham; the whole production is floured, dipped in egg and sautéed —superb meat, elegantly crusted and splendidly filled.

Good salads in tart dressings, including an excellent combination of spinach and mushrooms.

The cheese cake is a comedown; the Zuppa Inglese, buried in fluffy egg whites, is the very familiar sweet. The waiters are conscientious in the preparation of zabaglione here, dosing it with plenty of Marsala and beating it over the flame until it is frothy and hot. Unfortunately, this requires the use of burners in the dining room, and the principal shortcoming of this establishment is inadequate ventilation, yielding a smoky atmosphere that is aggravated by the alcohol fires. Asthmatics be warned.

A good restaurant. If you stick to the best dishes and wear your gas mask, a superb one.

★★ SAN MARCO

36 West 52nd Street
LUNCH, MONDAY TO FRIDAY; DINNER, MONDAY TO SATURDAY. CLOSED SUNDAY.
Reservations, CI 6–5340.
Credit cards: AE, CB, DC, MC, V.
Expensive.

This new 52nd Street San Marco is to the old place on 55th as a carefully selected second spouse to an impulsively taken first—perfectly suitable and all that, but lacking a certain capacity, recalled with some nostalgia, to infuriate. At the old you suffered a bit of crush at the bar for the thirty minutes between the hour of your reservation and the time you were actually inserted into your tiny allotted space; you endured your neighbors' loud camaraderie, the staff's conflicts; you longed for escape from intimate bedlam, dreamed of a comfortable and civilized setting for the vigorous food and sturdy Italian wines.

Well, you got what you thought you wanted. "Never pray for a new king," said the wise man, "he will be worse than the old one." How we miss that old despotism. The new San Marco is benevolent, like a well-run clinic.

The place is long, wide and airy, the large tables in well-spaced rows across the generous spread, the lofty ivory walls made less bare by numerous paintings that have no other purpose. As in the previous San Marco, the ledge above the banquette that rims the room is strung with bottles of wine; and tall étagères of dark polished wood, open front and back, one-wine-bottle-deep, display hundreds of bottles more, and serve as "room dividers," to break up the cavernous volume. But these displays, for all they ought to suggest of alcoholic abandon, are coolly architected and, therefore, sterile. Maybe the place would feel OK if it weren't an *Italian* restaurant, but the assertive food of Italy in these spare surroundings is like a hot pastrami on Arnold Brick Oven White.

Accordingly the customers, particularly at lunchtime—here or there the token beard, there or here a woman with men, and beyond those, little but pairs and quartets of suited executives, discussing, with studied squinted eyes, the games of corporate business as if they were the conflicts of states. At night, however, things loosen up, and the signs of life San Marco needs are provided by New Yorkers who can afford the restaurant and enjoy their prosperity—you see colorful duds on fetching folk, hear smart talk and tipsy laughter.

The menu is very much the old menu, at prices that are no less immodest, including, as a dinnertime appetizer, a little number called Spiedino Romana—a row of alternating layers of mozzarella cheese and bread, grilled until the bread is toasted and the cheese strong and pully, served in an oily and salty anchovy sauce. It is a terrific dish, at once coarse and well-balanced, the sharp flavors offsetting the solid weight of the food. One ordinarily avoids liver pâté in Italian restaurants, because it is usually imported. The lunchtime menu at San Marco, however, informs you that the pâté is "homemade," and you investigate by placing an order for same. Well, you should have figured that an Italian pâté will be oily where a French one will be buttery, and you might have anticipated that the difference, to a predisposed palate, will be off-putting. This may be an acceptable dish, it is herby and far from flat, but you will have to approach it with a wide-open mind.

Cappelletti in Brodo means chicken dumplings in chicken broth—little pasta pouches stuffed with ground chicken and herbs, in a broth which has the gamy quality of chicken fat and plenty of seasoning; the tender dumplings are just right in the sharp soup.

Good noodles, with a strong egg flavor, cooked to order so they are firm but tender, and in Fettuccine alla Veneziana they are moistened with a vibrant sweet-and-sour tomato sauce in which peas and bits of ham are apparent, the flavor of rosemary very subtle.

Veal dishes do not seem to be San Marco's strength. You can actually get a Veal Scaloppine al Limone in which it is difficult to detect either the flavor of lemon or that of sautéed veal. The obscurity of the lemon is miscalculation, that of the veal indolence —it is barely browned, only on one side (the side that is "up" on your plate), and permitted to stew for a while in bubbling butter. This is ruination of a good ingredient. The veal birds (Involtini di Vitello) are somewhat better—hefty loaves formed of veal around a strongly herbed and spiced stuffing of cheese and ham, served in a winy mushroom gravy. At lunchtime the serving is augmented with a dozen or so gnocchi —firm little potato loaves that make a better match for the gravy than the birds themselves.

Sausages and Peppers (billed as "farmers style") is the kind of dish one thinks of in those Italian restaurants with checkered tablecloths and waiters in shirt sleeves. The San Marco version is no less vigorous than what you get in neighborhood places, succulent and spicy, but there are touches of class—an admixture, in the sausages themselves, of an exceptionally fragrant black pepper which, despite its abundance, does not overpower the dish but adds an unexpected piquancy. The meat is garnished with sautéed red peppers and fresh mushrooms.

For perfect, elegant simplicity, have Branzino alla Pescatora—a great slice of immaculately fresh striped bass, moistened with a delicate tomato sauce that is lightly garlicked. Purists who insist that fish should be no more than buttered and lemoned are the losers.

San Marco has always made a lovely event of the simple act of serving up a dish of zabaglione. To begin with, your captain prepares the dish in the dining room, with much grand stirring over the flame; and the result is hot, sweet and winy. Moreover, it is served up in a handsome porcelain goblet, the thick golden foam mounded high above the rim, some of the excess coursing down the sides and stem. Don't worry, your fingers will not be made sticky. You eat it with a spoon. The cheese cake has a smooth, custardlike quality; it is heavy and moist, laden with chopped fruits—very nice.

○ SARDI'S

234 West 44th Street
LUNCH AND DINNER.
Reservations, 221–8440.
Credit cards: AE, CB, DC, MC, V.
Expensive.

You enter to the checkroom, the untidy little bar, and the stairway to the upper level. Upstairs the principal bar, the busy three-deep one, newspaper men and newspaper women, actors and actresses (though nary a star stands here), and all the desk people and go-fer people that fill out the middle levels of those industries. The drinking is gay, rarely boisterous. This attic level of Sardi's is a little dingier than the main floor, a function of the lower ceiling. The dirty-salmon walls are much like those downstairs, the massive air-conditioning ducts somewhat more oppressive by virtue of their being closer to your head. And of course there is the checkerboard of colored-in caricatures the height and length of every wall. There is no pleasure in being surrounded by hundreds of grotesque heads, some of them up close. Lucille Ball at five feet, gaudily grinning at you in primary colors, is actually frightening. Up here there are a couple of islands of gingham-topped tables set aside for drinkers who want to avoid the bar-side crush. You get a pot of Cheddar surrounded by Ritz crackers. The drinks are ample, the waiters city-wise. The place is patrolled by a tuxedoed gent with slicked-down hair, a beery complexion, jowls, and a constant preoccupation with a wad of gum. Things are a touch more gracious downstairs—all the tables under crisp white linen, the ceiling far enough away so that you hardly notice the patches in the cracked plaster that they mean to paint over one of these years. The overall feeling is of Old New York functionalism, rows of tables, plain chairs, wooden floor, nothing more than is needed to make eating possible—except those ghastly drawings.

You expect at least a decent shrimp cocktail in a place like this, but the shrimp are overcooked, and you are grateful for the horseradish and Tabasco that accompany the dish. Even the Smoked Brook Trout with Sour Cream and Horseradish Sauce, which every restaurant in town gets from the same few sources, is here so poorly handled that it is dried out by the time it reaches you—the horseradish sauce is useful, if lumpy, and the garnish of diced jelly is an irrelevance. As neither of these dishes is prepared to order, it is an astonishment to have them served ten minutes apart. Surely one would never take dining advice from any habitué of this place, but lovers of Sardi's do love Sardi's cannelloni (available as an appetizer or main course). Maybe the dish is all right early in the week—try it for Monday lunch perhaps—but it can be tough and rank, as though reheated on a radiator.

It is possible to get perfectly decent broilings in this place, and the lamb chops, for one, are very thick, tender, lightly charred and accurately prepared.

The specialties of the house on the regular menu are printed in capital letters, so you experiment with SUPREME OF CHICKEN SARDI, which turns out to be an abundance of tasteless chicken in a cheese sauce that has flavor only because it is burnt. This wretched stuff is served over asparagus that has been kept in hot water since early spring. Another fast-moving item here is the Deviled Roast Beef Bones. Though the title suggests that the bones themselves are deviled, there is nothing on them but a little meat, a lot of fat and too much breading, which serves to prevent much of the grease from running off—accompanying mustard sauce tastes as if it is made with Gulden's, which is to mustard as shells are to eggs. At lunchtime there are Fried Oysters—a tough crust around a lump of cotton wool. Avoid with care the so-called Fresh Spinach Salad. The spinach tastes as if it has been in cold storage since the last war, the mushrooms are tasteless, the zucchini plastic, the bacon overburdened with responsibility among these sorry partners.

Very ordinary desserts, for the most part, including sodden cheese cakes and tired pastries. But in this department the specialties are in fact superior to the rest of the list. The Frozen Cake, Zabaglione Sauce, is a splendid layered affair of good ice cream, startlingly tasty and berrylike strawberry sherbet, rich cake and silken icing, all moistened with a zabaglione that is loaded with Marsala. And the Bocconi Dolce is a more than tolerable and very picturesque combination of strawberries, whipped cream, dark cake and icing—when the berries are good, the dish is good, but you can't count on ripe berries every time.

The Sardi's dinner cycle is built around theater times—the place is quiet between curtain-up and curtain-down, busy before and after. You see pretty starlets with their gargoyle handlers (agents need not be good-looking). Much table-visiting and kissing. Yes, theater people do pronounce "darling" as "daaahling," and they do it a lot. Of all this establishment's faults, its contempt for the public is the most contemptible. Half a dozen pairs of desperate little ladies are standing around hoping to squeeze in a Sardi's lunch before the Wednesday matinee. They wait and wait. Along comes a customer with a familiar face, but no reservation. "Yes, Mr. X," says the host, "your table is ready, right this way."

★★ SAY ENG LOOK

5 East Broadway (at Chatham Square)
LUNCH AND DINNER.
Reservations, 732-0796.
Credit cards: MC, V.
Inexpensive.

When this establishment moved to larger, two-story quarters a few doors north of its original site, it elected to shift itself into quite another Chinatown genre. The food is just what it was in the old place, but, to attract the hordes of new customers that would be needed to fill the new one, Say Eng Look boldly chose to make itself the equal of anything south of Canal Street in terms of ugliness. If you remember the old place, you know that with its demise utilitarian chic was dealt a body blow. The new Say Eng Look has gone all the way: bronze dragons rampant on red suede walls, red-and-white "gingham" oilcloth on the tables, chairs that are the last word in North Carolina Ming (*so* much more hideous than those Grand Rapids imitations). The acoustic tiles on the beamed ceiling look like big Uneeda Biscuits. The antiqued mirror, with which certain walls are faced, is, happily, dark, so the scene is not exactly repeated. Upstairs is like downstairs, but substitute orange suede for red, and add red lanterns—they hang near the second-story front windows, which look out over Chatham Square.

As there are more than 150 dishes to choose from, you will want to commission an order or two of aromatic beef, to hold you while you consider the availabilities. You dip the cool slices of sweet-spiced meat into the fiery oil that is provided, and keep a bottle of cold beer handy. You will make most of your selections from the list of "special dishes" that is printed on yellow paper and taped to the front of the menu. You will select, for example, fried whole fish with seaweed, the crusty beast fresh and tender within its browned exterior, strewn with scallion greens and with rather dry seaweed that is only mildly gamy. That rather grainy seaweed may also be had spread across a big platter of sweet and crunchy sautéed shrimp. The dish for which the house is best known is fried roll fish with bean-curd sheet, in which the fish is formed into a roulade with the bean curd and fried in hot fat until the white meat is steamy, the bean curd crisp and parchment-like. (When, on occasion, the dish is made hastily, in fat that is not hot enough, it lacks its usual sparkle.) A singular exotic from the sea is the sea cucumber, a gelatinous mass served here, in giant chunks, as the principal bulk in the dish called sea cucumber with crabmeat. The sea cuke has a pleasant texture—like a slightly rubbery melon—and very little flavor, but it is a good backdrop for the occasional morsels of pink crabmeat and the strands of sharp scallion green that give the dish its character. More of those scallion greens are mingled with long strands of boned eel in the dish given as eel with Chinese vegetable—its sauce is dark and potently ginger-flavored.

Tai chi chicken is a spicy dish—chunks of boned white meat with mushrooms and red peppers in a thick hot sauce that is slightly sweetened. The closest thing to Western food on the menu is called lion head, giant pork meatballs flavored with anise and buried in hot cabbage and dark sauce. Perhaps because the dish is the favorite of the dilettantes, the moo shu pork is put forth in a desultory version. Among the vegetable dishes, consider the eggplant with meat in spiced sauce, a hot eggplant mush studded with the whites and greens of scallions; and black mushroom with puff, in which the pale, rather cartilaginous and dumpling-like vegetables called puffs are mingled with smoky mushrooms, crisp water chestnuts and sweet green peas, all in a thick and polished sauce.

You may skip dessert. Two beers are available: Tsing-Tao, from China—much flavor, but an occasional bottle is flat; and Budweiser. The service varies from the brusque to the avuncular.

★★ SEA-FARE OF THE AEGEAN

25 West 56th Street
LUNCH AND DINNER.
Reservations, 581-0540.
Credit cards: AE, CB, DC, MC, V.
Expensive.

This restaurant requires that men wear jackets, but if you arrive without one, you are provided with a limp, much-worn, pale-gray linen number, compared with which your basic animaled polo shirt is full dress. This is a system whereby the establishment can be a little snooty, but not at the risk of passing up a live customer.

Sea-Fare is known for its art, which is all over the place. Some of it is ancient, much of it is barely dry. In boxes that are carved into the walls, contemporary vases are displayed bathed in light, behind glass, like museum pieces. There are a couple of oils by someone who has chosen to be influenced by Walter Keane. Cézanne, you understand, is not represented.

The restaurant is meant to be grand. Big enough it is—a large front room that, by brass-balustraded stairways, divides into a lower level and a mezzanine at the back. But the effect is somewhat undone not only by the clutter on the walls but by such appointments as armchairs that are upholstered in frayed plastic—their wooden backs have been engraved in a style known as Grand Rapids Hellenic. The place is popular, often crowded, at least a little hectic when it is. The aisles are filled with staff, but on occasion you can wait twenty minutes for first sight of whoever it is that will be helping you. The shortage of efficiency, however, is compensated for by shows of it: A host studies his log with great seriousness before he seats you, but then is unable to lead the second half of your party to wherever it was that he led the first half; and your waiter very carefully asks who gets what when he takes your order, and then asks it again when he delivers the goods. But he delivers mostly good goods.

The clams and oysters are fresh and just opened. You get good tarama, the Greek spread of softened bread, red caviar and lemon—this version is light, somehow mild and salty at once, almost creamy. The clams Cassino are a big winner, tiny littlenecks adorned with bits of onion, tomato, green pepper, bacon, the clams tender in their seasoned juice. The Manhattan chowder is sharp and spicy, loaded with crisp vegetables, dominated by the sweetness and tartness of tomato—the many bits of clam are a good note in the sturdy soup. Mild red pepper, buttery hot milk and tender oysters make up the oyster stew—there is something palliative about the dish, whatever your condition.

It is suggested that when you first get hold of your waiter you refuse to release him until he lets you know which of the main courses is not available. Surely it is idiotic to spend ten minutes deciding on four varieties of fish and then be expected instantly to substitute three others while a man with a pencil and pad stands impatiently by.

Still, when you get your broiled whole pompano, all that may be forgotten, for the sweet meat is wrapped in elegantly crisped skin, and, moreover, your waiter has succeeded in separating the meat from 90 percent of the bones. The house has sometimes served swordfish that has been deprived, by an overlong stay in the broiler, of its natural moisture. The broiled flounder is delicate and sweet, and for a few extra dollars you may have the two halves of the fish converted into a kind of pillow into which is stuffed a mound of fine crabmeat that is mingled with minced red pepper—an abundant and very satisfying dish, superior, by virtue of its simplicity, to almost all the gloppy crabmeat-stuffed dishes around town. Sea-Fare bothers to obtain Dover sole, and then obscures its character by breading it and serving it in a "garlic" sauce. The garlic is remote, and the fish has been reduced to fish-and-chips, sans chips. The shrimp Santoríni-style are fine, served on a layer of good rice: The shrimp surround a grilled tomato that is surmounted by hot feta cheese, the entire production moistened with a mild tomato sauce—tasty food, albeit devoid of breed. You are better off with the striped bass Aegean-style, in which the crusted fish—snowy white and moist inside—and a couple of littlenecks in their shells are served in a red sauce that is sharp and herbed. Good cold dishes: a two-pound lobster in its shell, not cold, but cool, tender, garnished with a simple potato salad, crisp celery, slices of juicy tomato, and strong black Greek olives, and served with an exceptionally creamy mayonnaise; and salmon, a pattern of fresh dill across the firm pink steak, and more of that wonderful mayonnaise.

You will not be excited by most of the desserts. Not by the icy, clammy rice pudding, hard grains in every bite, liberally cinnamoned as if for purposes of disguise; not by the strawberry shortcake, which is syrupy, and not redeemed by its excellent whipped cream; not by the Aegean-style peach, which, your waiter assures you, is served in champagne sauce—the poached fruit is good, but do not hunt for bubbles in the sugary syrup. However, the custard is light, just delicately touched with caramel. The apple pie is cool and a little sour, its lard crust coated with browned sugar. And the baklava is fine—layers of honeyed nuts interleaved with flaky pastry.

★★ SHEZAN

8 West 58th Street
LUNCH, MONDAY TO FRIDAY; DINNER, MONDAY TO SATURDAY. CLOSED SUNDAY.
Reservations, 371-1414.
Credit cards: AE, CB, DC, MC, V.
Expensive.

The food at Shezan is authentic, but so removed from its natural setting—even from any pretense of its natural setting—that eating here calls to mind looking at exotic or ancient artifacts within the walls of a slick, contemporary museum. Shezan is subterranean, windowless. The starkness of its lines is relieved by the warmth of its materials and the softness of its low light. The place—floor and walls—is covered with a tweedy gray-brown carpeting, and the rooms are separated by walls of glass blocks (like big ice cubes) that, by unseen lights, are made to glow. The ceiling is of metallic acoustic tiles that have the color and dull sheen of pewter. They reflect, dimly, the tables below, which are set with beige linen, handsome copper service plates, and, on little brass stands on marble bases, glass-enclosed candles. You sit on banquettes of cocoa-colored suede or on tubular-steel armchairs upholstered with the same stuff. You are served by a cordial staff of gentlemen from the subcontinent.

Except for a couple of soups, the first courses seem to be items designed to seduce the reluctant indirectly into an Indian dinner. One of those soups is mulligatawny, which is thick, of an earthy vegetable intensity, flavored with sweet and hot spices, fragrant with its sprinkling of herbs. But most of the first courses are on the order of the crab cocktail, a ball of crabmeat, mingled with vaguely Asian herbs and spices, set in the hollow of a half-avocado. The dish is a not very promising first step toward an Indian-American cookery. If you must start slowly, start with the papaya, for the orange melon is ripe and firm and sweet—you may brighten it with lemon—and it is a fit approach, both cool and light, to the weightier matters ahead. On the other hand, if you want solid stuff right from the start, an order of jhinga shahi, divided between two, is for you. The dish consists of eight marinated shrimp grilled on a skewer, red and blackened, oiled and spicy, juicy and crisp, adorned with parsley.

Samundar ki shahzadi is the designation this house gives to any of various fish baked in a coconut sauce. Sometimes the dish is prepared with tilefish, which is fine in its sauce of spicy oil studded with sweet white raisins. It is strewn with slivered almonds that, too bad, are straight from the can. The chicken curry—murgh korma shahi—is of big chunks of the crisp-skinned bird in a yogurt sauce that is earthy, sweet-spiced, thick. Big chunks of superb lamb are the bulk of saag gosht, in which the tender meat is coated with a deep-green sauce of herbed and pungently spiced spinach. Some splendid meat-balls—called kofta jahangir—are both spicy and fruity, blackened on the outside and bright red within. They are served, accompanied by hardcooked eggs, in a yogurt sauce that is thick with onion and tomato. More ground beef, this time shaped like sausages, goes by the name of seekh kabab mughlai. The hefty rods of beef have been heavily seasoned, then cooked over flames, and they arrive hot and juicy. Among kidneys, lamb kidneys are the gamiest. Their commingling—in a dish called gurda kapoora—with sweetbreads, and their immersion in a thick and peppery dark sauce that is seasoned with garlic and ginger, does nothing to obscure their loud flavor—this is good food, but for some it is hard to take. Shezan's rice is substantial but light, a little spicy, very moist. The dahl is a hot, thick lentil mush, bits of spice in it. Raita, the cool yogurt mixed with crisp chopped cucumber, and sprinkled with herbs and spices, is perfect with virtually all the dishes here. Two good breads are offered—the naan is a little salty, very light, with a vivid wheat flavor; the paratha tastes just as strongly of grain, but it is sprinkled with sesame seeds as well and baked in butter, so that it is richer and more complex than the straightforward naan.

It is probably not what you want of a dessert, but halwa mumtaz mahal is the most interesting sweet offered. It is of ground vegetables, with a dominant taste of roots—the moist red paste is sweetened and nutted, and served hot. The kheer khas is one of those mystifying sweets of the East, a pistachio-sprinkled custard that seems distinctly soapy. Kulfi is the house ice cream—it is quite hard, icy, flowery rather than sugary, sprinkled with chopped seeds of sweet spice.

★ SHUN LEE PALACE

155 East 55th Street
LUNCH AND DINNER.
Reservations, 371-8844.
Credit cards: AE, CB, DC.
Medium-priced.

The place looks like the lobby of a Miami Beach hotel and, appropriately enough, it is loaded with tourists. They have perhaps never been frightened by golden wallpaper before and they shriek a lot—delightedly when their attention is diverted to the blue flame that burns on the top tier of their Assorted Appetizers. Dozens of young waiters wander around during the slow periods (when the place is only half filled) and you are likely to be asked about drinks and such half a dozen times. You are not, unfortunately, furnished with Do Not Disturb signs and no amount of heavily applied facial boredom deters these couriers from their persistent appeals. The place is huge, and despite its various levels and sections and the turns in the walls, it seems barnlike. In so immense a setting it is not surprising that none of the staff has much of an idea what the rest of it is doing. Or perhaps it is their unwillingness to care in the service of so inelegant a clientele, for this is the home of some of the most contented and boisterous diners in town, comfy on these Naugahyde gold shantung banquettes, under these gilded chandeliers.

But the place has a persistent reputation as one of the best Chinese restaurants in New York and it is true that if you visit it a dozen times with a dozen friends, you will be able to learn enough about the menu to put together nothing but fine meals. If the establishment, however, is to be judged by everything it is willing to purvey—more than seventy items on the menu—it is not one of the city's best.

The Hacked Chicken in Hot Sauce is composed of strands of white chicken under a thick sauce apparently composed of peanut and oil—a thick, lively sauce with a vague quality of smoke in it, but the not-so-secret secret of this well-known dish is the chicken itself, for without the distinct taste of meat there is no foil to the sauce, and this chicken is flat. If you do not know your way around this place and if you are unknown to the management, they size you up (sometimes wrongly) and decide how little trouble they can get away with. You order some Fried Dumplings. They arrive in eight seconds. Naturally, they are not fried dumplings. They are steamed dumplings; the crust on one side that is formed by last-minute frying, to form fried dumplings from steamed dumplings, has not been bothered about. Terrific dumplings, you understand, lovely spiced ground pork accented with bits of strong parsley, wrapped in a firm noodle casing, and served with a bowl of tart sauce. But they are not fried dumplings. Assumptions are made. When three people request two orders (eight dumplings), your helpful servant dispenses three to him, three to him, and two to her.

A dish styled Frogs' Legs Wang Style (Chef Wang is the culinary king of Shun Lee country) might as well be made of rice noodles or cardboard for all the flavor of frogs' legs that can be detected in the dish. The taste of frozen frogs' legs is at best obscure and, for all the little green peppers and sautéed onions in this dish, nothing can rescue it from its overpoweringly sweet sauce. Disaster. The Velvet Shrimp Puffs are another world, the shrimp pounded down to light cutlets and served in a pale, oily sauce, mingled with morsels of crisp vegetables—snow peas, water chestnuts, mushrooms. A lovely, delicate dish.

Veal is rare on the menus of New York's Chinese restaurants and this place lists but one dish, Sliced Fillet of Veal, Hunan Style, a heavily garlicked dish of slivers of veal —pale and tender meat—with snow peas and green peppers, hot and spicy, but not searingly so, the diverse elements very well balanced. Wang's Amazing Chicken is a bit less, again because the chicken itself tastes like nothing in particular. It is combined with well-cooked eggplant, crisp mushrooms and snow peas, all heavily accented with Chinese parsley; all fine, but the second-rate chicken makes for a second-rate dish. The Eggplant, Family Style, loses the quality of eggplant in its sweet sauce.

Naturally, there are desserts for these people who look like they are stopping off at this posh restaurant after a trip to the supermarket (or are they on their way to the hardware store?), but the desserts are nothing.

• SHUN LEE WEST

43 West 65th Street
LUNCH AND DINNER.
Reservations, 595-8895.
Credit cards: AE.
Medium-priced.

Ancient New York restaurant lore has it that if, on entering a Chinese restaurant, you espy no Chinese at tables therein, you should count yourself in the wrong place and quickly leave. Shun Lee West has had no trouble keeping the Chinese away, the advantage of which is that there is, therefore, plenty of room for those who will deduce nothing from their absence—the only crowd from whom repeat business is to be expected. But just to play it safe, Shun Lee has taken an additional step designed to keep the cognoscenti away: common wisdom has not yet grown up around the subject of Oriental restaurants in which you are greeted by Occidental hosts, but Shun Lee, in its determination to cater, in its new outlet, to the most indiscriminate clientele, has installed at the door a bearded Caucasian whose glib and mindless chatter goes with him (and you) all the way to your table, and then stays. He appears unable to distinguish between those he bores and those who would rather be out of their skins than within his earshot. Trying to get rid of him is like trying to brush away air. It has been suggested that, to get rid of him, Shun Lee Palace and Shun Lee Dynasty opened Shun Lee West.

But no sooner is he gone than you may wish for his return. For the menu, though it is composed of words—many of them English—printed in the Modern European alphabet, might just as well be in Chinese. And your captain's English, for all his good intentions, could not in an hour's time answer half the questions that logically arise from the cryptic listings. What is one to make of Honey Baby Spareribs, Heavenly Fish Fillet, General Ching's Shrimp, Chen Du Pork? Dishes that are hot and spicy are marked with a star. You ask your captain to tell you about Hunan Country Chicken (which is marked with a star). "Hot and spicy," says he. If you really want to know, you have two choices. Order the stuff and find out, or send for the beard.

The restaurant is huge, a bar and several rarely used tables in the large wallpapered entranceway, scores of tables in the main dining room further in. The big room is painted pearl gray. It is rimmed with a dark-red banquette. Smaller, semicircular banquettes help to subdivide the vastness of the space. The tables are covered with grape-colored linen, the floor with dark-red carpeting. The long walls are hung with lengthy oblongs of Chinese art. Potted palms stand here and there, and mirrored columns provide a bit of glitz. The customers are in silks and jewels, doubleknit suits and jump suits, zippered jackets over polo shirts, jeans and running shoes. Every third garment sports the emblem of its maker.

Be it understood that within the Shun Lee organization knowledge of how to prepare Chinese food well surely exists. Sometimes it filters down to even those chefs who cook not for esteemed customers, but for plebes. Accordingly, once in a while you will hit a terrific dish here. But not the hacked chicken, for this familiar item of cold shredded white meat, under a thick, spicy peanut sauce, depends, for its drama, on the contrast between the flavor of the sauce and the taste of the chicken. The drama fails when the chicken has no taste at all. The cool Szechuan noodles in their sesame sauce are timidly seasoned, so that the noodles, which are a foil to the spiciness of the sauce, are in this version a foil to nothing in particular. The cold Yunnan pork, with cucumber, is spicy and tasty, but cartilaginous. And a similar dish of kidneys with peppercorns suffers most decidedly from the imperfect washing of that organ meat. Something given as Szechuan wontons are warm, perfumed, spicy, but they seem like flavor without food, the gummy noodle lacks character. And the so-called crystal shrimp are slightly fishy little dumplings, pleasant but forgettable.

There are a few winners among the main courses, including "wonderful taste scallops," in which the morsels of rich seafood are browned and crisped and served with scallions and sliced peppers in a pungently seasoned sauce that is dark and meaty. The so-called iron fish with black bean sauce is, unnecessarily, "finished" on a side stand beside your table—which is to say it is transferred from one plate to another in the presence of a flame. When the sauce is poured over the fish it sizzles, and everyone says ooh. The fillets of fish were a little overcooked even before they were sizzled, but this is fresh fish, and the black bean sauce, with its Chinese vegetables, bits of fresh, sharp ginger and morsels of pork, tastes as good as it sizzles. But the alleged ginger on the sliced duck with young ginger root is as yet unborn, and the bird is as dry as stale bread —the spiced salt that accompanies the dish would probably be just the right zest to a well-made version. The tangy spicy lamb is of pungent meat, mingled with red and green peppers, asparagus shoots, crisp scallions. But Shun Lee West's orange flavor beef is probably the worst rendition of this dish in New York—bits of tangerine rind that provide the orange flavor are burnt to utter blackness, the sauce is a viscous and sugary syrup, and the total effect is of chewy candy.

At weekend lunches, and at night after 10, dim sum are served. These are the various morsels—many of them dumplings or fritters, or deep-fried meats or seafood—that, served in great variety, are the stock-in-trade of the dumpling houses that are showing up all over town these days. Here most of the items are leaden, or greasy, or tasteless, or combinations thereof. Some of these items—the stuffed bean curd, the five-spiced chicken, the crab claw—are perfectly decent food, but there is not a first-class dumpling house in town that fails to surpass this humdrum selection. Dim sum at Shun Lee West is just an effort to capitalize on a recent fad by peddling it to an indiscriminate clientele.

The almond cookie is soggy. The fried banana smacks of frequently reused frying oil. And the rice pudding, which, to his credit, your captain tried to talk you out of, is little more than hot sugar and canned fruit.

★★ SICHUAN PAVILION

322 East 44th Street
LUNCH AND DINNER.
Reservations, 986-3775.
Credit cards: AE, CB, DC, MC, V.
Expensive.

The singular distinction of this new establishment is that it is sponsored by—and boasts ten "master chefs" from—mainland China, a.k.a. "Red China," "Communist China" and "China." Naturally, everyone expected a staff uniformed in slippers, Mao caps and blue pajamas. But, unfortunately, in the matter of theme, Sichuan Pavilion is one big boat missed. Think what could have been done: anti-Russian and anti-American posters plastered up on the walls daily; the menu printed up as a Little Red Book, the names and prices of the dishes interspersed with examples of the late Chairman's culinary insights, e.g.: "A dinner without wine is like a day without the productive labor that fortifies man for his combat with the bourgeoisie and the revisionists, and propels him toward the consummation of his revolutionary goal." Consider for a moment the potential effect of loudspeakers on every wall, blaring forth, "The East is Red," to the rhythms of which, hourly on the hour, all present, brandishing chopsticks, perform unison calisthenics in the aisles. And of course the sticky question of what to do with the Gang of Four could have been resolved by shipping them here to bus tables.

Instead they put together a restaurant that would do just fine in Las Vegas, with

Formica walls and hanging red lanterns, carpeted floors and bamboo-pattern wallpaper, tufted Naugahyde banquettes and tuxedoed waiters. Calligraphic scrolls and depictive native art here and there (the Great Wall, families of pandas) do nothing to undo the effect. The big Chinese banquets that are accommodated in a fraction of this restaurant's space only add to it. The pond-size tables are surrounded by dozens of Chinese, well-fed and well-tailored. Dishes are carried in, and the great platters are later carried out, by the dozen. Throughout dinner every table remains adorned with quarts of Johnnie Walker Black and magnums of 7-Up. A dinner without wine . . .

It is claimed, by statements to the effect on the menu, that more than a dozen of the dishes served here have never before been served in New York, and that ten others have never before been served in America. Commercial considerations may have been at work in the delay, for though the food here is honestly made, of good ingredients, little of it reveals the lightness, simplicity, clarity that are the New York food fashions of this day. The food here seems not only foreign, but anachronistic, out of an era when complexity was a dazzling virtue, solidity a reassuring sign of value. Many things here are easier to praise than like, especially those dishes that have a heaviness akin to Central European cooking in its dumpling aspect.

Among those dishes are not, however, the dumplings themselves. Unlike most dumplings served in New York's Chinese restaurants, these are soft, like lightly packed pillows. They are somewhat scantily filled with a fragrantly garlicked meat stuffing, sprinkled with oiled sesame seeds, and served in a polished sauce, red and red-hot, in which not only the heat but the flavor of the peppers is vivid. Equally striking are the beef strips in a small steamer—they come in a little covered steel pot with a perforated platform built into the bottom, which kept the meat out of contact with the boiling water when the dish was prepared. The tender strands of peppery beef are mingled with bits of scallion green and breaded, but so lightly and crisply that the coating seems more like ground nuts than batter. The dish is at once light, perfumed and powerful. The spring rolls are exceptional here—they are the size of your thumb, they sparkle with minced chives, and they are both crusty and almost weightless. Of the cold appetizers, avoid the cold smoked fish appetizer, which is pallid, and try instead the shredded rabbit meat, the pale strands mounded up over shredded scallions—in its light sesame oil dressing, the meat is tantalizingly elusive, its flavor both fugitive and strong.

Then there are the dishes that will elude you without tantalizing you at all. Crispy rabbit meat, for one, crispy lamb chunks for another, both dishes composed of meat buried in rather flavorless batter—the dishes are probably rendered in perfect style, but you would have to grow up with food like this to love it. The crispy shrimp packs may give you a problem too. These "packs" are cut from a log—of shrimp forcemeat wrapped in bean-curd pastry. The shrimp flavor is remote, the dish consisting mainly of crisp textures, moistened and spiced. But the dry sautéed squid, which all the world seems to hate, is really a fascinating, albeit alien-seeming dish. It is made of dried, not fresh, squid, and if the universal and idiotic complaint (that it would be "better" if the squid were fresh) is set aside, and the dish is considered for what it is, its components are found to make up a set of dramatic contrasts (somewhere between assonance and cacophony). The squid is gamy and chewy, it is mingled with strands of meat, peppers of two colors, bean sprouts, all seasoned and bound in oil. It may grow on you.

The Chengdu-style whole fish is a sea bass, crusted, strewn with spiced ground meat and scallion greens, all in a dark-brown, almost meaty sauce that is suffused with hot pepper. The fish is perfectly cooked, light and moist, and despite its great size, its seeming weightlessness makes it easy to dispatch. The chicken chunks in garlic sauce and the sautéed boiled pork slices are hot and tasty dishes of good meats in strong sauces. But the smoked duck is both simpler and more appealing—the moist meat and crisp skin are permeated with the flavor of smoky tea.

Among the vegetables, the eggplant strips in garlic sauce are a rather greasy version of this familiar dish. The napa cabbage with golden shrimp, however, is a huge bowl of hot broth, crisp cabbage and crispy little shrimp that actually seem to have a powerful fresh-shrimp flavor—they set off the cabbage elegantly. The item listed as "double side golden fried noodles" is more complex than the title suggests—some of the noodles are crisp, some are limp and tender, and they are mingled with mushrooms, more of those lovely shrimp, slivers of water chestnut, and minuscule cutlets of meat. Yet each item stands alone—a wonderful noodle dish.

Desserts. Something listed as "crispy flower pastry" is a million layers of paper-thin pastry around a moist layer of perfumed sugar. The so-called "purée nuts," an amalgam of sweet rice, pulverized water chestnuts and ground walnuts, is like a hot and honeyed cereal. Few desserts available in Chinese restaurants in New York seem quite as right at the end of a Chinese dinner as these. There is also an item called "flowery date cake," which seems, unfortunately, like uncooked dough strewn with a few date flakes—still, you must wait fifteen minutes for it.

Sichuan Pavilion gets a good bit of business from the nearby UN, and the tables of Indians, Japanese or Africans are easy to identify. Occidental diplomats seem not to have found the place yet. On the subject of the political implications of this restaurant's presence in capitalist New York, your captain informs you that he himself is from Taiwan, that nevertheless he works amicably with the mainland chefs, and that he happily leaves what conflict may remain to be resolved to the exertions of Shultz and Reagan.

★ SILVER PALACE

50 Bowery (near Canal Street)
LUNCH AND DINNER.
Reservations, 964–1204.
Credit cards: AE, CB, DC, MC, V. No credit cards at lunch.
No liquor.
Inexpensive.

This is Chinatown's largest restaurant and one of the biggest in New York. Accordingly, for the first time, it is now possible for the annual, semiannual, quarterly and monthly celebratory dinners of Chinese political organizations, trade groups, sects, tongs, tribes and block associations to be attended by the entire memberships, their spouses, friends and relations on weekend vacations, visiting firemen from San Francisco and points east, and the press.

Up the broad carpeted stairway or, if you are infirm or enjoy rides, up the purring escalator of a lobby that would befit a Chinese movie palace of Hong Kong's Great White Way, if there were such a thoroughfare, or even if there weren't, decorated, as it is, with tiles and lights and glitter and gilt. You achieve the upper landing, whip out your field glasses and scan the scene, which is a healthy block long, brightly lit, packed with tables that are, in turn, packed with people. The extensive ceiling is supported by columns that are faced with antiqued mirror. There is a backlighted mural of Hong Kong's harbor, garish painted tapestries, a fish mural (aglow), an icebox (with 7-Up, Coke, Nedick's Orange Soda, and a few fingers of Cutty Sark in a bottle stowed away for after hours). The food flies through on little nurses' carts pushed by the waiters at a hustling clip, flash bulbs pop, beer cans pop (you bring your own beer), applause crackles. Applause crackles? Applause crackles. For when the back two thirds of this place is set aside for a mammoth "affair," the deadly serious eating that goes on during these rites is sometimes followed by amplified speeches, which, in turn, are followed by polite smackings of hands. To Occidental ears at the Bowery end of the Silver Palace, the speeches will sound like the loudspeaker announcements on New York subways. For a clearer rendition, repair to the facilities, into which the proceedings are piped. No escape Big Brother. The place opens in the morning. One assumes it is quiet then.

There is also an extensive menu. Violate the Chinese order of things by beginning with Chinese Parsley with Sliced Fish, which is a violation because it is a soup, which traditionally is eaten later in the meal. Whenever you eat it, it is a strong fish broth, perfumed with the scent of coriander leaves and studded with slivers of fresh ginger and hefty chunks of fried fish. If you prefer your fish unmoistened, there is available a Fried Sweet and Sour Sea Bass, the whole immense fish presented on a platter, hot and crusty, inundated in a sweet red sauce and slivered vegetables—this is more of a production than a delicacy, but there is no denying the freshness of the fish. The Sauté Flounder Balls are not spherical, neither are they good—on occasion the chunks of flounder have been a day over the hill. The carrots and water chestnuts that are part of the potpourri are OK, and the chunks of zucchini that were dry-sautéed in oil before they were mingled in are juicy and crunchy and almost save the dish.

Sticking with the house orthography we move on to Szechuan Style Sauté Shrimp, a huge mound of crisp crustaceans in a hot oily sauce, all under a liberal sprinkling of scallion greens—an impeccable dish, even if the shrimp lack the flavor of the unfrozen article.

The title Preserved Bean Curd with Watercress may mislead you, for this is mainly the cress, an immense mound of it, strong and grassy, bits of ginger here and there, in a broth that is thickened with bean curd—wherefore the name.

Good duck dishes, including Braised Duck with Mushrooms, hefty slices of a juicy crisped bird, surrounded by crisp broccoli and covered over with broad mushroom caps that are dark, firm and nutty, everything lightly moistened with a salty brown sauce.

Avoid such things as Crispy Fried Spare Ribs with Sweet & Sour Sauce, a grotesque array of tomatoes, pineapple, green peppers and too much more. Avoid just as assiduously the Chinese Style Broiled Beef, a leaden pot roast that satisfies certain hungers for slabs of beef.

★ SIMON'S

75 West 68th Street
LUNCH, SUNDAY TO FRIDAY; DINNER, DAILY.
Reservations, 496-7477.
Credit cards: AE, CB, DC, MC, V.
Expensive.

Simon's is very much the subterranean hideaway. You must go down some steps, around a corner, along a dark corridor to gain entrance to its dark, low-ceilinged intimacy. There is also something sassy about Simon's, serving, as it does, fancy food at high prices in a hole in the ground. The walls of its dining room are of brick or weathered wood. On them are mounted glitzy Deco mirrors of black and gray and silver. The small tables are covered with snowy linen, just as if this were any old ritzy spot. The illumination—if it can quite be called that—is from dim, naked, unfrosted light bulbs that protrude from porcelain fixtures mounted on the walls. The ends of the feeble lamps are silvered over the way exterior light bulbs were for wartime dimouts. These lights are visible, but they do not make other things visible, so the tiny candle on your table is indispensable. First of all, you read the menu by its light. And only with its aid can you discern the frontier between your meat and your potatoes. One evening your waitress is dressed in a black jumpsuit, Argyles and running shoes. Another night your waiter wears a Simon's T-shirt. Some nights the whole staff wears them (except for the guitarist at the front end of the room, who plinks softly and seems to lull himself to sleep as he does so).

If you must wait for a table, you do it at the tiny liquor bar-cum-oyster bar, behind which the bartender pours drinks, dispenses wine, cracks open mollusks and serves them to you on ice. You can have your oysters plain or with lemon (80 cents per oyster), or (at higher prices) with such admixtures as pickled ginger, sauce vinaigrette, horseradish, tomato and wasabi, caviar. All but the caviar work well with the blue-points. You select the preparation you want from the oyster menu.

From the regular menu (which changes from time to time and is always augmented by specials of the day), you select smoked duck breast with figs, firm little slabs of the rich, pungent meat and slivers of juicy dark fig arranged around a mound of duck meat and walnuts bathed in oil. Or you choose the rabbit-veal-and-pork terrine, a moist and well-flavored forcemeat wrapped in silken white fat, studded with hazelnuts, a core of sweet, fruity prunes at its center. You have had better carpaccio—this slice of beef has lost its bloom, the thin mustard with which it is moistened does not conceal the fact, and the three garnishes—pickled ginger, capers, a mound of chopped parsley—seem like the current stages of an ongoing experiment. An appetizer of sweetbreads is served with dressed vegetables, sometimes asparagus, sometimes string beans—the morsels of almost fluffy meat are artfully browned and crisped, and the vegetables are in a mustard vinaigrette that is laced with bits of tomato. The pasta has the strong, homey flavor of egg noodles at their best. The noodles are fine when they are served in a sauce of dried, oiled tomatoes, with pine nuts and cheese. But with smoked salmon, chives and cream, the egg quality of the noodles argues with the smokiness of the fish. At Simon's you get a salad after your first course—good watercress and lettuce in a light dressing, with a small slice of mild goat cheese.

The coho salmon grenobloise is the entire pink fish—its bones removed—floured and sautéed in its skin, and strewn with capers that have been warmed in butter and then mingled with croutons. This is a couple of steps away from what is usually meant by "grenobloise," but the variation is a good one, even if the fish is a little overcooked. The red snapper is filleted and browned—it is fresh, moist, perhaps a little mild for being prepared without its bones, served in a gentle sauce touched with tomato and basil. Wonderful bay scallops are sautéed and served in a buttery sauce that is flavored with Pernod. A strong sauce of roasted red peppers is served on the side, and you add it to the scallops according to your lights. What Simon's calls cassoulet you would call a stew of four meats—lamb, duck, sweetbreads and sausage—in a winy sauce, garnished with white beans that are combined with chopped celery and carrots. This is very nice food, but if you were expecting cassoulet, you will probably be surprised, maybe disappointed. The tournedos is billed as "with wild mushrooms," but it is served with button mushrooms to which a couple of wild ones have been added. The meat itself —filet mignon—is tender and perfectly cooked, but bland, as this meat often is. Many times better is the giant butterflied veal chop, stuffed with fresh spinach and served in a dark, char-flavored sauce that is thick with truffles. The rack of lamb (served for two) is good, strong-flavored meat, its surface herbed and crusted, the whole moistened with a light tomato sauce.

The apple pie with Cheddar cheese is dreadful. The coffee meringue—coffee ice cream on a chewy meringue under chocolate syrup—is a harmless sweet. A sometimes available apple tart is notable for the tangy, barely cooked crispness of its fruit, and for the lightness of its pastry. When you order sherbet you get three tennis-ball-size dollops of three different colors and flavors, mango and grapefruit often among them.

★ 65 IRVING PLACE

65 Irving Place (at 18th Street)
LUNCH, SUNDAY TO FRIDAY; DINNER, DAILY.
Reservations, 673-3939.
Credit cards: AE, CB, DC, MC, V.
Expensive.

Four connected rooms running west on 18th Street from the corner of Irving Place: a barroom, with a short bar, a few marble-topped cocktail tables, and a row of dining tables along a wooden banquette from which you may watch the youngsters in the windowed, tile-enclosed kitchen that occupies the inner corner of this room; and three dining rooms, the walls of which are covered with a dark, jungly wallpaper of greenery and pale blossoms. Framed mirrors hang here and there, plain chairs surround the white-linened tables. The restaurant is windowed all along its outer perimeter, hanging plants at the top of the glass panels, lace curtains below. You could mistake the place for fancy, and some people do. Accordingly, it gets its share of a certain crowd. One large group of achievers quickly reaches unanimity (in the affirmative) on the proposition "A good salesman can sell anything." But the restaurant also attracts an artsier, more tasteful Gramercy Park set.

You are served by comely young waitresses in black trousers, white shirts and black bow ties. Their formality, however, is only fabric-deep. Through an ajar door to the kitchen, you observe one of them idly appraising a sauce by dipping her fingers therein, then sucking the tips thereof, a pastime in which she is encouraged by one of the young men in kitchen whites who, while she samples, affectionately applies his open-handed approval to her posterior: 65 Irving is a cheerful place.

But you will not invariably cheer about the food. The mussels steamed with saffron, for example, have taken on a lot of saffron flavor and given up all their ocean sweetness in the process. The morels in pastry shells are $6.50, so you assume you will be getting morels, not a few of those and a lot of other mushrooms. The pastry is flaky, the morels tantalizing, and the pink, creamy and slightly acidic sauce is fine, but there is much between the billing and the reality. Very good carpaccio, but the tasty raw beef is carved by a microsurgeon, for the slices are about as hefty as Saran Wrap—you moisten them with a green sauce that is rich, tart, crunchy; or you roll the meat into a ball the size of a pea and devise a game for it: delicious food, but not to be shared. ($6.) The nutted duck pâté is cold and dry, the strong mustard with which it is served essential not only for flavor but for heat and moisture. It may be best to start with the Caesar salad, for even though you will not find therein the anchovies one reasonably expects from the title, the romaine lettuce is fresh and crisp and unblemished, and the dressing is vibrant with strong cheese.

Each day a pasta dish is served, on occasion carefully cooked green and white noodles in a rich ricotta sauce that is studded with fresh green peas, alive with crinkly parsley. But on occasion those same noodles, just as carefully cooked, are sauced with an apparently improvised collection of peas and peppers and herbs—good ingredients taken to no particular end.

Your host informs you that the breast of chicken en croûte is prepared with seeded Jarlsberg cheese and ham, and he is half right, yours arriving sans red meat. This is a niftily turned out dish: shining like a little loaf of just baked bread, sprinkled with seeds, in a white sauce that adds much needed moisture and richness, for the chicken is dry and bland—the ham would probably help; the seeds of the cheese are a misplaced note. The veal paillard is of good, tender meat, crisscrossed with faint black lines, just touched with the flavor of charring. Good pork chops, a pair of them, connected at the bone, a black paste of stewed prunes between them, are served with a sweet, dark sauce.

Escarole and garlic are listed as part of the liver dish, but the garlic is remote, the escarole simply a leaf on which the nicely grilled meat is served—a good, simple dish that is better than what it claims to be. You may get the rack of lamb "for 2" for one, and it is probably the best main course in the house—here the garlic is unmistakable in the herbed breading that coats the juicy, tender, plump red meat encased in the blackened ribs. Nowadays you are rarely served a tough steak, but 65 Irving remembers how. This steak is marinated in oil and herbs, and the charred herbs on the surface add a nice note. But they do not offset your labors.

The cheeses are not brilliantly chosen. A chalky, red-rinded so-called Fontina is almost inedible, and that seeded Jarlsberg is surely intended to be cut into dice and served on toothpicks with gin. Better selections are sometimes offered. The tarts are nice; the custard between the fresh fruit and browned pastry is lightly liquored—the one of raspberries and ground hazelnuts is exceptional. The linzer torte, with its latticework pastry over thick raspberry preserves, is close to perfect. And the lemon tart, a triangular wedge cut from a great circular wafer, is acidic and sugary, browned dark, the flavor of rind vivid. The chocolate cake—made with ground walnuts in place of flour—is crunchy and buttery, and it has an intensity of chocolate flavor.

Despite its shortcomings it is easy to enjoy this comfortable place; somewhat less easy, but quite possible, to eat well.

• SLOPPY LOUIE'S

92 South Street (near John Street)
LUNCH AND DINNER. CLOSED SATURDAY AND SUNDAY.
No reservations (952-9657).
No credit cards.
No liquor.
Inexpensive.

Once upon a time, this ramshackle old box of a store was the fairly well kept secret of its not insubstantial following. It was the quintessential hole-in-the-wall-with-surprisingly-good-food. You brought someone here to observe his dismay at first sight of the place, his subsequent relief and astonishment at his first bite of food. You will still elicit the dismay easily enough, but the relief and astonishment are more difficult to arrange.

Along each side of the primitive dining room a row of long communal tables of dark wood are set with paper place mats and equipped with dispensers of paper napkins and a bottle each of ketchup and hot sauce. Overhead the stamped-tin ceiling is undulant, like a choppy sea upside down. The floor is of asphalt tile. The walls are painted a cheerful tone of surplus-paint pea green, and they, and their built-in mirrors, are festooned with flounder-shaped paper posters, on each of which is written the name of an available variety of fish. There is a stopped clock on the wall, a hoary mounted fish, an old red lobster shell, dreary prints, coat hooks. Coffee urns occupy one rear corner, an ice machine stands in the other.

The waiters are as close to wordless as it is possible to be in that profession. One fellow simply closes his eyes and shakes his head when one of the items you order is not available. If you happen not to be looking right at him at that moment, you will expect the dish but not get it. As far as can be determined, food is brought to you and set down as soon as it is ready, whether or not you have finished your previous course. The young people who crowd this place do not mind. They just take another gulp of iced tea and eat faster. Louie's sells no alcohol. The popular drinks are iced tea, Coke, water. Cans of brought-in beer and an occasional bottle of wine are also seen, but this is not much of a setting for drifting into a hazy good mood.

The raw oysters and clams are fine, cold and recently opened. The meat in the crabmeat cocktail is only somewhat separated from its cartilage. The broth of the oyster stew is of milk imperfectly combined with butter, so the latter floats greasily upon the former. The fish chowder is ruinously thick with cornstarch.

Though this place is best at broiled fish, the talent does not much reveal itself in the broiled seafood combination—five small slices of saltwater fish, served in a tight little row with lemon and tartar sauce. The fish—bluefish, salmon, lemon sole among them—are all fresh and prettily browned, but because each slice is small, and because they are cooked together, inevitably a couple of them are overcooked and lose some of their moisture. But the restaurant makes splendid full portions of broiled snapper, gray sole, swordfish; and very nice broiled scallops, browned and a little buttery. The so-called shrimp creole is of sweet shrimp, but the rather obvious celery-onion-and-tomato sauce is not a sauce at all, just a combination of ingredients. Louie's vegetables are kept in a steam table, and show it. Louie's French fries cry out for ketchup.

The peach shortcake is made of canned peaches, the strawberry shortcake of frozen berries. Your obvious choice is the banana shortcake, which, like the others, is topped with excellent whipped cream. Ice cream is available.

★ SMITH & WOLLENSKY

201 East 49th Street
LUNCH AND DINNER.
Reservations, 753-1530.
Credit cards: AE, CB, DC, MC, V.
Very expensive.

An admirable audacity was at work when Smith & Wollensky was dreamed up, for the place violates, or seems to violate, a law of nature—that you cannot re-create the past. If some determined maniac came along and spent his life making up, say, a "Bach" cantata and finally succeeded in producing a work that was perfectly in the style, not a note wrong, every word apt, there would still be something missing: genuineness. This is not a conceit having to do with the mere fact that Bach did not write the cantata. The work will simply not wear well. Eventually it will sound wrong, even though at first it could not be faulted. Smith & Wollensky, however, which is only a couple of years old, is rapidly becoming the real thing. More and more the place seems to be out of the distant past. It is possible that in five years it will seem to be fifty years old, rather than what it is—a 1970s takeoff on restaurants that were born in the Depression.

There is nothing new in modern interpretations of old styles. But Smith & Wollensky is not that. It is, rather, very close to a steal, a ripoff. And yet the place does not offend. This is because the borrowings—of style and artifacts—were so lovingly assembled that the imitation became a tribute. Smith & Wollensky is a bit of the Palm, Christ Cella, Pietro's, Joe & Rose. Many details are strictly its own, but they are subsumed in the powerful old flavor of New York's durable steakhouses, places that seem to consist of little more than tables and chairs and aisles between, the only adornments relics that were passively accumulated over the decades. Walking into Smith & Wollensky for the first time is like discovering that your lover has a new body. What is important about new bodies for old lovers, you understand, is not the new body, but the old lover. If you love Pietro's, Joe & Rose, all those places, you will, willy-nilly, love this place. Smith & Wollensky is familiar even if you have never made love to it before. You do not have to get to know it. You already know it. And sure enough, habitués of the Palm, etc., have become regulars at this place too. They settled in as if they had been coming here for years.

The vast space that was the hideously adorned Manny Wolf's, now happily departed, has been cleverly cut up into rooms of odd sizes and shapes, one of them on a level slightly higher than the others. The intended impression is of a restaurant that grew over the years by the addition of now one room, now another. Each room is furnished a little differently from the rest, but all are well within the Plain Style.

You enter to an anteroom that is dominated by two huge clocks, their handsome circular faces in handsome wooden frames, each pair of hands stating the correct time, one in Roman, the other in Arabic numerals. To your left is the big barroom, the bar itself surfaced with polished copper, faced with dark marble and rimmed at its base with the standard brass rail. Ancient hanging lamps of white glass glow softly over the bar along its length. Behind the bar there is an island of liquor bottles, against the wall old wooden wine cabinets and glass liquor closets that look like the shells of Wurlitzer jukeboxes. There are little bowls of hot fried zucchini and cottage-fried potatoes on the copper counter, and most of the time there are plenty of people standing along its length, nibbling and tippling. The rest of the barroom is filled out with a dozen bare wooden tables, and during meal times some of those are spread with linen for people who want to eat where the drinking is. The restaurant's walls—of plaster, brick or stamped tin—are painted a warm pale beige, the lower portions faced with dark polished wood that is trimmed along the top with a broad band of marble. The large central room is spread with tables and chairs, and the raised room, which affords a nice view of the whole place, is fitted out with a row of commodious old booths. A rather barren room on the Third Avenue side of the restaurant is rimmed with a banquette of tufted simulated reddish-brown leather. There are sporting prints on the walls, old photographs of the hundreds in attendance at long-ago banquet parties. A glass-enclosed old fire engine model hangs on a wall of stamped tin. Antique breakfronts are the waiters' service stands, and a big wood-and-glass-doored icebox is filled with racks of chilled wine. The kitchen is open to your view, and a huge circular table occupies the space right outside its entrance, clearly an echo of the big table in the Christ Cella kitchen. The waiters, in putty-colored "linen" jackets and brown-and-white polka dot ties, stride around on plain hardwood floors. They are mostly young, eager, polite, helpful, except for a few standard New York bumblers who have apparently been retained for atmosphere. (They learned their trade in the old school, where a hardworking waiter was one who talked to three tables at once.) The place hums, but it is not noisy. There is no sawdust on the floor.

The problem here is that the food is not invariably wonderful. If you read on you will learn what to eat and what to avoid, and you will be able to assemble a sturdy dinner of good food. But the fact is that Smith & Wollensky has not mastered the much glorified but basically simple task of producing good broiled steaks. The ones you get here are okay, but not the equal of the best in town.

The place does, however, serve up the most elegant lobster cocktail of any restaurant in New York. It consists of a small lobster, bifurcated and spread out on a plate of ice, garnished with two halves of a lemon and a little ramekin of sparkling cocktail sauce. The shrimp cocktail is a joke by comparison, the crabmeat cocktail—substantial shafts of red-flecked fresh meat that are garnished like the lobster—a little bland, albeit very nice. When they broil those shrimps you get the benefit of peppery butter, but these are still contemporary shrimps and not worth the bother. Sometimes there is cold bass, and it is fresh, strong-tasting and served with splendid herbed mayonnaise. Good prosciutto and melon is served here, the meat smoky and strong, the fruit ripe and sweet.

Smith & Wollensky charcoals its steaks instead of searing them in gas flames. This imparts a carbon flavor to the meat that some adore, some abhor. That is merely a question of taste. The difficulty is that here at S & W the beef is not the ultimate in satiny, fat-streaked, juicy, tender solidity. One steak is a little grainy, another a bit dry, another slightly tough. They are accurately prepared, but the place never seems to serve up that wondrous chunk of blood-rich meat that is right at the heart of the good life. The lamb chops are the best broilings in the house, plump triple-rib chops, the flavor of well-fatted lamb sealed within charred crusts. The prime ribs are the best beef—the rare slices really rare, rather than painted with trick juices, the roasted crust a nice salty foil to the pink meat. The veal chops are simply nowhere.

And then there is the matter of chopped beef. Many a carnivore of discriminating palate finds ground beef the ultimate beef. You may think of it as the low-price item on the menu, what to foist on the kiddies if you bring them along. But a perfectly made chopped steak is a marvel of juiciness, flavor and texture. To make one right, you chop the meat (with a knife, ideally) just before you prepare it. The chopped meat at S & W is chopped well in advance, and so the chopped steaks are both dry and mushy.

Then there is the lobster. If you ask for a broiled lobster, you get a steamed lobster that is stuck under the broiler just before it is served. This way you steam away some of the lobster's flavor and then toughen it by broiling it after it is cooked. Broiling is the ultimate lobster preparation, but it is also the most demanding. S & W does not even undertake it, which is a pity, for the lobsters are of good quality.

Terrific hash brown potatoes, crusty and salty and firm, shot through with sautéed onions. The cottage fries are crunchy and salty, the French-fried zucchini a little limp, the French-fried onions crinkly, crisp, sweet and, like everything else in this place, abundant.

Sometimes you get first-class strawberries here, and they come with real—albeit excessively sugared—whipped cream. And sometimes there is apple pie, individual little pies that are warm, strongly flavored with cinnamon, studded with raisins and moistened with a milky, vanilla-flavored sauce. The cheese cake is a good version of the usual rich thing, the pignoli cake is a liquored mush and the fruit cup—of fresh fruits—is crisp, colorful and refreshing.

The crowd is decorous and largely male—admen, customer's men from the nearby brokerage offices, barristers from Paul Weiss, corporate success stories from every department (sales, manufacturing, finance), and self-made entrepreneurs from every commerce (goods, services, illusions). Says one gent to a lady lucky enough to be along for the feed: "You want to meet some important people? Okay. You'll meet important people. Next Tuesday."

All the wines except for the sparkling wines are American, and there are several good bottles on the brief list.

• SPARKS

210 East 46th Street
LUNCH, MONDAY TO FRIDAY; DINNER, MONDAY TO SATURDAY. CLOSED SUNDAY.
Reservations, 687-4855.
Credit cards: AE, DC, MC, V.
Very expensive.

A few years ago Sparks moved uptown from East 18th Street and thereby took on as competition the established steakhouses of so-called Steak Row, the famous collection of beef palaces clustered in Manhattan's East 40s. The Cetta Brothers, proprietors, had promoted their downtown place—in semiliterate block-letter advertisements—as a top-quality steakhouse, equal to the best, selling steaks and trimmings at half the price of the midtown spots. But when the Cettas moved to East 46th Street, the low-price aspect of their hard sell was dropped. Sparks did do some advertising when the new store opened, but the principal promotional ploy was a $2,000,000 lawsuit against the *Times* and its restaurant critic in response to an unfavorable review. That has proved very effective. For when *New York* magazine's Gael Greene finally delivered her giant work on New York steakhouses she not only took Sparks seriously, but treated it with the kind of respect that is usually reserved for dead heroes.

The new Sparks is done up in *fin de siècle* New Orleans Bordello. But instead of gaslights in the etched-glass chandeliers, there are pale pink incandescents; instead of a plump and friendly Madame, there is a bored host; and instead of sex on the customers' minds, there is absolutely nothing. Anybody who chooses this place in favor of its nearby competition would choose Goneril over Cordelia.

Sparks is a pretty big place, with broadloom carpeting, shiny trowel-marked walls that look like faded icing, dark wood, brass rails and plastic upholstery. Dim landscapes and rococo clocks adorn, presumably, the walls. And at the front of the room there is an immense, ornate, baronial breakfront of pale wood that would easily dominate the lobby of the Metropolitan Opera House. It is used for the storage and display of wine, some of it very good stuff, including Jeroboams of great Bordeaux. They must be mainly intended for display, for at 70° Fahrenheit and more, they are becoming less and less valuable with age.

Waitresses work one corner of the room, waiters the rest of the place. Most of both groups are willing and able, but a couple of the gents comport themselves like bitter thugs who would be out of this jail and away from this tedious work in a trice if the guards relaxed their watch.

The food is not vile so much as it is dead: raw clams that are fresh, but probably opened hours before serving, so that they are flat; baked clams that seem to be breaded with packaged bird stuffing; a shrimp cocktail of tasteless, frozen shrimp; and broiled shrimp that come with a lemon butter that lacks lemon. At Sparks you discover that unripe Cranshaw melon tastes like watermelon. The mixed green salad is crisp, but the house dressing is a thickened complexity that would befuddle analysis if it did not dull curiosity. The dish to start with is sliced tomatoes and onions—the tomatoes are pretty good for these days, the rings of red onion are crisp and strong, and the simple vinaigrette is impeccable.

The steaks here are sometimes dry near the surface, especially if cooked past rare, and both the filets mignons and the sirloins, though seared and accurately cooked, lack the juicy firmness and the high flavor of the best beef. At your command Sparks will degrade your meat even further—Beef Scallopini is a stewlike sauté of meat, peppers and mushrooms in an inspid sauce; and Steak Fromage (rhymes with *dommage*) is the regular tolerable sirloin surmounted by what seems to be cold, blenderized Roquefort foam.

The red snapper is a nameless white substance in a tasteless breading, the scallops little white lumps of denatured seafood. The lobsters, however, are not bad, though the so-called broiled lobsters are only broiled after steaming. Under those conditions you are better off with the steamed—they are occasionally a little overcooked, but are by and large the best main course in the place.

They bake lots of potatoes here, and toward the end of the evening they are leathery outside, powdery inside. The hash browns seem to be batter-fried—in place of potato flavor you get the taste of brown crust, which can be very good.

The cheese cake is the most insipid kind of goo, the strawberries are not invariably ripe and the whipped cream that is served with the berries is made with that miracle cream of perpetual shelf-life and no other life. The thing to have is the Bassett's double chocolate chip ice cream—perfect.

Sparks has a substantial following—people from the traffic side of industry, the financial side of communications and the bookeeping side of the professions. If you want to conduct a secret affair, this is the place. No one you want to know will ever spot you here.

★★ SUSHIKO

251 West 55th Street
LUNCH, MONDAY TO FRIDAY; DINNER, MONDAY TO SATURDAY. CLOSED SUNDAY.
Reservations, 974–9721.
Credit cards: AE, CB, DC, MC, V.
Medium-priced.

The neighborhood seems to be picketed, but the pickets are not carrying signs. In this part of town, hard by Eighth Avenue, there is much traipsing, up and down the streets, by bizarrely attired female humanoids whose leisurely gait tells much about their occupation. But assuming that the lure of raw fish is more compelling than their blandishments, or that by reason of gender the latter were not directed your way, you make it to and enter this humble restaurant in the humbler half of the humbler half of Manhattan's midtown. There are gilded paper lanterns hanging in the front window, but there the *luxe* ends. Within, there are splintery bamboo walls, yellow oilcloth on the dozen or so tables, rickety rice-paper lanterns. There are also adornments—a Kirin Beer calendar (scenic), a telephone (pay). Behind it all, the plinking and wailing of recorded Japanese music, and when that lets up, the murmur of the Japanese language. The place has a substantial Japanese clientele, including not just the neat and clean executives that habituate the swanker restaurants on the less humble, East Side half of midtown, but women and children and menials, too, drawn by the low prices and creating, in their aggregate, a more homey ambiance than the aura of officers' mess you experience when surrounded by dozens of close-tonsured black-haired men in impeccable suits.

The sushi bar that is the off-to-one-side hub of the dining room is manned by hirsute Japanese youths whose lank hair, casual white garb and offhand manner are no clues to the neat things they do with the fresh seafoods that are the principal ingredients in the sashimi and sushi served here. This is one of the best restaurants for raw fish in New York, and the place to enjoy it is on one of the half dozen stools at the little bar, where you can point at any item on display, ask its identity, struggle with the heavily accented polite answer, try it despite your lack of new information, and have a wonderful time.

You sit down to paper napkins, little chopsticks in a paper sheath; you are brought a warm moist square of terry cloth on a little bamboo canoe, and if you are at a table instead of at the bar or if you want hot food served to you at the sushi bar, a seven-page menu in a hangdog folder, the first page of which is an ardent paean to the pleasures of eating in Sushiko, albeit with some good advice: "Sushi is for the true connoisseur. . . . Eaten with beer, Sake or whiskey, there is no equal in this world." Hyperbole aside, those are the right beverages for this food.

You put yourself in the hands of the youngster behind the bar; he places a clump of moist pink pickled ginger before you, on a little board, the ginger shaped to a pyramid by his nimble fingers. (If you do not enjoy seeing the food you are about to get fingered, eat at a table.) You are started off with slices of dark-red tuna, soft and velvety, around moist rice and a sharp mustard that seems to clear the head. Then some mackerel, distinctly fishy compared to the tuna, also on rice, and sprinkled with sesame seeds on the silvery skin, for a crunchy, grainy accent. Next, though only for willing experimenters, raw abalone, a tough and inky-tasting and cartilaginous meat, with a stormy-oceanic flavor that calls for a calm interlude of raw squid—a very rich, almost buttery raw seafood that is enhanced by a moistening of soy sauce.

The second movement also begins with the tuna theme, but in this variation the fish and rice are formed into cylinders within a wrapping of crinkly seaweed sheet, and one-inch discs are cut off and served in pairs. Then we return to the abalone motif, but this time the resilient sinew has been tamed by boiling and made succulent with a sauce that is thick and brown, like warm chocolate—your server explains informatively that it is "special sauce." And if you have been swallowing everything placed before you without making a face, you qualify for some Japanese eel—it is salted and smoked in Japan, and it is behind the counter window in a little wooden box, and you will like it if you like smoked, rubbery, jellied salt.

Of course, you needn't go the whole route.

Having warmed up on seafood, you proceed to meat, which will, if you wish, be served to you at the sushi bar. And while you are waiting for it, you may observe an egg loaf, deep-yellow, lightly browned, being sliced behind the bar for delivery to some of the Japanese customers. Get a slice—it is steamy and sweet and firm, a rolled Japanese omelet, made in clear oil.

Now your Katsu Don arrives—thin slices of breaded pork, made in an eggy batter, served with onions and mushrooms, atop a bowl of rice. Or else your Gyu Don—beef that is barely steamed, very tender, with delicate slivers of sweet onion, on rice. Of course there are good versions of teriyaki and yakitori, and so on, but as the principal attraction of the place is the products of the sushi bar, a properly gluttonous approach to that may dictate a restrained one toward meat. You have to watch out for the man behind the bar. As you are about to wipe your lips for the last time, he hits you with some charcoaled tuna stomach, hot and sweet (you really do well here sampling what the knowing Orientals have made for them), and it is very hard to resist the oily fish with the sharp accent of the charred parts.

At the real end, someone will bring you a nice hot glass tea.

★ SWEETS

2 Fulton Street (near South Street)
LUNCH AND DINNER. CLOSED SATURDAY AND SUNDAY.
No reservations (344-9189).
No credit cards.
Medium-priced.

You can see the Brooklyn Bridge and you can smell the Fulton Fish Market from the street outside the ancient squat building that houses this 140-year-old relic. The restaurant is one flight up the iron stairs, and on occasion, at lunchtime, the waiting line extends down those stairs and into that street. The place attracts folks who are proud of their resistance to fads. They wear white shirts, smoke Lucky Strikes, drink Manhattans before, Budweiser with. Order a bottle of wine in this place, and your waiter looks around desperately for help. Once it was widely believed that the waiters at Sweets were the rudest in New York. But most of the members of the championship team of the sixties and seventies have been retired now, and the current crew specializes instead in absence, both of body and mind. It is not unusual to wait twenty minutes for the privilege of ordering a bottle of beer, another ten to get it. And however long it takes for your snapper to get cold may be how long it takes for your companion to be served his bass. One waiter here, trying to free a little room on a crowded table, pours the last couple of inches out of your bottle of Beck's into your guest's glass of Michelob. No one has ever pointed out to the busboys that violently flinging plates into a tub of dishes sometimes causes bemused diners to drop their forks and leap up in alarm. If you are seated at the west end of this restaurant, the din is augmented by the sounds of the kitchen, which are apparently amplified and pumped out at you.

The walls of the restaurant are faced with pale plastic "wood" paneling. The illumination is sufficient unto an operating room. The hardwood floors slope down from the outer walls. Air conditioning has not been introduced. A row of electric fans has been mounted on the long wall—they swivel, each to the beat of its own drummer, like a disorganized chorus line or a string section in which each player has his own ideas about the bowing—whence, on hot days, they blow hot air from one place to another.

Happily, the food, though often flawed, is better than anything else about the place. The lobster and crabmeat cocktails are of fresh, cool meat, served with decent cocktail sauce, though all that can be said of the house shrimp is that they are without the medicinal taste that seems to accompany them all over town. The fried oysters—battered and lightly browned in deep fat—are warm and tender within their quite delicate crust. You can have those oysters broiled—they are prepared out of their shells, on toast, and they are heavily buttered and browned, a treatment that does nothing for them. The abundance of butter on your plate (as in many of the dishes here) makes a greasy setting. You cannot be sure the house will not cook the clam stew too long in its hot milk (you can have yours in cream), and clams get tough when they are overcooked.

But the strength of this place is its broiled fish. Each huge serving is impeccably fresh, breaded, buttered, and prepared on the metal platter on which it is then served to you. You can get a salmon steak that is about the size of a one-inch center cut from a medium-size watermelon—it is pink, rimmed with blackened skin, succulent. A remarkable halibut steak has about two-thirds that diameter and twice the thickness—its white interior falls into sweet, moist flakes. For something louder, there is mackerel, the meat of which is oily and strong. The giant portion of snapper is fluffy, the equally immense serving of striped bass more resilient, but just as fresh and juicy. The broiled bay scallops (of which you are given about three dozen) are knee-deep in butter, which is too bad, and the breading and browning of these little morsels in that much fat does away with their character—still, this is decent food. Finnan haddie (smoked, salted haddock) is served several ways, including an alleged "au gratin." The strong, smoky fish appears simply to be breaded, buttered, baked, yielding a hefty plate of food, but without the cheese the title leads you to expect. The home-fried, lyonnaise and hashed-brown potatoes are splendid.

You may have pecan pie in which the nuts are vastly outnumbered by the corn syrup.

Nesselrode pie, the egregious rum-flavored concoction of custard and candied fruit, is offered in a perfect version. The cheese cake is a watery clay, the chocolate rum cake a gooey one. There are stewed prunes.

The wine list, though brief, has exceptional depth in Portuguese rosés.

★★ SWISS INN

882 First Avenue (near 49th Street)
LUNCH, MONDAY TO FRIDAY; DINNER, MONDAY TO SATURDAY. CLOSED SUNDAY.
Reservations, 758-3258.
Credit cards: AE, CB, DC, MC, V.
Medium-priced.

Though this restaurant has had three New York sites in its lifetime (which extends back to the sixties), it always manages to look as if it has been hidden away in its locale since the dawn of the neighborhood. Though sometimes busy for lunch, it is a sleepy place in the evening. The reasons are plain to see, for the homey establishment is out of place—seems to get lost—on this swinging avenue of garish matchmaking emporia-cum-food-and-booze. The Swiss Inn is a reliquary of Swiss kitsch, with framed flags of the Swiss cantons over the bar, a mountain climber's pick mounted on a brick wall, seriously intended hilarious oils (Boy with Cow, Still Life with Swiss Cheese), framed color photographs of Alpine vistas. But the place has all the comforts of a restaurant, including food that, if it is never inspired, is always decent, often yummy, and cheap.

For a mere $2.25 you will be brought a big, silvery slab of sour herring, firm and meaty, under a great dollop of sour cream that is laced with strong, crisp onions. The same fee may be exchanged for the wurstsalad, a mound of cool, pink and porky discs of sausage, over which marinated onions have been spread—they are tart, crisp, sharp. You get two slabs of headcheese for the money, a firm jelly studded with chunks of salty and cartilaginous organ meat, and moistened with a vinaigrette that is thick with onions and herbs. You get about ten thin slices of bündnerfleisch—the air-dried beef of Switzerland—arranged on a circular wooden board; the mahogany-colored meat is light and gamy. The Swiss Inn even turns out a creditable Russian egg, the shiny, hardcooked ovoid covered over with a garden salad—rich mayonnaise and crisp vegetables. The snails are the standard item in a rather obvious butter, to which too much alcohol has been added.

You can occupy yourself with cheese fondue and cool wine for a couple of hours, for the big pot of melted cheese—flavored with wine and garlic—is served to you on a burner, over which it simmers until you have had all you want. You impale a chunk of bread on a long fork and dip out the viscous substance. If you scrape bottom, you will come up with slivers of garlic. The fondue is served for two. Medallions of veal, beef and lamb, and a thin slice of liver, make up the mixed grill, in which the four good meats are arranged around a hot, juicy grilled tomato. More of that buttery veal, in thin slices, is served as medaillon de veau à la crème—fresh mushrooms are added to the wine-flavored cream sauce that coats the meat. On the prix-fixe side of the menu you will find ripple, smoked pork chops. You get two of them, fat and pink and glistening, leaning on opposite sides of a small mountain of very sour sauerkraut. Though no Swiss has ever set a lobster trap in his native land, this place offers lobsters from time to time, and they are fresh, of sweet ocean flavor, tender, not overcooked. And even if, for some reason, you hate every main course you get, you will go home content, for with dinner you are served rösti potatoes, in which partially precooked tubers are formed into a big pancake and pan-fried until they are browned and crusty —happily, if you finish your first serving, you may have another.

Most of the listed deserts are ice cream items or such standards as chocolate mousse and caramel custard in conventional versions. The apple tart is above average—the firm fruit is coated with an almost burnt caramelized sugar. If you want to go back to dipping, the chocolate fondue (served for two) becomes thicker and thicker as you diminish the amount in the bubbling pot by fishing out the hot brown syrup on chunks of pineapple, slices of apple, berries, grapes.

★★ SWISS PAVILION (Now closed)

4 West 49th Street
LUNCH, MONDAY TO FRIDAY; DINNER, MONDAY TO SATURDAY. CLOSED SUNDAY.
Reservations, 247–6545.
Credit cards: AE, CB, DC, MC, V.
Expensive.

This has always been potentially one of the best restaurants in New York. But there has always been one thing or another.

The food at the Swiss Pavilion is not only good but authentic. Even that is not necessarily a virtue, but this authenticity is more than just a matter of the right ingredients in the correct proportions; one has the feeling here that the food is prepared by people who grew up with it, people who care about its tasting the way it tasted in the original, who provide not just the technical quality called authenticity, but also authority grounded in tradition.

But the Swiss Pavilion seems to compromise itself, once it gets past the actual preparation of the food, by catering to certain popular tastes. The disproportionate number of flambés on the menu is one thing, of fondues another.

A third is the horseshoe bar, a before-dinner drink at which may lead you to suspect you have chanced into one of the many restaurant/dives in the neighborhood that make most of their money on the torrents of booze that pass over the bar during the cocktail hour. The customers, instead of the proprietors, run the place. It has become theirs, and it is noisy and sloppy, with empty bottles, messy-looking pots of cheese dip, stirrers, napkins and other assorted junk strewn about. You could overlook it, but sometimes the boys get a notion to have dinner here (not often), and when they do, they do not lower their voices.

In the handsome dining room, its walls hung with pennants, you are seated at settings of solid and graceful brown ware on soft, putty-colored linen. The service is not as professional as it once was (the dining room is no longer staffed by Swiss-trained Swiss, but by friendly and willing but still-learning South Americans of various nationalities). In the old days, for example, it would have been unthinkable for a captain to wave you back to the hatcheck room (if you got past it undetected and, thereby, got past the hostess); he would simply have seated you himself, or asked you to please wait while *he* went for the hostess.

But once the food starts coming, you are OK. You may begin with something called Ramequins—little quiches made with superior cheese and bits of meat and perfectly browned crusts; they are hot and aromatic, and they are delicious with cool red wine. Or you may start with Surprise au Céleri—a surprising and perfectly successful combination of poached apple, a delicate liver pâté, and crisp celery root, acidic, tasting almost raw, in a thick mayonnaise. If that does not seem ridiculous, take note that the dish is served with Cumberland sauce—lingonberries and orange—and that the sauce is delicious on these diverse ingredients.

The soups here are all very good, from the cold apricot soup to the hearty Basler Mehlsuppe, a beef-stock broth cooked with excellent strong-tasting flour. There is also one soup made on a base of chicken stock—it is called Schoppa Da Giuotta, and it is eggy, laden with big kernels of barley and bits of ham, and redolent of chicken fat—it is almost as thick as mayonnaise.

Among the flambés is one gaily entitled "Hühnerbrüstchen mit Orangen, flambiert." The chicken arrives at the serving stand already cooked—it is a chicken breast, stuffed with veal, nuts and honey. Your server combines this with orange, and he cooks it some more; he adds grapes and cooks it further, he tosses in some raisins and cooks and stirs again. Then he flames the event in Curaçao (after a couple of tries). The stuffing within the chicken breast is a little like a sausage, and the fruit-and-brandy sauce is very nice on the spicy meat. The dish is served with very good spinach, loud and salty.

The Tournedo aux Morilles is not invariably fashioned from a perfect slice of beef, but the sweet, crinkly mushrooms (morels) are spectacular, and the dish is served in a very good cream sauce made slightly sharp with a touch of brandy. The best things on the plate, however, are the almost unbelievable noodles—they are firm yet soft, the flavor of eggs is vivid without being in the least "eggy," and the butter they are moistened with is all they need—probably the best noodles in New York.

One very simple and good dessert: Öpfelchuechli. These (that's a plural) are apple rings that are deep-fried in beer batter right before your eyes (or under your nose, if you wish) and sprinkled with cinnamon and sugar. The inside is sweet and soft, the outside sweet and crisp—good stuff. The rhubarb pie is something else. It is quite tart, only slightly sweetened, and the excellent crust and good firm quality of the fruit notwithstanding, the dish requires learning to like.

★★TABLE D'HÔTE

44 East 92nd Street
DINNER. CLOSED SUNDAY AND MONDAY.
Reservations, 348-8125.
No credit cards.
No liquor.
Medium-priced.

The luxury of selecting your food, at a public eating place, from among a number of choices is a custom of comparatively recent origin—specifically, the late eighteenth century. Before then you showed up at the right time and place, and ate what everyone else ate. It must have been a pleasure not to suffer the decision-making process of your nearest and dearest. Questions like "Do you think I would like the duck" or "Do you think the sole is fresh" or "If I don't like my liver, will you switch with me" were not asked.

Get even with those who have made indecision a weapon and then turned it on you. Bring them to Table d'Hôte and watch them squirm. There is one fixed menu per night, no choices. The food is always good. And in such simple and charming surroundings an alternate form of torture may not suggest itself. Not responsible, however, for events of later in the evening.

Table d'Hôte is eight tables in an old store, in which nothing has been exactly renovated, but in which everything except the floor has been painted white: an ancient stamped-tin ceiling, patched in places—but not in others—where over the years fixtures and outlets were installed; the walls, which are of wood, and which are hung here and there with pans and pots and pottery and sundry utensils and old framed prints. The floor is barn red. The kitchen, off in one corner, and entered through a portal that is hung with a red cloth, is separated from the restaurant proper by partitions that do not reach the ceiling. Light that comes over the partitions from the kitchen, and the candles and lanterns on the tables, is all that illuminates the dining room. Withal, the place does not seem shoestring. Perhaps it is the unlinened tables, which, if they are not antique, are both old and in good repair; or the old patterned china; or the loose red cushions on the seats of the ancient chairs. The room is of a piece despite its seemingly random appointments. Only the single palm tree seems borrowed from someone else's notion of what goes into a restaurant dining room.

When the weather is fine, the front door is left open, with a string of cowbells hung across it. The bells ring when you unfasten the string. That is heard in the kitchen. So if no one of the staff is in the dining room when you come, you will be greeted promptly by someone who comes out of the kitchen for that purpose. There is one big plain store window on each side of the door, one choice table under each. The staff of three—two young women and a young man—apparently share all duties, though one of the women, presumably because of her exceptional charm and goodwill, is in the dining room more than the others.

You telephone to learn the components of the evening's fixed menu, and if you are interested, you reserve, obtain a bottle of wine and bring it with you.

Some of the dishes that have been served: a hot, clear chicken broth, its flavoring —of roots and herbs and seasoning—perfectly balanced and vivid, in it firm, meat-filled little tortellini; delicately poached leeks, still crisp, retaining a little of their onionlike strength, with a rich mayonnaise that is strewn with minced scallion greens; fresh and tiny bay scallops, crunchy shrimps, sweet and tender green peas, all in a delicate wine sauce, on rice, garnished with thin asparagus; slices of buttery veal, with slivers of sharp ham and mushrooms, in a wine sauce that is powerfully fragrant of strong sage. The salads are of fresh greens in an elemental oil-and-vinegar dressing that is seasoned with judicious restraint. If one evening's crème caramel seems, for its lightness and delicacy, like too little dessert, another night's chocolate mocha roll, of such freshness and lightness that it seems to have cooled from its preparation moments before you eat it, is more than ample.

It requires a bit of taking in, this odd storefront establishment on an Upper East Side block of formidable old brownstones. All evening long, locals pass by, read the posted menu, peer in the window. What they see, often, is every table taken by their neighbors, who are obviously comfortable and having a good time.

○ TAVERN ON THE GREEN

Central Park, at 67th Street and Central Park West
LUNCH AND DINNER.
Reservations, 873–3200.
Credit cards: AE, CB, DC, MC, V.
Very expensive.

When Frederick Law Olmsted built Central Park more than a century ago, he copied nature with man-made lakes, forests and meadows. The essential structures and roadways were invisible from most points in the park, as was most of the city outside. The place was truly bucolic then, right down to its birds and beasts. No Manhattanite was more than an hour from serenity. Eventually, of course, the park's horizon was disfigured by the huge buildings that became this city's specialty. And what are usually referred to as special interests managed to convert tracts of the park to nonpastoral uses.

But even if these 840 acres were thrown into permanent shade by a World Trade Center on Central Park South, and if the 79th Street Lake were drained, filled in and paved for stock-car racing, the insult to Olmsted's vision that is the new edition of Tavern on the Green would hardly be matched. This is the effulgence of vulgar ego, initials carved on a landscape. Tavern on the Green, however, is no greater threat to New York than the potentates who permitted it on city land. Hope rests with the citizens, and there are good signs—yes, the Tavern is packing them in, but the place is clogged not with New Yorkers, but with suburbanites, Texans and drunks (happily siphoned off from some of our town's more gracious eating places). The miraculous fact that some of the food served here is good makes no difference to them. Balloon strings in hand, they gobble down the tasty with the egregious in states of glazed, indiscriminate glee.

Fortunately, Warner Leroy has not yet devised a way to polka-dot the sky, and it is possible to avoid much of this establishment's posh honky-tonk by eating on the patio, which they call the Garden. Here there are several dozen white-enameled tables, many of them under fringed umbrellas. You are attended to by youngsters in garish yellow shirts, black bow ties and red aprons. They bring drinks (you pay when you receive, else you might escape over the low retaining wall into the freedom of the park), a bowl of iced raw vegetables, and a selection of foods from the Garden Menu, a brief version of the Elm Tree Room Menu, which is an expurgated rendition of the Crystal Room Menu. It is all hustle out here. A waiter takes your order, collects and goes off with, he hopes, a tip. Next round you are served by someone else, very likely. This minimizes customer-server bonds; and such niceties as clearing away the detritus of previous customers or your own accidents is attended to casually at best. At night, of course, it is dark out here, the illumination that is thrown on the bottom branches of the trees makes for little light on the ground, and hapless customers, some of them heavily sedated, have been seen stumbling and tripping over low-lying furniture and the borders of the swatches of earth that surround the trees. The Garden is L-shaped, and the best thing about it is that it is wrapped around the glass-walled Crystal Room, for the Crystal Room is a three-ring circus in one ring, which from outside looks like a silent movie of a three-ring circus in one ring, which is fun to watch.

The Crystal Room is a circular, glass-walled room containing ten crystal chandeliers that depend from a hard ceiling of pastel plaster, the petrified top of a birthday cake. Never mind that when you arrived at the Tavern you had to stand in line to tell a couple of arrogances that you were present, in hopes of being seated at the table you reserved for this very hour; never mind that this simply meant that you had to stand on yet another line; and never mind that these delays, which took you well past the hour of your reservation, led finally to a brief, escorted stroll to a table not yet made up. The simple facts are that people in glass houses shouldn't sing "Happy Birthday"; in this place you are sure to be serenaded with three or four shrieked, tuneless renditions of it per dinner; and within these hard walls every voice in the place is boosted to the tune of around eighty watts per channel. Glass, crystal, plaster, brick and hardwood floors —would anyone create a crowded restaurant room of these materials other than sadistically?

In much less demand is the Elm Tree Room (not far away, just down the corridor past the plaster reindeer). Here we have mostly wood, with brass and copper ornaments on the walls, partitions topped by long rows of golden globes the size of bowling balls, etched mirrors with park scenes of the nineteenth century. The room is roughly in two parts: the westernmost section, which includes the long curving bar, looks out on the parking lot, but when things are slow this is left unoccupied in favor of the several dozen tables near the kitchen. Now why do you suppose that is? Well, this room is a lot quieter than the Crystal Room, but when, as frequently happens, a busboy drops a tray of dishes when he collides with the dining-room side of the kitchen door, the unexpected report, like the sound of a hundred cannon in the newly improved acoustics of Avery Fisher Hall, is reflected at these very tables by a cannily positioned brick wall angled just for the purpose. Anyone who survives one of these events may sleep easy, for his cardiac arrest is not imminent.

To eat. Have a second choice ready, for half the things you order will be unavailable, often the very items the waiter recommends; and don't arrive too hungry, for there is no telling when you will be fed. Candidate for Worst Dish: Hot Pâté Périgourdine, rubbery sausages in a rubbery pastry—inedible. Contender: Quenelle of Pike with Sauce Nantua, a gelatinized and tasteless dumpling in a loud sauce that is only dimly of crayfish. Be smart: order the oysters, which are fresh; and command a pepper mill and use the lemon, for the horseradish was grated hours before and is moribund—who wants ketchup? (you get some in a thimble), and this third little cup that accompanies contains what must be a cleansing agent. Or a little less smart: Escargots Bourguignonne, about a dozen snails in a miniature frying pan that is laden with herbs in melted butter.

The menu informs you that "Tavern on the Green is proud to welcome as Chef de Cuisine the extraordinary Daniel Dunas, Recently Chef de Cuisine for 12 years at The Connaught Hotel, London." Like an idiot you therefore order Chicken Dunas, which is described as "Sautéed with Artichokes and Fresh Asparagus Velouté." You receive a half-cooked breast of chicken (it blushes within) drowning in a sauce that is little more than flour and water, some tolerable asparagus, and an artichoke heart that has been very gently simmered, for many hours, in a solution of brine and Tide. The Sweetbreads will put you in mind of the breaded veal cutlet you grew accustomed to when you were condemned to five school lunches a week.

And yet the fish is fresh, prepared to order and not overcooked, though the sauce that accompanies the Red Snapper Dijonnaise is little more than harsh mustard. And the Calf's Liver, Broiled Over Charcoal with Sage Butter is tender and accurately cooked, though the flavor of the charcoal is excessive, that of the sage imaginary.

Slivered almonds are added to the green salads, and that is not a bad note, though the dressing is too sour. A few cheeses are listed, but, as your waiter informs you at nine o'clock one evening, "Someone forgot to take it out of the icebox." Soufflés? "Sorry, we're not making them this evening." The sweet desserts are your basic plethoras. The Hazelnut Cheesecake with Strawberries must be eaten at once before it solidifies to concrete; the Chocolate Cake is insipid; something given as Praline & Strawberry Ice Cream Cake is a wedge-shaped sundae made with Hershey syrup; and the Banana Fritters come with a cinnamon sauce that tastes like a warm cinnamon lollipop soup, albeit the hot ripe bananas are pleasant in their crisp deep-fried batter.

Fashion note: diamond-studded cigarette holders are definitely in this season, as are little rhinestone butterflies directly on the lenses of the sunglasses that are on top of your hair. Dress flexibly, for the air conditioning is different things in different parts of the rooms.

The waiters are mostly young, earnest, well-meaning and really up against it in this madhouse. The wine list is extensive, and a couple of dozen of the wines have asterisks next to their names. The note informs you that these are "REASONABLY PRICED WINES." We may conclude that the others are unreasonably priced.

★ TENTH STREET CAFÉ

189 West 10th Street
LUNCH, SATURDAY AND SUNDAY; DINNER, TUESDAY TO SUNDAY. CLOSED MONDAY.
Reservations, 989-6765.
Credit cards: AE.
Expensive.

Things are slow, and the lady behind the bar, her gentleman friend, seated on the other side of the bar, and the hostess, seated beside him with her knees up against the armrest, are drinking and smoking and laughing it up at full throat, much in the manner of a set of talk-show panelists who have agreed in advance to appreciate one another's lines. As the Tenth Street Café is tiny, the carryings on more or less dominate the aural scene. You may either struggle hopelessly to enjoy the show, or carry on with equal vociferousness one of your own to drown it out. In fact much about the Café suggests that, as to the relationship between a place of public accommodation and its trade, this establishment could be labeled deviationist (if there were any sign that it was familiar with traditional standards in the first place). When your hostess is not on duty, your host is. His shirt is artfully unbuttoned, so as to provide just the teensiest peek at his navel. You get the distinct impression he would have got dressed up if he were not working this evening. One of his waiters goes around in the vest of a three-piece suit, from below the back of which his shirt billows. One and all they talk to you in the kind of conversational breeze which suggests that but moments before the flip of a coin determined which of you would carry and which eat. That style—or absence of style—is common these days, but it is even more tiresome than usual in a place that otherwise affects cool formality.

So cool, in fact, that even a crowd of people does not warm this place up. The restaurant is painted gray and it is softly lighted. The brightly colored and deadly modern art is behind glass, framed in metal. Just inside the restaurant's plate-glass façade hang vertical gray blinds. Gray carpeting cushions the floor. The high-backed chairs, of caning framed in black enamel, are the coldest note in the setting. The most amusing are the "vases" you will find on each table—they appear to be rocks, they are about the size of a small fish, and from holes in each of them protrude long stems bearing exotic flowers. A couple of tables for two are about the size of a large pizza. One chair at one of them is so situated that you cannot back away from your table in it when the table behind you is occupied. Instead you egress sideways, in the seated position, straightening up only when you are clear of your table top.

None of which seems to hurt the mostly good food that you select from the imaginative menu: about fifteen grilled mussels crowded back into five mussel shells that are prettily arranged on five leaves of fresh red lettuce—the mussels are moistened with a salty, lightly garlicked snail butter; so-called smoked salmon croustades, in which some rather ordinary, almost fishy smoked salmon is served in a couple of pastry boats with sour cream and dabs of black caviar—the dull pastry will make you long for a bagel, the dish itself for a slice of raw onion. A leek and prosciutto pie is a quiche in which most of the custard has been displaced by the meat and vegetable of the title— the hot, beautifully browned slice of pie is made with stout ham, sweet fresh leeks. A quattro formaggio pizza that outdoes itself some nights by being composed of five cheeses is about the size of a dinner plate, its base not pizza dough, but a light, flaky pastry; the ingredients with which it is topped (tomato, Parmesan, Port-Salut, Gruyère, mozzarella, Stilton) do not argue among themselves. Each day a pasta is offered, sometimes green and white noodles in a heavily parsleyed sauce of cream and Stilton —that particular cheese is odd-tasting with pasta, and the dish works best when there is only a little cheese in the sauce.

At $11.50 the pair, you figure the fish cakes will be something more elevated than college dining hall Friday lunch. They are composed of salmon as well as haddock, which makes them pink, but there the differences end. The light parsley sauce with which they are moistened, though not up to the task of ennobling the dish, does flatter it. But there is lovely freshness and lightness to the fillet of red snapper (skin on) that is backed over a light and lightly seasoned forcemeat of sole—the fish is livened by a sauce that is sharpened with chives. The Café's breast of chicken is browned, covered over with nuts and herbs, robustly flavored with garlic. It is a terrific bird, though sometimes a little dry, and the bits of sharp ginger you encounter are great startlements. The game dish varies from day to day. Sometimes you get a couple of quail in a wine-and-tangerine sauce that is thick with onions and other vegetables. It is much like a hunter sauce, but the tangerine seeds are a bitter nuisance. As to the birds themselves, they are not, of course, truly wild game, and though they are carefully roasted, they are mild. Bits of garlic adorn and fortify the pretty good steak, which arrives with a dollop of herbed butter melting over it.

Stilton cheese shows up cooked into a number of items on this menu. You may also have it straight, but the cheese has lost some of it sharpness—the tangerines, strawberries and tart apples with which it is served make a selection that is at once too acidic and too sweet to be right with cheese and wine. The surprisingly salty cheese cake is moist, solid but not heavy, browned, garnished with strawberries. The chocolate almond mousse cake is slightly citrus flavored, rich, leavened with chopped nuts, intense. The orange or lemon tarts are pastry cups filled with flavored custard and adorned with strands of rind—not bad. On occasion the hazelnut meringue cake has been waiting for you much longer than you for it, and has wilted and lost some of its chewiness—

strawberries are built in, whipped cream is added on, and the dessert is probably fine when it is fresh.

★ TOSCANA

246 East 54th Street
LUNCH, MONDAY TO FRIDAY; DINNER, MONDAY TO SATURDAY. CLOSED SUNDAY.
Reservations, 371-8144.
Credit cards: AE, CB, DC, MC, V.
Very expensive.

The restaurant is a small, boxlike room, neat and creamy white, brightly but gently lit. Windows high up on the walls are fitted with satiny white drapes that hang in luxuriant folds. One wall is mirrored, and under the length of the glass runs a banquette of glowing, golden-brown velvet. The room is carpeted. But you note that the white-linened tables are too small for such substantial pretensions. There are even spots, here and there around the room, where those tables are so proximate that a waiter addressing his charges at the table next to yours necessarily has his backside at your elbow. And when he goes off to a sidestand to perform a little hocus-pocus over a flame, the fumes of the fuel fill the air in half the dining room (though the aroma is gone in a trice when the fire is extinguished). Toscana can be a classy little spot, for sure, but except on your luckiest evening, you will have to overlook a thing or two to sustain the effect.

If you are unlucky enough to order the antipasto, it is a canned sardine you will have to overlook, and there is nothing else of interest in the standard assortment. Begin instead with the mussels of the house—they are fresh, and they are steamed in the oiled, garlicked and pungently seasoned broth over which they are mounded up and served. Or start with the grilled shrimp, which are big, crunchy, sweet-tasting, and moistened with an oil that is heavily peppered and herbed.

Occasionally a noodle here is over- or under-cooked. The pesto sauce is the creamy kind, and it lacks the wild herb flavor and sharpness that you have probably come to expect. But the simple spaghettini al pomodoro sports a good tomato sauce that has been artfully intensified.

Some utterly undistinguished cold salmon is almost rescued by a thick green sauce that is tart and lively with herbs. And some perfectly buttered cold veal, in the vitello tonnato, is completely sabotaged by a tuna sauce that is reminiscent of nothing but drugstore tuna sandwiches. Have the striped bass instead. It is firm and fresh, and its sauce livornese—though rather mild by the standard of most New York sauces of that name—is good, a little creamy, bits of olive and caper for sharpness and tartness. Scaloppine Toscana is more of the house's good veal, this time warm, with slivers of vividly flavored ham, quartered hearts of fresh artichoke, mushrooms and tender peas, all in a buttery sauce. What you call beef paillard, Toşcana calls battuta di manzo. The broad, thin slice of beef is perfectly juicy and pink within its blackened surface—as good a paillard as you will find.

One night you are served a lovely Caesar salad—utterly fresh greens and a very pungent anchovy and garlic dressing, thick with egg yolk. Another night you are served wilted endives with arugula that is just getting in under the wire. The dressings are made with first-class olive oil. When there is provolone on hand, it is firm, salty, sharp.

The zuppa inglese is obvious and cloying, not simply moistened with rum, but wet. But the chocolate cake is rich and strong. And the custard in the napoleon is lightly liquored and creamy within its flaky pastry.

Toscana has its following—people who have learned their way around the rather brief menu—and the place is cheerful most evenings, even comfortable if you manage to get a good-size table.

★★★ LES TOURNEBROCHES

153 East 53rd Street
LUNCH AND DINNER. CLOSED SUNDAY.
Reservations, 935–6029.
Credit cards: AE, CB, DC, MC, V.
Expensive.

Les Tournebroches, the French entry in the Citicorp Stakes, is the enterprise of Charles Chevillot, proprietor of the Upper East Side's estimable La Petite Ferme. M. Chevillot has always had a taste for simple food, and here at his new store things are plainer than ever. Most of the foods are cooked by little more than the application of heat to their surfaces: by grilling or by exposure—on skewers or spits—to the heat of open flames. And the restaurant turns out food of surpassing character, because this elemental cookery preserves and emphasizes the essential flavors of these excellent basic ingredients.

As this form of cooking *is* primitive, it can be prepared in the restaurant's dining room, before your very own unbelieving eyes, by young men who handle food and food implements with an absence of finesse—albeit with a certain awkward charm—that suggests techniques picked up the day before.

This is a modestly furnished place which does not quite achieve its intended country charm. Within walls of dusty rose there are tables with tops of painted tiles within plain wooden frames. They are surrounded by chairs of rattan and pale wood and by benchlike banquettes upholstered in a nubbly country cloth of dark-blue and white. The grilling and roasting area is within a kind of altar of green tiles, behind a low serving counter. Great sprays of wild and cultivated flowers are spotted about the room, and there are smaller sprays, in crockery mustard pots, on many of the tables. Your napkin, as at La Petite Ferme, is a coarse kitchen towel. Everything, however, is a bit too sleek for rusticity, and the earnest young waiters and waitresses, in folksy shirts and skirts and aprons, seem to be modeling country costumes in a city setting.

They bring you les hors d'oeuvre variés in an inch-deep white plate with fluted vertical sides. They include gentle ham wrapped around ripe melon; very smoky and tender tongue rolled into tubes; shredded carrots and crunchy dill-dressed pickles; good sardines; and a big dab of pungent mustard on a leaf of lettuce. Sometimes there is pea soup, and it has the strong flavor of unsullied wheat and a crunchy garnish of fresh parsley—earthy food.

Veal chops are served browned, juicy and tender, with large slices of herbed butter melting on the hot meat. Filet mignon is converted into a tasty steak by wrapping a belt of bacon around the rim of the tender meat and grilling it until its surfaces are crackling and blackened. Racks of lamb are roasted by hanging them within a few inches of flaming irons, and when the chops are cut apart you find that the fat has been drained away from the meat in this cooking, so the eyes of the chops are moist and pink without being greasy; this is superb lamb, gentle but a little gamy, crisped bits of meat and fat clinging to the edges of the meat and the ribs. The brochette de fruits de mer consists of plump and rich scallops, shrimp and chunks of fish that have been skewered and turned before the flames. This is impeccably chosen seafood, the clear fresh flavors of each item lightly accented with the slightly smoky flavor of the skewer cooking. Main courses are served with simple vegetables, shredded or whole, well buttered.

Extraordinary berry tarts: blueberries, blackberries, strawberries or raspberries on browned, crunchy butter crusts, the berries bursting with ripeness, the crusts slightly hard and crumbly; apple tarts that are the same crusts covered with crisp, cinnamoned, sugared fruit under slivers of crêpe. Too bad the tarts are sometimes cold.

★ TOUT VA BIEN

311 West 51st Street
LUNCH AND DINNER. CLOSED SUNDAY.
Reservations, 974–9051.
Credit cards: AE, CB, DC, MC, V.
Inexpensive.

This is a seedy little shop overseen by a hustling little craggy Gallic satyr—in a padded-shoulder, double-breasted suit—and a handful of family Gorgons—molded hair and one dubious eye apiece. The waitresses attend, address and carry with commendable forthrightness, the corpulence of a couple of them severe trials to their brief, snug uniforms. All this in a room of maple-stained pine paneling, a row of tables down the middle, a parallel row along one wall, maybe fifteen in all. Running half the length of the opposite wall, the bar, at which local French sit and gossip gutturally, behind which the color TV sometimes flickers. Occasionally a long-quiet tippler emits a stream of French invective. It is as if he has been constructing it during his silent, meditative drinking, and his knowing bar mates croak and cackle appreciatively. Tout Va Bien is a family affair, wrapped in habit and shipped here from any of a thousand French back streets, complete with French café music from the ancient jukebox. On occasion one of the overseers stops, looks around at every person and object in the place, like a primitive foreman. If the comic crockery, map of France, trophies or theatrical photos are in any detail out of place, it will be noticed, as surely as would the disappearance of the phone-booth-size air-conditioning machine that stands just inside the front door. This is the tangible source of livelihood, and it is watched over like the farm ox.

You receive a glass dish of celery, olives, carrot sticks and ice cubes, all crisp, and a menu, limp. From the latter you will learn that the selection of first courses is both limited and commonplace, including a pâté that is little more than high-class liverwurst, though good for that. Of the few other appetizers only the Haricots Blancs are of interest—you receive a substantial platter of the little white beans. They are thoroughly cooked, so they are tender, but they retain their crunchiness; they are blanketed by a layer of slivered raw onions, recently sliced and still strong, and the two vegetables are bound together in a vinaigrette that is mostly mild oil and strong mustard

—all very good. If neither the beans nor the pâté grabs you, share a main course as an appetizer—one of these orders of Moules Marinière will appetize as many as four. You receive a great mound of tender, steamed mussels, in their shells, piled in a deep plate, under it about a pint of primitive, briny broth, alive with chunks of garlic—this liquid may be slurped up with a spoon or soaked up with the chunks of toasted crust you will find in your basket of bread.

"Bouillabaisse" is emblazoned across the menu cover in big black letters, suggesting that it is an item in which Tout Va Bien specializes. And, in fact, their version of this dish justifies their pride, though for some reason, despite its being the best food in the house, it is served, in obedience to custom, on Fridays only. You are probably unaware that the conditions of the New York real estate market are responsible for violations of certain traditions in re the serving of bouillabaisse. New York rents are high. For adequate profits many restaurants compress numerous customers into compact spaces. To accomplish this requires that customers be seated at wee tables and, accordingly, there is insufficient room for a broad plate of bouillabaisse broth and another of fish and shellfish to be served simultaneously. You get the plate of broth first, a deep inch of steaming, vaguely orange liquid, oceanic, strong of lobster and lobster shell, spiced with saffron, hefty crusts of bread therein. You may, if you wish, intensify this broth with dabs of aïoli, for a huge glistening slab of the powerfully garlicked mayonnaise is served with the soup. When you have dispensed with that, a pot of solid food is brought and your waitress ladles onto your plate half a small lobster, mussels and shrimp, striped bass. It is not all perfect—on one occasion the shrimp are perhaps a bit overcooked, on another the mussels—but nothing is really bad, the bass is impeccably fresh, the lobster consistently tender and rich, all the ingredients well-flavored of the spicy broth. And if the first delivery doesn't take care of you, that pot holds enough for a second serving.

Tout Va Bien is relatively inexpensive. The food is not vastly less costly than at several other West Side French places, but many of the house dishes here are intrinsically cheap, among them Tête de Veau, not an item they stand in line for, because its translation is calf's head. This strong meat is rimmed with firm jelly; after a long soaking in cool water it is poached in stock, and several chunks of it are wrapped in linen and brought to you—you moisten the meat with a strong vinaigrette that has been laced with parsley, all of which makes for a rich and oily dish. It is served with some of New York's best French fries—tender, thin sticks, lightly crisped, lightly salted, nice foils for the soured fatty meat. Equally unappealing to casual visitors is the ivory-colored honeycombed substance known as tripe—stomach to you. It is served here as part of a gamy stew in which tomatoes, onions and peppers predominate—potatoes are added near the end of the cooking, which thickens the already sturdy dish. You can get a decent Steak au Poivre—not the primest meat available, but tender and accurately cooked, the coarse granules of black pepper embedded deeply and dominating the dish, the sauce of brandy, butter and pan scrapings tasty but relegated to the background by the pepper.

Dreary desserts, including Italian ice cream things; pastries that may as well remain in the refrigerator; a mousse that is without air.

If you have an anniversary coming up, know that "Happy Birthday" is on the jukebox, with a two-beat pause for the name of the celebrant.

★ TRES CARABELAS

314 East 39th Street
LUNCH, TUESDAY TO FRIDAY; DINNER, TUESDAY TO SUNDAY. CLOSED MONDAY.
Reservations, 689-6388.
Credit cards: AE.
Inexpensive.

This restaurant is not wholeheartedly intended for your patronage, unless you are a Spaniard in New York. The place is housed in Casa de España, the Spanish cultural center. When you telephone you may be asked to speak Spanish, please, by someone who simply assumes that you can. The menu is in Spanish, no printed translation. And though, with the courtesy that seems intrinsic to the Spanish character, you will be treated hospitably here, your host will sometimes except himself from that custom and short-answer your inquiries about the menu—he has a busy insider's impatience with a stray, harmless interloper.

You enter an unmarked building to a large anteroom that displays help-wanted and situations-wanted ads, on three-by-five cards, in Spanish; you pass through the barroom (furniture by Plastic City) to the restaurant proper, a starkly rectangular block of a room, its walls of smooth white plaster, dark crossbeams on the white ceiling, black wrought-iron sconces and chandeliers providing the bright illumination. Ornate chairs surround the white-linened tables. The still lifes on the walls are, like the paintings in the Prado, murky. When the place is busy, as it often is, it seems at once ecclesiastical and gay—and noisy, for the carpeting on the floor fails to dampen the noise that ricochets painfully among the hard surfaces.

Tres Carabelas has an underground reputation, partly because it does not call attention to itself, partly because its prices are low, and partly because the clientele seems so genuinely of the old country (gentleman Spaniards in stiff collars and dark suits, with cigarette holders and hothouse ladies; others, of the playboy generation, in cashmere turtlenecks and jeans, with foreign—American—girlfriends) that the visitor is convinced the cooking must be the real thing.

Much of it is, but, to dispose of the worst first, there is nothing real about these imitation-French snails; paella that simulates the pre-cooked, dry product of every second-rate sangría parlor on Columbus Avenue; a zarzuela of seafood with a glutinous white sauce that has no business near fish or shellfish in any cuisine.

Skip those and have the tortilla española, a peasanty potato pudding, peppered and eggy and solid; or the callos a la madrileña, innumerable slivers of tripe, and discs of sausage, in a thick red-pepper sauce; or the gambas al ajillo, spicy-hot shrimp in a heavy oil that reaches your table still bubbling; or the garlic soup, a winter dish, thick with bread and egg, and powerfully fragrant of garlic.

The hake is really cod, and what your host calls its "green sauce" is quite white, made with dried herbs, but the fish is flaky, fresh, garnished with clams and mussels—the dish manages not to be damaged by the frozen peas and canned asparagus that adorn it. You may have a chicken dish—pollo al chilindrón—of a half chicken under a foothill of red and green peppers, onions and mushrooms, black olives and cubes of ham—all in a tangy red sauce of tomatoes and hot red pepper. If you attend this place only once, order the lamb chops, salty and oiled, meat that is gentle and strong—the little chops seem to have no weight but their flavor.

The chestnut cake is a good rich dessert, sharpened with orange peel. The bread pudding is like a fortified custard studded with juicy raisins. The other desserts—coconut meringue pie, banana cake, chocolate mousse cake, flan, et al.—are sweets of no distinction.

★★★ LA TULIPE

104 West 13th Street
DINNER. CLOSED MONDAY.
Reservations, 691-8860.
Credit cards: AE, CB, DC, MC, V.
Very expensive.

The best food in the Village will cost you $45 per person, prix fixe; a bottle of wine will be $14 more at the least. For this you will endure a host whose mechanical thin smile has been carefully designed to let you know he has more important things on his lofty mind. Perhaps he is just shy with strangers, for he does ease up with customers he knows. But his captain is hard to alibi for. He is tall, slender, works in well-cut three-piece civvies. He positions himself at your table with one foot forward, as if to measure off the distance at which he wishes to keep you. He lowers his eyes to quarter-mast—he has been through this tiresome process so *many* times before—and, as they say, goes, "Madame will have? And then? Monsieur will have? And then?" And then he goes again—this time away—leaving a cleansing absence.

Once you know that La Tulipe is owned by Americans, you are struck by the elaborateness of its self-conscious Frenchness. That French captain is only a *par exemple.* The front room is equipped not only with French posters but with a zinc-topped bar, zinc-topped tables, the kind of straw chairs you see in street cafés in Paris. There is a little oyster bar in this front room as well, where nothing is shucked, of course, but Belons. It is a little embarrassing, as when you encounter someone from your past and discover that in the meantime he has taken on an English accent.

The dining room at the back is painted deep maroon, with severe rectangular mirrors built into the walls. Long, curved arms extend from the sconces, at their ends lamps that glow harshly against the dark background. But a handful of tasteful oils, and flowers fitted in where there is space in the crowded room, just about undo the depressing high seriousness that weighted this place down when it was new. Unless you get one of the chockablock tables for two, this is now a pretty comfortable room.

And there is no denying those Belon oysters, which are cold and sweet and sparkling, and which you dip into a spiky sauce mignonnette that is crisp with bits of shallot. You may have a slice of pâté that is a two-color candy-stripe swirl of pale foie gras and darker, thin-sliced tongue—rarely is anything to eat as rich, creamy and strong as this startling dish. Poisson à la nage, a hot fish-and-soup appetizer, is a small side of snapper, with crisp vegetables, in the briny—but not hard—slightly thickened stock in which it was cooked; the fish is steeped in the earthy flavors of the broth. A spinach-flavored sweetbread forcemeat is stuffed into La Tulipe's ravioli, which are served in a creamy sauce that is dotted with tomato and powerfully peppered. The lesser first courses include the gratin d'aubergine, baked eggplant of clear flavor under a layer of mild browned cheese; and the beignets de courgettes—fried zucchini to you—which come in a little basket, but are much like fried zucchini anywhere.

Your red snapper arrives in the paper balloon in which it was baked. The paper is removed, and you find that the fish is extremely juicy—but not wet—that it is strewn with the herbs and vegetables that heighten its delicate flavor, that it is moistened with a buttery broth. The shrimp are perfect sweet ones, and in the so-called shrimp ragout they are arranged, with bits of pimento and wild mushrooms, around a muffin of rice, in a creamy and winy sauce—the splendid dish is sprinkled with fresh chives and browned slivered almonds. Slices of rare squab, as rich as organ meat, blanket a hillock of fresh spinach that is studded with pine nuts and black raisins, and surrounded by a semolina grain (couscous) that is wonderful when flavored by the bird's sweet sauce. You get lovely kidneys here, clean and crunchy, in a light wine sauce that is touched with lemon, mustard, parsley. The elegantly cooked, thin-sliced calf's liver, grill lines on its surface, pink and juicy inside, is adorned with sweet-and-sour white raisins and sautéed onion. Three rosy lamb chops are cut from a grilled rack, their edges crusted with herbs and a garlicked breading—the lamb is strong, the garnish of white beans sturdy, the grilled tomato hot and juicy. And a big, tender veal chop cut from a braised rack—its edge dark, its eye pink and glistening—is served with a mound of woodsy cèpes, in a sturdy dark sauce.

You are offered a range of goat cheeses—from creamy-and-mild to just this side of randy—and they are in perfect shape. The two special desserts of the house are: a pear tart, which becomes an apple tart late in autumn and is unavailable in winter—the apple version is nicely caramelized, and the crust is fine, but it has little fruit flavor; and an apricot soufflé, which is exceptional, for it is moist but firm, light but substantial, and it retains the acid edge of the fruit—unless you prevent it, the center of the browned top will be cut away and whipped cream spooned in, an admixture that diminishes by dilution the soufflé's good flavor. La Tulipe's floating island is like a fluffy hazelnut cake served in a cool cream. The chocolate cake is rich, strong, edged with leaves of black chocolate, moistened with a cool green sauce flavored with mint. Coffee is $1.50 extra.

The place gets a prosperous clientele in tailored suits and one-of-a-kinds. Some casual folk come as well. The waiters and waitresses do their best, and it is probably not their fault that, especially for groups of four or more, not all the first courses or main courses are always served at the same time.

• "21" CLUB

21 West 52nd Street
LUNCH AND DINNER. CLOSED SUNDAY.
Reservations, JU 2-7200.
Credit cards: AE, CB, DC, MC, V.
Very expensive.

Jack and Charlie's, as the cognoscenti like to call it, is probably the most successful culinary sleight-of-hand ever carried out. It has been going on since Prohibition, and the flow of customers is inexhaustible. Yet anyone who attends this place once, and then voluntarily does it again, has got to have been fooled by the reputation, the glittering

292

clientele or the intensely masculine interior, because the food, frantically tended flames at the serving tables notwithstanding, is nothing but Stouffer's at three times the price, from the Pâté of Chicken Livers "21" (an airless mousse much like peanut butter) through the Terrapin Maryland (turtle à la king) to the Kersen Aardbeien en ys Van Urk (berries, including white strawberries, with pineapple and raspberry sherbet, in tutti-frutti sauce).

To the credit of the place, the ingredients are of decent quality, but the preparation of the food is so uniformly lackluster, and its service so pedestrian, that the only thing to be admired here, in fact to be wondered at in awe, is the list, lengthy and starry, of gourmets, epicures, columnists, dining-out authorities, travel books and restaurant guides that not only take "21" seriously but treat it with a respect usually reserved for the central figures in the world's religions.

Everyone "knows" that it's very difficult to get into "21." In fact, there is nothing to it: make a reservation and show up. It's true that the man at the desk will greet you coolly if he doesn't know you; that the coat-room attendant, if she sizes you up for a dodo, will give you your ticket and say "Don't lose it"; that you may be ignored for a while before you are transferred to one of the host's underlings; that the latter may be hard to follow as he leads you, without looking back, to a table through a thick crowd of black-jacketed captains (from whom he is impossible to distinguish); and that your captain will take your order willingly enough, but may well answer your questions, if any, with a degree of impatience that is only partly the result of his ignorance of the menu; but all that must be weighed against the security that comes of the certain knowledge that the food at "21," though tasteless, is harmless. This is a clean place.

It's best to pass up the more ambitious dishes for simpler food, though this is no guarantee of results. There is no faulting the clams or oysters, but the ratatouille appetizer, for example, is little more than a dish of poached vegetables, whereas, on the other hand, the clam-juice cocktail is certain not to disappoint. The Bismarck herring is firm and tart. There is much Caesar salad eaten here as an appetizer. To call it Caesar salad is to take a liberty; to serve it at all is to take license—decent greens in an eggless, overly sour dressing.

You can get good roast beef here; and the sautéed brook trout with capers is fresh and flaky, if not inspired. But "21" is supposed to be a big deal for game. If you order partridge, pheasant and quail, you can be certain that they will be given an all-American roasting to the point of stringy dryness of flesh within, limp dejection of skin without. The pitchers of currant jelly (Ann Page?) and white sauce (Wondra and milk) are actually welcome.

There is a "21" Burger listed as a *Spécialité*. (Your waiter may allow as how it is the most popular dish in the place.) This is the final triumph—the world's most ordinary dish, a hamburger, prepared without any imagination, served with a sheaf of hangdog string beans and peddled as a specialty of one of the most expensive restaurants on earth, for which board chairmen, pols, celebrities of stage, screen and tube point the noses of their liveried chauffeurs toward West 52nd Street.

You are cordially warned that soufflés take an hour. So you order the Crêpes Soufflées "21," which take only thirty minutes, except that they take an hour. (How long would the soufflé take? Is the rule to double, or to add, thirty minutes?) The Crêpes Soufflées turn out to be a bit of brandied soufflé filling in pancakes (so far not bad), served with a congealed crème Anglaise that lacks utterly the sharp flavor of cooked milk but tastes, rather, like an ulcer patient's custard. The apple pancake is better— the same pancake, filled with pretty good stewed apples.

There is a low-ceilinged barroom on the main floor, with a number of tables nearby —this is the informal part of "21." Upstairs there are wood-paneled walls, red linen, red leather chairs and banquettes, silver urns and plates on shelves and on the walls, sporting prints, horsy wallpaper—the effect is of a hunting lodge in the form of a mansion. Where else can you see, at a table for six, six gray suits?

★ UKRAINIAN RESTAURANT

140 Second Avenue (near 9th Street)
LUNCH AND DINNER.
Reservations for four or more, 533–6765.
No credit cards.
Inexpensive.

This establishment, occupying a back room on the ground floor in the Ukrainian National Home, has been here since the Year One, as has the Home. Recently, however, there has been a change—the place now announces itself to the public, by way of signs out front and advertisements. As the former status of Ukrainian Private Club has been changed to Place of Public Accommodation, the Ukrainian Restaurant, to repeat its eminently definitive title, is now fat for the fire. Sizzle, sizzle.

Follow your nose down the broad entrance hallway to a dining room done in Rural Motel, with plain wooden floor, knotty-pine walls and much in the way of mirrors. To the recorded tootling strains of the "Pennsylvania Polka" and other tunes suitable for accordion rendition, you escort yourself to a table of your choice. The red-and-white checkered tablecloths are protected from your carelessness by State Quiz paper place mats, in which outlines of the forty-eight continental states are printed helter-skelter on the place mat, instead of in their correct geographical relationships to each other. You are required to guess the names of the states *from their outline shapes alone.* (Each outline is numbered, and you turn the place mat upside down, if you dare, to learn the correct answers.) Obtaining the assistance of your waitress is no fairs.

Those waitresses, by the way, wear Ukrainian native blouses. And the menu lists native food, which attracts clusters of middle-aged Slavic entrepreneurs (plump men in porkpie fedoras), couples of elderly Slavs (he in his rough broadcloth going-out suit, she with a cameo at the throat of her black silken dress), younger, courting Slavs (his hair plastered down, hers plastered up), toward closing time the late-nighters (she gowned, he sharkskinned), and lone Slavs (they drag out their dinners with paperback mysteries until it is time to return to the little pad and the little TV).

Food. Like "Jelly Pigs Feet" (presumably feet from a jelly pig), which consists of a block of murky aspic, cool, gamy and salty, in which are embedded tender shreds of meat, the buckwheat cereal called kasha, chunks of carrot, and sections of the cartilage which, when boiled, produced the binder that forms the jelly from the broth. It is a cool and rather invigorating dish, but a bit off-putting to some, like one's first oyster. Like stuffed cabbage, an egg of warm, ground and flavored meat in a shell of tender cabbage leaves. Like pierogi, a mildly seasoned patty of meat and kasha enveloped in a noodle pouch. Like "Ukrainian Borscht," the nationalistic modifier suggesting, correctly, that the soup is hot; moreover, it is sour and strong, imbued with the deep flavor of long-cooked bones.

One genius orders "Lazanski," convinced it will turn out to be nothing but emigrated lasagna, and as the almost total decline of poetic justice would have it, is close. One order of this substance is ballast for a small boat, and the genius ate it all—the fact that it tastes wonderful playing only a small part in this gluttonous feat. Lazanski consists of noodles, fried onions, slivers of oiled cabbage, plenty of soft cheese, the entire production well-salted and seasoned with cinnamon. It is easy to eat also because it is slippery.

For something even earthier, there is boiled beef, served on kasha, all under a sweetish white sauce. (Suggest that the sauce be canceled.) The meat is abundant, fibrous and gamy, and the kasha, pebbly and grainy, is a fine foil to the beef. In much the same spirit, different only in the details, are the goulash, potted veal shank, roast pork, &c.

The listing is not replete with tempting desserts, nor, for that matter, with any other kind. Cherry blintzes are not strictly a dessert, and with this doughy wrapper around these insipidly sweetened fruits, do not try to reinterpret them that way. Nor, for that matter, is the "Home Made Apple Cake" much more than stewed and sugared apples between undistinguished pie crusts.

The waitresses confess that despite the ethnic character of their garb, they are neither Ukrainian nor anything neighboring it. They carry the food from the kitchen on rectangular plastic trays, which they balance on one hand as they serve you. This is hard to do, and instead of lowering your dish to the place in front of you by lowering the hand that is holding it, they do something like a curtsy, lowering everything, by bending the knee and hip joints. This is excellent exercise.

★★UNCLE TAI'S HUNAN YUAN

1059 Third Avenue (near 63rd Street)
LUNCH AND DINNER.
Reservations, TE 8–0850.
Credit cards: AE, CB, DC.
Medium-priced.

Squab, ham, rabbit, oysters, venison, lamb, pheasant, and captains in tuxedoes are rarities in Chinese restaurants in New York; for all but the last of which a bit of gratitude to Uncle Tai may be in order. The captains here are mechanical at best, and if you are a bit of a boor yourself, they have apparently been waiting for you, for there is nothing they like better than trading discourtesies with, say, the ill-dressed. When they see someone who looks like a displaced Pell Street noodle-shop frequenter, they stiffen. They are accustomed to families taking an hour or two off from homework and TV, discussing tales of Stuyvesant High and IBM and the difficulty of getting a cab outside Bloomie's at five.

The house is in on the act. They, too, wish to deny their origins. For example, they want to pretend that this is not a Chinese restaurant. Not only do they have these floor officials dressed in formal black-and-whites, but the wallpaper on the walls looks like something in a small-town rooming house (that is, an American, not a Chinese, small town); the hanging plants are very much the healthfood restaurant trappings of this day; the spotlights mounted under the ceiling cast the flashy glow of the steak-joint-and-rock-Muzak places that are dotted around the East Seventies. Perhaps it is all an experiment, for the grotesque icicle chandeliers, which illumined this establishment before its light renovation, are still in place. They do not turn them on, but presumably they could if the nostalgia movement catches up with Sino-Grotesk.

The Fried Oysters are battered and breaded, deep-fried until deeply browned, rapidly, so the oysters are warmed without being at all toughened. But unless you start with a tasty oyster, you will not end up with one, and this is just a well-made dish that suffers from its indifferent ingredient. Begin instead with Cold Peppered Rabbit: strands of oiled meat, sturdily spiced, over thin, crisp lengths of cucumber, the dish garnished with sprigs of fragrant coriander leaves—lively food. Or with Sliced Chicken with Hot Oil: moist slivers of good pale meat in a dark-brown sauce that is hot and winy, studded with scallion greens—this sauce has saturated the chicken, making the meat at once juicy and strong.

Proceed to Sliced Hunan Vegetable Pie, a peasant's imitation of Peking Duck, in which crunchy rectangles of browned vegetable wafer are wrapped in pancakes with hoisin sauce and florets of scallions; it is held between the fingers and eaten. The wafers have the crunchy warmth of hot fried vegetables done in good oil, and the sweet sauce and strong scallions set them off perfectly. Continue on to Sautéed Sliced Pheasant, a sweet meat here mingled with fresh ginger, snow peas, scallions, each texture and flavor clear, and yet wedded to the others in this heavily peppered sauce. Move along to Sliced Venison with Garlic Sauce, another sweet meat, this one mingled with crunchy red and green peppers, water chestnuts and scallions, big floppy mushrooms, all in a moistening of dark oil that is alive with the scent and flavor of fresh garlic.

Sliced Hunan Lamb is one of the dishes that made Hunan food a hit when it first hit town at the turn of the decade. It is nowhere made as well as it was then, but it is still good food in the version served here: substantial slices of meat, the size of silver dollars, oiled and tender and pungently accented with the hot peppers that are distributed among the slices, all flavored with garlic—the crisp taste of watercress and the sharp contrast of scallions point up the richness of the meat. Missing is the careful sautéing this dish used to get, so that each sliver of meat was browned outside, pink inside.

The Frogs' Legs Hunan Style are well-prepared, tender, moist, crusted and oiled, bits of scallion clinging to the morsels of meat. But these are frozen frogs' legs, their flavor has been tamed.

Dishes that take extra time to prepare are discouraged, particularly if ordered not long before closing, or if the place is busy.

You can do your shopping here. Every rack at the midtown department stores is represented of an evening, a touch of Barney's too.

○ UNITED STATES STEAKHOUSE CO.

120 West 51st Street
LUNCH, MONDAY TO FRIDAY; DINNER, MONDAY TO SATURDAY. CLOSED SUNDAY.
Reservations, 757–8800.
Credit cards; AE, CB, DC, MC, V.
Very expensive.

Rockefeller Center's United States Steakhouse is a theme restaurant. Its themes are the American peanut, the American hero, and meat.

The peanut. There is a pause at the end of the day's occupations known as the cocktail hour, and there is a big barroom here to which lots of the guys from upstairs in the Time-Life Building repair. They stand around the huge circular counter-height oak tables that bear giant bowls of unshelled peanuts, and they light their cigarette lighters, hoist long cold ones and crack peanuts, all without looking. They drop the peanut hulls at their feet, toss the seeds between their teeth and slowly grind them with their huge molars, their jaws rippling. After a while they are ankle-deep in peanut shells, and by seven o'clock this place looks like the elephant house.

The peanut also shows up on the menu, in cream of peanut soup, which has vegetables in it, and which is every bit as execrable as you fear; and it shows up in six-nut pie, which is every bit as etc.

The hero. Photographs of famous domestic and imported Americans hang on the walls. And boy, are they funny. Each and every one of them has the same caption, in comic-strip balloons, painted in over the head of the subject! And the constant caption (this will kill you) is: "Best £?&.* 0%!¢ steak I ever tasted!" Cute? For example, there is a picture of Marlon Brando in *The Godfather,* and instead of saying whatever it was he was saying in that particular never-to-be-forgotten scene, what he is saying is: "Best £?&.* 0%!¢ steak I ever tasted!" And believe it or not, there is a picture of John Vliet Lindsay looking down on the bean of Abraham Beame, and *Lindsay* is saying it. And then there is this very smiling picture of Eisenhower, Dulles and MacArthur (looking as if they just castrated Truman), and *they're* saying it. Well, you walk along the walls, and it goes on and on, a laugh a frame. Leo Durocher, Bob Hope dancing with Rocky Marciano, Marilyn Monroe flashing an acre of thigh, Franklin Roosevelt, Cardinal Spellman, Superman, Muhammad Ali, Sophia Loren in bed with Marcello Mastroianni, Dean Martin. All the greats and near-greats. The animal kingdom is spared.

Meat. Meat is served in the dining room, which features hefty wood partitions around leather-upholstered booths, big tables, thick red carpeting, and waiters and waitresses who wear aprons of chain mail, no less. Some take their work seriously, but many are between jobs, leaning on your booth or table with the insouciance of members of your party who just happen to be standing.

The best part of your dinner is on the house—a basket of warm potato chips that are crisp and not too greasy. Like all good potato chips, they are habit-forming, and efforts to restrain yourself for fear of "ruining your dinner" are ill-advised.

Everything else is fee-for-service, including an appetizer of tartar steak, a golf-ball-size dollop of raw beef, dry and underseasoned, though of freshly ground meat. The clams and oysters are usually fresh but rarely sparkling; and the shrimp are soggy and icy. The cocktail sauce with which these are garnished is itself garnished, with horserad-ish that was grated back when. Your waiter warns you that "Today's Stuffed Vegeta-ble" is hot. "Lemme warn you," says he, "it's hot." It's cold.

Cold steak salad, at its best, is one of the highest achievements of the lowly art of rescuing leftovers—crisp vegetables and a tangy dressing converting last night's exces-sive dinner into today's light lunch. Here the procedure is reversed. Steak broiled especially for the salad is made to seem week-old with strands of tired greens and bland cheese and a lengthy immersion in the vinaigrette, which makes the meat marinated, not dressed.

The broiled steaks and lamb chops are not bad (the latter served with a stainless-steel jigger of cold green jelly), but they do not approach the balance of firmness, tenderness and moisture you find in Manhattan's best steakhouses. The chopped steaks are mushy rather than ground, and by late in the evening the roast beef, bland to begin with, is no longer rare. Avoid the immense lobsters, which are dry and fibrous. What they call "Hashed Browns With Apple" are amorphous chunks of deep-fried potato to which the bits of apple are irrelevant. No civilized person would insert decent butter into this establishment's baked potatoes. The mysterious ingredient in your salad dressing is Yankee Stadium mustard.

Cakes and pies that might be tolerable to obsessively sweet teeth are served at ruinous icebox temperatures. You cannot quarrel with the listing "Fresh Strawberries," for the word "fresh" does not connote "ripe."

★★ UZIES

1444 Third Avenue (at 82nd Street)
LUNCH, SATURDAY AND SUNDAY; DINNER, DAILY.
Reservations, 744-8020.
Credit cards: AE, CB, DC, MC, V.
Expensive.

This place is the snazzier offshoot of the adjacent Hoexter's Market, but without the pack of singles desperadoes at the bar, and without the late-night disco dancing. Uzies gets a cooler crowd. There are people meeting people at the bar, sure enough, but they are not breathing hard. Jet setters in training come here, in carefully selected ensembles of denim and cashmere, or in Italian silk suits, or fishermen's sweaters and wet-look pants. At Uzies you should be absolutely smashing or seem absolutely not to give a damn. You must have money or seem to. You should be suntanned, irrespective of the season. When you spot someone you know, softly *shriek* with delight and crush him/her in a movie embrace, taking care not to mar anybody's make-up or tousle anybody's hair. Ask anyone at Uzies and he will tell you the same thing. He is having a *won*derful time. Not only in Uzies, but in life.

Uzies is dimly lit, but if you squint you may perceive that the place is done up in shades of cocoa, café au lait, cinnamon, chestnut, brown sugar, nutmeg, caramel, burnt almond and cognac. The front room houses the bar and tables, the back room tables only. Pinpoint lights in the ceiling cast circles of light on the white linen. The black-glass windows that look out on 82nd Street and the black floor-to-ceiling sheet mirrors are the glitzy notes; and a handful of paintings and prints—chosen, except for a Ferrari poster, for their superb irrelevance—are the touches of color. There is a glinting chrome eagle atop the huge chrome-plated espresso machine at the back end of the bar. The place is usually busy, and it is busily patrolled by waiters in casual formals—black-and-whites, but with long white aprons.

Yes, there is an Uzie, a swarthy, heavy-lidded, eagle-beaked suggestive smiler, the embodiment of insinuation in search of a motive. He half sits, half leans on a barstool, smirks as if in cocky display of his giant teeth, crosses one leg over the other, bringing into better view a black patent-leather loafer, with brass buckle, and a bare ankle. Perhaps he could insinuate himself a pair of socks. As a frontispiece, bring back Toots Shor.

But Uzie is very easy to ignore. And the food in this place is easy to admire: broad slices of tender raw beef (carpaccio), spread with an oily and crunchy sauce of capers, minced onions and parsley; spaghetti puttanesca, a winy, mahogany-colored, anchovy-flavored sauce which, in this version, is augmented with whole tender clams, the pasta, as in all the noodle dishes, firm but tender; fettuccine Uzie, green noodles and shrimp and scallops in a hot sauce that is creamy but not thick, the seafood fresh, the sweet flavors of each shellfish vivid; green noodles mixed with white in more of that tender cream sauce, this dish, called paglia e fieno ronis, shot through with morsels of smoked salmon and much fresh dill; meaty little tortellini, in a cream sauce that is thickened with strong Parmesan cheese, lightly herbed, and made fragrant with fresh nutmeg.

The fish of the day—there are usually two or three—are always fresh. The skate—angel wings, your waiter calls it—is not an especially tasty fish, but they sauté and brown it with care, and serve it in a creamy sauce of lime and butter that brings it to life. The swordfish is sliced thin, grilled hot and very rapidly, so that it is both crusted and juicy, and it is moistened with a lobster sauce that has the clear strong flavor of the fresh shellfish. The boned pompano comes off less well—it is nicely cooked, but the combination of eggplant duxelles (on which it reclines) and the lemon-flavored white sauce (under which it is concealed) just does not work.

The Tuscan chicken is a good bird, meaty and moist, broiled—and lightly blackened —with rosemary. The grilled veal chop is big, charred and juicy. And the sirloin steaks are of excellent tender beef, fibrous and bloody, accurately prepared.

Your coffee-flavored chocolate cake sits on a black crust under liquored whipped cream—a cool, sharp, strong, extremely sweet cake. The cheese cake is refrigerated too —it is made with ricotta, it is sometimes flavored with lemon, sometimes with anise, and it survives its refrigeration if you get it on a day when it is fresh.

★★ IL VALLETTO

133 East 61st Street
LUNCH, MONDAY TO FRIDAY; DINNER, MONDAY TO SATURDAY. CLOSED SUNDAY.
Reservations, 838–3939.
Credit cards: AE, DC, MC, V.
Expensive.

This is not Nanni's North, though Il Valletto is, in fact, the recent undertaking of Mr. Nanni, proprietor of the very popular Nanni's, of East 46th Street. But here (on the premises of the blessedly defunct Running Footman) Nanni has invested some of his midtown cash in uptown posh. If you dread this address for memories of the stuffy old Footman, be assured that no trace of that dreary mortuary remains. The Italian warmth has been transfused into the premises until the entire place glows pink and brown and gold. From the moment you become hooked on the mixed nuts (no peanuts) which accompany your apéritif at the massive polished bar, you grasp that Nanni is here expressing a side of himself that was never in evidence in the travel-poster-adorned little place downtown. Through the bar to the first room—small, softly lit, the walls covered with casually striped, glowing velvet, a handful of tables, a grouping of special places. Through that to the main dining room, forty pink-linened tables under chandeliers of lights in red shades hanging from a plum-colored ceiling a couple of stories over your head. There are heavy Italian murals set into the ivory walls—you need not look up at them. One thing in common with Nanni's: the place is an amplifier—a bit of conversation hits you from across the room, and a few minutes later, still bouncing around these hard walls, it hits you again. It makes everyone, even your host, cheerful, and he calls your companion *"Cara bambina,"* though she is well past weaning.

Another thing in common with Nanni's: much is made of what is not on the menu, and much of what is not on the menu is the best food in the house. As it is not on the menu, it may not have an official title, so the waiter suggests, with technical correctness, a hot antipasto which, on description, turns out to be a hot seafood salad—dozens of tiny scallops and a lesser number of shrimp, lightly floured, sautéed, with a bit of garlic, in oil and wine which have been simmered down to a smooth and oceanic broth. The little scallops are sweet and rich, the shrimp crisp, the dish just about perfect. Also not on the menu, but on display at the entrance to the large room, the cold antipasto— the principal attraction here is the *cold* seafood salad, a sparkling intermingled collection of chunks of lobster (!), tiny mussels, shrimp and onions, all in a limpid vinaigrette —the impeccable ingredients make this an extremely refreshing and stimulating appetizer. In nearby trays there are marinated artichokes and roasted peppers, good food, the artichoke leaves cured to the point where they have lost all their fibrousness, the peppers firm and sweet.

If you are granted one dish in this restaurant before you are added to the unemployed and consigned to your own kitchen, choose yet another that is not on the menu— gnocchi, with what the waiters have been trained to call "Nanni's special sauce." These plump potato dumplings are, miraculously, at once firm and ephemeral. The lightest pressure of your tongue and palate against the pale shells effects instantaneous disappearance. But the flavor of the sauce lingers, a slightly sour and yet creamy tomato sauce, with slivers of ham, tiny peas and herbs. The dish is sprinkled with cheese and very briefly put under the broiler before it is served, creating a lightly browned, gauzelike veil which adds a sharp, heady flavor to the otherwise gentle dish.

Your standard restaurant freak is, of course, frustrated by the almost universal "ordering off the menu" practiced at Il Valletto. Where is the inside-dopester appeal of ordering off the menu if everyone is doing it? Has been discovered, to fill this gaping gap, the practice of ordering *directly from the menu,* which has a return-to-innocence snob appeal, like the Mickey Mouse watch or forties musicals at 2 A.M. What you do is read the menu, select food you think you will like and instruct the waiter to bring those dishes. It's fun, and anyone can learn to do it. Start by ordering Trenette al Pesto. (Trenette is like linguine, but even more slender; pesto is a buttery green sauce of fresh basil and two or three cheeses.) This version is weighted toward cheese—crumbly nuggets and fine grains in among the fragrant green stuff—and it is served on just-cooked noodles that are tender but firm. You will require a spoon for the pool of flavored butter that remains at the bottom of your dish.

More from the menu: Zuppa di Clams—little clams, in their shells, steamed in wine and oil and garlic until they are warmed but not the least toughened, sprinkled abundantly with parsley and served mounded up over a deep plate of the briny broth they were steamed in. Sea Bass Marechiaro—a substantial length of fresh, resilient fish, lightly floured and then sautéed, to form a thin crust, moistened with a modest sauce of wine and tomatoes, with a little garlic and a bit of parsley, and garnished (nice note) with a few steamed mussels and a mound of crunchy spinach that is soaked in oil and garlic. Scaloppine alla Francese is a better than average version of this dish. The veal is pale, tender, crusted with a batter of eggs and flour, sautéed in butter and moistened with lemon—but despite the unusual sprinkling of strands of prosciutto ham, this is less than exciting. Pollo Scarpariello—chunks of chicken that are well-crisped but rendered a bit oily in the process; the dish is redeemed, however, by the flavors of fresh garlic and parsley. The chicken and the veal are served with artichoke hearts that are filled with buttered sweet peas and bits of bacon.

Il Valletto may well be the only restaurant in New York that makes available half a dozen or more imported Italian cheeses at room temperature: Gorgonzola, ivory veined with blue, smooth, creamy and sharp; Parmesan, hard and crumbly, with a strong bite and a scent that clears the head; Romano; Fontina; etc. The sweet desserts are a varying assortment of unabashedly rich cakes.

• VANESSA

289 Bleecker Street (at Seventh Avenue South)
LUNCH, SUNDAY; DINNER, DAILY.
Reservations, 243-4225.
Credit cards: AE, CB, DC, MC, V.
Expensive.

The wines on Vanessa's list are presented strictly in the order of their prices, the cheapest first, the most expensive last. Australian cabernets, burgundies, rieslings, all varieties and colors are side by side in a bacchanalia of class-conscious but otherwise ecumenical international neighborliness. You get the impression the management assumes that its customers know little more about what they want to drink than how much they are willing to pay for it. Look about you and you will probably conclude that the management is right, for Vanessa's success is a triumph of the publicity profession, and its customers are those who want to go to the places to which they ought to want to go. This is a Greenwich Village restaurant, but it is no more a part of the Village than are the nervous camp followers who come to it from out of nowhere in response to hot tips in the press.

Under the circumstances your host's contumely is easy to explain. He is perched on a stool near his desk. He is talking on the phone, smoking. Your arrival forces him to bring his conversation to an exasperated end. (When will they *ever* stop walking in the door?) He draws and slowly exhales a long last puff, turns to his tormenters and, a measurable moment later, switches on his charm, but only to low. He leads you to a terrible table. You demur. He finds a worse one. You demur and point to a better one. He does not look where you point when he tells you that that one is reserved. It goes unused all night.

Vanessa is a big purple place, dimly lit, with polished brass sconces of Deco inspiration mounted on walls that are in part covered with intricately patterned, murky cloth. The ceiling is a couple of stories above your head. You sit on pale chairs of bentwood and cane, the seats of which have been furnished with soft cushions. There is a single exotic flower on each table. A dark, giant orchid is emblazoned on one wall. It is difficult to know what they had in mind, but the result is a kind of sexiness that appears to have been learned about thirdhand.

You may learn about the carpaccio firsthand—the thin slices of just-cut raw beef are dressed with good oil, herbs, minced capers and strong grated cheese. Something called flan Vanessa is shaped like a muffin, tastes like a quiche, has all kinds of shellfish buried in its custard, is served in something like a sauce Nantua (a smooth substance flavored with lobster shell), is pretty good to eat. Snails of no particular distinction are, fortunately, buried in a thick, garlic-flavored tomato sauce.

Vanessa's linguine primavera whistles in the dark—the pistachio nuts will get your attention at first, but presently you will notice that this assemblage of carrots, peas, broccoli, green noodles and a garlicky cream sauce adds up to confusion. Chunks of plum tomato, plenty of good seafood and much Pernod make the spaghetti di mare a tasty if inelegant dish. The tortellini have a bit of nutmeg in their meat filling, and they are fine with the sautéed wild mushrooms and thick cream sauce with which they are served.

Your waiter, reading in the dark from a prompt sheet, tells you that the fish of the evening is swordfish—er—grenoise. Perhaps he means grenobloise, for its sauce, albeit red, is studded with capers—anyway, the thin slices are dry and tasteless. Eight nicely deep-fried oysters are served on fresh spinach in a pool of what appears to be melted butter rapidly congealing—good food that seems to be unfinished. Lots of fish and shellfish in the fish stew (the composition of which varies from time to time)—on occasion the production is a quasi-bouillabaisse, with a saffron- and Pernod-flavored broth in which giant croutons are buried. The broiled chicken is bloody near the bone (unintentionally, probably), and its mustard sauce separates before your eyes. A so-called scaloppine of veal au citron is in a lemon-flavored tomato sauce that seems to have been designed for an ocean-going fish—it overwhelms the mild veal. Your rack of lamb is less than half a rack (the standard portion), and by the time you decide that its menu description—"provençal"—has nothing to do with what you are eating, it is gone.

The crème brûlée is a heavy, airless custard, but its tender crust is like crystallized caramel. The chocolate cake is exceptional, intense and extremely creamy, strewn with bits of almond, and served with good whipped cream that is adorned with a sprig of fresh mint. There is crème de cacao in the sauce that is poured over the profiterole, but there is sogginess in the pastry. Exotic flavors of ice cream are served, including pumpkin ice cream, which comes, of course, with cranberry sauce. You may have dark chocolate mousse or white or a little of each—the sweet stuff is served in an almond pastry shell (also a little soggy), in a pool of raspberry purée. The purée is lifeless, but the white mousse is fluffy, the brown one of marvelously concentrated flavor and richness.

★★ VAŠATA

339 East 75th Street
LUNCH, SUNDAY; DINNER, TUESDAY TO SUNDAY. CLOSED MONDAY.
Reservations, 650-1686.
Credit cards: AE, CB, DC, MC, V.
Medium-priced.

The Czechoslovakian restaurant Vašata has been here for many years, serving the burghers of the middle-European community of Manhattan's East 70s. That population has diminished recently, as has Vašata's business and the length of its menu, but not the quality of its food. There are few places in town where the homey home-cooking of the Slavs is set forth so solidly and in such unabashedly bourgeois old-world surroundings. The timbered ceiling and wooden columns are gestures to farmhouse décor, as is the decorative china on the cream-colored rough plaster walls. But the big tables covered with white linen, the comfortable chairs and banquettes, and the thick carpeting are urban comforts. And the well-fed gentry who make up Vašata's clientele have smooth hands and well-fitted clothes. They are satisfied that their taste is good taste, their way of life irreproachable. At Vašata you are surrounded by contentment in several languages.

The best dishes include a marinated herring that is tart, almost biting, covered with strands of crisp onion in cool cream; head cheese of tender morsels of meat and organ meat in a cool jelly—you liven the dish with raw onions and a squeeze of lemon; pickled calf's brain on toast, the rich gray meat and its creamy sauce lovely against the crusty bread.

If you come here once, the thing to have is the roast duck. In fact you will sometimes see six of them heading from the kitchen to a table of six regulars. Ducks cannot be better roasted than these, their skins crisp and browned and crackling, the meat tender and juicy. The duck comes with a pitcher of sauce that is made from the roasting juices, not from fruit, and that additional richness may be more than you want. The pork chops Serbien are covered with a tomato paste that is pungent with the tartness of green peppers, and the chops themselves are sweet and tender. Vašata makes perfect breaded calf's brains, the crust as crisp as crackers, the brains steamy and soft.

But such dishes as the ham salad, breaded mushrooms, chicken paprikash, Wiener schnitzel and veal à la Vašata, though well prepared and all they are intended to be, may seem unrelievedly plain to the unaccustomed palate. With your main course you select a couple of garnishes from a long list of dumplings, potatoes, vegetables and salads, and usually the waiter will suggest the ones that are best with the food you ordered.

The desserts consist principally of palacinky—hot pancakes filled with apricot jam or chocolate—and fluffy pastries. They are fine but not memorable.

Pilsener Urquel, the wonderful beer of Czechoslovakia, is available here, but white wine is the best drink with most of this food. Several good wines are available at very reasonable prices.

★★★ LE VEAU D'OR

129 East 60th Street
LUNCH AND DINNER. CLOSED SUNDAY.
Reservations, TE 8–8133.
Credit cards: AE.
Medium-priced.

New York offers few prizes as coveted as a table in this legendary establishment when—at the little bar near the center of the long, narrow room—there is a crowd of people who wish they, too, had one, when still others are flowing in through the small front door, when the restaurant is, in short, its teeming self. Le Veau d'Or is the extra reward of life that is its own reward, the comfort that needs no trappings of comfort, familiarity, casual excellence. If you are condemned to eat in but one restaurant in this city for the rest of your life, choose this one. You can get better meals elsewhere any day of the week, in more luxurious surroundings, but this place is a stayer. Critics point to its flaws. It has flaws. God forbid it should be perfect.

The house colors are golden wood, red leather, white linen, the black uniforms of the waiters, all aglitter. The walls are crammed with framed and unframed objects— Paris street signs, white lettering on blue (Place de la Concorde, Boulevard St. Germain, Place Pigalle), glossy black-and-whites of Paris markets, engraved mirrors, travel posters, still lifes in gaudy hues. And there is the Golden Calf himself, in oils, asleep between the sheets, with his own private pun: *Le veau dort.*

There is something Chaplinesque about this restaurant when it is most crowded. Here is a waiter with a tray of food walking through an aisle through which no one, it is obvious, even without a tray of food, can possibly walk. Still, staring straight ahead, oblivious of his equally unseeing obstructors, he walks. Here is yet another tuxedoed madman, this one carving a duck on a serving cart that is in the middle of yet another all-but-invisible aisle, just as if half a dozen people were not hipping him as they make the turn around his posterior. It is wondrous how these men go on, as if they were working in the wide open spaces of the Four Seasons on a slow day. There is something fanciful about your host's behavior as well. He is a natty and cheerful chap, he likes to shake your hand if he thinks he has seen you once or twice before, and he suggests that you wait at the bar for a few minutes, just as if there were access to that part of the room by any method other than the knife. But reservations are taken, seating is at a fair approximation of the specified time—how it all works is a mystery, and no one seems to mind, for everyone is busy being civilized and cheerful. This is where the Upper East Side eats when they are not eating where the Stuffy Upper East Side eats. And their sons and daughters eat here when they are home from school. And sometimes the generations eat together. But—very big but—Le Veau d'Or is not a secret, and it is not a society, and it is not particularly expensive, and people have been coming here for decades, from everywhere.

Rouse yourself with Maquereau au Vin Blanc, hefty filets of strong fish in a marinade that is a little sweet and a lot sour. Or soothe yourself with Nova Scotia salmon, the genuine article, though it is a crime to serve it with this loud oil. Or warm yourself with Coquille "Veau d'Or," scallops and mushrooms in a shell, in a lightly tomatoed white sauce.

The saucisson chaud is disappointing—warm fatted sausage that lacks the sparkle and spice that can redeem this kind of leaden weight. Choose, instead, the saucisson d'Arles, a pungent salami of purple meat and white fat that is so gamy and high it is almost rank—you have to like that kind of thing. The pâté is very good, finely ground, moist and heavily seasoned. And the onion soup is one of the few versions of this dish around town that is made with onions that are cooked until they are dark—that makes for a hefty brew, and the topping here, of flavorful cheese deeply browned, is just right for the strong soup. The watercress soup is hot, thick with potato, suffused with the flavor of its strong chicken-stock base—it has little of the quality of fresh watercress, but it is an excellent cup of food.

It is not invariably on the menu, but when it is, you should not pass up this establishment's tripe à la mode de Caen. The little slices of tripe are gummy and yet tender, and they are served in a spicy red sauce that gives off a heady fragrance of country brandy. There is good chicken, served as Poussin Rôti en Cocotte, "Grand-'Mère," a very moist bird that has been cooked with browned onions, cubes of sturdy bacon, abundant mushrooms, all in a roasting-pot liquid that is redolent of the fat of the bird. The Boeuf Braisé Bourgeoise is little more than a good pot roast in a deep, sweet vegetable sauce—the sauce is wonderful on the salty noodles that accompany this dish. Crusty and tender frogs' legs Provençale are served here, with an extremely concentrated purée of tomatoes, and with Pommes Anna, thin slices of potato that have been baked in clarified butter until the potatoes are tender and oily, their edges lightly browned—altogether a simple and splendid plate of food. The not-so-secret secret of rack of lamb is good meat, accurately roasted. In this place you may get it a little rarer than you asked for—they do not want to harm this great lamb, the eye of each rib the most gentle and yet flavorful of morsels. It is served only for two, but men of normal proportions have been seen dispatching an entire six-rib production. It is served with crisp green beans that are sprinkled with bits of strong garlic and polished with butter, and with firm flageolets, the thick white beans that are somehow the ideal starch with lamb.

There is almost always some good cheese in the house—goat cheese or hard and creamy Roquefort. The big-deal dessert is Fraises "Romanoff," ripe strawberries in liquored whipped cream. The pear poached in wine is firm, stained red, winy and sweet —a very good version of this very common dessert. The mousse and fruit tarts are fine.

Le Veau d'Or could long ago have raised prices, moved to larger quarters and continued to fill every table. But a bigger, better Veau d'Or is a contradiction in terms. The excellence of this place derives from its decades of respect for tradition in the face of myriad fads, by which stationary route it arrived at its current state: it is the essence of New York—and yet few restaurants in town exude its relaxed worldliness.

★ VIENNA PARK

35 East 60th Street
LUNCH, MONDAY TO FRIDAY; DINNER, MONDAY TO SATURDAY. CLOSED SUNDAY.
Reservations, 758-1051.
Credit cards: AE, CB, DC, MC, V.
Expensive.

The three rooms of this place are softly lighted, carpeted, painted in mostly beiges and grays. There are little candles on the beige-linened tables, a few flowers. A gray-on-gray engraving (much enlarged) of old Vienna covers a long wall of the main dining room. The place is modern (but not *too* modern), tasteful, without character. It is designed to offend no one. The contented come here, confident that at the next table they will not spot the discontented.

Many of the waiters appear to have been imported from Vienna, where, it seems, practices are at variance from stateside customs. One fellow brings you a bottle of Beaujolais of a different year and different shipper from what you selected. When you remonstrate he assures you that "All Beaujolais Villages is the same." His comrade, when you order an $11 Côtes du Rhône, becomes avuncular, suggests a $20 Châteauneuf-du-Pape, which, he assures you, is from the same region and much better. Their mild contempt for their customers is perhaps understandable, for the place is crowded with a clientele that loves every bite of food here equally well, the good and the dull.

They love, and very well might, the matjes herring, firm and oily, salty and sweet, served with a dollop of sour cream, raw onion and crisp apple. They like the marinated salmon and bass—the slices of lovely fish are strewn with fresh dill, which is fine, but the mustard sauce is absurdly powerful for this delicate meat, and must be used sparingly or not at all. The headcheese is designed for this crowd—it is genteel, which is, of course, contrary to the very nature of headcheese. Four slices of sole dumpling, studded with salmon, are a little gelatinous—their sweet wine sauce helps. Some very plump and tender snails are served in a pastry boat under a fragrant and buttery tarragon sauce.

As you might well expect in a Middle European restaurant, the boiled beef is among the best dishes—the huge chunk of meat is moist, fibrous, tender, solid. It is served with a good enough horseradish sauce. But, surprisingly, the paillard of beef is just as good, rapidly grilled to a seared, lightly blackened surface, blood-juicy within its crust. The tender meat is pointlessly adorned with chopped tomato—which seems to water down the beef—and with tasteless onion rings. The grilled liver is fine. The breaded medallions of veal, with wild mushrooms in the paprika sauce, are solid and decent. Watch out for the whole baby chicken—you were hoping it would be moist, but instead it is wet. The sautéed peppers and paprika sauce do not convert the bird—to which they are proximate, but not otherwise related—into a dish.

The sachertorte is a good version of the genuine article—a rich chocolate cake under a velvety dark icing, a layer of apricot preserves within. The cheese cake is really cheese-flavored white cake, served with raspberry purée—an unambitious and entirely successful sweet. The apples in the apple strudel are little more than warm apple sauce. Warm fresh-fruit salad is served wrapped in crêpes, with vanilla and chocolate sauces

—the disparate elements of this dish seem unable to recover from their respective culture shocks. What goes as hazelnut parfait is a terrific ice cream with a bit of raspberry purée, which is valuable mainly for its brilliant color.

Jacket and tie required. Rule not enforced.

★ VIENNA 79

320 East 79th Street
DINNER.
Reservations, 734-4700.
Credit cards: AE, CB, DC, MC, V.
Very expensive.

Your host looks at his watch when you arrive at five minutes before the hour, and then he looks at you. He informs you that you are early, in a manner heretofore reserved for informing the unclean that their uncleanness is perceptible through several senses. You are ordered to the bar. Presently your appointed hour arrives, and presently it passes. Still you are not granted a table, though unoccupied ones stand unoccupied. Cleaner customers arrive and are seated at once (after being greeted warmly by name). It is the better part of an hour before, with unctuous apology for the delay, you are shown to a place in the dining room.

The problem, of course, is that you do not look like Vienna 79 material. Perhaps your coat is not of the same goods as your trousers (and neither is a pin-stripe worsted), or your silk blouse comes from last year's thrift shop, or your tresses are neither metallic of hue nor glued in place. Vienna 79 gets a stuffy crowd. This is Yorkville, after all. The Teutonic burghers and their fraus are sooo happy to have a place of their own that is pricey enough to keep the merely curious out. Ach, this publicity in the *Times* nearly ruined everything, people coming from all over. But that has passed, and the place is packed nightly with locals, captains of light industry and purveyors of nineteenth-century professional services and their doll-like wives, ladies who donate two hours a week of their time to wheeling books and magazines from room to room at the hospital.

The order was given: Load the place with atmosphere. Vienna 79 oozes candlelit supper-club intimacy. Except for the handful of barely glowing track lights that play on the smoky-gray walls, what illumination there is, is cast by the burning tapers, in little pottery holders, that stand—and drip romantically—on each table. A gray-on-gray detail map of ancient Vienna almost covers one gray wall. Against the opposite wall a few tables are nestled into shallow, mirrored alcoves. The place is carpeted, the linen is starched. The laughter is gay, never too loud, the tinkle of glasses seems somewhat more in evidence here than in most restaurants. There may be nothing Viennese about the place, but the brand of contentment is old-world. Some people come here just to carry out long-nourished fantasies in which they smoke cigarettes in long cigarette holders and gaze through the smoke at their dreamboats. You can do it either sex.

Some of the dishes on the menu are actually Viennese, at least vaguely. Among these is Rindfleischsalat, which, like many a cold dish here, is served in the bowl of a huge wineglass. This is marinated beef, long tender strips of it, tossed with crisp strands of green pepper, red pepper and onions, garnished with the eighth part of a ripe tomato, the fourth of a hard-cooked egg, all in a bright, light, tart and vibrant dressing. In an identical wineglass you are brought some quite different food, Krevettencocktail Lustige Witwe. The menu characterizes this as "Viennese shrimp cocktail," which, if it is not taken in good humor by all thereby defamed, surely justifies an international incident. It is a composition of chopped shrimp and canned asparagus, and it can only be successfully defended if medical benefits are established. But you get lovely cured salmon here, the velvety dark-pink fish—only faintly salty, and lightly flavored of dill —is served with a gentle mustard sauce. The breaded mushroom caps are hot and crunchy within their picture-book, golden-brown breading, but they are more texture than mushroom. The snails are the big winner—large tender ones in a creamy sauce that sparkles with parsley. They are served in a hole excavated in a decapitated roll, so the polished sauce is already soaked into the bread when you have eaten the snails.

One of the main courses takes cognizance of the extraordinary history of serious music in Vienna. It is called Forelle à la Mozart, a reference, presumably, to a trout Wolfgang Amadeus would have composed had not Schubert done it later. The fish is skinned and boned (which is a sure method of eliminating the flavor of trout), breaded, sautéed and inundated in shrimp and a creamy dill sauce. It is nice hot food, but it has no specific quality of trout.

The breaded chicken is, like the breaded mushrooms, perfectly done to a lovely crispness, but the moist chicken within is one of today's chicken-factory chickens—this is a nice preparation wasted on a nowhere bird. The Wiener schnitzel is composed of tender, pale veal encased in yet more of this restaurant's crisp and delicate breading. But Wiener schnitzel, of course, is not much of a dish to begin with—this one is elegantly prepared, and if you squeeze on the lemon, it actually comes to tame life. Much better is the boiled beef, slabs of meat that are at once coarse and tender, hefty and sharp—they arrive steaming, and you moisten them with a creamy horseradish sauce. Order an entrecôte medium-rare and it arrives blood-rare, surmounted with crisp julienned vegetables in mustard sauce. Like many of the dishes, the ingredients are fine, but the composition is artless, the whole no more than the sum of the parts. When game is in season, Vienna 79 offers some; venison, for example, which it carefully butchers in such a way that there is at least a touch of gristle in every morsel of the venison ragout —nor is the natural sweetness of deer meat evident in this preparation. The ragout gravy is thick, dark and smooth, and the dish is served with slices of fluffy dumpling that are veined with parsley, but the stew itself is a comedown.

Of course there is Sacher torte, and it is a perfect balance of chocolate, ground nuts and the polished sweetness of its thin, dark icing. And the place produces a splendid and unusual strudel of flaky pastry and creamy, raisin-studded cheese, served warm in a custardy vanilla sauce. Pass up the crêpes with chestnut purée, which have no chestnut flavor, just the soft solidity of Middle-European desserts at their most deadly —it is garnished, however, with real, rich whipped cream. As is the raspberry purée, a sweet, purple, pleasantly seedy froth.

On occasion a zither player stations himself between the barroom at the front and the dining room, and plinks. "The Third Man Theme" comes up around every third number, "Mona Lisa" almost as often. The patrons just love him.

A couple of dozen Austrian wines are listed.

★★ WALLY'S

224 West 49th Street
DINNER. CLOSED SUNDAY.
Reservations, 582–0460.
Credit cards: AE, CB, DC, MC, V.
Very expensive.

Wally's was started up, around ten years ago, by Walter Ganzi, scion of a founding family of the restaurant once known as Ganzi & Bozzi—it is now called the Palm. Walter is no longer connected with Wally's, but the place still sports a menu that is derived from the Palm's. Moreover, this place actually prints it up! And at Wally's you do not have to suffer Second Avenue indignities to sample it.

Even the staff and clientele will seem familiar to Palmists. You are greeted by a corpulent gent whose hoarse, croaking voice is of the type traditionally developed by twenty years, boy and young man, of street-corner hollering, refined, perhaps, by an athletic career marred by an overabsorption of hooks to the Adam's apple. (His backward-leaning posture suggests not only the need to pull back his forwardly placed center of gravity, but also the defensive stance of the glove-shy.) At the massive bar on your right the middle-aged boys are mostly round. Brightly colored ties flow down their ample tummies. The rings at the bases of their plump pinkies can only be removed by cutting. At the snugged-in tables under the stairway on your left, and in the pale-green dining room at the back, many of the male diners tuck napkins into the collars of their shirts. Their equally well-nourished female companions are notable for their gleaming carapacial garments (which call to mind the shells of the gigantic lobsters the ladies dispatch with dispatch), for their brilliantly enameled fingernails (which call to mind the claws), and for the defiantly primary tints of their superbly molded hair.

Wally's is a steakhouse, and no steaks in New York are much better than the huge, crusty, tender, accurately grilled boulders of beef that are planted before the carnivores who keep the place busy. The sirloins are a couple of inches thick (when rare), the double sirloins the size of a heavyweight's flexed biceps. Even milady's comparatively delicate filets mignons are made he-manly by their hefty proportions and charred, glistening exteriors. A Palm specialty that is also available at Wally's is steak à la stone, a slightly Italianate production in which an immense sirloin is served, sliced, over slices of toast that are surrounded by sautéed onions and red peppers. If you eat a steak a day, as some do, steak à la stone makes an excellent, special-occasion, pinguid departure from the Spartan grind. Other broilings include: a sextet of lamb chops, served as three doubles—big rib chops of strongly flavored meat that is suffused with the loud taste of lamb fat; a duet of veal chops, served as two singles, the great slabs of pale and tender veal moistened with a blunt, slightly oily red sauce—solid food; a chopped veal steak, served as two hamburger-size patties, the flavor of the gentle meat unalloyed except for the bright-green adornment of chopped parsley; a large chopped steak of freshly ground beef, its juiciness sealed within seared surfaces.

Do not, however, conclude that Wally's is the perfect eating place. Its giant lobsters, which go for $40, are either tough or very tough. And the Italian food, except for some simply prepared fish, is humdrum.

If red meat and a baked potato will not hold you, you may begin with clams, which are usually fresh; an excellent crabmeat cocktail, which is unfortunately served at icebox temperature; or a splendid Caesar salad of crisp greens and a strong cheese dressing—it is studded with lots of plump capers and crunchy knobs of crouton. The best potatoes in the place are the hash browns—they arrive as a great pancake of potato chunks, the outer ones browned, a few almost blackened, and the charred bits are like a zest to the weighty food. The place also does French-fried onions, and they are dark, crisp, crinkly, heavily salted and still moist of the frying oil.

The rum cake and chocolate mousse cake are cold and candylike, but fine if you like intense sweets. The cheese cake is of cream cheese, rich, sugared and heavy.

Wally's is a comfortable jernt. The waiters are city cool.

★ WINDOWS ON THE WORLD

1 World Trade Center
LUNCH AND DINNER.
Reservations essential, 938–1111.
Credit cards: AE, CB, DC, MC, V.
Very expensive.

Weeks after you make your reservation and ninety seconds after you board the nonstop elevator to the 107th floor (having cleared your ears on the trip up with three violent swallows), you disembark to a low-ceilinged bronze-and-marble sanctum, complete with the only restaurant cigar stand in New York at which you may purchase a meerschaum pipe. Such transparent tourist titillations should not necessarily steer you to the next car down, for this lofty spot sometimes transcends its own pretentiousness—which is going some.

You are early and you are invited to wait in the "Living Lounge," a somber red-and-beige chapel with four thrones and a view of New Jersey. Instead, in an effort to nurture the festive spirit that brings you to this celebratory spot, you elect to pass your waiting time in the bar—it looks over Brooklyn and beyond, and unlike the view of Jersey—gigantic neon signs and sequined apartment houses—the vista to the east is of a trillion fallen gems, swatches of translucent light cutting through massive blocks of stone, lengthy pearl-strung bridges repeated in bottomless black water. This barroom is like a bottle-lined womb, the bar itself under a canopy of mirrors. You confidently toss a $5 bill on the counter and call for a couple of highballs. Hefty drinks and all that, in handsome crystal, but the fin will not cover two ordinary Scotches. And if you prefer to sit at one of the tables—tiers of them descend from the bar toward lofty windows and the distant views—there is a cover charge.

Your time comes, and you slip through a futuristic maze of marble tunnels—faceted with mirrors and photomurals—until you reach a clearing, whereat your imperious host, standing at a great book. He is talking very slowly on the telephone, while a circle of supplicants attends on his first free moment.

The spacious curved room is shrewdly terraced so that one has at least a teeny view from any seat, though of course you may have to turn your head to find your favorite spire. The place is modern, but passively so, neutrally: soft brick-colored carpeting, beige banquettes, simple chairs of cane and clear wood, brass railings that accent the lines and turns of the room. Spotlights throw mottled effects on the white walls, a cascade of wine bottles provides a bit of color here, a cluster of brass-studded columns does it there. It is cool.

French bread in a silver bowl, curls of cold butter on a saucer-size china tray. You spread the latter on the former with gleaming, plated flatware, while you consider the gleaming crystal and the little open dishes of coarsely ground pepper and salt. All is well until your adenoidal captain addresses you with a manner designed to help you relax: "Good evening, I'm Jay, your captain for the evening." (To protect the innocent, no names have been changed.) Soon he brings you a bottle of the very young wine you ordered and continues his helpful ways: "I think we should let this breathe for a while." "What if it stubbornly holds its breath?" Laughter only from Jay.

There is a prix-fixe menu and an extensive à la carte array. You may begin with Terrine of Veal and Pistachios, a coarse and spicy, garlicky and well-herbed amalgam of much meat and a remoteness of nuts. It is cloaked in tender fat and adorned with cool diced jelly and a sprig of crisp watercress—simple and satisfying food. Up a step of ambition to Ragout of Duck Livers and Raisins in Brioche, a hot and sweet little sauté of white raisins and the livers in fresh warm pastry. The livers are not invariably sautéed to crispness outside, pinkness within, but the moist raisins are always to the rescue. The Tortellini of Shrimp in Cream arrives in a six-inch silver pan with a fitted lid—the crescents of pasta are stuffed with ground shrimp and moistened with cream and strong cheese. The dish is hot and heavily seasoned, and the pasta is firm, but the flavor of the shrimp is distinctly less than that of the clear fresh article, and the dish seems contrived—someone's not very clever variant of a classic. The Pike and Spinach Pâté is an excessively salted item of little finesse, in which a sauce Aurore—tomato-flavored velouté—goes far toward taming the hard-edged pâté.

If you are on the table d'hôte side of the menu, you would do well to opt for the Roast Prime Sirloin: ample slices of good meat, tender and rare, garnished with a superb purée of mushrooms that is earthy and redolent of strong stock. On the facing à la carte page there is listed Squab Tabaka, a perfectly roasted bird, cooked through, yet with none of its moisture lost, the filmy skin browned to a crackling parchment. This is a rich bird, and the fruit sauce that accompanies it—largely of prunes, thick and acidic—is lovely against the oily meat.

But the Frogs' Legs Sautéed Provençale are plastic legs in a tomato-and-garlic sauce that seems to belong on pasta—the dish just does not add up. If you must have seafood, you will do somewhat better with Marinated Bluefish with Toasted Sesame—the marination adds a bit of herb and spice to the fish, but at the expense of its natural oiliness. The fish is carefully broiled, flaky and slightly crusty, but the sesame seeds are beside the point. Of the à la carte vegetables, the Baby Eggplant Grilled with Soy Sauce and Ginger reduces this vegetable almost to its essential vapor—it is salty and earthy and memorable. The simple green salad is of good greens and a delicate vinaigrette, but the Beefsteak Tomatoes, Basil Dressing, is, surprisingly, garlicked in the manner of garlic pizza; and you leave wondering where the basil may be.

Incredibly, it is possible to be brought a tray of petrified cheese—Brie that flowed once but never will again, blue cheese that is brown from exposure, little soft-ripening cheeses in fossilized crusts. If you put up a fuss they will find something much better. There are a couple of marvelous desserts—a Golden Lemon Tart in which paper-thin slices of lemon are atop an airy lemon mousse that is studded with clumps of sweetened pastry crumbs, the whole thing on a superbly browned crust. The Cold Sabayon is flavored with a heavy dose of white port and served onto plump, ripe berries—the effect is of sugared berries in a liquor in a cloud. Lots of elaborate ice cream concoctions are available.

The place has had plenty of time, and it is not up to its claims for itself. In the course of clearing your table, rolls are dropped, water is dribbled across your sleeve, crusts of bread are left behind. Too much management in evidence, whispered disputes, dramatic pointings, running off and running on—one begins to take sides.

An extraordinary wine list of around a hundred wines. What is most extraordinary about the selection is that almost nothing is offered that is not ready to be drunk, unlike 90 percent of New York's restaurants, where they will sell anything they have, ready or not.

• WINGS

76 Wooster Street (near Spring Street)
LUNCH, SUNDAY; DINNER, DAILY.
Reservations, 966-1300.
Credit cards: AE.
Expensive.

Wings is probably no pinker than lots of other places, but it is illuminated with a cold light that gives it a fuchsia glow of sufficiently painful severity to put you in mind of snow blindness achieved through rose-colored glasses. Very sleek, and presumably inspired by the revelrous delight the movie industry took in color when the silver screen first got the gift of the rainbow, this emphasis on so narrow a band of wavelengths makes of the intended restaurant and bar an infantile sensory event instead. It is impossible to imagine a crowd other than the habitually narcoticized that would make a habit of this place.

You enter to the (you guessed it) pink bar (with a silver-colored "brass" rail) at which destitute singles sip and glumly ogle. This street level is actually one flight up, for beyond the bar you are at the top of a two-bank staircase (silver banister) that leads down grandly, like the stairs that give onto a stage set in a movie musical, to the dining room below. The ceiling is pink (a tube of fluorescent light pursues an irregular path across it), the walls are pink, the linen is pink, the baby grand is pink. Sometimes the last is played. The idiot, however, who denies you a large table because they are all "reserved" (the restaurant remains half empty through closing time) is white. The upholstery on the banquettes and chairs is a rather deep rose, as is the carpeting. You look down to rest your eyes. The place gets a long-haired crowd (except for a few rebellious brush-cut girls), many of whom must toss back their tresses before each bite of food. The first microskirts of the new fashions are here. You will spot a number of intellectuals in rimless glasses and leather, as well as ladies who have modeled their imagoes on the depictions of heroines on the covers of mass-market paperback romantic novels.

Even some of the food is pink. The menu promises smoked and fresh salmon, but you are delivered only the former. Four florets of the mild fish are dressed with oil and strewn with slivered almonds—not bad. And some warm fresh vegetables, allegedly "scented" with ginger, are actually suffused with it—they are lightly buttered, crisp, more than decent. But the rather cold sweetbread terrine, with its tough core of beef, is so powerfully flavored of dill and pepper as to render the other ingredients mere carriers. And the spaghetti with morels and mushrooms is in a soupy sauce so strongly seasoned as to obliterate the chives that are billed as part of the dish.

Wings has steamed some fresh bass perfectly, and strewn it with crisp vegetables, but the fish is without the flavor of the seaweed the menu mentions, and it arrives without the oysters that the menu has led you to expect. A nicely roasted (medium-rare) duck is garnished with kumquats and apples, chestnuts and cranberries, and moistened with a smooth, sweet sauce. Some rather leaden veal is in a basil sauce that would do nicely on a plate of spaghetti. And an otherwise perfectly prepared filet mignon is graced with bone marrow that was left in a warm place over the weekend.

The pleasant dacquoise is a chewy, coffee-flavored sweet. The ganache is a chocolate item that seems to be composed of chocolate cake, chocolate mousse and chocolate— unfortunately it is cold. An icy kiwi tart on a claylike pastry is garnished with a white cloud of something spewn from a metal device.

★★ WISE MARIA

210 Spring Street (at Sixth Avenue)
LUNCH, SUNDAY TO FRIDAY; DINNER, DAILY.
Reservations, 925-9257.
Credit cards: AE, MC, V.
Expensive.

In all of New York there is no snappier setting for the consumption of pizza pie. Wise Maria is posh, but Wise Maria is casual. Its dining rooms are sleek and aglow, but its host greets you in shirtsleeves. The place sells fancy food, but the place sells sausage platters. It puts you in mind of the lover who one minute wants to be playfully toyed with, and then wishes to be taken very seriously for certain qualities of mind. Wise Maria, however, is not that kind of lover at all. She never shifts position. She is a different Maria to different people, to be sure, but all at once. For this is SoHo, where whatever you seek is right, where the style is any style. The high prices this establishment exacts, however, do tend to scare off the youngest, most exhibitionistic members of the downtown set.

You enter to the barroom, a pink-marble-topped bar on one side, a triptych of big plain mirrors behind it, framed by massive beams of dark wood. There is seating for dinner over the partition. This room is mostly putty-colored wainscoting, with pink lights in the ceiling casting their glow on an old terrazzo floor. There are a handful of booths, as well as tables surrounded by Thonet chairs. Spend a little time at the bar here, and watch your host at work when, as often happens, tables are very much in demand. You will note that couples unknown to him are not seated—reservations notwithstanding—until a suitably tiny table for two is available. But if the couples are friends of the house, they may well be shown to a commodious booth in this front room. The front room is perhaps not where you want to sit anyway, for the hard surfaces all around guarantee that it will be painfully noisy when the crowd is at all boisterous. Pray that you are not in a reverie when, as seems often to happen, a slippery plate cracks into the terrazzo floor. Farther back are two small connected rooms, pink, bare-walled, gray-carpeted, softly lit by recessed lights. You are seated on gray-upholstered side chairs, or on a mauve banquette, before tables set with white linen. The only adornment back here is the array of appetizers, desserts and wines, garnished with a huge spray of wildflowers, all brightly lighted by a spotlight directly above, that makes a colorful centerpiece in the back room. The place is patrolled by young waiters and waitresses in white shirts, narrow four-in-hands, and long white aprons—mostly they are pleasant and helpful, though a few of them deliver their information as if they had crammed for this oral exam, and know the words but not the substance.

The substance—from an often revised menu—includes sliced tomatoes with smoked mozzarella cheese and fresh basil. There is something soapy about the cheese, but by its smoking it has taken on a nice burnt gaminess that is in striking contrast to the juicy tomato and the fragrant herb. Not much to the carpaccio—thin slices of just-cut raw beef, drops of light mayonnaise thereon. Or you may start with roasted peppers—dark red, skinned, imbued with oil, salty and sour. They are served with roasted whole baby eggplants, which are about the size of large eggs, soft and oily, delicately spiced, and with sharp green olives and rich little black ones, both from the lands near the Mediterranean. On the sausage platter, one hard sausage is fragrant with fennel, another is studded with strong black peppercorns, yet a third is intensely garlicked. The meats are served with salty Gorgonzola cheese and a firm chunk of good—albeit not aged—Parmesan, more of those olives and a fiery-hot red pepper. That pizza is for real, though unlike pizzas you have known. It is made without cheese. The thin crust, which is about as big across as a dinner plate, is dark and crisp, and it is spread with thin circles of tomato that are moistened with oil and strewn with fresh herbs—a good, elemental dish that sometimes suffers from bland dough. Similar dough is used to form the calzone, a great hollow crisp pillow; when you break into it you find at the bottom a steaming layer of seasoned and herbed ricotta cheese—the hot cheese is wonderful with the crusty pastry. Sometimes the house offers littlenecks with herb butter—the tiny clams are very gently warmed, so they are tender, and the butter and herbs enrich and liven them.

A couple of pasta dishes are offered each day, and from their descriptions you might well suspect that their recipes were found in *Discover Yourself Through Pasta,* if there were such an opus. Spaghetti with fresh tomatoes, onions, pancetta and ginger, for example, sounds unlikely, but the ginger spiciness is splendid with the other flavors, and the pasta itself is artfully cooked—tender but firm.

Perfectly fresh bass is grilled until lightly browned, and it is served in a gentle sauce that is just touched with Pernod. But the mustard vinaigrette and basil on the steamed lobster call more attention to themselves than to the otherwise well-prepared crustacean. The cold vitello tonnato is of meat that is at once fibrous and buttery, under a puréed tuna sauce—tart and salty—that is studded with capers. The veal is garnished with cool rice, lightly oiled, which is mingled with pine nuts and bits of red pepper, and adorned with cool white grapes. The principal problem with the rice is that the grains fall between the well-separated tines of your broad three-pronged fork. It is expected that a veal chop the eye of which you could stick in your eye will hold you. This is a splendid chop, crusty and juicy, and a small dollop of mixed Gorgonzola cheese and butter, which is melting upon it, and a sprinkling of oregano, are fine with the tender meat, as is the whole roasted shallot that tags along. But there is simply no rational explanation for the fact that a single lamb chop of this size would never be masqueraded as a main course, while one such veal chop often is. A roasted baby chicken is served bifurcated. As more than two chickens may well be in the works at one time, you will not always be served two halves of the same chicken. In fact on occasion you are given a half-chicken and an unrelated half-Cornish hen. Cornish hen is the only bird around these days than which chicken has more flavor, which this easy opportunity for comparison dramatizes. The roasted bird(s) is moist, and it is served with an herbed pine-nut dressing and a hot fresh fig—good food, despite the slightness of the flavor of the bird itself. Splendid liver—thin, tender slices—is served with sweet strands of sautéed onion, bits of Italian bacon, much moisture and tang and gentleness in the meat. The salads are of crisp greens, their dressing made with a good, strong olive oil.

In the poaching of pears at Wise Maria, more is boiled away than gained. The fruit is served in a zabaglione that is mostly whipped cream—a cloying dish. Some raspberries are a little soft, some strawberries less than uniformly ripe. The latter are served with mascarpone, a mild, firm cream cheese that is fine with fruit. What the menu refers to as cold ricotta soufflé looks like and tastes like, and is, a lemony cheese cake, at once elegant and pudding-like, sugared, delicately browned, light—a wonderful sweet. The almond cake is nutty, almost weightless, touched with lemon. And the chocolate torta, served in a pool of vanilla sauce, is wonderful in the way the texture of the ground nuts leavens the weight and intensity of the almost black chocolate.

• WOODS

718 Madison Avenue (near 64th Street)
LUNCH AND DINNER. CLOSED SUNDAY.
Reservations, 688–1126.
Credit cards: AE, CB, DC, MC, V.
Very expensive.

Woods is a restaurant for a nice, clean date. Make sure your date is nice and clean and go to this nice, clean place, where everything is nice and clean. Dirt, you understand, they do not have. If anything in this place had a smell, everyone would faint.

You are greeted by a neatly tonsured and tailored gentleman who draws your coat from your shoulders with the seriousness of a master removing the drape from a just-painted corpse. Effete religiosity pervades. Some of the waiters discuss the menu with you as if they were sharing wisdom picked up in the Himalayas.

Woods is long and narrow, softly lighted, all beige and natural wood. Beige is this year's color, so the women here, particularly blondes, are invisible.

The menu changes frequently, so that as soon as regular customers have learned which dishes to avoid, new traps are in place. Herewith, a sampling from three bills of fare.

The hors d'oeuvres from the trolley (their word)—such things as mousse of smoked trout and chicken salad—are sandwich spreads raised to a low art. A listed vegetable tart turns out to be a reheated mushroom quiche, but a crab quiche is browned, fluffy and thick with sweet crabmeat. Some asparagus, happily, are peeled, firm, buttery, and nicely lemoned. But something given as watercress soup does a terrific imitation of blenderized salted peanuts.

Every trace of character is drained from the fish Woods serves—it can murder halibut, bass, salmon, each in its own pointless preparation. And it can roast lamb so that it is very rare and extremely tough, and serve it with an absurd garnish called mint hollandaise. The winner is steamed liver. Steamed liver, be informed, gives vivid meaning to the words "organ meat." But when the liver is sautéed and served with shallots, it is fine. The vegetable garnishes are fresh, but somehow they are made tough rather than crisp. Kale, cauliflower, green beans, broccoli, carrots—all tough. You probably could not do it if you tried. The herbed roasted potatoes are lovely.

Wonderful desserts: tarts—one time orange, another time strawberry—of ripe, juicy fruit on gentle custard and browned, crumbly crusts; splendid chocolate roulade, with chunks of black chocolate and a layer of mocha cream that is thick and intensely coffee-flavored; rich cheese cake; good Stilton cheese with crisp Granny Smith apples.

Woods is a bloodless restaurant, but its mannerly pretensions have caught on with a very proper crowd, and it is busy.

PLEASE NOTE...

A newsletter supplement to this book is published every month. It is called *Seymour Britchky's Restaurant Letter,* and it is now the most influential restaurant periodical in New York.

In this handsomely printed newsletter Mr. Britchky writes about New York's newest restaurants—eating places that have opened too recently for inclusion in this book. Mr. Britchky also writes about established restaurants at which new ownership, or new chefs, have instituted major changes of policy.

Seymour Britchky's Restaurant Letter is available by subscription only.

Suscribe today. Send $20 for a one-year subscription (12 monthly issues) or $35 for a two-year subscription (24 monthly issues) to:

Seymour Britchky's Restaurant Letter
Post Office Box 155A
New York NY 10276